Victorian Anthropology

Victorian Anthropology

George W. Stocking, Jr.

THE FREE PRESS
A Division of Macmillan, Inc.
New York

Maxwell Macmillan Canada
Toronto

Maxwell Macmillan International
New York Oxford Singapore Sydney

The Free Press
A Division of Macmillan, Inc.
866 Third Avenue, New York, N.Y. 10022

Maxwell Macmillan Canada, Inc.
1200 Eglinton Avenue East
Suite 200
Don Mills, Ontario M3C 3N1

Macmillan, Inc. is part of the Maxwell Communication Group of Companies.

First Free Press Paperback Edition 1991

Printed in the United States of America

printing number

1 2 3 4 5 6 7 8 9 10

Library of Congress Cataloging-in-Publication Data
Stocking, George W.
Victorian Anthropology.

1. Ethnology — Great Britain — History — 19th century.
2. Social Evolution — History. I. Title.
GN308 . 3 . G7S76 1987 306'. 0941 86–18370
ISBN 0–02–931551-4

For Carol

Contents

Preface xi

Prologue: A Precipice in Time 1

1. *The Idea of Civilization Before the Crystal Palace (1750–1850)* 8

   The Progress of Civilization in the Enlightenment 10
   The History of Culture in Germany 20
   The Science of Progress in France 25
   The Problem of Civilization in England 30
   Civilization as an Issue of Attitude and Method 36
   Biblical Anthropology and the *Vestiges of Creation* 41

2. *Ethnology on the Eve of Evolution (1830–1858)* 46

   James Cowles Prichard and the Ethnological Problem 48
   From Popular Antiquities to Folklore 53
   Linguistic Paleontology: The Aryans as Primitive Men 56
   Anglo-Saxonism, Polygenism, and Physical Anthropology 62
   The Revolution in Human Time 69
   The Crisis of Prichardian Ethnology 74

3. *Travelers and Savages: The Data of Victorian Ethnology (1830–1858)* 78

The Benevolent Colonial Despot as Ethnographer 81
A Methodist Missionary in Cannibal Feejee 87
The Gentleman Traveler as Social Darwinist 92
Primitivism, Polygenism, and Natural Selection 96
Ethnographic Data, Racial Attitudes, and Ethnological Theory 102

4. *The History of Civilization Before the* Origin of Species *(1851–1858)* 110

The Triumph of the Laws of Intellect over the Laws of Nature 112
Retracing Historically the Social Progress of the Aryan Race 117
Making the Associationist Tradition Evolutionary 128
Redefining the Basis of Human Psychic Unity 137

5. *The Darwinian Revolution and the Evolution of Human Culture (1858–1871)* 144

Filling the Gap in the Fossil Record 146
Tracing Up the Origin of Civilization 150
The Natural Development of Spiritual Culture 156
The "Comparative Method" and the Antiquity of Man 164
Evolutionary Argument and Polemical Context 169
Continuity and Disjuncture in Classical Evolutionism 179

6. *Victorian Cultural Ideology and the Image of Savagery (1780–1870)* 186

Animistic Religion and the Progress of Human Reason 188
Primitive Promiscuity and the Evolution of Marriage 197
Savagery and Civilization in Early Victorian England 208
Reason, Instinct, and the Problem of Moral Progress 219
A Cosmic Genealogy for Middle-Class Civilization 228
Colonial Otherness and Evolutionary Theory 233

7. *Evolutionary Ideas and Anthropological Institutions (1835–1890)* 238

The Protection of Aborigines and the Advancement of Ethnology 240
The Emergence of Anthropology as an Alternative to Ethnology 245
The Darwinian Resistance to "Anthropology" 248
Organizational Struggle and Institutional Compromise 254
The Anthropology of the Anthropological Institute 257
The Limits of Institutionalization in Victorian Anthropology 262
The Victorian Anthropological Compromise 269

Epilogue: The Extinction of Paleolithic Man 274

A Prospective Retrospect: The Historical Significance of Victorian Anthropology (1880–1980) 284

The Anthropological Reputation of Victorian Anthropology 286
The Historical Reputations of Victorian Anthropologists 294
Classical Evolutionism and the Idea of Culture 302
Classical Evolutionism and Disciplinary Discourse 314
The Ambiguous Heritage of Evolutionary Anthropology 324

Notes 331

A Note on Manuscript Sources 356

References Cited 357

Index 411

Preface

This book has been long in the writing, and its final form reflects its history. To orient readers to some underlying assumptions (and limitations) of method and structure, it may help to offer a brief retrospect.

Work began in 1969, when Robert Young invited me to come to England to participate in a seminar on "history and science" at King's College, Cambridge. I decided to take advantage of this chance to do research in primary sources in the history of British social anthropology, as a means by which a predominantly anglophone researcher might add a comparative perspective to prior work focusing primarily on American cultural anthropology.[1] During a second six-month trip in 1973, when I was a guest of the Department of Anthropology of the London School of Economics, I again worked in various manuscript archives.[2] At this point, I was still planning to cover the history of British anthropology from the late-eighteenth to the mid-twentieth century, as I had already begun to do in my teaching. Several essays treating earlier phases were published in the early 1970s, and others on the twentieth century that have recently been published were first drafted in this period.[3] By that time, my conception of the book had expanded from one volume to three, under the general title *Scholars and Savages: From Evolutionism to Functionalism in British Anthropology*. The first volume was to treat the emergence of what I have called "classical evolutionism"; the second, the later sociocultural evolutionists and the early-twentieth-century crisis of the evolutionary tradition; the third, the emergence of modern social anthropology. In that conception—which may still eventually be realized—what is now *Victorian Anthropology* was to have been the first volume. By the end of my year at the Center for Advanced Study in the Behavioral Sciences in Palo Alto, California (1976–1977), all but two of its present components (chapter 6 and the "prospective retrospect") existed in drafts variously approximating their present form. However, I did not finish this volume at that time, and the manuscript was deposited in a file cabinet—from which over the next few years it was removed only occasionally for reference purposes in teaching and for perusal by a few students and colleagues.

Of the various reasons for this delay, there are several that illuminate the character of the present volume. In part, it had to do with a predisposition toward a certain style of historiography. Briefly stated, my goal as historian is to be as interpretively suggestive as possible without knowingly doing violence to historical particulars. Although I aspire to more than "merely" narrative or descriptive history, I feel very strongly that historical generalizations must grow out of and directly relate to concrete historical materials. However, in seeking a more general understanding of historical phenomena, I am reluctant to commit (or to limit) myself to a single interpretive point of view. Deliberately eschewing the discussion of "causes," I prefer instead to view historical phenomena in a variety of different "contexts." (Readers will note that the former morpheme—as noun, if not as conjunction—scarcely appears in my writing; the latter word, sometimes to the point of stylistic redundancy.)

Heretofore, these historiographical predispositions have in fact discouraged the production of large-scale interpretations. My major prior work, *Race, Culture and Evolution,* was a set of essays salvaged from the collapse of a more ambitious structure; my other books have been edited volumes.[4] But despite a penchant for the vignette rather than the panorama, I do aspire to make far-reaching statements about far-reaching problems in the history of anthropology. While the present volume is perhaps something less than a general historical synthesis, it is also something more than another series of "essays in the history of anthropology." Perhaps it might best be characterized—without claiming any methodological innovation—as an experiment in multiple contextualization.

As I make explicit on page 239, *Victorian Anthropology* is an attempt to look at an episode in the history of a particular discipline, and more generally in the history of western European anthropological thought, in a nested series of contexts: three broad traditions of inquiry into the general problem of civilization from the middle of the eighteenth century; several specific currents of inquiry which in the 1840s were to merge in the study of "ethnology"; the kinds of empirical evidence available in the 1850s for scholars inclined to speculate about the developmental significance of "savages"; discussion in that decade of the progress of civilization; the role of developmental studies of savages in the more general scientific debate about Darwinian evolution in the 1860s; the way in which discussions of savages became institutionalized first as "ethnology" and then as "anthropology" between 1837 and 1871; and, in an appended discussion (on which I will comment further), the history of social evolutionary thought in anthropology, in both Britain and the United States, over the following century. To symbolize the grounding of my contextualizations in a particular historical moment, I have framed these varyingly panoramic perspectives with two vignettes, in which many themes of the book are concretely manifest.

In attempting this multiple contextualization of what I will call (with caveats noted below) "classical evolutionism," I have constantly had in mind a book published three years before I began my research: *Evolution and Society: A Study in Victorian Social Theory*—whose author, John Burrow, was also a participant in Bob Young's seminar. Burrow's book was an extremely stimulating departure from the mainstream historiography of anthropology, much of which had been (and continues to be) genealogically oriented: seeking analogues to present thinking in the work of prior writers, it traces ideas backward in time in order to establish lineages—albeit sometimes interrupted—for contemporary theoretical viewpoints. By contrast, Burrow took as his problem the explanation of what has traditionally been a major discontinuity in that historiography (the period between 1800 and 1860), and in approaching this problem he significantly broadened the immediate contextual framework in which mid-nineteenth-century social evolutionism must be understood. But if his work was very suggestive, Burrow's major theses (the discontinuity of mid-nineteenth-century social evolutionism from earlier developmental traditions, its independence from Darwinism, and its relation to "the crisis in utilitarian social theory") seemed somewhat problematic. In arguing the last, he gave inadequate attention to more traditionally "anthropological" contexts (cf. chapters 2 and 3 of the present book); in arguing the second, he neglected the more indirect influence of Darwinism in transforming problems, rather than in providing models of explanation (cf. chapters 4 and 5 of the present book); and in arguing the first, he did not grant sufficient weight to longer-run historical forces that sustained a concern with the relationship of civilization and savagism, and to the perdurance of certain major alternative anthropological orientations over long stretches of intellectual historical time (cf. chapters 1 and 6 of the present book).

While I hope that my attempt at multiple contextualization speaks to each of these issues, it is only fair to note that the last of them remains somewhat problematic. This is reflected in my occasional (and somewhat ambivalent) use of the term "paradigm." When Thomas Kuhn's *Structure of Scientific Revolutions* appeared at the very beginning of my own scholarly career, I found its argument for discontinuity in the development of scientific thought also extremely suggestive—not as a model of how that development "actually" takes place, either in the natural or the social sciences, but as an orientation toward certain aspects of certain episodes in the history of the latter (which, in its original formulation, were not in fact assumed to have been covered by Kuhn's model). Since then, a considerable philosophical and historiographical controversy has developed around the term "paradigm," and a friendly critic of my manuscript felt that I would save myself some trouble by rewriting the two dozen or so passages in which the word is used so as to avoid it entirely.[5] I have, however, resisted this advice, because I still find "paradigm" more suggestive in certain contexts than many of the readily available alternatives, insofar as it emphasizes certain disjunctive features of major anthropological orientations—especially, their coherence at a level prior to theory or evidence—as they have succeeded one another at particular historical moments. But I am well aware that, even as a lightly held historical metaphor, the idea of "paradigm" is problematic, especially in an argument that is as interested in exploring continuity as disjunction. The fact that the assumptions of what I have upon occasion referred to as different "paradigms" may be found in the work of a single writer confirms their status as an historian's abstractions; the fact that these "paradigms" are recurrent alternatives in the history of anthropological thought suggests that they might better be thought of as "traditions" of inquiry or interpretation.

This terminological ambiguity, however, in fact expresses a tension that my multiple contextualization is designed in part to evoke (especially in chapter 5, and in the appendix): that between systems of ideas as they are abstracted from the flow of intellectual debate—whether by their advocates, their critics, or their historians—and as they are much more complexly manifest either in specific polemical contexts or over the longer reaches of intellectual history. From this point of view, "paradigm" and "tradition" might be used to emphasize, respectively, the synchronic/disjunctive and the diachronic/continuous aspect of major anthropological orientations that are both perduring and historically specific. Each term expresses an aspect of the intellectual transition that my multiple contextualization seeks to illuminate.

This augmentation of context beyond that normally attempted in the history of anthropological thought has required me to venture into areas well beyond the bounds of my greatest specialist competence. Given my rather strong perfectionist inclinations, this caused me no little methodological angst, especially in relation to chapter 6 and the "prospective retrospect." That these should have been problematic is not surprising. They were the most ambitious (and in the end the longest) components of the book; they were also the ones in which my ambiguous disciplinary identity was most at issue. The one was an attempt, by an Americanist with no prior training in British intellectual or social history, to define the broadest possible framework of contemporary cultural historical significance—in relation to issues on which the literature has grown very rapidly in the last decade. The other was an attempt, by an imperfectly acculturated immigrant from another disciplinary culture, to speak to the problem of subsequent anthropological significance.

These essays were the more difficult because, in rather different ways, they required me to reconsider a position I had affirmed rather strongly at the very beginning of my career. My reputation as an historian of anthropology was to some extent founded on a critique of disciplinary histories written from a "presentist" perspective, and a defense of "historicism" in the historiography of the behavioral sciences. Although the present structure of contextualization reaffirms my commitment to an historical understanding that emphasizes contexts prior to or contemporary with the phenomenon being studied, it also reflects my greater appreciation of the manifold ways in which historical understanding "presupposes a continuing tension between past and present—not only between an historian's present and the past he studies, but that past present and its antecedent past, and between that same past present and all of its consequent futures"—among which our own present is, if only for the moment, the most important.[6] Because the attempt to turn that last tension to contextualizing purpose did in fact create a problem in the temporal structure of the manuscript, I relegated my somewhat tentative essay on "The Historical Significance of Victorian Anthropology" to the status of an appendix. Certain readers may nevertheless find this schematic "Prospective Retrospect" useful in defining social evolutionism as an historical phenomenon.

Although I am satisfied that *Victorian Anthropology* provides the basis for a more adequate historical understanding of "classical evolutionism" than any existing volume, there are some limitations of coverage and perspective that should be noted. It is perhaps worth making explicit that "classical evolutionism" refers to "social" or "cultural" (or "sociocultural") evolution and not to biological evolutionism—although my argument in fact insists on their interrelation. Similarly, while *Victorian Anthropology* may illuminate to some extent the historical roots of contemporary sociobiology, it is not a book about biological thought in the social sciences.[7] So also, while I have a good bit to say about race, this is not a book about racial relations, or about the role of evolutionary racialism in British imperial expansion.[8]

There is one other orienting comment, regarding usage. In part as a consequence of the reaction against evolutionary assumption in anthropology, by about 1930 the word "savages" had ceased being acceptable in the mainstream of Anglo-American anthropology, either as an analytic category or a descriptive term. There were of course sound anthropological reasons for this rejection (as for that of its less frequently used conceptual mate, "barbarian"); and these have been reinforced in the interim by the changing historical role of the peoples once so stigmatized. If I have used such terms without quotation marks in *Victorian Anthropology* it is because the book attempts to recreate the thought world of scholars who took for granted their descriptive if not in all cases their analytic validity. The same reasoning led me to reproduce such now rejected ethnic categories as "kaffir," and to use "man" or "mankind" when referring to the human race. And by the same token, I have not felt it appropriate to comment along the way on all the ways in which evolutionary racial assumption has been subsequently criticized—although to some extent the "Prospective Retrospect" serves this function.

Finally, in view of my strongly held feeling that historical understanding may be both distorted and informed by commitment to a present anthropological viewpoint, I should perhaps comment on my own somewhat eclectic intellectual orientation, which is the residue of a number of formative experiences: a seven-year commitment to a rather vulgar Marxism, four years of training in a social science-oriented American Civilization program, seven years of teaching historiography and American social history at Berkeley, and now eighteen years in a department known as a center of "symbolic" anthropology[9]—during the last six of which I have served also as director of the Morris Fishbein Center for the History of Science and Medicine.

My own anthropological perspective might best be described as "Boasian," insofar as Franz Boas (who was my earliest preoccupation as historian of anthropology) embodied and articulated what I suspect is an "eternal tension" between two approaches to the study of human phenomena—one seeking to subsume a variety of them under a general law, the other seeking to penetrate the secrets of the individual phenomenon "until each feature is plain and clear."[10] While my historiographic style is perhaps more consistent with the latter, I respect the efforts of those who pursue the former—and am quite willing to draw on generalizing assumptions or theses when they seem to facilitate the understanding of particular phenomena.

Although I am inclined to feel that a "Boasian" orientation is a good basis from which to seek historical understanding, it is also one that highlights my status as "outsider" to the tradition that I seek to understand. For modern British social anthropology may be viewed as emerging in explicit opposition to Boasian cultural anthropology, and even British social anthropologists who today are moving toward a more "cultural" approach have little knowledge of Boas. Despite a year's residence among the natives, a friendly acquaintance with many of the now passing generation of tribal elders, a continuation of contact since my departure from the field, and a favorable reception for some of my previous publications, I know that I am marked as "American"; and although I do not share the nihilism of some of my Chicago colleagues toward the traditional subject matter of social anthropology, I have not mastered the language of kinship analysis.[11]

On the other hand, it is one of the assumptions of modern anthropological inquiry that a position of cultural marginality is a privileged one from which to understand not only the rules and regularities of native behavior, but also the "native's point of view." From this perspective, my position as an historian with almost two decades of membership in a major American anthropology department with long-standing ties to British social anthropology may be a fairly good one from which to undertake the present enterprise.

More could be said about the limitations—or the advantages—of my perspective, but this is perhaps enough to give the critical reader a starting point. What remains is to acknowledge at least a few of the many debts that I have accumulated over the long period that this volume has been in process. I would like to thank the following institutions which have supported or otherwise facilitated my research and writing: the Department of Anthropology of the University of Chicago (through the Adolph and Marian Lichtstern Fund for Anthropological Research); the Wenner-Gren Foundation for Anthropological Research and King's College, Cambridge (for my trip to England in 1969); the National Endowment for the Humanities, the National Science Foundation, and the Department of Anthropology of the London School of Economics (for my second research trip in 1973); the National Endowment for the Humanities and the Center for Advanced Study in the Behavioral Sciences (for my stay there in 1976–1977, during which a major portion of the present text was written); and the John Simon Guggenheim Memorial Foundation (for enabling me to devote 1984–1985 to its completion). Along the way there were of course a large group of archivists and librarians, and several research assistants (notably Larry Carucci, Deborah Durham, and David Koester), who facilitated my research. Among the various students who have pursued research topics relevant to my own, or who have reacted to materials I have used in teaching courses, I would like to single out Greg Schrempp, Mark Taylor, Richard Parmentier, Mark Francillon, and Ira Jacknis. I am especially grateful to the anthropological and historical colleagues who read all or portions of the manuscript, including Keith Baker, Barney Cohn, Jan Goldstein, Peter Novick, John Peel, Robert Richards, Barbara Rosenkrantz, Sheldon Rothblatt, and David Schneider—as well as to Bob Young, for his invitation to come to England back in 1969. And although my subject is a bit outside his own area of expertise, Alan Richardson helped immeasurably in enabling me to complete the writing of it. Finally, and always, there is my wife Carol, to whom the book is dedicated.

Prologue: A Precipice in Time

South entrance to the Crystal Palace—1851
The Illustrated London News 18 (May 3, 1851):366–67

IN Thomas Hardy's Wessex, the year 1851 seemed to older men "an extraordinary chronological frontier"—"a precipice in Time." Suddenly, ancient and modern were brought "into absolute contact," as in a geological fault. The temporal disjuncture was most dramatically evident miles away in London, the origin of the railway that had just reached out to Hardy's Stickleford. There, in a glass cathedral to the Goddess Progress, its transepts and its nave filled with icons of the Industrial Revolution, was celebrated the first of all "world's fairs": the Great Exhibition of the Works of Industry of All Nations. For the more philosophically minded celebrants, like the Reverend Dr. William Whewell, Master of Trinity College, Cambridge, wandering the corridors and galleries of the "Crystal Palace" provoked speculation on its deeper "meaning, power, and spirit." Not surprisingly, its symbolism spoke in many voices.[1]

A glorified greenhouse 1,800 feet long and tall enough to enclose a group of Hyde Park's great elms, the very building itself mirrored the "triumphs of the useful arts over external nature." Its mutually interchangeable cast-iron girders, columns, and sashbars were a harvest gathered from the machine shops of the Industrial Revolution; its sparkling exterior, a tribute to free trade, which had recently encouraged the removal of an excise tax on glass. Its conception and organization, too, were a triumph of the liberal entrepreneurial spirit. Deriving from a half-century tradition of French industrial exhibitions, it took on its special character when Henry Cole, a leading planner, learned that the French had rejected a proposal to make their 1849 exposition international. Filled with visions of "Peace, Abundance and Prosperity" in a world where "industrial aggressiveness would in time replace military aggression," Cole conveyed the same suggestion to Prince Albert, who as President of the Royal Society of Arts had helped initiate plans for a British exposition. The Prince Consort responded favorably: since manufacturing, science, and taste belonged "as a whole to the civilized world, particular advantage to British Industry might be derived from placing it in fair competition with that of other Nations." In good liberal fashion, the whole project was carried on "without one shilling being drawn from the national resources," and the Royal Commission supervising construction in fact eventually realized a handsome profit.[2]

Coming only a few years after Engels had chronicled the desperate *Condition of the Working Class in England* and Disraeli had seen the country divided into "two nations" between whom there was neither intercourse nor sympathy, the Exhibition had great symbolic political import.

Although Chartism was on the wane, and England had escaped unscathed from the revolutionary events traumatizing Europe in 1848, the shock waves were still strong enough to touch the Exhibition. Rumors on the Continent saw London swarming with Red Republicans bent on assassination, and it was only after some debate that the inaugural ceremonies were opened to the general public. *Punch* felt they were a "magnificent lesson" for the Prussian princes—" a splendid example of that real freedom . . . and perfect security . . . which are the result of our constitutional monarchy." Concern that the lower classes who came later at cheap weekday rates might carve their initials on the displays proved equally unfounded—although 93,000 of them roaring delight at the Duke of Wellington's appearance on October 7 caused great alarm that the collapse of the whole structure, long feared by some, had finally begun.[3]

The very size of the crowds symbolized processes rapidly transforming British traditional society. The railway boom of the forties had reticulated the provinces with 6,500 miles of track, and country folk who had lived in a walking world were now sped fifty miles an hour on cheap excursion trains to the metropolis. Images of Manchester streets and Cumberland villages depopulated were the stuff of journalistic humor, and it is estimated that almost one-fifth of Britain's population actually attended during the six months of the Exhibition.[4]

But as Dr. Whewell suggested, the crucial symbolism of the Crystal Palace lay in the material objects confronted by this massive audience. According to the classificatory system worked out by the chemist Lyon Playfair, the major exhibit categories—Raw Materials, Machinery, Manufactures, and Fine Arts—were each subdivided, so that one could locate "Mangles, Washing Machines, etc." as Subdivision 19, Division C, Class XXII (Iron and General Hardware). In an excess of the free trade spirit, Prince Albert had proposed that grouping be without reference to national origin; however, the actual arrangement was national and geographical, each nation insofar as practicable arranging its products according to the general system.[5]

Although Queen Pomare sent pandanus mats from Tahiti and the King of Dahomey contributed a chief's throne, the staunch self-help principles of the organizers made it hard for the "less advanced aborigines" to participate. Contributions from the British colonies and dependencies were for the most part in the Raw Material category. However, the large display organized by the East India Company included items in all thirty classes—the most dramatic a large stuffed elephant, complete with human figures in an ivory howdah, given to Queen Victoria by the Nazim of Moorshedabad. Perhaps disdainful of the whole endeavor, the Chinese Empire requested only 300 of the 5,000 square feet it had been allocated; by contrast, the United States requested extra space for an exhibit which, in addition to such major attractions as the McCormick reaper, included gimcrack inventions like the "air-exhausted" coffins and fruitboxes offered by one New Yorker to preserve both corpses and comestibles from putrefaction. According to the *Official Catalogue,* the largest contributions outside of Britain came from the German states (where "craftsmanship" was emphasized rather than heavy industry) and from the French (whose well-developed industry was devoted more to luxury objects "of minute art" than to those "of more ordinary character and extensive demand").[6]

Appropriately, the fullest expression of the European spirit of civilized industry was found in the west wing. There, in the rooms filled with machinery in motion, one could watch the power looms, the model locomotives, the centrifugal pumps, the horizontal and vertical steam engines—"a thousand iron monsters snorting and clattering." Foreign visitors were overwhelmed, and English farmers, dusty from the distance they had come, stood with mouths agape, as the British Industrial Revolution, pandemonic in its noise, but cleansed for the moment of its pain, went twirling and thrusting away before their very eyes. Here it was that the moral of the Exhibition was most sharply drawn.[7]

In the words of Prince Albert, the Exhibition was founded on the great complementary principles of "the unity of mankind" and "the division of labor," through which mankind approached the fulfilment of its "great and sacred mission"—the use of God-given reason to discover the laws by which the Almighty ruled creation, so that by applying them man might "conquer Nature to his use." The purpose of the Exhibition was to "give a true test and a living picture of the point at which the whole of mankind has arrived in this great task, and a new starting point from which all nations will be able to direct their further exertions."[8]

The most obvious lesson of the Exhibition, however, was that in pursuing their sacred mission, not all men had advanced at the same pace, or arrived at the same point. Reflecting on this fact, Dr. Whewell affirmed man's unity as artificer and artist—even the rudest savages shared a generic human capacity for invention. Nor was there "really anything *barbaric* in the skill and taste" of the ornamental works of the Orient. What distinguished the "stationary" civilizations of the East from the "progressive" West, and above all Britain, was a social principle. Here, "the machine with its million fingers works for millions of purchasers, while in remote countries, where magnificence and savagery stand side by side, tens of thousands work for one." Men with less sanguine views of the British social order spoke the same message in different tones. Henry Mayhew, even then at work documenting the horrors of "slopwork" and of the London "rookeries," saw the Exhibition as "one huge academy for teaching the nobility of labour," and for proving that the "industrious poor instead of the idle rich" were "the really respectable men of this country." But it was nonetheless *British* labor that had made the Crystal Palace—"no other people in the world could have raised such a building": "one glance was quite sufficient to account for the greatness of the nation to which it belonged!"[9]

Despite the hopes of its more exuberant sponsors, the Great Exhibition did not inaugurate an era of amicable industrial competition and international peace, nor did it, as Mayhew predicted, signal the transformation of factory laborers into "the artists of our manufacturers." Nevertheless, the Crystal Palace does in retrospect seem to have marked the opening of the mid-Victorian "age of equipoise"—a temporary balance between the powerful and sometimes conflicting forces remolding British society. The discovery of gold in Australia and California marked the beginning of an unprecedented economic boom that continued until 1873. Agricultural prosperity, rapidly growing industrial output, rising prices and profits, higher incomes for many segments of society, including portions of the working classes—all contributed to decreased political tension and relative social tranquility in a society which to those who shared its benefits seemed a model for the world to emulate. As Lord Palmerston suggested: "We have shown the example of a nation, in which every class of society accepts with cheerfulness the lot which Providence has assigned to it; while at the same time every individual of each class is constantly striving to raise himself in the social scale—not by injustice and wrong, not by violence and illegality, but by preserving good conduct, and by the steady and energetic execution of the moral and intellectual faculties with which his Creator has endowed him."[10]

Not everyone in Britain profited by Palmerston's example. Indeed, the balance of the age of equipoise bore down heavily upon the urban poor, the unorganized working classes, the tenant farmers, the agricultural laborers. Beneath the placid surface of mid-Victorian society there were "ugly depths of fanaticism and savagery." If the major problems of social order seemed solved, "respectable" men "did not for a moment assume that the nation was safe on a platform of godliness: their insistence on the need for honesty, chastity, temperance and thrift was dictated by the threats of dishonesty, sensuality, drunkenness and improvidence." When the Victorian era began, "the old harsh wild world of the eighteenth century was only just disappearing." Any person "who was over thirty in 1850 had lived in a world in which there were not only no railways, but also no police to speak of." Those middle-aged at the time of the Crystal Palace would not only have seen "great changes," but would also have been "used as a matter of everyday fact to much that we would consider very brutal and primitive."[11]

We are back, then, at Hardy's "precipice in Time." The urban and industrial social order symbolized by the Crystal Palace was a very recent phenomenon in 1851, a transformation in the lifetime of the men who had made it, a transformation not yet accomplished for many of those who witnessed it—and for millions in Britain who did not. For just as the transformation created new cankers of urban suffering and savagery, so did it leave many rural areas little touched. Until late in the progress of industrialization, "the social structure of the English countryside changed much less than might be expected." "Traditional England" was not so much transformed as gradually diminished in relation to "industrial England," until it was "finally reduced to an insignificant fringe."[12] In this context, the sense of temporal disjunction could be very sharp indeed, and many who witnessed the Exhibition—whether as the summation of their own experience or as foreshadowing a world yet to be experienced—must have felt themselves standing at a precipice in time.

It is hardly surprising, then, that the Exhibition forced some to think about the origins and progress of the civilization it epitomized. Much in the Crystal Palace encouraged speculation of a more specific sort: the overall system of classification, which forced jurors to compare the same functional object in a variety of national forms; the character of the different national exhibits, which led one along a line of progress from the Tasmanian savage through the "barbaric" civilizations of the East, northwest across the European continent toward an apex in Great Britain; even the copper coal scoops of Joseph Tylor and Sons, which were arranged so as to demonstrate "the changes in their patterns" and their "different improvements from 1780 till the present time." Whether the later evolutionary interests of Tylor's nineteen-year-old son Edward owe any direct debt to the Exhibition can only be a matter of speculation. But there is evidence to suggest that the two great ethnological collections of the evolutionary period—the Christy and the Pitt Rivers—were stimulated by the Great Exhibition. Henry Christy (the London banker who was Tylor's chance companion on his trip to Mexico in 1856) began his study of primitive habits and customs as a result of his visit to the Crystal Palace. General Pitt Rivers—then still Captain Lane Fox of the Grenadier Guards—began his collection about the same time, and its special principle of classification by form (with spears, bows, clubs, etc. each grouped in series from simple to complex) bears an obvious resemblance to that employed in judging at the Exhibition.[13]

In his contribution to a series of lectures on the results of the Exhibition, Dr. Whewell speculated on the relationship of space and time. Different nations had reached different stages in the progress of "the useful and ornamental arts," and all of these stages could be seen at once "in the magical glass which the enchanters of our time have made to rise out of the ground like an exhalation." There, "the infancy of nations, their youth, their middle age, and their maturity'' all appeared ''in their simultaneous aspect, like the most distant objects revealed at the same moment by a flash of lightning in a dusky night.'' Thus ''by annihilating the space which separates different nations, we produce a spectacle in which is also annihilated the time which separates one stage of a nation's progress from another.''[14]

Whewell is not a figure one associates with ''evolutionism.'' His general philosophical viewpoint was antithetical to that embodied in the British evolutionary tradition; and although he later admitted feeling the weight of Darwin's argument, he would not allow the *Origin* on the shelves of Trinity College library. All this perhaps makes it even more significant that his consideration of ''The General Bearing of the Great Exhibition on the Progress of Art and Science'' should have led him to formulate the basic principle of the ''comparative method'' of sociocultural evolutionism.[15]

The classic works of British sociocultural evolutionism were all products of the age of equipoise. If one were to encapsulate in a phrase their most general contextual definition, one could do worse than to describe these works as an attempt to understand the cultural experience symbolized by the Crystal Palace.

ONE

The Idea of Civilization Before the Crystal Palace (1750–1850)

The first locomotive passing Great Grimsby church—1848
The Illustrated London News 12 (April 15, 1848):24

By the time of the Crystal Palace, the idea of "civilization" had been problematic for a century. To understand mid-nineteenth-century sociocultural evolutionism, some examination of this prior period is necessary—especially in view of a discontinuity that has long marked the history of anthropological thought. While the Enlightenment has traditionally been a fertile source of ancestors for anthropologists seeking to anchor their own ideas more deeply in time, the early nineteenth century has been a kind of "dark age," barren of theoretical interest save for figures like Auguste Comte who kept the developmental tradition alive.[1] The only monographic study of British sociocultural evolutionism has interpreted the early-nineteenth-century hiatus in terms of the eclipse of the earlier tradition of Scottish "conjectural history" by an essentially ahistorical utilitarianism. In this view, the efflorescence of sociocultural evolutionism around 1860 was neither a transfer of biological evolutionism to the social sphere (as the historiographical catchphrase "social Darwinism" suggests), nor simply the reemergence of a tradition that has been traced beyond the Scots back to the Greeks. Rather, it was a response to an intellectual crisis within the utilitarian tradition dominating British social thought, "the outcome of a tension between English positivistic attitudes to science [and] a more profound reading of history, coming . . . from German romanticism, which made the older form of positivist social theory, philosophic radicalism, seem inadequate."[2]

This view has much to commend it to those who, rejecting a more linear intellectual history, emphasize the tangled interrelations of ideas and thinkers in particular contexts. But while it has the virtue of relating social evolutionary theory to the immediately preceding dominant form of social thought, there are other perspectives from which to view the intellectual discontinuity it seeks to explain. If the tradition of progressive developmentalism went into decline after 1800, it is nevertheless still true that the half century before the Crystal Palace produced a considerable body of British writing (including utilitarianism itself) that was somehow concerned with "the progress of civilization." Furthermore, both within the British tradition and in Continental traditions that influenced it, there were currents of thought that fundamentally conditioned the way progress in civilization was conceived: ideas about non-European "savages," who defined "civilization" by contrast; ideas about the physical nature and differentiation of man, which raised the problem of its universality; ideas about the nature of social order, which defined the specific content of civilization; and ideas about the methods appropriate to the study of human life and history, which defined the extent to which it might be subsumed within the rubric of natural science.

No doubt many of these issues are implicated in the influence of "German romanticism" on a central idea of the Enlightenment. But early-nineteenth-century thinking about civilization took place in the shadow of other broad forces of historical change: notably, the Industrial Revolution, the changing class structure, the revival of traditional Christianity, and the French Revolution. Each of these forces made the achievement and maintenance of civilization more problematic; each had the effect of introducing discontinuities into a general universal process—so that by 1850, the linkage of "civilization" with particular European cultural forms was somewhat differently conceived from the way it had been in the Enlightenment.

All of these matters are an essential part of the background of Victorian sociocultural evolutionism. At the risk of some methodological discomfort, it will therefore be necessary to sweep hurriedly across a century of European history, stepping briefly into areas where specialists might spend a lifetime, in order to review some of the ways intellectuals approached the problem of civilization, and some of the subtle changes which that idea had undergone, from the time the word began to assume its modern meaning. And since beginnings in history are always regressively problematic, it will be necessary also to take several backward glances beyond the point we have selected for our running start.

The Progress of Civilization in the Enlightenment

The cultural contrast implicit in the idea of "civilization" is surely as old as civilization itself. And some of the words by which it has been expressed go back to Greece and Rome. "Barbarian" derives from the Greek contrast between those who spoke intelligibly and those beyond the pale of civil life whose language seemed simply reiterative mumbling—notably the Scythians, who for centuries were the archetype of the barbarian nomads of the Eastern steppes.[3] A second contrastive term derives not from language but from habitat: "savages" (from the Latin "sylva") were those who lived in the woods, rather than in the city—and who, with the era of discovery, were more apt to be encountered by seafaring Europeans venturing West than to thunder out of the East on horseback.[4] Similarly, the tradition of seeing such contrasts in progressive developmental terms can be traced to the Greeks, reemerging at various later points when pride in human cultural achievement was particularly strong, as it was in Italian cities in the late sixteenth century.[5] A century later, the ''battle of the ancients and the moderns'' opened a new phase of speculation on human ''progress,'' and by the middle of the eighteenth century, when ''Europe'' rather than Christendom had become the encompassing rubric of Western cultural identity,[6] the changing sense of the broader historical processes molding that identity was expressed in a redefinition of the word that subsequently formed the third term of a developmental triad: ''civilization.''

The word ''civilization'' already existed as a legal term, referring to the conversion of a criminal proceeding into a civil one; and the verb ''civilize,'' the participle ''civilized,'' and the noun ''civility'' had long been used to express a contrast between European and ''savage'' or ''barbarous'' manners and social life. Although the earliest appearances of ''civilization'' in the newer sense approximate this meaning of ''civility,'' the longer word had from the beginning a more embracive potential, combining in a single form the ideas of both status and process. Rejecting Boswell's Scottish special pleading, Dr. Johnson refused to put ''civilization'' in his dictionary. But his preferred ''civility'' was soon to lose its original connotational reference to the status of citizenship, and came to refer rather to the quality of human social intercourse—if not to manners merely. By contrast, the meaning of civilization was to broaden, becoming in the Anglo-French tradition the generic term for both the overall process of human progress and its cumulative achievement in every area of human activity.[7]

By the time Dr. Johnson published his dictionary in 1755, more systematic speculation on the process of civilization had already begun in the work of a group of Scottish and French thinkers whose writings may be taken as the proximate source of many of the assumptions that a century later were to structure thinking about the evolution of human society and culture.[8] These writers drew of course on many earlier notions, in addition to the idea of progress itself: ideas about ''the Great Chain of Being'' that linked all forms of creation in a finely graduated hierarchical series; ideas about the changes that modified the natural and the social world through time; ideas about human psychology and the social condition of man in a ''state of nature''; ideas about the contrast between Europe and the ''despotism'' of the great Asiatic societies.[9] For the most part, these ideas belong to traditions of speculation that may be traced backward to classical antiquity, and which from the revival of ancient learning are intertwined with the lineage of modern social developmentalism. But in the century before 1755, what we would now consider developmental ideas were often also complexly linked with ideas deriving from the other major source of Western thought—the Judeo-Christian religious tradition.[10]

For the Bible, too, offered a framework for speculation about the process of civilization—one which was to be a major conditioning influence on the development of social evolutionary thought through the middle of the nineteenth century. While the idea of progress has been interpreted as a secularization of the history of salvation, the actual historical account contained in the first chapters of Genesis—the Creation and the Fall of Man, the Flood, the Tower of Babel, and the Genealogies of Nations—is quite a different matter. That account may be interpreted as defining an anthropological paradigm whose temporal framework was both finite and confined, whose psychological and epistemological assumptions were innatist and apriori, whose principle of social order was patriarchal, whose principle of human diversification was genealogical, whose principle of temporal change was degenerationist, and whose privileged reconstructive data were those of linguistic relationship—and which, in many if not all of these respects, contrasts sharply with the paradigm that may be derived from the developmental tradition.[11]

Although the historicity of the biblical account of human genesis was widely accepted down to the time of Darwin, the much longer chronologies of other ancient peoples had always presented a challenge for Christian apologetic writers. By the later seventeenth century, atomistic and mechanistic tendencies within the Scientific Revolution were posing problems for the sacred account of the history of the earth, and by this time also the discovery of the populations of the New World had raised issues regarding the history of its peopling. Among the writers responding to these trends was the French Calvinist Isaac de La Peyrère, who sought to rationalize the biblical account with "the most ancient records of the Egyptians, Ethiopians, and Scythians," and with the existence of peoples in "the world newly discovered" who he felt "did not descend from Adam." Published in 1655, his *Praeadamitae* argued the plural origin of mankind, the much greater antiquity of gentile peoples, and the local character of the Noachian Deluge.[12]

Along with Spinoza and Hobbes, La Peyrère belonged to a "triumvirate of devils incarnate in an age that knew Satans when it saw them." Forced to abjure both his preadamite theory and his Calvinism, he spent his later years in a monastery; and the "flood of books and pamphlets" answering him continued throughout the rest of the century. But rationalism in the defense of orthodoxy could also lead onto slippery terrain; as a result, some of those whose primary motivation was the defense of biblical assumption found themselves arguing positions that had traditionally been associated with the Graeco-Roman developmental tradition.[13]

One line of defense sought points of identification between the conflicting histories. Thus, by comparing the *Customs of American Savages* with those of the nations of classical antiquity, the Jesuit missionary Joseph Lafitau sought to establish the derivation of American Indians from the Old World in the years after the Flood (arguing, for instance, that a Huron divinity corresponded to Jupiter, "which is identical with the ineffable name Jehova"). A second line, pursued in the *New Science* of the Neapolitan historian Giambattista Vico, involved the rejection of the histories of all gentile nations as "fabulous" creations of the irrational poetic mind of mankind fallen into a nearly bestial state in the aftermath of the Flood. But the effect of this defense was not only to encourage Lafitau's equation of contemporary savages and ancient Greeks; it also buttressed an image of primitive mankind resembling that of Thomas Hobbes, and a subsequent course of history resonant of the natural development hypothesized by the ancient progressivists, which had passed into the early modern world largely through Lucretius' *De Rerum Natura*.[14]

Although Vichian assumptions about human nature, the early history of nations, and the possibilities of human self-knowledge were not without influence in early-nineteenth-century historical thought, Vico's work was little read in eighteenth-century France or Britain. One whose work was widely influential—though it has scarcely been appreciated by historians of anthropology—was John Locke. Just as Lockean assumptions are fundamental to the modern liberal tradition, and to so many of the other human sciences (including psychology, economics, and political science), so have they been to anthropology, especially in its social developmental form. If Locke did not systematically pursue the developmental sequence implied in his suggestion that "in the beginning all the World was America," his associationist psychology nevertheless provided the basis for a conventionalist explanation of the origin of language that stood in sharp contrast to the biblical account of Adam's divinely inspired linkages of name and essence. The same psychological assumptions were to provide also the basis for a great deal of speculation on the progress of the human mind. Similarly, Locke's ideas about the social contract and the natural harmony of human egoisms—contrasting sharply with the biblical patriarchalism of Robert Filmer—were the primary basis for thinking about the problem of social order within the British utilitarian tradition.[15]

While later eighteenth-century speculation about the progress of civilization may be seen as continuing earlier debate on the history of gentile nations, and while it reflected in varying degrees the influence of Lockean assumptions, the discussion seems to have had a definite moment of beginning. Paradoxically, the immediate stimulus was provided by a work which, although often invoked as an eighteenth-century precursor of social anthropology, is not easily encompassed within the developmental tradition: Montesquieu's *De l'esprit des lois* (1748). Montesquieu was little interested in the primitive forms of the social state. He did distinguish between "savage" hunters, who lived dispersed in clans, and "barbarous" shepherds, who lived "in small nations capable of being united," but he did so in the course of discussing the quality of land as a variable affecting the form of the state. Savages and barbarians differed from the groups he was more concerned with in that they were governed almost solely "by nature and by climate." Elsewhere he tended to argue the dominance of moral over physical causes in the formation of the *esprit général*: thus, while climate and topography impelled Asia to despotism, there were numerous other contributing factors that could be manipulated in the interest of political stability. But if Montesquieu was far from being a simple environmental determinist, he nevertheless tended to conceptualize the social world more in spatial than in temporal terms. And while the thrust of his whole work was to elucidate the variety of factors governing the historical development of nations, that development was still viewed in terms of repeated patterns of growth and degeneration, rather than of unilineal progress. Nevertheless, Montesquieu's social typologies and systematic comparisons helped to direct social inquiry beyond Europe to the total range of social phenomena, greatly stimulating the search for their general causes.[16]

During the winter of 1750–1751, Adam Smith in Edinburgh and Baron Turgot at the Sorbonne each gave lectures attempting a more general or scientific formulation of the idea of progress in civilization. While Smith's do not as such survive, Turgot's clearly reflect the stimulus of Montesquieu, with one profound difference: Turgot's comparison is structured by time. An early passage provides a clear statement of what was later to be called the "comparative method" of sociocultural evolutionism: "thus the present state of the world . . . spreads out at one and the same time all the gradations from barbarism to refinement, thereby revealing to us at a single glance . . . all the steps taken by the human mind, a reflection of all the stages through which it has passed." Paeanist to the progress of the century of Louis, Newton, and Reason, Turgot arranged in time what Montesquieu conceived in spatial terms. The move was far from unprecedented: Lucretian developmentalism, postdiluvial histories of the gentile nations, even the history of salvation offered models of linear development, just as Lafitau and others provided precedents for historical reconstruction on the basis of cultural comparison. Nevertheless, Turgot's work does represent a change of some importance in the history of social anthropological theory. Although later eighteenth-century progressivists often acknowledged a great debt to Montesquieu, between him and them the primary axis of cultural comparison had been displaced by ninety degrees, from the horizontal (or spatial) to the vertical (or temporal).[17]

Turgot worked out his argument more systematically in two discourses "On Universal History." The first traced the "Formation of

Governments and the Intermingling of Nations'' in the context of a more elaborate theory of socioeconomic stages. Reduced to savagery in the aftermath of the Flood, men had lived widely dispersed in small groups of wandering hunters, until they finally discovered that they could herd certain animals rather than chase them. From here, Turgot followed the development of man through the pastoral or barbarous stage, with its cycles of migration and conquest, to the agricultural stage, in which a stationary population with a disposable surplus and the need for defense provided the basis for more complex social differentiation, and the city came to dominate over the countryside. From there on, Turgot sketched a generalized view of the development of government, emphasizing the pressures leading to the growth of despotic empires on unbroken plains, and the rarer growth of small republics in areas of broken topography. In the second discourse, Turgot traced ''The Progress of the Human Mind.'' Beginning in the reasonings of men who searched for causes beyond the capacity of their understanding, science gradually disentangled itself from error and moved toward the goal of truth—unless, as among the Asiatics, it was forestalled by ''precocious maturity.''[18]

In all of this Turgot was inclined to give a large role to individual men of genius and to the essentially diffusionary process of the intercommunication of ideas. Nevertheless, much of later sociocultural evolutionary thinking (including Comte's law of the three states and Tylor's animism) was contained in these two short discourses. From 1750 on, developmental problems were central to the agenda of social theoretical speculation. Following Turgot, similar themes and variations were elaborated in the works of Jean-Jacques Rousseau, Antoine-Yves Goguet, Charles de Brosses, Lord Kames, Adam Ferguson, Nicolas-Antoine Boulanger, Cornelius de Pauw, Abbé Reynal, John Millar, Jean-Nicolas Demeunier, Adam Smith, William Robertson, and others—down through the culmination of the tradition in Condorcet's *Sketch for a Historical Picture of the Progress of the Human Mind* in 1795.[19]

French and Scottish writers shared a belief in human progress, a notion of ''civilization'' as its encompassing expression, and the idea that its development might be studied philosophically. They also shared the basic assumption of what is often referred to, somewhat anachronistically and rather too specifically, as *the* comparative method: the idea that in the absence of traditional historical evidence, the earlier phases of civilization could be reconstructed by using data derived from the observation of peoples still living in earlier ''stages'' of development—which may be regarded as the methodological expression of the displacement of Montesquieu's axis of comparison.[20] Nevertheless, there were differences between the French and Scottish natural historians of progress; and if we are to understand the special character of Victorian evolutionary thinking, it is necessary, even at the risk of oversimplification, to suggest some distinctions.

The most basic of these is a difference in psychological assumptions. Starting from the Lockean *tabula rasa*—naturalized as Condillac's statue with the single sense of smell—French writers tended to view the human mind as a response to the external world, built up from sensations by the laws of association. By contrast, Scottish progressivists—profoundly disturbed by the skeptical implications their countryman David Hume had educed from Lockean principles, and following in the "moral sense" tradition of Shaftesbury and Hutcheson—insisted that there were mental principles which were not the products of observation and experience; in general, they conceived the mind as founded upon inherent "active powers," appetitive needs, and intuitive perceptions.[21] Correspondingly, the French tended to see human development as the progress of human reason, gradually extricating itself from superstition and error; they were particularly interested in the nature of primitive mentality and the evolution of religious belief. By contrast, the Scots tended to see progress as grounded in the passional nature of man, and in the conditions of social and economic life—subsistence modes, the division of labor, and the institution of property. Whereas the Scots emphasized the unintended consequences of human action, the French emphasized the conscious creative capacity of the human mind, and made progress part of an activist political program, which led toward utilitarian liberalism. The Scots were rather more conservative, showing at the same time a certain precursory affinity to Marxism.[22]

Underlying these distinctions, however, was a broader movement unifying French and Scottish attitudes toward the progress of civilization. Until rather late in the eighteenth century, there was a strong tension between progressivist ideas and more traditional modes. Whether based on the biblical idea of the Fall, on classical notions of a primitive Golden Age, or upon revived conceptions of the cyclical movement of social life, the dominant inherited intellectual models emphasized processes of degeneration and decay.[23] The "cosmic optimism" that emerged in the earlier years of the eighteenth century was not so much a hopeful creed as a vindication of the status quo founded on the static hierarchy of the age-old Chain of Being. The reversal of assumption involved in the development of a systematically progressivist conception of civilization was not easily accomplished. History—recorded rather than conjectured—provided plenty of evidence of decline, but there was no secular historical model for indefinite progress.[24]

Furthermore, while the cultural and social change of their own lifetimes buttressed progressivist assumptions, there was a sense of loss as well as of gain in the lived experience of progress. Scots and Frenchmen both bemoaned the decay of virtue and the growth of luxury and vice. The ambiguous "noble savage" of Rousseau's "Discourse on Inequality" was not the only manifestation of primitivism or historical pessimism among the French philosophers of progress.[25] A similar ambivalence is evident among Scots who worried lest the manly virtues be sacrificed to the development of commercial and industrial society. When James MacPherson "discovered" his fraudulent odes of Ossian in 1761, Lord Kames and Adam Ferguson became staunch defenders of these foundation "documents" of the romantic movement, with their picture of ancestral Scots—otherwise quite primitive—whose manners were "so pure and refined as scarce to be paralleled in the most cultivated nations."[26] All of which is simply to suggest that it took some time for primitivist assumptions to be disentangled from the idea of progress in civilization, and for the "noble savages" and the Chinese sages who provided the weaponry of social criticism among the *philosophes* to be relegated to their eventual positions on the ladder of civilization.[27]

Optimism, however, grew stronger with each passing decade. There is a rough correlation of cosmic attitude and date of birth among these precursors of the social sciences. Vico (1668) and Montesquieu (1689) never entirely abandoned older cyclical views; Kames (1696) still spoke of a "progress" of decay and corruption; Monboddo (1714) even defended the ancient metaphysics against the Newtonian. The first systematic promulgators of progressivist assumptions, Smith and Turgot, were born in the 1720s; and among both Scots and French, the most unambiguously progressivist were the latest born: John Millar (1735), who despite his more explicitly sociological orientation, was in other respects the Scotsman closest to the French; and Condorcet (1744), who was able to contemplate the ultimate perfectibility of man while hiding from the guillotine.[28]

That this intellectual movement was in a general sense precursory to modern anthropology seems clear enough. But it is important to insist on the embracive singularity of this prototypical "Science of Man": it was the laws and potentialities of human nature in general that focused attention. William Robertson stated the goal clearly in suggesting that "to complete the history of the human mind, and attain to a perfect knowledge of its nature and operations, we must contemplate man in all those various situations wherein he has been placed, [and] follow him in his progress through the different stages of society."[29]

This focus on generic human nature had important implications for the "anthropology" of the Enlightment. By and large, eighteenth-century anthropology did not seriously question the basic unity of all the diverse groups who had been contacted in the age of discovery—a unity which was also the heritage of the Christian tradition. This is not to suggest that the Enlightenment lacked a sense of human differences as a problem to be explained, nor to deny the widespread evidence of a negative evaluation of non-European groups. The emerging idea of progress in civilization was closely linked with a heightened self-consciousness of European identity and cultural superiority, which Voltaire had expressed in the image of Europe as "a kind of great republic" with a common set of religious and political beliefs "unknown in the other parts of the world."[30]

Not only did "civilization" tend to have a definite geographical location, but various widespread ideas about human difference also gave it a quasi-racial aspect: traditional humoral and environmental notions of the formation of human character and physical type; the idea of the Chain of Being, in which the Huron and the Hottentot were links between the European and the orangutan; the Buffonian theory of the degeneration of all animal species in the New World—which until quite late in the century remained the locus classicus of savage man.[31] Such ideas have stimulated scholarship on the "racism" of the Enlightenment, and there were in fact those—like Kames—who followed La Peyrère in arguing that only a separate "local creation" could account for the population of America.[32] But in general it seems fair to say that the eighteenth-century writers did not conceptualize human diversity in rigidly hereditarian or strictly physical terms, if only because comparative anatomy and physical anthropology were barely beginning to provide the basis for such thinking.[33] Furthermore, developmental speculation was still severely constrained by traditional biblical limits of human time and biological species. Although earth history had been stretched considerably in the preceding century, resistance to the expansion of human existence continued very strong; if Rousseau speculated that "many thousands of centuries would have been necessary to develop successively in the human mind the operations of which it was capable," he still felt it necessary to characterize his reasoning as merely "hypothetical and conditional." And although there were several exceptions among the French, the "evolutionism" of the progressivists was essentially social and not biological. Arguments that orangutans were in fact men assumed a considerable modification of mankind in the civilizing process, but they did not assume a crossing of species boundaries, nor any fundamental modification or differentiation of human nature.[34] Allowing something for the effects of prolonged environmental influences, what separated savage man from civilized man was not a difference in inherent mental makeup so much as the progress of refinement and of civilization itself.

By the same token, civilization, like man, was singular: the plural of the noun did not appear until the nineteenth century.[35] This, too, had important limiting implications for eighteenth-century anthropology. It was not simply that the nascent impulse to relativism was constrained within a single hierarchical framework. A case can be made that the progressivists were not interested in the data of cultural variety for its own sake. Among the French especially, the savage was important as a counter in current polemic: as a pawn in the quarrel between the ancients and moderns, as a proxy in the battle against institutionalized Christianity, or as a foil in the critique of contemporary social forms. One studied the "sociology of error"—or perhaps better, its social psychology—in order to establish the meaning of rational progress. Although the *philosophes* had an implicit idea of culture as a generic human characteristic, they had no real notion of culture as the constituting medium of different thought worlds. All that intervened between the essential rationality of basic human needs and the potential rationality of social institutions to satisfy them was superstition and error—encouraged of course by despots and priests. Despite differences in psychological assumption, the same might be said of the Scots. What was critically problematic in their social thought was not the origin of civilization in savagery, or the variety of its forms, but the progress of civilization in Europe. If the point is overdrawn, it nonetheless highlights the fact that for the Enlightenment, there was civilization, but no culture in the modern anthropological sense.[36]

Despite these limitations, there emerged in France and Scotland in the years before the French Revolution a dual tradition of social theoretical speculation in which the problem of civilization was of central importance. We have not attempted to consider the extent to which it represented a peculiarly "bourgeois" vision, the ways in which it reflected the historical circumstances of racial and cultural contact, or how its variants were conditioned by specific national experience. The point has been rather to characterize eighteenth-century intellectual currents that attempted to formulate in general typological and causal terms the development of human ideas and institutions from some primitive or "natural" state. Many of the methodological assumptions, general developmental sequences, and specific substantive conceptions of later sociocultural evolutionism can be found within these currents: the idea of human "psychic unity"; the "comparative method"; the "stages" of intellectual and socioeconomic development; the shift from military to commercial society; the ideas of primitive fetishism, static oriental despotism, and the vigor of man in European temperate zones. At the same time, we have hinted at certain differences of attitude and assumption that will later take on greater significance. For the present, however, let us see how the problem of civilization was approached in different national intellectual traditions in the early nineteenth century, in relation to their characteristic modes of inquiry in the human sciences.

The History of Culture in Germany

During the period when "civilization" took on its modern meaning in France and Scotland, a parallel process of social redefinition was taking place in Germany. The characteristically German term for the development and cumulative achievement of human capacity was not "civilization" but "culture"—a more concretely metaphorical word, with an already long traditional reference to the process of personal cultivation. "Civilization" was also incorporated into German usage, but the German reaction against the cultural imperialism of the French Enlightenment, and a growing sense of economic and political backwardness to France and England, were expressed in a complex historical tension between the two terms. At times synonyous, often overlapping, but in general somewhat antithetical in meaning, "civilization" came to connote the universal "external" phenomena of material progress and social organization; "culture," the varied "inward" moral and aesthetic manifestations of the human spirit.[37]

The specific character of German thought on human cultural development is manifest in Johann Gottfried Herder. One can find in Herder's thought a certain conception of universal human progress and an implicit hierarchy of cultural achievement—as well as the "comparative method." But although influenced by them, Herder reacted sharply against French models; and although the Scottish commonsense philosophy was more congenial to the German mind than Anglo-French associationism, he wrote a sharply critical review of Millar's *Origin of Ranks*. Bitterly contemptuous of those who saw their own age as "the summit of human culture," Herder was much more pluralistic, relativistic, and historicist than the French or Scots.[38] He emphasized the variety of national characters, seeing each as the unique outcome of a people's environmental and historical experience, embodied in its own mythology, which was the characteristic religious, esthetic, and ethical expression of the *Volksgeist*. Never fully commensurable, these national spirits were all equally manifestations of divine immanence realizing itself in the spiritual development of humanity as a whole. Formed far in the past, each national spirit unfolded organically from an "internal prototype": Jews, scattered through the world, remained spiritually the same as in the land of their fathers; blacks, fired with "boiling passions" by the burning tropic sun, were permanently denied the "finer intellect" of Europeans. Only the "well-formed" men molded by temperate climes could have produced the "cultivation and humanity" peculiar to Europe. Paradoxically, Herder is thus not only a source of cultural pluralism and anthropological relativism, but also of nationalist and even racialist assumptions.[39]

More significantly for present purposes, Herder represents perhaps the most important individual source of German romanticism in all its varied manifestations. The positive evaluation of mythopoeic mentality, the historical conception of national individuality, the interest in traditional German folklore, the search for the oriental roots of Western culture, even the program for a comparative study of languages, as well as the historical movement in a narrower sense—all can be traced to Herder. Oversimplifying, one might say that during the period of the Revolutionary and Napoleonic Wars Herder's personal rebellion against "Gallomania" became a generalized reaction against the French Enlightenment—the "revolt of outraged history," in Lord Acton's words, which made "the ages of faith and imagination a defense from the age of reason."[40]

In this context, the early nineteenth century saw the blossoming of humanistic inquiry in Germany, as the spirit of historicism and stricter conceptions of method combined to transform a relatively undifferentiated philological tradition into a series of specialized fields in which German scholarship won international preeminence. We will focus here on only two of these in which certain attitudinal and methodological issues bearing on the study of civilization are clearly expressed: historical scholarship in the strict sense and comparative philology.[41]

In the words of the great classical historian Barthold Niebuhr, historians were "attracted to many forgotten and decayed institutions by the sound of their downfall"—and by the revolutionary attempt to reconstruct them. Rejecting the "impulse of fabrication" that made or unmade laws at the whim of the legislator, Karl von Savigny—the other founding figure of the "historical school"—echoed Herder in insisting that the substance of law "proceeded from the inner nature of the nation and from its history." The basic problem of jurisprudence was therefore to trace that history "back to its origin, in order to grasp the core of our law conditions." In the aftermath of the end of the Holy Roman Empire in 1806, both Savigny and Niebuhr turned to the study of Roman institutions. Because the German "races" had enjoyed the fruits of Roman cultural forms at second hand, by conquering nations formerly under imperial rule, they had been able to rise from barbarism without smothering the "noble peculiarities" of their "national genius." Pursuing the "ideas on which the institutions of the Roman state" were founded, Niebuhr produced a history of Roman origins that ended where Gibbon began; by contrast, Savigny traced the influence of Roman law beyond the Fall of Rome into medieval and early modern Europe.[42]

The characteristic idealist assumptions of German humanistic inquiry, although not yet formalized in the distinction between the *Geistes-* and the *Naturwissenschaften,* were already implicit in the historicist viewpoint. Niebuhr suggested that the difficulty Asiatics had in conceiving the "idea" of a republican constitution was no greater than that facing modern historians of early Rome. Only by sweeping their minds free of "habitual associations" through "critical and philological studies" could historians hope to enter a thought world in which apparently familiar ideas had different meanings. Thus in the sphere of human spiritual activity, knowledge was not a matter of formulating general laws, but rather an empathetic process of understanding.[43]

Other attitudinal and methodological considerations, however, were in fact to limit the range of human experience in which the historical school attempted to apply this understanding. Although Niebuhr began his history with an ethnographic survey of the ancient peoples of Italy, he mocked the developmental notions of the philosophical histories "with which we were surfeited during the latter half of the last century." Savagery was a degenerative state that provided no basis for reasoning about ultimate origins; the true historian should in any case "confine himself to going backward from one step of time to another."[44] Given the documentary orientation and the critical methods of classical philology which Niebuhr and later Leopold von Ranke propagated among historians, this historicist principle of continuity worked to exclude many non-European peoples from the purview of history entirely. Furthermore, the very concept of the "nation" had undergone redefinition since the time of Herder. Remolded in the fire of German resistance to the French, nationalism was no longer cosmopolitan, but divisive, and national identity had come to be equated with the "state," conceived in "power-political" terms. In this context, Rankean history, although written on a canvas that swept across Europe, was much narrower in subject matter than the "universal" histories of the late-eighteenth-century Göttingen school.[45]

There were, however, other currents of German romantic historicism in which broader views of human history flourished—although here, too, attitudinal and methodological constraints were to have a narrowing impact. From the time the British jurist Sir William Jones organized the Asiatick Society of Bengal in 1784, a continuing stream of publications based on ancient Persian and Sanskrit texts sustained a literary and scholarly interest in the Orient in which German writers played a leading role. From the beginning, the assumptions embodied in orientalism ran counter in important respects to those of the philosophers of progress. Jones' presidential discourses to the Asiatick Society attempted to fit the history of the ancient East into a framework of traditional biblical assumption, with the races dispersed from the family of Noah each retaining an underlying knowledge of primitive monotheistic revelation, but gradually degenerating into polytheism. It was in this context that Jones argued that the gods of Greece, Italy, and India were actually the same, and that Greek, Latin, and Sanskrit were related languages derived from "some common source, which, perhaps, no longer exists." At the same time, Jones held a much more positive view of Indian civilization than Montesquieu and his progressivist heirs, at least as far as its past glories were concerned.[46]

For a brief period in the German romantic movement, this positive evaluation produced a kind of "Indomania," as the spiritual coherence of the Middle Ages was rediscovered in a primitivist Indian Golden Age. Paradise was shifted eastward from Mesopotamia; God himself was said to have invented the Sanskrit characters; and India was seen as the birthplace of all wisdom and art. In this spirit, Friedrich Schlegel went to Paris in 1802 to immerse himself in manuscript sources and learn the Sanskrit language. By 1805, however, H.T. Colebrooke's essay on the much older Vedas had called into question the monotheistic image derived from Jones' *Laws of Manu,* and Schlegel's enthusiasm waned considerably before he published *On the Language and Wisdom of the Indians* in 1808. Although still insisting that the doctrine of emanation was a "perverted conception of revealed truth," he now emphasized the "savage errors" of its subsequent degeneration into astrology and materialism. What remained in the aftermath of Indomania was orientalism—and historical linguistics. Elaborating Jones on the affinities of Sanskrit, Schlegel offered a prospectus for the science of comparative philology: "that decisive factor which will clear up everything is the inner structure of languages, or comparative grammar, which will give us altogether new insights into the genealogy of languages, in a manner similar to that in which comparative anatomy has shed light on higher natural history."[47]

Within a short time, Schlegel's program began to be realized. In 1816, Franz Bopp produced the work usually taken to mark the beginning of comparative philology, *The Conjugation System of the Sanskrit Language,* in which the relations of what Bopp later called the Indo-European languages were explored by systematic analysis of their verbal inflections. Other scholars, fired by romantic interest in national cultural origins, approached comparative philology from the outer branches of the Indo-European tree. When Schlegel's brother August criticized the early folklore studies of the Brothers Grimm for their "ignorance of linguistic laws," Jacob Grimm formulated the most famous of such laws: "Grimm's law" of the sound shifts in the Germanic languages. By 1833, when the volumes of Bopp's monumental *Comparative Grammar* began to appear, Schlegel's vision had been fulfilled: the genealogical classification of languages had indeed given comparative philology a place within the human studies analogous to that of comparative anatomy within biology.[48]

The new comparative philology—later to be distinguished more sharply from classical philology as comparative "linguistics"—often tended to be assimilated to the natural sciences, because it revealed a natural human capacity expressing itself in deterministic manner, beyond the control of individual human will, but susceptible to a rigorous systematic study that demonstrated underlying laws. In contrast to comparative anatomy, which still conceived the sequence of biological forms in discontinuous pre-evolutionary terms, comparative philology had a more clearly dynamic diachronic character. But if it offered a law-governed model of branching development in time, it, too, was in a sense pre-evolutionary, since human linguistic capacity tended to be sharply (even divinely) differentiated from purely animal faculties. In this context, early-nineteenth-century comparative philology, like other humanistic inquiries in this period, still reflects various assumptions characteristic of the biblical tradition.[49]

Although older etymological approaches tracing the degeneration of languages from an original Hebrew tongue had gone out of fashion, the underlying model of early comparative philology was still degenerationist. True, there was a subcurrent of "morphological" or "typological" classification, stemming also from Schlegel and elaborated by Wilhelm von Humboldt, which had an ambiguously progressivist character. In this framework, all languages were classified into three or four groups according to their essential grammatical principle: the "isolating" (Chinese); the "agglutinative" (a vast residual category from which the American Indian languages were sometimes separated as "incorporative" or "polysynthetic"); and the "inflectional" (Indo-European and Semitic)—which some writers saw as standing in a developmental sequence. But Bopp refused to do so, and the basic thrust of comparative philology was toward the study of demonstrable genealogical relationships, which tended still to be seen in terms of degenerative processes modifying older structurally more perfect forms. Similarly, the persistance of such categories as Semitic, Hamitic, and Japhetic (the latter one of several competing names for the Indo-European family) suggests the continuing influence of the biblically based conception of world historical process as a sequential migration of populations from a central geographical point. In this context, comparative philology seemed to lend the potential of its methodological rigor to an attempt, on the basis of linguistic and other similarities, to trace the affinities of all the various "races" of man, and if possible to reduce their present diversity to a primitive unity analogous to that of the Indo-European language family—an approach that for several decades provided the methodological underpinning for a study called "ethnology."[50]

But there was also a diversifying thrust within the intellectual movement of which comparative philology was a part. In this context world history was conceived in migrational terms, with a sequence of peoples moving across the face of Europe from a primitive Aryan homeland.

However, in contrast to the dominant monogenetic tendency of the ethnological tradition, the emphasis was not so much on reducing present variety to original unity as on the preservation of racial essence. In the context of the earlier romantic orientalist effort to de-Judaize Christianity, in the aftermath of Johann Fichte's appeal to the German *Urvolk* against the French *Mischvolk*, comparative philology was sometimes influenced by emerging racialist assumption. Indeed, it provided a major intellectual buttress for the German tendency, from Herder through Schlegel to Hegel (and beyond), to visualize the progress of culture (or civilization) as a movement from East to West across Asia, conceived in racial terms, with the Germanic peoples as the carriers of the purest or highest manifestations of the divine spirit.[51]

The conceptualization of human progress that developed in Germany in the decades before 1830 was thus in various ways strikingly different from that which had emerged west of the Rhine prior to 1800. The influence of traditional religious belief was more directly manifest, and primitivist attitudes which in France and Scotland were gradually excluded from the concept of civilization were to some extent incorporated into the culture/civilization duality. In the context of the post-Kantian idealist tradition in German philosophy, this contrast between inward spiritual growth and external hedonist utility was paralleled by an epistemological duality, in which the phenomena of human historical development tended to be separated from rather than integrated into the model of knowledge appropriate to the natural sciences. There was, however, an evaluational ambiguity contained within the culture idea. While in a sense more relativistic than the Enlightenment conception of a universal civilizing process, the pluralistic organicism of German culture had not only a nationalist but even a racialist potential. In a period in which humanistic scholarship in Germany began to be seen as offering a model of disciplined inquiry, these trends in German cultural thought were to have considerable impact on Anglo-French thinking about the problem of civilization.[52]

The Science of Progress in France

By 1830 the intellectual currents of the revolutionary epoch had affected speculation about the problem of civilization in France as well. Condorcet's successor prophets of progress carried on the eighteenth-century tradition, but in doing so they moved ''from equality to organicism.'' This shift was evident as early as 1803, when Saint-Simon argued that the revolutionaries had erred in applying ''the principles of equality'' to blacks. Had they consulted the ''physiologists''—Vicq-d'Azir, Bichat, Pinel, and particularly Cabanis—they would have learned that "the negro, because of his basic physical structure, is not susceptible, even with the same education, of rising to the intellectual level of Europeans."[53]

Although he was closely associated with the *idéologue* heirs of Locke and Condillac, and remained in general an environmentalist, Cabanis in fact modified the sensationalist tradition at its source, by arguing that the sensations of the external world on which all thought processes depended were not the same for all humans, but varied with age, sex, temperament, health, regimen, and climate. Those who were inclined to question traditional psychological assumptions were offered an even more staunchly determinist and physicalist viewpoint when Franz Gall and his collegue J.C. Spurzheim settled in Paris in 1807. Their new science of phrenology saw human intellectual and moral capacity in strongly determinist terms, with different human faculties localized in particular regions of the brain and reflected in the external form of the skull—at a time when the racial variation of the human skull was beginning to be the subject of systematic comparative anatomical concern.[54]

When Linnaeus first included man in his *System of Nature,* his division was still grounded in the age-old humoral tradition, with skin color corresponding to psychological type. By 1800, some comparative anatomical material had been collected; Samuel von Sömmering had dissected blacks and Europeans; Charles White had made anthropometric comparisons; Peter Camper had developed a measure of the facial angle; and Johann Blumenbach had begun the publication of his *Decades Craniorum.* Although White was a polygenist, investigation was still largely carried on in terms of the orthodox monogenetic assumption that all men were one species. The underlying biblical model is quite evident in Blumenbach's racial classification, which was the most widely accepted in the pre-Darwinian nineteenth century: all five races were the offspring of a single primeval Caucasian type, which had "degenerated" in two directions under the influence of environment—on the one hand, through the American toward the Mongolian; and on the other, through the Malayan toward the Ethiopian.[55] But when the great French comparative anatomist Georges Cuvier offered his own tripartite racial classification in 1817, the impact of the phrenological movement and the general shift away from egalitarianism were clearly evident.

Although his own early views on the capacity of blacks had tended toward egalitarian environmentalism, Cuvier now spoke of "that cruel law which seems to have condemned to an eternal inferiority the races of depressed and compressed skulls," and came as close to embracing polygenism as his profound establishmentarianism would allow. Given its emphasis on the structural correlates of organic function, its narrowly limited view of the modifying influence of environment, its impulse to classification, and its static teleological conception of biological "type," the implicit thrust of Cuvierian comparative anatomy—for those not inhibited by religious orthodoxy—was clearly toward a polygenetic view of human racial differences. In the 1820s, this impulse was strikingly manifest in France in the work of such men as Bory de Saint-Vincent, Desmoulins, Virey, and William Edwards, a naturalized Jamaican physiologist who lectured Restoration historians on the inadequacies of the traditional linguistic view of race.[56]

Over time, the inegalitarian assumptions of the emerging racialist physical anthropology had a considerable impact on thinking about the progress of civilization. But the most influential form of early-nineteenth-century developmentalist thought—Comtean positivism—was less affected by notions of human hereditary inequality than by more generalized biological ideas about "life," "organization," and the problems of classification and comparison. And perhaps as important as the new biology in the shift toward "organicism" was the influence of French analogues of the romantic historicists beyond the Rhine: the émigré Catholic traditionalists Joseph de Maistre and Louis de Bonald. From their perspective, the Revolution's systematic attack on the monarchy, the estates, the church, the guilds, and the family had left society without any institutional restraint upon the centrifugal atomism of liberal individualism other than the centripetal tyranny of the revolutionary state itself. In reaction, they returned to medieval Europe for the model of an organic society—an ordered hierarchy of social groups morally integrated by religion.[57]

It was in this dual context of early-nineteenth-century biological thought and the social ideas of theocratic conservatives that first Saint-Simon and then his rejecting (and rejected) young disciple Auguste Comte reworked the progressivism of Condorcet to create a new "positive" science of social man. In 1822, in his "Plan of the Scientific Operations Necessary for Reorganising Society," Comte sought to resolve the prolonged crisis of the "most civilized nations" by inducing liberal spokesmen to abandon their purely "negative" critical attitude toward the old Catholic-feudal system. Although the downfall of the old order was "the necessary consequence of the progress of Civilisation," it was chimerical to assume one could construct a new "social system" in a few months, since society was only possible on the basis of a uniform "system of general ideas." The dogmas of liberty of conscience and popular sovereignty—natural manifestations of the "critical" phase—were obstacles to the positive "organic" attitude that could alone end the present anarchy. Fortunately, there was one group with both the capacity and the moral authority to "terminate the Revolutionary Epoch": the men of science.[58]

Comte saw scientific knowledge evolving through three successive states: the theological or fictitious, in which a small number of isolated observations were linked by supernatural ideas; the metaphysical or abstract, in which a larger number of facts were linked to ideas conceived as personified abstractions; and the scientific or positive, in which great numbers of facts were connected by the smallest possible number of general laws, each in turn suggested or confirmed by facts. In one science after another—astronomy, physics, chemistry, and, most recently, physiology—observation had conquered imagination, until only politics remained behind on the metaphysical level. The key to the solution of the present crisis was for scientific men "to elevate politics to the rank of a science of observation." Ignorance might lead some to oppose and even temporarily forestall the inevitable progress of civilization, but since "no one is so foolish as knowingly to place himself in opposition to the nature of things," the demonstration and the propagation of the "law of progress" was both the first task and the major mechanism of social reorganization.[59]

But if Comte turned the lost medieval order of the traditionalists into further evidence that human progress was governed by purely natural laws, he did not subordinate his positive science of politics totally to biological imperatives. Although "social physics" was a branch of physiology, there was an important distinction: for physiology, the significant organic entity was the individual; for social physics, it was the race. Physiologists did not need to concern themselves with this difference, since animals were not progressive and had no history. But once language had given the first impulse to civilization, the condition of each human generation depended on that of the preceding, and any deduction of regularities of collective behavior from laws of individual physiology was doomed to failure. In this context, the primary method of social physics was comparison, and especially that variant of comparison Comte later spoke of as the "historical method." The former compared the "different states of society coexisting" in the present; the latter, the "consecutive states of humanity" through its total development.[60]

Even so, Comte's social physics was strongly biological in character. Rejecting mathematical analysis on the ground that Bichat had shown its inapplicability to organic phenomena, he was far from pleased when the Belgian astronomer Adolphe Quetelet applied the Laplacian calculus of probabilities to empirical social data and (independently of Comte) used "social physics" in the subtitle of a very influential argument for the deterministic character of moral and social phenomena. It was in this context that Comte differentiated his own inquiry by the neologism "sociology." Similarly, Comte excluded psychology from his hierarchy of sciences, preferring to incorporate into physiology a ''positive theory of cerebral functions'' that had a strongly phrenological cast. Comte's essential biologism was reflected also in his later distinction between social statics and social dynamics. The ''master thought'' of the former—''the radical consensus proper to the social organism''—was the ''consequence and complement'' of a fundamental idea already established in biology; and although social dynamics was differentiated from biology by ''the master thought of continuous progress,'' Comte still argued that the ''whole social evolution of the race must proceed in entire accordance with biological laws.''[61]

This did not, however, imply a belief in biological evolutionism. It was rather that, standing at the head of an essentially static organic hierarchy, mankind added to it a dimension of change in time, so that in prolonging the biological series, the terms of the sociological series were successive rather than coexisting. Neither did it imply much concern with the differences between human races. Although human progress was reflected physically in an increased cerebral capacity, and there were suggestions that race was a factor affecting its rate, Comte tended to emphasize the ''necessary invariableness of the human organism'' at every degree of the social scale. Nor, indeed, was Comte much concerned with cultural variability, except in terms of his hierarchy of social development, which had been defined by contrasting the medieval order with the Europe of his own day. Though he eventually elaborated his periodization to differentiate ''fetishism,'' ''polytheism,'' and ''monotheism'' within the ''theological'' stage, non-European savage man played both a minimal and a culturally undifferentiated role in Comte's sociological thought. Comte's vision was in fact largely limited to the white race, and his conception of civilization, though in principle universally human, was in practice Europocentric.[62]

In one form or another, the problem of civilization was the concern of numerous publicists, economists, philosophers, and historians in France around 1830. Some, reflecting an old French tradition that conceived class differences in quasi-racial terms, or influenced by German romantic thought, tended toward pluralistic racial views (although race, in these contexts, was usually more a linguistic than a physical category). Others, like François Guizot—with whom the idea of civilization was perhaps most prominently identified—thought more in terms of a unified conception of European progress, reaching its apogee of course in France. But it was the successive volumes of Comte's *Positive Philosophy,* finally completed in 1842, that offered the most systematic and influential model for an ostensibly *scientific* study of human progress in civilization. Uniting the traditionalist conception of ''Order'' with the eighteenth-century conception of ''Progress''—''as rigorously inseparable as the ideas of Organization and Life in Biology''—the hierarchy of positive sciences provided both the essential mechanism of the civilizational process and the principles for understanding it.[63]

The Problem of Civilization in England

According to Michel Foucault, the human sciences as we know them are the product of a radical rupture at the end of the eighteenth century in the unconscious metastructures of western European thought, which gave new meaning to the empirical phenomena of language, life, and labor. Although it would carry us too far afield to interpret the problem of civilization in Foucault's terms, it is worth noting that the positive disciplines associated with these three phenomena after 1800 were tied to specific national traditions: comparative philology was characteristically a German, comparative anatomy a French, and political economy a British inquiry. Not surprisingly, thinking about the problem of civilization in Great Britain was strongly conditioned by ideas about human labor, and more generally by the thought modes of political economy.[64]

But if the idea of civilization developed in Britain in the shadow of the Industrial Revolution, it did not escape the impact of the political revolution whose effects we have noticed already in Germany and France. For a whole generation, the fate and character of European civilization hung in the balance, and from the beginning the idea itself was implicated in the crisis. Thus for Edmund Burke, to whom the French Revolution recalled the spectacle of ''American savages'' returning from the ''murders'' they called victories, European civilization had depended for ages on ''the spirit of a gentleman, and the spirit of religion,'' both of which had nurtured the pursuit of learning. Commerce, trade, and manufacture had grown up under ''the shade in which learning flourished,'' and would decay if its supporting principles were extinguished. In sharp contrast, Thomas Paine found the ''savagery'' of modern life in the wretchedness of the masses, whose state was ''far below the condition of an Indian.'' For him, the achievement of ''more perfect civilization'' involved the elimination of government and the freeing of the forces of economic individualism. The issues implicit in this confrontation—the locus of modern savagery, the orientation of civilization toward the past or toward the future, and the relation of civilization to the institutions of class, of religion, of government, and of economic life—reflected general historical processes transforming British society. But after 1792, cultural awareness tended to be displaced, as it were, upon the French Revolution, which conditioned the discussion of ''civilization'' in Britain for much of the early nineteenth century.[65]

The center of that discussion shifted south within the British Isles. Young Englishmen continued to come to Edinburgh, where many of them heard the lectures of Dugald Stewart, heir to Adam Ferguson in the chair of moral philosophy. But Stewart's biographical efforts on behalf of earlier Scots from whom his own thought was derivative suggest that he was in fact the residuary legatee of the eighteenth-century Scottish tradition. The political reaction against the French Revolution, which forced Paine to leave England, may have been a factor in its decline: both Stewart and Millar were subjected to political attack in the 1790s. But the tradition of "conjectural history" was already weakening when Stewart coined its name in 1793. His own efforts were directed to the study of the human mind, in which he followed the "common sense" psychology, and to political economy, in which he followed Adam Smith. As the nineteenth century progressed, the former became more parochially Scottish, at least within the British Isles. In contrast, political economy was a very successful intellectual export.[66]

Below the Tweed, however, discussion took place in a distinct philosophical milieu. There the Lockean psychological tradition had been developed by David Hartley along lines paralleling Condillac, and Joseph Priestley had attacked the assumptions of Scottish "common sense." Combining Hartley's associationism with Hume's principle of utility, Jeremy Bentham in 1789 enunciated the doctrine of utilitarianism: pleasure and pain were the two "sovereign masters" of mankind, and the principle of utility (or greatest happiness) founded on their governance was the sole standard of morality and the basis for establishing morals as an objective science of human behavior. There is no need here to retrace the history of utilitarianism—its problems with the natural as opposed to the artificial identification of individual human egoisms, its incorporation into Smithian political economy, its transformation under the influence of James Mill into a democratic political doctrine, its later history as philosophical radicalism, or its relation to the theological utilitarianism of Bishop Paley, which was more diffusely influential in molding the character of British thought. The problem is rather the fate of speculation on the progress of civilization in this utilitarian milieu.[67]

The conflict between psychological assumptions and the philosophy of history in utilitarianism has been a subject of controversy—whether Bentham had a real appreciation "Of the Influence of Time and Place," or whether the legislator could deduce his political principles directly from a human nature assumed to be everywhere the same. Although it has been suggested that there is an "inherently unhistorical or antihistorical bias in associationism," one suspects that what made Benthamite thought ahistorical was not so much the abstract logic of its psychology as the situational logic of its self-conceived historical mission.[68] In France, where the fabric of history and social order had been ripped apart, philosophers of progress turned to the past in order to reweave it. In Britain, where the reaction against revolution threatened to entangle progress in the web of history, philosophers of progress turned from history in order to accomplish the reformation of the political and economic system in the present. In both cases, however, the underlying goal may be posed in similar terms, as the definition of the political and economic conditions of a fully civilized life.

Various early-nineteenth-century movements in British thought may thus be regarded as arenas in which the problem of civilization continued to be discussed by writers preoccupied with other matters than establishing a developmental interpretation of human history—and whose thinking (like that of German historians and philologists) in some respects led to a separation of modern civilization from earlier stages. The economic and political components of philosophical radicalism may both be viewed in these terms.

Although economic analysis came to be carried on within a narrower historical framework, its relation to the problem of civilization was still apparent. In *The Wealth of Nations,* the "rude state of society" provided the basic reference point in explicating the benefits of the division of labor, and Smith frequently distinguished "nations" of hunters, shepherds, and husbandmen from "opulent and civilized nations." Already, however, the consequences of man's natural propensity to "truck, barter, and exchange" were analyzed primarily with reference to the political economy of modern European nations.[69] In Stewart, "barbarous nations" played little role once he reorganized his lectures on moral philosophy in 1800 to give separate status to political economy. David Ricardo, whose *Principles* of 1817 marked the real establishment of the British school, still occasionally referred to "the early stages of society" in his opening discussion of the labor theory of value. However, the introduction of money, "the general medium of exchange between all civilized nations," introduced a discontinuity between the economics of savage and civilized man; and the great bulk of Ricardo's argument was an analysis of the economic conditions of civilized life. The arena of free trade in which the pursuit of individual advantage operated automatically for the good of all was quite explicitly the "universal society of nations throughout the civilized world."[70]

James Mill, in whom the Scottish tradition was united with and then dissolved into the Anglo-French, may be read as introducing a parallel discontinuity into the political development of civilization. In the *History of British India,* Mill argued that Sir William Jones had wrongly described the Hindus as "highly civilized"; Mill now relegated them to a lower place on the scale with all the other "half-civilized," "stationary" Asiatic peoples. Despotism was the mode of government appropriate to their "level of civilization," and under utilitarian influence, British rule in

India took the form of a benevolent administrative despotism. It was only for fully civilized Europeans that the radical political principles of utilitarianism were appropriate. Although the word "civilization" appears only once in Mill's *Essay on Government,* the point of the essay was that "the middling rank" formed the sole appropriate guarantors of representative government because they were "the chief source of all that has exalted and refined human nature"—which was to say that they contributed most to civilization. In this context, the *Essay* may be regarded as an analysis of the political conditions of civilized life.[71]

Turning from what may be called, loosely, the lineage of Paine to that of Burke, it is clear that a concern with the conditions of civilized life also preoccupied more conservative thinkers. William Wilberforce's *Practical View of Christianity,* the charter of the Evangelical Revival, was among other things a disquisition on the place of Christianity in civilization. Attacking William Robertson as a lukewarm Christian and Adam Smith as an apologist for Humean skepticism, and pointing to the French as exemplars of the moral depravity that infidelity inevitably produced, Wilberforce urged his readers not to imagine vainly "that our state of civilization must prevent moral degeneracy." Although the vices that "naturally infest the darkness of a ruder and less polished age" had receded "on the approach of light and civilization," there was a countervailing tendency for the "relaxed morals and dissipated manners" of the "higher orders" to diffuse downward in the social scale, and even for religion itself to decline. This was not, however, due to any antagonism between civilization and *true* Christianity—which was in fact the guarantor of peace and prosperity, the buttress of social order, and the means to arrest "the progress of political decay." Indeed, in an advanced period *only* Christianity could serve this function, and Wilberforce called on the higher orders to reform themselves and to make Britain a "sanctuary" from which Christianity would "be again extended" to the world at large.[72]

As in the realm of economic and political thought, revitalized religion may be seen as introducing a discontinuity into the progress of civilization. Insistence on such discontinuity was in fact one means of accommodating progressive developmentalism to the reasserted claims of divine revelation. Rejecting French and Scottish arguments of the purely human origin of language or of savagery as the original human state, the evangelical churchman John Bird Sumner's *Treatise on the Records of the Creation* saw savagery rather as the consequence of cultural and physical degeneration in the wake of the Deluge. But while some men had degenerated after the Flood, others had progressed along the lines traced by the Scots, until Europe was now "the centre, from which the rays of civilization are diverging in every direction." Although Sumner insisted that all men were one in origin and nature, the effect of his argument was to place the savage not at the foot of a single upward ladder of progress, but at the bottom of a diverging ladder of degeneration. Such views were in fact the common currency of popular religious belief and the missionary movement.[73]

Sumner's book has been described as the means by which a generation of English churchmen were able to reconcile the principles of political economy—and particularly the arguments of Thomas Malthus—"with their reviving concepts of a Christian society"; and it is in fact in the debates around Malthus that the utilitarian and the evangelical streams converge and the various facets of the discussion of the problem of civilization in Great Britain before 1830 begin to come together. Malthus wrote in explicit answer to Condorcet and all others who would overthrow every "present establishment" in the vain pursuit of "the perfectibility of man." But drawing heavily on the Scottish writers, he also saw human development as a progress from savagery to civilization, in which the pressure of population provided the dynamic force. The issue was simply whether at any point in the "natural progress in civilization" the "mass of the people" could ever be free from distress "for want of food." Malthus' answer in 1798 was profoundly pessimistic; and in softening some of his "harshest conclusions" for the second and later editions, he introduced another discontinuity into the discussion of civilization. Among savages and barbarians—whose generally wretched, Hobbesian existence Malthus now documented at some length—it was the "positive checks" of war, famine, and disease (as well as infanticide) that kept population within the bounds of food. Only in "modern Europe" did the "preventive check" of "moral restraint" operate to any considerable degree, as more and more people chose to delay marriage for prudential reasons.[74]

Like Marx in a later period, Malthus was the specter haunting the discussion of social issues long into the nineteenth century. Debate focused largely on the efficacy of the "prudential restraint," and on "the total social and economic conditions" that made it possible. In contrast to earlier writers who had seen a link between luxury and low fertility as evidence of social degeneration, liberal Malthusians like Nassau Senior began to conceive material wants in more positive and relativistic terms: "as wealth increases, what were the luxuries of one generation become the decencies of their successors." Senior concluded that in civilized societies men postponed marriage not from fear of want but from the desire to raise themselves. With other writers, he suggested a similar diffusion of notions of comfort down the social scale, and looked forward to the possibility that middle-class models of social aspiration and sexual restraint might operate among the laboring classes as well.[75]

Malthusian thinking was particularly salient, of course, to the science of political economy. As developed by Ricardo and his followers, the "dismal science" was founded on the law of population which, in the face of "nature's decreasing response to human effort to increase the supply of food," led inexorably to falling net returns to industry, to more or less constant real wages whose natural level was the subsistence minimum, and to ever-increasing land rents. The ultimate tendency of economic development was thus toward a state of stagnation; and although Ricardo saw that "stationary state" as yet "far distant," James Mill could still insist that even in the present "the general misery of mankind" was a fact following from the laws of human nature and economic growth. At the same time, the Ricardians shared the practical optimism of the merchant and manufacturing groups for whose interests they were spokesmen, and the long-run pessimistic logic of economic ideas was countered by the short-run logic of practical interest. The demand for free trade in corn, the reform of the poor law, and the encouragement of colonization were all ways of cushioning the immediate impact of the Malthusian principle; and over a longer period the diffusion of the prudential restraint down the social scale (or even the daring possibility of birth control) might even nullify it entirely.[76]

But if political economy could thus sustain the progress of civilization against the logic of population, it was one more factor modifying the eighteenth-century idea. Political economy posed much more sharply the implicit antagonism of civilization to nature, whether external or internal to man. The problem was to "realise all the progress that is possible" under "physical conditions which are unfavourable to progress." Human nature was still essentially progressive, but for its potential to be realized, human instinct had to be overcome by foresight. Furthermore, not all men had succeeded equally in the labor of overcoming nature, both outside and within themselves. It was the middle classes of modern European civilized society in which the liberation of human reason from the forces of instinct had progressed furthest. They were at once the guarantors of future progress and the group capable of the greatest present happiness; and the aim of social and economic policy should be to secure their status and maximize their number.[77]

This convergence of issues of economics, politics, morality, and class in the discussion of the problem of civilization produced a subtle transformation in the idea itself, giving its usage after 1830 an implicit content more specific than that which had emerged in the eighteenth century. Although the ostensible reference was still to a generalized progress of knowledge, technique, social organization, and morality, civilization often tended to imply a number of things that were more specific reflections of recent British experience: the factory system and free trade; representative government and liberal political institutions; a middle-class standard of material comfort and the middle-class ethic of self-discipline and sexual restraint; and the Christian religion in its Protestant form. And although civilization tended to be conceived in terms of external manifestations, its various elements were the expression of a relatively integrated system of cultural values. Just as evangelical discipline had been secularized as "respectability," so was political economy evangelized in the "gospel of work."[78] The two were linked, in a sexual context, by the doctrine of prudential restraint; the ability to delay gratification, to exercise rational control over one's baser instincts, was in turn the basis for individual liberty and political responsibility.

Extended to the larger history of mankind in the context of other tendencies we have been discussing, this class vision of human progress greatly sharpened the antithesis between savagery and civilization. Although religious orthodoxy and humanitarian sentiment inhibited men from accepting the radical racialist conception of plural human origins, savages were nevertheless generally conceived in negative terms by progressionists and degenerationists alike. Indeed the process of degeneration itself had been in a sense transvalued: previously associated with a European fall from primitive cultural simplicity, it was now more often associated with a savage fall from primitive religious grace. By linking civilization to middle-class virtues rather than aristocratic vices, the evangelical and utilitarian impulses had given it precisely that moral underpinning that still seemed questionable to many eighteenth-century writers. Not yet, or no longer, able to subject themselves to the discipline of labor and delayed gratification, indulgent of their instinctive passions, savages were at the mercy of the forces of nature. By contrast, civilization, whether one viewed it as a natural outgrowth of human capacity or as a divinely assisted process, tended to be seen as a triumph over rather than an expression of the primal nature of man, just as it was a triumph over external nature. In short, the traces of residual primitivism that still complicated the late-eighteenth-century concept of progress in civilization had been exorcised. The Noble Savage, fantasy of a precapitalist mentality that saw labor as the curse of fallen man exiled from the Garden, found it ever harder to survive in the prospective Eden of a civilization produced by the gospel of work.[79]

Civilization as an Issue of Attitude and Method

By about 1830, then, cultural ideology in Great Britain had begun to reflect a conception of civilization integrated around ideas about human labor, or in a broader sense, human productivity. There were, however, others more critical of the new industrial society who, like Coleridge, saw "civilization" as "but a mixed good," standing in "permanent distinction" and "occasional contrast" to "cultivation." The contrast suggests the German idea of culture, and in this period there were in fact a number of British thinkers who felt the influence of German historical and philosophical thought. Among them were Thomas Arnold and the "Liberal Anglican" historians, and that related group of scientists and broad churchmen centering around William Whewell, which Arnold suggested might be called the "Cambridge Movement."[80]

Responding to the stimulus of Niebuhr's *History of Rome,* the Liberal Anglicans tried to build a comparative "science" of history based on Vico's conception of development in terms of organic cycles of growth and decay. Behind or beyond the Vichian cycles of profane history, however, the Liberal Anglicans felt that there was a progressive moral development which they conceived in essentially Herderian terms—and with a similar ambiguity of cultural relativism and racial determinism. Rejecting the associationist uniformity of human nature, they saw *history* as composed of a plurality of cultural worlds, each to be understood in its own terms. *Progress,* on the other hand, had moved historically westward across the earth, transmitted from race to race, until now in Britain "the crisis of civilization" must be faced, and only the saving power of Christianity offered hope that the natural cyclical order of periodic national calamity might finally be broken. From a methodological point of view, there was thus a distinction between those aspects of history governed by God's general Providence, which could in a certain fashion be studied scientifically, and those aspects governed by his special Providence, which were beyond the realm of scientific determination.[81]

This methodological discontinuity, which applied particularly to the origin and early stages of civilization, was similar to that propounded in William Whewell's writings on the history and philosophy of science. Whewell lectured at Cambridge on moral philosophy and political economy, attacking both Bentham and Ricardo; but except insofar as his Kantian epistemology involved a rejection of sensationalist psychology, he did not rely on the moral sciences in developing his philosophy of scientific method. But if his anti-uniformitarianism was elaborated primarily in relation to geology, it nonetheless applied in principle to all the "palaetiological sciences"—those whose "fundamental idea" was that of "historical causation." Among these were comparative philology, archeology, and the "philosophical history of the human race," viewed with respect to "the progress of Mythology, of Poetry, of Government, [and] of Law."[82]

Whewell argued that *no* palaetiological science could "arrive at a beginning which is homogeneous with the known course of events." They were all therefore peculiarly dependent on history and tradition, and especially on those historical writings which "have the strongest claim to our respect as records of the early history of the world." Furthermore, although man and his works might be viewed as part of "the

Natural Course of Things,'' man was ''a moral as well as a natural agent,'' and therefore aware of his subjection to a higher moral government. There was thus ''a *Providential* as well as a Natural Course of Things,'' and *it* was ultimately ''consistent and intelligible'' only in terms of the Sacred Narrative. Any attempt ''at present to include the Moral Sciences in the same formulae with the Physical'' opened up ''far more controversies'' than it closed. In short, one finds both in Whewell and the Liberal Anglican historians a distinction analogous to that which was to develop in Germany between the *Natur-* and the *Geisteswissenschaften.* And although these writers represented minority currents in British intellectual life, the prevailing religious atmosphere in this period tended to support their resistance to those who would subsume the phenomena of human moral life within the natural sciences.[83]

The most important such attempt was John Stuart Mill's ''On the Logic of the Moral Sciences,'' which was the culmination of his *System of Logic*—and which, ironically, seems in the process of translation to have elicited the first use of the term *Geisteswissenschaften* in German. Published in 1843, Mill's *Logic* was to become a ''kind of sacred book for the students who claimed to be genuine Liberals,'' and in the last half of the century ''the groundwork of natural science in the Universities.[84] Since liberalism and natural science were both central to the later evolutionary impulse, it is worth considering for a moment the background and argument of Mill's defense of the sciences of human nature and civilization.

Although Mill was bred to a utilitarianism which by his own account lacked any meaningful historical dimension, the ''problem of civilization'' was made a focus of his intellectual concerns from early childhood. His father's *British India,* Ricardo's *Economics,* and Malthus' *Population* all helped to form the Benthamite sectarianism of his late adolescence. He was of course untouched by any directly religious influences, but in the aftermath of his oedipal crisis of 1826 he turned to the Germano-Coleridgians, discovering that human nature included other principles than those of reason; that self-cultivation in the fullest sense was essential to true civilization; that every people—even ''unmitigated savages''—had ''their own education, their own culture''; and that the civilization of the present was in a profound sense the product of past history.[85]

Whatever Mill acquired from the romantic reaction to eighteenth-century rationalism, however, it did not include ''the romantic philosophy of mind.'' For Mill, the notion of innate ideas was simply the ultimate means by which ingrained prejudice whose ''origin is not remembered'' could ''dispense with the obligation of justifying itself by reason.'' When he turned to the philosophy of history, it was not primarily to the Scots or to the Germans—both of whom were contaminated by "intuitionism"—but rather across the channel to the lineage of Condorcet: the Saint-Simonians, Guizot's *History of European Civilization*, and most importantly, Comte's *Positive Philosophy.*[86]

True to his utilitarian heritage, Mill, in contrast to Comte, grounded the moral sciences in the science of individual human nature. Although he did not deny that mental phenomena had a basis in cerebral structure, and that a "portion of human nature" was instinctual, Mill was skeptical of the claims of phrenologists and physiologists. He founded his own psychology rather on a version of the "Laws of Association" set forth in his father's *Analysis of the Phenomena of the Human Mind.* True, in moving from the "Laws of Mind" to actual human behavior, Mill reflected the Germano-Coleridgian influence by proposing a "Science of Character" to explain how a common human nature was expressed in specific cultural and historical situations. But he remained true to the tradition of his father by regarding his "Ethology" merely as a "system of corollaries" of psychology. The laws of human nature were already well enough known that any "competent thinker" could deduce from them "the particular type of character which would be formed, in mankind generally, by any assumed set of circumstances."[87]

If his psychology thus reflected his intellectual patrimony, the impact of subsequent influences was stronger when Mill turned from "the science of the individual man" to "the science of man in society." To Mill, the "interest-philosophy of the Bentham school" was "the mere polemics of the day" disguised as science. He granted the validity of isolating a single human motive—"the desire for wealth"—to construct an abstract science of political economy. But he insisted that its practical application, and the establishment of other "departments" of a "general Science of Society," would depend on the development of a "Political Ethology," the science of the causes which determine the type of character belonging to a people or to an age. And "the more highly the science of ethology is cultivated, and the better the diversities of national character are understood, the smaller, probably, will the number of propositions become, which it will be considered safe to build upon as universal principles of human nature." Following Comte, Mill went on to speak of the "universal *consensus,*" or interrelation of "the different parts of the social organism," characteristic of each "state of society." "Social Statics" was the theoretical study of such consensus, and Mill quoted at length from his own appreciation of Coleridge to define the prerequisites of any stable social order: a system of education or "restraining discipline," the "feeling of allegiance or loyalty," and "the active principle of nationality."[88]

This tentative approach to a more organic or functionalist—indeed, even cultural—social theory was, however, short-circuited when Mill went on to subordinate the study of "Social Statics" to that of "Social

Dynamics." Although foreshadowed in Comte, this shift was consistent with a pattern in Mill's work that also reflects longer-run tendencies in the British sociological tradition. Just as he had subordinated ethology to psychology, just as the "laws of the phenomena of society" were "nothing but the laws of the actions and passions of [individual] human beings united together in the social state," just as in his own career Mill was to forego the study of ethology for the *Principles of Political Economy,* so also did he argue that "the mutual correlation between the different elements of each state of society" was "a derivative law, resulting from the laws which regulate the succession between one state of society and another." Thus it was that "the fundamental problem of sociology" was "to find the laws according to which any state of society produces the state which succeeds it."[89]

True, the Germano-Coleridgians had also subordinated the analysis of present social order to the past, producing "a philosophy of society, in the only form in which it is yet possible, that of a philosophy of history." Mill's philosophy of history, however, was rooted in the French tradition. Ultimately, it was the march of human reason that enabled him to shortcut the difficult process of combining "the statical view of social phenomena with the dynamical." In principle, it would be necessary to consider the contemporaneous condition, interrelation, and simultaneous change of each and all of the separate elements of society. But fortunately, "one social element" predominated among "the agents of the social progression": "the state of the speculative faculties of mankind." Thus "the order of human progression in all respects" would be a "corollary deducible from the order of progression of the intellectual convictions of mankind."[90]

In this context, Mill proposed a study that in important respects foreshadowed the sociocultural evolutionism of the 1860s. The "initial stages of human progress" could only be deduced from "the laws of human nature," since they left "no direct memorials." After "the first few terms of the series," the problem became so complex that direct deduction was no longer possible. Fortunately, however, "since both the natural varieties of mankind, and the original diversities of local circumstances, are much less considerable than the points of agreement, there will naturally be a certain degree of uniformity in the progressive development of man and of his work"—as was evident by comparing the "various states of society now existing in different regions of the earth." Furthermore, this uniformity became greater as society and civilization advanced, and "the evolution of each people" interacted with that of every other. To determine the "order of human progression" as an empirical law, however, it would not be enough to examine only a portion of social progress; it would be necessary rather "to take into consideration the whole of past time, from the first recorded condition of the human race."[91]

Mill's model of dynamic sociological inquiry was conceived as a study of history, not of prehistory: and the achievement of his program would present rather different problems after the transformation of human time that took place at the end of the 1850s. Nevertheless, his influence on the major sociocultural evolutionary thinkers was evidenced in many ways—most importantly, in their conception of the conduct of scientific inquiry. In the present context, however, the point to emphasize is the manner in which the historical and sociological influences of the early nineteenth century were assimilated by English utilitarianism. Its antihistorical bias—a reflection perhaps of the political activist phase of philosophical radicalism that ended by 1839—had to a certain extent been exorcised. History, however, had been reintroduced in the generalizing positivist guise of the "inverse deductive method," and the influence of historicism was further constricted by a basically rationalistic worldview, and by the assumptions of British associationist psychology. Furthermore, the possibility of a functionalist study of social systems was already subordinated to a methodologically individualist study of their progressive development. In short, the Germano-Coleridgian and the Comtean impulses had been domesticated to the dominant English utilitarian tradition.[92]

Biblical Anthropology and the *Vestiges of Creation*

But however much of Victorian sociocultural evolutionism was implicit in Mill's program, it was not yet evolutionist in the biological sense. The environmental plasticity of the human mind did not imply its simian origin. Few British thinkers in this period publicly entertained such a notion, and the most notable advocate—the Scotsman Robert Chambers—published his work anonymously. The controversy precipitated in 1844 by his *Vestiges of the Natural History of Creation* is thus a final crucial element in contextualizing the problem of civilization on the eve of Darwinism.[93]

Chambers' *Vestiges* saw the origin of man and the early progress of human civilization as part of a broader, cosmic developmental sequence in which it had "pleased Providence to arrange that one species should give birth to another, until the second highest gave birth to man." But such manifest deism did not save Chambers from violent attack, and although both Darwin and Huxley found the biological argument naive, the reaction of many scientists was clearly conditioned by nonscientific ideological factors. As the geologist Adam Sedgwick put it, "the world cannot bear to be turned upside down." The "glorious maidens and matrons" of Britain must not "poison the springs of joyous thought and modest feeling" by listening to the "seductions" of an author who argued "that their Bible is a fable when it teaches them that they were made in the image of God—that they are the children of apes and the breeders of monsters—that he has *annulled all distinction between the physical and the moral*—and that all the phenomena of the universe" were merely "the progression and development of a rank, unbending, and degrading materialism." If the *Vestiges* were true, "the labours of sober induction are in vain; religion is a lie, human law is a mass of folly [and] morality is moonshine."[94]

Sedgwick's rhetoric—symbolic of an intellectual challenge the sociocultural evolutionists would later have to meet—recalls that of an earlier era, when the French Revolution seemed to many in Britain to threaten similar dire consequences. By association, it raises a more general historiographical problem: the impact of the Revolution upon scientific thinking generally, and more particularly upon speculation in the sciences Whewell called "palaetiological." Much historical scholarship on the idea of biological evolutionism has emphasized the continuity of its development. But there are also more radically discontinuous views of the historicization of the human world, and the present discussion would seem in some ways to sustain such discontinuity. Furthermore, it would suggest that this discontinuity was profoundly conditioned by the French Revolution, the intellectual reaction it provoked, and the stimulus it gave to religious and moral revival.[95]

Although the impact of the Revolution has not been adequately studied from this perspective, it seems worth suggesting that the image of Voltaire as "ape-demon" and of the French as a "nation of baboons," which haunted the British national mind for decades, is more than metaphorically related to the general antievolutionary reaction that had begun in British thought by 1800. For those who saw the Revolution as threatening the very foundations of European civilization, the book that, more than any other, formed the basis of that civilization took on a new—or reassumed an old—meaning. The deistic evolutionary speculations of Erasmus Darwin, which had seemed innocuous enough in 1793, were within a decade widely condemned as an attempt to substitute the religion of nature for the religion of the Bible.[96]

For many years after that, science in Britain felt the pressure of revolutionary paranoia and evangelical bibliolatry. This did not mean that science had to conform in all respects to the literal Word. In most areas there was plenty of leeway for religious men of science to pursue their inquiries without direct intellectual hindrance, and even in some more sensitive areas the evidence of science could easily be interpreted as actually sustaining the biblical account. Thus, although it required a metaphorical interpretation of the days of Creation, Cuvierian catastrophist geology provided support for the Deluge until the 1830s; and even after that time geology might be pursued by believing scientists without too much epistemological strain. But there were distinct limits to the "curious providential materialism" that characterized British scientific thought in this period. The Bible, after all, was not a textbook in geology, but a book about God and Man; and if there was no conflict between Genesis and geology that could not somehow be reconciled, the problem of "man's place in nature" was a more explosive one. Here a discontinuous view of natural processes was not simply an intellectual convenience but a social and theological necessity.[97]

Although traditionally less sharp in British than in French thought, the line between man and animal was now rigorously insisted upon. The two decades after 1800 witnessed a general reaction in British natural historical thought against the old idea of the Chain of Being, which had tended to blur the distinction. Those who rejected the Chain did not abandon all analogical argument from the rest of nature to the nature of man, but to press such analogy too far risked more than scientific criticism. When William Lawrence published his *Lectures on the Natural History of Man* in 1819, his insistence that life could not be discussed independently of animal body nor mind independently of brain nearly ruined his career as physiologist. He was widely reviled as an atheist and materialist, a "fellow-labourer" of Voltaire and the other *philosophes* in "the infamous attempt of demoralizing mankind." Virtually without defenders in the scientific community, Lawrence withdrew his book from circulation, only to be denied the right to suppress a pirated edition on the ironic ground that the law of copyright gave no protection to blasphemy.[98]

Lawrence was little influenced by conjectural history, and was only in a very precursory sense part of the tradition of biological evolutionism; but in the postrevolutionary period the issues he treated were easily linked to those of human origin and the growth of civilization, and any attempt to treat such phenomena in naturalistic terms also risked association with the dangers of French atheism and materialism. Although conjectural historians had not in general placed the development of society in a biological framework, the early expressions of biological evolutionism tended—as Chambers did in *Vestiges*—to take for granted a developmental view of "The Origin of Society" (which was in fact the subtitle of one of Erasmus Darwin's offending evolutionary poems).[99] For those who felt the foundations of their social order shaking, there was an obvious connection between the assumptions that mind was a function of the brain, that man had evolved from an animal, and that religious ideas had developed naturally from savage polytheism. In the logic of evangelical anti-Jacobinism, they were all equally threats to the immortality of the soul, which was the essential buttress of human morality and social stability. Although the matter clearly requires further study, it seems safe to say that the early-nineteenth-century decline of conjectual history should be understood in the context of this unfavorable milieu.

Doubtless, the vast majority of British men of science felt the impact of antirevolutionary reaction and revived religion through the internalization of cultural values rather than through repressive external social control. But whatever the mechanism, it seems clear that these conjoint movements profoundly affected speculation in all areas of palaetiological thought through the period of Chambers' *Vestiges*. It may well be, as some recent scholarship would have it, that the more openly religious approach in science actually laid the basis for the first really comprehensive view of the history of life. But there is no denying that a resurgent Christian belief strongly conditioned British anthropological thought in the pre-Darwinian nineteenth century.[100]

From a very broad historical perspective, in which the history of anthropological thought may be seen as an alternating dominance of the biblical and the developmental traditions, the pre-Darwinian period in Britain is one in which, after a century in retreat, the biblical tradition reassumed a kind of paradigmatic status. Within this framework, all men were presumed to be descended from one original pair, who had been formed by God as the final act of Creation, and to whom he had revealed the one true religion and certain other fundamental institutions of civilization. Implicit in this view were more specifically "anthropological" assumptions: the unity of man, the recency of his appearance on earth, the degeneration of non-Christian savage peoples, and a sharp distinction between man and other animal forms. These assumptions were in fact interlocking. The qualitative distinction between man and animal reinforced the rejection of a plurality of human origins, which would tend to fill the gap between ape and man with a hierarchy of biologically differentiated forms. Correspondingly, degeneration, conceived in physical and cultural terms, provided an alternative explanation for the manifest human diversity that increasingly forced itself on anthropological observers in this period. Thus could hierarchy and unity coexist in anthropological thought, just as aggressive ethnocentrism and Christian humanitarianism coexisted in the general cultural attitude toward non-Western peoples.

The assumptions of biblical anthropology were most strongly evident in the work of clerical writers such as Sumner, Whately, Wiseman, Whewell, and Sedgwick.[101] But in a more diffuse way, they affected the thinking of men who in retrospect we would be more inclined to regard as anthropologists. As we shall shortly see, this thinking was both Whewellian in assumption and Germanic in its intellectual affinities, and it was relatively unconcerned with the origin and progress of civilization. Rather, it focused on the question "is mankind one or many?"; and it sought to show that, despite their manifest cultural and physical diversity, all men were in fact one species. From this perspective, biblical anthropology stands in sharp contrast to the proponents of a natural scientifically oriented study of the progress of civilization, who were less interested in the actual cultural or physical diversity of mankind.

To simplify matters somewhat, the emergence of the sociocultural evolutionary viewpoint that characterized British anthropology after 1860 may be seen as the bringing together of two hitherto separated concerns: on the one hand, a study of the variety of mankind that had yet to free itself completely from the constraints of biblical assumption; and on the other, a study of the progress of civilization for which a positivistic program was already well established.[102] This convergence could take place only in a context that legitimated a naturalistic study of the phenomena of human origins. The longevity of Chambers' *Vestiges,* which despite the odium it aroused went through twenty editions by 1860, is in a sense the measure of the emergence of that context. By that date, the intellectual buttresses of antievolutionism had been greatly eroded, and the rapid passage of another European revolutionary threat had confirmed the stability of the social order evolved in Britain since the earlier revolutionary period. The same years were to witness the decline of biblical anthropology and the legitimation of naturalistic approaches to the variety of man. Systematic evolutionary speculation became thus both a less threatening and a more viable enterprise.

In this context, the problem of civilization was once again reformulated. Indeed, one might say that for several decades after 1851, civilization in Britain was not so much a problem as an assumption. Insofar as it was problematic, the primary question was no longer how to accomplish it or defend it, but rather to explain its development, and why it was that not all men had shared equally in the process—why it was that though the whole world had been invited to attend, the Crystal Palace had been a uniquely British creation.

TWO

Ethnology on the Eve of Evolution (1830–1858)

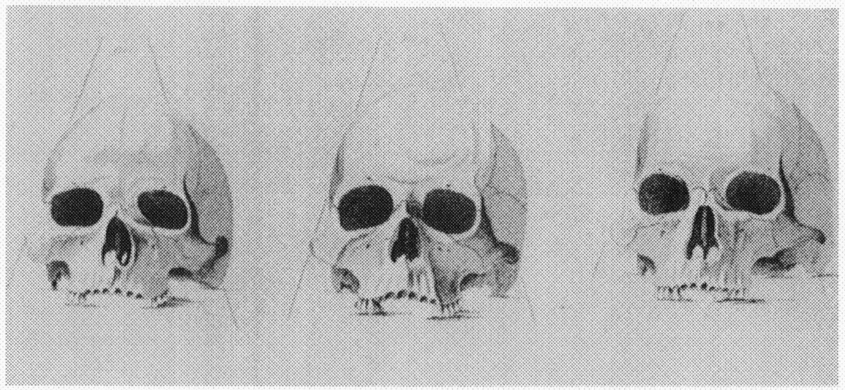

Dr. Prichard's skulls from Kongo, Louisiana, and Canton—1855

James C. Prichard, *The Natural History of Man: Comprising Inquiries into the Modifying Influences of Physical and Moral Agencies on the Different Tribes of the Human Family.* 4th ed., Edwin Norris, ed. (London, 1855), vol. I, between pp. 110–11.

THE uncivilized tribes of the world were little represented at the Great Exhibition. They were more in evidence after the Crystal Palace was sold to private speculators in 1852, dismantled, and reassembled in Sydenham. Among the other fauna in the newly established Natural History Department were thirteen life-size groupings of savages—the Eskimos across the aisle from the polar bear, the Red Indians next to North American birds, the West African Negroes alongside the chimpanzee, and so on through the Bushmen, Kaffirs, Malays, Dyaks, Papuans, Australians, and Maoris. Although included under the rubric "Natural History," these exhibits were illustrations of a particular subdiscipline: "Ethnology," or "the Science of Human Races." New enough that the guidebook spent some time discussing the meaning of the word, "ethnology" was nonetheless sufficiently well established to have produced the five-volume third edition of a work recommended to interested readers as a general synthetic treatment: Dr. Prichard's *Researches into the Physical History of Mankind.*[1]

In Britain in the 1850s, "ethnology" was in fact the most general scientific framework for the study of the linguistic, physical, and cultural characteristics of dark-skinned, non-European, "uncivilized" peoples.[2] As such, it is the most relevant focus for inquiry into the proximate origins of evolutionary anthropology, and the more distant origins of the anthropology of the twentieth century. For etymology notwithstanding, the historical unity of the tradition which in the Anglo-American sphere is called "anthropological" has been defined primarily by its human subject matter, which—allowing for differences of terminology and attitude—has for the most part been essentially that of pre-Darwinian ethnology. Although the questions asked of this subject matter have changed, the dichotomy between the European civilized observer and the culturally distant (and objectified) "other" has always been central to the anthropological tradition—as indeed current attempts to surmount it testify.[3] Whether they observed dark-skinned non-Europeans better to understand their own civilization, or simply to explain the variety of mankind, what unifies the scholars we retrospectively include in the anthropological tradition is the fact that they studied peoples who were once called "savages." On these grounds as well as on those of institutional continuity, "ethnology" is perhaps more clearly a part of the history of Western anthropology than the eighteenth-century precursors for which it has customarily been neglected by historians of the modern discipline.

Despite the fascination that savagery had long exerted on the European mind, the emergence of its systematic study in the nineteenth century was a complex and somewhat indirect process. The emergence of the human sciences is often seen as a process of fission, in which specialized disciplines developed out of an earlier undifferentiated moral philosophy. In this process of differentiation, technical elaboration conspired with ethnocentric motive to narrow the focus of inquiry to the phenomena of civilized life: the economy of money, the political science of the state, the psychology of rational consciousness, or the history of written sources. In this context, ethnology may be viewed as a science of leftovers or residues. It was not so much a product of fission as it was a fusion of diverse styles of inquiry, derived from the natural historical, the moral philosophical, and the humanistic traditions—in relation to a particular subject matter that was being excluded from other emerging human sciences. Thus although its subject matter was marginal and even alien to them, many of ethnology's methodologies were drawn from traditional forms of inquiry, and its central problem—the unity or diversity of mankind—derived from deep-rooted European "anthropological" concerns. Nevertheless, ethnology was the science of savages in the sense that it was the only scholarly discourse that took them seriously as subject matter.[4]

Although post-Darwinian social evolutionism placed savagery in a very different explanatory context, it, too, was a science of savages, insofar as it was founded on the comparative analysis of descriptive accounts of dark-skinned, uncivilized men. To understand social evolutionism as a generalized mode of inquiry into a particular body of empirical data, then, we must first understand the immediately preceding model of inquiry into the same body of data. We must first understand ethnology.

James Cowles Prichard and the Ethnological Problem

Ethnology in Britain was primarily associated with the name of the Bristol physician James Cowles Prichard, and one may trace its growth in the development of Prichard's thought from the time of his medical dissertation in Edinburgh in 1808 to the completion of the third edition of his *Researches* in 1848. Indeed, Prichard—who attended Dugald Stewart's lectures on moral philosophy—goes a long way toward bridging the historiographical gap that has separated the developmentalism of the eighteenth century from the social evolutionism of the mid-nineteenth. A consideration of his work will illuminate both the specific historical character of pre-Darwinian ethnology and the nature of the intellectual transition in which Victorian evolutionism emerged.[5]

Prichard's *Researches* originated as a response to a scientific challenge within a particular religious and political milieu. The scientific challenge was created by the emergence of comparative anatomy as the dominant life science of the early nineteenth century, in the aftermath of the explosive growth of data on biological diversity produced by the explorations of the late eighteenth. Given the tendency within comparative anatomy toward a radically diversified view of man, the impulse was strong to define the dark-skinned savages of the earth as separate species of mankind—especially in the context of the debates over Negro slavery, and of an aggressively expansive European civilization whose rapidly growing technological superiority was revolutionizing the terms of race contact all over the world. Although this "polygenist" impulse can be traced back at least as far as Paracelsus, it had always run counter to Christian orthodoxy, and was now in Britain held in check by the revival of evangelical religion. But in France, where the monster of atheism thrived on the blood of revolution, there were avowed polygenists, and some religious men of science in Britain therefore felt it necessary to counter the doctrine intellectually. It was to this effort that Prichard devoted his life.[6]

The specific stimulus came from Lord Kames, whose polygenetic interpretation of American Indian origins had been discussed in Dugald Stewart's lectures. Prichard had inherited from his Quaker parents a strong commitment to the doctrine of human unity, and he was profoundly disturbed not only by Kames' polygenism, but also by the view of religion Kames shared with other Enlightenment developmentalists. Following a then well-traveled path from Quakerism to the Anglican church, Prichard had been touched by the Evangelical Revival while studying at Cambridge and Oxford after leaving Edinburgh, and his religious commitment would no more allow him to accept Kames' primitive polytheism than his aboriginal polygenism. Prichard believed that just as in the beginning all men were one, so had God in the beginning revealed to all men the one true religion. Although he did not escape the influence of the Scottish philosophers, he would not follow them when their developmentalist speculations seemed to lead toward the atheism of the *philosophes*. His concern with civilization was not to trace its origins but to defend its foundations, and in defending both primitive revelation and human unity he was in fact defending the principle that all mankind had once been and were rightfully subject to a single ethical dispensation. Over the next four decades Prichard's religious commitment seems to have attenuated somewhat, and the commitment to human unity became, as it were, the functionally autonomous motivation of his ethnology. But in the years in which his ethnological viewpoint was defined, religious belief and the defense of the Bible were clearly primary determining factors.[7]

Thus it was that Prichard dissociated himself from those aspects of Enlightenment anthropology that ran counter to revived Christian orthodoxy, returning instead to an earlier current of anthropological thought whose manifestations we have already noted: the biblical anthropology which for centuries had structured European views of the early history of mankind, and which had provided the framework for the antique discipline of historical chronology. Implicit in the 1813 edition of his *Researches,* Prichard's ties to the chronological tradition were clearly evident in 1819 in his *Analysis of the Egyptian Mythology,* which attempted to harmonize "the historical records of the ancient Egyptians and those contained in the Sacred Scriptures." Although the chronological tradition was already moribund in the Enlightenment, there are manifest continuities between chronological and ethnological inquiry. Starting from the confusion of languages at the Tower of Babel and the subsequent dispersion of the descendants of Noah, the fundamental problem of ethnology was to fill the gap until the first historical records of each present "nation," "people," or "race," and in the process to show how all the observed differences between them could have been produced in the descendants of a single family—all within the traditional biblical chronology, which allowed only 6,000 years as the span of human existence.[8]

This is not to say that Prichard was uninfluenced by newer currents of scientific thought. From the beginning his work reflected the stimulus of comparative anatomy, and it is possible to read major portions of it as part of the development of a naturalistic view of man. But this naturalistic impulse in Prichard was always constrained by the framework just defined, which found its characteristic scientific expression in comparative philology rather than comparative anatomy. Thus Prichard's medical dissertation of 1808, although heavily endebted to Blumenbach, also reflects the influence of Sir William Jones, and over the long run the tradition associated with Jones was to prove more powerful.[9]

These two influences correspond to two phases of ethnological inquiry. What we may call "the ethnological problem"—demonstrating the unity of the human species—had both a biological and an historical aspect. Thus, on the one hand, Prichard discussed the physical differences among men and the biological mechanisms that might have produced them; on the other, he discussed the present racial distribution of men, and tried to trace them all back historically to a single root. Both tasks suggest a relationship to biological evolutionism, and Prichard's earlier attempts to explain physical differences in monogenetic terms led him to speculations that have been regarded as foreshadowing Darwin. Over the years, however, his explanations took on a more traditionally environmental cast: races had gradually become different physically under the direct influence of the environments into which they migrated.

But whatever the differentiating process, Prichard's biology was always antievolutionary in the sense that it assumed an unbridgeable gap between apes and humans. What Prichard studied was the "evolution of varieties" within a single human species created by God.[10]

Similarly, although developmental assumptions are also reflected in his treatment of the second phase of the ethnological problem, Prichard's historical orientation was essentially un- (if not anti-) evolutionary. His task was to establish connections between the races of men on the basis of similarities of physical type, religion, political institutions, customs, and above all, language, which he insisted was the most reliable indicator of racial affinity. But although comparative, Prichard's approach was quite different from the developmentalist "comparative method." True, in other cultural spheres than religion, he tended to assume a generally progressive development from the savage state. And in 1813 he in fact suggested that this was correlated with a racial development from black to white—although in later editions he retreated from this heterodoxy, which, by making Adam black, was perhaps offensive to more traditionally degenerationist biblical anthropologists.[11]

From the beginning, however, the central concern of Prichard's historical inquiry was not development but derivation, not progress but origin—conceived in terms of source rather than causal process. Thus he suggested in discussing the political systems of Egypt and India that he had "no concern with the causes that gave rise to these establishments." *His* comparisons were rather intended to "determine whether they are of separate derivation and growth, or manifest congruities so clear and extensive as to leave no doubt of their common origin." In Prichard's early work, independent invention—which was to become one of the assumptional markers of social evolutionism—was linked to polygenism. If one accepted the idea that the religious notions of the Egyptians were "peculiar to themselves"—that is to say, independent inventions showing no "mark of foreign improvement or innovation"—then one might also "infer that the Egyptians were a race peculiar to Africa, and originally distinct from the posterity of Noah and Adam." Prichard's ethnology was fundamentally diffusionist rather than developmentalist, because diffusion (in a broader sense which included both the migration of peoples and the diffusion of culture) was a better means for linking separated nations to a single source: if one could not prove identity, one could at least establish contact.[12]

Toward the end of his career, Prichard elaborated what was in effect the social evolutionary concept of "the psychic unity of man," arguing the similarity of human mental productions as one more body of evidence for the unity of the human species. In this context, he in fact began to reason from independent invention, and even to conceive the growth of religion in developmental terms. But to overemphasize this similarity with sociocultural evolutionism obscures the sharp transition that was involved in its emergence. For Prichard, psychic unity was not the starting point for speculation about the development of civilization, but the end point of speculation about the unity of man. In contrast to E. B. Tylor, for whom psychic unity was a necessary premise in tracing a uniform sequence in the evolution of religion, Prichard used uniformities of religion to establish the psychic unity of man. His overriding purpose had always been to prove all men were originally one, and if at the end of his life he abandoned traditional biblical chronology for the 20,000 years suggested by his friend, the Egyptologist Baron Bunsen, it was because this allowed more time for all races to develop from a single root.[13]

The essential point is the historical unity of Prichard's ethnology, and the discontinuities that mark it off from the developmentalisms that preceded and followed it. All of Prichard's work may be viewed in terms of one implicit visual metaphor: that of a tree, with contemporary tribal twigs linked by major racial branches to the trunk of a single human species, rooted—for this metaphorical tree had a precise location—near the point where Noah's ark had come to rest in Southwest Asia. By the third edition of the *Researches,* a proliferation of ethnographic data and more rigorous methodological criteria had combined to blur the structure of the tree. But if the actual historical unity of mankind became more problematic, Prichardian ethnology continued to be governed by the image of the tree. When in 1847 Prichard defined the task of ethnology, it was simply a slightly more open-ended formulation of the underlying ethnological problem: "To trace the history of the tribes and races of men from the most remote periods which are within reach of investigation, to discover their mutual relations, and to arrive at conclusions, either certain or probable, as to their affinity or diversity of origin"—a question which Prichard, to the end of his career, answered in monogenetic terms.[14]

Prichard's career was thus one long series of approaches to the solution of the ethnological problem, and when at the end he defined the study to which he gave his life, his definition reflected the breadth and variety of these approaches. Anatomy, physiology, zoology, physical geography, history, archeology, and philology were all among the departments of knowledge that "contributed to the cultivation of ethnology." However, Prichardian ethnology did not weigh all these approaches equally. Over the course of his career, the physical anthropological approach to race was systematically subordinated to approaches in cultural and especially in linguistic terms. In 1848, Prichard went so far as to object to the inclusion of ethnology within the natural history section of the British Association for the Advancement of Science because it was "more nearly allied to history than to natural science."[15]

If Prichard's ethnology was widely embracive, it was because a broad range of anthropological data were unified in the solution of the ethnological problem, and subordinated to the ultimately historical purpose of showing that all migrating tribes, nations, and races of mankind could be traced to a single source.

Prichard died in 1849, a year after the completion of his magnum opus; but the ethnological orientation he exemplified outlived him. In the 1850s its most prominent advocate was Robert Gordon Latham, whose early training in both medicine and comparative philology had prepared him for both aspects of the ethnological endeavor. In 1850 Latham published a frankly Prichardian *Natural History of the Varieties of Man,* and it was he who was in charge of setting up the ethnological exhibits when the Crystal Palace was moved to Sydenham. Over the next decade, Latham maintained his position as Prichard's heir in numerous ethnological publications, culminating in the two-volume *Descriptive Ethnology* of 1859.[16]

During this same period, however, the ethnological paradigm was subjected to various stresses and strains that ultimately led to its replacement by social evolutionism as the dominant model of anthropological inquiry. On the one hand, there were further pressures on the biblical framework underlying the ethnological approach: human unity was increasingly called into question; the chronology of human existence was radically revised; and mankind was more and more brought within the purview of naturalistic explanation. On the other, the historical focus of anthropological inquiry broadened to include once more as a central concern the origin and growth of European civilization. These developments may be traced in various areas of anthropological study, all of which were to feed into the evolutionary synthesis of the 1860s.

From Popular Antiquities to Folklore

Although Prichard devoted one volume to "the history of European nations," and drew on "ancient traditions" in his ethnological argument, the present customs of the European peasantry—which were to be methodologically and substantively integral to social evolutionism—were not a matter of central concern to him. During his lifetime, however, the contrast had become very sharp between the civilized lifestyles of modern industrial England and the traditional modes that still survived in rural enclaves and on the Celtic fringe, and by 1850 a number of scholars were searching out and recording the fast-disappearing beliefs and customs of the "folk."[17]

This British folklore movement grew out of an antiquarian tradition that can be traced to the sixteenth century, where it was in fact linked to the tradition out of which ethnology emerged—one of the concerns of the early antiquaries having been to establish a genealogical connection between some putative national ancestor and the family of Noah. Ties to later anthropology are also evident in the antiquaries' source materials, which included "popular" as well as "physical" antiquities: following the example of the great Elizabethan antiquary William Camden, many antiquaries used contemporary oral traditions to supplement the archeological remains of Anglo-Saxon churches, Romano-British forts, Celtic burial grounds, and "Druidic" megaliths. And of the various currents that fed into anthropological inquiry, the antiquarian tradition was the first to achieve permanent institutional form, with the founding in 1717 of the Society of Antiquaries—which by 1770 had begun to issue a regular journal entitled *Archaeologia.* The sociology of antiquarian knowledge was more clearly manifest, however, in the *Gentleman's Magazine,* which from 1731 on included a large amount of antiquarian material. Although eventually classified and republished in thirty volumes in the late nineteenth century, these antiquarian tidbits were originally scattered among the birth, marriage, and death notices of the landed gentry. Sustained in the present by estates inherited from the past, they occupied their leisure by noting traces of the past that survived in the present lives of the uneducated dependents surrounding them.[18]

Their attitudes toward these survivals tended to be purgative. The Reverend Henry Bourne's collection of *Antiquitates Vulgares* of 1725 included "proper reflections" on each custom, "shewing which may be retain'd and which ought to be laid aside." In general, "popular antiquities" represented the continuity of error and superstition in an enlightened age, and were explained in terms of the impact of Roman Catholicism on prior pagan belief. This attitude dominated the reworking of Bourne's compilation published in 1774 by Reverend Joseph Brand, then secretary of the Society of Antiquaries. Although "erased by public authority from the *written word*" during the Reformation, the "popular notions and vulgar ceremonies" of the British countryside had been "snatched out of the smoking ruins of Popery" and committed "to the keeping of *oral tradition.*" Protestant authorities might even have connived at this, just as Roman Catholic monks, from baser motives, had once weaned pagans gradually from heathen practices by encouraging a "profusion of childish rites, pageants, and ceremonies" in order "to twist flowers" around the "shackles" of Popery. Supplemented and republished down to the later nineteenth century, Brand's *Popular Antiquities* were grouped into three major categories: those ceremonies and beliefs relating to the annual calendric cycle; those relating to the rural life cycle from christening to wake; and miscellaneous superstitions relating to witchcraft, charms, ghosts, and the like. Most of them were drawn from printed sources, ranging from Roman Catholic Rituals of Worship and the "Demonology" compiled by James I, through the late-eighteenth-century *Statistical Account of Scotland, Drawn up from the Communications of Ministers in the Different Parishes,* right on down to clippings from nineteenth-century provincial newspapers, such as the item from the *Inverness Courier* in 1845 describing an attempt by Scottish peasants to cure a young girl of witchcraft by hanging her above a blazing fire.[19]

By that time some gentlemen antiquaries, influenced by the romantic movement and stirred by nostalgia for a rapidly disappearing way of life, had begun to see the culture of the folk in a more positive light. Following the lead of Sir Walter Scott, they now began to collect tales, legends, and ballads from the folk themselves. Although Scott habitually reworked the tales he had been told by family servants and peasants of the Scottish border, his lengthy prefaces and frequent footnotes provided the model of a more "philosophical examination" of "the origin of popular fiction, and the transmission of similar tales from age to age, and from country to country." While Scott himself did not systematically pursue this investigation, others followed up his leads. In the early 1820s Thomas Crofton Croker carried out "the first intentional field collection" among the Irish peasantry, and in the 1830s his collaborator Thomas Keightley explored certain methodological issues. Confessing that he, too, had previously embellished tales, Keightley insisted on the sanctity of oral tradition as a precondition for the study of the geographical distribution of plots and incidents, and explicitly posed an issue later central to social evolutionism: whether the similarities of legends were the result of transmission, or of "independent formation" based on "the original sameness of the human mind." Keightley felt the issue could be decided only by considering both the number of similarities and the order of their occurrence in particular tales; but in general he adhered to the prevailing diffusionary viewpoint, arguing that "fairy belief descended from the primitive Gotho-Germanic religions and then spread to the weaker Celtic-Cymric peoples."[20]

Keightley, Croker, and other antiquary-folklorists such as Thomas Wright were all active in a group of literary and antiquarian societies formed in London in the decade after 1834 for the purpose of editing and publishing historical and literary documents of various sorts. Prominent in this interlocking directorate of the British antiquarian movement was William John Thoms, who took advantage of his position as a clerk in the House of Lords to pursue a variety of antiquarian literary labors. In 1846, writing in the *Athenaeum* under the pseudonym Ambrose Merton, Thoms suggested the term "folk-lore" as a "good Saxon compound" to refer to "what we in England designate as Popular Antiquities." Insisting that "the belief in Fairies is by no means extinct in England," he proposed that in districts "where steam engines, cotton mills, mail coaches, and similar exorcists have not yet penetrated, numerous legends might be collected." Thoms went on to outline a methodology for their study, which the leading historian of the field has described as including "direct field observation, accurate reporting, communication of specific data, and the comparative commentary by 'Merton,' if this were beyond the resources of the writer." Within three years Thoms' columns had become so successful that he founded a separate journal, *Notes and Queries,* which for three decades served as the primary organ of the British folklore movement.[21]

But although Thoms and his colleagues succeeded in legitimating "folk-lore" as something more serious than the casual leisure pursuit of country gentlemen, they did not provide much in the way of theoretical orientation, beyond showing the pagan origins of British folklore and tracing it to German roots. Indeed, German scholarship was the ultimate court of appeal, and Thoms' comparative comments on his correspondents' items usually took the form of noting that the same thing could be found somewhere in the Brothers Grimm. He bemoaned the fact that Brand—still the "textbook" of most English students—was no more than a "huge mass of imperfectly digested materials," but he was never able to complete the English equivalent of Jacob Grimm's *Deutsche Mythologie* that was his life's goal. Such theoretical speculation as the material of British folklore elicited was largely carried on in terms of diffusionary processes similar to those of contemporary ethnology.[22] Nonetheless, its study had already suggested to some men issues of an evolutionary sort, and within a few years Brand's fragmentary *Antiquities* were to become an integral part of Tylor's interpretation of *Primitive Culture.* Before then, however, a fresh infusion of German thought had transformed the basis of British folklore studies.

Linguistic Paleontology: The Aryans as Primitive Men

By 1850 the new comparative philology had been known in Britain for a generation. It continued, however, to be thought of as a German discipline, and was for a time popularly identified with a single German émigré scholar: Friedrich Max Müller, who throughout the later nineteenth century was to maintain an interesting contrapuntal relation to the development of British anthropology.[23]

Although he later consciously adapted himself to English cultural norms, Müller was by birth the inheritor of two major German cultural traditions: Lutheran pietism and romanticism. His father, a poet and "fellow worker of the Brothers Grimm," died when Müller was only four, and the boy grew up under the influence of his deeply religious mother's "passionate love." During his university days at Leipzig in the early 1840s the "higher criticism" of the Tübingen school had begun to shake the historical foundations of Christianity, and many of Müller's later views on primitive mentality seem clearly to reflect the mythopoeic principles underlying Strauss' *Life of Jesus.* But on the foundation of his mother's "subjective revelation" he was able to erect an enduring framework of belief that survived every intellectual shock of the next half century. Grounded in German idealist philosophy, his thinking was elaborated in the study of Sanskrit and the sacred books of India, in which Müller found a universal basis for religion in man's intuitive perception of the unseen divine power constituting the visible natural world.[24]

From Leipzig Müller went first to Berlin, where he heard the lectures of Franz Bopp, and thence to Paris, where the Sanskritist Bournouf encouraged him to undertake the study of the hymns of the Rig-Veda. For the next two decades Müller worked on the first authoritative edition of what was then thought to be "the oldest book ever composed." Traveling to London in 1846 to consult East India Company records, he established contact with the Prussian minister, the Anglophile intellectual Baron Christian Bunsen, who long before had been his father's friend. Bunsen, too, was a German pietist seeking new foundations for belief, and his massive efforts to document God's progressive self-realization in history were influential in the emergence of a more liberal theology in England.[25]

Taking Müller under his wing, Bunsen introduced him to English intellectual circles in 1847 at the Oxford meetings of the British Association for the Advancement of Science. Müller then settled there to supervise the publication of his Veda volumes by the University Press, and quickly found a place in Oxford life. By 1851 he was lecturing on comparative philology, and in 1854 he was elected to a chair in modern languages. Five years later he missed election to the chair in Sanskrit, in part because the conservative country curates who dominated the electorate felt him implicated in the controversy over the liberal Anglican manifesto *Essays and Reviews,* one of which was an extended explication of Bunsen's biblical researches. However, Müller's naturalization into the British intellectual aristocracy had already been ritualized by marriage to a woman whose aunts had wed James Froude and Charles Kingsley; and by 1868 it was completed when a chair in comparative philology was founded with the express proviso that it be offered first to Müller.[26]

When Müller arrived in England, comparative philology and ethnology were closely related disciplines. Both had begun, as it were, at the Tower of Babel, and both tended to assume that linguistic relations were evidence of racial affinity. Prichard's *Eastern Origin of the Celtic Nations* had helped in 1831 to establish the western boundaries of the Indo-European family; Latham's *Comparative Philology* in 1862 challenged then prevailing orthodoxy—to the lifelong detriment of his own reputation—by arguing that the original Indo-European speakers came from Europe rather than Asia. Similarly, the work of Bunsen and Müller in the 1850s may be regarded as an extension of the Prichardian ethnological tradition. Thus Bunsen argued that the "scaffolding for the primeval history of religion" was to be provided by a linguistically based "genealogical tree of the families of mankind"; and Müller in 1851 suggested that the "great discovery" of Bunsen's Egyptological researches had been to show that man in Africa developed gradually by degeneration from the Asiatic stock.[27] All four scholars gave papers to the ethnological subsection of the British Association in 1847, and Müller later recalled that it was then "taken for granted" that comparative philology "would in the future be the only safe foundation for the study of Anthropology."[28]

Müller's major work of philological apprenticeship appeared in this context. Indo-European philology alone would not complete the scaffolding Bunsen required for his *Philosophy of Universal History,* since many of the world's languages could not be tied genealogically to the Indo-European tree. In 1847 Bunsen had subsumed most of them in the category he called "Turanian"—which included not only the bulk of Asian languages, but also the American, Malayian, Polynesian, and even (possibly) the Papuan and Austrialian as well. By pairing the Turanian with the Iranian as two branches of a single "Japhetic race," which he then posed against the Chamitic and Semitic as "three steps of development of one and the same stock," Bunsen was able to embrace all the languages of the world in a single monogenetic framework.[29]

The "Letter on the Turanian Languages" which Müller contributed to Bunsen's *Universal History* was intended to document this hypothesis. The difficulty was that the Turanian languages were so various, so poorly preserved in written documents, and so little studied that it was hopeless to establish genealogical relations among them. Müller therefore fell back on the "morphological classification" of Wilhelm von Humboldt, hypothesizing a series of migrations out from "the common centre of mankind." The first had gone to China, where language was "arrested at the first stage of its growth," the primitive root words being simply juxtaposed without modification. This was followed by a series of Turanian migrations, whose genealogical relations were obscured precisely because the unifying structural principle of agglutination led to the rapid differentiation of dialects under the conditions of nomadic life. Finally, there were the migrations of the Semites and "Arians," whose languages had passed out of the stage of "mechanical crystallization" to achieve "such settled principles and such intense individuality in grammar and dictionary, that the national character . . . of its descendants . . . could never obliterate or efface the stamp of their common parent."[30]

Although this early excursion into Turanian philology later proved an embarrassment to Müller, he soon produced other philological works that had a lasting impact on English intellectual life. His essay on "Comparative Mythology" in 1856 and the *Lectures on the Science of Language* he gave to large and distinguished audiences in London in 1861 and 1864 were important not only in terms of their specific subject matter, but more generally in propagating the notion of the "Aryans" as the primitive ancestors of modern European civilized populations. The notion that a single community of language and race existed at the base of the Indo-European linguistic tree was coeval with comparative philology itself, and by 1850 the notion of a series of migrations out of Southwest Asia was a commonplace among both comparative philologists and ethnologists. But it was apparently Müller who first gave the older term "Arian" the spelling associated with modern racialism, and for some years he was the most vocal "Aryanist" in Britain.[31]

Later in life, after several decades of controversy over the "origin of the Aryans," Müller was to ridicule those who used the word as a racial category, insisting that from an early date he had argued the independence of ethnological and linguistic classification. But in the 1850s he habitually referred to the Aryans in terms that implied a community of language and race. Furthermore, there was an ambiguity of attitude as well as assumption in Müller's Aryanism. On the one hand, the notion implied the brotherhood of dark-skinned Hindus and light-skinned Teutons; and Müller, like his mentor Bunsen, believed that linguistic study would ultimately reaffirm that all men were "children of the same father—whatever their country, their colour, their language, and their faith." On the other hand, Müller felt that Kant's philosophy represented "the perfect manhood of the Aryan mind," and many of his more rhapsodic passages are similarly resonant of Aryanist racial ideology, which in this very period was given its classic formulation by the French orientalist Count Arthur de Gobineau.[32]

In the 1850s, when the span of mankind's existence had just begun to be stretched beyond the traditional biblical chronology of 6,000 years, Müller's inquiry had a reconstructive as well as a genealogical interest. In studying the Vedas, Müller hoped to find "a picture of what man was in his most primitive state." Comparative philology was in fact a form of prehistoric archeology, since the surviving words of antique languages were "the most ancient monuments of the human race." To reconstruct the life of the "primitive and undivided family of the Aryan nations," Müller used (though he did not invent) a technique later called "linguistic paleontology": any natural object, human artifact, or social relationship described by the same root form in all Indo-European languages could be assumed to be part of the primitive Aryan heritage; any for which there were two or more different roots must be a later innovation. The roots for sea being different, one assumed the Aryans lived inland; the root for door being the same, one assumed they lived in houses with doors. On this basis Müller described the undivided Aryans as "agricultural nomads" who could plow, weave, build roads, and count to one hundred, who "recognized the bonds of blood and the laws of marriage," who "followed their leaders and kings," and who were "impressed with the idea of a Divine being."[33]

In this context, Müller hypothesized a general "mythopoeic age" that explained the "ridiculous" creation myths of the Greeks in a manner consistent with the "regular progress of the human intellect." Each common Aryan word was "in a certain sense a myth"—an appellation that by "a kind of unconscious poetry" expressed in language only one "out of the many attributes which seemed characteristic of a certain object." Mythology was the unintended metaphorical product of linguistic processes operating on these primitive appellative forms. Terminations of gender forced the sexual personification of nonhuman forces; absence of auxiliary verbs forced the attribution of active behavior to personified phenomena; synonymy allowed two persons to spring from a single object; polyonymy allowed two objects to be inhabited by a single person. Müller later spoke of these processes as "disease of language": "Whenever any word, that was at first used metaphorically, is used without a clear conception of the steps that led from its original to its metaphorical meaning, there is danger of mythology; whenever those steps are forgotten and artificial steps put in their places, we have mythology, or if I may say so, we have diseased language."[34]

On such assumptions Müller argued that all of Aryan mythology was built on a common ground plan based on the observation of those natural phenomena that "bear the character of law, order, and wisdom impressed in them," and particularly on the "whole solar drama" reenacted "every day, every month, every year, in heaven and earth." The idea of divine powers sprang from the "wonderment" with which the "forefathers of the Aryan family" gazed upon the "bright powers" that each day came and went from nowhere. The interpretation of Aryan mythology was largely a matter of making equations in the roots of names (Greek Zeus = Sanskrit Dyaus, from the verb *dyu*, to shine) and following out the solar pattern in each myth. Thus, the idea of a young hero, whether called Baldr, Sigurd, Sifrit, or Achilles, who died in the fullness of youth, was "first suggested by the Sun, dying in all his youthful vigor, either at the end of a day, conquered by the powers of darkness, or at the end of the sunny season, stung by the thorn of winter."[35]

Müller's essay on comparative mythology is said to have swept all the materials of British folklore "into its orbit" for almost two decades. For George Webbe Dasent in 1859, the mythological and philological affinity of the Indo-European peoples was "now the first article of a literary creed." More broadly, the comparative philological methods Müller epitomized to British intellectuals in the years around 1860 offered a model for inquiry into the early stages of civilization generally.[36]

This is something of a paradox, because despite his references to the progress of the human intellect, Müller was at the deepest level profoundly antievolutionary. There were numerous overtones of degenerationism in his work, and in 1856 he had argued that the idea of "humanity emerging slowly from the depths of an animal brutality can never be maintained again." When Darwin soon suggested precisely that, Müller continued to maintain that "language is our Rubicon, and no brute will dare to cross it." Derisively rejecting all naturalistic explanations of the origin of language, he argued that the "bow wow" (or onomatopoeic) and the "pooh-pooh" (or interjectional) theories favored by evolutionists could never account for more than a small portion of the primitive roots that were the constituent elements of all language. These basic "phonetic types" were simply "ultimate facts," given—as Plato had suggested—"by the hand of God."[37]

At the same time, there was much in Müller that could be read in evolutionary terms. He himself later suggested that all his labors were connected by a single thread tying together "the origin of thought and language with the origin of mythology and religion." Despite his refusal to regard man as simply "a more favored beast," he quickly adapted the Darwinian idea of natural selection to describe the process by which, from numerous candidates, only certain words were preserved. He was enough of an intellectual opportunist to emphasize the points of contact between his ultimately idealist Germanic thought modes and the empiricism of his adopted compatriots, and for a time he loudly trumpeted the notion that the science of language was "one of the physical sciences," because it was governed by laws beyond the control of individual man.[38]

Thus it was that in reviewing Müller's work in 1866, E. B. Tylor attributed to him "the merit of having taken up the problem on the principle applied with such success to geology by Sir Charles Lyell, that of working back from the processes whose action we can trace in modern times and under similar conditions, and arguing that, where we find like effects in late and early periods of history, it is probable that the causes we know to produce them in the one case were also at work producing them in the other." Müller, who became involved in a bitter dispute with Tylor's followers over the interpretation of Greek mythology, came eventually to realize there were profound differences between his methodological assumptions and those of sociocultural evolutionism; and over time there was a drawing back on Tylor's part as well.[39] But in the early 1860s, Tylor built on Müller's work in developing his own evolutionary viewpoint. Furthermore, not all inquiry into the development of civilization was evolutionary in character, and the assumptions of comparative philology were also congenial to scholars whose interests were more traditionally historical. In short, whether considered as science or as history, comparative philology around 1860 was a highly salient field for British intellectuals concerned with the early history of mankind.

Anglo-Saxonism, Polygenism, and Physical Anthropology

By the time Müller arrived, there was already in England a flourishing tradition of Anglo-Saxon racialism, the roots of which go back to the antiquarian movement, when scholars searched for native English precedents to justify the break with Rome and then the defense of parliamentary power against royalist pretension. From the beginning, Anglo-Saxonism was part of a broader tradition of European thought that validated national, religious, or class interests by linking them with specific populations of the early medieval period—most notably in France, where the nobility claimed dominion by right of the Frankish conquest of a Gallo-Roman populace. By the early nineteenth century, Anglo-Saxonism had begun to take on a more distinctly racial meaning, with the emphasis less on Saxon resistance to the Norman yoke than on the common Teutonic origin that separated all Englishmen from their Celtic neighbors. Antiquarian and folklore studies offered new evidence of the historical unity of the "northern nations," and by the 1830s Müller's precursors in the propagation of comparative philology, Benjamin Thorpe and John Kemble, were tying Anglo-Saxons firmly to their Germanic ancestors in the Indo-European language family. Ethnology had begun to provide a framework in which this linguistic identity could be expressed in explicitly "racial" terms, and by the late 1840s, the idea of the Anglo-Saxon "race" was an intellectual commonplace. Thomas Arnold at Oxford was already influencing a generation of Saxon historians; Kemble at Cambridge had just completed his study of the land-holding and political institutions of *The Saxons in England;* Disraeli had published a series of novels rife with Saxonist assumption; and the short-lived *Anglo-Saxon* magazine was propagating the world Christianizing mission of the Anglo-Saxon "race."[40]

By the middle years of the nineteenth century, Anglo-Saxon racialism did more than define the positive content of national identity. The enterprising, liberty-loving Saxon, self-reliant and self-controlled, who had for some time been juxtaposed against the impulsive, imaginative, violent, and somewhat childish Celt, was now on a broader stage contrasted with the savages of the non-Western world, in whom the Celtic character was painted with a darker brush. Even humanitarian, monogenist, and environmentalist writers like Prichard accepted many long-traditional notions about the content of particular "racial" characters. Thus the Germanic nations were superior "in moral energy" to the rest of mankind; the Celts, in contrast, were unchaste, fickle, quick to fight, and wanting in "firmness and self-command." Given such "physical and moral degradation," it was no surprise that the outcome of their contact was invariably "the complete and final subjugation" of the Celts. Defending "African nations" against the charge of mental inferiority, Prichard drew on the Celtic analogy: exposed for two centuries to hunger and ignorance, the "two great brutalizers of the human race," the descendants of the Irish expelled from Armagh were remarkable for their "projecting mouths," and their "advancing cheekbones and depressed noses" were evidence of their "barbarism." If one could reverse the environmental conditions that had produced this degradation, it was probable that "a few generations would obliterate the effect" for Irish and Africans alike.[41]

Within the broader social and colonial context conditioning these Anglo-Saxon racial attitudes, the mid-century years have special significance. There were a number of events that sharpened the sense of separation of Europeans from dark-skinned colonial peoples. The controversy surrounding Rajah Brooke's suppression of the "pirates" of Sarawak in 1849 led others besides Charles Kingsley to question the humanity of the Dyaks and the Malays. Within a few short years, the "Indian Mutiny" led a larger number of Britons to reject the notion of common Aryan brotherhood with Hindus, who thenceforth were increasingly to be assimilated within a generalized dark-skinned racial fraternity stigmatized by the epithet "nigger." By the end of the decade, the issue of Negro slavery, in which so much of the nineteenth-century discussion of race had been ideologically enmeshed, came once again to prominence with the outbreak of the Civil War in America. And within Europe itself, the "racial" nationalism of the revolutionary epoch of 1848 gave the idea of race a greatly heightened saliency, even for men of unquestioned humanitarian commitment. Thus Prichard's obituarist, the Quaker physician Thomas Hodgkin, described that year as having been "disgraced" by the "savage atrocities" of "the wars of races."[42]

Although the political connotations of the race idea suggest to twentieth-century readers a rigidly biological determinist approach, in 1850 this was far from necessarily the case. The process by which "race" took on a clearly biological meaning was by no means complete, and contemporary biological assumption in fact justified a confusion of physical and cultural characteristics. The notion that acquired characteristics could be inherited was widely accepted, despite the general rejection of the evolutionary ideas associated with the much-ridiculed Lamarck. Given the belief that the habitual behavior of human groups in different environments might become part of their hereditary physical makeup, cultural phenomena were readily translatable into "racial" tendencies. From this point of view, the determinism implicit in the race idea was biological only in a secondary way. Much of Anglo-Saxon and other forms of "racial" nationalism, as well as Müller's Aryanism, may best be understood in this context.[43]

Well before 1850, however, there were also those who treated racial differences in a more strictly physical way, who emphasized the biological determination of cultural characteristics, and who tended to see human races in rigidly hierarchical and even polygenetic terms. Although stronger on the Continent, by mid-century this physical anthropological impulse was beginning to assert itself against the Prichardian ethnological tradition in Great Britain. The year 1848 saw the establishment (and quick demise) of an *Ethnological Journal* in which Luke Burke openly advocated the polygenist viewpoint. Two years later a book appeared arguing hereditarian racial doctrine in an extreme form: Robert Knox's *The Races of Men.*[44]

After studying medicine in Edinburgh, Knox had served as an army surgeon at Waterloo and the Cape, where he had dissected the bodies of fallen blacks. Going thence to Paris to study comparative anatomy under Cuvier and Saint-Hilaire, he had returned to Edinburgh to begin what promised to be a brilliant career in anatomy. In 1828, however, he was implicated in the infamous activities of Burke and Hare, unwittingly accepting sixteen murdered bodies as the "legitimate" merchandise of the grave-robbing traffic that regularly supplied the needs of anatomical demonstrators. Although legally exonerated of complicity, Knox was burned in effigy by an angry populace; eventually the odium roused by the murders and by his radical political and religious views forced him to leave Edinburgh. From 1842 he supported himself largely by public lecturing, and *The Races of Men* was given as a lecture series in various English cities.[45]

Like Gobineau and many other racialists, Knox projected on the screen of history a pessimism engendered by his own life experience. All theories of "human progress in time" seemed to him illusory: "Man's gift is to destroy, not to create." Arguing that "race is everything in human history," Knox insisted that no race could overcome the limits of its hereditary makeup—not even the dominating Saxon democrats, whose pragmatic virtues were counterbalanced by a certain intellectual dullness. Although Europeans might exterminate the dark-skinned races in portions of the globe, Knox felt that insuperable barriers to acclimatization would make permanent colonization of the deep tropics impossible.[46]

Clearly regarding himself as an advocate of a novel viewpoint, Knox insisted that although "the word, *race,* is of daily use," he was using it "in a new sense"—not in casual reference to differences that might arise from such "fanciful causes" as education, religion, or climate, but rather to designate physical entities unchanged since the beginning of recorded time. The polygenist character of Knox's racial views was somewhat obscured by the "transcendental" biology he had adopted from Saint-Hilaire, with its mystical notion of the "unity of type" pervading all animal life. But even in the first edition, Knox made it clear that his primary target was the "illustrious" Prichard, who had so long "succeeded in misdirecting the English mind as to all the great questions of race." And when a second edition appeared in 1862, Knox argued explicitly that certain of the races of men were "entitled to the name of species."[47]

While Knox is marginal to the mainstream of nineteenth-century British anthropological thought, the physical anthropological viewpoint was by no means without influence. Nourished in the shadow of Cuvierian comparative anatomy and the phrenological movement, physical anthropology by the 1840s had begun to emerge as a distinct approach to the study of human variability. Although much of its data had been collected in loosely descriptive natural historical or purely anecdotal terms ("a gentleman in Bombay assures me . . . "), a considerable amount of comparative anatomical material had also been collected, and various measures developed that seemed to give precision to racial comparison. The most important of these was of course the cephalic index originated by the Swedish anatomist Anders Retzius, which was to be the most widely used measurement in later-nineteenth-century physical anthropology. Distinguishing between dolichocephalic (narrow-headed) and brachycephalic (broad-headed) races, Retzius used his system to reconstruct European racial history, and by 1849 his influence was felt in England among men of less extreme racial views than Knox. After Prichard himself had sent a number of skulls to him in Sweden, Retzius forwarded to the British Association a paper in which he argued that the original British population, like that of Europe generally, had not been Celtic long-heads, but a broad-headed "Turanic" race whose remnants were to be found among the Basques and Lapps.[48]

Although the linguistic categories of the ethnological tradition are still evident in this exchange, over the next decade several other British medical men, following Knox, began to deal with physical differences among humans in terms that led them into conflict with the assumptions of Prichardian ethnology. This process can be traced in the diaries left by two of the most prominent British physical anthropologists: Joseph Bernard Davis and John Beddoe.

As a young man, Davis had shipped as surgeon on an Arctic whaler, but by 1845 he had been settled for two decades as a medical practitioner in Staffordshire. His diaries at that time reflect rather diffuse antiquarian interests of a fairly traditional sort, as well as a strong interest in the phrenological movement, then near the height of its influence in Great Britain. These two concerns came together in 1849 when, after visiting the museum of the local squire, Thomas Bateman, Davis remarked that the numerous ancient British skulls it contained ought to be turned to scientific use. Bateman, an antiquary of some repute, encouraged him to make the attempt; and by 1851 Davis was excavating barrows with Bateman, collecting skulls with an enthusiasm Beddoe later described as "ghoulish." Davis' ethnological opinions by this time were decidedly polygenist. He felt that Prichard's own data refuted the monogenist hypothesis, and in 1856 recorded a conversation in which the aging William Lawrence confided that since the days of his "blasphemous" *Natural History of Man* he, too, had become convinced of the diversity of human origin. By this time, Davis had already joined forces with another polygenist medical man, Joseph Thurnam, for a systematic study of ancient British skulls. Modelled on the work of the American polygenist Samuel Morton, their *Crania Britannica* was founded on the "fundamental axiom" that the form of the human head was "not transmutable in the different Races."[49]

The diaries John Beddoe kept as a young man in Bristol begin with similar generalized antiquarian and natural historical interests, but an entry of 1848 suggests that revolutionary nationalisms had stimulated a "racial" interest: "The cowardly and treacherous Italians must have changed much, if they can permanently withstand the steadfast Teuton and the impetuous Slave." These racial interests were placed in a more rigorous comparative anatomical context when Beddoe went to London to prepare himself in medicine. At University College in 1851, he attended lectures by Robert Grant, who drew on the French polygenist Bory de St. Vincent to characterize the "sub-species" of man. During further medical training in Edinburgh, Beddoe carried on anthropological studies of Highland Scots; and when he finally returned from the Crimean War to practice in Bristol, he became Davis' "ally, assistant, and fellow-labourer." Beddoe approached the question of "permanence of types" through the study of eye and hair color, which could be observed in large numbers of people "without the concurrence of the subject," and by this means constructed a primitive statistical "index of nigrescence." Following up a scheme of Davis' for a national inquiry by questionnaire into the physical characteristics of the British people, Beddoe was able to get data from two hundred correspondents, most of them doctors who followed his own life-long example by collecting data from their patients. By 1868, Beddoe had put together a manuscript on "The Origin of the English Nation," which was later to become his magnum opus, *The Races of Britain.*[50]

Despite the contributions of Davis and his co-workers, Britain was not a major center of physical anthropology, and British practitioners tended to look abroad for intellectual and methodological models: to the United States and the so-called "American School" of Morton's followers; to Germany, where what was soon to be a flourishing physical anthropological tradition was then emerging; and most of all to France, where another polygenist physician, Paul Broca, was remodeling anthropological inquiry along anatomical lines. But wherever the physical anthropological viewpoint was manifest, it contained a strong polygenist impulse. On the basis of skeletal and cranial evidence, polygenists insisted that blacks were physically distinct and mentally inferior; on the basis of the racial representations on "ancient Egyptian monuments" they argued that races had remained unchanged throughout the major portion of human history; on the basis of the mortality of whites in tropical areas they hypothesized that different races were aboriginal products of different "centers of creation" and could never fully "acclimate" elsewhere; on the basis of anecdotal evidence they asserted that the hybrid offspring of blacks and Europeans were only partially interfertile. On all these grounds they argued that mankind was not one but several biological species—the number varying with different polygenist writers.[51]

By the time of the *Origin of Species,* polygenism had had a considerable impact. The German physiologist Rudolf Wagner suggested that "just before Darwin's book appeared, the theory of the possibility or probability of the different races of mankind having descended from a single pair was thought perfectly antiquated, and as having lagged behind all scientific progress." And even Darwin, whose own theory was to redefine the framework in which such issues were discussed, felt that a naturalist confronted for the first time with specimens of Negro and European man would doubtless call them each "good and true species."[52]

At one level, the more strictly physical anthropological approach to race that emerged in Britain in the 1850s may be viewed as a more naturalistic variant of the traditional ethnological approach. Physical anthropologists were interested in classifying the "types of mankind" rather than in reconstructing their "physical history." Ethnology, however, also contained a classificatory impulse, albeit conceived in more nominalist terms. In a sense, the issue was one between "lumpers" and "splitters," and monogenism and polygenism were competing answers to a single question: "is mankind one or many?"[53] But in fact a sharp challenge had been raised to the ethnological conceptualization of human variation. It was not simply that the monogenist viewpoint inherited from the Bible was increasingly called into question. Physical anthropologists questioned the assumptions as well as the conclusions of Prichardian ethnology.

At its most extreme, Prichard's argument involved the assumption that one could reason systematically from the nonphysical to the physical: if two unlike physical types were linguistically related, Prichard tended to assume that their physical differences had arisen historically under the influence of environment. The same assumption underlay Müller's suggestion that one blood flowed in the veins of British soldiers and Indian "mutineers." But this depended on the priority of language as an index of racial affinity, and medical men who devoted themselves primarily to the measurement of skulls and the observation of pigmentation were likely to question this assumption.[54]

Although it continued to influence both scientific and popular thinking about race for years to come, the ethnological priority of language had already begun to be criticized not only by physical anthropologists, but by some philologists as well. The earlier hopes that comparative philology could be generalized beyond the Indo-European family to establish genealogical or morphological connections between all the languages of man were becoming somewhat tarnished. The French orientalist Renan now argued the absolute disparity between even the Aryan and the Semitic families; Müller's attempt to establish the unity of the Turanian tongues was being widely attacked; and some philologists, like August Pott, were now themselves embracing polygenism on purely linguistic grounds. In this context, the earlier alliance of linguistics and ethnology was greatly attenuated, and Müller himself came to insist that race was a purely physical category.[55]

Underlying the attack on monogenism and the linguistic view of race was a more fundamental issue: the extent to which it was appropriate to consider man in purely naturalistic terms. The barriers to such a view, which in some respects had been raised higher in the earlier nineteenth century, were by 1850 being seriously eroded. Prichardian ethnology and the emergent physical anthropology occupied somewhat ambiguous positions in relation to this movement. Prichard himself was by no means totally rejecting of physical anthropology; although he was always skeptical of phrenology, he did use craniological evidence to help decide issues of racial affinity. Much of his general argument in fact rested on "analogical" reasoning from the characteristics of all animal species, and looking back it is easy to find in his work a more dynamic and potentially evolutionary view of physical man than that of physical anthropology, which was entangled in the static categories of the pre-Darwinian period.[56]

But from the perspective of that period itself, it seems clear that Prichard's work as a whole should be regarded as an outgrowth of biblical anthropology, not only in its commitment to monogenism, but in its tendency to maintain the separation between man and the rest of animal creation. So at least it seemed to many physical anthropologists, who saw themselves as partisans of science against religious orthodoxy, and who, in Knox's words, insisted that "no good reason exists for regarding man as a distinct creation from the living world." This is not to say that physical anthropologists anticipated or readily embraced Darwinism. In fact they tended rather to resist it as a new form of monogenism, or simply to dismiss it as a restatement of themes already manifest in Lamarckian or German transcendental biology. But they did share with Darwinians the assumption that mankind must be studied as part of the animal world. Unlike Prichard, they would not have objected to being included in the natural history section of the British Association. As we shall see, what disturbed them was rather the feeling that it was not possible within the traditional rubric "ethnology" to study mankind simply as a physical entity, as one (or more) species in a natural world of biological species.[57]

The Revolution in Human Time

If the incorporation of mankind into the tradition of comparative anatomy marked an important step in the development of a naturalistic anthropology, the culmination of that process came only with Darwinism, which not only allowed present and past mankind to be studied as an animal species, but the very origin of humankind to be treated without reference to supernatural causation. This culmination, however, took place in a context of changes in the surrounding framework of religious belief, as well as in the study of archeology—an area of anthropological inquiry which in 1858 experienced its own independent intellectual revolution: a revolution in human time.

In the 1830s, when the Bridgewater Treatises were published to demonstrate the "Power, Wisdom, and Goodness of God, as manifest in Creation," Christian men of science could still offer serious intellectual defenses of the reality of miracles. When William Whewell asked if man, "with his thoughts and feelings, his powers and hopes, his will and conscience" was simply "the ultimate result of the condensation of the solar atmosphere," the very statement of the question implied a negative answer. Even Charles Lyell's geological "uniformitarianism" could not conceive of the "leap" from "an irrational to a rational animal" as part of any "regular series of changes in the animal world."[58]

The framework of belief that made Whewell's question rhetorical, however, was seriously undermined in the next two decades. The phrenological movement, which in this period influenced many British intellectuals, helped to break down the barrier between instinct and reason by grounding all mental and moral faculties of man in the organic structure of the brain. While the Deluge was still accepted as an historical event even after geologists had abandoned its universality, German "higher criticism" was beginning to undercut the Bible's general claim to historicity. If at first only those minds were troubled who were in some way "anxious for trouble," the controversy over Chambers' *Vestiges* troubled many who would have preferred to remain at peace. By 1851, in Harriet Martineau's *Letters on the Laws of Man's Nature and Development,* Victorian Britons were confronted publicly by the "full creed" of scientific materialism, which a very troubled Charlotte Brontë described as "the first unequivocal declaration of disbelief in the existence of a God or a future life I have ever seen." In this changing context, Whewell's query about the origin of man could no longer be treated as rhetorical, and the time was soon coming when many would answer "yes."[59]

In defending miracles, Whewell appealed to the "Law of Continuity," arguing that there was one great historical chain of causation that explained the entire history of the cosmos, ranging up from those causes which regulated "the imperceptible changes of the remotest nebulae in the heavens, to those which determine the diversities of language, the mutations of art, and even the progress of civilization, polity, and literature." But if, as Whewell suspected, the latter were "quite inexplicable by the aid of any natural causes with which we are acquainted," then "the result of our investigations, conducted with strict regard to scientific principles," would require us "to contemplate supernatural influences as part of the past series of events." Whewell argued, in effect, that a continuous historical sequence of causation "took rational priority over the supposed universal efficacy of secondary causes and therefore that a miracle would be scientific if it were needed to maintain historical continuity." But although phrased in terms of the historical continuity of causes, Whewell's argument assumed major discontinuities, most particularly that separating ape and man. Because science could not point to a convincing set of secondary causes to account for the emergence of man as a culture-bearing animal, one could as scientist believe that the process was, as the Bible suggested, miraculous.[60]

If Darwinism bridged for its believers this historical discontinuity, its ability to do so depended in part on developments in archeology. The need for supernatural causes to maintain historical continuity of causation depended also on the shallowness of the archeological record. So long as the span of human existence was limited to the historical period, and so long as archeology focused on the remains of relatively civilized man, it was hard to provide a strictly uniformitarian development for those cultural phenomena for which Whewell insisted on the intervention of God. Not only was the evidence inadequate, but the span of human time was simply too short to make a uniformitarian process convincing.

In 1850, however, British archeology was only beginning to stir from the doldrums of antiquarianism, and seemed hardly likely to play a central role in a scientific revolution. Focusing primarily on the relics of the medieval period in Great Britain, it was parochial both in space and in time. True, the years around 1850 did see a burgeoning interest in ancient civilizations overseas. But if Wilkinson's account of ancient Egypt, Layard's of Nineveh and Babylon, and Stephens' of the Maya were widely read, the impact of such works can actually be seen as anti-evolutionary. For those who still accepted biblical chronology, the effect of archeological investigations such as these was to preempt almost the entire 6,000-year span for human groups who were fairly highly civilized. There was little time left "in the beginning" for these groups to have raised themselves from savagery. On the other hand, there was plenty of time available for nineteenth-century savages to have fallen from an originally higher state; and the romantic aura of decay and destruction emanating from broken ruins, toppled monoliths, and sand-swept or vine-covered pyramids tended to sustain a degenerationist rather than a progressivist view of human history.[61]

Although there were indications of heightened activity in the archeology of Britain itself, that study, too, was only beginning to break out of the older antiquarian tradition. Stimulated in part by discoveries made in the construction of railways, local archeology had become quite fashionable, and in 1843 a British Archaeological Association was formed—the Society of Antiquaries having been for some time stagnant. The roots of the new organization in the generalized antiquarianism that nourished the folklore movement are evident in their overlapping personnel. Indeed, scholars trying to support themselves by their own intellectual activity were forced to cut a rather broad swath, with divisive consequences for archeology. When Thomas Wright, a founder of the Archaeological Association, printed some of its proceedings in a private publishing venture, the animosities aroused split the Association into two parts, one of which became the Archaeological Institute in 1846. Both groups, however, focused primarily on the physical antiquities of medieval Britain. Prehistory barely existed, and the "blessed word Celtic covered everything pre-Roman." Looking back thirty years later when the Institute met for a second time in Salisbury, General Pitt Rivers recalled that no one present at the 1849 meeting "had the least idea that beneath his very feet were to be found relics of man's worksmanship at a time when he was contemporary with the elephant'' and other animals long extinct in Britain.[62]

Evidence for the existence of prehistoric man in Britain had in fact been reported to the Society of Antiquaries as early as 1797 by John Frere; and in the years around 1830 there was a series of finds in Britain, Belgium, and France. But such evidence was resisted by the leading geologists, into whose growingly professional province the issue naturally fell, and who regardless of theoretical persuasion were agreed on the recency of man. Although the scripturalist catastrophism of the 1820s in principle allowed for antediluvial man, it did not allow for him in Europe, but only in the Asian ''cradle of the race.'' John McEnery, a Catholic priest who dug at Kent's Hole in Devonshire, was so cowed by geological orthodoxy that he was inclined to regard the flints he found with extinct animals as somehow deposited *after* the Flood.[63]

When in the 1830s the Deluge ceased to be regarded as the last grand catastrophe of geological history, both ''progressionists'' and ''uniformitarians'' continued to reject the idea of antediluvial man—which in usage if not etymology came to refer to any humans before the very recent period. Charles Lyell himself struck the characteristic note of resistance in commenting in 1833 on Schmerling's discoveries at Liège: ''He has found human remains in breccia, embedded with extinct species, under circumstances far more difficult to get over than I have previously heard of. . . . '' Whatever their private questionings, the public resistance of geologists continued unabated into the 1850s. When in 1847 Boucher de Perthes published the first volume of his *Antiquités celtiques et antediluviennes* (which attacked but did not yet reject the framework of biblical anthropology), French geologists rejected it as amateurish speculation; and when he sent a paper on his Abbéville researches to the British Archaeological Association in 1849, it made little impression.[64]

Despite their resistance to antediluvial man, British archeologists did respond to another innovation which, although less revolutionary, redefined and stretched existing categories: the ''three age'' system Christian Thomsen had developed to organize the collections of the Danish National Museum. In 1849 the folklorist Thoms prepared an English edition of the *Primeval Antiquities of Denmark,* by Thomsen's pupil J. J. Worsaae. Developed in the 1810s, the Danish system was pre-evolutionary in both a Darwinian and a cultural sense. The time perspective was shallow, and the central hypothesis was cast in diffusionary racial terms that saw the Bronze and Iron Ages carried into Denmark by more highly cultivated intruding races, rather than developed independently by the nation's Stone Age aborigines. Even so, much of Worsaae's argument was cast in developmental terms. At various points he offered comparative asides on the artifacts of Tierra del Fuego and the South Seas, and he tended to associate technology with ''stages of civilization.'' When he visited England for the second time in 1851, Worsaae in fact predicted that the three age system would "apply to the British remains" as well as to the Danish.[65]

For those who would accept it, Worsaae's book offered a framework of relative chronology to order the large number of physical antiquities and human remains that had been discovered in the barrows, tumuli, and round towers of Great Britain. Although some, including Thomas Wright, refused to accept the idea of a pre-Roman Bronze Age, others quickly adopted the Danish scheme. According to Daniel Wilson, an engraver whose interest in the civic history of his native Edinburgh led eventually to a general work on *The Archaeology and Prehistoric Annals of Scotland*, the three age system offered a "new historic chronometry," which he proceeded to apply to Scotland in four phases: the Primeval or stone; the Archaic or bronze; the Teutonic or iron; and the Christian.[66]

Biblical assumptions still hung heavily over Wilson's vista of human history. He suggested that the primitive Caledonians had become "untutored savages" in the course of nomadic wanderings in which "they had forgotten all the heaven-taught knowledge of Eden, and had utterly lost the antediluvian metallurgic arts." But in many respects, Wilson's argument broke from tradition, not least in coining the word that was used to describe the new "prehistoric" archeology of the 1860s. If he insisted on the special creation of man, he was inclined to interpret Egyptian civilization in progressivist terms. If he still saw archeology as providing a more comprehensive picture of European racial migrations, when it came to comparing the artifacts of British barrows and Mississippi mounds, he saw their similarity not as evidence "of an affinity of race, or of mutual intercourse," but of "some cause operating naturally at a certain stage of development in the human mind." Finally, his work suggests a convergence of a number of emergent disciplines on the single problem of human prehistory. Although only archeology could reveal the traces of the "unknown Allophylian [i.e., Turanian] race" that preceded the Celts in northern Europe, Wilson granted the "essential dependence of Archaeology on the kindred sciences," which in his own work included geology, ethnology, physical anthropology, folklore, and philology.[67]

The 1850s saw a number of important discoveries bearing on prehistory. The very dry winter of 1853–1854 revealed remains of prehistoric Swiss lake dwellings, and in 1857 the bones of Neanderthal man were discovered in a limestone cave in Rhenish Prussia. Even so, Lyell could still affirm as late as 1855 that "we have every reason to infer that the human race is extremely modern." The real break came in 1858, when a new fissure was opened during quarrying operations near Kent's Hole. Brixham Cave was immediately called to the attention of the Geological Society of London, which appointed a committee of prominent scientists to investigate. When the carefully supervised excavations subsequently revealed numerous human artifacts *in situ* with extinct animals, the grounds for rejecting the evidence were very slim indeed. In this context De Perthes' earlier discoveries were reevaluated. Reporting to the Society of Antiquaries on a visit he and several others made to Abbéville at Easter in 1859, John Evans concluded that it was now beyond doubt that "in a period of antiquity, remote beyond any of which we have hitherto found trace, this portion of the globe was peopled by man." When Lyell announced his own conversion at the Aberdeen meeting of the British Association later that year, the revolution in archeology was well-nigh accomplished. Its impact on anthropological thought was to be enormous.[68]

The Crisis of Prichardian Ethnology

Speculation about early European history had for decades been structured in terms of a model of racial movement—a series of migrations from the East into the European continent. We have seen expressions of this view in each of a number of areas of anthropological inquiry: in diffusionary interpretations of European folklore; in archeological ages explained in terms of racial intrusion; even in physical anthropology, despite the polygenist thrust that ran counter to migrationism; and most obviously in comparative philology, from which many of the basic categories and assumptions of this viewpoint were derived. This conception of history as racial movement from the Orient had its source in a biblical tradition of anthropological speculation, which in early-nineteenth-century Britain was transformed in the work of James Cowles Prichard into the science of "ethnology."[69]

Using a controversial term in a loosely metaphorical way, we may find in Prichardian ethnology a number of the characteristics of a scientific "paradigm."[70] For the scientific community of its adherents, Prichard's *Researches into the Physical History of Mankind* provided a concrete exemplar of ethnological research. Built on a set of both articulated and implicit assumptions that had the a priori character of a disciplinary worldview, generating a series of particular ethnological puzzles, Prichardian ethnology drew on a variety of traditions of inquiry to establish ethnic connections within the framework of the underlying image of the racial tree. But by the 1850s, many inquirers into human diversity, troubled by what within a Prichardian framework seemed anomalous evidence, called into question both the explicit and implicit assumptions of Prichardian ethnology, and began to consider alternative modes of explanation for the same body of data. In a sense that is more than merely metaphorical—since some of the actors seemed aware of it—the ethnological paradigm may be said to have been in a state of crisis in the years after Prichard's death in 1849.

In this context, suddenly in 1858 the oldest evidence for man's existence was found not in the East, but in Europe itself, and at a much earlier point in time than traditional sources of ethnology could document. While this did not lead to a total rejection of the conceptualization of human history in terms of racial movement, it did have a profound impact on historical speculations carried on under the aegis of comparative philology. One result was a debate that raged for several decades as to whether the Aryans had originated in Asia or in Europe.[71] But the issues confronting traditional ethnology went much deeper than this. Before 1850, the comparative anatomical and the comparative philological orientations had coexisted within ethnology in a kind of asymmetrical tension, the static diversifying impulses of the former constrained by the historically unifying tendencies of the latter. But in the 1850s this uneasy balance was seriously threatened, as comparative philologists no longer took for granted that all languages could be related genealogically, and physical anthropologists attacked the use of language as the primary criterion of racial affinity. Now, to make matters worse, the revolution in human time threatened to undercut the claims of linguistic ethnology to cast light upon the primitive origin of mankind.

Founded on the Bible, conceptualized as a history of racial movement, and buttressed largely by the evidence of comparative philology, the historical argument for human unity depended for its prima facie plausibility on a relatively short chronology. The longer the period of human migrations, the more unlikely that they could be traced to their origin. Prichard had long been sensitive to the difficulties of the historical argument. Even before he accepted Bunsen's 20,000-year chronology, he had concluded that "historical investigations" were "entirely unavailing" when it came to outlying races "whose isolated existence and peculiar aspect and manners are most calculated to excite our curiosity and doubt." But the great expansion of human time opened up in Brixham Cave obviously compounded such difficulties. Insofar as scholars took seriously the new antiquity of man, they must have found the project of tracing human migrations to a single source increasingly hopeless. Coming at a point when the methodological assumptions of Prichardian ethnology were already under attack, the revolution in human time posed almost insurmountable problems for the Prichardian paradigm, viewed as an approach to human history.[72]

But the crisis had its paradoxical aspect: for if the temporal revolution greatly weakened the *historical* argument for human unity, its effect on the *biological* argument was quite the opposite. As Lyell suggested, it in fact answered one of the strongest arguments against monogenism: "So long as physiologists continued to believe that man had not existed on the earth above six thousand years, they might, with good reason, withhold their assent from the doctrine of unity of origin of so many distinct races; but the difficulty becomes less and less, exactly in proportion as we enlarge our ideas of the lapse of time during which different communities may have spread slowly, and become isolated, each exposed for ages to a peculiar set of conditions. . . . "[73]

Furthermore, although it had occurred without reference to the virtually contemporaneous publication of the Darwinian hypothesis, the archeological revolution established at least two essential preconditions for the development of a Darwinian view of man. It helped to bridge the temporal discontinuity that had developed in paleontology between man and supposedly separate creations of earlier animal forms. And in doing so, it provided the expanded temporal framework that made the gradual evolution of a culture-bearing animal from an apelike creature seem, if not likely, then at least not prima facie implausible. Although there was still a considerable leeway for the survival of polygenist racial assumption in the new Darwinian context, the ultimate unity of the various races of man soon no longer seemed seriously at issue to most British students of human diversity. Paradoxically, the same temporal revolution that made the historical solution of the old ethnological problem seem a hopeless project made its biological solution seem no longer problematic.[74]

The end result was the transformation of "ethnology" and the emergence of the synthetic disciplinary rubric that in the Anglo-American tradition has been called "anthropology."[75] Freed from the constraints of biblical anthropological assumption, the study of man could now in principle, if not always in practice, be carried on in strictly naturalistic terms. The historical dimension was not eliminated from anthropological inquiry, since its central problem still involved the delineation of change through time. The content of this problem, however, was quite different. The strains within the Prichardian paradigm had begun to be felt just as the cultural changes symbolized by the Crystal Palace were compelling new attention to the growth of European civilization. Its supercession occurred when the process of civilization generally was cast within the new archeological and biological framework that had emerged by 1859. Anthropological inquiry, which for decades had focused on the problem of human unity, was now refocused on the problem of the origin of human civilization. Oversimplifying a reorientation whose complexities will take many pages to disentangle, one might say that "the natural history of man," which had been interpreted primarily in terms of movement in space, was now to be understood in terms of development in time. Brought within the compass of the positivistic philosophy of progress in civilization, this developmental history of man was now conceived in "scientific" terms. Although anthropologists did not abandon the study of migration and diffusion, change in time was now conceptualized primarily in terms of repeated events governed by lawful processes regularly producing the same effects from the same causes, rather than in more particularistic terms. The regularity of the cultural evolutionary ladder was superimposed upon the irregular outlines of the ethnological tree as the governing visual metaphor. Substantively, the focus of anthropological inquiry was still on the cultural and physical diversity of the human species; but the data of contemporary savage peoples were now to have a different significance.

THREE

Travelers and Savages: The Data of Victorian Ethnology (1830–1858)

"An Exhibition of the Native Club-Dance"—Fiji, 1840
Charles Wilkes, *Narrative of the United States Exploring Expedition during the Years 1838, 1839, 1840, 1841, 1842* (Philadelphia, 1850), vol. III, facing p. 190.

ALTHOUGH articles in early ethnological journals sometimes reflected personal experience overseas, Prichardian ethnology was essentially an activity of the study, not the field. Except for some bones and artifacts that came into his possession, observations he gathered from patients in his medical practice, and information in letters from a network of correspondents abroad, the material on which Prichard built his ethnology came largely from the printed pages of books. Many of these were very old ones: the ancient historian-geographers who described the peoples at the margins of the classical world; the chroniclers of barbarian invasions of the Roman Empire; and the early antiquarian accounts of the national histories of Europe—testimony to the continuity of Prichardian ethnology with deeply rooted traditions of speculation about human diversity. From the beginning, however, Prichard also drew on more contemporary travel accounts; and as the years and the editions went by, his volumes became more and more compendia of the travel literature of nineteenth-century Europeans abroad.[1]

Prichard was not unconcerned with the quality of the ethnographic information on which he drew. Thus he felt that because they usually made short visits, "naturalists" were less to be trusted than missionaries, many of whom through long residence had become "intimately acquainted with the languages of the natives." In 1839 he was the moving spirit behind an ethnographic questionnaire circulated by the British Association for the Advancement of Science, and his last published ethnological writing was a guide "prepared for the use of Her Majesty's Navy and adapted for travellers." Neither of these, however, seems to have elicited much systematic information, and the sources of ethnographic data remained very much the same in the two decades after Prichard's death. Books on the experiences of travelers, explorers, naturalists, missionaries, and colonial officials continued to flow from the presses, to be noted in the annual listings of accessions to the library of the Royal Geographical Society. Such ethnographic materials as were to be found here and there in these accounts provided the basis for the theoretical arguments both of ethnologists and of the social evolutionary writers who succeeded them. Indeed, it might be argued that there was no fundamental change in this respect until the end of the century: with the exception of a few regular correspondents from the field like Lorimer Fison and Baldwin Spencer, the ethnographic sources of E. B. Tylor and James Frazer are of a piece with Prichard's.[2]

But if the major Victorian anthropological writers were "armchair" anthropologists, this does not imply that their speculations were unconstrained by the ethnographic material available to them. The character of available ethnographic "data"—always keeping in mind the somewhat anachronistic and always problematic character of that term—had a great deal to do with the theoretical revolution that occurred after 1860. Contradictory and redundant data contributed to the stress in the ethnological paradigm, and the range of possible theoretical alternatives to it was limited by the types of ethnographic data available. These data were not of course the unconstituted, directly observed "facts" of Gradgrindian or positivist epistemological myth. Prior assumption—whether in the form of theoretical commitment or of unconscious or explicitly articulated cultural values—constrained their collection as well as their selection and interpretation. But if European travelers perceived dark-skinned "savages" through blinders of ethnocentric preconception, this did not mean that they were unaffected by their experiences abroad, even if these did not lead them to adopt a modern anthropological viewpoint on racial and cultural differences.

To understand the emergence of social evolutionism, it therefore seems worthwhile to look at the attitudes, experiences, and writings of some of those who provided the data of Victorian ethnography. George Grey, Thomas Williams, Francis Galton, and Alfred Russel Wallace all published works in the 1850s that were frequently referred to by ethnological writers of this and the following decade. Of varied personal backgrounds, they encompass the major professional categories of the authors of travel accounts—being, respectively, a colonial administrator, a Methodist missionary, a gentleman explorer, and a scientific traveler of more modest origins. The peoples they studied, and the "colonial situations" that both facilitated and constrained their inquiry, span the earth from the Pacific through Africa to Ireland and on to the New World. Although all were confident of their own cultural or racial superiority, they illustrate a number of possible theoretical and attitudinal postures, ranging from a post-Enlightenment imperialist progressivism, to an evangelical monogenetic assimilationism, to a pessimistic racialist eugenicism, to a paradoxical polygenistic primitivism. Treated in temporal sequence, they illustrate the movement from Enlightenment developmentalism to biblical degenerationism and then toward evolutionism—to which Galton and Wallace of course contributed in a major way—and the parallel degradation of the status of savages in the minds of Europeans.

Beyond this, the experiences of these four Britishers overseas provide a series of biographical microcosms of the historical experience of actual contact between nineteenth-century Europeans and the "savages" whose origin, status, and fate social evolutionism would attempt both to explain and to justify. From this broadly contextual point of view, as well as from the narrower perspective of the role of ethnographic data in a major theoretical reorientation, these rather concretely descriptive vignettes may carry substantial exemplary weight.

The Benevolent Colonial Despot as Ethnographer

Sir George Grey was a benevolent administrative despot whose iron-willed public personality fused anomalous ideological elements into what was to become one of the archetypical modes of the British colonial proconsul. A social radical with the instincts of an autocrat, he pursued liberal humanitarian policies with resolute dogmatic zeal—and a dissembling, manipulating opportunism. An idealistic visionary of multiracial social harmony in a period of rising racial antagonism, he was also a systematic propagator of Anglo-Saxon imperialism in a period of colonial retrenchment—and therefore periodically in trouble with both colonists and the Colonial Office. The cornerstone of his public career was his native policy: combining naive humanitarianism and imperialist realpolitik, it sought the advancement of native welfare through the systematic confiscation of tribal lands and the destruction of tribal institutions. Paradoxically—for those who see anthropological empathy as necessarily premised on the acceptance of cultural diversity—Grey was one of the more perceptive ethnographers of his day, and author of some of the most influential ethnographic work of the century.[3]

Son of an army colonel with aristocratic family connections, Grey was born just after his father's death in the Peninsular campaign of 1812. His Anglo-Irish mother, daughter of a clergyman, chose her second husband (a baronet) from the same profession, and Grey was indelibly marked by her evangelical piety. Although he profited intellectually from a family connection with the Liberal Anglican scholar Richard Whately, his early education was erratic, and in the end, he followed his father into the military. For several years after he was commissioned an ensign in 1830, Grey served in Ireland, searching for illicit stills, maintaining order at political meetings, and protecting the officials who forcibly collected Anglican tithes from the Catholic peasantry. Although later in life he was able to carry out such ''dirty work of empire'' without apparent qualm, in Ireland his adolescent heart went out to those whose aspirations he had been sent to repress. He saw enough ''to give a bias to my mind forever as to the necessity for change and reform''—which in the 1830s took the form of emigration, a social panacea advocated by Edward Gibbon Wakefield as a solution to the Malthusian dilemma. For Grey, however, the goal of ''systematic colonization'' was not to reproduce the old world in the new, but to create an egalitarian society in which the poorer classes of Britain could lead simpler natural lives free from the tyranny of landed aristocracy.[4]

In 1836 Grey proposed to the Colonial Secretary and the Royal Geographical Society an exploration of northwestern Australia, hoping to open the interior for settlement. In July of the next year, Grey embarked in the H.M.S. *Beagle*, only recently returned from the voyage that had taken Darwin around the world; at Cape Town, he chartered a schooner, loaded her with livestock, and sailed for Australia with a party of twelve, landing in December 1837 at Hanover Bay, southeast of Timor. The following February, the ill-planned and ill-fated expedition was attacked by aborigines, leaving the badly wounded Grey to ponder the cruel necessity of self-defense, and the "tenderness and solicitude" with which the man who had speared him was carried off by his comrades to die with Grey's rifle ball between his shoulders. Although his own wound was slow to heal, Grey carried on exploring, discovering a mountain peak he named for Charles Lyell, and a river that conjured up visions of a thriving settler population trading cotton in the nearby Malay Archipelago. When laudanum no longer sufficed to keep him going, Grey made his way back to the coast, where he was picked up by the *Beagle* and taken to Mauritius to recuperate. Upon his return to western Australia later that year, his boats were smashed by storms near Bernier Island, and his party was forced to walk southward toward Perth. When it became evident that their meager supplies would not last at the pace of the slowest, Grey went ahead alone for help. Sustained by "frequent perusal and meditation of the Scriptures," and by the belief that soon "civilization would have followed in my tracks," he covered the 300 miles back to Perth in three days without food or water.[5]

Within several months after his return to England in 1840, Grey put together a two-volume account of his explorations, including 200 pages on the languages, tribal laws, and customs of the Australians—which he treated with a certain empathy. When, like some other Europeans, he was taken as the ghost of a long dead son by a native family who had never seen a white, he tried not to dispel his new mother's "dream of happiness"—since he realized that he could not stay long enough to replace "this vain impression by a consoling faith." In southwest Australia, where he stayed for some months, Grey had been able to learn the local dialect and gain more intimate knowledge of the natives than the fleeting contact of his northern explorations allowed. He made it a point to attend funeral ceremonies extending over several days, investigating native beliefs that the deaths had been caused by sorcery, recording verbatim an interview with his chief informant, and translating a number of native songs. Although he found no sight in the world more "revolting" than natives feasting on "the carcass of a putrid whale," he offered a long and sympathetic account of hunting and food preparation. Grey argued that, contrary to popular belief, aborigines could collect all the food they needed each day in two or three hours;

given the exhilaration of the hunt and the sociability of the family meal around the campfire, he was not surprised that "it should be so difficult to induce a savage to embrace the customs of civilized life."[6]

The most remarkable aspect of Grey's account was his treatment of Australian social organization. Due to the rigidly enforced avoidance of the names of the dead, it was only with considerable sensitivity and indirection that he was able to collect a mass of genealogical material. Starting with those dead long enough for the prohibition to have weakened, he worked on individual natives of "loquacious humour," finally managing "round their fires at night" to "involve them in disputes regarding their ancestors." Grey only began to unravel the complex social structure of the area, and generalized his statements far beyond; but he did call attention to phenomena that were long to be the foci of anthropological inquiry and debate. The aborigines were divided into a small number of "great families," perpetuated and spread over wide areas by "two remarkable laws": that children always took the family name of the mother, and that a man could not marry a woman of his own family name. Each family adopted as their *kobong* or crest some animal or plant species, to which they felt themselves mysteriously connected, so that they would only kill it with great reluctance. While writing up his materials in England, Grey apparently came across the copy of Albert Gallatin's *Synopsis* of American Indian tribes that Prichard had presented to the library of the Royal Geographical Society; in it Grey found descriptions of matrilineal clans and "*totams*" that seemed remarkably similar. But although he thereby juxtaposed for comparison social phenomena that were to preoccupy anthropologists on into the twentieth century, and in fact noted that "civilized nations, in their heraldic bearings," preserved "traces of the same custom," Grey was far from interpreting exogamous matrilineal kinship, totem, and tabu in social evolutionary terms.[7]

Grey was more interested in biblical than American Indian comparisons. He found a "similar law of consanguinity" implicit in Genesis, where one could also find the custom of naming children "from some circumstance connected with their birth." Grey was sharply critical of the "closet" reveries of "deistical writers" who imagined that savage man "urged on by his necessities, and aided by his senses" might "step by step" mount to the "pinnacle of civilization." But if his account savors slightly of traditional Christian degenerationism, he nonetheless rejected the idea that the Australians "were originally in a state of civilization" and had "gradually sunk to their present condition." It was rather that God had willed that they should remain savages "until a certain period." Indeed, aboriginal life was filled with "evidences of design." If the men of this own expedition, equipped with iron tools and in full possession of their faculties, could almost die of hunger "from ignorance of the natural productions'' of the continent, then clearly the Australians, who lacked those tools, must have been provided in advance with the knowledge that enabled them to survive. Since it was beyond the capacity of any savage patriarchs to invent, alone or in assembly, social forms so complex and ''well adapted to the wants and necessities of the savage state,'' clearly they must have had a divine origin. Indeed, they were so ''ingeniously devised'' as to work together to ''annihilate'' any effort to overthrow them: thus the law that men ''connected by blood on the female side'' must join in avenging crimes meant, in a polygamous society, that one man's children were ''repeatedly all divided amongst themselves''—a custom that by itself would ''prevent this people ever emerging from a savage state.''[8]

On the other hand, aboriginal institutions, allowing ''no scope whatever'' for the development of intellect or benevolence, were surely not beneficial to human beings as rational creatures. These institutions systematically degraded the rest of society for the benefit of the stronger, older males, who were exempt from many of the food prohibitions and monopolized the women. The latter suffered most of all: betrothed in infancy to old men, driven by loveless marriage to amorous intrigue, punished for infidelity by spearing if not by death, they were liable to be carried off violently at any moment, so that the ''early life of a young woman at all celebrated for beauty'' was one continued series of ''ghastly wounds'' and ''captivity to different masters.''[9]

However ''ingeniously devised'' by the Deity, such a state of society could not have been intended to last indefinitely. Fortunately, the same divine power had in fact set in motion a ''progress of civilization'' governed by laws ''as certain and definite'' as those of planetary movement. Christianity and civilization marched hand in hand around the world, and the ''wizard wand'' of British commerce had in fifty years already ''laid the stable foundations of six empires.'' Cities were rising in the trackless forests; strongholds of superstition were being cleansed by the Gospel; and the English tongue alone was now heard where ''ruder languages'' once held sway.[10]

Grey was aware that cultural contact could have deleterious effects. Even one European living in the habitat of an aboriginal group destroyed the delicate balance with nature on which their lives depended. But in fact their lands were being massively expropriated, and it seemed that if they survived extinction, it would only be as ''a despised and inferior race.'' Small wonder they did not embrace civilization, when it offered only irregular labor at low wages, when they experienced British law only as punishment, and when no exertion of their own seemed likely to overcome the unfounded prejudice that their capacities were ''on a level with the brutes.'' Rather than live a ''hopeless, joyless'' servant's life, they returned to the habits and friends of their childhood—and Grey himself would "have done the same."[11]

But as Grey suggested in a report to Lord John Russell, then Colonial Secretary, the problem was one of human policy and not divine plan. As a result of misguided "philanthropic motives," colonization had been founded on an "erroneous principle," which applied British law only to native crimes against European person and property, leaving natives otherwise free to follow their customs with impunity. Grey had seen a native woman speared in the streets of Perth without interference. Such a policy of benign neglect left younger savages, who were more adaptable to European habits, unprotected from the violence of their elders. Although Australians were as intelligent as any race, no race could emerge from savagery while subject to such a "peculiar code of laws" as their native customs. Gradually, but firmly, a new system of institutions had to be introduced to enable them to take "their rank among the civilized nations of the earth": a special force of mounted police, court procedures appropriate to native comprehension, apprenticeships to individual settlers, and rewards of money and land for those who served faithfully (and embraced monogamy). Grey's actively interventionist policy of what was later to be called "direct rule" had thus an ambiguous double potential: on the one hand, British law, humanitarian social policy, and the hope, however naive, of rapid amalgamation into a harmonious and egalitarian multiracial society; on the other, the force of the police, the systematic extirpation of traditional institutions, and the possibility of self-interested abuse.[12]

With the aid of his childhood mentor Whately, Grey won appointment in 1841 as Governor of South Australia, where Wakefield's "systematic colonization" scheme had gone awry. Despite settler opposition, Grey improved the colony's economy and finances, and in 1845 the Colonial Office sent him off to save another colony on the verge of disaster. Wakefield's New Zealand Company was at loggerheads with missionary interests over land policy, and an accumulation of grievances had led to the "rebellion" of many Maori tribes. By a combination of personal diplomacy and military repression, Grey established his *mana* (charismatic power) with the Maori chiefs. Vigorously following up both tendencies of his native policy, he defended Maori land rights under the treaty of Waitangi; at the same time he acquired by purchase or seizure tremendous areas of Maori land in the futile hope that it could be saved from land speculators to carry out a checkerboard policy of racially integrated settlement. Even so, he managed to maintain his *mana* with the Maori, and despite his constant evasion of Colonial Office instructions, his reforming activity in New Zealand won him appointment as Governor of Cape Colony and High Commissioner for South Africa in 1854.[13]

With the eighth "Kaffir War" just over and the Crimean War just begun, the British government favored a policy of stabilization and retrenchment in South Africa, leaving the natives and the Boers to themselves beyond the colony's frontiers. But Grey's imperialist humanitarianism was irrepressible. Adroitly taking advantage of the "cattle-killing delusion"—an anti-British prophetic movement—he was able to take over large areas of African land, leaving the scattered fragments of the Xhosa people eventually to be reduced to the status of a rural proletariat. Although threatened with recall when he pushed plans for a general South African federation, Grey's reputation with the Colonial Office was high enough in 1861 to take him again to New Zealand, which was then on the brink of racial war, brought on by years of land jobbery and the neglect of Maori welfare. Although he served through seven years of fighting, Grey was finally dismissed from the governorship, spending the rest of his life on the margins of New Zealand politics as an advocate both of Henry George's "Single Tax" and of British responsibility to forestall all other imperialisms in the Pacific by acquiring territories themselves.[14]

Throughout his years as colonial governor, Grey maintained his ethnological interests, and was instrumental in the collection and publication of a large body of ethnographic material. Finding that the speech of rebel Maori chiefs was larded with allusions "resting on an ancient system of mythology," he set about recording Maori traditions, largely through Maori intermediaries. In addition to several volumes of textual material in Maori, he published his own translation of the *Polynesian Mythology and Ancient Traditional History of the New Zealand Race,* so that the European reader could listen directly "to a heathen and savage high-priest . . . unfolding the religious opinions upon which the faith and hopes of his race rest." Grey's "faithful translation" was in fact somewhat bowdlerized and reworked, and he could not resist moralizing prefatory comment: prevailing across the Pacific for 2,000 years, the religious system underlying the "puerile" Maori mythology had been responsible (at the rate of 2,000 annually) for the sacrifice of four million human beings to "false gods"—although he hastened to reassure readers that the perpetrators were in no way deficient in intellect or "incapable of receiving the truths of Christianity."[15]

Grey had less time to ethnologize among the "Kaffirs"—who were less likely than the Maori to stir any residual feelings of Noble Savagery that the Evangelical Revival had left in the souls of ardent Christian Britons. He regarded their tribal government as little more than "organized pillage" by tyrannical chiefs, sustained by witchdoctors playing on the superstitions of the people "to reduce them to a terrified submission." Even so, he seems to have played a role in instigating Colonel John MacLean's remarkable *Compendium of Kafir Laws and Customs*—in which the papers of the missionary H. H. Dugmore in fact showed how the power of chiefs was hedged by obligations of reciprocity. More generally, Grey encouraged the collection of ethnological and linguistic data by correspondence with missionaries, settlers, and officials throughout Africa—materials which he entrusted to the scholarly care of Wilhelm Bleek, a protégé of Baron Bunsen who had come to South Africa as philologist with a party of Liberal Anglican missionaries. Upon receiving the first volume of the descriptive and analytic catalogue Bleek published in 1858, Bunsen described it as a "treasure trove" of facts for African ethnologists and comparative philologists, particularly of the "Historical" school.[16]

Grey's ethnological reputation was not limited, however, to the Prichardian school; his work, especially the *Polynesian Mythology,* was also frequently cited by social evolutionists. When he returned for several years to England following his dismissal in 1868, he spoke to the Ethnological Society on the social life of the Maori, drawing comparisons with ancient Britons and defending Maori rebellion with allusions to the British uprisings against Roman Christianity. Even so, when John Lubbock attacked Archbishop Whately's "degenerationism" at the British Association the following year, Grey offered his own experience of savages to show that his childhood mentor had been "mainly right." *True* civilization and Christianity were synonymous, and though men had often fallen into idolatry, it was beyond human capacity to rise to civilization without divine assistance, either direct, or through the mediation of races that had already received the truth.[17]

A Methodist Missionary in Cannibal Feejee

Before Livingstone made it fashionable for university men to venture overseas to convert the heathen savage, British missionaries were often self-educated men of artisan origins. Along with the tremendous spiritual energy released by the "practical Arminianism" of the Evangelical Revival, they took with them a strong commitment to the Protestant virtues—impulses as congenial to their own social as to their converts' spiritual uplift. Many suffered terribly, but those who survived the difficult early days of mission building often came to enjoy a position of theocratic prestige they might never have found at home, frequently ending their lives in relatively comfortable colonial circumstances. Although they were full of the spirit of self-abnegation and Christian love, these motives were compromised somewhat by an aggressive ethnocentrism. When confronted with peoples whose cultural values seemed at polar variance, they assumed that because they themselves had risen from ignorance and low estate by their own exertions and by embracing vital Christianity, the natives to whom they offered education and the word of God would do likewise. When these expectations were frustrated, they were quite capable of portraying fallen savage man in rather bleak terms, whether to vindicate their own disappointed efforts or to exhort those at home to greater ones.[18]

What little is known of his early life suggests that Thomas Williams was typical of these early-nineteenth-century missionaries. Born in 1815 in the Lincolnshire town of Horncastle, he grew up in a staunchly Methodist household, training as a carpenter in his widowed father's workshop. Although not "a cultured man," he was "endowed by nature with a wide range of gifts" and a "masterful temperament." After a conversion experience in his early youth, he preached in nearby villages in his young manhood, before volunteering as a missionary to the Fiji Islands in 1840.[19]

The Wesleyan Methodist mission in Fiji was an extension of earlier missionary labors on Tonga, which in 1834 were "blessed" by the Holy Ghost with the conversion of King George Tubou and thousands of his subjects. Traditional Tongan ties to the Fijian archipelago turned the missionaries then to the island of Lakemba, which had a considerable Tongan population. Despite some Tongan converts, the efforts of the two missionaries who settled there in 1835 were little rewarded, although the Fijians were always anxious to obtain iron trade goods the missionaries offered for labor (and for pilferage). When after several years' efforts the Fijians seemed to be "growing more debased and devilish than ever," the Methodists on Tonga drew up an appeal to British Methodists on behalf of "Cannibal Feejee." Since Williams' uncle was then president of the Methodist Conference, the call may have been conveyed to him with special urgency. Accompanied by his bride, young Williams arrived in Fiji in July, 1840 after a voyage of 300 days.[20]

The next thirteen years were very trying ones. After recovering from spiritual doubts that assailed him upon his arrival at Lakemba, Williams was sent in 1843 to "dreadful" Somosomo, where his predecessors closed their blinds "to shut out the revolting scene" of cannibal feasts next to the mission station. Undaunted, Williams barged into native ceremonials, mocking Fijians for sacrificing to their gods only scant portions in filthy bowls—only to be told "it is our way," and threatened with the burning of his mission station. When the old king died, Williams rushed to prevent the ritual strangling of his widows, only to discover that two were already gone, and that the old king, still breathing, was to be buried alive. While his successor Tuilaila agreed to stop the widow strangling at two, and later on ordered his favorite wife to *lotu* (embrace Christianity), he accepted the missionaries only on sufferance: "Our business was to do as he directed us, and give him knives and axes." When Williams tried to prevent Christian converts from taking up arms for Tuilaila in time of war, that sufferance ended, and in 1847 the Somosomo station was abandoned.[21]

Williams was then sent to Mbua Bay on Vanua Levu, where earlier mission work had been more successful, and a revival occurred shortly after his arrival. Preaching one Sunday "with much liberty," he aroused some of his audience to writhe on the ground in convulsions; but if such religious ecstasy recalled revivals back in England, his attitude toward the convulsive shaking of possessed Fijian priests was strictly rationalistic, and he accused them to their faces of fakery. As was often the case, missionary successes led to strife between Christian and traditional Fijians, who at Mbua Bay confronted each other across a river: on the heathen bank "a blackened native carrying in glee a cooked joint of human being"; on the Christian, "a neatly dressed youth reading the Feejeean New Testament under the shade of a palm tree." Williams' last three years in Fiji were wracked by almost continual warfare—or rather, by violent assaults upon Christian Fijians, who until toward the end were restrained by pacifist policy. Again plagued by doubt, Williams left the islands in broken health, consoling himself that the mission had held its ground under "often afflictive circumstances.[22]

Early on in this history of frustration, Williams began to collect ethnographic material in the hope that details of custom along with native phraseology might help "catch a number of straggling words" for a dictionary the missionaries were compiling. The ultimate product of his endeavors, *Fiji and the Fijians,* was long regarded as the principal authority on Fijian culture at the time of European contact. Caught between despair at their present fallen state and confidence in their future salvation, between overpowering ethnocentric horror and incipient empathic understanding, Williams struggled to interpret "the strange and almost anomalous blendings of opposite traits in Fijian character." He seems to have spent years trying to decide whether the Fijians were "without natural affection" beyond "mere animal attachments"—in the end concluding that if one made allowance for custom and training, this natural human principle could indeed develop in a manner radically different "from that to which we are accustomed." Thus it was simply "misdirected affection" that led sons to kill their widowed mothers, and daughters actually to weep when Christian charity forestalled the murder. Although such "abominable practices" must arouse disgust in "sensitive minds" fresh from "highly civilized" society, "personal intercourse seldom fails to produce at last a more favourable impression."[23]

In this context, Williams saw a systematic contrast between the natural capacities of the Fijians and those aspects of their character produced by living "for many generations, under the uninterrupted power of influences different from any which we daily feel." There was much that was positive in Fijian life. Despite the "wildest savagism," they were excellent agriculturalists and artisans; and unlike other savages, they "could give reasons," and carry on "a connected conversation." Indeed, they were "so strong minded, so enterprising, and so versatile," and their language so vigorous and flexible, that there was no reason why Fijian literature should not eventually "take rank with the noblest."[24]

On the other hand, the "innate depravity" common to all men was in Fiji "fostered into peculiar brutality" by the character of their religion, and by all their "early training and associations." Proud, ungrateful, deceitful, covetous, and cowardly, they were horrible in rage and implacably cruel in revenge. Cutting off the limb of a living victim, they would cook and eat it before his very eyes, "sometimes finishing the brutality by offering him his own cooked flesh to eat." One chief had personally consumed over 900 victims in his lifetime and, as recently as 1851, fifty bodies had been cooked and eaten on a single occasion. Cannibalism, like patricide, was a social institution, "interwoven in the elements of society." The very gods they worshipped—irregularly, from fear and greed—were simply "demonized heathen, monster expressions of moral corruption." And what Williams recounted only scratched the surface; beyond lay licentious sensualities and fearful atrocities "which I *dare* not record."[25]

Like Grey, Williams clearly regarded Fijian customs relating to women, marriage, and the family as critical links in a never-ending chain of degradation. Mere beasts of burden subject to the tyranny of old men in polygamous marriages that robbed them "of the domestic pleasures springing from reciprocated affection," Fijian women were "led literally 'to bite and devour one another.'" Polygamy was the rotten core of Fijian society—an institution that virtually dissolved "the ties of relationship, and makes optional the discharge of duties which nature, reason, and religion make imperative." From it followed infanticide that eliminated two-thirds of the female children at birth (an apparent demographic contradiction Williams did not explain). From it followed also the child neglect that recreated the pattern of Fijian personality in the next generation. Deprived of proper discipline, subject to fitful attempts at parental mastery, Fijian children grew up "without knowledge, without good morals or habits, without amiability or worth, fitted, by the way in which they are reared, to develop the worst features of heathen life."[26]

Williams was not explicit about how the vicious cycle of Fijian social institutions and cultural personality had begun. Although he read the ethnological materials resulting from the United States Exploring Expedition that landed on Fiji in 1840, he was little concerned with traditional ethnological issues. He felt that the Fijians were related to the darker races of Asia, and had been isolated on Fiji since the peopling of the American continent; but he offered only scattered hints of their subsequent history. Although at one point he suggested that they had developed from patriarchal society to a form of feudalism in the last century, in general he would have nothing to do with views of history as "an improvement ever developing itself with all the certainty of fixed law." The movement of Fijian moral history was "uniformly from bad to worse": old men spoke of recent atrocities as "far surpassing the deeds of cruelty which they witnessed fifty years ago."[27]

On the other hand, the "wild and contradictory" Fijian traditions shadowed forth "some of the great facts in the history of mankind, of which the Bible contains the exact and standard records." Thus the chief Fijian god, Ndengei, had created a man and a woman whose offspring peopled the earth; and when their descendants angered him, he sent a universal flood, from which eight people (the biblical number) had been saved. When they later tried to build a large tower to make astronomical observations, it had fallen to the ground. What emerged in Williams' account was thus a traditional Christian degenerationist view of savagery as the degradation of wandering tribes of fallen men in the aftermath of Babel. Having lost all but the barest traces of true monotheism, Fijians illustrated a kind of moral evolution in reverse, until their heathenism, "by its own uninfluenced development," had "reached the most appalling depths of abomination."[28]

Although its deliverance from the "tyranny of the Devil" had begun before Williams left Fiji, it took more than the word of God to accomplish it. "Sermons alone" would not do "the thorough heathen much good"; they might be preached at forty years and "be no wiser in the end." Fortunately, the word of "Jiova" was supported by European trade goods, Western medicine, and the force of British arms. The first made missionaries sought after by heathen kings; the second helped prove the power of Jiova, when priestly ministrations were less efficacious than missionary medication; the last was the ultimate court of religious appeal. When asked if he believed missionary preachings, the son of Somosomo's king responded: "Everything that comes from the white man's country is true; muskets and gunpowder are true, and your religion must be true." After British warships visiting Fiji staged exhibitions of naval artillery, Thakombau, the most powerful Fijian chief, concluded in 1849 that "if we offend these people," they would "destroy us and our town at once." The prospect of Christian help in his ten-year war against neighboring Rewa gave Thakombau positive reasons to *lotu*, and after he defeated his heathen enemies with Christian Tongan support in 1855, Fijians converted by the thousands.[29]

By that time, Williams had settled in Australia, where his distinguished pastoral career culminated in the presidency of the Australian

Methodist Conference. His monograph on Fiji was published in London in 1858, supplemented by a fellow missionary's account of the history of the mission, so that Christian consciences, at once shocked by the horrors of savagery and reassured by the victory of Christ, could be exhorted to further efforts in the cause of Christianity and civilization: "The wail of suffering and the savage yells of crime still mingle with the 'new song' which has begun to rise from Fiji. Shall the gospel, which has already cleansed so many of her stains, complete the work? . . . Let the Christians of Britain and Australia make answer to God and their consciences."[30]

The Gentleman Traveler as Social Darwinist

Between Grey and Williams one senses already a fall in the status of savages. As the century progressed, the distinction between the practices and the natural capacities of savages became more tenuous, especially perhaps for men of scientific inclination who were losing their religious belief, such as Francis Galton.

Descended from successful Quaker businessmen on his father's side and from Erasmus Darwin on his mother's, Galton trained for medicine in Birmingham and then in mathematics at Trinity College, Cambridge (where he was a close friend of Henry Maine). When his father's death in 1844 gave him permanent financial independence, Galton—having "many wild oats left to sow"—put aside his career goals and set out for the Middle East. Traveling up the Nile he encountered a French Saint-Simonian exile who urged him to depart from "English routine" and go by camel across the desert. Although he later saw the proposal as the start of his "scientific wanderings," at the time Galton's caravan travel led him no closer to ethnography than the discovery that while you could not strike a Berber, you could beat Egyptians with sticks "as much as you like." On the other hand, his experience of religious diversity in the Muslim world—where he learned to speak a "fairly fluent" Arabic and lived "a very Oriental life" in Syria—may have laid the basis for his own later fall from Christian orthodoxy.[31]

Upon his return from the Middle East, Galton spent four years learning "the A B C of the life of an English country gentleman" by devoting himself to hunting and shooting. After phrenological analysis failed to give him direction, he finally ended his "fallow" period by returning to Africa in 1850 as leader of an expedition in the region west of Lake Ngami, which Livingstone had discovered the preceding year. Galton's experiences during the next sixteen months among the tribes of southwest Africa were to fix a set of racial attitudes and preoccupations that shaped his scientific work for the rest of his life.[32]

In a certain immediate sense the effect was relativizing. After joining a Hottentot punitive raid on some wandering Damaras who had stolen two of his oxen, Galton could see what such excitement might mean to "savage minds," and even had a glimpse of "what fearful passions exist in our own minds [once] they are thoroughly aroused." He was struck by the sharp contrasts between tribes. Though beautifully featured, the nomadic Damaras were "filthy and disgusting in every way," and without "perceptible notion of right and wrong." In a passage later cited by many writers on the savage mind, he compared their mental abilities unfavorably to those of his dog Dinah, who kept track of her puppies more easily than the Damaras kept track of their cattle. Like many savages, they seemed literally "to court slavery": "engage one as a servant, and you find that he considers himself your property." In contrast, the agricultural Ovampo, although much uglier, were an "inquiring race," with a "high notion of morality in many points"—though Galton clearly felt a moral as well as aesthetic distaste in refusing the temporary wife they offered. Without paupers, and all of them "well to do," the Ovampo were an obvious point of leverage for philanthropists "anxious to promote African civilization." To enslave *them* would be "a crying shame."[33]

Paradoxically, however, Galton felt ill at ease among the monarchical Ovampo, "as a savage would feel in England," because he was "no longer [his] own master." He actually felt relieved to return to anarchically republican Damaraland, where he could "go when I liked and where I liked." Like many Britons in "savage" lands, he found exhilaration in the liberation of the aggressive individualism of his cultural personality—in almost single-handedly imposing peace and a code of laws on fractious Hottentot raiders, in leading his caravan several hundred miles through dry and hostile Damaraland, perhaps even in the floggings he administered to thieves and laggards of his own party. In the end, his own cultural identity and standards were profoundly reinforced, and what stuck with him most was not the respect and care with which the Ovampo treated their elders, but the "horrors of savagedom" among the Damaras, who "as a rule" smothered sick relatives, and once left a "wretched native" to die in the bush, his head rolling horribly from severed muscles in the back of his neck. If the variety Galton found among Africans was a factor stimulating his later inquiries into hereditary human capacity, it was the Damaras, generalized, who came to stand for the Negro race, essentially the same—and vastly inferior to Europeans—in all environments and social situations.[34]

The volume Galton published in 1853 was primarily narrative, but there was ethnographic material scattered here and there. His most rigorously quantitative physical anthropology was an attempt (using his surveyor's sextant from a discrete distance) to obtain accurate measurements of the buttocks of a veritable "Venus among Hottentots." But he also included incidental descriptions of physical types, offering the confident opinion that the Bushmen and Hottentots were in fact the same "yellow, flatnosed, woolly-headed" people, differing only in "dirt, squalor, and nakedness." He also compiled (though he did not publish) dictionaries in several languages, learned to speak a barely adequate Setswana, and recorded miscellaneous details of behavior and belief. His six-page description of the Damaras included, among other information, an example of the "jumble of ideas, which, for want of a better name, must be dignified by that of their religion or creed"; several of the "vast number" of their superstitions, "all stupid, and often very gross"; and a smattering of information about their *eandas* (descent groups) and their meat tabus. But this was enough to establish Galton's *Travels* as an important source for the ethnologists of the 1850s—Latham named it as a reference work in the Crystal Palace guidebook, and cited it again in his *Descriptive Ethnology.*[35]

In 1857, while serving a five-year stint as secretary of the Royal Geographical Society, Galton authored a handbook for travelers, in which he suggested that since most savage countries were "Hobbesian," travelers might often have to take the law into their own hands. But the real turning point in his life came the following year, when his cousin Darwin "demolished a multitude of dogmatic barriers in a single stroke." The period of Galton's reorientation—which involved the abrupt shedding of his religious belief—seems to have been marked by psychosomatic maladies leading eventually to a mental breakdown in 1866, and he published little in these years that casts light on his intellectual development. In 1863, however, he offered a Darwinian explanation for "The First Steps towards the Domestication of Animals," which he thought could easily have been accomplished by savages. Despite their brutality, they shared with civilized children the "taste for taming and caressing young animals"; given wild breeds with appropriate characteristics, a "half-unconscious" selection for tameness would produce the domestic breeds known today.[36]

During these same years, Galton carried on a "purely ethnological inquiry into the mental peculiarities of different races." Apparently also in the context of his growing realization of the sterility of his own marriage, he turned to the general problem of human heredity, with the goal of showing that just as man by selection controlled the quality of animals, so also "human mental qualities are equally under control." After many months of labor, he produced in 1865 a two-part article on "Hereditary Talent and Character," which contained the germs of all his later polymathic labors in anthropometry, experimental psychology, statistical method and theory, the biometric study of heredity, and eugenics.[37]

For present purposes, what is interesting about Galton's social Darwinist manifesto is the way in which his African experience, transformed, informed its argument. On the one hand, there was the generalized Negro race, juxtaposed against the American Indian to prove the heredity of character type, just as the statistical analysis of biographies of eminent men proved the heredity of intellectual power. Thus the Indian was patient, reticent, dignified, and lacking in passion; the Negro was impulsive, warm-hearted, gregarious, "always jabbering, quarrelling, tom-tom-ing, or dancing." On the other hand, there was the generalized "savage," posed against civilized man to illustrate how even under conditions of civilization natural selection operated to develop certain peculiarities of innate character. "The requirements of civilization" had bred into advanced Europeans "the instinct of continuous steady labour" and bred out the "wild, untameable restlessness" that was "innate with savages." Civilization also prolonged individual development, so that starting out as infants on a par with savages, civilized men continued to develop, while savages remained "children in mind, with the passions of grownup men."[38]

And yet it is remarkable how recent and fragile a thing Galton felt civilization to be, and how little natural selection had yet operated to mold men to its requirements. If the "feeble nations of the world" must give away "before the nobler varieties of mankind," their very extinction evidenced the inability of mankind in general to meet "the requirements of incoming civilization." We, too, were starting to show ourselves "incapable of keeping pace with our own work." Beyond steady labor, tameness, and prolonged development, there was little to distinguish "the nature of the lower classes of civilized man from that of barbarians." Like animals "suddenly transplanted among new conditions," our instincts could not cope with our "altered circumstances." Because natural selection had not yet caught up with "religious civilization," man's "whole moral nature" was still "tainted with sin." Indeed, the idea of original sin was simply our own consciousness of this maladaptation—evidence that, far from having "fallen from high estate," man was rising in moral culture faster "than the nature of his race could follow."[39]

The very operation of natural selection had in fact become problematic. True, "the social requirements of English life" were destroying the "Bohemian" spirit of adventure inherited from our nomadic savage past, because men who could not settle down either left fewer children or emigrated. But it was also true that civilization had diminished the "rigour" of natural selection, the simple fact of inherited wealth alone preserving "very many rightful victims." Society might produce a race of geniuses by using state subsidies to encourage those with the greatest natural gifts to marry early and only among themselves. But far from taking selection into its own hands, modern society was in fact at the mercy of "numerous social agencies" operating in "precisely the opposite direction." While the "active and ambitious classes" followed the Malthusian prudential maxim and delayed their marriages, the "improvident and unambitious" reproduced themselves disproportionately. So it was that in established civilizations, "the race gradually deteriorates," until eventually "the whole political and social fabric caves in" and society lapsed back into barbarism.[40]

In all this, there is clear evidence of the transmutation of personal experience. Galton himself had yielded to the bohemian spirit, even glimpsing the passions beneath the civilized veneer. Returning to England to settle into a late and childless marriage, he found for himself a place in the then emerging "intellectual aristocracy." Not surprisingly, his idea of the "best form of civilization" was a utopia of the middle-class intelligentsia: society would not be costly; incomes would derive from "professional sources" rather than inheritance; every gifted lad through education could enter "professional life"; and the weak would find refuge in "celibate monasteries or sisterhoods." But in contrast to some other evolutionists of similar background who managed to remain fundamentally optimistic about the progress of Victorian society—and perhaps therefore less inclined to social Darwinism—Galton was led toward a pessimistic view of civilization in which biological mechanisms were centrally problematic.[41]

Primitivism, Polygenism, and Natural Selection

Galton embraced Darwinian evolution; Alfred Russel Wallace was coauthor of its basic mechanism—and for both men, evolutionary issues were closely tied to the problem of "race." But although Wallace's racial theory in fact verged on the polygenetic, the experiential attitudes on which it was based were quite different from Galton's. A gentle maverick among Victorian intellectuals, Wallace by personality and social background was much more susceptible than his more respectable scientific colleagues to intellectual enthusiasms—and among these was a rather un-Victorian romantic primitivism.[42]

Born in 1823, Wallace was the eighth child of a family whose independent means had long since begun to dwindle. At fourteen he visited a brother who was an apprentice in London, joining him in the evenings at the Mechanics' Institute. Coming under the influence of Owenites, he developed a lifelong identification with the working classes, and began to shed his religious belief for a naturalistic determinism. For six years he assisted another brother surveying in Wales, until the family broke apart upon his father's death in 1843, and Wallace turned to teaching school in Leicester. There he became interested in mesmerism and phrenology, and the natural historical interests he had developed while surveying took more definite form when he became friendly with the aspiring entomologist Henry Bates. Wallace had already been captivated by Darwin's Beagle *Journal,* and he now found in Alexander von Humboldt's *Narrative* of Latin American explorations a second role model of the scientific traveler. He also read Malthus on population, Lawrence's *Lectures on Man,* and Prichard; but the book that affected him most strongly was Chambers' *Vestiges.* Wallace in fact used Chambers' "ingenious" evolutionary hypothesis to gloss Prichard's ethnology in polygenetic terms: "If the theory of the 'Vestiges' is accepted, the Negro, the Red Indian and the European are distinct species of the genus Homo."[43]

Seeing no real prospects for himself at home, and having already conceived the notion that systematic collection of similar species might provide a test for Chambers' evolutionary hypothesis, Wallace decided in 1847 to use £100 he had saved to undertake a joint expedition with Bates to the Amazon. The two men separated shortly after arriving in Brazil, where Bates remained for eleven years. Wallace was back in England in 1852, after extensive travels on the northern tributaries of the Amazon, very near the southernmost point of Humboldt's wanderings a half century before. Although most of his collections and notes were lost when his returning ship burned and sank, Wallace was able to put together *A Narrative of Travels on the Amazon and Rio Negro.*[44]

Among the materials Wallace salvaged were vocabularies from ten "hitherto unknown" languages, which he decided to show to Robert Latham—the "greatest philologist of his time." Finding Latham in the Crystal Palace surrounded by Italian artisans at work on the ethnographic displays, Wallace offered the advice of an eyewitness to make their South American Indians look less like figures of classical sculpture. Latham reciprocated by adding a philological appendix to Wallace's book, which he then cited in the guide to the exhibits.[45]

Those who followed up Latham's citation would have found some scattered ethnographic observations, and an extended discussion of the tribes of the river Uaupes. Unlike the "noble races" of the North American prairies whom they resembled, these tribes were agricultural and had a "permanent abode"—the *malocca,* or long house, where a number of families formed "a sort of patriarchal community." Free from "the encumbrance of dress," they regarded paint "as a sufficient clothing"; in contrast to civilized fashion, but "imitating nature," the males appropriated all the ornaments. Lacking marriage ceremonies, they took as many as three wives, carrying them away by force, real or feigned. Because they could hardly believe "that death can occur naturally," they were constantly revenging imagined murders by poisoning their enemies. Wallace could not "make out" any belief he would call religion, but he did observe numerous "prejudices" regarding women, which were held "with much tenacity" even by nominally civilized and Christian Indians. His only venture into ethnological theory came when he commented on resemblances to customs in Borneo and New Guinea, but he reserved judgment as to whether these proved "remote connection" or were simply "accidental coincidences, produced by the same wants" in similar climates and "an equally low state of civilization." Although education and good government might form these tribes into a "peaceable and civilized community," Wallace expected rather that they would be reduced to the state of other half-civilized Brazilian Indians, who had "lost the good qualities of savage life" only to gain "the vices of civilization."[46]

As the last passage suggests, there was much ambivalence in Wallace's racial and cultural attitudes. He often remarked on the characteristics of groups he called "races": the "fresh-coloured" English, the "swarthy" Portuguese, the "apathetic but finely formed" Indian, and between these "a hundred shades and mixtures" only an "experienced eye" could detect. And he saw Brazilian frontier society through the eyes of an upright and industrious British Protestant. The "widespread immorality" ("too disgusting to be committed to paper") was the logical outgrowth of Portuguese national character, unchanged since the early days of Portuguese overseas expansion. In the drab Amazon frontier towns, their wandering spirit, distaste for labor, and passionate love of trade led to gambling, drink, and a "whole host of trickeries, cheatings, and debaucheries." Although geography had deprived the country of the "long winter nights, with blazing hearths" that were the foundation of domestic tranquility in Britain, the environment had potentialities that "the energy of Saxon races" could take advantage of. Given a "half-dozen friends disposed to work," Wallace could show Brazilians how to convert virgin forests into "an earthly paradise." Indeed, the prospect of living "free from all the money-matter cares and annoyances of civilization" was almost enough to make him abandon his beloved England. He did not wish to escape the "struggle for existence" that called forth "the highest powers and energies of the race." But if this struggle produced a society where millions suffered "dread miseries, while but a few enjoy the grateful fruits," then he would rather live as an Indian and watch his children grow "like wild fawns"—"rich without wealth, happy without gold."[47]

The impact of his encounter with the "true denizens of the forests," the "real uncivilized inhabitants of the River Uaupes," remained with Wallace to the end of his life. Totally different from the trousered and nominally Christian Indians he saw during his first three years on the Amazon, they were "as original and self-sustaining as are the wild animals of the forest," living "their own lives in their own way, as they had done for countless generations before America was discovered." Despite his never really questioned Anglo-Saxon attitudes, this "unique and not to be forgotten" experience of an integrally functioning native culture, in the context of his own alienation from industrial civilization, brought Wallace closer than most Victorian travelers to the perceptive modes of modern anthropology.[48]

Lacking independent means, Wallace had no real prospect of pursuing his science in England, and with £200 insurance from his lost Amazon collections and free passage provided by the Royal Geographical Society, he set off in the spring of 1854 for another expedition to the tropics. For the next eight years he traveled in the Malay Archipelago. Living often in native huts, sometimes for extended periods with native families, frequently suffering from hunger, fever, and infection, he was often the only and sometimes the first European in the areas he visited. His narrative account is full of anecdotes that convey a sense of the pathos of primal cultural encounter. In a Celebes village the sight of his white skin was enough to set dogs barking, children screaming, and buffalos running amok, so that he had "to creep about like a thief." When he responded to queries of the Aru Islanders as to whence he came, they cried out in disbelief: "Ung-lung! Anger-lang! Ang-lang! . . . You are playing with us. N-glung! Who ever heard of such a name?" When he could not give a convincing explanation of why he collected shells, insects, birds, and animals, he was "set down as a conjurer, and was unable to repel the charge." When he could not tell them what had happened to their ancestors who had been carried off to sea (as he later surmised, three centuries before by Portuguese explorers), they felt confirmed in their belief. No doubt in the next generation he would be transformed into "a demigod, a worker of miracles, and a being of supernatural knowledge." Such transcultural isolation was "very unpleasant to a person who does not like to be disliked"; and Wallace's efforts to make friends and his sensitivity to local custom are two of the leitmotifs of the narrative.[49]

Wallace had not however abandoned all the cultural baggage of European progressivism. Indeed, this further field experience was in some respects disillusioning of his earlier primitivism: savagery now "seemed a more miserable existence than when it had the charm of novelty." True savage life was almost Hobbesian—or Malthusian—in character: "small isolated communities at war with all around them, . . . drawing a precarious existence from the luxuriant soil, and living on from generation to generation, with no desire for physical amelioration, and no prospect of moral advancement." Wallace tended to measure progress in simple terms of population increase, which he linked causally to the condition of women, so that the way to promote a higher civilization was "by inducing women to confine themselves to domestic duties." He defended the "paternal despotism" of Dutch indirect rule on the grounds that the relations of "an uncivilized race and its rulers" were not merely analogous but identical to those of child and parent. The Dutch recognized that there were "certain stages through which society must pass in its onward march from barbarism to civilization"—whereas the English tried to force all things at once, so that "we demoralize and we extirpate, but we never really civilize." Similarly, he preferred the Dutch system of monopoly to English free trade, which invariably resulted in the degradation or extinction of "the lower race." Indeed, Wallace saw the latter as the inevitable—and early—fate of all races in the area save the Malay.[50]

But Wallace insisted that all savages were not the same: "there is in fact almost as much difference between the various races of savages as of civilized peoples." And in the end his message was that civilized European man could "learn something from the savage." Moral progress had not kept pace in Europe with intellectual achievement—indeed, "our whole social and moral organization" was still "in a state of barbarism." In contrast, the "perfect social state" envisioned by "our best thinkers" (Wallace had in mind Herbert Spencer's *Social Statics*) was in fact nearly realized among "the better class of savages," who lived in virtual equality and harmony, governed only by "the public opinion of the village freely expressed." Doubtless there was cultural preconception underlying even Wallace's questioning of progressivist assumption. But the Noble Savage was not a piece of cultural baggage often carried by tropical travelers in the mid-Victorian period; nor did many of them cast their experience of dark-skinned savages in these terms.[51]

Wallace's Malaysian ethnography was no longer an incidental aspect of more general natural historical observations. He was consciously collecting data to solve problems of racial affinity in terms of the ethnological paradigm or its emerging physical anthropological counterpart. But unlike the contending schools at home, he placed little weight in the end on either linguistic or cranial evidence, arriving at conclusions he felt would "astonish Latham, Davis, & Co.!" Orthodox philologists, including Prichard, had argued that all Oceanic races were "modifications of one type"; by contrast, John Crawfurd, a polygenist philologist, maintained that there were many distinct ones. Rejecting language as a primary taxonomic device, Wallace distinguished "two radically distinct types" with "no traceable affinity to each other": the Malay, related to the races of the Asiatic mainland; and the Papuan, who with the closely related Polynesians were the surviving island remnants of the aboriginal population of an Oceanic continent that had recently subsided.[52]

Wallace's heterodoxy, however, was not based primarily on physical characteristics. The Polynesians and the Papuans, whom he grouped together, in fact differed sharply in skin color and hair form. Rather, the critical evidence for the "absolute diversity" of Malay and Papuan was the contrast in their "moral features," which could be observed only by the ethnographer in the field: "one must see the savage at home to know what he really is." Previous ethnologists had been led astray by travelers who never stayed long enough to become "acquainted with peculiarities of national character." Arriving at the Ke Islands in January, 1857, after long experience with the Malay race, his "first view of Papuans in their own country" gave a contrast so sharp that had he been blind, Wallace would have known they were not Malays: "The loud, rapid, eager tones, the incessant motion, the intense vital activity manifested in speech and action, are the very antipodes of the quiet, unimpulsive, unanimated Malay"—even his Malay servants could not help but note the contrast. In the end, then, it was "little traits" like the "nigger grin" of Papuan children that led even this gentle and empathetic man of primitivist inclinations toward what seemed like a polygenetic view of race.[53]

And yet Wallace remained ultimately monogenist. An evolutionary viewpoint, which in 1844 had suggested to him that mankind might in fact have become differentiated into distinct species, eventually provided a framework for unifying all the races of man. And the establishment of this evolutionary view was related to Wallace's ethnographic researches. When he went to Malaysia, he still had no hypothesis to explain the process by which one species emerged from another. Like Darwin, he found the key in Malthus, whose work he recalled during a siege of fever on the island of Gilolo in February, 1858. One of the subjects uppermost in his mind at this time was the origin of human diversity. His notebooks for the three preceding months had been heavily ethnographical, and he later said that it was on Gilolo that he found "the exact boundary between the Malay and the Papuan races." Lying there with nothing to do but think, he recalled Malthus' "clear exposition of 'the positive checks to increase'—disease, famine, accidents, wars"—which kept down the population of savage races. Transferring this model from man to animals, which bred so much more rapidly, he was "vaguely thinking how this would affect any species," when "there suddenly flashed upon me the idea of *the survival of the fittest*."[54]

Wallace's flash of insight helped to transform the terms in which speculation on racial diversity was carried on. He sent off to Darwin a paper "On the Tendency of Varieties to Depart Indefinitely from the Original Type"; and Darwin, fearful that twenty years' work might be forestalled, was forced to publish his own evolutionary hypothesis along with Wallace's.[55] The impact of all this on ethnological speculation was profound. By changing the context in which the debate between monogenists and polygenists was carried on, it established the basis for what seemed a new monogenism, but was actually, as Wallace himself suggested, a synthesis of the two older points of view. But more than this—as we shall see—it helped to define a different set of anthropological issues, and thereby to establish social evolutionism as an alternative to the ethnological paradigm.

Ethnographic Data, Racial Attitudes, and Ethnological Theory

The explosive growth of ethnographic data collected from the frontiers of nineteenth-century European expansion created serious problems for Prichardian ethnology. We have already noted how contradictions between the data of language and of physical type strengthened the polygenist impulse; more generally, one might say that the problem of a human taxonomy was greatly complicated. And there was a rapidly increasing amount of information which in terms of the dominant classificatory criteria was simply residual: material on sociology, religion, and other aspects of cultural life. There is evidence to suggest that in the 1850s the accumulation of anomalous and irrelevant data in these residual areas began to be perceived as a problem.

As the successive editions of Prichard's *Researches* grew from one to two and then to five volumes, his work took on the character more of an ethnographic compendium than of an ethnological argument. And not only was there a mass of data that had no clear bearing on the ethnological problem; some data were actually problematic for it. Prichard found similar customs and beliefs in peoples so widely separated or manifestly distinct racially that contact or affinity seemed unlikely. As the biblical comparisons of Grey and Williams remind us, such difficulties had not always in the past inhibited the imaginations of men tracing the ten lost tribes of Israel. But to those trained in the more rigorous comparative methods of anatomy and philology, such data were, from the point of view of establishing racial connections, increasingly anomalous. Prichard was aware of Grey's *kobongs* and *totams,* and could in fact add further instances of what we would call matrilineal descent groups—but not to his ethnological purpose. True, he was able to incorporate some data of cultural similarity in areas widely apart into his overall monogenist argument by quietly reversing his earlier position on independent invention: the fact that men who were apparently unrelated geographically or racially held similar beliefs was simply another body of evidence for the essential unity—the psychic unity—of mankind. But if this new argument subordinated refractory data to the ethnological problem, it was something of a methodological anomaly within the ethnological tradition, which remained essentially diffusionistic. Nor did it solve the larger problem of irrelevant, redundant, or anomalous data.[56]

When Robert Latham published *Varieties of Man* in 1850, he justified following so closely in Prichard's footsteps on the grounds that "the accumulation of facts, even in the eleventh hour, has out-run the anticipations of the most impatient." Latham still hoped to cope with this data within the ethnological paradigm: classification, in terms of connection by descent and affiliation, was his "*chief* end." But as the decade wore on, Latham's data seemed to overwhelm him. Describing the Crystal Palace exhibits in 1854, he suggested that "few ethnological phenomena deserve more attention" than the reappearance of "similar customs in different parts of the world." But he offered no general explanatory framework for them, and was often reduced to describing them merely as "curious." And at the end of the decade, he prefaced his last major ethnological work by saying that his object was merely to describe: "If a certain amount of classification accompany the description, well and good"; but speculation would "form no notable portion of this work." With Latham, ethnology had thus virtually retreated into a purely descriptive "natural history" of the sort pursued by early-eighteenth-century botanists.[57]

There are hints in Latham's work, however, of a different possibility. Latham's descriptions of particular groups contained considerable information on their religious creeds and on such sociological matters as their marriage customs and tribal divisions. Indeed, he evinced a recurrent interest in issues that were to preoccupy John McLennan (who in fact drew heavily on Latham's work). Thus the Magar people of Nepal were divided into twelve "thums," each "supposed to be descended from some male ancestor," and within each of which "there is no marriage." Indeed, Latham noted that the phenomenon which McLennan was later to name "exogamy" was "so common as to be almost universal," and might be inferred "in many places where the actual evidence of its existence is incomplete." But although he also noted instances of "polyandria," Latham refused to pursue such problems—presumably because they belonged to the "Natural History of Civilization," which, although allied to ethnology and anthropology, was for Latham a distinct inquiry. But it was in fact the "natural history of civilization," redefined in a Darwinian context, that was to provide the framework in which the anomalous and redundant data of the ethnological paradigm would take on new meaning.[58]

To understand better the form that framework took, it may help to consider the constraints that the ethnographic data available in this period placed on ethnological theorizing. According to Latham, "an ethnologist must take what he can get in the way of information without asking too minutely whether each particular fact tallies with the rest."

His informants rarely examined phenomena "from the same point of view": one traveler described dress, another customs, another manners, another religion; some noted facts because they were common, others because they were rare. "Let one writer note what the other omits," and two tribes "so closely allied as to have, in all fundamental points, the same ethnological character" might not seem to the ethnologist even similar.[59]

However, traditional ethnological issues of ethnic classification and affinity could at least be approached through the kinds of data collected by Wallace and Galton: vocabulary lists, observable details of physical appearance, and miscellaneous manifestations of belief and behavior. But if anthropological theorizing within the ethnological paradigm was possible on the basis of superficial data on a large number of groups, the ethnographic information that might sustain a more holistic or a functional anthropological theory was not so easily obtained. Residing right among the natives of Aru, Wallace could not through his Malay contact language find out much about social or religious matters. He realized at a certain point that there was warfare going on between two neighboring villages, but he had more to say about the shields the men carried than about the motives of the quarrel ("some matter of local politics I could not understand"). And during his relatively short stay, he could not see "any signs of religion at all."[60]

Recalling Prichard's preference for long-resident missionaries over briefly-visiting naturalists, we may see Williams (and perhaps Grey) as foreshadowing a more intensive ethnographic style whose data would in fact sustain a more holistic interpretation. Both men tended to see native society and culture as integrated systemic phenomena, in which different social institutions worked together to maintain the existing social order within a given environmental setting—as in the case of Grey's Australians—or in which a distinct cultural personality was recreated in each generation by a form of marriage and a pattern of child rearing—as in the case of Williams' Fijians. But such "functionalism" embraced only a portion of native life, and that from a particular ethnocentric perspective. Williams had little light to shed on the *vasu* relationship or the Fijian system of *tabu:* the right of the *vasu* to despoil his mother's brother's property at whim was simply "the most prominent of the public notorieties of Fiji" and a discouragement to individual industry; *tabu,* simply the secret principle of despotic rule and the justification for months of idleness.[61]

What Grey and Williams offered was a functionalism of the abhorrent. Confronted by institutions and behavior that did violence to their own value systems, and committed to rapid cultural change, they tended to see the customs and beliefs that frustrated their reforms not simply as isolated manifestations, but as part of a *system* of savagery, a *system* of heathenism, and to look for the critical linchpins of the system they opposed. Significantly, both found these in customs governing the relations of the sexes. Indeed, it is worth noting that the data later central both to evolutionary theory and functionalist social anthropology—those of religion and kinship—were precisely the foci of their ethnocentric abhorrence and the targets of their attack. Consequently, insofar as such phenomena tended to be seen in either functionalist or evolutionary terms, it was from an inverted perspective that denied them positive value: the system of savagery, the progress of human degeneration.[62]

While it comes as no surprise that there should have been profound attitudinal or ideological constraints on the collection and interpretation of ethnographic data by Britons overseas in the Victorian period, their nature is worth more specific comment. Offspring of the Evangelical Revival and the Industrial Revolution, these men traveled in a period when the differential in sheer physical power between civilization and savagery was growing rapidly wider, and when the self-assured moral values of Protestant respectability had not yet been seriously corroded by relativist doubt. Sustained by that power and those values, British travelers overseas carried with them a powerful sense of personal self-confidence and cultural rectitude. Men whose value systems and behavioral norms seemed to their own descendants highly repressive, they could hardly help but be disturbed by systems that molded the most powerful human instincts in ways that were very different from those they took for granted. If their century was more humane than the eighteenth, it was much less tolerant, and their revived Christianity surely did not teach them cultural relativism. Yet in a world much more radically differentiated culturally, they witnessed modes of behavior which even the staunchest modern relativist might have trouble coping with: cannibalism, patricide, widow-strangling, wife-spearing, and infanticide. If their Christianity taught them that all men were brothers, other ideological influences conspired with historical experience to make that brotherhood problematic indeed. In this context, the sheer visual impact of encounter could lead otherwise humane men to question human brotherhood. After meeting with a group of Fuegians, naked in a storm—"poor wretches . . . stunted in their growth, their hideous faces bedaubed with white paint, their skins filthy and greasy, their hair entangled, their voices discordant, and their gestures violent"—Darwin could hardly make himself believe that they were "fellow-creatures, and inhabitants of the same world."[63]

Extending to these travelers an empathy similar to that anthropologists now extend to native peoples, one can perhaps understand (without sharing) the distaste and horror they often evinced in situations of culture contact—especially if one bears in mind that the cognitive modes by which modern anthropology interprets human difference, as well as the perceptive modes by which it observes them, are themselves historical products. While many writers of Darwin's time interpreted human behavioral differences as the cumulative expression of life experience in different social or physical environments, they did not conceptualize what they saw in terms of the modern anthropological idea of culture. What Darwin observed among the Fuegians was a kind of hurried, unanalysed ethnographic gestalt, in which paint and grease and body structure blended into a single perception of physical type, perceptually unseparated from what he heard as discordant language and saw as outlandish behavior—a gestalt that he subsumed under the term "race." This was in fact quite consistent with the natural historian's treatment of other animal species, in which body type, cries or calls, and habitual behavior were all data to be used in distinguishing a variety or "race." Given the somewhat "Lamarckian" notion of adaptation which Darwin at that time still shared with so many of his contemporaries, this idea of "race," when applied to humans, inevitably had a mixed biocultural character. "Nature, by making habit omnipotent, and its effects hereditary, has fitted the Fuegian to the climate and the productions of his miserable country." In this context, "culture" was simply a way of specifying the cumulative hierarchical aspect of human racial differences—as when Darwin compared his Fuegians to "a race a little more advanced in culture." Expressed in hierarchical terms and linked to a vaguely biocultural conception of race, it was part of a different worldview from that of modern anthropology.[64]

Such Lamarckian racialist thinking was quite pervasive in this period, even after "natural selection" offered an alternative mechanism of adaptation. Nor was it limited to natural historians. Indeed, Christian humanitarians and secular radicals were almost invariably racialists in this sense. But it is necessary to go behind the umbrella category of "pseudo-scientific racism" that is sometimes used to describe nineteenth-century racial thought. By present scientific standards, no doubt they were all "pseudo-scientific"; but if our ethical or political commitment reinforces this judgment, we may still usefully distinguish different currents of racial assumption—all of them manifest in Darwin's reflections on his Fuegian encounter.[65]

In addition to the diffuse Lamarckianism we have just described, it is worth noting that there are traces also of the traditional Christian view, which insisted on the common humanity of savages, and explained their inferior status and capacity in terms of degeneration or design—but which saw social and physical environment as the critical factors in determining their past history and future prospects. Thus Darwin's rhetoric upon occasion suggests that he still thought of savage man as fallen man, who must redeem himself (or be redeemed) through progress.

In contrast to both of these, there was an emerging racialism of a harsher, hereditarian sort, which rejected Lamarckian biocultural interactionism and subordinated culture to race. Denying the common origin of savages, it saw their status as the expression of permanently inferior capacity, impervious to social influences in the present. Later to be manifest in Darwin's imagined naturalist's perception of the Negro and the European as distinct species, this view is already there in his hesitation to believe the Fuegians "fellow-creatures."[66]

But there was still another framework available to Darwin for conceptualizing "man in his lowest and most savage state." Inherited from the Enlightenment, it, too, is evident in his *Beagle* journal: "One's mind hurries back over past centuries, and then asks, could our progenitors have been men like these?—men, whose very signs and expressions are less intelligible to us than those of domesticated animals; men who do not possess the instinct of those animals, nor yet appear to boast of human reason, or at least of arts consequent on that reason."[67] In the 1830s such thinking was less intellectually acceptable than it had been a half century earlier or was again to be a half century hence. By that later time, in a radically changed temporal and biological context that Darwin himself helped to create, it had become the dominant anthropological framework for conceptualizing the observed (and imagined) differences between savages and civilized men—although in doing so it incorporated elements of the other views we have been discussing.

That evolutionism, rather than some viewpoint more consonant with modern holistic or functionalist anthropological approaches to sociocultural phenomena, became the dominant viewpoint in later Victorian anthropology may be discussed in many contexts. The issue is not entirely idle historically, since we have already noted in Comte and Mill theoretical frameworks that might have provided the basis for a more functionalist anthropology. But even if other factors to be discussed later (both theoretical and ideological) had not influenced the outcome, one wonders if the existing traditions of empirical study would have been adequate to sustain a more integral approach.[68]

By contrast, social evolutionary speculation was easily carried on with ethnographic data of the sort normally provided by Victorian travelers abroad. It still allowed a place for the linguistic and physical data that had been the primary building blocks of speculation governed by the ethnological paradigm. It could and did incorporate such exceptional collections as Grey's *Polynesian Mythology,* and made abundant use of monographs such as Williams' on the Fijians. But it could also take more fragmentary materials and put them to constructive purpose. Building heavily on the residual data of the ethnological paradigm, it gave meaning to the oddments of sociological and cultural material Latham recorded but left unexplained. The critical evidence for establishing a series of stages in human social and cultural development was precisely those cultural similarities in widely separated areas which were anomalies for the ethnological model. In a sense, what social evolutionism did was to take the large masses of ethnographic data that filled the pages of Prichard's *Researches* without contributing directly to the solution of the ethnological problem, and to classify them for another evidential purpose.

Although social evolutionists did not pose the matter in just these terms, they were in fact quite conscious of the need to classify already existing ethnographic data. In 1868 E. B. Tylor attributed the "now backward state of the science of culture to the non-adoption of the systematic methods of classification familiar to the naturalist." Early the next year, the Ethnological Society set up a Classification Committee to establish a "fixed terminology," collect data on columned register-sheets especially prepared for the purpose, classify it systematically, estimate "the relative value of all evidence," and prepare maps "marking the geographical distribution of the several classes." Significantly, the committee felt that materials relating to physical type and language "having been made the subjects of study for some time," its main efforts should be devoted to facts relating to religion, folklore, sociology, and material culture.[69]

From this point of view, then, what social evolutionism did was to reclassify the existing ethnographic data on the savage peoples of the world, juxtapose it to the rapidly accumulating data of European folklore and prehistoric archeology, and construct on this evidential basis a new framework for interpreting savage man. If this was indeed largely an activity carried on in the study, if not in the armchair, there was nonetheless good precedent in Victorian science, especially in the fieldwork disciplines, for a comparative inquiry based on data collected by men whose observations were incidental to some other activity. Darwin and other "eminent men of science" joined Prichard in contributing to the Admiralty's *Manual of Scientific Enquiry,* edited by Sir John Herschel—who had been the first leading Victorian scientist to give systematic philosophical formulation to the methods of scientific inquiry. All of the contributors seemed to take for granted that science could make systematic use of data collected by persons "of good intelligence and fair acquirement" whose life experience carried them to corners of the world established scientists visited, if at all, only in the years before they became established.[70] And if, like Darwin's, their own theories were grounded in observations they themselves carried out, the most eminent among them accepted many of the comparative speculations of ''armchair'' anthropologists as legitimate contributions to a scientific understanding of man's place in nature. To understand why they should have done so, we must turn away from the traditional data of ethnology to consider in greater detail the ways in which British intellectuals treated the problem of civilization in the 1850s.

FOUR

The History of Civilization Before the *Origin of Species* (1851–1858)

"The Great Exhibition—Official Award of the Prizes"—1851
The Illustrated London News 19 (October 25, 1851):529—where the engraving appears beneath the quoted caption.

EVEN before the Great Exhibition had opened, a writer in the *Economist* described it as "a fitting close" to the "wonderful half-century gone by"—confidently predicting that the next fifty years would surpass the last by as much as those had surpassed all the years that had gone before. "All who have read, and can think" must now believe that endless and ever-faster progression was "the destined lot of the human race."[1] While not everyone who thought about the Exhibition was so sanguine, the Crystal Palace—and the social experience it symbolized—did stimulate a number of men to speculate about the progress of civilization.

They did so in the context of several available intellectual traditions: notably eighteenth-century progressivism and various early-nineteenth-century intellectual currents that stood in differing relations of tension to it—including, on the one hand, English utilitarianism and Comtean positivism and, on the other, a congeries of related intellectual orientations emanating largely from Germany. To characterize all of this speculation as "evolutionary," however, would be to sacrifice a meaningful historical specificity that is in fact the focus of our concern. For if sociocultural evolutionism, too, must be understood as an attempt to understand the encapsulated historical experience of the Crystal Palace, it was still possible in the early 1850s to think about European progress in terms that were not yet fully "evolutionary," in the sense we seek to define, or that even ran counter to it.

One of the critical issues in this historiographical judgment is the relation of these 1850s progressivists to the assumptions about human nature that, according to John Burrow, were called into question in the "crisis of utilitarianism."[2] Another and related one is the role played by non-European savages in their writings: just as savages were virtually unrepresented at the Crystal Palace, they did not bulk large in the works we shall be considering here. For the most part, these writings were concerned with the progress of civilization in Europe, and the more immediately relevant contrast—as in the Exhibition itself—was with the "static" societies of Asia.

Before the first decade of the age of equipoise had passed, however, the cultural-cum-chronological contrasts suggested by the Crystal Palace were placed in a new context. Brixham Cave and the Darwinian revolution provided a totally different temporal and biological framework for the progress of civilization, in which the savages of the world played a much more prominent role, and the variability of human psychic nature took on a very different meaning.

To reassess the role of the Darwinian revolution in the emergence of sociocultural evolutionism, it is necessary therefore to consider first some mid-Victorian writings on the problem of civilization whose genesis reflected the experience of the Crystal Palace but not yet that of Brixham Cave or the *Origin of Species*. The early works of Henry Thomas Buckle, Henry Sumner Maine, and Herbert Spencer will serve this purpose well. Almost exactly contemporary by birth, they were close to forty by the time Darwin published, and had already formulated their characteristic viewpoints. Although in quite different ways, they were each influenced by the heritage of eighteenth-century progressivism, and attuned to the major intellectual currents of their day. Each wrote works that were among the most influential of their age, although their subsequent fates were quite different. There is good reason to argue that this varied outcome had something to do with the way each of them related to the utilitarian tradition, and the way each man's thought could be accommodated to the Darwinian revolution—to which of course Spencer's may be regarded as a major independent contribution. By considering the development of their thinking in greater detail, we may cast some light on the emergence of sociocultural evolutionism.

The Triumph of the Laws of Intellect over the Laws of Nature

Standing outside the normal processes by which intellectual traditions are transmitted, the autodidact may embody the spirit of his age in an unusually direct way. For the same reason, his relation to the past is apt to be distorted: his intellectual roots descend haphazardly, putting down feelers here and there as they happen to find nourishment. In Buckle's case, the result was to link the England of the Crystal Palace closely to the French Enlightenment.

Son of a prosperous London shipowning merchant, Buckle was so sickly as a child that doctors feared mental exertion might injure him permanently. He attended school only briefly, and his contact with the world of traditional learning came largely from his mother, who taught him to knit quietly while she read to him from Shakespeare and the Bible. From adolescence, however, Buckle seems to have taken an interest in religious and political questions, following his Calvinist mother on the former and his Tory father on the latter. In 1839, when he was almost eighteen, his health improved enough that he started work in the countinghouse of the family firm. Within a few months, however, his father's death and a £20,000 inheritance allowed him to define his own life.[3]

Having at this point little more than "reading and writing English and proficiency in chess," Buckle persuaded his mother to take him abroad to learn languages, and during the next year made a start toward the nineteen he later claimed to know. In France, he became a radical; in Germany, a freethinker—although he continued to speak of himself as a Christian, and never abandoned his belief in an immortal soul. Upon his return, Buckle pursued his education by "desultory and irregular" reading, until late in 1842 he found his vocation in "the flattering hope" that the industrious application of "talents certainly above mediocrity" might enable him to make a mark in the relatively unstudied field of medieval history. He spent the next few years plowing through the books which, at the rate of more than £300-worth annually, gradually filled the library of the London house he lived in with his mother.[4]

Judging from his commonplace books, Buckle's mature historical viewpoint was slow emerging. His medieval interests early shifted to the sixteenth and seventeenth centuries, and his affinity for the Enlightenment is suggested by frequent citation of Hume, Gibbon, and Robertson, as well as religious writers involved in the eighteenth-century discussion of deism. Many entries suggest a rather naive antiquarian approach—what he recorded primarily were etymologies, first appearances, origins, and archaic customs, often with a rationalist anti-Catholic bias. Significantly, his entry on climate and national character in fact minimized the relationship between them.[5]

Buckle's reading moved haphazardly, as he was led here and there browsing in bookstalls, or followed a particular historical spoor from one reference to another. Sometime after the appearance of the Paris edition of 1846, however, Buckle read Guizot on the history of French and European civilization, and discovered there a model for his own later inquiry—though he found the epitome of civilization not in France, but in that "great and splendid nation" of which it was his "pride to count myself a member." Whether by chance or by comparative design, Buckle's interest at this point shifted away from Europe, and he was led, through the works of the Göttingen historian Heeren, to readings in Asian and African history and ethnography. This excursion into Prichardian ethnology led Buckle to geographical determinism and back to Montesquieu; it also led him to a very negative (although monogenetic) view of savagery. Dominated by the physical world, savages *had* no "national character"—"all of them being equally vain, crafty, cruel, superstitious, and improvident." Their extinction, as Darwin had suggested in his *Beagle* journal, was inevitable, and provided for Buckle the model of the eventual "triumph of intellectual over physical laws."[6]

Toward 1850, Buckle turned to political economy, citing McCulloch, Mill, Malthus, and the early nineteenth-century Russian economist Storch, "the first writer who saw the connection between the study of political economy and that of the history of civilization." All of this seems to have reinforced a prior interest in the problem of population, which now led Buckle to medical, statistical, and physiological writers—including Simon's *Animal Chemistry.* It was apparently while reading the latter in June, 1850 that he began to see physiology, "through the medium of food," as the critical link in the causal chain he later was to argue between the "laws of climate" and those of population and wealth. Even so, Buckle seems still to have been planning a rather conventional history of the reign of Elizabeth, and it was not until May, 1851 that he definitely conceived his own enterprise as a "history of civilization." Given the fact that Buckle served as judge of a chess tournament held in conjunction with it, the Great Exhibition seems a likely catalyst.[7]

Be that as it may, there is another influence, critical to his posture and his purpose, which is not directly reflected in his commonplace books: his readings in the "great masters of method," from Aristotle, Bacon, and Descartes to Comte and Mill. A fragment from the early 1850s suggests that it was especially Mill's "Logic of the Moral Sciences" that helped define Buckle's enterprise. Buckle distinguished two traditions in logic—the deductive Aristotelian and the inductive Baconian—which were related to the "idealist" and "sensualist" traditions in epistemology. Although he was later to write an extended critique of the deductivism of the Scottish intellect, Buckle was nonetheless disturbed by the extreme antideductivist bias in English thought. The Baconian focus on "externals" facilitated the accumulation of wealth, and had in turn been reinforced by "the progress of what may be called our *economic* civilization"—but at the expense of corrupting philosophy with its "mechanical and prosaic spirit." The corruption affected even the writing of history, which Englishmen wrongly conceived in terms of *external* acts rather than the *internal* development of opinions. Fortunately, however, there were countervailing tendencies: one of the contributions of women to the progress of knowledge was by loving cultivation to transmit to their empiricist sons their own imaginative (and apparently genetic) tendency to reason deductively. In this context, the special virtue of Mill was that, although a sensualist, he was the first logician ever to transcend the inductivist/deductivist antithesis.[8]

Buckle's own proclivities, molded by an almost lifelong intellectual relationship with his mother, were essentially deductive: "all he wanted was the great outline of history, which furnished him with data for some of his speculations, and the proof of others."[9] When it finally came to giving order to all those antiquarian entries in his commonplace books, Buckle did so by appealing to a few general assumptions derived from his reading, his family background, and the cultural presuppositions of his age—all developed in neatly dichotomous fashion.

Citing Adolphe Quetelet and other statistical sources on the regularity of suicides, marriages, and misdirected letters, Buckle began by arguing that all human behavior was governed by law. All historical events sprang from the reciprocal modification of man by external nature and of nature by the mind of man. The laws of nature could be divided into two categories: the influences of climate, food, and soil, which governed the accumulation and distribution of wealth; and the "general aspect of nature," which governed the accumulation and distribution of thought by directing "the association of ideas." When expressed in "hurricanes, tempests, earthquakes, and similar perils," nature's power constantly threw the mind "into a timid and anxious state," so that imagination predominated over understanding and superstition stifled the growth of knowledge. But where nature was less formidable, greater confidence encouraged "an inquisitive and analytic spirit," and gradually the laws of nature were superseded by the laws of mind.[10]

The latter, too, could be doubly divided. The principles of morals, like the laws of nature, were essentially invariable, and therefore contributed nothing to human progress, since "a stationary agent can only produce a stationary effect." But the principles of intellect were essentially cumulative, and gradually triumphed over moral laws just as mental laws in general triumphed over physical. Thus it was that although he began by asserting "the intimate connection between the physical and the moral world," Buckle ended by resolving progress into "an encroachment of the mind of man" upon "organic and inorganic forces of nature." Once free of those forces, the history of every civilized people was solely dependent on three things: "the amount of knowledge possessed by their ablest men"; "the direction which that knowledge takes"; and "the extent to which the knowledge is diffused, and the freedom with which it pervades all classes of society."[11]

In this framework, the history of human civilization divided itself into two great parts: the European, where the tendency was "to subordinate nature to man"; and the non-European, where it was "to subordinate man to nature." The latter was quickly disposed of. The savages of the world received scant attention, and India, Egypt, Mexico, and Peru served simply to illustrate the "immense mischief" of the powers of nature, which everywhere outside Europe produced "one-sided and irregular civilizations"—wasteful, caste-ridden despotisms in which both wealth and thought were unequally distributed. Subject to internal stagnation and decay, they were toppled by any "unfavourable circumstances" arising from without. Everything truly "worthy of the name of civilization" had in fact originated in Europe, and within Europe England was the one nation that by its isolation and mild government came close to offering the "experiment ready-made" of a "civilized people who had worked out their civilization entirely by themselves."[12]

Paradoxically, however, the laws of civilization were more easily explicated in "those other countries where social disease is more rife"—where the laws governing "each separate element" were made more obvious by a hyperactivity that threatened the harmonious composition of the whole. Thus it was that Buckle proposed to begin his *History of Civilization in England* by studying German history to determine more precisely "the laws of the accumulation of knowledge," American history for its diffusion, French history for the "occult tendencies" of the "protective spirit," Spanish history for the laws of ecclesiastical development, and Scottish history for the influence of the "method of investigation that its ablest men habitually employ."[13]

Buckle never got to English civilization. When the second of sixteen projected volumes appeared in 1861, he decided to recoup his strength by travel in the Middle East. After sailing on the Nile and crossing the Sinai Desert clad in flannel and a swallow-tailed black coat, he died of typhoid in Damascus, rejecting until the end the ministrations of a French doctor. His history of civilization ended with the Scots, whose conjectural histories he attacked as "purely speculative" deduction. Although he owed a considerable debt to Adam Smith, Buckle's own history was rather a blend of Montesquieu and Condorcet, recast in the mold of Cobdenite radicalism—a "sort of vast Anti-Corn-Law agitation," with knowledge substituted for cheap bread, a struggle between the "protective spirit" sheltering error and superstition and the spirit of skepticism impelling the progress of civilization.[14]

Leslie Stephen recalled Buckle's book as one of two "great intellectual shocks" received by "the generation which was growing to maturity in the 1850s." In the later editions of his *Logic,* Mill attributed largely to Buckle the new English willingness to see the "collective series of social phenomena" as "subject to general laws"; and the contemporary historian of British rationalism credited Buckle with a major role in liberating England from "the religious terrorism which has been weighing on her since the Peace of 1814." One might think that such a contribution would be seen by contemporaries as part of the Darwinian revolution. But Buckle's moment quickly passed. Henry Maine later said he knew of "no modern reputation which had declined so much in so short a time." Although Buckle's private correspondence suggests that he was receptive to Darwinism, his contemporaries were in retrospect inclined to attribute his decline precisely to its impact—which in Stephen's words left Buckle "stranded on a shore from which the tide of speculation has ebbed." The assumptions that had governed English thought since the time of Locke—the uniformity of human nature molded fresh in each generation through the laws of association by the power of environment—were no longer tenable once Darwin showed "the supreme importance of inborn and hereditary tendencies."[15] The significance of this understanding of Buckle's fate is a matter to which we shall return.

Retracing Historically the Social Progress of the Aryan Race

If Buckle was left stranded by an ebbing wave of thought, Maine was caught up on a flowing one. Despite the fact that Maine's thinking was defined in a pre-evolutionary epoch, and in nonevolutionary terms, it quickly found a place in the postevolutionary milieu. Moreover, there are compelling contrapuntal reasons for including him in a study of the emergence of sociocultural evolutionism. Although his insistence on the patriarchal origin of marriage was a factor in his longtime marginality to the British anthropological tradition, the dominant evolutionary view of the development of human marriage was elaborated as an alternative to Maine's views. Furthermore, his distinction between kinship and territory as underlying principles of social organization, and his conception of the village community were to have a continuing relevance. In the longer run, his ideas on corporate groups were to become quite influential in modern British social anthropology. And his very marginality to the anthropological mainstream in the nineteenth century helps to define it: by contrast, he illuminates its character; by inclusion, its limits.[16]

The leitmotif of Maine's life, as of his thought, was that of progress within established structures—progress conceived in terms of the leadership of elites of wealth, power, and natural ability. For Maine, the critical factor was the last, which he possessed in almost wasteful abundance. Long before Lord Annan had defined it historically, he saw himself as a member of the "intellectual aristocracy" that emerged in England as he grew to maturity—though it took him no small effort to make his way into a group that some others entered from financially more secure middle-class families. While hardly lowly, Maine's origins were humble (and anomalous) enough to make him a bit secretive about his past; they were also "precisely such as to stimulate his desire for prestige and financial success." His father was an M.D. from Aberdeen, and his father's brother (whose daughter Maine later married) was a leading figure in the Scottish border town where the Maine family had long lived. His parents migrated south to England two years before his birth in 1822; two years later, his father mysteriously abandoned them. His "doting mother," however, was by no means bereft of resources or connections. Her own Oxfordshire family had East India Company investments, and her cousin, the same John Bird Sumner who authored the

Treatise on the Records of Creation, was eventually to become archbishop of Canterbury. As Maine's godfather, Bishop Sumner procured a nomination for him in 1829 to Christ's Hospital, a prestigious charitable school with a long tradition. From that point on, the young man's natural brilliance, personal charm, and great ambition propelled him upward.[17]

At Pembroke College, Cambridge, where he read classics and mathematics, Maine virtually monopolized the university prizes that usually went to St. John's or Trinity men. His friend Galton recalled Maine as one of the few outsiders "who became thoroughly at home in Trinity itself," and in 1842 he was invited to join the intellectually exclusive secret society, the Apostles, most of whom came from Whewell's Trinity. Their weekly meetings focused on philosophical and historical topics, with a strongly utilitarian emphasis and a considerable input of German historicism. Niebuhr had long been "their god," forming "all their sentiments"; but the Apostles were also whirled "this way and that" by the ideas of Bentham and Mill. At one meeting during Maine's membership they voted unanimously that "the system of expediency" was no derogation of the moral dignity of man.[18]

Maine's undergraduate years were not only intellectually formative; he also established personal connections that were extremely helpful in furthering his career. When he was barely twenty-five, and had served three years as junior tutor at Trinity Hall (de facto, the Cambridge law college), the influence of the politically powerful father of one friend helped win him the Regius Professorship of Civil Law. Supplementing its not onerous duties with legal practice, Maine added in 1852 the Readership in Roman Law and Jurisprudence at the Inns of Court, one of five such positions established after parliamentary commissions urged the reform of legal education.[19]

Over a longer period, Maine's own legal writings were also to help remold legal education; but there is little evidence that his characteristic viewpoint had emerged by 1852. He must have been well versed in the "analytical" approach of John Austin, whose Benthamite *Province of Jurisprudence Examined* was the leading work in a field that was "little more than [a] branch of utilitarianism" in the twenty years before 1850. And as a student of Roman law with a Germanizing bent, Maine doubtless read Savigny, whose volume on the Roman law of contract in 1853 marked the culmination of a half century's research in historical jurisprudence. But the syllabus of Maine's early Cambridge lectures was quite traditional, following directly the headings of an analysis of Roman civil law published in 1779 and revised in 1836 by his predecessor in the Regius chair.[20]

Maine was, however, part of a growing group in the British legal profession who felt the need for reform, and in 1855 he joined in the formation of the Juridical Society of London, for which he prepared his first published legal writing: "The Conception of Sovereignty, and its Importance in International Law." Writing as an Austinian, Maine was nevertheless critical of Austin's treatment of the sovereign as absolute proprietor of a "national territory." Until late in modern history, sovereignty was based rather on the idea of the tribe—"a patriarchal society, a nomad horde, merely encamped for the time upon the soil which afforded them subsistence"—or, when the monarch departed from "the special relation of chief to clansmen," upon the "idea of universal dominion" inherited from the Roman Empire. The idea of *territorial* sovereignty—of sovereignty over a limited portion of the earth's surface—"was distinctly an offshoot, and a tardy one, of Feudalism."[21]

Although the germ of Maine's subsequent historicization of utilitarian theory is implicit in this argument, a contrasting aspect of his later thought was expressed the following year in an essay on "Roman Law and Legal Education." Despite the manifest influence of Savigny's *Roman Law in the Middle Ages,* it was now Maine's mathematical rather than his classical training, his Benthamite inclination to analytical systematization, that predominated. The power of the Roman legal tradition in the modern world was not simply historical but logical as well. Analogous to the benefit "which a geometrician derives from mathematical analysis in discussing relations of space," its relevance for modern law lay in the model it provided for codification. One studied Roman law not because our own jurisprudence had once been like it, but "because all laws, however dissimilar in their infancy, tend to resemble each other in their maturity." Here was the germ of the other half of Maine's thought—what might be called the utilitarianization of history. *Ancient Law,* however, was still a way off; one finds perhaps as much of it in another of the papers of the Juridicial Society: Patrick Colquhoun's "Rise and Progress of Roman Civil Law."[22]

Maine was a highly political animal, and one place to look for catalyzing influences is in his journalistic writings. Although his earliest unsigned articles on French topics for the *Morning Chronicle* have not been identified, the antidemocratic bias of his later writing suggests that he, like his close friend Fitzjames Stephen, was profoundly disturbed by the Revolution of 1848. Later articles in the *Saturday Review* on the Crimean War and the Indian Mutiny offer more definite clues. Again, there are illuminative contrasts. His domestic political sympathies lay with the free-trade Peelite group of the unreformed Tory party, and when the aristocratic political and military establishment came under Benthamite attack for mismanagement and corruption in the Crimean War, he rallied to its defense—throwing up the recent financial difficulties of the Crystal Palace as evidence of the miscarriages of middle-class, "un-aristocratic enterprise." If the great families had a virtual monopoly on political office, it was "one which even political economists call a natural monopoly." With the exception of a few men trained in the anti-Corn Law agitation, the only other segment of society with an equivalent political education was his own "literary class."[23]

But when the Indian Mutiny led to aristocratic attacks on the governance of the East India Company, Maine leapt to the defense of this middle-class and traditionally Benthamite establishment. The issue of Indian government was one that could "fairly be treated as a question of classes." Since the aristocracy dominated Parliament, the call for direct parliamentary control was simply a euphemism for control by the aristocracy, which was in fact seeking to enhance its power by "shutting off the only walk of public life in which the rest of English Society can learn the arts of Government and give proof of its capacity for applying them."[24] The apparent disharmony of Maine's Crimean and Indian polemics is resolved in the thematic unity of his life and work. In the one case he defended an aristocratic establishment into which he sought entrance as an intellectual aristocrat; in the other he defended the middle-class establishment (in which his maternal family had investments) that until then provided the only regular means for men of his background to enter into the domain of public life dominated by the aristocracy.

The antinomies of Maine's thought are further illuminated by issues of racial relations raised by the Indian Mutiny. He had no sympathy for the "moral depravity" of the Sepoy rebels: those who did not believe greased cartridges had caused the mutiny simply did not understand the "immemorial superstition which has ravelled up the mind of the Oriental into a maze which defies all the ingenuity of the West to penetrate." But if this was a moment when "the thirst for revenge and the purpose of chastisement blend[ed] into each other," Maine was still strongly critical of those who "condemned the idiosyncrasies of their dark-skinned fellow creatures" and called them "Niggers." He even charged Lord Palmerston with attempting to create an Anglo-Saxon plantation oligarchy on the model of the American South. Drawing heavily on John Stuart Mill's anonymously authored official defense of the East India Company, Maine argued that planter interests were seeking to overthrow the traditional village community—"the only true organisation of which the Hindoo race is capable"—because the large quasi-feudal landholdings of Bengal *zemindars* lent themselves more easily to exploitation. Similar motives led planter interests to wreck the company's attempts at legal codification through the introduction of

English common law, thereby risking the disruption of "one of the most symmetrical administrative organisations the world has ever seen." Paradoxically, this paragon of Benthamism had been the outcome of Burkean processes—a unique historical solution to the problem of "how a free country can administer an alien dependency at once despotically and successfully."[25]

Maine spoke of the discovery of the village community as "like the first glimpse of a great truth in a course of physical experiment." Readings stimulated by the Crimean War had already familiarized him with a similar social form in Europe. He later spoke of the accounts of the Russian commune in Haxthausen's *Russian Empire* as "the revelation of a new social order, having no counterpart in the West."[26] He was apparently already at work on an historical treatment of law in the ancient world, but his essays of 1855 and 1856 reflect no interest in any stratum of legal history underlying Roman law, nor any significant comparative dimension. The Indian and the Russian data, juxtaposed against the Roman, led him to such a stratum, but in the context of a new methodological approach. To the analytic impulse of Benthamism and the historical impulse of German jurisprudence was now added the impulse of comparison.

Specifically, it was the comparative philology of Indo-European languages that now provided Maine's methodological exemplar. He could have been led via Elphinstone's and James Mill's histories of India back to Sir William Jones; or through his friendship with the Celtic scholar Whitley Stokes, who had trained with a Tübingen philologist before coming to the Inner Temple in 1853—or perhaps from the *Cambridge Essays,* which contained his own essay on legal education, to the analogous Oxford volume, which contained Max Müller's essay on comparative mythology. But he could scarcely have pursued an interest in Indian scholarship without being led to comparative philology, the influence of which is frequently and at several points explicitly manifest in Maine's later work.[27]

When *Ancient Law* was published early in 1861, the structure of its argument reflected the variety of its intellectual sources. The first four chapters attacked modern assumptions obscuring the growth of ancient law: the Benthamite conception of positive law and the Rousseauistic conception of the state of nature. Against the Benthamites, Maine argued that codified law was only the last stage of a development that moved from the judgments of the heroic king through the customary law of a juristical oligarchy. Once achieved, codified law was subject to "the conscious desire of improvement" only by a further three-stage historical process of indirection. At first, legal fictions performed the "two-fold office of transforming a system of laws and concealing the transformation"; then the civil law was brought in line with a body of rules claiming "superior sanctity" through the notion of equity; only latterly did the Benthamite mechanism of legislation become a means by which written codes were modified to bring law into harmony with "advancing society."[28]

Implicit in the idea of equity was that of "natural law" which, by providing a model of "absolutely perfect law," had long been a major factor in Western progress. Recast in the form of the "state of nature," the concept of natural law had in the modern period led political thought astray. The villain was Rousseau, in whose speculations "the central figure, whether arrayed in English dress as the signatory of a social compact, or simply stripped naked of all historical qualities, is uniformly Man, in a supposed state of nature." Although this "non-historical, unverifiable condition of the race" had since fallen into disrepute, its "subtler guises" continued to distort the thinking of writers on the growth of law, who characteristically took "no account of what law has actually been" in epochs prior to their own. While they were careful enough observers of "the institutions of their own age and civilization, and those of other ages and civilizations with which they had some degree of intellectual sympathy," when they turned to "archaic states of society which exhibited much superficial difference from their own, they uniformly ceased to observe and began guessing."[29]

A truly scientific jurisprudence could only be founded on an historical basis. It must begin with "the simplest social forms in a state as near as possible to their rudimentary condition"—determined not by a priori speculation, but by penetrating "the history of primitive societies." Fortunately, the very conservatism of human nature made this possible: "the resistance it opposes to change is such that, though the variations of human society in a portion of the world are plain enough, they are neither so rapid nor so extensive that their amount, character, and general direction cannot be ascertained." By examining the surviving records of ancient legal systems on principles similar to those "which have led to such surprising results in comparative philology," Maine felt he could determine the "rudiments of the social state" and locate "the germs out of which has assuredly been unfolded every form of moral restraint which controls our actions and shapes our conduct at the present moment."[30]

The picture of primitive society Maine derived from "comparative jurisprudence" turned out to be the same patriarchal conception Locke had attacked two centuries before in his polemic against Sir Robert Filmer. Rather than being buttressed by analogy with the savages of America, it was already "familiar to most of us from early childhood"—because it was in fact the same as that contained in Genesis. Founded on the *Patria Potestas*—the absolute dominion of the father over the person and property of his children—this elementary social form was the family based on kinship through males. Uniting "all those who are under the same Paternal Power, or who have been under it or who might have been under it if their lineal ancestor had lived long enough to exercise his empire," the "agnatic" family was a "perpetual and inextinguishable" corporation, whose sacred unity was regularly commemorated by family sacrifices and ceremonies that were "the pledge and witness of its perpetuity." In this primitive society, no single person could ever be regarded as a separate social unit; all individuality was "swallowed up in his family," which was collectively responsible for the crimes of any individual member.[31]

Following up "the hint provided us by the Scriptural example," Maine suggested that permanent communities "began to exist wherever a family held together instead of separating at the death of its patriarchal chieftain." The history of political ideas began "with the assumption that kinship in blood is the sole possible ground of community in political functions"; all larger social units were formed on the principle of descent "from one original stock." Social development was thus a process of aggregation, of families uniting into gens (or houses), of houses into tribes, of tribes into a commonwealth—with adoption and fictive kinship preserving a mythical consanguinity, until finally, in a revolutionary change of profound implications, "local contiguity" replaced kinship as "the basis of common political action."[32]

Arriving thus at a social state whose relics were preserved in the commentaries of Gaius that Niebuhr had discovered in 1816, Maine saw in the subsequent annals of Roman law "a nearly complete history of the crumbling away of an archaic system, and of the formation of new institutions from the re-combined materials." Gradually, the "empire of the father" was whittled away by fictions, equity, and legislation, as personal rights and property were removed "from the domestic forum to the cognizance of public tribunals." Starting "from one terminus of history," from a "condition of society in which all the relations of Persons are summed up in the relations of Family," one moved steadily "towards a phase of social order in which all these relations arise from the free agreement of individuals." Using the term "status" to designate all personal conditions derived from "the powers and privileges anciently residing in the Family," Maine argued that "the movement of the progressive societies has hitherto been a movement *from Status to Contract.*" Relying heavily on Savigny, Maine went on from here to trace the development in the later Roman tradition of specific legal conceptions central to the transformation that had produced modern civilization: inheritance, property, contract, and crime.[33]

Despite its catalytic role in the development of his thought, the evidence of "Sclavonic" and "Hindoo" village communities played only a subordinate role in the argument of *Ancient Law.* At once an "organized patriarchal society and an assemblage of co-proprietors," the Indian village community was the still existing analogue of the Roman gens. The fact that "similarly compounded" but slightly variant societies existed in Russia and the Balkans was evidence that for each step in the development of family forms there was an "analogous alteration in the nature of Ownership"—thus confirming the implicit thesis of the whole book: that the linked development of the law of family and of property reflected the central dynamic process in the growth of civilization.[34]

Soon after *Ancient Law* appeared, however, Maine's life took a turn that gave the village community a more central role in his thought. The book's favorable reception—and certain political connections—led to his appointment as Law Member of the Viceroy's Council in India, and for the next seven years he resided in the country whose observation he felt critical to the understanding of human progress. Despite an intense dislike of Calcutta, however, his actual experience of life outside the British capital was rather limited. He learned neither Sanskrit nor any local vernacular, and his further understanding of the village community came largely from his familiarity with judicial materials, and from the written reports and oral testimony of fellow administrators with local experience. Despite his earlier attacks on the planter interest, his superiors in London felt him generally "inclined to side with his fellow-countrymen"—not being the sort of man easily "to face unpopularity."[35]

Maine's Indian experience brings more sharply into focus the double tendency of his earlier thought. Some commentators have emphasized his support of "the claims of prescription over change as the basic ingredient of wise public policy," and he has been seen as a progenitor of Cromer and Lugard and the later imperialism of "indirect rule." But Maine was also a strong advocate of active central government and legislative reform. Suggesting in his first speech to the Governor's Council that social progress was "almost mysteriously dependent" on the "completest freedom of contract," he did all he could to facilitate that progress in India by breaking down "existing barriers to individual personality and property rights." To Europeans who saw themselves as "exclusively children of the age of free trade and scientific discovery," India offered the lesson that "most of the elements of human society, like most of that which goes to make up an individual man, come by inheritance." But in India itself, where only "the empire of the English race" restrained the "pent-up flood of barbarism," the weight of the past was "an inheritance of nearly unmixed evil." Willy-nilly, British power was dissolving "the ideas and social forms" underlying native Indian society, and it therefore must assume "the duty of rebuilding upon its own principles that which it unwillingly destroys."[36]

These principles were, in a broad sense, utilitarian. At the end of his life, Maine looked back upon a half century in which England had undergone a peaceful revolution along Benthamite lines, in which property and contract were made "the agencies by which the material existence of the entire community was to be improved." What was wrong with Bentham was not his economic ethics, but his politics. Granting with Bentham that the "greatest happiness of the greatest number" was the proper standard of law and morality, this did not mean "that the opinion of the greatest number is conclusive as to what is best for their happiness." In Victorian England as in British India, the opinions of the multitude were in fact the greatest enemy of progress—as they had been since the dawn of history.[37]

The central question underlying Maine's inquiry in *Ancient Law* had in fact been the same as Buckle's: how to explain the great difference between the "stationary societies" of the East and the "progressive societies" of the West. Rejecting Buckle's climatic interpretation, he had focused on the internal world of custom and law, arguing what was in effect an analogue of Müller's "disease of language." Although in the beginning the usages of barbarous society were those "best suited to promote its physical and moral well-being," the multitudes were "incapable of understanding the true ground of their expediency," and therefore invented "superstitious reasons" for their permanence. On this foundation "irrational imitation" generated a body of customary usage which, given a religious authority and ultimately codified as law, acted everywhere as a brake on the progress of material civilization. Only in western Europe had law escaped stagnation, allowing the gradual evolution of the legal system which provided the basis for realizing the utilitarian ideal. But once the processes of material civilization had achieved this liberation, European power over stationary societies was irresistible, and there was no viable alternative to the conscious adaptation of their cultural forms to a more utilitarian model.[38]

The view of human history Maine elaborated in *Ancient Law* and implemented in India seems in many respects evolutionary, and he is sometimes spoken of as a "unilinear evolutionist." He was indeed a staunch advocate of the "Comparative Method" as a means of placing "parallel phenomena" in the present in an "order of historical succession," and he did speak of "laws" and "stages" of development. Nonetheless, Maine's inquiry had been defined in a framework that differed from that of sociocultural evolutionism in important ways. Far from reasoning from the data of contemporary savages, he regarded them—in terms echoing his godfather's degenerationism—as the "mere waifs and strays of humanity." But he had no hesitation to reasoning from "the Scriptural history of the Hebrew patriarchs": by extending his argument from the Indo-European to the Semitic races, the Bible suggested that the first society among *all* "races of men" had been "originally organised on the patriarchal model." This reliance on Scripture, with its very shallow depth in time, confirms that Maine's viewpoint was defined without regard to the archeological revolution, which in fact undercut his implicit equation of "ancient" and "primitive." As he later acknowledged, the societies he studied were no longer "primeval," given "the vast antiquity now claimed for the human race"; and by the time he returned from India his picture of primitive patriarchal society had been called into question on the basis of "an altogether new kind of testimony" derived from "the ideas and usages" of contemporary savages. Thus it was that Maine's later works all reflect a continuing attempt to sustain the argument of *Ancient Law* in a postevolutionary temporal and developmental context.[39]

With his membership in the intellectual aristocracy validated by a knighthood in 1871, Maine was to hold academic positions at both Oxford and Cambridge. In addition to a vituperative attack on *Popular Government,* and posthumously published lectures he gave in 1888 as, appropriately, the Whewell Professor of International Law, Maine wrote three more books elaborating themes of *Ancient Law*—each of them based on some new body of evidence from within "the extreme Easterly and the extreme Westerly branches of the Aryan race." Together they formed in effect a single study of "the process of feudalization" by which, from germs "deep in the more ancient social forms of the Aryans," the modern modes of European individual ownership had developed through the aggrandizement of powerful leaders at the expense of the common holdings of the village community.[40]

In all these later works Maine was quite willing to emphasize the links between his own and evolutionary thinking, when such links sustained his argument. But his more general strategy was to differentiate his study from that of "the school of so-called prehistoric inquiry" by accepting and insisting on certain limitations of race, time, and method that had in fact originally defined it. He was willing to extend his argument to the Semitic and if necessary to the Uralian races, and to make occasional comparisons with groups farther afield—citing the evidence of Kaffir laws to sustain his analysis of the relation of chief to clansman in Ireland. But in general he was very dubious of any connection between "barbarous Aryan usage and savage non-Aryan practice." Although he was willing to accept the American evolutionist Lewis Henry Morgan's evidence that other races had different notions of kinship, he saw no reason to assume that "the kinship of the higher races" had "grown out of the kinship now known only to the lower."[41]

The emergence of "progressive" societies was a quite exceptional historical phenomenon, the product of nonrecurring events within the Graeco-Roman tradition. The essential method of Maine's inquiry was "to trace [this] history backwards" on the basis of surviving written records "belonging to races with which we have some affinity." True, "direct observation" could sometimes come "to the aid of historical inquiry," especially in India, where the process of feudalization had never been completed, and the "dry bones" of the ancient village community were still articulated and functioning. But if Indian villages cast light on the origins of European civilization, it was not because of a general principle of the psychic unity of mankind (which Maine thought a rather dubious proposition). It was rather because comparative philology had shown that both groups were offshoots of the same "Aryan" race and had originally shared the same culture.[42]

It has been suggested that Maine's Aryan hypothesis was "merely a facade," hiding the fact that his historical method "required for its validation the typically positivist assumption of general laws of social development"—else how could he guarantee that Aryan institutions would develop "in parallel fashion" after the branches of the race had lost contact? But Maine required no such guarantee. Indeed, it was "quite inconceivable" that, acted on by "all kinds of influences," the surviving remnants of the patriarchal family should "have come down to us in exactly the same shape" in each of the Aryan races. For Maine, the function of the comparative method was "to determine whether [these remnants] have sufficient similarity to suggest a common parentage and to say what the parent institution is." By recombining "the separated elements," the comparative historian showed that "what we call property, what we call marital right, what we call parental authority were all originally blended in the general conception of patriarchal power." His ability to do this depended on the fact that certain Aryan peoples had *not* developed, but had preserved the older institutions more or less unchanged.[43]

Maine's method depended also on the idea of survivals. But his survivals, which derived from Savigny's historical jurisprudence, differed in emphasis from E. B. Tylor's, which derived from folklore and geology. It is not simply that Maine distinguished between "*mere* survivals," which had no present function, and "those relics of ancient thought and conduct which have been kept alive longest" precisely *because* they "have generally had a usefulness of their own." For Tylor, the methodological utility of survivals depended on the psychic unity of man, which enabled the present inquirer to reason back from irrational tradition to the rational behavior underlying it; for Maine, their utility depended on an underlying historical connection: a specific group of earlier men behaved historically in a particular way, and the practice survived in different forms among their various descendants.[44]

While it is true that Maine was touched by positivist assumption, his inquiry was always in a fundamental sense historical. Tracing the roots of modern civilization *backward* in history, not *forward* from an assumed prehistoric state, he had no interest in the problem of "absolute origin," and always retained a Whewellian distaste for "inquiries which, when I have attempted to push them too far, have always landed me in mudbanks and fog." His purpose was to study the "real" and not the "imaginary" history of civilized institutions, and he was caustically critical of any assumed universal parallelism: "there is nothing in the recorded history of society to justify the belief that, during the vast chapter of its growth which is wholly unwritten, the same transformations of social constitution succeeded one another everywhere, uniformly if not simultaneously."[45]

Despite these basic differences of assumption between Maine's inquiry and sociocultural evolutionism, it is nonetheless true that in a post-Darwinian milieu his argument took on an evolutionary significance. Maine's willingness to grant that the patriarchal family was "by no means universal among savage men" did not satisfy social evolutionist antagonists who argued the one-time universality of matrifocal forms. In defending himself, Maine argued convincingly that the *Patria Potestas* was more consistent with a Darwinian picture of primate behavior than the primitive promiscuity assumed by his opponents. Beyond this, a "social Darwinist" rhetoric was quite congenial to Maine's elitist view of history; his later writings contain a number of references to "the law of the survival of the fittest." Perhaps as a result, Leslie Stephen had no difficulty incorporating Maine retrospectively into the evolutionary canon: "Coming soon after the publication of Darwin's great book," *Ancient Law* had "introduced a correlative method into the philosophy of institutions." There were more compelling reasons for this intellectual cooptation; but they should not blind us, as they did Stephen, to the distinction Maine later insisted on between *his* comparative method, which derived from traditional historiography and comparative linguistics, and that of the sociocultural evolutionists, which was conditioned in a fundamental way by the Darwinian revolution.[46]

Making the Associationist Tradition Evolutionary

Despite his tremendous influence on the intellectual life of the second half of the century, Herbert Spencer—like Maine—was marginal both to the contemporary community of British anthropology and to its subsequent tradition. But in contrast to Maine—and to Buckle—his viewpoint was of course clearly evolutionary. Indeed, it is largely due to his influence that the term "evolution" eventually became the rubric to designate a natural developmental viewpoint in both the organic and the "superorganic" spheres; his writings, already evolutionary quite independently of Darwin and Wallace, helped define the intellectual milieu in which anthropological evolutionism flourished. Precisely because his evolutionism emerged before the *Origin of Species,* its consideration may help us to understand the impact of the Darwinian revolution.[47]

Spencer was born in 1820 in Derby, one of the smaller Midlands towns that in the preceding half century had been the *mise en scène* of the Industrial Revolution. His intellectual character was molded by two contrasting influences: a severe moral code of self-help and diligent industry inherited from the Wesleyan Methodism of his four grandparents; and a deistic rationalism inherited from his schoolteacher father, secretary of the Philosophical Society which Erasmus Darwin had founded in Derby in 1783. Linked by utilitarianism, these same two influences defined a provincial radical culture which, despite growing antagonism between its middle and working-class elements, was for a time able to unite "Unitarian and Primitive Methodist, manufacturer, greengrocer and artisan, Benthamite and Godwinian" against the traditional aristocratic political order and cultural ideal.[48]

By the 1830s, this provincial radical culture was beginning to break up, as the internal pressures of class division were heightened, and the developing railroad network began to destroy its relative autonomy. Spencer himself participated in the latter process. Having gained a practical scientific education from his father and from his uncle (an evangelical, albeit radical, minister with whom he lived for three years), at seventeen Spencer began a career as a civil engineer, and for a decade played an active role in the last great battle of the Industrial Revolution.[49]

He was also active in the politics of provincial radicalism, which, despite the forces undermining it, continued fairly strong throughout the 1840s. Like the metropolitan radicals, and the working-class movement that eventuated in Chartism, provincial radicalism turned away from traditional political channels after the frustration of the expectations that had been aroused by the Reform of 1832. But in contrast to the more militant Chartists, it still saw the middle and the working classes as linked together in opposition to the aristocracy. And in contrast to metropolitan radicals, who sought to turn the state into "an organ of benevolent, disinterested administration," provincial radicalism applied "the logic of laissez-faire to the polity as well as the economy"—minimizing the functions of the state and emphasizing the role of "public opinion" in the shaping of social institutions. For some time Spencer served as local secretary to the Complete Suffrage Union, and his first political writings were a series of letters to Edward Miall's *Non-Conformist* on "The Proper Sphere of Government," in which he argued that "the laws of society," like those of nature, were such that "natural evils" would rectify themselves by virtue of a "self-adjusting principle." Indeed, much of Spencer's later sociology, including the concept of the social organism and the opposition of militant and industrial societies, was already foreshadowed in the rhetoric of provincial radicalism.[50]

One phase of provincial radical culture was of course the phrenology movement, which for many middle-class radicals offered a bridge between traditional religious belief and a purely secular reformism. As preached by the Scottish lawyer George Combe, phrenology's hereditarian implications were somewhat softened. Combe not only allowed a considerable adaptive activism in the exercise and development of mental faculties, but assumed that the effects of such activity were transmissible to offspring. Spencer had become a convert at the age of twelve after hearing Spurzheim lecture in Derby, and in 1846 designed a "cephalograph" he hoped would place the science on a firmer comparative foundation. Although soon thereafter he became skeptical of certain points of phrenological doctrine, its influence, like that of provincial political radicalism, was very much evident in the "System of Social and Political Morality" he conceived in 1846 to answer his father's expressed belief that "the declared will of God is the only possible standard of morals."[51]

Conflating Bentham and the deistic natural theology of Bishop William Paley (neither of whom he had read) into a single "doctrine of expedience," Spencer began *Social Statics* by discussing his dissatisfaction with utilitarian ethical theory. Though the "greatest happiness" maxim defined the "creative purpose" of human existence, it could never provide a rule of practical conduct. Given the manifest variability of human nature "in instinct, in morals, in opinions, in tastes, [and] in rationality," the maxim could never have any definite meaning, since "no fact is more palpable than that the standard of happiness is infinitely variable." Spencer, however, was not about to rest satisfied with either moral relativity or human psychic diversity. Arguing that "morality knows nothing of geographical boundaries, or distinctions of race," he suggested elsewhere in *Social Statics* that human nature was after all constant in its "elements," if not in their "ratios." The resolution of the paradox, and the basis for a scientific ethics, was found in the Scottish moral philosophy, recast in phrenological terms.[52]

The moral forces on which social equilibrium depended were "resident in the social atom—man.'' However, they were not, as utilitarians thought, a matter of intellect, but rather of feeling, sentiment, and ultimately of instinct—in short, of the ''Moral Sense,'' which was an amalgam of two other ''faculties'': the ''instinct of personal rights,'' and Adam Smith's ''sympathy.'' Like all faculties, the moral sense was subject to the law that ''a faculty to which circumstances do not allow full exercise diminishes; and that a faculty on which circumstances make excessive demands increases.'' It was therefore variously manifest in different men, and the equilibrium between its two components varied systematically ''with race and epoch.''[53]

The moral sense, however, was necessarily realized in the course of human history. For Spencer, the notions of ''evil'' and ''civilization'' were dynamically antithetical: evil was ''the non-adaptation of constitution to conditions''; civilization was ''the adaptation that has already taken place.'' But since the adaptation of life to circumstances was a law of nature, the gradual perfection of the moral faculty and the completion of civilization ''were removed out of the region of probability into that of certainty.'' Thus it was that the relativity of Spencer's first ''lemma'' (''change is the law of all things'') was balanced by the absolutism of his second (''unable as the imperfect man may be to fulfil the perfect law, there is no other law for him''). Thus it was that the moral law must be deduced from the endpoint of human development and not from the beginning.[54]

Social Statics was therefore a study of ''the equilibrium of a perfect society.'' Founded on the freedom of every man ''to do all that he wills provided he infringes not the equal freedom of any other man,'' it elaborated this ''first principle'' along two different lines: the specification of individual rights and the limitations of state action. The first line gives us a radical libertarian Spencer, arguing for the right of all to the use of the earth (and therefore against the individual ownership of land), for the full equality of women, and even for ''the rights of children.'' The second gives a more familiar Spencer, arguing for private initiative and laissez-faire in trade, religion, education, social welfare, and even in the delivery of mail. Whereas the first focused primarily on the definition of human rights in an ideal society, the second emphasized the qualification these were subject to in less perfect stages of civilization. Because in man's ''original predatory state'' the ratio of self-preservation to sympathy in human nature was very high, and it was only the ''multiplication of the race'' that forced humans ''to live more or less in the presence of each other,'' society was possible only on the basis of coercive authority, and in the beginning all government was despotic. Gradually, however, the development of sympathy and ''self-restraining power'' made possible the ''diminution of external restraint,'' until for "the rightly constituted man" all "external help" would be unnecessary. Civilization was thus "the evolution of a being capable of conforming to it."[55]

The later portions of *Social Statics* were one long argument on the interrelation of social institutions and individual character: "in the social organism, the seemingly fixed framework of laws and institutions, is moulded by the seemingly forceless thing—character." Because the institutions of any stage of civilization must correspond to the state of national character, which was a summation of individual characters, it was futile to attempt to change human behavior by legislation. Indeed, Spencer saw social institutions as mechanical crutches for as yet imperfect character; the reflection of the "non-adaptation of man to the social state," they would die out when all men possessed "an active instinct of freedom, together with an active sympathy." At that point, "all still existing limitations to individuality" would disappear, and men would live together naturally in "perfect individuation and perfect mutual dependence."[56]

One can find in *Social Statics* the germs of each of what have been called Spencer's "three sociologies": the contractual individual, the social organic, and the cultural. The first is evident in his conception of society as an aggregation of individual social atoms, whose individual natures determine by summation the character of the social whole; the second, primarily as an occasional metaphor—the "social organism" tacitly opposed to the "mechanism" of state administration; the third, implicit (as it was to remain) in the relation of social forms and national character. But if Spencer had written no more social theory than *Social Statics*, he would scarcely be thought of as a sociologist, nor as a figure in the emergence of evolutionism, whether biological or sociocultural. Despite his polar types of savagery and civilization, he made no systematic use of the data of savagery, his stages of development were minimally elaborated, and the whole process had virtually no depth in time. Spencer's preoccupation was not the origin of civilization in savagery, but its completion in the present. Still part of the polemical weaponry of middle-class radicalism preparing for the final victory over aristocratic power, *Social Statics* was not an account of how civilization had arisen so much as a manual of how to fulfill it.[57]

Nevertheless, the book already reflected a shift critical to the emergence of Spencer's subsequent evolutionary thought. He later saw his whole enterprise as an attempt to provide a "scientific basis" for ethical judgments, "now that the moral injunctions are losing the authority given by their supposed sacred origin." In *Social Statics* this secularization—or more particularly, biologization—of morals may be seen in process. As Spencer moved from specifying the ideal rights of man to discussing human adaptation in a less than perfect state, Nature replaced God as the active force. It was her "stern discipline" that, "partly by weeding out those of lowest development, and partly by subjecting those who remain to the never-ceasing discipline of experience," achieved "the growth of a race who shall both understand the conditions of existence, and be able to act up to them." It was in this context, too, that the notion of social organism was given somewhat greater elaboration in the last pages of the book. Indeed, Spencer ended *Social Statics* by suggesting that moral truth "proves to be a development of physiological truth"—"a species of transcendental physiology."[58]

Spencer's writings of the 1850s were further steps in this secularization, as the autodidactic provincial radical found a place for himself first in the metropolis and then in the cosmos. From late 1848 on Spencer lived mainly in London, supporting himself by journalistic and literary work, and establishing connections with important intellectuals. Always "an impatient reader," he was never able to go beyond the first pages of any book "the fundamental principles of which I entirely dissent from"—as he remarked of Kant's *Critique*. Now, however, he came more directly in touch with wider frameworks of thought, partly by a kind of intellectual osmosis—as when G. H. Lewes and George Eliot, both Comteans, expounded the "positive philosophy" in conversation—and partly by readings his new friendships stimulated—as when Lewes brought along a biological volume on a walking trip, and Spencer found in it the pregnant phrase, "the physiological division of labour."[59]

In this context, Spencer developed the various lines of inquiry that were to merge in his general evolutionary thesis. During 1851, when he also attended Richard Owen's lectures on comparative anatomy and spent many days "with pleasure and profit" at the Crystal Palace, he collected materials to refute the Malthusian theory of population, which was clearly a threat to the utopian equilibrium of *Social Statics*. Fortunately, the "inherent tendency of things towards good" assured that the forces of intellect would take over from those of reproduction, and population pressure, which had been the spur to human progress, would eventually reach a stable equilibrium.[60]

While working on his population essay, Spencer came across Von Baer's formula for embryological development—"every organism in the course of its development changes from homogeneity of structure to heterogeneity of structure"—and concluded that the same law must hold for "the ascending grades of organisms of all kinds." Spencer had inclined toward the "development hypothesis" in biology since 1840, when he read *The Principles of Geology* and found Lamarck's thesis more convincing than Lyell's refutation. Early in 1852 he published an essay in which he rejected Special Creation, and suggested that "complex organic forms may have arisen by successive modifications out of simple ones." By this own account, Spencer then went on to apply Von Baer's formula "first to one and then to another group of phenomena, until all were taken in as parts of a whole."[61]

By this time, Spencer had become more familiar with the major European traditions in epistemology and psychology, largely through his friend Lewes' *Biographical History of Philosophy.* In 1852 George Eliot gave him a copy of Mill's *Logic*—one of the few books Spencer read from cover to cover—and he became entangled in Mill's dispute with Whewell over the basis of logical certainty. Naturalizing, as it were, what he found worthwhile in the innatist assumptions of German idealism and Scottish moral philosophy, Spencer was able to come to terms with the dominant associationist tradition in English psychology by uniting his "development hypothesis" with the associationist "experience hypothesis." On this basis he elaborated an evolutionary associationism that sought to explain "the way in which Mind gradually evolves out of Life." Spencer argued that "the so-called forms of thought" were "the outcome of the process of perpetually adjusting inner relations to outer relations"—"fixed relations in the environment producing fixed relations in the mind." Applying the Lamarckian notion of "use-inheritance" to the law of association, he gave associationism a cumulative depth in time: "not only in the individual do ideas become connected when in experience the things producing them have repeatedly occurred together," but the effects of such repeated associations were "transmitted as modifications of the nervous system" in the next generation, so that they accumulated in "successions of individuals." On this basis Spencer could finally rationalize utilitarianism and the moral sense: innate moral intuitions were simply "the results of accumulated experiences of utility, gradually organized and inherited," so that "they have come to be quite independent of conscious experience."[62]

Late in 1854, Spencer conceived an article that was to be the first synthetic statement of his evolutionary viewpoint. But as the essay was "the subject of some anxiety," he put it aside while he worked on his *Principles of Psychology.* As he was completing that book, he suffered a crisis that left him permanently plagued by insomnia and periodic nervous difficulties. The first symptoms of breakdown appeared while he was writing the chapters explaining the higher mental faculties of reason and will in terms of evolutionary associationism. Spencer had intended to write one more section in which the argument he had so far carried on in terms of mental function would be related more systematically to the developing physical structure of the brain. Such an argument was in fact incorporated in the second edition of 1870; but in the first, he referred to it only indirectly as material that "might prejudice some" against the rest of his thesis. It seems likely, however, that he was unable to write it at this time, and that his breakdown was symptomatic of how profoundly hesitant even this rigorously nonconforming developmentalist was to take the final step in displacing supernatural by naturalistic evolutionary causation. For eighteen months Spencer found all intellectual work impossible, and when he was finally able to take up and complete the general essay on "Progress: Its Law and Cause," its difficulty may be measured by his own later calculation that it had been written at the rate of half a page a day.[63]

The essay opened with a critique of the "current conception of Progress"—including by implication his own in *Social Statics*—as a "teleological one" that interpreted development "solely as bearing on human happiness." Spencer now tried to show that quite "apart from our interests" the law of all change—"whether it be in the development of the Earth, in the development of Life upon its surface, in the development of Society"—was "an evolution of the simple into the complex, through successive differentiations." The cause of this universal transformation of the homogeneous into the heterogeneous lay in the fact that "every active force produces more than one change—every cause produces more than one effect." Starting from the original "nebulous medium" of the solar system, Spencer sketched this "multiplication of effects" through the inorganic, the organic, and the superorganic worlds. At the end of 1857, after postulating the "instability of the homogeneous" as the antecedent cause of the whole transformation, Spencer projected a series of volumes elaborating his scheme. After circulating a prospectus for his "synthetic philosophy" to potential subscribers early in 1860, he spent the four decades until his death in 1903 in its realization.[64]

Spencer's evolutionism was thus formulated quite independently of Darwin, and in terms of a different causal process than natural selection—although he easily found a place in his essentially Lamarckian scheme for what he himself christened "the survival of the fittest." By that time a more systematic sociocultural evolutionism was already part of his general evolutionary viewpoint—most notably, perhaps, in his essay on "Manners and Fashion," in which he hypothesized the development of all law, religion, and manners by differentiation from a common source of reverence for authority, urging "a protestantism of social forms" to combat usages "that have ceased to facilitate and have become obstructive." Indeed, much of the argument of his 1857 essay dealt with the evolution of various human sociocultural phenomena: government, manufactures, commerce, language, literature, science, and art.[65]

But the very fact that Spencer's "superorganic" evolutionism developed independently of Darwin in the context of his own broader scheme of inorganic and organic evolution sets his thinking apart from that of other sociocultural evolutionists. True, by 1860 he had for some time been drawing on the ethnological and anthropological writings of his day—as when he cited Galton's Damaras, "whose conceptions of number scarcely transcend those of a dog," as evidence for the continuity of mental life from "the automatic actions of the lowest creatures" to the "highest conscious actions of the human race." But although he argued that "the adult mind of the savage" was a convenient point of departure in tracing "the genesis of science," he did not systematically use the data of contemporary savagery to reconstruct the phases of sociocultural evolution. *His* comparative method was based instead on the fundamental analogy between "low types of organisms and low types of societies" (that each "consists of many like parts severally performing like functions") and on the analogical application of a model of embryological development to the evolution of societies. Because Spencer was preoccupied by the more general problem of establishing an overall evolutionary development in all realms, analogies of structure and process played a critical role in his argument.[66]

By contrast—as we shall shortly see—the evolutionism of Lubbock, Tylor, and McLennan was a solution to problems posed by the already accomplished biological and archeological revolutions. Tylor later felt it "most strange" that Spencer did not place "in its proper niche the evidence of pre-historic archaeology." Spencer, however, had moved from the shallow time of *Social Statics* to the indefinite time of *First Principles* without apparently feeling the impact of the newly discovered antiquity of man; and the method of reconstructing human history in a vastly extended temporal frame was never problematic for him in the way it was for Tylor, Lubbock, and McLennan.[67]

These differences of context, purpose, and method affected Spencer's relation to other sociocultural evolutionists in another way. Although he had formulated his basic viewpoint by 1860, Spencer's writings were still not such as to define him primarily as a sociologist; and for the next decade he was preoccupied with other aspects of his evolutionary philosophy. In 1867, he hired an assistant to search the travel literature of the world for data on uncivilized peoples, which over the next decades he published in tabular form in a series of folio volumes entitled *Descriptive Sociology.* His first important sociological publication, a methodological treatise on *The Study of Sociology,* was in a general sense evolutionary, but it derived its specific empirical content from contemporary society. It was not until 1876 that he finally published the first volume of the *Principles of Sociology*; and when he did, he became embroiled in controversy with McLennan, who felt he had failed to qualify himself "to hold an opinion" on the universality of polyandry, and with Tylor, who went so far as to charge him with plagiarism.[68] The point is not to deny Spencer's contributions to sociocultural evolutionary theory (especially in the area of psychological assumption); it is rather to suggest that by the time Spencer got around to systematic evolutionary sociology, sociocultural evolutionism in British anthropology had already been well established by other writers, in a somewhat different context.

Redefining the Basis of Human Psychic Unity

To appreciate the specific historical character of sociocultural evolutionism, let us briefly reconsider the relationship of Buckle, Maine, and Spencer to the three major intellectual movements to which it has been linked in previous historiography: eighteenth-century progressivism, utilitarianism, and Darwinian evolutionism.

From the perspective of the broader history of progressivist thought, which at each of its major historical moments has been concerned with something analogous to "the problem of civilization," all three writers might be seen—along with the sociocultural evolutionists to be considered in the next chapter—as part of a single intellectual tradition which also includes the eighteenth-century progressivists. Of the three, Buckle seems the closest to the eighteenth century, insofar as Montesquieu and Adam Smith defined the poles of his progressivism. In the case of Spencer, however, the influence of Scottish thought, mediated by phrenology and provincial radicalism, seems to have been rather diffuse; and while among French progressivists he knew the work of Comte, he took great pains, on the whole convincingly, to deny any significant debt.[69] For the university man Maine—in contrast to the two autodidacts—the eighteenth century was already relegated to the past, there to be conceptualized in terms of more recent intellectual modes critical of the Enlightenment. On the whole, it would seem that if our interest is in the specific historical character of a particular moment in the progressivist tradition, motivating influences are better sought in more contemporary intellectual currents and events.

Certainly, all three men responded to the political and social developments of the 1830s and 1840s, and to the recent intellectual movement most obviously embodied in the cultural symbolism of the Crystal Palace: utilitarianism. Each was conscious of difficulties facing the utilitarian point of view. Even Buckle, who has been described as caught "in the Utilitarian cul-de-sac," expressed dissatisfaction with the broader empiricist tradition of which utilitarianism was a part. Maine's writings were one long debate with Bentham and Austin, and the inadequacies of utilitarian ethical theory were the starting point of Spencer's early work, which was later elaborated in specific relation to epistemological and psychological issues confronting the utilitarian tradition. As far as these three figures were concerned, it does seem useful to regard that tradition as undergoing a "crisis." However, the recollection of the younger Mill's personal crisis of the 1820s makes the timing of that crisis somewhat problematic. And one may wonder also about any interpretation of this crisis that tends to dissociate it from the emergence of Darwinism.[70]

Buckle's intellectual fate is particularly revealing. Once the Darwinian revolution had been accomplished, men who had at first responded favorably to Buckle had second thoughts—most notably Leslie Stephen, who as early as 1880 advanced the view that social evolutionism had offered a solution to problems confronting utilitarian thought. Stephen was particularly disturbed that for Buckle (as for Bentham) man was an "unvarying entity of constant properties." In Stephen's view, Buckle (like John Stuart Mill) had lacked any viable middle way between accepting human differences as evidence for "absolutely fixed types" and rejecting "all the characteristics of a race or class as mere external appendages." But since Darwinism "made it possible to accept evolution without mysticism," it was no longer necessary for empiricists to regard the specific qualities of an organism as "mere external additions, superinduced upon a uniform stock." They could now be seen rather as "properties of a type, fixed for the moment, although slowly changing" in "continuous growth under determinate conditions." In arguing against Buckle's notion that there had been no moral progress, Stephen suggested that although men were little modified by moral preaching, they were "most profoundly modified by being born into a vast and complex organization, and thus undergoing from their earliest days an elaborate system of drill, and imbibing, unconsciously, not only knowledge, but innumerable modes of feeling."[71]

From a present perspective, Stephen's words may suggest that the utilitarian tradition had failed to provide an anthropological concept of culture. For Stephen, however, it was not culture but "race" that was the rubric for "the influences by which society is moulded through beliefs and customs." That something other than a rigid hereditarianism was at issue is indicated by the fact that in 1900 Stephen was willing after all to follow Buckle and Mill in excluding organic race from sociology. But he would not exclude "the influence of the 'moral' element in building up the social structure." In short, he insisted on what an anthropologist today would call "culture"—although he still spoke of it in terms of "moral and social evolution."[72] The point, of course, is not to belabor Stephen for failing to employ a concept unavailable to him, but by contrast to explicate one that was. Carrying much of the meaning that "culture" does today, "race" was a kind of summation of historically accumulated moral differences sustained and slowly modified from generation to generation. Threatened with rigidification by polygenist hereditarianism, this ''cultural'' sense of race seemed once again viable within an evolutionary framework in which ''Darwinism'' was not incompatible with the inheritance of acquired characteristics.

As if to confirm Stephen's hindsight, there is evidence that in the early 1850s Buckle did toy with racial explanation, but in the end joined Mill in viewing race as the ''most vulgar'' of the modes of evading inquiry into ''the effect of social and moral influences on the human mind.'' But Stephen's dissatisfaction with Buckle, and with utilitarianism, reflected his feeling that this inquiry had in fact been evaded. Buckle was not in practice seriously interested in the causes or the role of cultural differences in human history, except as evidence of the influence of climate or as factors distorting the progress of human knowledge. Retrospectively, we might suggest that what bothered Stephen about Buckle was the stillbirth of Mill's proposed ''science of ethology,'' which, as a ''science of causes which determine the type of character belonging to a people, ''might have provided the means for including the influence of ''the 'moral element' in building up the social structure.''[73]

From his own perspective, however, what bothered Stephen—and many contemporaries—about Buckle was not simply his failure to take seriously the ''moral'' differences among mankind, but his rejection of the idea of ''moral progress.'' In a pre-Darwinian world, in which mankind as a moral creature was clearly differentiated from the realm of brute creation, Buckle's insistence on the static character of human morals need not disturb one's moral certitude. If in retrospect Darwinism seemed to Stephen to provide the answer to Buckle's inability to cope with human moral differentiation, at the moment of its emergence Darwinism seemed to many rather to make Buckle's insistence on the static character of human morals much more problematic. For men now alone in a timeless universe governed by naturalistic processes, an evolution of morals seemed doubly necessary: on the one hand, to explain how human virtues might arise from the instincts of the brute; on the other, to reassure that there was some meaning in the life-generating process after all. From this perspective, the temporally shallow cultural determinism implicit in Mill's ethology scarcely seemed adequate. One wanted a moral reassurance that had a more profound and more organic directionality in time.[74]

In this context, the fate of Mill's ethology seems to have been related to the advent of Darwinism. In the aftermath of the *Origin,* cultural variety came to be viewed in a Darwinian framework. This did not necessarily imply the notions of struggle and conflict connoted by the catchphrase "social Darwinism," although such tendencies surely existed. More importantly, the softer monogenetic form of pre-Darwinian racialism, which already tended to biologize human cultural differences in terms of change in time, took on a new meaning. It was no longer a matter of a few score generations modifying an essentially unchanging human type, but of changes accumulating over a vastly increased span of human life on earth, stretching back to Brixham Cave and beyond to apelike forms. In such a context, even an environmental view of "race" implied a much greater depth of cultural difference in time, a difference which time, acting now through selection as well as the inheritance of acquired characteristics, had given a profoundly organic aspect.

Thus to say Buckle was pre—evolutionary reflects more than the fact that he died before he was forced to come to terms with Darwinism. It reflects also the limitations of his conception of human time, which remained essentially that of the biblical chronology. And it reflects also the relative insignificance of "savage races" in his historical inquiry. It was not simply that the data of savagery did not weigh heavily in his argument, but rather that the differences between savages and civilized men carried, as it were, no evolutionary weight.[75] If today we find Buckle's views on this issue more congenial than Spencer's, they are nonetheless a measure of the distance that separated Buckle's thinking—which in this respect was still that of the eighteenth century—from the sociocultural evolutionism that was emerging at the time of his death.

Maine was of course pre-Darwinian in several of the same ways as Buckle. He, too, had defined his problem within the biblical time scale; and savages had little place in his argument, which was based on different methodological assumptions from those of sociocultural evolutionism. But if both men sought to explain the civilization that seemed so special to the West, Maine's was a very different view of human history from Buckle's. On the one hand, Maine explicitly intended to demonstrate "moral progress as a substantive reality."[76] On the other, his Germanic emphasis on the deeply rooted internal spiritual determinants of cultural forms—whether conceived as an immanent unfolding or the cumulative expression of cultural tradition—gave human mental and moral differences a much greater temporal weight. It was thus not merely the pull of polemical context that led Stephen to regard Maine's work as a social correlative to Darwin's. Although deriving more from the Germanic than the utilitarian current in Maine's thought, there was an underlying intellectual affinity that made his ideas more compatible with Darwinian evolution than were Buckle's.

Buckle chose the left horn of Stephen's utilitarian dilemma; Maine rested comfortably between—accepting significant human mental differences without feeling the need to treat racial types as "absolutely fixed." Spencer is worth considering in greater detail, since it was he who provided what Stephen felt to be a resolution of the problem—although from a present perspective it might seem that in doing so he seriously compromised the possibility of an anthropological cultural determinism. In 1855, while struggling with the synthesis of the empiricist and innatist traditions, Spencer seemed little troubled by the issue of human psychic unity, asserting without apparent qualm that "no one contends that there is any absolute distinction between . . . the faculties of the civilized man and those of the savage." Nevertheless, Spencer did insist on considerable variation in racial mental makeup: "We know that there are warlike, peaceful, nomadic, maritime, hunting, commercial races—races that are independent or slavish, active or slothful. . . ." Taking for granted their common origin, he reasoned from this mental diversity to the Lamarckian processes that must have created it: "there can be no question that these varieties of disposition, which have a more or less evident relation to habits of life, have been gradually induced and established in successive generations, and have become organic."[77]

As we have seen, the same principle of use-inheritance, combined with Spencer's version of the laws of association, underlay his scheme of "the growth of intelligence." On this basis Spencer went on to suggest that the human brain "represents an infinitude of experiences received during the evolution of life in general." These included the experiences of human progress in civilization, so that Europeans presumably had "from ten to thirty cubic inches more brain than the Papuan." Although he extended the principle of psychic unity to the animal world, Spencer fundamentally qualified it for mankind: while there was no reason to suppose "any specific difference between brute reason and human reason," it was nonetheless true that the difference between "the highest forms of brute rationality" and "the lower forms of human rationality" was less than that separating the Hottentot from Laplace. In such a context, Spencer later characterized the assumption that "human nature is everywhere the same" as an "error" his generation had been taught "in early life." For it must be substituted the "truth" that "the laws of thought are everywhere the same."[78] Spencer thus resolved Stephen's dilemma by giving the utilitarian view of human nature a depth in evolutionary time, in which the cultural differences separating savage and civilized man—become organic through the inheritance of acquired characteristics—could be arranged in hierarchical racial terms that provided what seemed an assured framework for the continuing belief in both intellectual and moral progress.

It is perhaps a moot point how widely Stephen's dilemma was consciously perceived as a problem confronting utilitarianism in the 1850s. But there is no doubt that the psychic unity of man was being threatened by the growth of more rigidly hereditarian racial assumption. And it is clear that the logic of sociocultural evolutionary argument required psychic unity as a premise upon which evolutionary sequences could be reconstructed. Sociocultural evolutionists might find that premise in other places—in a still untroubled utilitarian assumption, or as the conclusion of Prichardian ethnology. But insofar as the conception of human psychic unity was to have an evolutionary rationale, Spencer's evolutionary associationism was the most likely source in the post-Darwinian period. His solution to the problem drew heavily on commonly accepted ideas about savages, and on pervasive Lamarckian notions of biological process that were not distinctively Darwinian. But in the absence of an adequate treatment of human psychology by Darwin himself, Spencer's became the basic psychological orientation of Darwinians. That Darwin himself viewed it as an integral part of the Darwinian revolution is evident in the later editions of the *Origin,* where he modified his original suggestion that "psychology will be based on a new foundation" by noting that it had already been "well laid by Mr. Herbert Spencer."[79]

Interestingly enough, Mill—who read the *Principles of Psychology* three times, each time with greater appreciation—accepted Spencer as carrying on his tradition in British psychology. Along with Alexander Bain, Spencer was successfully "affiliating the conscious operations of the mind to the primary unconscious organic actions of the nerves, thus filling up the most serious lacuna and removing the chief difficulty in the association psychology." While Spencer's "doctrine of Heredity" was impetuously conceived, it would "very likely prove true." What Mill did not live to appreciate was that this shift to a more physiological psychology conceived in an evolutionary framework further forestalled the possibility that his "science of ethology" would be developed once he himself put the project aside.[80] Even if ethology had been successfully defined as an empirical rather than deductive study, it would have become entangled in the biosocial confusion engendered by the assumed heredity of acquired characteristics.

The implications of all this for scientific conceptions of the mental characteristics of non-European peoples were of course profound. In the eighteenth century, savages had still been generally assumed to share essentially the same psychic nature as Europeans. In the first half of the nineteenth, this essential unity was eroded by a developing hereditarian racialism. When the systematic study of non-European peoples and the systematic study of the development of civilization, which became largely separate undertakings during this period, were integrated after 1860, it was in the context of Spencer's evolutionary associationism. The result may be regarded as a compromise between eighteenth-century unitarian environmentalism and nineteenth-century pluralistic hereditarianism; but it also compromised any possibility of a purely cultural interpretation of human psychic differences. Although conceived as products of environmental influences in which cultural factors were included, these differences tended to be thought of as hereditary, and the cultural factors defining them were so hopelessly enmeshed in the framework of biological evolutionism that men like Leslie Stephen had difficulty conceptualizing them except in terms of "race."

FIVE

The Darwinian Revolution and the Evolution of Human Culture (1858–1871)

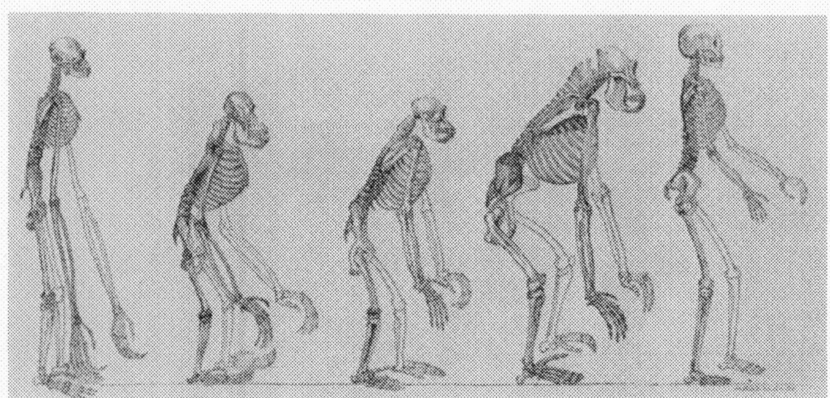

Gibbon, Orang, Chimpanzee, Gorilla, Man—1863

Thomas H. Huxley, *Evidence as to Man's Place in Nature* (London, 1863), frontispiece, where it is indicated that the drawings are from specimens in the Museum of the Royal College of Surgeons, and that the gibbon is represented at twice the scale of the others.

GIVEN the manifestly revolutionary impact of Darwin's work upon the Western intellectual tradition, it is not surprising that a variety of intellectual and ideological trends in the years after 1858 should have been interpreted as reflections of his influence. To social scientists looking backward for markers on the road to the present, and to general historians glancing to the side in search of intellectual influences, the *Origin of Species* has been a most convenient intellectual reference point.[1] The subsequently problematic relation of biological and social theory—especially in the early twentieth century and again in the recent debates on "sociobiology"—has encouraged this tendency, and there is no denying that the "interaction between biological and social theory" is an important historical problem. There is, however, a strong current of scholarship in the history of the social sciences that tends to reject the idea that sociocultural evolutionary thought developed in direct response to a Darwinan stimulus.[2] There is also evidence to suggest that the ring of historical contemporaneity emanating from the category "social Darwinism" is a bit problematic. Some have questioned whether the extreme laissez-faire notions often thought of as "social Darwinist" are really Darwinian, or whether they are not more appropriately associated with Herbert Spencer, or whether the flow of influence should not be reversed, and Darwin's scientific views seen as a reflection of the economic ideology and practice of Victorian society.[3]

It seems clear enough that Darwin's published work lent itself to "social Darwinist" interpretation, just as his personal opinions tended in the same direction. And one can certainly find English writers in the 1860s who might well have been called "social Darwinist," even if they were not. One thinks immediately of Francis Galton, and also of Walter Bagehot. However, Bagehot's "Thoughts on the Application of the Principles of 'Natural Selection' and 'Inheritance' to Political Society" were in fact more Lamarckian than Darwinian.[4] And the "eugenics" movement that grew from Galton's work—which some feel is the historical phenomenon most appropriately labeled "social Darwinist"—was, like the label itself, a later development. It was the product of a period when traditional liberalism, threatened by forces of democracy and collectivism at home, and by those of nationalism and militarism abroad, was no longer the optimistic creed it had once been. Rather than a positive application of the principles of natural selection to the interpretation of social phenomena, eugenics was an attempt to compensate for the failure of natural selection to operate under the social conditions of advanced civilization.[5] All of which suggests this is an area where the historian must be particularly sensitive to the problems involved in labeling and tracing intellectual influences.

We may distinguish, for instance, between what was explicit or directly implied in the *Origin* and the range of metaphysical, moral, or ideological notions deriving from other sources that were intermingled with Darwinism—thereby facilitating the intellectual acceptance of a theory whose implications were for many Victorians quite disorienting, or legitimating social phenomena whose moral basis required buttressing. From this point of view, the sociocultural evolutionary teleology of progress may better be thought of as "Darwinistic" rather than "Darwinian." Taking a more narrow textual view—and a cue from the historical philosopher R. G. Collingwood—we might look for the questions to which men's ideas were answers. On the one hand, questions raised in prior scientific (or extrascientific) contexts might be "Darwinized." On the other hand, Darwinism might raise new questions which had not been relevant in previous contexts. And the answers in both cases might be either Darwinian or Darwinistic.[6]

From this point of view, the impact of Darwinism on anthropological speculation becomes much more complex. For just as the anthropological questions to which Darwinism provided answers were not all Darwinian, neither were all the anthropological questions raised by Darwinism answerable in a strictly Darwinian framework. But in the context of the Darwinian debate, some of these questions were nonetheless compelling for all that, and men answered them as best they could. It is therefore necessary to pay close attention to the interplay of questions and answers in the developing Darwinian debate if we would understand its relation to the emergence of sociocultural evolutionism.[7]

Filling the Gap in the Fossil Record

For present purposes, the most important questions raised by Darwinism in the narrow sense were those suggested by Darwin's one cryptic reference to the problems of anthropogenesis: "Light will be thrown on the origin of man and his history." Implicated in that phrase was a whole range of issues having to do with the physical evolution of humankind, the evolution of human capacity for culture, the history of the varieties of the human species, and the history—or evolution—of human civilization. Bishop Wilberforce's celebrated query, at the Oxford meeting of the British Association in 1860, about Huxley's personal primate ancestry is evidence that contemporaries were quite aware of such issues from the very beginning of the Darwinian debate. Darwin's hypothesis was widely referred to as "the ape theory," and the centrality of the issue of natural as opposed to supernatural anthropogenesis is manifest in historical accounts of the Darwinian revolution.[8]

Some of the questions implicated in Darwin's threateningly tantalizing aside had in fact been long debated; others now forced their way into the center of scientific discourse for the first time. But in either case, they were now discussed in a new context, which included the revolution in human time following upon the discoveries at Brixham Cave. Although the latter was in a sense an independent development, it had largely merged with the more general Darwinian revolution by the time Lyell published *The Antiquity of Man* in 1863. Lyell could still argue human antiquity without committing himself to a Darwinian view of human development, but not without discussing the latter problem at length. And one could scarcely accept a Darwinian view of man save on the basis of a greatly lengthened human chronology; indeed, there were in fact pressures generated by Darwinism itself to make this chronology much longer than that indicated by Brixham Cave.[9]

The Darwinian revolution was a rapid one. As early as 1863, Charles Kingsley suggested to a friend that "Darwin is conquering everywhere and rushing in like a flood"; and it has been argued that a generally evolutionary viewpoint was widely accepted "among the educated classes" even before *The Descent of Man* was published in 1871. But resistance was strongest on the matter of anthropogenesis, and it took a while for certain critical issues to come to the forefront of debate. For the first several years, attention focused on the physical relations of man and ape—most notably, in the vitriolic debate between Richard Owen and Thomas Huxley over the uniqueness of the *hippocampus minor* as a feature of the human brain. The critical evidence for Huxley's insistence that it was not unique was offered at the British Association in 1862, and in the following January Huxley drew together the anatomical evidence on *Man's Place in Nature*—the first published statement to the general public applying the Darwinian hypothesis systematically to man.[10]

Huxley's case was strongest at a general level—in arguing the slow gradation of physical differences from the lowest animal up to man, and in demonstrating certain anatomical similarities between men and apes. But as Huxley was well aware, there were serious gaps in the argument. If the structural differences between man and gorilla were "not so great as those which separate the Gorilla from the lower apes," it was also true that "in the present creation, at any rate, no intermediate link bridges over the gap between *Homo* and *Troglodytes.*" Nor were past creations so helpful as they might have been. Huxley was forced to conclude that the fossil remains "hitherto discovered do not seem to me to take us appreciably nearer to that lower pithecoid form, by the modification of which [man] has, probably, become what he is."[11]

Faced with these gaps in the fossil record, Darwinians adopted various expedients. One was to force the newly established antiquity of man even farther back. If a really primeval man had not been found in Engis or Neanderthal—which, like Brixham Cave, were both postpliocene—then one might look to the pliocene or even the miocene. Huxley thus concluded his book by urging that "we must extend by long epochs the most liberal estimate that has yet been made of the antiquity of Man." Another expedient was to appeal to the results of pre-Darwinian physical anthropology—to use old answers to a new question—and to throw living savage races into the fossil gap. Thus Huxley argued that "the difference in the volume of the cranial cavity of different races of mankind is far greater, absolutely, than that between the lowest Man and the highest Ape."[12]

Similar expedient minglings of older and newer ideas can be found in the thinking of Alfred Russel Wallace. Provoked by Lyell's continuing refusal to commit himself to Darwinism, Wallace turned to the problem of human evolution in 1864. Attempting to solve an older anthropological problem in Darwinian terms, he tried to "harmonize the conflicting views of anthropologists" on the unity of man. All now agreed that man had been around for 100,000 years, but there was no reason not to assume 10,000,000. If so, the observed racial stability of the last 5,000 years meant nothing—provided one could find causes that at some point "would check any further physical change." Wallace found these in the basic mental and moral characteristics of man, which once evolved enabled him to adapt to environmental changes by inventing new tools, dividing labor, and working cooperatively with foresight for the future—thereby taking from nature "that power of changing the external form and structure which she exercises over all other animals."[13]

In this context, Wallace argued that mankind had indeed once been a single "homogeneous race"—but at a point so far in the evolutionary past that it lacked even the power of speech. Natural selection operating on this creature "scarcely raised above the brute" had produced the physical differences distinguishing present races, which were so deeply rooted that one might "fairly assert that there were many originally distinct races of men." Although selection had long since ceased to operate on their bodies, it had continued to have an effect on their minds, because increased mental ability would always be of adaptive value. Selection had raised even "the very lowest races" far above the brutes they still resembled physically; but it had raised the Germanic races of the temperate zones much further still, and in the end would lead to the "inevitable extinction" of "those lowly and mentally undeveloped populations" with whom Europeans were now coming into contact. Mankind would thus be once more racially homogeneous, with mental faculties so ennobled that all would live in perfect freedom and mutual sympathy in the utopia of Spencer's *Social Statics.*[14]

Although polygenists were not enthusiastic about Wallace's compromise, he had in principle resolved the old issue of human unity through the new mechanism of natural selection operating in a new expanse of human time. In doing so he also offered an explanation for the anomalous (from the Darwinian viewpoint) fact that the fossil men so far found were large-brained: it was simply that man "in his last, his intellectual phase," was "a very persistent and ancient type."[15] But in the process he had in fact accepted the polygenist view of human racial differences, and had also drawn upon some rather timeworn notions of the stages of human sociocultural development. And perhaps most importantly, he had shifted the focus of interest in the debate over anthropogenesis from the physical to the mental and social evolution of man.

Other influences were contributing to the same shift. Huxley's book had elicited a sharp response from the anti-Darwinian party, in the course of which the Duke of Argyll formulated the issue around which much of the subsequent debate on the evolution of man focused. Whatever structural analogies existed between apes and men, these had no "practical bearing at all on the question of the proper origin and nature of mankind," since "the real distinctive characteristics of man begin just where these resemblances of structural organisation leave off." Among these "distinctive" human features the Duke enumerated "the gift of articulate language,—the power of numbers,—the power of generalisation,—the power of conceiving the relation of man to his Creator,—the power of foreseeing an immortal destiny,—the power of knowing good from evil, on eternal principles of justice and truth." Though he spoke in terms of the origin of human faculties, the Duke in fact tended to assimilate the origin of faculties to their expression in human achievement. His challenge was thus in effect a more general statement of the issue Archbishop Richard Whately had posed shortly after the *Origin* appeared: "the impossibility of the *last* step of all—the advance of savage *man* into the civilized, without external help."[16]

In Whately and Argyll, the degenerationist assumptions of biblical anthropology surfaced to become, perhaps for the last time in the realm of serious scientific discourse, central issues of debate. Indeed, they may be regarded as providing a kind of program for sociocultural evolutionism in the later 1860s. Proponents of Darwinism were challenged to offer a naturalistic developmental explanation for those specifically human manifestations for which anti-Darwinians insisted on a divine origin. They were asked to show that language, science, religion, morality, and law—and by extension, other divinely ordained institutions such as human marriage—had grown up naturally as part of man's development from savagery to civilization.[17]

To approach such questions was no easy task. Despite Darwin's optimism, his work had done more to redefine the problem of man's early history than to solve it. From a present perspective one may perhaps speak of the "triumph of the Darwinian method." But in the 1860s, when his critics were attacking the adequacy of natural selection, Darwin defended his general evolutionary argument by relying more heavily on other explanatory mechanisms, some of which are, from a present perspective, less characteristically Darwinian—notably, the inheritance of acquired characteristics. In this context, it is hardly surprising that men whose interests involved them in the anthropogenetic problems posed by the Darwinian revolution approached these in terms that were not necessarily Darwinian. The major issue was to keep out the hand of God—to provide a purely naturalistic explanation of the development of human capacities and human civilization. To accomplish this, men resorted to intellectual expedients that were not in all respects consistent with what is now seen as the "Darwinian method."[18]

The point, then, is that although sociocultural evolutionism was not a simple transposition of biological thinking to the social realm, it was nonetheless deeply implicated in the Darwinian revolution. In view of the eighteenth- and nineteenth-century antecedents we have traced already, one might say that sociocultural evolutionism offered old answers to some new questions raised by Darwinism. The matter is not, however, quite as simple as that, since the traditions of debate about old questions and the polemical context in which the new were raised both affected the way in which the old answers to new questions were formulated.

Having examined the work of several writers whose intellectual orientations were fully formed before the Darwinian revolution began, let us turn to a slightly younger group whose intellectual development reflects its catalytic impact: John Lubbock, E. B. Tylor, and John McLennan. Although their backgrounds and early intellectual interests were quite diverse, there is evidence that each, in his own way, responded to the questions of anthropogenesis raised as the Darwinian revolution progressed. Furthermore, there is a unifying tendency in their responses: in each case, there is an intellectual discontinuity—a shift from traditional ethnological, comparative philological, or historical orientations toward a more systematically "developmental" point of view, in which the characteristic assumptions of sociocultural evolutionism become clearly manifest.

Tracing Up the Origin of Civilization

Insofar as one could be born and bred to Darwinism before 1858, John Lubbock was. Eldest son of a prominent London banker who was distinguished also as a mathematician and astronomer, young Lubbock was close to Darwin from the time he was still a young boy, when his family moved to an estate in Kent scarcely a mile from Darwin's Down House.

Lubbock's father was a somewhat forbidding patriarch, and the boy seems to have found a more nurturant relationship with Darwin, who guided his early interests in natural history, and apparently also contributed to his quiet loss of religious orthodoxy—though Lubbock remained a regular churchgoer save for "one short interval of insistent scepticism." With Darwin his friend and confidante, and his father treasurer of the Royal Society, Lubbock's entry into the world of science was an early and easy one. In 1855 he was congratulated by Lyell and Darwin for discovering the first fossil musk-ox in England; and that same year, at young Lubbock's request, Lyell proposed him for membership in the Geological Society. Two years later, barely twenty-three, Lubbock was elected to the Royal Society. He was one of the very small group who knew of Darwin's theory before 1858; and when Bishop Wilberforce tried to kill evolution with ridicule at Oxford, Lubbock responded with embryological evidence in Darwin's favor. When Huxley that same year asked him to join the editorial board of the *Natural History Review* so that "the young men with plastic minds" could control a journal of their own, Lubbock was quick to agree. All of which is to say that he was from the very beginning part of the Darwinian inner circle.[19]

From the time he was taken from Eton at fourteen to join the family banking business, Lubbock was also active in the world of trade, and he soon entered the world of Liberal politics as well. Forbidden by his father to stand for Parliament in 1863, defeated in 1865 in part because of his scientific views, and again in 1868 despite the support of John Stuart Mill, Lubbock was finally elected in 1870. His greatest parliamentary triumph was the creation of the bank holiday—the first legal holiday of a purely secular character, popularly called "St. Lubbock's Day." But he was also active in such causes as shortened hours of labor and the introduction of scientific education into endowed schools. Although Gladstone's Irish Home Rule Bill drove him from the Liberals in 1886, he remained a Cobdenite free trader to his death. Early in life he had told Darwin he hoped to achieve three goals: to be president of the Royal Society, Chancellor of the Exchequer, and Lord Mayor of London. Rejecting Darwin's advice that he could be any one if he gave up the other two, Lubbock lost them all. Even so, he was Vice-Chancellor of the University of London, first president of the Institute of Bankers, and second chairman of the London County Council. In 1899, his career in public life was rewarded with a peerage; he chose his title, Lord Avebury, from a prehistoric site whose megaliths he had studied, and which he subsequently purchased to save from demolition for new buildings.

In his later years, much of Lubbock's writing was of a distinctly popular character: works on the geology and scenery of England and Switzerland; books on economic and political questions; and collections of moral platitudes and quotations on how to achieve happiness. As an "expositor of science" and "moral mentor to the general public," he had a vogue "almost without parallel." From the beginning, his prevailing public tone was one of unswerving utilitarian optimism. Modern life had increased our pleasures and lessened our pains a thousandfold; utopia, far from being impossible, was "on the contrary the necessary consequence of natural laws." Lubbock was apparently troubled by periods of depression, in which he often turned to Darwin personally for support; and it seems likely that his sociocultural evolutionism also served a reassuring function. In a literature where the line between "scientific" anthropological views and personal cultural values was often blurred, Lubbock's pages are mustier than most. But if they seem especially dated today—and did even at the time of his death—he was nevertheless a serious contributor to the Darwinian debate, and his works were clearly a response to scientific issues raised there.[20]

After a tour of the Somme gravels in 1860, Lubbock quickly became a leading member of what its adherents spoke of as the "prehistoric movement." Although primarily an interpreter and synthesizer of the work of others, Lubbock visited all the important Continental sites, either alone or in the company of such leading prehistorians as John Evans, Henry Christy, or Joseph Prestwich; and he also maintained regular correspondence with the leading Continental prehistorians. His accounts of the major sites—several of them sent first to Darwin for comment—were published in the *Natural History Review,* and in 1865 were brought together with other material in a synthesis of all the evidence for human antiquity. Coiner of the distinction between "neolithic" and "palaeolithic" as further subdivisions of the Danish three-age system, Lubbock was second only to Lyell as an expositor of man's antiquity to Victorian intellectuals.[21]

The full title of his book in fact embodies the basic principle of "the comparative method" of sociocultural evolutionism: *Prehistoric Times, as Illustrated by Ancient Remains, and the Manners and Customs of Modern Savages.* For the most part, however, its general tenor is closer to the diffusionist ethnological tradition that interpreted cultural change in terms of the migration and contact of races. Thus Lubbock specifically rejected the notion that the European Bronze Age was an indigenous development, endorsing instead the Aryanist view that it was introduced by a "new and more civilised people of Indo-European race, coming from the East." Only at the very end of his book, in relation to "the simpler" weapons and implements, did Lubbock adopt the hypothesis of independent invention. Taken in the context of the book's overall structure, this suggests a good bit about the emergence of sociocultural evolutionism.[22]

Rather than moving forward in time from savagery to civilization,

Prehistoric Times moved backward from the present, starting from the Bronze Age, back through the Swiss lake-dwellings and the Danish kitchen middens, to the caves and the river-drift gravel beds. This structure reflects Lubbock's purpose: to establish the extreme antiquity of man, he led his readers farther and farther back into the past, until, suffused with a ''vague and overpowering sense of antiquity,'' they were prepared to take seriously his suggestion that man ''must have had representatives in miocene times.'' It was only then that he turned to modern savages, and he did so for a specific reason: the inability of either history or tradition to cast any light at all on a period so deep in time. Here the archeologist could only ''follow the methods which have been so successfully pursued in geology,'' and look elsewhere in the world for the living representatives of species extinct in Europe. The key to their comparability was provided by material culture: it was the analogy of their ''crude implements and weapons'' that made the Van Diemaner and South American ''to the antiquary what the opossum and the sloth are to the geologist.''[23]

What followed was a rather grim Cook's tour of savagery, sweeping eastward from the Hottentots in Africa through the Veddahs, the Australians, the Tongans, the American Indians, down to the Fuegians at the tip of South America. Lubbock belonged to what one might call the ''too offensive for description'' school of ethnography; his account of savage nations is a one-hundred page elaboration of that apocryphal nineteenth-century ethnographic account: ''manners, beastly; religion, none.'' The general tenor is conveyed by Lubbock's summary: ''the true savage is neither free nor noble; he is a slave to his own wants, his own passions; imperfectly protected from the weather, he suffers from the cold by night and the heat of sun by day; ignorant of agriculture, living by the chase, and improvident in success, hunger always stares him in the face, and often drives him to the dreadful alternative of cannibalism or death.''[24]

This starkly ignoble view of savagery is worthy of comment. Even more than other evolutionary writers, Lubbock carried his cultural values emblazoned on his scientific standard. His pioneering study of the behavior of *Ants, Bees, and Wasps* is at points quite amusingly anthropocentric, its comments on the ''character'' of different ant species reading quite like a Victorian traveler's judgment of the character of different native races. On the other hand, his insect study attests to his appreciation of the problems of the scientific observation of behavior, and the critical caution of his archeological studies proves him sensitive to the problems of using data collected by others. Furthermore, Lubbock thought of himself, and was regarded by others, as an opponent of ''that prejudice against inferior races now so current in England.''[25] If, then, he seems to have relaxed his critical standards when discussing human savagery, this may have reflected something more than his complacent acceptance of Victorian value assumptions.

In fact, Lubbock's view of savagery reflected the demands—and the structure—of his argument. His purpose at this point was to give a picture of what Stone Age men were like. In the absence of adequate archeological data, he turned to contemporary savagery, focusing on what from his viewpoint were its most primitive aspects. He did this by a kind of argument from opposites, emphasizing the absence of what Europeans took for granted, the presence of what they regarded as offensive. But when his argument required a more favorable view, Lubbock's picture of the savage changed somewhat. This change is not unrelated to the way in which the Darwinian controversy developed after 1865.

Momentarily revitalized in the Darwinian context, the degenerationist assumptions of biblical anthropology posed a serious methodological threat to those committed to an evolutionist view of human origins. By insisting that savages were "the degenerate descendants of far superior ancestors," rather than the contemporary remnants or equivalents of the primitive ancestors of civilized man, anti-Darwinians made it impossible to use savages to fill the place of the "missing link"—thus keeping wide the gap between ape and man. Lubbock attempted to answer the degenerationists in papers given to the British Association in 1867 and 1868. In the first he responded to Archbishop Whately's insistence on the impossibility of the "last step of all" by suggesting that "there are indications of progress even among savages," and that "among the most civilized nations there are traces of original barbarism." In the second he responded to the Duke of Argyll's contention that savages were "mere outcasts of the human race" driven by stronger races to the harsher environmental corners of the earth. Insisting that the world had been widely populated even when all mankind was still in a savage state, Lubbock suggested that the Eskimos did rather well for themselves in their difficult arctic environment. But it was not enough simply to find signs of progress among savages. What the degenerationists rejected was not savage progress per se, but the possibility of their "independent progress" without the help of civilized men or the intervention of the deity.[26]

Thus it was that when Lubbock published his *Origin of Civilisation* in 1870, its structure was clearly evolutionist, rather than diffusionist. Lubbock began by considering Maine's three methods of studying the "rudiments of the social state"—contemporary observation of "less advanced" civilizations, historical records, and ancient law—and suggested that Maine might have avoided errors had he relied more on "the laws and customs of modern savages." Systematic comparison of travelers' accounts would have revealed a "remarkable similarity between different races''—a similarity ''so striking'' that ''different races in similar stages of development often present more features of resemblance to one another than the same race does to itself, in different stages of its history.'' In this context, the repeated movement of Lubbock's *Origin* was *from* the past *to* the present, as he ''traced up'' each of the major social institutions or cultural forms—art, marriage, kinship, religion, morality, language, and law—from its first manifestations in savagery toward its fullest flower in modern Europe. Thus marriage was ''traced up'' from communal marriage to individual marriage by capture to exogamy; religious ideas, from atheism to fetichism to totemism to shamanism to idolatry and finally to monotheism. The stages were not always clear-cut, but the descriptive process was essentially the same in every case.[27]

It is worth considering the implications of the phrase ''tracing up.'' The diffusionist traces back, not up—back in time through one historical connection after another. But as Lubbock suggested at several points, the origin of civilization was too deep in the void of time for history to help. One could only approach the problem indirectly, by comparison. As Lubbock argued in a later edition, ''the lower races of man'' today were in a social state ''ruder and more archaic than any which history records as having ever existed among the more advanced races.'' By comparing savage tribes belonging to different portions of the human race, and by eliminating from the picture customs peculiar to certain groups, one could get back to a core that was common to all men in the primitive state. And if this did not reach far enough, Lubbock seems clearly to have felt that one might imagine the absence or the opposite of some European custom or belief, and reason forward from there. For in the absence of documentary evidence, that was what one must do: reason forward, by comparison and conjecture, tracing or sketching how civilization must or might have developed from these beginnings, not in historical detail, but as a sequence of stages or phases. This reconstructive procedure required a rather different savage from the brutish creature of *Prehistoric Times*—one who, however inferior, however disgusting, however stupid, was essentially rational. Just as an ignoble savage seemed necessary to paint a convincing picture of the primitive state, a rationalistic savage seemed necessary to get man out of that state—and to allow us to reconstruct the process. As Lubbock suggested, savages ''do not act without reason, any more than we do, though their reasons may often be bad ones and seem to us singularly absurd.''[28] It was this basic human rationality that enabled us to recreate the intelligible cultural practice behind the absurd survival. But it not only made possible the reconstruction of sociocultural evolution, it was also, by a kind of analogical extension, its essential mechanism. If one could not establish historically how man progressed from one stage to another, one could at least imagine how a rational creature, being on one level, might think himself to the next—how he might independently invent whatever was next in the sequence one had recreated by one's own rational processes of comparison and conjecture.

So it was that the *Origin of Civilisation*, in contrast to *Prehistoric Times*, placed greater emphasis on processes we associate with sociocultural evolutionism: "independent invention," the "psychic unity" of mankind, and the "parallelism" of development (although without using these terms). Thus it was that tree worship was practiced among such widely separated geographical groups that one must conclude it was "simply one of many illustrations that the human mind, in its upward progress, everywhere passes through the same or similar phases." Lubbock's whole purpose, as he later suggested, was to show that "the development of higher and better ideas as to Marriage, Relationships, Law, Religion, etc. has followed in its earlier stages a very similar course even in the most distinct races of man," and that they had each "independently raised themselves" from a similar condition of "utter barbarism."[29]

In short, between 1865 and 1870 Lubbock shifted his orientation considerably in the context of the developing Darwinian debate. In 1865, he was still concerned with establishing the antiquity of man, not yet with recreating his evolution; and his comments on cultural development were still largely from a diffusionary ethnological point of view. By 1870, however, the characteristic emphases of the sociocultural evolutionary viewpoint had all emerged. Not perhaps so systematically as this argument has suggested—since Lubbock was not a very systematic ethnological thinker. The *Origin* was almost as much an ethnographic hodgepodge as the last portion of *Prehistoric Times*. But insofar as it implied a systematic argument, it was that we associate with sociocultural evolutionism; and this was to become even more strikingly manifest in later editions.[30]

The Natural Development of Spiritual Culture

Direct ties to Darwinism are not so immediately evident in the case of Edward Burnett Tylor. In some respects, he seems better viewed as a survival of the Enlightenment, a latter-day *philosophe* attacking theology, superstition, and "all the practices of civilized life for which common sense can find no justification." But if one follows the details of Tylor's intellectual development, both his links to the contemporary anthropological milieu and the impact of the Darwinian revolution are clear enough.[31]

Born in the year of the first Reform Bill (1832), Tylor was the fifth child of Quaker parents—although like many other young Friends in this period he seems early to have given up the distinctive Quaker dress. Educated for a time in a Quaker school in Tottenham, he entered the family brass firm in London at the age of sixteen. However, his business career was cut short in 1852 after the death of both his parents, when he developed symptoms of consumption. Over the next decade, during which he traveled widely, his intellectual development was influenced primarily by two men: his elder brother Alfred, and the Quaker ethnologist-archeologist Henry Christy. Manager of the family firm, juror at the Crystal Palace, and geologist of minor note, Alfred was interested also in archeology, the history of technology, political economy, and industrial education; his staunchly uniformitarian and anti-idealist epistemological views were clearly manifest in his younger brother's anthropology. Tylor met Christy in 1856 on a tram in Havana, during a year he spent in North America; the two went on to Mexico together, where they traveled for four months on horseback. For the ten years until Christy's death, Tylor followed "all the details of his ethnological researches," as his older friend moved from collecting antiquarian and ethnological specimens to an active role in the prehistoric movement.[32]

Although the account of his Mexican excursion (his first published work) did not appear until 1861, Tylor began keeping a series of notebooks in 1858 which, read in the context of *Anahuac,* give glimpses of his intellectual development. Before meeting Christy, Tylor had traveled in the Mississippi Valley, apparently with the thought of settling and setting himself up in business; his letters to his brother were full of observations on economic, political, and philanthropic matters. Similar concerns are reflected in *Anahuac,* within the framework of a rather conventional travel account. Preoccupied with the inhumane, illiberal, and un-English elements of Mexican life—which he tended to interpret in terms of the ill-effects of racial mixing—Tylor ended by predicting that the country would become a United States protectorate, as "every intelligent Mexican" must hope. Once back in England, however, Tylor began to devote himself to systematic reading on Mexico, as well as along certain comparative lines. These interests, too, are reflected in *Anahuac*—particularly in several scholarly appendices, including a note on Dasent's recent essay on comparative mythology as a way of supplementing "ethnological and philological research" into the "relations of the early races of Man."[33]

Led thus to the tradition of Prichardian ethnology, Tylor seems for a while to have been particularly preoccupied with linguistics. In addition to readings in "general philology," he had by the winter of 1860 learned the elements of Sanskrit and "got some knowledge" of Russian, Greenlandish, and Fijian. For the next two years, his lists of books to be read had a heavily Germanic cast, with emphasis on comparative philology and comparative mythology. In the winter of 1861, he noted that Max Müller was "read aloud"—presumably with his wife Anna Fox, whom he married in 1858, and who throughout their childless marriage shared his anthropological interests. But there were also more general ethnological works, including "Dr. Prichard," as well as notes relating more directly to the early history of man: sketches of a geological site, notes and sketches of the artifacts in Swiss museums, and notes on conversations with Christy. By late 1862, it is clear that these latter concerns—the early history of man in the context of the archeological revolution, rather than comparative philology, comparative mythology, or diffusionist ethnology—were to be predominant. Immediately following a book list for autumn 1862 is one labeled "Primeval Man"; thenceforth, Tylor began another series of indexed notebooks, which he continued in numbered sequence throughout the rest of his career.[34]

This would suggest that once Tylor arrived at his central problem, the continuity of his intellectual life was unbroken. But the matter is not quite so simple. Beginning his anthropological career within the linguistic ethnological tradition, Tylor never abandoned it entirely; and his first major anthropological work is in effect a transition between the two projects implicit in its title: *Researches into the Early History of Mankind and the Development of Civilization.* As the similarity of title in fact suggests, Tylor's *Researches* may be seen as an attempt to carry on Prichard's *Researches* in a new temporal context. Tylor sought to "establish the ethnological argument from beliefs and customs"—to apply all of Latham's unusable data to a quite traditional ethnological purpose. But he was also very much influenced by Buckle's attempt to look "through the details of history to the great laws of Human Development which lie behind." Coming, however, from Prichardian ethnology, Tylor felt that it was "not enough to have in view the more advanced races"; one must draw also on ethnological data. From this perspective, his book was an attempt to qualify Buckle's "rash generalizations" by a more extended history which, avoiding "too hasty an appeal to first principles," would draw on such "indirect evidence" as "Antiquities, Language, and Mythology." Tylor's *Researches* were thus in a sense a methodological exercise—an attempt to see how far a study of cultural similarities might carry one toward reconstructing the actual early history of mankind.[35]

Granting that "when a general law can be inferred from a group of facts, the use of detailed history is very much superseded," Tylor insisted nevertheless that reasoning from the general laws of the human mind was only possible with facts that "have not, so to speak, travelled far from their causes." The data of independent invention had "no historical value whatever"; the only similarity of culture one could use for purposes of historical reconstruction was one resulting either from "blood relationship" or "intercourse, direct or indirect, between the races among whom it is found.'' In this context, all of his essays were ''various cases of a single problem'': distinguishing ''things which are merely similar'' from those which, ''having at some spot of the earth their common source and center of diffusion, are really and historically united.'' It was the great virtue of comparative mythology, upon which Tylor drew heavily, that each year it furnished new clues ''by which common descent or intercourse is to be traced.'' Indeed, ''the mass of analogies in Art and Knowledge, Mythology and Custom, confused and indistinct as they at present are, may already be taken to indicate that the civilizations of many races, whose history even the evidence of Language has not succeeded in bringing into connexion, have really grown up under one another's influences, or derived common material from a common source.''[36]

Tylor was still very much concerned with the traditional ethnological problem of human unity—an issue then the subject of considerable debate in the Anthropological Society of London, which he briefly served as foreign secretary until the ''pugnacious'' racism of its president offended his humanitarian Quaker principles. When he drew the strands of his *Researches* together by relating them to ''some widely circulated Ethnological theories,'' the first (although not so labelled) was polygenism: ''the facts collected seem to favour the view that the wide differences in the civilization and mental state of the various races of mankind are rather differences of development than of origin, rather of degree than of kind.''[37]

Up to a point, then, Tylor's *Researches* may be regarded as an attempt to solve the old ethnological problem in a new temporal context, using evidence derived from the history of ''the complex whole which we call Civilization.'' But if we may interpret a certain portion of the argument of *Researches* in Prichardian ethnological terms, the thrust of the book was toward a developmental viewpoint. Five early chapters treated the development of language, starting with gesture language—the study of which had brought Tylor into direct contact with the Enlightenment interest in ''Wild Men and Beast Children''—proceeding then to the relation of gesture and word language, to picture writing, and to word writing. All of this led to a discussion of the relation of images and names, in which Tylor discussed the primitive inability to separate ''the external object from the mere thought or idea of it in the mind'' along lines foreshadowing his later theory of animism. The central chapter was a cautious weighing of the evidence for ''Growth and Decline of Culture,'' in which Tylor concluded that decline was rather a phenomenon of ''the history of particular tribes, than the history of Culture as a whole''; three further chapters dealt with the development of technology. Substantively, the bulk of the book thus focused on developmental rather than diffusionist topics.[38]

Furthermore, Tylor's five general conclusions, taken together, had a manifestly developmental import. The first two insisted on the psychic unity of mankind and the progressive rather than degenerative character of human history. The next, restating the alternative of independent invention and diffusion, cast doubt on the possibility that diffusionary explanations would *ever* succeed in establishing that "the civilization of the whole world has its origin in one parent stock"—which was in effect to say that, even when approached from the perspective of a new type of data, the traditional ethnological problem might prove insoluble. The fourth conclusion argued that all attempts to "trace back the early history of civilization" reached an "ultimate limit" in a state "somewhat resembling" that of contemporary "savage tribes," and that this actually observed state provided a basis more "convenient to reason upon than a purely theoretical one." The last—which reflects Max Müller's notion of a "mythopoeic age" recast in terms of Tylor's empiricist epistemology—suggested that many facts in "the history of custom and superstition" had "their common root in a mental condition underlying anything to be met with now," in which "objective and subjective relations" were systematically fused. Having reached this point, the next task was clearly to trace human mental evolution forward from this mythopoeic age.[39]

As Alfred Wallace pointed out, this task "required researches of a very different nature" from those of traditional ethnology. Nevertheless, Tylor's *Researches* may be read as providing the logical basis for such an attempt, and there are several passages that suggest he already had in mind pursuing it. In the end *Researches* must be regarded as breaking from the ethnological tradition rather than exemplifying it. In the opening pages, Tylor noted that "accounts of the culture of lower races" were "mostly unclassified."[40] The rest of the book may be regarded as an attempt, on the basis of methodological distinctions Prichard had not elaborated, to sort out the accumulated ethnographic data of Prichard's five volumes into two piles: those that fitted an ethnological model and those that fitted an evolutionary one. When six years later Tylor published *Primitive Culture*, there was no doubt that it exemplified the latter.

In the meantime, the problem of "the last step of all" continued to be lively debated. Argyll attacked Lubbock in a series of articles in 1868, reprinted the next year as *Primeval Man*. That same year an article summarizing the status of the controversy appeared in the *Contemporary Review*. Restating the issue of degenerationism, it insisted in effect that the problem could not be met by diffusionist arguments, since the question was whether savages could rise without any outside assistance. Furthermore, the real issue was not "the origin of industrial arts," but "the origin of moral culture." "Spiritual progress" was a "very different thing from material"; its laws lay "beyond the jurisdiction of science" and were in fact "traceable to a direct divine communion as their source."[41]

Although such issues were clearly linked to the degenerationist tradition of biblical anthropology, they resonate of other currents as well: the Liberal Anglicans, Whewell, and the Germanic tendency generally. The latter point is worth emphasizing, since Tylor's debt to German thought has recently been strongly insisted upon, and there is no doubt that he became familiar with a broad range of German scholarship during his Prichardian phase. But writing *Primitive Culture* in response to the demands of a debate he spoke of as developing "month by month," Tylor returned to his empiricist roots. The influences associated with Prichardian ethnology receded into the background, to be replaced by those of the British and French positivist tradition. Tylor's purpose now was not simply to refute degenerationism, but more generally to rebut the argument that man's spiritual life was not governed by the same natural laws of progress as his material existence: "The history of mankind is part and parcel of the history of nature," and "our thoughts, wills, and actions accord with laws as definite as those which govern the motion of the waves, the combination of acids and bases, and the growth of plants and animals." It was not accidental to Tylor's purpose that over half of the book was devoted to the evolution of religious beliefs, where more than anywhere else one might have expected a development by "direct divine communion."[42]

In this context, the historical and diffusionary assumptions of the ethnological tradition would no longer suffice. True, diffusion continued to play a subsidiary role in sociocultural evolutionary thought, spreading and consolidating the general upward progress. But insofar as the issue was *unassisted* savage progress, diffusion might actually be seen as damaging to the developmental case. Perhaps for this reason, Tylor was no longer concerned in *Primitive Culture* with determining whether specific similarities of culture were the result of diffusion. The problem was not now the history of "tribes or nations," but rather the "condition of knowledge, religion, art, custom and the like among them." The way to solve it was to classify "the phenomena of Culture" and to arrange them "stage by stage, in a probable order of evolution." In making such comparisons, "little respect" need be had "for date in history or for place on the map," or for "the question of race." It was "no more reasonable to suppose the laws of mind differently constituted in Australia and in England, in the time of the cave-dwellers and in the time of the builders of sheet-iron houses, than to suppose that the laws of chemical combination were of one sort in the time of the coal-measures, and are of another now." All the world was one country, and the similarity and consistency of human cultural phenomena could be attributed to "general likeness in human nature on the one hand, and to general likeness in the circumstances of life on the other."[43]

In the case of the mechanical arts, the notion of development was so much "at home in our minds" that we might "reconstruct lost history without scruple, trusting to general knowledge of the principles of human thought and action as a guide in putting the facts in their proper order." When it came to the rest of culture, the first problem was to get a "means of measurement" by which "to reckon progress and retrogression." Fortunately, a "rough scale of civilization" was readily manifest to any Englishman in the age of equipoise. Without a hint of irony at its easy ethnocentrism, Tylor suggested that "the educated world of Europe and America practically settles a standard by simply placing its own nations at one end of the social series and savage tribes at the other, arranging the rest of mankind between these limits according as they correspond more closely to savage or to cultured life." Thus "few would dispute" that the Australian, Tahitian, Aztec, Chinese, and Italian "races" stood in precisely that ascending "order of culture"—although its implied but missing apex might give pause to those south of the Alps. Defining civilization as "the general improvement of mankind by higher organisation of the individual and of society, to the end of promoting at once man's goodness, power, and happiness," Tylor had no hesitation in measuring "power" as embodied in "material and intellectual culture." And if he granted that progress was "harder to reckon" in regard to "goodness" and "happiness," he still felt that "the general tenour of the evidence" showed that "on the whole the civilized man is not only wiser and more capable than the savage, but also better and happier, and that the barbarian stands between."[44]

With the general order established, Tylor applied the comparative method to reconstruct the outlines of development in the major areas of spiritual culture. But as an added guide and safeguard, he employed the "doctrine of survivals." Arguing that "general laws of culture" could be elicited even from "antiquarian relics," Tylor insisted that there was nothing arbitrary or meaningless in culture. Things that seemed so to civilized man had a practical intention "when and where they first arose," but were "now fallen into absurdity from having been carried on into a new state of society, where their original sense has been discarded." The doctrine of survivals was thus the obverse of the idea of independent invention—a principle of intellectual conservatism rather than creativity. Expressed in the idea of independent invention, psychic unity enabled one to reason up the scale of civilization; expressed in the doctrine of survivals, it enabled one to reason back down—"to declare that the civilization of the people they are observed among must have been derived from an earlier state, in which the proper home and meaning of these things are to be found."[45]

Tylor was not the only scholar in this period to conclude that surviving forms or relics of the past could help to reconstruct the course of man's development. It was an obvious inference from geology, archeology, linguistics, law—or, as in Tylor's case, from folklore. But in *Primitive Culture* he made the doctrine his own, and offered back to folklore a new intellectual synthesis that gave unity to that study till the end of the century. For Tylor, the doctrine of survivals opened up all of European folklore as data to support an evolutionary argument, and portions of *Primitive Culture* reflect fairly directly the categories of material collected in Brand's *Antiquities*. The European peasantry now served as a crucial link between modern civilized and primitive savage man. In good uniformitarian fashion, survivals united the causal processes of the present with those of the past. Those who accepted Tylor's methodological argument in praise of folly had only to look about themselves for evidence that "the savage state in some measure represents an early condition of mankind, out of which the higher culture has gradually been developed or evolved, by processes still in regular operation as of old."[46]

In elaborating this strongly positivistic viewpoint, Tylor was brought at a number of points directly (or by implication) into conflict with Max Müller, whose ideas he had responded to quite sympathetically during his more Germanic phase. He now discussed the origin of language explicitly in terms of the interjectional and imitative theories Müller had so ridiculed. More generally, his ties to the British empirical tradition were strongly reasserted. In treating the origin of mathematics, he sided with Mill against Whewell, offering ethnographic data to support the view that "the fundamental truths of that science all rest on the evidence of sense." Similarly, when it came to mythology, he emphasized the role of sense experience; Müller's "disease of language" was simply a "secondary formation" affecting myths which primitive men, reasoning by analogy, had invented to account for natural phenomena.[47]

In every area of culture, the point was that development had proceeded "by the exercise of purely human faculties in purely human ways," as part of a process Tylor himself frequently spoke of as "mental evolution." Although he later made a point of emphasizing that his argument had been developed independently of both Darwin and Spencer, its genesis in the Darwinian debate is confirmed by the striking parallel between his major topics and the distinctive human features the Duke of Argyll had enumerated eight years before. That parallel did not escape the attention of prominent Darwinians: after having *Primitive*

Culture read aloud to him by his wife, and finding it "most profound," Darwin himself wrote to Tylor that "the Duke of Argyll ought never to hold up his head again."[48]

The "Comparative Method" and the Antiquity of Man

In contrast to Lubbock and Tylor, whose links to sciences implicated in the Darwinian revolution are easily established, John Ferguson McLennan had stronger ties to the utilitarian tradition in social theory. However, he also felt the impact of the developing Darwinian debate, and the changes in his thinking roughly parallel those we have already noted.

The eldest son of an insurance agent in Inverness, Scotland, McLennan later recalled growing up surrounded by people who lived one family to a room in houses with rough clay floors and raggedly thatched roofs, whose lives were filled with the violence and cruelty of "untutored savages." McLennan, however, managed to escape from all this to take a first degree at Aberdeen; and in 1849, at the rather tardy age of twenty-two, he went to Cambridge—apparently because his parents feared the Romanizing tendencies at Oxford. Although he impressed all who knew him at Trinity with his brilliance, and won a wrangler's place in the math tripos, McLennan did not take a degree—apparently because he was even then plagued by ill-health. He spent several years in London, where he was part of the pre-Raphaelite circle and wrote unsigned articles for a liberal periodical (Lewes' *Leader*). He must also have studied law at the Inns of Court (where he would have heard Maine lecture), since he was admitted to the Scottish bar in 1857.[49]

For the next thirteen years, McLennan practiced law in Edinburgh, where he was active in scientific and literary life, and in attempts to reform the Scottish legal system. After the death of his first wife (daughter of the utilitarian economist McCulloch) McLennan returned to London in 1870, where he obtained the post of parliamentary draftsman for Scotland. With the fall of Gladstone's government in 1874, he resigned, and spent the rest of his life ministering to his tubercular condition. Tended by his second wife and by his brother, he spent winters in San Remo and Algiers, where he caught the malaria from which he died in 1881. According to Tylor's obituary, his career had suffered because he refused to play "the legal game according to the accepted rules"; and though he often hoped for a university position, McLennan was "too erratic to run along the academic groove." Even as an institutional outsider, however, his views had considerable impact.[50]

McLennan's first contribution to social theory was the article on "Law" in the eighth edition of the *Encyclopaedia Britannica*—testimony either to his brilliance as a law student or to his Scottish connections. A compendium of the social theoretical possibilities available to him in 1857, it contained an underpinning of Scottish developmentalism in the discussion of "the origin of civil society," a smattering of Savigny and a touch of Whewell on the relations of law, morality, and national character, and by implication a good bit of Maine, including the assumption that society commenced in the patriarchal family. But the essential framework was utilitarian, recast in terms of positive sociology as enunciated in Mill's "Logic of the Moral Sciences"—whose position on several disputed issues McLennan chose over that of Comte. Apparently untroubled by any crisis in the utilitarian tradition, McLennan argued that "critical morality in the relative form, with the greatest happiness of the whole society for its standard of right" must still be the "guide of law." If in Turkey "purity" was "consistent with polygamy," McLennan still believed that legislative action could be grounded in "the sciences of human nature and society" in the form of Mill's "political ethology." If the laws of different societies must differ as their social states differ, the underlying principles of lawmaking, resting on "the general laws of human nature," were "everywhere the same." As applied in Britain, these laws brought McLennan into conflict with Herbert Spencer, whose views on "Over-Legislation" were a focus of his concern for the codification and reform of English law.[51]

A similar reformist spirit pervades an article McLennan published in 1861 on the English and Scottish laws of marriage—an issue regarding which he had been publicly active. There was then a lively debate centering on problems of bigamy and inheritance—with English peers fearful lest dukedoms be lost to bastard issue through the informality of Scottish marriage. McLennan was an ardent defender of Scottish common law marriage, arguing that laws enacted the preceding century in England to enforce publicity and formal ceremony as a condition of marriage had gradually been reduced to a mere "hedge of forms." Easily breached by the unscrupulous, they were still, while they "survive," of sufficient force "to convert those who have honestly misinterpreted them into paramours merely." As the reference to surviving forms suggests, the article foreshadowed many of the concerns of McLennan's anthropology—but not, however, its specific argument: far from seeing marriage in evolutionary terms, he appealed specifically to its "Divine Founder."[52]

Apparently while studying Roman law for the *Britannica* article, McLennan had become interested in "the early history of civil society." Like Tylor, he turned first to Prichardian ethnology and comparative philology. In May of 1863, he reviewed several accounts of "The Hill Tribes in India" in conjunction with Prichard's *Researches,* Latham's *Descriptive Ethnology,* and Müller's *Lectures* on language. McLennan felt that these tribes helped to illustrate "the divisions, the movements, and the progress of mankind"—which, glossed as classification, diffusion, and development, represent the three major viewpoints involved in the transition then in process in mid-Victorian ethnology. Similarly, his primary concern may be regarded as a problem generated by tensions within the traditional ethnological paradigm: how, in a geographic area where there were at most two races, considered from a physical standpoint, there could be such a variety of languages and customs. Although he found a partial explanation in the sequence of population movements, there was a residue of unexplained cultural differences, which McLennan treated in terms of the "perfect" analogy "between law and language." Just as dialects varied more or less accidentally in small isolated groups, so would customs, "the rudimentary forms of law"—especially in view of the general "fluidity" of primitive institutions. Because the same end could be achieved by various means, a fixed rule emerged only by trial and error, holding "only so long as there is sameness of circumstance." Reflecting Müller's ideas on dialect variation, this view of social process is logically quite Darwinian. But while there were by now hints of an evolutionary view of marriage, it is clearly *not* the one McLennan was to advance eighteen months later in *Primitive Marriage:* matriliny, polyandry, and marriage-by-capture were still for him simply abnormal or exceptional social forms, whose origin would be "hard to explain."[53]

McLennan's own retrospective awareness of the development of his thought was evident in 1867: after commending this essay to John Lubbock, he wrote again urging Lubbock not to read it, because his own rereading had "shocked" him to discover how poor it was.[54] That McLennan should have been caught up by the development of his thought is not surprising. Between "Hill Tribes" and the preface to *Primitive Marriage* in January, 1865, there had been a change in his problem, its context, his method, and in the substance of his argument.

Primitive Marriage began with a version of the doctrine of survivals: symbolic forms in the present represent corresponding realities in the past; where we now find the symbolic forms, we may infer that the realities previously existed. Finding a symbolic representation of marriage-by-capture in the rites of peoples all over the world, McLennan concluded that at some past time "it must have been *the system* of certain tribes to capture women for . . . wives." Both the actual practice and the ceremonial representation of marriage by capture were correlated with "a rule which prohibited marriage within the same tribe"—for which McLennan invented the term "exogamy." Reasoning backwards, he explained the origin of exogamy in terms of the practice of female infanticide, which had adaptive value in the state of perpetual hostility characteristic of primitive men. Killing off many of their own female children, who were "a source of weakness" in warfare and the quest for food, primitive tribes were forced "to prey upon one another for wives." McLennan went on to characterize primitive sexual relations as at first promiscuous, and then (of necessity) polyandrous, with kinship recognized only through the female, since paternity would be impossible to determine. Having reconstructed the most primitive form of marriage, McLennan reversed the direction of his reasoning and suggested a sequence of stages by which female kinship might develop into male kinship, exogamous groups become endogamous, and the undifferentiated tribe evolve into the gens and then the family.[55]

From this summary, it should be clear that between mid-1863 and the beginning of 1865 McLennan's problem had changed dramatically. Rather than seeking to explain the variety of customs in a particular area, he sought now to explain the origin of the single custom most critical to human social order. And in contrast to Maine, who had appealed to Scripture as a model for the origin of society, and who accepted a view of human history that opened "with perfect marriage, conjugal fidelity, and the certainty of male parentage," McLennan sought to explain its origin in naturalistic developmental terms.[56]

Although he dealt with the matter only in an aside, the context in which McLennan's central problem was posed was clearly that of the Darwinian revolution—specifically that of prehistoric archeology, with its greatly lengthened span of human existence. In contrast to Maine, McLennan now explicitly rejected help from comparative philology. Its "so-called revelation" was "void of instruction," now that the institutions of the Aryans were revealed to be "post-pliocene, separated by a long interval from the foundations of civil society, and throwing back upon them no light."[57]

To approach his evolutionary problem in an indefinite prehistoric time span, McLennan offered "one of the clearest, most elaborate, and least apologetic" expositions of the comparative method of sociocultural evolutionism. Nor was it a matter of extending the method of Maine. Although what was to be McLennan's method was one of the three Maine had discussed in *Ancient Law,* Maine had rejected it for one explicitly modeled on comparative philology. Like comparative philologists, Maine compared phenomena that were presumed to be genetically related, relying heavily on surviving historical documents, and trying to establish verifiable historical sequences of cause and effect; his use of contemporary ethnographic sources was almost always constrained within these limits. By contrast, McLennan's comparative method drew on phenomena spread throughout the world; its very conception was designed to circumvent the total lack of documentary historical data; and it was intended to recreate generalized stages rather than specific historical sequences. McLennan's laws of development were based on the assumption that once a given effect could in principle be explained in terms of some hypothesized cause, and a certain amount of data could be collected from different groups to suggest the widespread existence of the assumed causal sequence, then all other instances of the effect could, by an inversion of reasoning, be explained in terms of the hypothesized cause. In short, once McLennan had abandoned the confined geographical area of the hills of Munipore for the sweeping panorama of human antiquity, his comparisons were constrained only by the doctrine of survivals, which assumed that a practical reality always necessarily preceded its symbolic formal manifestation.[58]

Similarly, the substance of McLennan's argument involved a radical departure both from Maine's and from his own earlier position. Although a thesis in some respects similar had (unknown to him) been independently advanced by the Swiss jurist, Johann Bachofen, in 1861, McLennan's was quite rightly thought of as a revolutionary innovation. In contrast to the traditional European conception of monogamous marriage that Maine still took as his starting point, McLennan postulated an initial condition in which marriage did not exist, but the sexes cohabited promiscuously. Furthermore, he saw Victorian monogamy as having evolved from a prior state that patriarchal Victorians would surely have regarded as antithetic—polyandry. And in sharp contrast to his earlier argument from the fluidity of primitive society, McLennan now emphasized "universal tendencies," and regular "stages of development" from "lower to higher." Accidental variation was all very well to explain local varieties of custom in the Indian hills, but by 1865, the change in his problem and context impelled him to seek explanations that left less room for accident.[59]

In short, the Darwinian revolution posed the problem of the history of human marriage very differently from the way it had been posed for Maine. For those who sought to treat the emergence of human culture in a Darwinian context, it was necessary to deal with precisely those questions of "absolute origin" Maine felt so uncomfortable with, and to deal with them in a purely naturalistic way. In this context, historical accident seemed a weak barrier to the intervention of divine providence. What was needed was an explanation in terms of regular, lawful process. As McLennan, quoting Dugald Stewart, suggested in the last line of his book, regular stages of development were the alternative "to that indolent philosophy which refers to a miracle whatever appearance both in the natural and moral worlds it is unable to explain."[60]

It seems likely that McLennan's dramatic reorientation was precipitated by what he later called Lyell's "yielding" in 1863, "after long resistance," to the extreme antiquity of man. More brilliant than Tylor or Lubbock, and more given to intellectual enthusiasm, it was McLennan who first applied the new developmentalism systematically. In less than two years, at a time when Lubbock was still documenting the antiquity of man and Tylor debating the relative merits of the historical and comparative methods, McLennan put together what was substantially the full sociocultural evolutionary argument. He even attempted to create a cooperative intellectual venture to pursue the common inquiry. In 1867, he wrote to Lubbock saying he had been working on a summary view of human progress that might best be "the work of several persons." Between Lubbock and Huxley in the south, and himself and the Sanskritist S.T. Aufrecht in Edinburgh, a "tentative scheme" might be agreed upon as a summary of results so far and a guide to future inquiry. He himself was at work on a large chart which would show "all the stages of progress in Arts and Sciences etc. that have been found concurring with each phase of Social Organisation." In a subsequent letter he went on to suggest the need for a "sharper" and more sociological definition of "civilisation." When he offered it in print two years later, it focused on the ways men were organized into domestic and political groups, the arts and sciences on which their subsistence was based, their means of "intercommunication and common action," and the social bonds of their religion.[61]

This article on "The Early History of Man" is perhaps the best single summary view of the sociocultural evolutionary position as it emerged in the mid-1860s. McLennan dealt with the problem under three headings: "The Antiquity of Man," in which he attacked the biblical chronology; "The Primitive State," in which he argued against degeneration and for progress; and "The Method of Studying Early History," in which he explicated the comparative method and the doctrine of survivals. Taken together, these three headings provide a schematic summary of the emergence of sociocultural evolutionism, both substantively and chronologically. Confronted by the extreme antiquity of man, the evolutionists of the 1860s drew upon those existing forms that seemed structurally (or otherwise) more archaic in order by comparison to reconstruct the evolution of human civilization.

Evolutionary Argument and Polemical Context

Having traced its emergence in three leading figures, what can we say more generally about what is sometimes called "classical evolutionism"? In the absence of explicit definitional statements from the historical actors themselves—which would by no means solve the problem of historical definition—what can we say that might help to "define" it as an intellectual historical phenomenon? One approach might be to abstract from the concrete historical material a set of systematic and logically related definitional propositions. Thus one might suggest that classical evolutionism embraced the following interrelated assumptions: that sociocultural phenomena, like the rest of the natural world, are governed by laws that science can discover; that these laws operate uniformly in the distant past as well as in the present; that the present grows out of the past by continuous processes without any sharp breaks; that this growth is naturally from simplicity to complexity; that all men share a single psychic nature; that the motive force of sociocultural development is to be found in the interaction of this common human nature and the conditions of external environment; that the cumulative results of this interaction in different environments are manifest in the differential development of various human groups; that these results can be measured, using the extent of human control over external nature as the primary criterion; that other sociocultural phenomena tend to develop in correlation with scientific progress; that in these terms human groups can be objectively ordered in a hierarchical fashion; that certain contemporary societies therefore approximate the various earlier stages of human development; that in the absence of adequate historical data these stages may be reconstructed by a comparison of contemporary groups; and that the results of this "comparative method" can be confirmed by "survivals" in more advanced societies of the forms characteristic of lower stages. For certain purposes—theoretical, critical, pedagogical, even historiographical—it may indeed be helpful to define "classical evolutionism" in some such terms as these.[62]

There are, however, certain problems with any such construct. There are other ideas commonly associated with sociocultural evolutionism (notably, "independent invention" and "race"), and we may reasonably ask how these are to be related to the set. But even assuming that we have isolated a coherent and adequate set—even, perhaps, a "theory" of "classical evolutionism"—we can have done so only on the basis of some distinction such as John Burrow has suggested between a writer's "theories" and his "views." And in the "real world" of historical texts, it is not so easy to distinguish the propositions "necessary" to a particular theoretical viewpoint from the qualifications, contradictions, and irrelevancies that caution, inconsistency, ambivalence, or various residues of personal intellectual history may have lodged within the larger body of thought from which "necessary" propositions must be extracted.[63]

Even making this distinction, the problem remains that the "necessity" of such central propositions is heavily conditioned by the "logical" requirements of specific historical contexts. They will therefore be variously perceived, ignored, distorted, stereotyped, or extrapolated to some further "logical" conclusion by different actors on the stage of intellectual history: the sociocultural evolutionists themselves, before they achieved the appellation "classical," their immediate opponents, their followers and subsequent critics, and their various historians. All of which suggests that when it comes to such major intellectual historical categories as "classical evolutionism" (or, indeed, "Darwinism") any attempt to define a single model of articulated assumption must necessarily be historically problematic. Though we risk a loss in immediate clarity and precision, our understanding may in fact be enriched by trying to unravel some of the obfuscating complexities of particular polemical contexts.

To begin with, we may note that the assumptions specified above were not unique to sociocultural evolutionism—as an intellectual historical label attached to each ("positivist," "uniformitarian," "associationist," etc.) would easily suggest. For the most part, they had been around for some time. Many were surely present in the eighteenth-century progressivist or nineteenth-century utilitarian traditions. But if both of these are intellectual "sources" of sociocultural evolutionism, it would be a mistake to tie "classical evolutionism" too directly to either. McLennan knew Dugald Stewart's moral philosophy from his Aberdeen curriculum, but it was only when he turned systematically to developmental issues that the Scots really became salient to his argument. In this context, he returned to eighteenth-century writers, citing Kames and Stewart, and discovering Millar for the first time in 1871. A similar turn to eighteenth-century French writers is symbolized on the title page of Tylor's *Primitive Culture,* which is adorned with an epigram from De Brosses' *Culte de dieux fétiches.*[64] The conclusion, then, would seem to be that although the eighteenth-century progressivist and earlier developmental traditions were available, they became relevant in the context of contemporary intellectual problems.

Closer to their own time, all three men may be regarded as part of the utilitarian tradition, and as speaking to problems that had arisen in it. Thus there is a sense in which the doctrine of survivals universalized utilitarianism by showing that customs without apparent utility today could be retrospectively explained in utilitarian terms. More generally, sociocultural evolutionism spoke to a general ethical crisis of confidence in which utilitarian assumptions were very much at issue. And in terms of specific influences, one could do worse than to explore the debt of all three writers to Mill's "Logic of the Moral Sciences." But one wonders whether in emphasizing the ties of sociocultural evolution to utilitarian social theory we risk losing sight of a major intellectual discontinuity—whether the framework of discourse had not changed so as to force attention to new questions and give old ones a very different significance.

Because he was initially so close to the utilitarian tradition, McLennan makes the point well. His later work remained utilitarian in a general epistemological, psychological, and ethical sense. But between

1857 and 1865 he shifted from the problem of constructing a science of legislation to that of reconstructing the origins of major human social institutions. Both are problems of social theory, broadly construed, and both can be derived from Mill's "Logic of the Moral Sciences." But they are rather different problems nonetheless; and once McLennan turned to evolutionary problems, he never returned to the questions of political ethology that had engaged him in 1857.

Despite a considerable shared intellectual heritage, Lubbock, Tylor and McLennan were engaged in rather disparate intellectual enterprises in 1857; a decade later they were all clearly part of a single intellectual movement, which retrospectively we may call "classical evolutionism." What unified them was the fact that they spoke to a common problem, in a particular context, in terms of the same body of data, and with a similar methodological approach—as well as an underlying commitment to a naturalistic uniformitarian explanation. Although there had been a cultural push in the early 1850s toward a developmental view of European civilization, and there were important intellectual precedents for such an inquiry, it was only when Brixham Cave established the great antiquity of man, and Darwinism linked man to some antecedent primate form, that this interest was translated into a systematic investigation of human sociocultural origins. In this project, the comparative study of the evidence of contemporary savagery—which had been the subject matter of the preevolutionary discipline of "ethnology"—became critically important.

By varying routes, Lubbock, Tylor, and McLennan had each arrived in the early 1860s at the conjunction from which sociocultural evolutionism emerged: on the one hand, the data of contemporary savagery; on the other, the antiquity of man. The latter played an ambiguous role in the Darwinian revolution. Although it was a boon to Darwinism in providing time for gradual human development, from a methodological point of view human antiquity was very problematic: having got man back to the pliocene, or even the miocene, it was necessary to get him out, without asking or allowing any assistance from his erstwhile creator. But as Henry Maine later suggested, the imperfection of the geological record was a "mere trifle" compared to the gaps that existed in the archeological record.[65] If prehistoric archeology established a bare outline for primitive technological development, it had virtually nothing to say about the origin of the distinctive human capacities and institutions the Duke of Argyll would have attributed to God. In this context, writers committed to a naturalistic explanation of human development threw whatever they could lay their hands on into the breach of time and culture.

Just as pre-Darwinian physical anthropology provided a racial hierarchy to fill the physical gap between ape and man, so did pre-

Darwinian ethnology provide a mass of cultural data—already roughly ordered hierarchically and conceptualized in terms of change in time—that could be used to fill the cultural gap, once it was freed from the incubus of traditional degenerationist assumption. Even before Brixham Cave, archeological discoveries had begun to establish closer links between archeology and ethnology. The similarities between European lithic remains and stone tools still in use among savages, or between the Swiss lake dwellings and the shoreside stilt houses of Wallace's New Guineans, compelled attention. Given the readily accessible biological idea that age could be conceived in terms of structure as well as in terms of chronology, the leap from visible material homologies to an assumed analogy of nonmaterial cultural forms was an easy one, whether or not one drew on assumptions available in the progressivist tradition. The breach in cultural time could hardly be allowed to remain an empty void simply because history could not fill it. Contemporaneity in space was therefore converted into succession in time by rearranging the cultural forms coexisting in the Victorian present along an axis of assumed structural or ideational archaism—from the simple to the complex, or from that which human reason showed was manifestly primitive to that which habitual association established as obviously civilized.

In filling this temporal gap, Lubbock, Tylor, and McLennan did not rely heavily on processes usually associated with either biological or social Darwinism. Although they appealed occasionally to natural selection, it did not provide a systematic dynamic of sociocultural development for them.[66] And although race did play a structural role in their argument insofar as it explained the currently existing developmental inequalities that enabled them to reconstruct the early history of civilization, they did not interpret human progress primarily in terms of racial conflict. Indeed, process was critical to sociocultural evolutionism primarily as a negative constraint: man must be got out of the miocene by mechanisms that guaranteed an *unassisted* progressive development. In meeting the degenerationist argument, there was in fact a tendency, especially at the lower end of the developmental scale, to rely on a process which, represented visually, seems rather more polygenist than Darwinian: the idea of independent invention. Instead of assuming the historical and genetic relationship of similar forms, it assumed their separate and independent origin: like minds in similar circumstances would invent (or copy from nature) the same cultural forms. Rather than connecting similar forms together as the branches of an evolutionary tree, it saw them arising separately and advancing in parallel through time.

Evolutionary process did not need to be conceived in terms of independent invention. But to exclude divine intervention it had to be regular, continuous, gradual, and essentially unidirectional. Since nature did not make leaps, there must be no gaps into which a supernatural causation might be inserted. In this context, evolutionary process tended to be conceived metaphorically in terms of growth, and especially in terms of the cumulative growth of human reason. Although there were manifestations of a more Germanic notion of the unfolding of inherent potentiality, and a certain tendency toward what might be called a materialist viewpoint, it is a mistake to interpret sociocultural evolutionists as either "cultural idealists" or "technoenvironmental determinists."[67] Allowing for a few residues of the Scottish philosophy or touches of German idealism, they were part and parcel of the empiricist and associationist traditions. The fact that they saw human rationality as a response to the stimuli of the outside world did not, however, prevent them from conceiving the evolutionary process primarily as a cumulative development of ideas. And whether invented once or many times, these ideas were the product of basically uniform mental processes. Thus it was that the processes of savage thought were recapitulated in the minds of children and could be recreated in the minds of evolutionists. Psychic unity made it possible to think oneself out of the miocene, both for the primitives who had been there originally, and the evolutionists who attempted to reconstruct the process by the "comparative method."

But as we have already suggested, it would be a mistake to assimilate the "comparative method" of sociocultural evolutionism too readily to the methods of comparison employed in comparative philology or comparative anatomy. As Maine later suggested in criticizing McLennan, the comparative method as employed in those fields had certain controls built in that were lacking in sociocultural evolutionary comparison: on the one hand, the documentary evidence that could establish actual historical relationships; on the other, "the multiplied dissections and observations of the living and the dead, from which the scientific enquirer infers the structure of the lower forms of life, and connects them with the structure of the higher." Such controls gave reason to believe that the forms compared were actually related. But in the case of sociocultural evolutionary comparison, there was no attempt to guarantee this. Nor, indeed, was there any attempt to make sure they were historically *un*related—as Francis Galton later suggested they must be if one were to generalize from the frequency of co-occurrence of specific sociocultural phenomena.[68] In effect, for purposes of recreating evolutionary development, the issue of historical relationship was simply put to one side.

This is not to say that sociocultural evolutionists were unaware of a distinction between history and evolution, or that in certain contexts they were not interested in historical or diffusionary questions.[69] It is rather to say that in the polemical context in which their model of explanation was defined, history was of limited use. It was all very well for Maine to speak of historical controls so long as he eschewed inquiry into ultimate origins. But for those who felt impelled to just such an inquiry, a less rigorous approach seemed justifiable. Did not Darwin himself say that comparison among collateral lines offered evidence of the gradations by which complex instincts were formed, even where the actual transitions in lineal ancestors were inaccessible? To regard modern savages as representing collateral lines in human development seemed plausible enough in 1865 to those who, rejecting degenerationism, were committed to extending the evolutionary viewpoint. Similarly, survivals—analogues to residual organs in the biological realm—seemed to provide a measure of chronological control in the attempt to make comparison do the work of historical or stratigraphic sequence. With many survivals, there was a built-in time factor, since the sequence could not be inverted and still make sense: so long as one thought in associationist and utilitarian terms, there seemed no question that every "symbolical form" was preceded by a "corresponding reality," or that a "practical purpose" in the past underlay every irrational custom in the present.[70]

But to grant the plausibility of the venture need not blind us to certain problems involved in sociocultural evolutionary comparison. Some of these were such as to be little noticed by writers of the period—as, for instance, the casually ethnocentric assumptions often taken for granted in substituting structure for chronology. But other issues were in fact argued by contemporary critics. Maine pointed out some of the implications of pillaging travel accounts in order to compare particular cultural items without regard to their specific contexts. True, he did not pose the matter in terms of the fragmentation of integrated cultures, nor make the case for anthropological fieldwork in functioning cultures as the equivalent of the anatomist's dissection—perhaps because he felt that in general "savage usages and savage ways of thought" were "a very slippery basis for conclusions." But he did remark on the dangers of taking one usage from Australia and another from Tibet to "construct a theoretical series of institutions, one growing out of the other": "The theory may be so plausible as to settle on the brain of some gentlemen, and persuade them that, wherever there is evidence of one of these customs, the remainder are present, or must have been present of old"—when in fact "there may be no real connection between these practices."[71]

In a sense, Maine was attacking a stereotype—from which he probably would have exempted Tylor, whose general methodological caution earned almost universal intellectual respect. But stereotyping, by carrying men's "theories" to conclusions their "views" do not allow, may offer a kind of intellectual surreality which reveals things that a fully textured representation would otherwise conceal. The perceptive antagonist senses where the theory must *really* lead, despite the qualifications strewn along the path by cautious advocates. Thus sociocultural evolutionists might grant—indeed, insist—that no existing savage tribe really represented primeval man. But contemporary and subsequent critical "stereotyping" correctly sensed that the reconstructionist enterprise depended on that equation being true, in a general sense. And, so implicitly did Tylor: one of the continuing problems of his later anthropology was whether any contemporary tribe could stand as "living representatives of the early Stone Age."[72]

In the end, Tylor settled on the Tasmanians. But the fact was that no existing tribe would adequately serve the purposes of evolutionary reconstruction. Thus it was that evolutionists were forced to fall back on conjectural expedients similar to Lubbock's method of reasoning by opposites. As McLennan suggested, "we can trace the line of human progress far backwards towards brutishness; finding as we go the noble faculties peculiar to man weaker and weaker in their manifestations, producing less and less effect—at the last, scarcely any effect at all—upon his position and habits." Paradoxically, this kind of reasoning involved the sociocultural evolutionists in rather un-Darwinian speculations about primitive man.[73]

Thus McLennan's stripping of nobler qualities led him back to the "gregarious animals" and to sexual unions that were "loose, transitory, and in some degree promiscuous." But Darwin, reasoning from what was known "of the jealousy of all male quadrupeds" and from what was known of the behavior of anthropoid apes, was more than a bit dubious, proposing instead a sequence of marriage forms in which promiscuity and polyandry were later developments. McLennan, in response, used an extremely revealing phrase: "the inquiry is, remember, a *human* one"—that is to say, one could not assume the same psychic makeup in men as in gorillas. Similarly, writing a few years later to a friend, he suggested that he was working "on the origin of laws of incest—which more than anything else, except speech, distinguish man from the brutes."[74]

At this point we are confronted with an ultimate ambiguity in sociocultural evolutionary thinking. The problem defined by Darwinism was to explain how the distinguishing human characteristics had originated by natural processes. But as Colonel Lane Fox put it, because "a line must be drawn somewhere, man's origin, in the proper acceptance of the term—man as a progressive being—has become indissolubly linked with the origin and development of culture." One required, therefore, a conception of man's precultural place in nature, as a basis to reason from. In attempting to conceive this state, one could model it on that of a presumed animal ancestor, or one could reason backward from man himself. For various reasons, reflecting the state of empirical knowledge, the character of their intellectual interests, their own heritage of religious assumption, and the polemical context of their inquiry, which required immediate answers to questions still debated today, sociocultural evolutionists chose the latter path. The tendency was to work backward from some implicitly assumed set of distinguishing human characteristics, by stripping down, or by opposites, to a hypothetical precultural state from which to think man forward once again. But if this approach served well enough in establishing a generally uniformitarian naturalistic process, the result in some instances was not so much to link man to the observed animal world as to separate him from it. Darwin obviously felt the difficulty. So did Maine, who insisted that his own patriarchal theory, with its emphasis on sexual jealousy, fitted better than McLennan's with the evidence of biology. So, eventually, did later critics of "primitive promiscuity" like Edward Westermarck.[75]

In the polemical context of the 1860s, however, the crucial problem was not to maintain on every point a neat Darwinian consistency—whatever that might have been—but rather to defend the idea of human sociocultural evolution itself. Many of the "ambiguous, discrepant, and even contradictory" ideas found in classical evolutionism reflect this fact. The much mooted issue of "unilinear" evolution—often attributed to evolutionists by their critics, but denied by their defenders—may perhaps be better understood in this context. Thus McLennan could say that we were not to assume that the progress of all races from savagery proceeded through exactly the same stages, and granted to Darwin a considerable empirical variation in the marriage forms of primitive man. But in doing so, he nevertheless suggested that "*for the purpose of thinking,* we may assume them all to have been of this [one] type." The italicized phrase is extremely illuminating: for purposes of *re*thinking primitive man out of the pliocene, one must show that "*every conceivable phase* of progress" has been "somewhere recorded," and one must then show that these phases "shade into one another by gentle gradations." Although parallelism at the lower stages strengthened the case for regular natural progression, it was not necessary that every race should in fact climb the ladder to the top. Quite the contrary: the comparative method required that they should not have; the evidence of ethnography and history showed that they had not; ethnocentric assumption suggested that they could not; and European expansion made it clear that they would not. All that was necessary was that there be a single cultural ladder by which man could have climbed unassisted from brute savagery to European civilization; and that the sociocultural evolutionists attempted to provide.[76]

As Maine might have pointed out, their position was analogous to that of earlier political philosophers who, attempting to create a purely secular basis for human social order, appealed to a hypothetical state of nature and a social compact which had little basis in historical reality. Similarly, Victorian evolutionists, seeking a secular developmental explanation of human cultural forms, were not only forced to go considerably beyond any verifiable historical reality, but appealed to processes that were rather tenuously related to Darwinism, and in some cases clearly ran counter to Darwinian assumption. For although it had been posed by Darwinism, their anthropogenetic problem was in a sense itself un-Darwinian. In recreating human sociocultural evolution, classical evolutionists did not in the first instance require a theory of differentiation, which would focus on the processes by which human cultural capacity in *un*like environments would produce *un*like cultural forms. In contrast to animals, both mankind and the process of civilization seemed essentially to be one. What was therefore required was not an origin of cultural species but an evolution of human civilization—an explanation that was uniformitarian not only in process but in outcome.

From this perspective, the similarity of sociocultural evolutionary assumptions to those of eighteenth-century progressivists is not surprising. Although the context that elicited their speculations, and into which they were interpreted, was very different, many of the constraints upon speculation were similar, and from a specific methodological and substantive point of view, there is great continuity. The doctrine of survivals and the emphasis on the evolution of human marriage would seem to be distinctive of Victorian evolutionism. But many other aspects of classical evolutionary argument—notably the discussion of the evolution of religion—would have seemed familiar to eighteenth-century writers. Although the classical evolutionists wrote in response to the demands of the Darwinian revolution, they were led by the demands of that polemical context toward speculations that had been elicited in a previous one, and were still available to them. In filling the void in cultural time with the data of contemporary savagery, they were carried back into close contact with an earlier developmental tradition, to which their own sociocultural evolutionism was in many respects closer than it was to Darwinism.

Thus it was that Tylor, responding to readers who thought it strange he had not mentioned Darwin or Spencer "in a work on civilization insisting so strenuously on a theory of development or evolution," could say that *Primitive Culture* was "arranged on its own lines, coming scarcely into contact of detail with the previous works of these eminent philosophers." When Tylor wrote his book, the *Descent of Man* had not appeared, and the realization of Darwin's promise in the last pages of the *Origin* had been left to the classical evolutionists. And if in fulfilling that promise they were led along pre-Darwinian lines, this did not prevent Darwin from accepting their contribution. In the interim, he himself had retreated somewhat on the role of natural selection in biological evolution, falling back on other expedients to guarantee his central argument. Thus whatever his reservations about the sexual jealousy of anthropoid apes, Darwin was quite willing to accept the sociocultural evolutionists' contribution to *The Descent of Man*—which incorporated almost fifty references to the work of Lubbock, Tylor, and McLennan.[77]

Continuity and Disjuncture in Classical Evolutionism

Having left the problem of historical definition in such a fluidly contextual state, it seems paradoxical to have invoked, even incidentally, the metaphor of paradigm—with its deceptive phonetic resonance of conceptual precision—to characterize the retrospectively constituted interplay of old and new questions and answers in a specific polemical context. The more so, since we have done this on the basis of only three writers, who differed among themselves in ways not dwelt on here; one need only double this small sample to discover that not all ethnological writers responded to the Darwinian revolution in the same way. Nonetheless, it is clear (even before pursuing the history of their reputations) that Lubbock, Tylor, and McLennan came to be regarded (and to some extent regarded themselves) as representatives of a single anthropological viewpoint. To recapture the elusive historical coherence of "classical evolutionism," it may therefore help to consider its boundedness as well as its fluid contextuality. One approach may be to look briefly at three writers whose relation to "classical evolutionism" is in some way problematic. In each case, the exception can perhaps be shown to prove the rule, and help give further definition to a mode of inquiry which, although deriving from a particular debate, profoundly conditioned the subsequent history of anthropology.

Daniel Wilson, who had coined the term that gave the "prehistoric" movement its name, treated the problem of *Primeval Man* in 1862. Accepting human antiquity, he argued that the growth of civilization in the pre-Columbian New World offered "striking confirmation" of the development revealed by European prehistoric archeology. But in certain critical respects, Wilson still wrote within the pre-Darwinian tradition. Rejecting the "monkifying process"—which he associated with polygenism—he insisted on the special creation of man, his capacity for moral degeneration, and the derivation of all races from the three sons of Noah. Although Tylor found things to praise in the second edition, Wilson's book never found its way into the evolutionary canon.[78]

By contrast, we may consider a figure recently resurrected from anthropological obscurity: C. Staniland Wake. Undaunted by the new antiquity of man, Wake felt that he could still solve the old ethnological problem in the new temporal context. Employing all the traditional criteria of affinity, he attempted to trace the races of the world back to a lost continent in the Indian Ocean, whose disappearance was recorded in the universal tradition of the Deluge. Rejecting Darwinian evolution as materialistic, insisting that between organic, animal, and human life there was no continuity, Wake drew upon idealist, intuitionist, teleological, and explicitly theistic assumptions to build his own scheme of mental evolution. If Wake later changed his position on a number of these matters, and eventually turned out to be more "right" than McLennan on issues relating to the evolution of human marriage, it is perhaps less a measure of his foresight than of his isolation from what became in his day the dominant theoretical framework in anthropology.[79]

That framework may be further clarified by a third case: Colonel Lane Fox, who in this period had not yet inherited the huge Wiltshire estate for which he changed his name to Pitt Rivers—and which must have given retrospective confirmation to his strongly-held belief that Providence governed history. Lane Fox even suggested that the timing of the discovery of evolution was itself evidence of "an overruling power," since within a few more decades the extermination of savage races would have made it impossible to use the comparative method to reconstruct "the sequence of ideas by which mankind has advanced from the condition of the lower animals to that in which we find him at the present time." Although his own uniformitarian progressionism had been defined in the 1850s—when he had sought to solve the problem of "the monogenesis or polygenesis of certain arts and appliances"—Lane Fox easily adapted it to the Darwinian revolution. Classifying the "various products of human industry" into "genera, species, and varieties," he discussed their development explicitly in terms of Spencerian evolutionary psychology and the processes of natural selection. Perhaps because he dealt with material forms, which lent themselves to more rigorous comparative treatment, Lane Fox was in fact rather more consistently Darwinian than his sociocultural evolutionary confreres. Rather than adopt the expedient of independent invention to introduce regularity and order in the prehistoric void, he insisted in effect that uniformitarian processes were better preserved by continuity than by repetition. Wherever possible, he tried to carry back a given material form to a single geographical source, even at the cost of criticism by his friends Tylor and Lubbock. But despite the fact that in many respects he continued to think in terms of the diffusionary ethnological viewpoint that still prevailed when his collection had begun, his status as a sociocultural evolutionist has never been in doubt.[80]

The fact that both Wake and Wilson faded from view, while Lane Fox Pitt Rivers always retained an important secondary place in the evolutionary pantheon, may tell us something about the conditions of membership. It is true that both Wilson and Wake ended their lives in Canada—the former as one of the leaders of Canadian anthropology, the latter in relative obscurity. By contrast, Lane Fox was a key activist of the British prehistoric movement, whose substantial social position enabled him later as Pitt Rivers to endow an anthropological museum at Oxford. And yet one cannot help feeling that relative institutional and social marginality was correlated with intellectual position in determining their respective fates. Although each man's developmentalism remained tied to preevolutionary traditions, Lane Fox was distinguished by his willingness—nay eagerness—to view human sociocultural development in the Darwinian context.[81] Once again, we are led to the conclusion that this context was critical to the definition of "classical evolutionism."

In this framework, we may consider the much-mooted issue of the place of independent invention and diffusion in the sociocultural evolutionary scheme. Although we have spoken of the ethnological "paradigm" as diffusionist, and of independent invention as a tendency within the evolutionary viewpoint, logically (as Lane Fox suggested), independent invention implied a "polygenesis of arts." By contrast, both diffusionary ethnology and Darwinian evolution were given temporal structure by a genealogical tree. But just as independent invention in Prichard's hands could become a defense of human unity, so could it become in the polemical context of the 1860s a defense of uniformitarian development. For unless one was willing to speculate about lost continents, the diffusionist approach to the early history of man broke down at a certain point. Even Lane Fox was left with a residue of forms that could not be traced to any single source.[82] But it was this area beyond the limits of historical reconstruction that was critically problematic in the Darwinian debate. Indeed, even if one could have traced every cultural form to a single source, anyone committed to naturalistic explanation would still have to find there an "independent invention"—that is to say, a causal process by which it could be generated by no other means than the interaction of external environment and "such processes of mind as stood for reason" at that phase of human evolutionary development. From that point on, diffusionary mechanisms could be easily incorporated into an evolutionary framework; but in the absence of convincing historical connections between cultural phenomena, independent invention guaranteed processual regularity, just as "stages of development" guaranteed the continuity of temporal sequence. In this sense, there was within sociocultural evolutionism a tendency to privilege independent invention over diffusion, despite the fact that from a broader conceptual point of view diffusionism was closer to the branching Darwinian model.

Franz Boas was to note this anomaly in 1896, when he drafted (but did not send) a letter to Tylor in which he suggested that it was "a most characteristic sign of the diversity of our present methods of thinking in physiological [i.e., biological] and psychological [i.e., ethnological] science that in the former we are inclined to derive genetically similar forms from *one* source; while in psychological science we are inclined to believe that an idea can develop independently in different communities or individuals."[83] That an assumption whose "necessity" seems heavily conditioned by a particular polemical context could still a generation later be a factor in anthropological debate raises interesting metahistorical questions about the articulation of specific situational determinants and perduring intellectual structures in intellectual history. Did the idea of "independent invention" achieve a kind of functional autonomy from polemical determination once it was integrated into the evolutionary argument—or was its salience for Boas a reflection of other, later polemical contexts? While these questions lie outside the temporal scope of the present argument, a consideration of a related problem—the continued relevance of diffusionary assumptions after the triumph of evolutionism—can perhaps add to our understanding of the impact of the Darwinian revolution on anthropological speculation.

Once the battle for naturalistic developmentalism had been won, Tylor's old diffusionary interests resurfaced; until the end of his career, he was concerned with borrowed elements in middle-American civilization. More generally, characteristically "ethnological" lines of inquiry continued to be pursued by anthropologists throughout the later nineteenth century. Just because human antiquity had so complicated the attempt to trace them to a single source, scholars did not cease to wonder about the histories and ethnic relationships of the diverse tribes of man. At the level of practical ethnography these were often the questions first asked of any given group: where did they come from? who were they related to? At a more general level, the question of human racial genealogy had an obvious continued relevance in a post-Darwinian context, since Darwinism—as Boas pointed out—assumed that similar forms must be genealogically related to each other.[84]

Similarly, it may be helpful to our understanding of post-Darwinian anthropology to think also of the continuity of the polygenist as well as the ethnological tradition. For if Darwinism deprived the unity debate of much of its meaning, particular polygenist assumptions and a general polygenist style survived in the static typological (and very un-Darwinian) view of race adopted by many physical anthropologists. Beyond this, many aspects of sociocultural evolutionism itself—in addition to "independent invention"—can be interpreted as reflecting polygenist assumption: the emphasis on classification in biological terms; the correlation of physical type and cultural achievement; the incorporation of a static racial hierarchy into a dynamic evolutionary sequence; the rejection of biblical assumption; and the insistence that man be studied as part of the natural world so that anthropology could take its place among the natural sciences. In the 1850s and 1860s, all of these were positions held by polygenist anthropologists.[85]

From this point of view, classical evolutionism may best be interpreted not as a "paradigm" but as a synthesis of elements from various preexisting intellectual orientations—Prichardian ethnology, the emerging physical anthropological alternative, and the tradition of progressivist cultural developmentalism—in an attempt to answer the new questions posed by the Darwinian revolution. Reverting to the visual metaphor hitherto employed, we may still see the outline of the old ethnological tree, its branching structure blending organically into the Darwinian landscape. But because its lower branches had been obscured in the mist of human time, Darwinians used the ladder of cultural evolution to get from the presumed ground level of human antiquity to a point higher up the trunk that led to European civilization. Although they sometimes tended to see other peoples as having climbed not so far on shorter ladders, they were generally aware that the unorganic rectilinearity of the ladder was merely an intellectual expedient, and that the tree beneath had a very different shape. The contemporary historical relevance of this visual model is attested by Lane Fox: the tree was "the grand type of progress," and the existing human races were "the budding twigs and foliage"; but because the dearth of knowledge of their early history made it impossible "to place them on their proper branches," one had to rely instead on a generalized rectilinear sequence of civilization based on the comparative method.[86]

Viewed in these terms, the methodological assumptions of the old and new anthropological orientations may be seen as complementary rather than conflicting. In correspondence with the American evolutionist Lewis Henry Morgan in the late 1870s, Henry Maine drew the distinction previously noted between his own and the comparative method of sociocultural evolutionism. He felt, however, that "the two lines of inquiry promise more and more to connect themselves together." In a subsequent letter in response to Morgan's *Ancient Society,* he suggested a specific point of contact in the problem of the nature of the Roman gens, which he went on to discuss in terms of the insights provided by Morgan's descriptions of the Iroquois Indians. At the furthest reaches of history, the comparative method (of evolutionary ethnology, not of comparative philology) became a recourse even for thinkers who in the first instance had not been interested in human antiquity and contemporary savagery.[87]

Similarly, it was possible for men whose characteristic argument had been defined in response to the Darwinian revolution to incorporate a good deal of the substance of arguments developed in a pre-evolutionary context as they moved forward in evolutionary time. If they did not accept Maine's assertion that primitive patriarchy was more consistently Darwinian than any notion of universal female promiscuity, they could still include his patriarchal state as a later phase of evolutionary development, accept the village community as a characteristic feature of the barbaric stage, and view the movement of progressive societies in terms of the shift from kinship to territory and from status to contract. As Tylor suggested in reviewing Maine's *Village Communities,* "within the present special subject . . . diverse theories of the origin of society scarcely clash." Thus it was that Lubbock, anticipating a similar retrospective cooptation by later historians, could refer in 1878 to "the school of Tylor and Sir Henry Maine."[88]

And yet to talk in terms of synthesis and complementarity does not do full justice to the manifest disjuncture between the Prichardian and the evolutionary points of view. There were fundamental differences in problem, context, assumption, and method. Prichardian ethnology had been unified around the problem of human unity, approached within a static biological and a limited temporal context; classical evolutionism was unified around the problem of human sociocultural development, within a dynamic biological and vastly expanded temporal context. The religious assumptions that had provided the underlying basis of ethnological explanation were now among the major phenomena to be explained. Conversely, the psychic unity of man was no longer a conclusion supporting the single origin of mankind, but rather a premise for establishing the human invention of cultural forms. The similarities of these forms, which had been subordinated to the tracing of racial affinities, became now the critical data for establishing a developmental sequence. Comparison, which had been used to establish connection in both time and space, was now subordinated to the reconstruction of generalized temporal sequence. Furthermore, the sequence of time itself had a very different character now that its vast extension was structured primarily in terms of regular stages governed by generalized processes and only secondarily by diffusionary and migrational processes of a more particularistic historical character.

Although there is no compelling reason to speak of this disjunction as a shift in paradigms, certain features of the paradigm metaphor are reflected in the process by which classical evolutionism emerged. Facing increasing criticism of its fundamental assumptions and a burgeoning of recalcitrant data, the Prichardian paradigm might well be spoken of as in a state of crisis in the 1850s. The new paradigm of sociocultural evolutionism promised to subordinate these anomalous data to a very different problem—to which attention was compelled in part by manifestly revolutionary changes in related intellectual realms. The change was brought about by younger men who came to ethnology from other disciplines, and who—as we shall later see in more detail—were united in a definite community life. Once the change had been accomplished, the disciplinary world was transformed, and the disciplinary memory was subject to systematic distortion. Prichard's work quickly lost current anthropological significance, save as an encyclopedic compendium of ethnographic data. In time, he faded into virtual obscurity, and anthropology was conceived as having begun with Darwin, whose actual influence, in turn, was largely misconstrued. Already by 1875 Lane Fox could say that "it would be sheer moonshine, in the present state of knowledge, to study Anthropology on any other basis than the basis of development." In view of what has been suggested as to the continuity of ethnological and polygenist assumption in the daily practice of anthropology, it is questionable to what extent evolutionism produced anything that might be called "normal science." But despite the continuity of alternative orientations, there seems little doubt that for the next generation or so the dominant anthropological viewpoint—or, to use a term Dell Hymes has suggested, its theoretical "cynosure"—was, at least in the Anglo-American sphere, that which we have called "classical evolutionism."[89]

Within this new evolutionary context, contemporary savages no longer stood at the margins of human history as the degenerate offshoots, the waifs and strays of mankind. For better or worse, they were incorporated into the main movement of civilization. But if savages still existed in the present, their developmental significance was relegated to the distant past, and in the context of evolutionary associationism and racialist assumption, that relegation had far-reaching implications. In the beginning, black savages and white savages had been psychologically one. But while white savages were busily acquiring superior brains in the course of cultural progress, dark-skinned savages had remained back near the beginning. Although united in origin with the rest of mankind, their assumed inferiority of culture and capacity now reduced them to the status of missing links in the evolutionary chain. Their cultural forms, although at the center of anthropological attention, had still only a subordinate interest. One studied these forms not for themselves, or in terms of the meaning they might have to the people who created them, but in order to cast light on the processes by which the ape had developed into the British gentleman.

SIX

Victorian Cultural Ideology and the Image of Savagery (1780–1870)

"Australian Aboriginal Marriage Ceremony"—1870

John Lubbock, *The Origin of Civilisation and the Primitive Condition of Man* (London, 1870), p. 74—from which the caption is taken.

IN reviewing Spencer's *Principles of Sociology* in 1877, Tylor suggested that it was the "besetting sin" of all who studied primitive man "to treat the savage mind according to the needs of our argument, sometimes as extremely ignorant and inconsequent, at other times as extremely observant and logical."[1] This double image of savagery, especially evident in Lubbock, is worthy of further consideration. When what is ostensibly the same phenomenon is treated in apparently contradictory ways, there may be other motives involved than the immediate demands of argument. Indeed, one suspects that the need Lubbock and his confreres felt to fill the cultural gap between the inhabitants of Brixham Cave and those of Belgrave Square, and the consequently un-Darwinian character of much of their evolutionary argument, may reflect more general historical processes than the polemical logic of the Darwinian debate.

What have been called the "ulterior motives" of Victorian sociocultural evolutionary anthropology have been suggestively discussed in terms of the need to exorcise the specter of relativism threatening British intellectuals after "the collapse of systematic utilitarianism and the weakening of traditional religious belief." Evolutionism has also been seen as the ideological reflection of economic exploitation and class conflict in an age of rapid capitalist economic development and imperial expansion. While evolutionism surely offered intellectual balm for minds sorely anguished by philosophical and religious doubt, and no doubt functioned ideologically to buttress hierarchical and exploitative relationships both at home and abroad, neither the "bogey of relativism" nor the "apology for domination" do full justice to the complex and ambivalent motives of those who wrote the major works of sociocultural evolutionism.[2]

To get at the motives of historical actors is an inherently speculative matter; to speak of some of them as "ulterior" introduces further difficulty, since it implies the possibility that actors may somehow deceive us as to their motivation, or that they are not fully aware of its complexities. Although we have ample reason in the world of daily experience and in the literature of dynamic psychology to accept both these possibilities, there is also good reason to be cautious in approaching intellectual history in these terms. Psychohistory is a risky venture even for the initiate; the sociological equivalent, which conflates "ulterior personal motive" with "latent ideological function," is equally problematic. And yet a history of evolutionary thinking which did not attempt to consider the possibility that it was molded by the broader cultural experience of evolutionary writers, or that it served other purposes than to answer certain scientific questions, would scarcely do justice to a viewpoint which its advocates were inclined to see as relevant to all spheres of human life. As a relatively unpresumptuous starting point for such contextualization, we may perhaps take a methodological hint from recent slang, and ask what it was that seems to have been "bugging" them: what were the gnawingly irritating contemporary concerns that required extended intellectual scratching?

Regarding their works as appendices to the *Origin of Species*, one might expect the sociocultural evolutionists to have been interested in the evolution of every manifestation of human faculty. But a glance at their tables of contents suggests that not all things human were of equal interest to them. Two-thirds of Lubbock's *Origin of Civilisation* was devoted to two particular human institutions: religion and marriage—which were respectively the primary interest of Tylor and of McLennan.[3] Nor is this to be explained in terms of the polemical logic of the Darwinian debate. Human marriage was at best of peripheral interest to that debate; and if the institution of religion was more centrally implicated, its overriding importance clearly reflects certain broader processes at work both in Victorian culture and the psyches of Victorian anthropologists.

Thus one way to get at "ulterior motives" may be to look more closely at the specific substance of the evolutionary argument, and to relate it to the life-historical experience of the evolutionary generation. With apologies to specialist historians of the period, and without venturing too far into the methodologically uncertain grounds of psychohistory or ideological analysis, perhaps we may also offer some speculations about the general psychological, social, and cultural processes implicated in sociocultural evolutionism, and even about its latent functions. In the end, we may come back to relativism and domination. But along the way, we may cast further light upon that paradoxical double image of savagery.

Animistic Religion and the Progress of Human Reason

The eagerness with which some men embraced Darwinism, and the need they felt to defend a natural rather than a supernatural causation in the realm of culture, suggests a considerable prior weakening of religious belief—a personal prefiguring of the more general "Victorian crisis of faith" to which Darwinism was a major contributing factor. What Tylor called "the great intellectual movement of the last two centuries" had not been reversed, but only channeled, by the religious revival that did so much to mold British society and culture in the early nineteenth century. As the contrast between Whewell and Mill suggests, there were in the 1830s strongly conflicting trends within what has been called the "common context" of early Victorian thought. And by the end of that decade its fabric was already beginning to fray, as the woof threads of natural theology were stretched by developments in natural science, and the warp threads of biblical revelation were stained by the corrosive of "higher criticism." True, the scientific pull was exerted largely by men who still accepted God's providential role, and the source of the corrosive was quite far off beyond the Rhine. But there were other more readily accessible grounds for questioning traditional belief. Paradoxically, the heightened moral sensibility of the evangelical period sometimes led the younger generation to wonder about such fundamental dogmas as eternal damnation and substitutionary penal atonement. Many came to feel with Herbert Spencer that it was "absolutely and immeasurably unjust" for all of Adam's guiltless descendants to be damned for a piece of disobedience "which might have caused a harsh man to discharge his servant."[4]

In the 1850s such doubt was still a very personal problem. Although the irreligion of the urban masses was a matter of some concern, organized skepticism was barely beginning to ripple the surface of the culturally pervasive religiosity. Even so, influences sapping traditional religious belief were already at work within the Church itself—where they were expressed in an attempt to reinterpret Christianity in a form that doubt could not so easily assail. Convinced that it was "no longer possible to ignore the results of criticism," certain Broad Church heritors of an earlier Liberal Anglican generation sought in German thought—as mediated by Max Müller's mentor Baron Bunsen—the means to demonstrate to educated Britons the compatibility of the critical spirit with an enlightened Christian belief. Drawing heavily on Bunsen's biblical researches, the seven prominent Anglican liberals who published *Essays and Reviews* in 1860 offered a doctrine of gradual spiritual progress, in which the "lesson of humanity" was at each point adapted to man's developing faculties: in its childhood, the human race was governed by the positive rules of the Mosaic Law; in its youth, by the example of Christ; in its current manhood, by "the teaching of the Spirit within." The form of belief was therefore to be adapted to the national character, which in Britain in "an age of physical research like the present" took for granted "the grand foundation of universal law." In this context, even Darwin's *Origin* could be incorporated into the divine plan, and the moral lesson of the Bible could be identified with the "voice of conscience."[5]

But if all this was reassuring to religious liberals, it was more than a bit unsettling to the leaders of the Church of England. Threatened on the one side by a resurgent Roman Catholicism and on the other by Nonconformist attacks on its Establishment position, they were not inclined to encourage an attempt to accommodate religious truth to the evolving human spirit. It was one thing to find, as some searching Victorians did, traces of more general religious truth in the myths of other peoples; it was quite another to reduce the Christian Bible to the general category of myth. Maine's evangelical godfather, now Archbishop Sumner of Canterbury, spoke for all the bishops in questioning how the authors—six of whom were clergymen—could honestly subscribe to the Thirty-Nine Articles. Two of them were in fact found guilty of heterodoxy in ecclesiastical courts; and although that decision was subsequently reversed by the Privy Council, their theological liberalism did not become really acceptable within the Church of England until the 1880s.[6]

It was in the larger context focused around the controversy over *Essays and Reviews*, as well as that of the Darwinian debate itself, that the sociocultural evolutionists dealt with the problem of religion. What we know of their early life indicates that they all grew up in religious homes, that in varying degrees they were all touched by doubt, that some among them were involved in the defense of the "Septem contra Christum," and that all of them were active propagators of the new orthodoxy of positive science. It is important not to lose sight of this active role. The sociocultural evolutionists did not merely respond to intellectual revolution; they marched in its ranks.[7]

Although we no longer accept simplistic views of the "warfare of science with theology," there is a danger that an historiography sensitive to the manifold ways in which traditional beliefs condition the emergence of new viewpoints may lose sight of real historical discontinuity. Victorian doubters did not question the traditional grounds of faith without ambivalence, or advocate heterodoxy without caution. Intellectual accommodations, either in process or in retrospect, softened the edge of controversy on both sides: at the ultimate metaphysical margin, Spencer found only "the Unknowable"; in the end, most theologians were able to accept the notion that evolution offered simply "a grander view of the Creator." But the issues were still sharp enough to lacerate the minds of contemporary actors, and even disinterested historical retrospect must acknowledge that "all that pain, doubt, fear, and confusion were not based on nothing." In the 1860s Tylor sometimes reassured his readers—and perhaps still even himself—that there was no conflict between true Christianity and the results of modern science. But in 1883, when Huxley's "agnosticism" had gained a certain degree of intellectual respectability, and theology, forced from the field it had so long shared with science, was taking to itself the burden of accommodation, Tylor was able to acknowledge—albeit in stanzas contributed anonymously to Andrew Lang's "Double Ballade of Primitive Man" —that the "mild anthropologist" had a more frankly "revolutionary" impulse: "Theologians all to expose,—'Tis the *mission* of Primitive Man."[8]

Even so, there is evidence to suggest that the heterodoxy Tylor propagated may have functioned as a substitute for the more traditional belief of his youth. There is a hint of the substitutionary atonement offered by natural science in the record of his experiences with spiritualism. For some Victorians, the spiritualist movement was the post-Darwinian analogue to phrenology, providing a bridge back from a soulless secular meliorism toward the spiritual world they had lost. Alfred Russel Wallace was one such—but not, however, Tylor. In 1872, when recent spiritualist manifestations attracted notice in the public press, Tylor came up from his home in Somerset to investigate them at first hand. In the course of seances with leading mediums, he witnessed phenomena that seemed to contravene the laws of nature: table rappings, clairvoyance, and even levitation. Much he felt was merely legerdemain—"except that *legerté* is too complimentary for the clumsiness of many of the obvious imposters." But there was a residue which, although largely dependent on the testimony of others, was in fact attested by respectable middle-class gentlemen whose judgment he was not inclined to question: "I admit to a prima facie case on evidence, and will not deny that there may be a psychic force causing raps, movements, levitations, etc." Nonetheless, he concluded his "Notes on 'Spiritualism'" by affirming that "seeing has not (to me) been believing"; and despite his evident private perplexity, he used this first-hand experience in his published work only to document the general fraudulence of spiritualist phenomena.[9]

The point is not to argue that they were authentic, but merely to suggest that the evidence had not been such as to convince Tylor of this, and that his avowed incredulity, like the spiritualist believer's acceptance, may have been conditioned by ulterior emotional needs. Tylor paid a price for his scientific naturalism: "he who believes that his thread of life will be severed once and forever by the fatal shears, well knows that he wants a purpose and a joy in life, which belong to him who looks for a life to come." Having paid this price, Tylor was not about to abandon his naturalistic rationalism easily. For some Victorians spiritualism offered a surrogate for the emotional security provided by unquestioned religious belief; but for the confirmed scientific rationalist, spiritualist phenomena could be agents of doubt rather than reassurance. For those unwilling to follow Wallace in hypothesizing an extension of scientific law to include them, the only alternative was to dismiss the phenomena themselves. In this context, seeing could hardly be believing, and there was at least a touch of unintended irony in the definition of faith with which Tylor closed his diary: "Blessed are they that have seen, and *yet* have believed."[10]

What was at issue was the very essence of religion, which Tylor had defined as "the belief in Spiritual Beings," and which he saw as fundamentally antithetic to "Materialistic philosophy." He had in fact elaborated his theory in the context of prior familiarity with the spiritualist movement, and he had chosen the term "animism" to designate the essential core of all religion because the more directly descriptive term "spiritualism" had been preempted by the modern sect. Like his own experience with spiritualism, his whole evolutionary scheme may be regarded as an attempt to explain away the apparently irrational or supernatural.[11]

Even at its most primitive level, religion was far from "being a rubbish-heap of miscellaneous folly," but was built on principles that were "essentially rational, though working in a mental condition of intense and inveterate ignorance." It seemed to Tylor "as though thinking men, as yet at a low level of culture, were deeply impressed by two groups of biological problems"—the difference between a living body and a dead one, and the nature of the human shapes that appeared in dreams and visions. From these two groups of phenomena, the "ancient savage philosophers" made "the obvious inference" that every man, in addition to his body, had a life and a phantom. By a second inference these were combined into the notion of a "ghost-soul"—a "thin unsubstantial human image," the "cause of life or thought in the individual it animates," capable "of leaving the body far behind," and "continuing to exist and appear to men after the death of that body." Far from being "arbitrary or conventional," these doctrines answered "in the most forcible way to the plain evidence of men's senses"—as the continuity of animistic thought in the modern world attested.[12]

It was as though primitive man, in an attempt to create science, had accidentally created religion instead, and mankind had spent the rest of evolutionary time trying to rectify the error. Culture—a term that Tylor used always in the singular and usually in a developmental sense—was a dual process. Religion itself had evolved "upwards from the simplest theory which attributes life and personality to animal, vegetable and mineral alike—through that which gives to stone and plant and river guardian spirits which live among them and attend to their preservation, growth, and change—up to that which sees in each department of the world the protecting and fostering care of an appropriate divinity, and at last of one Supreme Being ordering and controlling the lower hierarchy." But parallel to this development there was another: "through all these gradations of opinion we may thus see fought out, in one stage after another, the long-waged contest between the theory of animation which accounts for each phenomenon of nature by giving it everywhere a life like our own, and a slowly-growing natural science which in one department after another substitutes for independent voluntary action the working out of systematic law."[13]

If religious belief was the theoretical science of primitive man, religious ritual was its utilitarian application. Rites and ceremonies were "means of intercourse with and influence on spiritual beings, and as such, their intention is as directly practical as any chemical or mechanical process." Like the beliefs on which they were based, the "absurdities" of primitive sacrifice had their origin not in fraud, but "rather in genuine error": "if the main proposition of animistic natural religion be granted, that the idea of the human soul is the model of the idea of deity, then the analogy of man's dealing with man ought *inter alia,* to explain his motives in sacrifice." Just as the common man offered gifts to the great, to gain good or avert evil, so did the savage to his deity. All that was necessary to "produce a logical doctrine of sacrificial rites" was "proper adaptation of the means of conveying the gift." The irrationality of sacrifice was a secondary development, the reflection of the "usual ritualistic change" from "practical reality to formal ceremony." Thus men invented new ideas about their deities, but kept up old sacrifices nonetheless, "in spite of their having become practically unreasonable." Whereas new rites were seldom introduced "without rational motive," old ones were kept up by force of habit "after their meaning has fallen away."[14]

The irrational was thus the outcome of a twofold process: on the one hand, it was created by invention, when primitive men, like Locke's madmen, reasoned soundly from false premises or inadequate experience;[15] on the other, it was a product of survival, when things that were originally rational in motive became meaningless or absurd as they persisted by the sheer force of conservatism into a new intellectual context. By contrast, scientific rationality itself, like the conservatism of habit, was an unanalyzed category in Tylor's thought. That men should seek to understand and control the forces of nature, that they should persist in outmoded ways of thought, required no extended explanation. To the heritor of utilitarian liberalism, these were the forces that defined the polemical field; the one was self-validating; the other could be given no more than a contingent justification.

And yet the problem of the positive functions of religious belief could not be entirely ignored. Traditionalists insisted that without it social order was impossible—that morality and law could be validated only by divine authority, without which chaos would ensue. Against this, secular rationalists, echoing the words of George Eliot, might have argued their own experience: though God was "inconceivable," and Immortality "unbelievable," Duty was still "peremptory and absolute." But there remained the problem, as Tylor put it, that "unbelievers in [a] second life share ethical principles which have been more or less shaped under its influence." To establish an independent basis for moral behavior, he insisted on an evolutionary separation between morality and religion. The evidence of savage religion in fact disproved "the popular idea that the moral government of the universe is an essential tenet of natural religion.'' But if savage animism was ''almost devoid'' of ethical content, this did not mean that ''morality is absent from the life of the lower races.'' Far from it: ''without a code of morals, the very existence of the rudest tribe would be impossible.'' True, religion and morality had subsequently *become* intimately linked through the idea of retribution in a future life; and looked at ''from a political point of view,'' it was clear that this linkage had been a powerful influence on human history, providing just the sanction which traditionalists required. But just as the linkage was not original, neither was it irrevocable—among the most advanced sectors of British society there were many like Tylor who believed in ''a positive morality which shall of its own force control the acts of men.''[16]

In the end, the study of *Primitive Culture,* far from undermining law and morals, helped to place them on a sounder basis than ever before. The ''practical import'' of Tylor's study was to determine ''how far are modern opinion and conduct based on the strong ground of soundest modern knowledge, or how far only on such knowledge as was available in the earlier and ruder stages of culture where their types were shaped.'' It was the function of ethnography to ''bridge the gap'' between those laws and maxims that a people ''made fresh, according to the information and circumstance'' of a ''particular stage of its history,'' and those which became current merely ''by inheritance from an earlier stage, only more or less modified'' to make them compatible with new conditions. Fortunately, the oft-closed gates of discovery and reform'' were now open at their widest, and though they might be shut once more, it was also possible that scientific method would ''start the world on a more steady and continuous course of progress.''[17]

Toward that end, ethnography had a double task. By impressing men's minds with the ''doctrine of development'' it would encourage them ''to continue the progressive work of past ages.'' Seeing reason operating in history, they would take hold of it consciously as a weapon and undertake the second ''harsher, and at times even painful, office of ethnography'': ''to expose the remains of crude old culture which have passed into harmful superstition, and to mark these out for destruction.'' Active thus both in ''aiding progress and removing hindrance,'' Tylor's science of culture was ''essentially a reformer's science.''[18]

In relation to traditional Christianity, its implications were more radical than Tylor's peroration might suggest. He tactfully declined to take up personally the ethnographer's second ''harsher task,'' limiting himself to a ''slight allusion'' here and there, and leaving it to the ''educated reader'' to ''work out their general bearing on theology.'' But his allusions in fact indicated that this bearing was ''very close,'' and that the ''actual truth of religious systems'' was at issue. Insisting on ''the connexion which runs through religion, from its rudest forms up to the status of an enlightened Christianity,'' he proceeded to show that the human soul, the hope of immortality, and the very idea of God were products of human reason gone astray, and that the major rituals of modern Christendom had rational meaning only within the framework of an earlier barbaric philosophy. Natural caution and ingrained respectability led Tylor to imply that *some* current religious doctrines might survive ethnographic criticism, but it was by no means clear which, if any, these might be. No doubt many ''educated readers'' finished *Primitive Culture* with their faith intact, but the logical thrust of the book was clearly to reduce Christianity to the same category of ''mythology'' with which Tylor prefaced his discussion of the development of animistic belief. Rather than God having created man in His image, man had, through evolutionary time, created God in his; and his ritual relations with his slowly created Creator were modelled on his social relations with other human beings.[19]

As Max Müller later suggested, with just a touch of irony, the science of culture was ''Mr. Tylor's science''; and the question may be asked to what extent his thinking about religion was representative even of that small group whom we have treated as *the* sociocultural evolutionists. Clearly, they did not all equally share Tylor's heterodox impulses. Pitt Rivers had not banished God from history entirely—though he recognized that in this he was unrepresentative of his fellow evolutionists, and he did not write about the evolution of religion. Lubbock, whose real interest in the established social order was also quite large, was not inclined to affront tradition directly, and emphasized the positive role of science in elevating and purifying religious belief. McLennan's heterodox impulses found outlet for the most part in other areas, and Spencer was more inclined as he grew older to recognize the positive functions of religion. Quite aside from these differences of impulse, there were differences in argument as well. Lubbock felt that savage religion might better be discussed as ''superstition,'' since ''it differs essentially from ours''; and although he felt it was ''to a great extent a matter of definition,'' he later came to the conclusion that ''the lower races have no religion.'' Stimulated by a book treating *Tree and Serpent Worship* in diffusionist and racial terms, McLennan became preoccupied with the traditional ''problem of idolatry,'' which he transmitted to later Victorians in the form of ''totemism.'' Spencer gave a central place to ancestor worship, and in contrast to Tylor saw religion and ethics as ''originally one'' and thenceforth progressively differentiating, until in modern times they had become ''quite distinct.''[20]

But despite these differences of impulse and argument, there was a substantial unity underlying the sociocultural evolutionist approach to religion. Whether by diffusion or independent invention, they all accepted an essentially Tylorian view of the origin of religious belief. Though he did not refer to Tylor, Lubbock discussed "the religious theories of savages" in terms of the spirit which "seems to desert the body" during sleep. McLennan explicitly acknowledged his debt to Tylor's "animation hypothesis"—though he followed terminologically in the tradition of De Brosses and Comte by defining totemism as "fetichism" plus certain sociological "peculiarities" (notably, exogamy and matrilineal inheritance). As for Spencer, his ancestor worship was predicated on a "ghost-theory" so similar to Tylor's animism that the two engaged in a rather acrimonious dispute as to its originality and priority.[21]

All of them, in short, may be regarded as members of what later social anthropologists were to call the "English" or "intellectualist" school, which approached religion in terms of individual rationalistic psychology, neglecting its emotional bases, its symbolic and ritual aspects, and its social functions.[22] While such an approach no doubt reflected more general aspects of the English intellectual tradition, it had its basis also in the religious experience of the sociocultural evolutionists. Coming from staunchly Protestant Low Church or Nonconformist backgrounds, they naturally gave priority to belief rather than ritual—which by unstated definition (or the juxtaposition of the modifier "merely") was that which had no present function, though it may once have had a rational utilitarian basis. Belief was not only prior, but critically problematic in their own lives, since they were losing it, along with the emotional security it had once provided. In a culture where religious commitment was still a measure of respectability, this loss threatened them with reprobation and even with guilt—since by savoring too much of the fruit of science they had connived in their own disillusion. It was psychologically essential that this whole process be given some ultimate validation, and this evolutionism provided. If religious belief had never been divinely inspired, but was only a product of the human mind, there could be no guilt involved in replacing it with a better product of the human mind. Thus the loss of faith could be vindicated by the upward march of human reason.

They were aware, to some extent, that as an approach to the understanding of religion their viewpoint was a limited one. As Spencer put it: "while the current creed was slowly losing its hold on me, the sole question seemed to be the truth or untruth of the particular doctrines I had been taught." Later, he had gradually come to realize that there were other questions as well. Similarly, Tylor was aware that ritual had an "expressive and symbolic" aspect as well as a utilitarian one, and that he had failed almost completely to deal with the "religion of vision and passion." He justified himself on the grounds that selectivity was at times necessary for "scientific progress." And "scientific progress" was of course absolutely essential to his worldview. Having helped to undermine belief, it took upon itself the burdens belief had carried. It gave meaning to human life and direction to human history. Human reason, fallen into primitive animism, was slowly redeemed by science, culminating in the evolutionary viewpoint. And as the Creator retreated from the stage, sociocultural evolutionists themselves could take on the creative role, explaining to mankind how all that God had given had in fact been wrought.[23]

Primitive Promiscuity and the Evolution of Marriage

One of the most important of God's gifts to man was holy matrimony—an "honourable estate, instituted of God in paradise, in the time of man's innocency," to be used not "to satisfy men's carnal lusts and appetites, like brute beasts that have no understanding; but reverently, discreetly, advisedly, soberly" for the procreation of children, the avoidance of fornication, and for "mutual society, help, and comfort." Thus was marriage described in the Book of Common Prayer, whose rite was until 1836 the only form of legal marriage in England (save for Jews and Quakers); and we have already seen in the case of McLennan that even advocates of Scottish informality did not in 1860 question the divine institution underlying it. But as McLennan's article on the law of marriage suggests, that institution was by then not quite so stable as the dominant cultural ideology would have had it.[24]

The historiography of marriage, family, sexuality, and gender has burgeoned so explosively in recent years that any attempt to use their early Victorian manifestations as a stable "patriarchal" reference point must give even the nonspecialist historian pause. The declining importance of kinship ties beyond the nuclear core and the increasing emphasis on affective bonds as opposed to economic functions have been traced to 1500; and the "more companionate and egalitarian nuclear family of the eighteenth century" has been contrasted with the heightened patriarchalism characterizing internal family relationships in the two preceding centuries. But the attempt to get behind the stereotypic notions that are our heritage from the first post-Victorian generation has yet to produce a satisfactory synthesis; and even allowing for all the complexities that such a synthesis would encompass, it still seems safe to say that the dominant attitudes in matters relating to gender and sexuality in the early Victorian era were by present standards patriarchal and repressive.[25]

Patriarchal ideals still governed much of British social and political life in the early nineteenth century and, in the context of religious revival and the fear of revolution, had in fact been strengthened in certain areas—including most notably the home. As far as Henry Maine was concerned, legal conceptions governing the family were still in principle as patriarchal as in ancient Rome: he suggested to his readers that "the nature of the ancient Patria Potestas" could be brought "vividly before the mind" merely by "reflecting on the prerogatives attached to the husband by the pure English Common law." Although marriage itself was a form of contract, the relations it defined were those of status, in the sense that various rights and disabilities were imposed on the parties by virtue of their standing in the legal relationship of husband and wife. According to Christian tradition, marriage united two individuals in one person, and English law defined that person as the husband. As Blackstone had put it, a wife's "very being or legal existence" was incorporated into that of her husband. Unless there was specific contractual provision to forestall it, marriage brought her personal and real property under his complete control, and she herself became in effect his chattel in both an economic and a physical sense. Just as she *belonged* to him, so did the children that she bore him—he could, if he chose, deny her all access to them, even to the point of giving them over to his mistress. His powers included the right to vent aggressive impulses on her person for the purpose of legitimate chastisement: he could beat her, so long as he did not do it "in a violent or cruel manner." Nor were these perquisites and penalties much affected by the early movement against inherited privilege—the Reform Act of 1832 in fact gave sanction to female political disabilities that had previously been only customary.[26]

There was of course a difference between legal status and either the cultural ideology or the actual behavior of family relationships. But if early Victorian women were placed on an ideological pedestal, they were in many respects more constrained than they had been in the eighteenth century. A critical indicator was the restriction of the economic activities of middle-class women, as the home became separated from business premises constantly increasing in scale, and growing wealth sustained the withdrawal of women into a purely domestic sphere. With the sharper differentiation of the domain of work and the domain of love, the middle-class family home came to be seen as a refuge from the harsh male world of competitive individualism—in Ruskin's words, "the place of Peace," a sacred "temple of the hearth" sheltered from terror, doubt, division, and all the other anxieties rampant in the "hostile society of the outer world." Outside, it was the role of the husband to "encounter all peril and trial," and he would often be wounded or subdued, and "*always* hardened." Inside, it was the role of the wife to create an oasis of peace and emotional stability—not only to maintain the outward appearance of order and comfort, but to build around every domestic scene "a strong wall of confidence, which no internal suspicion can undermine, no external enemy break through." She was priestess of the Victorian religious cult of hearth and home, and on her shoulders "fell the burden of stemming the amoral and irreligious drift of modern society.''[27]

Fortunately, God and Nature had conspired to fit women for this holy role. Age-old Christian tradition and contemporary physiological assumption both sustained the view of woman as a being destined for a purely domestic sphere. The literal interpretation of Genesis mandated self-sacrificing devotion to human reproduction as punishment for all ill-conceived female pursuit of knowledge. Contemporary medical opinion sustained the view that woman was a being ''little capable of reasoning, feeble and timid,'' and naturally subject to the governance of the stronger and more rational male. But if her ''far more sensitive and susceptible'' mental makeup left her liable to a variety of nervous disorders, the instincts associated with ovulation underwrote the ideal characteristics that her role as priestess of the home demanded: domesticity, passivity, affection, nurturance, and intuitive morality.[28]

There was, however, a worm of ambiguity in the bud of ideal womanhood. Prisoners of their reproductive cycles, women were beings ''both higher and lower, both innocent and animal, pure yet quintessentially sexual.'' A creature so constituted might be expected to be the subject of massive cultural ambivalence. The explicit cultural ideology idealized her ''angel instincts'': she was ''the hope of society,'' on whom depended ''the righting of wrongs, the correcting of sins, and the success of all missions.'' But if the ideal wife and mother was ''so pure-hearted as to be utterly ignorant of and averse to any sensual indulgence,'' the alternate cultural image of the ''fallen woman'' conveys a hint of an underlying preoccupation with the threat of uncontrolled female sexuality. Thus a writer in the *Westminster Review* in 1850 found it fortunate for society that women, ''whose position and education have protected them from exciting causes, constantly pass through life without ever being cognizant of the promptings of the senses.'' Had nature not enacted and education not reinforced this ''kind decision,'' the consequences would be ''frightening.'' To avoid them, a considerable cultural effort was expended to keep the forces of human sexuality under firm control.[29]

The well-known cultural paraphernalia of Victorian sexual repression require no extended reiteration—though it may help to recall that they did not emerge full-blown in 1837. Deeply rooted in aspects of the Christian and specifically the Puritan tradition, more explicitly elaborated during the moral reformation of the middle and upper classes in the Evangelical Revival, the sexual values and attitudes we call Victorian were already established by 1830—quite soon enough to shape the personal character of their most eminent cultural exemplar, Queen Victoria herself. Although there was later elaboration in some areas and loosening in others, the basic structure of taboos was already defined: the renunciation of all sexual activity save the procreative intercourse of Christian marriage; the education of both sexes in chastity and continence; the secrecy and cultivated ignorance surrounding sex; the bowdlerization of literature and euphemistic degradation of language; the general suppression of bodily functions and all the "coarser" aspects of life—in short, the whole repressive pattern of purity, prudery, and propriety that was to condition sexual behavior for decades to come.[30]

The structure did not of course weigh equally on both sexes. The persistence of an older male-oriented ethos of aggressive sexuality may be glimpsed beneath its sublimation in the idea of "muscular Christianity." And for many of the males who did not live up to the cultural ideal, the age-old double standard of possessive patriarchy could justify if not legitimize a certain amount of premarital and even extramarital participation in a sexual underworld populated largely by lower-class women whose social situation, economic circumstances, and subcultural tradition did not sustain the image of angel innocence. It seems likely also that their sisters farther up the social scale were not so constrained as retrospective stereotype would have it. But despite the recent discovery of their role as agents of modernization in the home or as functionaries in the highly formalized "Society" that emerged to maintain the social coherence of the governing elite, there seems little doubt that the sexual and personal freedom of middle- and upper-class women were the focus of a powerful effort of cultural control. If child rearing and adolescent enculturation did not adequately internalize the values of the "perfect wife," then educational deprivation, economic dependence, demographic processes, legal tradition, and myriad forms of informal social control conspired to enforce them. And if their male counterparts did not always maintain dominion over the "mischievous wild beast" within, there seems little doubt that similar if somewhat less oppressive influences enforced upon many of them, too, a high degree of self-control.[31]

By the time John McLennan became interested in the evolution of marriage, however, the Victorian middle-class family was feeling the impact of pressures which, in the context of religious doubt, might well tend to make its divine institution seem somewhat problematic. As rising living standards and levels of aspiration made the paraphernalia of gentility ever more costly, the age of middle-class males at marriage rose significantly between 1840 and 1870. In the context of changing mortality rates and emigration patterns, this meant that a substantial number of "redundant women" were never to achieve the estate for which God had intended them. Within the middle-class family, the increasing economic cost of children, and the disinclination of some women to bear the physical cost, had begun to make its procreative purpose problematic, and by the 1860s one finds the first hints of an actual decline in family size. Already by mid-century, manual labor within the family was becoming increasingly the function of a rapidly increasing class of domestic servants, and the older domestic virtues were beginning to lose their hold. A few middle-class women, chafing against the triviality that filled the leisure hours of the "perfect lady," had begun to question aspects of the patriarchal tradition, and the 1850s saw the emergence of a movement on behalf of certain women's rights. Although the most important early activity centered on questions of education and employment, the issues of married women's property and female suffrage were already in the air. All these matters occasioned considerable public interest, which extended to related issues bearing on human sexuality. Widespread concern with the growing incidence of prostitution led to the passage of a series of Contagious Diseases Acts, which subsequently became the target of feminist attack against the double standard; there was similar public upset at the prevalence of infanticide and abortion.[32]

During the same period, breaches began to appear in the principles of the absolute indissolubility of the marriage vow. From the 1840s on, the question of permitting marriage to a deceased wife's sister was constantly before Parliament; and though it did not pass until 1907, opponents were well aware that what was at issue was whether marriage did indeed create two individuals of one flesh, or whether it was merely a contract terminable by death, and perhaps by other means as well. The 1850s also saw the first general legal recognition of such other means. Complete divorce (as opposed to a form of judicial separation granted in ecclesiastical courts) had hitherto been possible in Britain only by special Act of Parliament; and due to the great cost and the double standard, this meant that it was for practical purposes available only to aristocratic males, at a rate of roughly one a year since 1697. Acting on the earlier report of an investigative commission, in 1857 Parliament finally passed the first Matrimonial Causes Act, which enabled the middle classes generally to seek divorce in secular courts—although only for adultery, which if the wife were plaintiff had to be aggravated by some further abuse such as sodomy or rape. This act marked the beginning of seventy-five years of legislative reformation of the estate which God had instituted—most of it to the end of modifying its traditional patriarchal character.[33]

That these years were also very nearly the exact period of the anthropological debate over the evolutionary priority of "matriarchal" marriage seems scarcely an historical coincidence. Certainly, McLennan's *Primitive Marriage*—the first assertion of that priority in Britain—shows evidences that its argument was conditioned by the contemporary concern with problems of human sexuality and by the processes of social change affecting the institution of human marriage. Although McLennan offered no explicit definition of marriage, and showed a certain relativity in the recognition of its different "species," it is perfectly clear that "marriage proper" meant proper Victorian marriage. Its purpose was to control human (and especially female) sexuality, so that there might be "certainty of male parentage." Its critical diagnostic features were "the appropriation of women to particular men" and the "conception of conjugal fidelity." By the sociocultural evolutionary mode of reasoning from opposites, it followed that the first stage of its evolution was one of "promiscuity in the connection of the sexes"—even to the point of systematic incest. The actual evidence for the existence of such a stage was provided in a single ethnographic footnote, which referred to wife lending among the Chukchee and the Eimauk, the "licentious wantonness" of Patan women, the "incredible immorality" of the Gungorees, "frequent divorces" among the Bedouin, marriages of specified duration among Chinamen, and "similar or worse customs" that McLennan left unspecified. In the absence of any ethnographic evidence for a primitive state of general promiscuity, a mélange of ethnocentrically evaluated departures from the Victorian cultural norm served as proof of its possibility.[34]

That McLennan also had in mind deviant behavior in his own society is clear enough: "Savages are unrestrained by any sense of delicacy from a copartnery in sexual enjoyments; and indeed, in the civilized state, the sin of great cities shows that there are no natural restraints sufficient to hold men back from grosser copartneries." As he explained to Darwin subsequently, "promiscuity" denoted "the general conduct as to sexual matters of men without wives," and "our own time and towns" showed that many such men "just do as they can, and are neither over-nice nor over-scrupulous as to the manner." Savages were even less so: among the Australians, when a man found a desirable woman, "he forces her to accompany him by blows, ending by knocking her down and carrying her off." Indeed, McLennan's argument makes it clear that primitive marriage was in his mind little more than "rape." But if marriage by capture was associated with the aggressive and violent sexuality of the primitive male, the character of primitive marriage was also related to the laxity of female savage morals. Women "among rude tribes" were "usually depraved," and it was by means of polyandry, not polygyny, that humanity advanced from the originally promiscuous state. Here again, various aspects of the process reflect contemporary concerns. The "grosser copartneries" of Victorian prostitution were an obvious model for primitive polyandrous marriage. The latter, significantly, was the result of demographic imbalance, though among savages it was men who were made "redundant" by female infanticide—a phenomenon which McLennan elsewhere made clear also had its modern urban analogue. By this process of inversion, even marriage with the deceased wife's sister found a place in McLennan's scheme: the levirate, or marriage to the elder brother's widow, became critical evidence for the former existence of polyandry and the "successive stages" of its decay.[35]

The evolution upward from promiscuity and polyandry was essentially the evolution of the "ideas" of kinship, fatherhood, wifehood, and propriety. In good empiricist fashion, McLennan argued that these ideas were not "innate," but had "*grown* like all other ideas related to matters primarily cognizable only by the senses." But they were also clearly subject to a teleology reflecting their outcome in the Victorian family. Although blood ties through females were "obvious and indisputable" even in a state of primitive promiscuity, it was only when men *perceived* what women *experienced* in childbirth that, following these ties through their mothers and other "females of the same blood," they arrived at "a system of kinship through females." Once female infanticide, wife capture, and exogamy had combined to produce the system of polyandry—and particularly the higher Tibetan form in which a group of brothers cohabited with one woman—the basis then existed for the idea of fatherhood, since paternity, although collective, was within these limits certain. From there the power and the example of chiefs monopolizing women to themselves, the "influence of ideas of propriety, which grew up under the improved marriage system," and, above all, the "growth of property" led gradually but inexorably to a full system of agnatic kinship. For, as McLennan suggested elsewhere, once the marriage system allowed a man to be certain of his parenthood of specific children, "nothing but the effect of custom" would prevent the system of female kinship from dying out: "Born to him in his own house; by blood and circumstance the nearest and dearest to him; all his natural feelings would prompt him to leave them his wealth."[36]

On the one hand, then, McLennan had written an account of the rise of the idea of fatherhood; on the other, he had written an historical treatise on the "position of women." If they had lost the sexual freedom of "the early world," and the power that sometimes accompanied polyandry, they were protected by the progress of "refinement" from the violent sexuality of the primitive male. Polyandry—the earliest form of the marriage "contract"—had been a kind of training ground for men, giving them both the "idea of a wife" and "obligations in matters of sex." The relationships thus established were the ultimate basis for the Roman concept of the permanent consortship of one man and one woman, "with interests the same in all things civil and religious"—the idea which, "despite all woman's rights movements to the contrary," was "that destined to prevail in the world."[37]

McLennan's views of the evolution of human marriage were controversial even among evolutionists. Lubbock regarded polyandry as an "exceptional phenomenon" rather than a "necessary stage in human development," and preferred to see exogamy and infanticide as consequences of marriage by capture, rather than vice versa. Spencer, although drawing heavily on elements of McLennan's argument, found "reason for doubting [the] theory taken as a whole," and preferred to see endogamy and exogamy as alternative and coexisting adaptations to the perpetual hostility of primitive life—a captured wife becoming a "badge of social distinction" among the more aggressive tribes, while the weaker ones were of necessity endogamous. Tylor, who was inclined to leave questions of kinship and marriage to "legal minds used to the problem of contingent remainders," nonetheless indicated that considerable discussion with his friend McLennan had not enabled him to see the levirate as evidence of the prior existence of polyandry.[38]

At a more general level, however, McLennan's conception of the development of human marriage was in fact accepted by the major sociocultural evolutionists. They all tended to view marriage in terms of the control of human sexuality, and took for granted some early condition of primitive promiscuity. They all accepted the general priority of matrilineal forms—although they also incorporated Maine's patriarchy as a later evolutionary phase. And of course they all saw the evolutionary process culminating in a monogamous family resembling that of mid-Victorian Britain. Because he was the least involved in the elaboration of this orthodoxy, Tylor is a good measure of its acceptance. Reviewing the debate between Maine and McLennan in 1885, he felt that "converging research" had established the "early general prevalence of the system of kinship on the female side, which seems so strange to the modern European, with his long-inherited patriarchal tendencies." And in an earlier article, he had suggested that it was admitted "by all students" that female kinship was itself evidence of marriage having previously been "in a low and promiscuous state."[39]

But as Tylor's correspondence with Lorimer Fison would later reveal, primitive promiscuity proved itself a will-o'-the-wisp for late Victorian ethnographers: try as he might, Fison could not find the actual ethnographic exemplar toward which those deviations from monogamy in McLennan's footnote seemed to lead. As early as 1891, Edward Westermarck's *History of Human Marriage* (which rejected the notion of primitive promiscuity and the priority of matrifocal marriage) indicated that Tylor's consensus of "all students" was beginning to break down, and in 1896 Tylor himself noted that a "reaction" against the theory of "primitive matrimonial anarchy" was likely to cause it "to pass away altogether."[40]

Without attempting to trace the process here, we may say that by the 1920s, the priority of matrilineal kinship was no longer taken for granted in mainstream anthropology, and the problem of primitive promiscuity had been replaced by the universality of the incest taboo.

"Matriarchy," which had rarely in fact been argued as a systematic social organizational alternative to "patriarchy," had been returned to the mythological realm of the Amazons—from which Johann Bachofen, its main proponent, had derived it in the first place. Although a breath of life has been infused into the matriarchy idea by some recent feminist writings, their influence in anthropology has been reflected rather in the concern with the impact of European expansion on gender relationships. From the perspective of modern anthropological theory, the nineteenth-century discussion has long seemed quaintly "dated"; from the viewpoint of a culturally contextualized historiography of anthropology, the grounding of this discussion in ulterior Victorian assumption seems undeniable.[41]

It has been suggested by one feminist historian that the "matriarchal" orthodoxy was a conscious ideological construction, an attempt to create a new evolutionary foundation for traditional male dominance once Maine's effort "to prove the timeless and inherent nature of patriarchal authority" had run aground on methodological difficulties. No longer the original form of the family, patriarchy became instead the goal of evolution; and lest modern women should take Bachofen's "matriarchy" as a primitivist golden age, later British evolutionists were at pains to show that women had at no time wielded domestic and political power. On the contrary, the pedestal of Victorian domesticity was the high point of evolutionary progress. As Herbert Spencer put it, "the moral progress of mankind" was in no way more clearly shown than by contrasting the "position of women" among savage and civilized nations: "At the one extreme a treatment of them cruel to the utmost degree bearable; and at the other extreme a treatment which, in some directions, gives them precedence over men." In this context, Spencer in fact later justified the limitation of women's political rights on evolutionary grounds: because the vital needs of reproduction arrested their individual mental evolution at an earlier age, and their characteristic mental traits (notably intuition and dissimulation) were those adapted to "dealing with infantine life" and relating to the stronger male, their present hereditary mental makeup would incline them to support authoritarian government and incautious (i.e., maternal) social policy.[42]

The interpretation of social evolutionism as a conscious defense of the marital status quo, however, does not do justice to the complexities of intellectual connection, of ideological significance, and of ulterior motive. On the first point, suffice it to say that Bachofen's *Mutterrecht*, which was published in 1861, was neither a response to Maine nor a stimulus to McLennan, who did not read it until 1866. On the second, one notes that far from showing patriarchal authority "timeless," Maine in fact saw the increasing personal freedom, proprietary independence, and political privilege of women as a "law of development" that had almost "finally and completely assimilated the legal position of women to the legal position of men"; and his work was circulated (with his permission) by feminist groups. Along similar lines, one might argue that if, as Tylor suggested, *Primitive Marriage* cost McLennan half of his law business, it seems unlikely that it was because it was perceived as reaffirming on evolutionary grounds the patriarchal basis of marriage; rather, it must have been because its evolutionary rejection of divinely instituted patriarchalism was felt to be subversive of existing domestic order.[43]

In speculating about ulterior motives, it would be a mistake simply to rely on later statements such as McLennan's comment about women's rights movements or Spencer's reference to the "screaming sisterhood." Spencer's chapter on "The Rights of Women" in *Social Statics* had been so radical that Harriet Taylor sought to reprint it in some feminist essays she brought out in 1867. Spencer, however, did not agree; nor was he willing to support Mill's parliamentary petition for women's suffrage in the same year. Despite Spencer's protestations to the contrary, his later conservatism on this (and several other) issues would seem to represent a real shift of position, and not simply the revalorizing transformation of surrounding historical context that has been convincingly argued in relation to his early radicalism in general. Perhaps in the aftermath of that lost law practice, such a shift may also have taken place in McLennan, whose earlier work shows evidence of a more positive attitude toward "the equality of rights" between the sexes.[44]

But granting that they may have become more conservative in later years on this and other issues, to see the social evolutionists as seeking to preserve "the essence of patriarchal theory" by eliminating its "archaic harshness" seems an oversimplifying interpretation of their views on "the position of women." Like many contemporary feminists, the social evolutionists accepted the culturally pervasive view of women's nature—which was in fact given a kind of scientific legitimation by Spencer. And no doubt their somewhat varied domestic lives reflected prevailing norms—perhaps especially in the case of Lubbock, who upon his father's death maintained the "traditional patriarchal character" of the family house, even assuming a "quasi-paternal position" in relation to his younger brothers. But insofar as the evolutionists incorporated into their thinking Maine's progress from status to contract, they placed modern marriage in the context of a general movement that was eroding patriarchal authority in all areas. And despite its obvious basis in ethnocentric assumption, the use of the modern status of women as a measure of progress in human marriage reflected values that in cultural context were both humane and antipatriarchal. What was being proclaimed, after all, was the replacement of relationships based upon "violence and unwilling submission''—for which Grey's Australians were taken as the archetype—by those of ''mutual affection'' and ''consent.'' If Lubbock echoed the prevailing domestic orthodoxy in praising ''the Angels who make a Heaven of home,'' it was in the process of condemning the ancient Greeks for treating women ''rather as housekeepers and playthings.'' And though later he still found ''traces'' of the idea of forceful enslavement in contemporary marriage law, he felt these were ''curiously inconsistent with all our avowed ideas,'' maintaining that, in practice, English domestic relations were ''more advanced.''[45]

Although far from sharing Mill's radicalism, the classical evolutionists, when viewed in the context of contemporary attitudes, were far from standing in the rearguard on issues relating to gender and marriage.[46] Insofar as they contributed to undermining the notion of divinely instituted patriarchalism, the immediate contemporary cultural impact of their writings on the origins of marriage might well be regarded as revolutionary; and if their account of its subsequent evolutionary development could be read as reaffirming patriarchal relations, that reaffirmation had, to say the least, a certain contingency, given the generally antipatriarchal character of recent evolutionary processes.

It is true, however, that once past those early radical statements of Herbert Spencer, there is nothing in social evolutionist writings on marriage as systematically radical in its implications as Tylor's quiet subversion of the principles of Christian belief. Even more than in the realm of religion, their atitudes and motives in relation to gender and sexuality were marked by ambiguity and ambivalence. For if the pursuit of human reason in the evolution of religion had threatening implications for psychological security and social order, this was even more the case in the realm of sexuality, where the evolutionary dynamism was not that of reason unbound but of instinct repressed. But to see that problem simply as a matter of controlling the ''position of women'' narrows its significance unnecessarily. In the realm of sexuality, the forces that had to be controlled existed also within the human male. Although Maine's methodology was pre-evolutionary, on this point he may stand as illustrative. According to Maine, the reason the position of women was a measure of civilization was because it was also a measure of ''self-control''—''that same control which produces wealth by subduing the natural appetite of living for the present, and which fructifies in art and learning through subordinating a material and immediate to a remote, intangible, and spiritual enjoyment.'' Civilization was only possible on the basis of curbing ''the strongest, because the primary, impulses of human nature.'' If these impulses were unspecified, Maine's use of women as his touchstone of control makes clear what Victorian reserve might otherwise obscure: they were the instinctive forces of human sexuality. Although the social evolutionists rejected Maine's picture of man's primeval social state, they shared with him an appreciation of the repression involved in its transcendance.[47]

Savagery and Civilization in Early Victorian England

To bring together the philosopher savage of religious evolution and the bestial savage of sexual evolution it may help to look at the cultural experience of the evolutionary generation from a somewhat broader perspective. For just as evolutionary writings on religion and marriage reflect specific aspects of that experience, so did discussion of the overall evolution of human culture reflect the broader processes of sociocultural change transforming English society in the early nineteenth century.

Let us begin with a commonplace of Victorian historiography: British intellectuals born in the early decades of the nineteenth century saw the world of their adulthood as a product of unprecedentedly rapid and far-reaching historical change—so rapid and far-reaching that the world into which their fathers had been born seemed a radically different one. There was a strong tendency to telescope change into polarity: "it was only yesterday, but what a gulf between now and then." "Now," as Thackeray put it, was the era of railroads; "then" was the era of "stage coaches, . . . riding horses, pack-horses, highway-men, knights in armour, Norman invaders, Roman legions, Druids, Ancient Britons painted blue, and so forth" —two millennia of life within the British isles thus compressed into a single image of the "old world" before the "age of steam."[48]

As their intellectual heirs, we share this polarizing tendency: back before the Industrial Revolution, or the "great transformation," lies "traditional society," or "the world we have lost." Many of the social theoretical tropes that still shape our understanding of the emergence of the modern world are in fact part of this inheritance—despite the fact that several major episodes of critical reexamination have long since called into question their simple polarity. And yet granting that in the historical world polarity is never simple, it may nevertheless be heuristically fruitful to sketch in some of the characteristics of Thackeray's "then" before the age of steam.[49]

To begin with, we must accept its temporal indeterminacy. The disappearance of "the world we have lost" was both a revolution and an encroachment. Although the transformation of traditional England had begun early in the eighteenth century, the generation born in the 1820s and 1830s would still have been able to experience many features of the older world autobiographically as well as historically. At the same time, because they came of age at a late stage in the process, when the more traumatic accompaniments had begun to recede into the background, the evolutionary generation experienced the change not so much as a wrenching asunder but as a transformation accomplished.[50]

Whether located in the memories of their fathers or in the further reaches of contemporary Britain, the "old world" was an overwhelmingly rural one. When the first British census was taken in 1801, two-thirds of the population still lived in the countryside, and as late as 1851, when the Industrial Revolution was accomplished, agriculture was still the largest sector of the work force. As a rural world, the "old world" was closely tied to the processes and rhythms of nature. Despite the quickening pace of technological progress, mankind's power over nature was still for the most part manifest directly through the activity of the human hand, wielding tools of a relatively simple character. The "agrarian revolution" of the late eighteenth century was more a matter of the enclosure of open fields and the introduction of new crops and farming practices than of agricultural machinery, and agricultural work remained mostly manual and very labor-intensive until at least 1850.[51]

Because movement over land was restricted by the power of the human or animal leg, the "old world" was a very slow-moving and localized one. While there was in fact considerable migration, and the rural hinterland was linked through a network of minor market centers to the vast metropolis which was the arena of national public life, most inhabitants spent their lives in face-to-face village communities the size of those characteristically studied by modern anthropologists. "Everything physical was on the human scale," and "everything temporal was tied to the human life-span"—which, for the large bulk of the population, was short enough to make mortality an ever present preoccupation, and the continuity of social structure somewhat problematic. As the one large-scale institution regularly impinging on the day-to-day lives of a population of literal Christian believers, the Church played a critical role in maintaining authority relations in a society where "stable poverty" was the resigned expectation of most.[52]

The primary threads of the social tapestry, however, were familial: people rarely found themselves in groups larger than family groups, which were the basic units of economic activity and social structure. The sphere of individual agency was limited by family status, and for most people was subsumed in that of someone to whom they stood in a relation of dependence. In a world of great disparities in wealth and power, the most important families (enlarged by earlier marriage and the presence of dependent servants) were those of the country gentry, whose houses were the visible manifestation of the social continuity provided by the inheritance of landed property.[53]

Due to the larger size of landed families and the principle of primogeniture, the not inconsiderable social mobility was more likely to be downward than up. The finely graded hierarchy of status was broken by one major horizontal discontinuity, above which stood the "gentleman"—who in a society with few labor-saving devices was able to delegate to others the necessity of working with his hands. Insofar as class may be said to have existed, it was the single class of those whose wealth, status, literacy, and family position enabled them to participate actively in the national political sphere—a group dominated by the titled aristocracy. Below that ruling class, the major social linkages were vertical rather than horizontal, and the patriarchal principles governing intrafamilial life were extended by analogy upward toward the top. Power flowed downward and outward through family connections and ties of patronage until it touched ground among the illiterate laboring poor in each local village community at the base of the multiplex social pyramid; and from the bottom, deference flowed back up.[54]

Alternatively, deference may be viewed as part of a balanced reciprocity of customary relationships going back to the medieval period, in which the social cohesion of village communities was reinforced at critical moments in the calendric cycle by raucous rituals of status reversal and exactions of largesse by bands of laboring poor perambulating the parish. Buttressed by a rich fund of oral tradition, embellished by drink, licentiousness, rough play, and blood sports, the "vulgar and provincial customs, ceremonies, and superstitions" of village community culture filled the pages of Brand's *Popular Antiquities*, providing a continuing "primitive" base point for the "civilizing" processes that were transforming them.[55]

Although the patriarchal principles of this Filmerian rural world continued to be strongly manifest even into the nineteenth century, they had long since been countered—and corrupted—by the Lockean forces of possessive individualism. Even in its heyday, the patriarchal "world we have lost" in Britain differed in important respects from preindustrial society in other areas of Europe, where feudalism was still a living reality and status was more rigidly determined by birth. Although the word "peasant" continued to be used, the feudal category it designated had by the eighteenth century largely been "replaced by the new capitalist relationships of landlord, tenant, and laborer"—save at the Celtic fringe, where the rural population was "half immersed in tribalism, dominated by near-feudal or alien landlords." The "middle ranks" of the English social hierarchy were larger in number, had greater freedom of occupational choice, were generally better off, and enjoyed some possibility of transforming the fruits of their labor into higher status. Just as there was no English national peasant costume, there was no English word for "bourgeoisie," perhaps because the possibility existed for the richer tradesmen of the towns to transform themselves into country gentlemen through the acquisition of land. And at the top of the hierarchy, among the single class privileged to participate in the national public sphere where Lockean political principles were given practical manifestation after the Glorious Revolution, Lockean economic principles were ever more powerfully active: favored by the "absolute, categorical, unconditional" concept of property, seeking "their own profit by all the means which their special position had made available to them," the owners of landed property created the "climate and conditions in which a spontaneous industrial revolution could take place.[56]

Like Buckle, many Victorians looked back on that revolution as a transformation of the relation of mankind to nature. Since the mid-eighteenth century, the ease and speed of movement through nature had been greatly facilitated by the improvement of roads, the construction of canals, and the advent of the railroad. The efficacy of human labor in reworking natural products into human ones had been vastly multiplied by the steam engine and the new machinery it powered, with consequent changes in the locus, organization, and scale of productive activity: the domestic system, in which the craftsman's household members were the unit of production, had gradually given way to the factory system, with its "scores or even hundreds of highly specialized operatives and £40–£50 of fixed capital per worker." In this context, the numbers and distribution of human beings within the natural world had changed dramatically. The first censuses made it clear that, contrary to the fears of earlier depopulation theorists, the population of England and Wales was rising rapidly; and although the early stages of the Industrial Revolution took place in the countryside, each successive census confirmed the rapid increase in the number and size of towns and cities, and in their relative proportion of the total population.[57]

Just as the transformation involved a redistribution of population in space, so also did it involve a redefinition of the traditional social structure and the emergence of self-conscious class groupings characterized by "horizontal solidarity" and "vertical antagonism." The process has been described both as an "abdication on the part of the governors" and an "alienation of the middle and lower ranks." Committed to the pursuit of profit, the landed elite were less willing "to pay the price of paternal protection in return for filial obedience." In the aftermath of the anti-Jacobin reaction of the 1790s, they passed Combination Acts designed to render organized popular resistance ineffective, and in the repressive atmosphere of the wars of the French Revolution proceeded to the systematic dismantling of centuries-old legislation protecting wages and conditions of work. Frustrated in efforts to sustain the traditional paternal system or to resist by force the new machinery of industrialization, workers in rapidly transforming traditional crafts turned in the early postwar period to massive radical agitation for parliamentary reform. Provoked by the wartime restrictions on trade and the passage of Corn Laws which protected the rents of landowners at their expense, and responding to the economic and political writings of Benthamite philosophical radicals, commercial and entrepreneurial groups also moved toward collective assertiveness in the cause of parliamentary reform. Although the shift from the plural to the singular in "the language of class" had only begun, the heightened sense of opposition between the middle and the working classes was confirmed by the rejection of manhood for propertied suffrage in the resolution of the Reform Bill crisis of 1831–1832. The gentry long continued to dominate the political life of the countryside, and the major positions of national power continued through most of the Victorian era to be held by members of the aristocracy. But the repeal of the Corn Laws in 1848 symbolized the fact that aristocratic rule was now, so far as the middle classes were concerned, consensual rather than prescriptive, and that the entrepreneurial ideal of free trade and individual competition had become the dominant cultural ideology.[58]

The birth of class did not signal the end of hierarchy, of paternalist ideology, or of the validation of social status by traditional criteria. But the efficacy of the patriarchal principles of patronage and dependency was greatly attenuated, and the sphere of effective independent agency, both individual and collective, was considerably broadened—although to varying degrees for different groups. Serving both as the midwife and the governess of class, sectarian religion simultaneously reinforced and brought under control the leveling ideology of the age of democratic revolution. Undermining the dependency which in traditional society had been buttressed by the established church, affirming the possibility of universal salvation by the assertion of free individual will and diligent good works, Methodism provided models of effective individual agency and class organization—at the same time that it contributed to industrial discipline and helped to restrain class violence. If by 1850 the revolutionary impulse among the working class had been defused, the spirit of independent agency (domesticated by respectability) remained strong among the labor aristocracy of the craft unions. And for the middle-class groups who reaped the economic benefits of laissez-faire and the political benefits of parliamentary reform, the sphere of effective independent agency, individual as well as collective, was greatly enlarged. By the energetic exercise of their own abilities, enough of them were able to climb the ladder of social status to give substantial reality to the mythology of the "self-made man"—and to enable some among their offspring to join an emerging "intellectual aristocracy."[59]

However, for those who remained at the bottom, and who could not yet be reassured by the retrospective optimism of many modern historiographers, the actual experience of economic and social transformation was often very grim indeed. Artisans or domestic workers who languished in declining crafts, and whose wives and children were forced to adjust to the mechanical work rhythms of the factory—from which traditional interspersing elements of play had been eliminated—experienced the change rather as a loss than as a gain of independence. Villagers whose traditional right to glean had been preempted by the landlord's pigs, or whose common fields were included in the thousands of Enclosure Acts passed between 1760 and 1820—and some of whom participated in the incendiarism of the Swing Riots in 1831—did not see themselves as the beneficiaries of "agricultural improvement." Laboring poor excluded from the benefits of outdoor relief or paupers who deliberately committed offences that caused their removal from the workhouse to the gaol may have questioned the ideology of "independence" that motivated the Poor Law reform of 1834. Poverty-stricken immigrants from the English or Irish countryside who packed the hellish slums of the new industrial towns—many of whom had lost the consolations of religion without enjoying the spiritual uplift of radical working-class culture—might well have questioned the benefits of their liberation from the traditional ties of family and community.[60]

From the perspective of contemporary middle-class observers, the primitivism at the bottom of the social scale now had a dual character. On the one hand, there was the rural primitivism of the preindustrial world, marginalized in England and still flourishing on the Celtic fringe; on the other, there was the urban primitivism of preindustrial London, metastasizing in every industrial town and city. The first, which was to be the subject matter of the science of folklore, could still be looked at through an elegiac filter of "soft" primitivism, the more so as the blood sports of the villages were outlawed and the raucous visitations of Plough Monday were transformed into Plough Sunday services. But there were no traces of "Merrie England" to be found in the new city slums, which provided the subject matter of the urban reformer's science of social statistics. They remained, even in the process of reformation, a disturbing and alien phenomenon—so far removed from the amenities and the morality of civilized life that many observers, including Friedrich Engels and Henry Mayhew, were impelled to use racial analogies to capture the sense of difference. Thus for Engels the working classes were "a race apart"—physically degenerate, robbed of all humanity, reduced morally and intellectually to near bestial condition, not only by economic exploitation, but by competition and association with the coarse, volatile, dissolute, drunken, improvident Irish, who slept with their pigs in the stinking slums of Manchester. And for Mayhew, the street folk of London were a "nomad race" without "the least faculty of prevision," flouting the middle-class ethic of sexual restraint and hard work, reduced to the terrible alternation of "starvation and surfeit."[61]

The survival of such "savagery" in a world of unprecedented progress was one of the more disturbing of the cultural paradoxes experienced by thoughtful members of the Victorian middle classes. For the successful middle-class entrepreneur, contemplating the purchase of a landed estate that might in time validate his own rise in terms of the traditional status system, the paradox might be dissolved in self-congratulatory hypocrisy. But judged in terms of the more radical attitudes of his own upward striving youth, or from the perspective of offspring who felt freer to question some of the motivating values of a world they had not made, the paradox was not so easily resolved.[62] Retrospectively, however, we may suggest several ways by which its gnawing force was diminished: by attempts to improve the condition of those at the bottom of the social scale; by efforts to control the threat that it presented to the emerging industrial order; by attempts to keep the reality or the knowledge of it at a distance; and by efforts to interpret it in ways that gave it a less threatening meaning.

By the time of the Crystal Palace, a number of reform initiatives had begun to ameliorate some of the more appalling aspects of the transformation. Some of these—like the temperance movement—sought the moral reformation of the individuals whose lives had been wrenched by social change. Others sought by legislation or administrative measures to improve the conditions in which their lives must now be led. Thus a series of Factory Acts shortened the working hours first of children, then of women, and finally of all workers to sixty hours; a series of acts relating to public health began to cope with some of the more blatant problems of urban sanitation. But if the efforts of temperance advocates and factory and sanitation reformers may be seen as early assertions of the necessity of governmental intervention in the processes of laissez-faire, they probably had less ameliorative effect upon the living conditions of the lower classes than the threefold rise in real wages between 1800 and 1850.[63]

Early Victorians were perhaps more successful in policing the lower classes than in uplifting them. Although the new social order had been shaken by episodes of actual or threatened collective violence in the first decades after the Napoleonic wars, the passing of this dangerous phase of transformation was symbolized by the peaceful outcome of the last great Chartist demonstration of April 1848, when its leaders yielded to the warnings of the London Metropolitan Police that the procession should not march across the bridge from Kensington Common to Westminster. Since the formation of the London "peelers" in 1829, the new police had been extended to many provincial towns after the Municipal Reform Act of 1835; in the same period rural property and person were also made more secure with the establishment of professional constabularies, which in 1856 were made compulsory throughout the nation. By that time, social order seemed assured, and even the delinquents who sallied forth from urban "rookeries" were "becoming less blatant in their approach to those from whom they begged and stole." Walking the streets with less fear of molestation, middle-class citizens could also congratulate themselves that the treatment of criminals was more humane: gaols had been reformed (though prisoners inside them still walked treadmills); capital crimes had been reduced from 200 in 1808 to only 4 in 1861, and after 1868 even these were no longer made the occasion of public "hanging matches."[64]

But if a great distance had been traveled since 1780 toward "the organization of a civilized social life," the distance between the upper and the lower reaches of the social scale had not narrowed but widened in that period. Despite the increase in real wages, the Industrial Revolution had in fact made the distribution of income among different social groups considerably more unequal. And there are indications that the distance of day-to-day social relations had also increased as the vertical links of patriarchal hierarchy were replaced by the horizontal lines of class. The day had passed when a lady shared a bed with her servant at an inn, and would soon also pass when agricultural laborers joined the well-to-do farmer's table for Harvest Home. The separation of the growing numbers of domestic servants from the classes that employed them was one of the governing principles of the domestic architecture of the Victorian upper classes. Similarly, the segregation of social classes into different urban and suburban residential areas helped to keep the slum world out of sight and mind—so that the facts of Chadwick's Sanitary Report of 1842 could seem as strange to persons of the wealthier classes "as if they related to foreigners or the natives of an unknown country."[65]

Insofar as it could not be reformed, controlled, or distanced, the savage remnant of the Industrial Revolution could be reinterpreted. Accepting the Malthusian premise that population growth was antithetical to civilization, it was possible to reread the processes of economic change, social transformation, and material progress in moral terms and thereby not only to ease the burden of upper-class responsibility, but to shift it to the lower orders themselves. Nor was such ideologizing accomplished without reference to historical reality, as it has been subsequently interpreted: the role of demographic factors in the Industrial Revolution, and the fact that it was accompanied by a revolution in morals, are accepted commonplaces of modern British historiography.[66]

In 1780, the moral model of the socially dominant group was the aristocratic ideal of the gentleman. Free by birth, blood, and inherited landed wealth from the necessity of manual labor or contamination by the money-grubbing pursuits of commerce, free also to enjoy the private vices of gambling, drunkenness, and sexual indulgence, the gentleman was governed by a paramilitary code of honor which required any insult from another gentleman to be defended in a duel—which half the prime ministers of the transitional period actually fought at some point in their lives. The aristocratic ideal of the gentleman was not (nor was it intended to be) shared by all social ranks; the moral revolution was an attempt to generalize to the rest of society a transmuted version of the ascetic puritan work ethic that had previously been dominant only among sectors of the middle ranks. Evangelicals undermined the aristocratic ideal from within, convincing many among the upper ranks that the defense of property was better accomplished by moral regeneration than by force; dissenters and secular evangelical utilitarians "worked together to reinforce the moral superiority of the middle class and to impose its puritanism on the rest of society."[67]

By 1850, the attempt had been largely successful. Although the slaughter of game still remained a major preoccupation of the landed gentry, and the 1830s and 1840s had seen a revival of chivalric forms, dueling had been banished from the repertoire of gentlemanly behavior. It was now asserted by such middle-class spokesmen as Samuel Smiles that the "true gentleman," like the "self-made man," would be "honest, truthful, upright, polite, temperate, courageous, self-respecting, and self-helping." In fact, of course, the slowly changing criteria of gentlemanly status had not simply collapsed into those of respectability; nevertheless, it was by this time generally accepted that gentlemen, like every other social group, ought to conform to the norms of respectable behavior.[68]

Although "continent" was not among the adjectives of Smiles' enumeration, it has been suggestively argued that by the time he wrote the virtue of sexual continence had been integrated into the normative standard of respectable behavior—not simply as one more in a list, but in a way that drew together the realms of sexuality and political economy. In Victorian economic ideology, Homo Economicus was governed by opposing motives: the desire for wealth, comfort, and status on the one hand, and the aversion for labor and the desire for indulgence on the other. Save for those with inherited wealth, the two sets of motives were in conflict: in the respectable middle-class man, the tension was resolved by a prudent self-denying industry in the present in the hope of future reward; among those sectors of the lower classes who had not yet achieved respectability, the tension was resolved in favor of present self-indulgence. Similarly, in Victorian sexual ideology, Homo Sexualis was in tension between the motives of immediate gratification and sublimation of the sexual appetite; and here, too, there was a respectable middle-class and a lower-class resolution. The economic and the sexual models were in fact linked in contemporary physiological theory, which saw the amount of vital force as fixed: if one "spent" it on sex, one could not direct it to work. Nor were these virtues natural; rather, they were the result of rigorous self-discipline of opposing instinctual tendencies, which alone enable men (in John Stuart Mill's words) to sacrifice "a present desire to a distant object." Large groups of humankind—among whom Mill instanced both savages and "nearly the whole of the poorer classes," as well as by implication the unreformed aristocracy—were by defective training and life experience unable to exercise such foresight.[69]

The respectable middle-class ideology of economic sexuality did not of course emerge full-blown in the 1850s. Well before Victoria assumed the throne, Victorian sexual morality was already a powerful cultural force; and the close relationship of sexuality and economics was a central assumption of Malthus' *Principle of Population*, the book which more than any other defined the terms of social discourse in Britain for the next half century. It was Malthus' principle of population that made political economy the "dismal science"; and it was a central principle of that science that the pressure of excessive numbers against the means of subsistence was the major cause of poverty. But if Malthusianism "succeeded in de-moralizing political economy," it did not thus "demoralize" the issue of poverty. As a social phenomenon poverty might be viewed as a corollary of the "laws of nature," but individuals among the poor could always choose to exercise "moral restraint"; and if they did not, society could endeavor to enforce it upon them—as the reformed Poor Law of 1834 attempted to do. Those who did not submit sexual impulse to the governance of utilitarian economic motive could thus be seen as choosing to be poor; and even those who, like Mill, would not have made that judgment, nevertheless saw the poor as possessed of a different (and deficient) moral character. Like Lubbock's savages, they were slaves to their own wants and passions; constantly staring hunger in the face, because, in the word of Samuel Smiles, they could not sacrifice "present gratification for a future good."[70]

But if the "lesson of self-denial" was "one of the last that is learnt," the spread of respectability among the working classes held forth the prospect that it might yet be learned—and the paradox of surviving savagery thus eventually eliminated. In the meantime, those who had learned the lesson might enjoy the rewards of rational self-improvement, social mobility, and unprecedented progress in civilization—which were, in cumulative effect, ideological equivalents. Just as self-denial, industry, continence, and foresight were the means of individual upward mobility, so were they the mechanisms of social progress. Civilization—as Herbert Spencer's *Social Statics* made abundantly clear—was self-improvement writ large.[71]

Although the lives of the major figures of sociocultural evolutionism reflect the social processes of the Industrial Revolution in rather different ways, the theme of middle-class social mobility is a recurrent one. McLennan's career was one of hard fought and frustrated upward striving. Asking in 1870 for Lubbock's help in obtaining a position Gladstone had at his disposal as Prime Minister, McLennan noted that he had "never had a farthing" he had not earned "by my own exertions in the open struggle for life"—contrasting his own active efforts on behalf of the Liberal party with the "family influence" of his rival, who had an inherited annual income of £600. Although Lubbock at that time was himself already a baronet, the theme of social mobility, transposed into a higher key, is also evident in his career. Assuring Lubbock that the family were not of cockney origin—as his parliamentary opponent had apparently maintained in 1865—his banker father suggested, somewhat uncertainly, that they belonged "to the race of tenant farmers; or yeoman, or a mixture of both." Lubbock eventually reduced this ancestral indeterminacy by tracing his lineage back four centuries to Robert Lobuk, and ended his life as Lord Avebury, proud possessor of a castle in Kent. So also Tylor: as the son of an industrial entrepreneur, he was able to pursue his intellectual interests living as a country gentleman in Somerset; he ended his career with a knighthood, and a personal professorship at Oxford, which his early Quaker beliefs would have barred him from entering.[72]

Although the connections are less striking than in the case of the specific institutions of marriage and religion, the writings of these three men also reflect at critical points the experience of social change symbolized by their own social mobility. Thus the last sentence of Lubbock's *Origin of Civilisation* looked forward to a day when "the blessings of civilisation" would be extended not only to savages in other countries, but to "countrymen of our own living, in our very midst, a life worse than that of a savage." But the connection exists at a deeper level than perorational exhortation. That Tylor had in mind the phenomenon of social mobility in thinking about human progress is evident from a fragment preserved in his papers. Everyone knew "how families go up and down in the world": "A family may now be poor and ignorant either because the parents were once still lower and have not risen much, or on the contrary because the parents may once have been better off, and the household may have fallen through misfortune or ill-conduct." Although "the general result is a good deal the same in both cases, on looking closely one may make out what is the true history, for the appearance and ways of people who have fought their way up in the world do not show the symptoms of former prosperity. . . ." Perhaps because in this instance "survivals" might have documented decline as well as progress, the passage broke off; more generally in Tylor's work, that concept resonates to the experience of progressive social change. Although survivals like "the practice of salutation upon sneezing" might exist in the highest levels of civilized society, it was among the lower orders, especially in the countryside, that they are more likely to be found—as the virtual synonymity of "survival" and "superstition" suggests.[73]

The heuristic value of contemporary social experience was most systematically stated, however, by McLennan, who suggested that "in a progressive community all the sections do not advance *pari passu*, so that we may see in the lower some of the phases through which the more advanced have passed." Echoing Mayhew, he suggested that in London, the very center of "arts, sciences and intelligence," one could find "predatory bands, leading the life of the lowest nomads," as well as illustrations of every phase of the progress of the family, "from the lowest incestuous combinations of kindred to the highest group based on solemn monogamous marriage." And what was true of the large towns generally was still truer of the nation at large. In Cornwall and Devonshire "we discover remains of pre-Christian customs and superstitions, as well as modes of life of striking rudeness"; in the Highlands of Scotland "tribal and clan ties were till very lately in full force." Far from being merely folkloric curiosities, such "inequalities of development" were essential aids "in the investigation of the unrecorded history of a people." And because "inequalities of development" would be "indefinitely more numerous and striking for the totality of races of men than for any one of them," it was possible that "every conceivable phase of progress can be studied as somewhere observed and recorded," and that these could be shown "to shade into one another by gentle gradations," so that "a clear and decided outline of the progress may be made from the rudest phase to the highest." Extrapolating from the lived, observed, or reported experience of recent life in Britain, McLennan was able to derive (or to justify) a methodological principle which we may metaphorically reformulate in the language of Haeckel's "biogenetic law": phylogeny—the race-differentiated progress of the human species over the last hundred millennia—recapitulated ontogeny—the class-differentiated progress of British civilization over the last hundred years.[74]

Reason, Instinct, and the Problem of Moral Progress

Moving to a frankly metaphoric level of historical interpretation, we may perhaps bring together the philosopher savage and the bestial savage by reconsidering their dominant underlying psychological characteristics—reason and instinct—in relation to the movement from eighteenth-century developmentalism to Victorian sociocultural evolutionism. Among the many shared assumptions that link these two intellectual viewpoints, one of the more striking is of course a great confidence in the power of human reason—including, especially in the nineteenth-century version, the power to understand and control the forces of external nature. From this point of view, the Industrial Revolution may be regarded as the practical implementation of the eighteenth-century belief in human rationality, and nineteenth-century sociocultural evolutionism was a reformulation, in terms appropriate to the later British utilitarian tradition, of eighteenth-century accounts of the progress of the human mind. At every level, human beings tried to understand and control the world around themselves and adapt their behavior to it. Progress in positive knowledge—and therefore in effective rationality—consisted in a closer coordination of the external world and internal mental representations of it, largely by the elimination of reasoning that was either erroneously founded or no longer adaptive.

Among the various discontinuities that separate nineteenth-century evolutionary progressivism from its eighteenth-century precursors, none was more powerfully disjunctive than that introduced by Thomas Malthus. Letting loose the animal force of instinct into the orderly world of rational progress, Malthus in effect called into question the power of human rationality to control those forces of nature that were internal to humankind itself: thus agricultural production (the fruit of human knowledge) increased only by orderly arithmetic steps, while population (the fruit of human sexual instinct) increased by geometric leaps and bounds. The Malthusian savage lived in a Hobbesian world in which human rationality was constantly at the mercy of sexual instinct; and in the natural course of things the inherent tension between human reason and human biology was reducible only by continuous suffering or recurrent disaster.[75]

From this point of view, the moral revolution—although in origin antedating Malthus—was a means by which the natural course of history could be reclaimed for optimistic rationality. Thus it was that Malthus' second edition allowed the possibility that constant suffering and periodic disaster could be averted by the encouragement and diffusion of "moral restraint"—which differed from merely "prudential restraint" in that it did not simply delay marriage "from prudential motives, [but did so] with a conduct strictly moral during the period of this restraint." Whether merely prudential or fully moral, such restraint implied a model of both individual and racial development: like self-improvement, progress consisted not simply in a growth in reason, but in a repression of sexual instinct. And the two were in fact linked, not merely insofar as the repression of sexual instinct might be rationally motivated, but in the more profound sense that progress in reason would always be in jeopardy without a parallel progress in morals. Material progress and spiritual progress were opposite sides of a coin, insofar as the control of external nature depended on the control of nature within.[76]

Without some resolution of the Malthusian dilemma, the revival of developmentalism in the form of sociocultural evolutionism would have been difficult indeed—although Lubbock in fact dealt with the matter simply by asserting that "under civilisation, the means of subsistence have increased, even more rapidly than the population." In the case of McLennan, the resolution eventually took the form of a starkly amoral utilitarianism: in a posthumously published essay, he suggested that female infanticide, to reduce the pressure of population upon food, was "the most important [step] that was ever taken in the history of mankind"—the first fruit, as it were, of foresighted human reason risen beyond the stage of blind animal instinct. With its resonance of biblical degenerationism and its premonition of Freud, the idea that civilization had originated in crime was not easily compatible with mid-Victorian evolutionary optimism; and in 1852 Herbert Spencer had in fact offered a solution to the Malthusian dilemma more congenial to the morality of Victorian respectability.[77]

As he turned from the still programmatic *Social Statics* toward the elaboration of his cosmic evolutionary scheme, one of Spencer's first self-imposed intellectual tasks had been to put the Malthusian barrier to developmental optimism permanently behind him. Although he had planned to write a book on the topic, his alternative "Theory of Population Deduced from the General Law of Animal Fertility" was published as an article in the *Westminster Review*. In it, Spencer suggested that there were two forces that preserved the life of any organic form—one tending to the maintenance of individual life and the other to its reproduction. Since organic tissue and vital force used for one purpose could not be used for the other, these forces were of necessity inversely correlated. Insisting that there was a systematic opposition between individuation and reproduction in the organic world, Spencer argued that the former was tied directly to the increasing complexity of the nervous system. Although the pressure of population had previously been a constantly stimulating factor in the evolution of life forms, the time would come when the evolution of the nervous system would make such pressure unnecessary. Already in man the opposition of fertility and intellect could be demonstrated in the enlargement of human crania evident between the Australian aborigines and Englishmen. And if the Irish potato famine was evidence that the pressure of fertility still operated in modern life, Spencer nevertheless looked forward to a day when the discipline of labor to gain a living would have produced a race in which each pair would have only two children to reproduce themselves, and the pressure of population would disappear entirely.[78]

That Spencer may have been raising the respectable Victorian ideology of economic sexuality to the level of biological determinism is suggested by the fact that at the time he began work on this article he was actively contemplating the place of marriage in his own life. Giving numerical values to the advantages of emigrating to New Zealand against those of remaining in England, he added 100 points for "marriage" to the winning side of emigration. He later argued this as evidence that "a state of celibacy was far from being my ideal"; but at the time he chose instead to remain in England and work out the problem of the inverse correlation of reproductivity and intellect. Although Spencer granted that the selection incident to Malthusian disaster would have played a role in the process, a more significant guarantor of progress was the inheritance of acquired characteristics, which in his fully developed schema was the primary mechanism of the continuing evolution of the human brain. On this basis, the opposition between biology and reason could eventually be completely overcome, since in the Spencerian view, the results of human rationality could over time be incorporated into the organic structure of the human brain. The greater foresight and ability to delay gratification that civilized men showed relative to savages was not merely a cultural achievement, but was wired into their more highly evolved nervous systems.[79]

By the time the major works of sociocultural evolutionism were produced, the issue of moral progress, long simmering in the frictional heat of pre-Darwinian intellectual movements, had again bubbled up to demand attention. Malthusian assumption—not in the reassuring guise of "moral restraint," but once again in the raw form of the "preventive check"—had been transformed into the *primum mobile* of evolutionary change: "natural selection." And natural selection threatened to take all ethical meaning out of temporal process, not simply by postulating evolutionary change independent of God's direction, but also by premising it implicitly on vice rather than virtue. For in traditional moral terms, the implicit Darwinian injunction to "multiply, vary, let the strongest live, and the weakest die" could be interpreted as an exaltation of sexual indulgence, avarice, and aggression—a possibility of which Darwin may have had a premonition when, in an early evolutionary notebook, he commented on the instinctual origin of mankind's "evil passions": "the Devil under form of Baboon is our grandfather!"[80]

A generation later, Victorian anthropologists were willing to contemplate the possibility that the world as they knew it was the result of purely natural processes, and even to join in extending the revolt against patriarchal authority to the cosmos as a whole. But the weakening of their religious belief had not been accompanied by a loss of moral commitment. Like some other thinkers in the utilitarian tradition, they had felt the relativizing impact of "a more profound reading of history, coming to a large extent from German romanticism," and been forced by the rapid accumulation of information on non-European peoples to consider why it was that different groups of mankind found pleasure and pain in very different things. But granted that moral values varied in time and place—perhaps, in Darwinian terms, were "adapted" to different environmental situations—this could not mean that there was no standard by which they might be evaluated. Just as the "dismal science" of political economy required the consolation of "moral restraint" to be ideologically palatable to an optimistic industrializing society, so did evolutionary science—which some have seen as an ideologization of Victorian economic processes—require the cosmic consolation of moral progress. If the devil in form of baboon was to be our grandfather, then the moral guides and goals that had once been provided by the Creator had to find some evolutionary derivation and justification. The requirement was not simply imposed from without by the defenders of supernatural creation, who demanded an alternative theory for the origin of man's spiritual culture; it was also imposed from within, by the need evolutionists themselves felt for reassurance that processes whose origin was purely natural would somehow lead to a moral outcome.[81]

So it was that, unlike Buckle (who was pre-Darwinian), the sociocultural evolutionary writers were all concerned to argue the reality of moral as well as material progress. Thus McLennan, noting that it was "a favourite idea of some that man's progress has been material merely," insisted that "the moral sentiments of men can be seen improving with the domestic institutions." From this point of view, *Primitive Marriage* may be regarded as an account of the early moral evolution of humankind. Although Lubbock suggested that his "preconceived ideas [had] led him to doubt that [any human race could be] almost entirely wanted in moral feeling," his study of savagery had forced him to conclude that "Man has, perhaps, made more progress in moral than in either material or intellectual advancement." And while he admitted that there was no "atrocious" crime or vice recorded by a traveler that "might not be paralleled in Europe," he argued that what was punished as criminal behavior in civilized society was often—like parricide in Fiji—merely customary behavior among savages.[82]

Tylor, too, accepted the equation of civilized crime and savage custom: although "the ideal savage of the 18th century might be held up as a living reproof to vicious and frivolous London," in "sober fact, a Londoner who should attempt to lead the atrocious life which the real savage may lead with impunity and even respect, would be a criminal only allowed to follow his savage models during his short intervals out of gaol." And with Lubbock, he felt that the "oft-repeated comparison of savages to children" might be applied "as fairly to their moral as to their intellectual condition." Thus it was that even "the better savage life" was always "in but unstable equilibrium, liable to be easily upset by a touch of distress, temptation, or violence," and to become "the worse savage life, which we know by so many dismal and hideous examples."[83]

But in Tylor the relativist impulse was stronger than in Lubbock. He was willing to admit moral loss as well as gain with the progress of civilization. Thus the virtues of courage, honesty, and generosity might suffer, "at least for a time, by the development of a sense of value of life and property." And when, in response to Darwin's urging, Tylor looked more systematically at the problem of moral evolution, he took as a basic principle that the difference between lower and higher morality was less a reflection of abstract ethical ideas than of "unlike conditions of life." Morality was largely a matter of conforming to the customs of the society a person belonged to, and if anything, savages were more custom-bound than civilized men. Under favorable conditions, many of them had a "fair idea of virtue," and even realized it in ways that would put a "more cultured nation" to shame. Nonetheless, Tylor felt that a general survey showed that the lower the culture, the stronger the selfish and malevolent as opposed to the unselfish and benevolent impulses. Even if each culture grade should be judged by its own standard, the changes of moral standards from age to age were no mere shifting, but represented a progress in morality. Furthermore, what had been unconscious evolution was now giving way to conscious development.[84]

Herbert Spencer, the first and the most systematic of the evolutionary moralists, put the matter most succinctly in 1876, in discussing the sphere in which morality was most centrally at issue. There was both "a relative and an absolute standard by which to estimate domestic institutions in each stage of social progress." Judging them relatively, "by their adaptations to the accompanying social requirements," we might regard arrangements that we found "repugnant" as "needful in their times and places." But judging them absolutely, "in relation to the most developed types of life, individual and national," we might still "find good reasons for reprobating them." Although Spencer did not specify these "most developed types," there could be little doubt which they might be; sharing his ethnocentric identification, Spencer's readers would surely agree with his suggestion that a "preliminary survey reveals the fact that the domestic relations which are the highest as ethically considered, are also the highest as considered both biologically and sociologically."[85]

Although Spencer's immediate intellectual historical context differed from that of Lubbock, McLennan, and Tylor in terms of their respective relationships to the Darwinian revolution, there are certain critical points at which he may be regarded as their spokesman. Coming from within the same philosophical tradition, and dealing with evolution from a more comprehensive point of view, he sometimes explicitly and systematically articulated positions not fully stated or only implicit in their work. Just as his Lamarckian evolutionary associationism provided a means to reconcile the psychic unity of man with a hierarchical racialism, so did his insistence on both a proximate ethical relativism and an ultimate ethical absolutism help to resolve another (and related) tension in sociocultural evolutionary thought. In each case differences were arrayed along an extended temporal scale, so as to preserve human unity while simultaneously insisting on racial hierarchy. Mankind was one, as John Burrow has suggested, "not because it was everywhere the same, but because the differences represented stages in the same process."[86]

That process was both an intellectual and a moral evolution. Cast in the terms of Spencer's more systematic evolutionary theory, the picture he drew together in 1876 of "Primitive Man—Emotional" and "Primitive Man—Intellectual" may stand as a representation of its starting point. What Spencer offered under the former heading was in fact a picture of the moral character of primitive man—abstracted, as he suggested, from the variations to be found among existing "inferior races" as the result of their contrasting habitats, unlike modes of life, and differing forms of social discipline. The predominating trait was "impulsiveness"—the "sudden, or approximately-reflex, passing of a single passion into the conduct it prompts." Following necessarily from this was "improvidence"—the result of "desire go[ing] at once to gratification." Unable to conceive the future, thoughtlessly absorbed in the present, uncivilized man—like the "improvident Irishman"—was full of "childish mirthfulness." Intolerant of restraint, vain and vengeful, driven by a strong but irregular "philoprogenitiveness," his "moral nature" was best judged by his "habitual behavior to women"—which was "frequently brutal" and at best unsympathetic. In compensation for this otherwise erratic character, primitive man was "conservative in an extreme degree": "His simpler nervous system, sooner losing its plasticity, was still less able [than the common people of today] to take on a modified mode of action."[87]

Just as the moral character of primitive man was premised on a direct, unmediated expression of internal passional nature, so was the intellectual character of primitive man premised on a direct, unmediated apprehension of external nature. "Nearly everyone" who described savages testified to the "acute senses and quick perceptions of the uncivilized," to their powers of "active and minute observation," and to their "great skill in those actions depending on immediate guidance of perception." But in proportion as savage "mental energies go out in restless perception, they cannot go out in deliberate thought." The opposition of "perceptive activity" and "reflective activity" was further evidenced in their obsession with "meaningless details" and their imitativeness—the tendency to "ape" implying a "smaller departure from the brute type of mind." Unable to "see the likenesses which unite [phenomena] notwithstanding their unlikenesses," they were unable to rise "from the consciousness of individual objects to the consciousness of species," and quick to tire of any conversation that required "thought above the simplest." Having no general ideas, they had no "idea of a causal relation''; unable to distinguish between the ''natural and unnatural,'' they were victims of credulity incapable of ''rational surprise.'' Because they lacked curiosity and constructive imagination, their inventions had arisen unobtrusively ''without any distinct devising.'' Although developing rapidly, the savage intellect quickly reached its limit, and ''presently stop[ped] short from inability to grasp the complex ideas readily grasped by European children.'' The savage had, in short, ''the mind of a child with the passions of a man''—or, in terms of the present metaphorical opposition, the reason of a child and the instincts of a man (although not those of a civilized man, which would have been modified and constrained by reason).[88]

Perhaps because his sociocultural evolutionism was explicitly and systematically part of a broader cosmic process, and therefore required a greater degree of continuity with the subhuman level, Spencer—unlike Tylor—did not portray primitive man in the first instance as an ''ancient savage philosopher.'' Dissociating himself from ''current ideas respecting the thoughts of the primitive man''—who was ''commonly pictured as theorizing about surrounding appearances''—Spencer insisted that ''in fact, the need for explanations of them does not occur to him.'' But as soon as primitive man started to evolve, he quickly took on the guise of the philosopher savage, whose ''physical conceptions,'' at first ''few,'' ''vague,'' ''inconsistent and confused'' were nonetheless ''rational'' in ''the conditions in which they occur.'' The primitive mind, like ours, proceeded by assimilating ''states of consciousness'' with ''their likes in past experience''; but uncivilized men were led into error because their judgments of ''likeness and unlikeness'' were based on surface similarities rather than ''essential characters.'' Because the savage's actual experiences of the mutations of the inorganic world showed repeated ''transitions between the visible and the invisible,'' he was led inevitably, by ''the laws of mental association,'' to primitive notions ''of transmutation, of metamorphosis, of duality'' which, articulated by an ''unconscious hypothesis,'' were gradually systematized along essentially Tylorian lines—and then modified over time with ''the advance in reasoning power.''[89]

Similarly, Spencer's formal theory of instinct was more complex than the metaphorical opposition of reason and instinct suggests. He in fact insisted that there was no sharp hiatus, but a gradual transition between instinctive and rational actions. His Lamarckian view of mental evolution facilitated a complex interweaving of the two. Thus there was a gradual incorporation of habitual experience into the instinctual structure of the brain, so that the ''actions we call rational are, by long-continued repetition, rendered automatic or instinctive.'' His resolution of the conflict between intuitionism and empiricism involved a similar process, by which ''those instinctive mental relations constituting our ideas of Space and Time," although originally based in experience, had become "forms of intuition"—"elements of thought which it is impossible to get rid of."[90]

But the transition between instinct and reason also worked in the opposite direction. Whenever "from increasing complexity and decreasing frequency, the automatic adjustment of inner to outer relations becomes uncertain or hesitating," the "actions called instinctive [could] pass gradually into actions called rational." In general, as the "instincts rise higher and higher, they come to include psychical changes that are less and less coherent"; compound reflex actions become "less decided" and ultimately "lose their distinctly automatic character." Thus, in the long run "that which we call Instinct must pass insensibly into something higher." Over evolutionary time, there was a constant increase in the "proportion of actions that take place with deliberation and consciousness, as well as an increase in the amount of deliberation and consciousness."[91]

In both the intellectual and the moral sphere, the law of mental development was "an adjustment of inner to outer relations that gradually extends in Space and Time, that becomes increasingly special and complex, and that has its elements more precisely co-ordinated and more completely integrated"—so that there was an ever closer "correspondence between changes in the organism and coexistences and sequences in the environment." But if the correspondence became closer, it also became less immediate and more indirect: "Mental evolution, both intellectual and emotional, may be measured by the degree of remoteness from primitive reflex action." At one extreme, there was the formation of "sudden irreversible conclusions on the slenderest evidence"; at the other, the formation of "deliberate and modifiable conclusions after much evidence has been collected." At one extreme, "the quick passage of simple emotions into the particular kinds of action they prompt"; at the other, the "comparatively-hesitating passage of compound emotions into kinds of conduct determined by the joint instigation of their components." At one extreme, the primitive, uncivilized man—still a step below Tylor's failed philosopher savage—responding directly and immediately to the stimuli of external environment and internal nature. At the other extreme, the middle-class Victorian philosopher of civilization, who—by giving systematic theoretical articulation to one of the central presuppositions of the ideology of his class—formulated an evolutionary proposition even more fundamental than "the survival of the fittest": that the repression of immediate impulsive response was the essential mechanism of evolutionary progress in both the intellectual and the moral sphere. By marking off those who were intellectually capable of conceiving the future consequences of their behavior, and who were morally capable of bringing instinctive impulse within the control of this rational conception, this proposition provided the ultimate criterion of fitness. Those who were more able to control the forces of nature internal to themselves were also those more able to control the forces of nature that impinged upon them from outside. And because the results of such foresight were (whether by Darwinian selection or Lamarckian use-inheritance) built into the structure of the evolving human brain, both intellectual and moral progress were in fact given a biological guarantee—in a universe in which, for many, the Creator was no longer able to play the role of guarantor.[92]

Stepping back from Spencer's specific evolutionary argument, we may thus see the opposition between the philosopher savage and the bestial savage as a representation of conflicting potentialities of human (cum animal) nature, gradually brought together in the course of evolution—as in fact the parallel movement from polytheism to monotheism and from polygamy to monogamy suggests. On the one hand, the progress of initially erring human reason, an ever more perfect correlation of internal representations and external nature, bringing the latter under ever-greater control; on the other, the progress of initially bestial human instinct, in which internal nature was brought under ever-greater rational control. Mankind, which was now to be understood as natural rather than divine in origin, was nonetheless subject to rational moral purpose; evolution, which linked us to brute creation, enabled us also to transcend it. Even without the assurance of God, it was still possible to envision the movement of history as a triumph of the spiritual over the material.

A Cosmic Genealogy for Middle-Class Civilization

One of the striking things about sociocultural evolutionary assumption is its metaphorical extendibility—a quality clearly related to its very great ideological adaptiveness. That extendibility is evident in analogies or equations of both process and status. On the one hand, there is the analogy/equation between the biological evolution of the human species, the civilization of humankind, and the education of the human individual—evident particularly in Herbert Spencer's writings on the latter topic. The three forms of development were not only analogous, but could also be viewed as sequentially cumulative—especially in the context of the implied or explicit assumption of the inheritance of acquired characteristics. Other biological assumptions (''recapitulation,'' ''degeneration'' and ''arrested development'') facilitated analogizing up and down the developmental scale.[93]

In the post-Darwinian milieu, certain biological writers elaborated more systematic deterministic frameworks for such analogizing. Thus, the German biologist Ernst Haeckel's "biogenetic law" interpreted the ontogenetic development of the individual as a rapid "mechanical" recapitulation of the phylogenetic sequence of adult forms. But similar analogizing could be derived from pre-Darwinian biological traditions (German *naturphilosophie* or French transcendental morphology), and even from biologists quite critical of certain recapitulationist assumptions. Spencer's analogizing had its biological source in the work of Von Baer, who insisted that parallelism of embryological development did not imply the repetition of adult stages; but Spencer nevertheless had frequent recourse to the child/savage equation. And among most writers in the sociocultural evolutionary mode, such analogizing would seem to reflect simply an unexamined traditional tendency to equate different forms of "development," or to subsume them under a single metaphor of "growth," rather than any systematic set of biological assumptions.[94]

Indeed, one suspects that the metaphorical extendibility of sociocultural evolutionism may have been more a matter of analogies of status than of process. Consider the social categories that were metaphorically equated—if not directly, then through their mutual likeness to savages, or departure from the civilized norm, or sharing of some "primitive" attribute. The equation might be only implicit, as in Tylor's suggestion that what was customary among savages would be criminal in London; or it might be more systematically elaborated, as in Spencer's suggestion that the intellectual traits of primitive man were especially evident in "women of the inferior ranks" of our own society—who "quickly form very positive beliefs"; whose thoughts, "full of personal experiences," lacked "truths of high generality"; who could never detach an "abstract conception" from a "concrete case"; who were "inexact" and "averse to precision"; and who went on "doing things in the ways they were taught, never imagining better methods, however obvious."[95] Although lower-class women and criminals might differ in many respects, they shared a similarity to "savages." The list of social categories thus equated was quite extensive: in addition to criminals, women, and children, it included peasants, rustics, laborers, beggars, paupers, madmen, and Irishmen—all of whom were at times likened to savages or to "primitive" man.

What they shared, with each other and with savages, were certain mental characteristics—characteristics that placed them at a lower point on the unitary scale of intellectual and moral development: governed more by impulse, deficient in foresight, they were in varying degrees unable to subordinate instinctual need to human rational control. But beyond this—and some might have said because of it—there were certain common factors in their social position. Along different lines—of domestic life (woman, child), of socioeconomic status (laborer, peasant, pauper), of deviancy (criminal, madman), and of "race" (Celtic Irishman, black savage)—they all stood in a subordinate hierarchical relationship to those who dominated the economic life, who shared the political power, or who most actively articulated the cultural ideology of mid-Victorian Britain. Many of these relationships were not simply hierarchical, but exploitative as well, in the sense that the life possibilities of a single individual higher up were sustained by the labor of a number of people lower down the pyramid—one thinks of Tylor, carrying on research by having his wife Anna read to him, in a country house made possible by the income from the family brass foundry, with at least the minimum of domestic servants necessary to maintain "respectable" status in mid-Victorian England. Finally, these categories had in common that their individual freedom of action was in one way or another restricted: they were kept in a status of dependency or tutelage and denied the rights of full participation in the political processes of modern civilization.

Insofar as they remained subordinate, exploited, and unfree, these social categories must have been problematic for those who identified "civilization" with the triumph of "liberal" principles and the equal freedom of all human individuals from arbitrary customary or legal restraint—as did all of the sociocultural evolutionists (as well as Sir Henry Maine). Inequalities of status within civilized society might be a methodological convenience in reconstructing the course of human development, but in a period when middle-class liberals had achieved a substantial share of political power, their continued existence was from a moral and political point of view somewhat paradoxical, if not anomalous.

Living in a society which was, and saw itself, in rapid transition, Victorian intellectuals managed to live with paradox, and even to savor it. But this paradox was one for which evolutionary thinking in fact provided a resolution. If there were still residual inequalities based on gender, class, or race in mid-Victorian society, this was a reflection of the inevitable unevenness of the processes of development, whether individual, civilizational, or biological. If those whose status was unequal were also those whose mental development had not yet achieved the rational self-control and foresight on which individual freedom ought to be premised, then there was no paradox in denying them full participation in civilized society, until such time as (if ever) their mental development justified such participation.[96]

If paradox is the intellectual side of the coin of cultural ambiguity, ambivalence is its emotional obverse. In the classic analysis of the Victorian frame of mind, the opposition was treated in terms of the conflict between "the emancipated head" and the "traditional heart"—or the "critical spirit" and "the will to believe." Similar themes have been implicit throughout the present discussion of Victorian cultural ideology—notably in the response to Darwinism, in which the search for a natural origin was balanced by the yearning for an ethical goal. Those inclined to psychohistorical interpretation might also suggest, on the basis of the earlier discussions of religion and of marriage, an ambivalence about paternal authority—with sociocultural evolutionism dethroning the father in the heavenly realm of religion, yet enthroning him in the earthly realm of marriage (where one might aspire to inherit the father's position). Be that as it may, the previous account of the experience of ontogeny and phylogeny in early-nineteenth-century England suggests a certain ambivalence in the cultural challenge to traditional forms of authority, an ambivalence which may be conceived in both psychocultural and sociopolitical terms.[97]

If only at a symbolic level, we may suggest that there was an implicit psychological tension between two major cultural movements associated with the emergence of middle-class consciousness in the early nineteenth century. On the one hand, there was a political-philosophical movement which, by attacking all purely customary or traditional authorities, attempted to generalize the eighteenth-century pursuit of unrestricted rationality and individual liberty; on the other, there was a moral movement which implied certain rather severe restrictions on individual human liberty. Conceived psychologically, the goals of the middle classes thus involved simultaneously liberation and repression: on the one hand, rationality uninhibited; on the other, rationality which was explicitly inhibiting and on which the achievement of individual self-improvement, social mobility, and civilization must ultimately depend. Insofar as these processes involved the rational repression of instinctual tendencies, they involved also a sense of loss as well as gain and were the subject of ambivalence. To recapitulate those processes as evolution was at once to give a cosmic vindication to the sacrifice that repression involved, and to distance oneself from those who were unable or unwilling to make it.

A similar dualism of impulse can be seen at the sociopolitical level, where the emergence of a middle-class consciousness had both a revolutionary and a conservative dimension. On the one hand, it involved a challenge to the traditional hierarchical structure of status and authority; on the other, a grasping of the possibilities of mobility within it. Simultaneously called into question by social mobility and reasserted as measures of it, markers of class became in some respects more sharply delineated and insisted on. As the middle classes reaped the benefits of the attack on aristocratic power, and at the same time shared at least some of the benefits of an aristocratic lifestyle, they sought to distance themselves from those below. With the emergence of a "viable class society," their increasing stake in the status quo was paralleled by the attenuation of their revolutionary impulse. With the achievement of the "Victorian Compromise," they became increasingly conservative of a social order which, although retaining much of its traditional hierarchical structure, had not only accepted their social mobility, but was accommodating to them both politically and ideologically.[98]

This pattern of incorporation was reflected in the realm of social theory. Earlier in the century, when middle-class groups were still struggling to achieve political power and social status, the attack against aristocratic power and feudal institutions was carried on in terms of an ahistorical utilitarianism which had no need for gradualist arguments, which rejected intuitionist and nativist assumptions as excuses for that which present utility called into question, and for which relativism was the means of attacking customs and institutions that had nothing but tradition to justify their existence. John Burrow has suggested that after mid-century, "what was required from a philosophy of history was not that it should be an engine of radical reform, but that it should provide something much more like cosmic reassurance."[99] But the need for reassurance had a worldly as well as a cosmic dimension: as middle-class groups achieved a larger stake in the political and social status quo, their intellectual spokesmen found an evolutionary gradualism more congenial to their social situation, which was directly or indirectly sustained by many of those residual inequalities of status for which sociocultural evolutionism provided an intellectual justification.

The shift can be illustrated in the career of Herbert Spencer. While he was critical of Benthamite assumption in *Social Statics*, the impulse of his own provincial radicalism was still very strong: bent on attacking feudalism and aristocracy, he actually advocated the nationalization of land. But within a few years he had backed off from this—much to the dismay of Henry George—and he modified his views on other questions as well. Tylor, Lubbock, and McLennan were also political men, active in varying degrees in the politics of the Liberal party. But they were a half generation younger, and committed to liberalism when it was the political orientation of an established rather than a rising middle class. If an antipatriarchal impulse still motivated Tylor's writings on religion and was reflected to some extent in the debate on the evolution of marriage, the radical spirit that motivated Spencer's early writings on civilization seems otherwise not much in evidence. One suspects that with the passage of time—and such events as the Second Reform Bill, the Paris Commune, and Gladstone's Irish policy—they, like many other Liberals, were increasingly troubled by the threat of mass democracy. In the case of Pitt Rivers—whose stake in the existing social order had become very large indeed—the political implications of evolutionary gradualism were made quite explicit, when he expressed the hope that public display of his sequences of artifacts would prove to the working classes that progress must come slowly: "The law that nature makes no jumps can be taught by the history of mechanical contrivances, in such a way as at least to make men cautious how they listen to scatter-brained revolutionary suggestions."[100]

Beyond evolutionary gradualism lay a further moment in the development of evolutionary social theory: the more pessimistic social Darwinism of those who, like Galton, saw in modern society not so much an affirmative model of evolutionary process, but the evidence of a recent disjunction between social and biological evolution. Preoccupied still with the Malthusian problem, and unwilling to accept Spencer's optimistic Lamarckian gloss of the middle-class ideology of economic sexuality, they feared that modern society had facilitated what was in effect an ''unnatural selection''; and to counter the tendency of the intellectually fittest to control their fertility while the lower classes multiplied like rabbits, they advocated the necessity of positive ''eugenic'' intervention in the evolutionary process.[101]

By contrast, the classical social evolutionists—although conscious of what Frazer later called ''the volcano underneath''—saw modern civilization in more positive terms. Their evolutionism remained an essentially optimistic faith. It vindicated the rational repression of instinctual behavior that made individual mobility and social progress possible; it justified the residual inequalities of sex, class, and race which progress had not yet overcome; and insofar as it linked social processes with biological change—conceived rather more in Lamarckian than in Darwinian terms—it gave that progress an evolutionary guarantee. Theirs was an activity not unlike that of the successful early Victorian entrepreneurs who occupied their declining years ''hunting up genealogies'' to justify their children's entry into the landed gentry. Similarly, social evolutionism was a kind of cosmic genealogy for middle-class civilization, ''hunted up'' by men whose parents included such businessmen, several of whom were themselves candidates for entry in the ''intellectual aristocracy'' that was emerging from similar social sources in this period.[102]

To suggest that sociocultural evolutionism was conditioned by such ulterior motives and served such ideological functions is not to reject the prior argument that it was an attempt to answer certain questions posed by the origin of species and the antiquity of man. It is rather to suggest that the answers to such intellectual questions could also help to provide answers to questions pressing upon evolutionists from other realms. In explaining the origin of human culture, one also explained the cultural experience embodied in the Crystal Palace Exhibition. It is therefore not surprising that answers to both sorts of questions should have been conditioned by personal and family history, class and political identification, and religious, marital, and social concerns.

Colonial Otherness and Evolutionary Theory

By the same token, to look for ulterior motivation and latent function in the domestic social experience of nineteenth-century Britain is not to deny the relevance of British experience with non-European "others" overseas, either as a source of evolutionary assumption or as a field for its application. A number of the writers we have discussed spent time outside Europe at some point in their lives, and in the cases of Galton, Wallace, and Tylor, the formative impact of overseas experience on their anthropological viewpoints seems to have been considerable. But quite aside from personal experience, there were any number of channels through which the European experience overseas could have been a source of anthropological assumption, including the anti-slavery and missionary movements, the debates over such major colonial events as the Indian Mutiny, and all the literature they engendered. Even a confirmed stay-at-home like Spencer would have been familiar with missionary, travel, and natural historical literature long before he began having it combed for comparative data.[103]

There was, in short, a close articulation, both experiential and ideological, between the domestic and the colonial spheres of otherness. Those who went out to confront (and to convert, to uplift, to exploit, or to destroy) "savages" overseas did so in the context of the domestic cultural experience we have been discussing. Thus the "systematic colonization" of New Zealand and Australia in the 1830s and 1840s was explicitly justified as an attempt to forestall domestic Malthusian crisis by exporting surplus population. Both those who traveled overseas and those who read the literature they produced reacted to the experience of "savages" abroad, whether direct or vicarious, in terms of prior experience with the changing class society of Great Britain. And for Englishmen at home and abroad, domestic class and overseas colonial society were linked by the "internal colonialism" of the Celtic fringe. Thus Ireland, especially, had since Elizabethan times provided a mediating exemplar for both attitude and policy in relations with "savages" overseas.[104]

Emphasizing the articulation and translatability of domestic and colonial otherness, however, should not cause us to forget that there were certain fixed points and relationships on the scale by which otherness was measured. If Irishmen were portrayed in the popular press as apelike, and savages overseas sometimes compared favorably with Irish peasants, there was no real doubt about who was at the bottom: other social categories might be like savages, but with true savages it was not a matter of similitude but of identity. And while the relative position of different savage peoples was a matter of debate—with the Fuegians, the Australians, the Andamanese, the Tasmanians, and several others included among Spencer's "Types of Lowest Races"—the general characteristics of savages were clear enough. Dark-skinned and small of stature, unattractive, unclothed and unclean, promiscuous and brutal with their women, they worshipped the spirits animating animals or even sticks and stones—their smaller brains enclosing and enclosed within the mental world described in Spencer's chapters on the mind of primitive man.[105]

Whatever their similarity to savagery, all manifestations of otherness within British society were contained within the bounds of what had long been regarded as a single large linguistic-cum-racial group—the Celts, the Anglo-Saxons and the Normans being all white-skinned members of the Indo-European family. But beyond the British Isles there was a larger scale of otherness on which differences were marked in racial terms, and color became an indicator of culture. Tylor's arrangement of "races" in order of their culture—Australian, Tahitian, Aztec, Chinese, Italian—was also an arrangement in terms of color saturation, from dark to light, as well as a selection from major racial groupings of mankind.[106]

The national specificity of Tylor's highest category is worth noting—not simply because it implied an unstated higher reference point northwest across the English Channel, but because it most strikingly instances the ambiguity of the cultural and the biological in Tylor's scale. From our present anthropological perspective "Italian" denotes either a language or a nation; it is a cultural rather than a biological category. That Tylor should have spoken of the Italian (or, for that matter, of the Tahitian) "race" no doubt reflected a more pervasive looseness in the usage of the term. But like much of that usage, it could also have an implicit biological rationale in the Lamarckian (and Spencerian) assumption of the inheritance of acquired characteristics, which—as we have several times previously noted—provided a mechanism by which habitual behavior became instinctive, and cultural inheritance became part of biological heredity. Even Walter Bagehot, a writer whom we associate with "social Darwinism," and who doubted the direct influence of environment on the formation of major races, tended, when it came to mental or cultural characteristics, to blur the distinction between race and nation, and between the processes that formed them—insofar as he assumed that behavior socially transmitted by "imitation" could become part of hereditary physical makeup. In this context it is obviously oversimple to speak of "racial" as opposed to "cultural" "determinism," since what was biologically hereditary could itself be the result of cultural processes.[107]

On the other hand, there were also "social Darwinists" like Galton who more systematically rejected Lamarckian assumption, for whom the relationship of race and culture was much less interactive (allowing, of course, for the interaction involved in eugenic intervention). For them, and others more directly in the polygenist racialist tradition, the label racial determinist seems quite appropriate. Even in the case of those whose usage seems consistent with Spencerian assumption, one must keep in mind that once cultural habit became hereditary, it manifested itself as racial instinct—as in the case of those "races" Spencer had described as "independent or slavish, active or slothful." Thus insofar as Spencerian Lamarckians emphasized the cumulative effect of past heredity over the moderating influence of present experience, they, too, might be appropriately called racial determinists. Certainly, race played an important subsidiary role in social evolutionary argument, insofar as it helped to explain how those present inequalities of development which made possible the use of the comparative method had arisen—why it was that although mankind was one in origin and the laws of mind were everwhere the same, not all groups had progressed to the same level, or were likely to in the future. Such differences were simply the cumulative results of varying cultural experience in different environments, which, having become racial, limited the developmental capacity of different groups. And although Lamarckian thought lent itself to the notion that instinctual mental patterns formed in earlier stages of development might gradually be modified by education in the habits of civilization, Spencer himself, when consulted by a leading Japanese statesman as to whether Japan should encourage marriage with foreigners, urged its prohibition on the grounds that interbreeding between varieties that over "many generations" had become "adapted to widely divergent modes of life" invariably produced offspring to neither.[108]

While systematic exploration of the role of evolutionary thought in the relations of Europeans and "others" lies beyond the scope of this study, we may offer a few thoughts along these lines. The fact that Arthur Gordon carried Maine's work to the Pacific and attempted to apply Mainian principles to the government of Fiji suggests that the evolutionary literature may have been directly functional to the colonial enterprise. But the fact that it was Maine rather than McLennan that Gordon found useful is worth noting, not only because Maine was marginal to the evolutionary school, but because he was the writer who had most to say about the kinds of problems colonial administrators had to cope with: village organization, landownership, and codes of law. By contrast, A. W. Howitt, the Australian explorer and police magistrate who collaborated with the missionary Lorimer Fison on the analysis of aboriginal social organization, clearly regarded McLennan's writings as closet speculation, albeit the product of a fine "logical" mind. Fison himself dismissed Lubbock's work as the sort of compilation that could be put together by anybody who could afford "to give an ordinary clerk a pound a week to make extracts from works on savage tribes in any good library." Tylor's work on religion and mythology might seem relevant substantively to the work of missionaries; but if we may judge from the case of Robert Codrington, who spent years with the Melanesian Mission (and who in fact attended Tylor's lectures), they were uncomfortable with the hypothesis of animism on empirical as well as on theological grounds.[109]

But whether or not evolutionary writings provided specific guidelines for colonial administrators and missionaries, there can be no doubt that sociocultural thinking offered strong ideological support for the whole colonial enterprise in the later nineteenth century. Pre-evolutionary buttresses were of course still in place—among them, for instance, the idea that savages merely wandered in small groups on the surface of the earth, without attempting the systematic cultivation that was required to fulfill God's injunction to be fruitful and multiply, and had therefore no territorial claims that Europeans must respect. European penetration could also be justified in the philanthropic terms of antislavery and Christian mission, and effective abolition and conversion might in fact require extended European presence. But in an era when science was taking over many of the ideological functions religion had long served, a more secular justification was required: savages were not simply morally delinquent or spiritually deluded, but racially incapable. And while this racial incapacity, too, had previously been argued in nonevolutionary, polygenetic terms, these had never provided a satisfactory explanation of its origin. Evolutionary racialism did not merely assert the existence of a hierarchy of distinct races, it offered a secular explanation of how that hierarchy had arisen, and gave to it the accumulated weight of evolutionary processes in a greatly extended span of time. Cast in the terms of "natural selection" and "survival of the fittest," evolutionary racialism was, from the European viewpoint, a grimly optimistic, but morally ambiguous doctrine, which could be used to justify the worst excesses of expropriation and colonial rule. But the peculiar advantage of a more Lamarckian evolutionism was the opening it left for an uplifting philanthropic meliorism. Civilizing efforts on behalf of dark-skinned savages could, over time, eliminate savagery from the world, not by destroying savage populations, but by modifying their hereditary incapacity. In the meantime—which might be shorter or longer depending on the weight one gave to present as opposed to cumulative past experience—it was both scientifically and morally respectable for civilized Europeans to take up the white man's burden.[110]

SEVEN

Evolutionary Ideas and Anthropological Institutions (1835–1890)

Andaman Islanders, photographed (and measured) for the Anthropological Institute—1882

E. H. Man, "On the Aboriginal Inhabitants of the Andaman Islands, Part II," *Journal of the Anthropological Institute* 12 (1882): facing p. 174.

UNTIL this point, our attempt has been to understand historically a major intellectual reorientation—the emergence of "classical evolutionism" in the decade of the 1860s—by placing it in a variety of historical contexts: three national traditions of thinking about the problem of civilization during the century before the Crystal Palace; the several currents of inquiry which between 1830 and 1850 were subsumed under the new disciplinary rubric "ethnology"; the kinds of empirical evidence that were available in the 1850s about non-European peoples; thinking stimulated by the Crystal Palace about the progress of European civilization; the implications of the Darwinian revolution for speculation about human cultural development; and the formation of Victorian cultural ideology in the pre-Darwinian nineteenth century. The strategy has been one of multiple contextualization rather than of causal explanation. A series of interpretive nets has been cast around an historical phenomenon to capture as many of its scurrying significations as possible. Other nets might have been cast, and others will no doubt come along to cast them. For after all our efforts to contain it contextually, the quarry remains still elusive, and contextualization has in fact contributed to this.

So many of the assumptions of "classical evolutionism" can be traced back into prior contexts, or shown to be conditioned by those of immediate (and subsequent) polemic, that its concrete paradigmatic exemplification becomes highly problematic. Similarly, so many of the assumptions of the prior "ethnological" orientation persist beyond the 1860s (even into the twentieth century) that the idea of revolutionary paradigmatic succession becomes equally debatable. But the limitations of the paradigm metaphor do not alter the fact that a major transition in the history of anthropology took place in the decade of the 1860s, and it may even be that further exploration of these limitations can help further to illuminate that change. Let us therefore cast yet another net of contextualization, this time around the institutionalized interaction of the community of scholars who in retrospect we may call the "anthropologists" of the early and mid-Victorian periods—although, as we shall see, it was only after considerable controversy that they accepted that term as their self-designation.

By examining the emergence of a "relatively dense interaction" among scholars concerned with dark-skinned "savages"—the subject matter that has given anthropology its maximal historical unity—we may get a better idea of the changing day-to-day practice of anthropology, as it reflected the transition of the 1860s. If we discover little that might be regarded as "normal science" within an evolutionary "paradigm," we may nevertheless learn something about the relationship of ethnographic data and social evolutionary theory, about the complex processes of "institutionalization" and "professionalization" in anthropology, and even about the changing relation of anthropological research and humanitarian concern in the context of colonial expansion.[1] For what may be regarded as the oldest lineal ancestor of modern British anthropological institutions was devoted not to the disinterested study of non-European peoples, but to an active humanitarian defense of dark-skinned fellow humans threatened with extinction by "the gigantic efforts of modern commerce" and the "system of modern colonization as hitherto pursued." And the still-extant institution that emerged in the course of the Darwinian revolution assumed its distinctive character not only in the process by which "ethnology" was transformed into "anthropology," but in a parallel process by which humanitarian concerns were disengaged from intellectual, and the goal of scientific understanding displaced that of "protecting the defenceless, and promoting the advancement of uncivilized tribes."[2]

The Protection of Aborigines and the Advancement of Ethnology

Organized anthropology in Britain emerged during a particular phase in the history of British colonial expansion—that once seen as the liberal anti-imperialist interregnum between the mercantilist "old colonial system" and the "new imperialism" of the later nineteenth century. More recently, however, the decades before 1870 have been reinterpreted in terms of the "imperialism of free trade" as the "decisive stage" in an essentially continuous process of overseas expansion by the world's first industrializing nation.[3] In the aftermath of the Napoleonic Wars, which "set the seal" on the preindustrial empire in India, Canada, the West Indies, Australia, and the Cape, the explosive forces of industrial and demographic growth let loose a flow of products and people from the British Isles, which ran to the corners of the earth under the protection of an unchallenged sea power.

For several decades, the organization and the ideology of empire were in a state of irresolution, as humanitarians, colonists, colonial reformers, and free traders pushed their respective concerns in the metropolitan political arena. But by 1853, when Lord Grey published his commentary on *The Colonial Policy of Lord John Russell's Administration*, the basis had been established for a system of "informal empire." The doctrine of trusteeship justified the continued dominance over dark-skinned "uncivilized" populations, and the tropical colonies faded to the background of political consciousness for a generation; the doctrine of responsible self-government established a more stable relationship with the colonies of white settlement, which were granted an increasing degree of control over their own native populations. Although there was some continued resistance to the annexation of new territories, the radical option of dismembering the empire was never very seriously advocated; and both the thrust of commercial penetration and considerations of imperial security ensured an unbroken continuity in the geographical expansion of British colonial power. After mid-century the Crimean War, the Indian Mutiny, and a series of small wars and protests against European rule foreshadowed a new period when British hegemony could no longer be left so confidently to the forces of free trade periodically ''gingered up'' by government. By that time, however, the issue was not the propriety of empire, but how to defend it.[4]

Within this longer period, the impact of humanitarian sentiment on colonial policy was greatest in the 1830s, when the Quaker and Evangelical philanthropists who met in the Exeter Hall headquarters of the missionary societies were a force to be reckoned with—especially after 1835, when two heirs of the Clapham sect, Lord Glenelg and James Stephen, controlled the Colonial Office. The abolition of slavery by Parliament in 1833 had not ended the enslavement of Africans by other nations nor improved the relations of British and Boer settlers to Hottentots and Bantus in South Africa; and in 1835 Thomas Fowell Buxton, the evangelical Quaker who inherited Wilberforce's mantle as leader of the parliamentary antislavery group, succeeded in getting established a Parliamentary Select Committee on Aborigines. Besides investigating the sixth ''Kaffir War'' begun the year before, it was to inquire more generally into the problem of ''what measures ought to be adopted with respect to the Native Inhabitants of Countries where British Settlements are made, and to the Neighbouring Tribes, in order to secure them the due observation of justice and the protection of their rights, to promote the spread of Civilization among them, and to lead them to the peaceful and voluntary reception of the Christian Religion.''[5]

The thousand-plus printed pages of testimony gathered over the next several years had a slightly ambiguous double thrust. Witnesses from all over the empire testified to the evil consequences of colonization, which in Buxton's words had been ''little else than one uniform system of cruelty, rapacity, and murder.'' In contrast, there was a body of testimony, largely from missionaries, as to ''the favourable effects of fair dealing, combined with Christian instruction,'' which showed that ''those nations which have been exposed to our contamination might, during the same period, have been led forward to religion and civilization.'' Indeed, as the committee suggested in an aside, there was evidence to indicate that justice and self-interest were interdependent: the Kaffir Wars had interrupted a trade in European commodities amounting to at least £30,000 a year. This tension between the protective impulse, implicitly pushing toward the maintenance of aboriginal isolation, and the civilizing impulse, with its undercurrent of economic self-interest, ran through the committee's report. The same tension was reflected in the doctrine of trusteeship, which was to be the humanitarians' contribution to the mature ideology of empire. And though the committee opposed further "encroachments" on aboriginal territories, their humanitarian concern was also a major factor in the very growth itself of empire. On the one hand, "missionary imperialism" was a major type of informal penetration; on the other, the extension of formal rule was often justified to protect savages from the ruthless buccaneering of Europeans beyond the control of government.[6]

Nor was this the only ambiguity characterizing the protection of aborigines in this period; there was also a tension between strictly humanitarian concerns and an emergent scientific interest that also motivated some of Buxton's followers. Among these was the Quaker doctor Thomas Hodgkin, who before turning to philanthropic activities had done research on the disease later given his name, and who in 1837 took the lead in reorganizing the informal group supporting the Select Committee's activities into a permanent Aborigines Protection Society. The goals of the Society were defined by the paradoxical contrast between the devotion to "civil freedom," "moral and intellectual improvement," and the furtherance of "sacred truth" shown by Britons at home, and the "injuries we have inflicted, the cruelties we have committed, the vices we have fostered, [and] the desolation and utter ruin we have caused" in colonial areas overseas. Although committed to evangelism abroad as the only "effectual method to civilize" dark-skinned savage peoples, in practice the Society's evangelical role was directed primarily to people who were already civilized and Christian. Its "first object" was to collect "authentic information concerning the character, habits and wants of the uncivilized tribes." By disseminating this information widely, it hoped to create a public opinion that, "correctly taught, extensively spread, and expressed with deliberate firmness," would act first on the government at home and then on colonists abroad, not to halt European colonization overseas, but to change its character. Thus if the impulse of the Society was in the first instance humanitarian, some of its central activities were, in a broad sense, "anthropological." Not only did its early publications contain a good bit of ethnographic material, but many of its activities might be regarded as "applied anthropology"—among them, the preparation of a model "System of Legislation" that was in effect a program for directed cultural change "by persuasion rather than by force."[7]

This interest in "anthropological" issues did not, of course, arise simply as a by-product of evangelical and philanthropic concern. By the early 1830s, there were others besides James Cowles Prichard with serious scholarly interest in the dark-skinned non-European races of the world. Topics we would now regard as anthropological were discussed in the meetings of several groups—notably the Geographical and Philological Societies—as well as in various journals of the period. Hodgkin himself had argued before the Philological Society the "importance of studying and preserving the languages spoken by uncivilized nations, with a view of elucidating the physical history of man." But despite the multiplication of scientific and scholarly societies in the 1830s, the study of non-European uncivilized man still lacked an independent institutional locus.[8]

It is thus not surprising that among some of the members of the Aborigines Protection Society, the scientific impulse outweighed the humanitarian. When Prichard wrote to Hodgkin at the organization's anniversary in 1839, he made only a quick bow to its humanitarian goals before turning to the "curious and interesting problems" of philosophy and science that would be left unsolved "if the various races of mankind become diminished in number." Later that same year Prichard gave a paper to the British Association for the Advancement of Science "On the Extinction of Human Races," in which he predicted the extermination of most savage races and argued that, since Christian nations would not intervene to save them, "it is of the greatest importance, in a philosophical point of view, to obtain much more extensive information than we now possess of their physical and moral characters." In response, the Association set up a committee to prepare and circulate an ethnographic questionnaire. In presenting its report two years later, Hodgkin appealed for support of the activities of the Aborigines Protection Society; but the questionnaire itself contained little that related to the Society's humanitarian interests. By this time, however, the Society itself was undergoing changes that were to lead to the segregation of its scientific from its humanitarian concerns.[9]

One much later account suggests that a split developed between the "student party" and the "missionary party," and that the former was forced to withdraw. It seems clear that a conflict, if not of faction, then at least of purpose, developed within the Society, and that this conflict was affected by the waxing and waning of its fortunes. Shortly after its formation, the Society's prospects were bright enough to inspire imitation: the founding, after a visit by Hodgkin to Paris, of the Société Ethnologique de Paris in 1839. Although the change in name was attributed simply to the fact that France had "few aborigines requiring protection," the early success of the Paris society clearly provided an alternative model, especially in the context of the somewhat defensive and disappointed tone that crept into the reports of the Aborigines Protection Society after the first year or so. The Society had its successes—including the formation of auxiliary societies in the Port of London which, by appealing to sailors, would "excite proper sentiments in the minds of those likely to be brought in contact" with aboriginals. But a different public response is suggested by the Society's recurring need to emphasize that it was *not* opposed to European colonization in principle and it did *not* wish to maintain aborigines "in the purity of their race" as "objects of interest to the natural history of man." By 1842, there was clearly a feeling that the opportunity provided by the Parliamentary Select Committee had been lost, and that some reorientation was necessary.[10]

The situation within the Aborigines Protection Society reflected a reconsideration of strategy within the humanitarian movement. On the basis of the presumed natural incompatibility between the slave trade and free trade, Buxton developed a scheme to supplement the existing naval blockade against slave trading by an active encouragement of legitimate commerce through treaties with tribal chiefs and the development of native agriculture in West Africa. Although the Colonial Office opposed this actively expansionist scheme, Buxton, with the support of the newly founded African Civilization Society, was able to win government support for an expedition up the Niger. The disastrous fate of the Niger expedition in 1842, following upon the failure of the humanitarians to stifle at its birth the "new system of slavery" which the Indian coolie trade established in a number of British colonies, marked a drastic falling off of humanitarian influence on issues of colonial policy. The increasing pessimism within the Aborigines Protection Society and the gradual disengagement of the scientific impulse seem clearly related to this more general ebbing of the humanitarian tide. In this context, the printed statement of the Society's object was changed in 1842: rather than "protecting the defenceless," it would "record the[ir] history," and a resolution was passed to the effect that the best way to help aboriginals was to study them.[11]

Despite this reorientation, there were some who felt that the natural history of man was not thriving within the Aborigines Protection Society—including the secretary, Richard King, who had been a pupil of Hodgkin's at Guy's Hospital before going on a two-year expedition to the Arctic. In July 1842, King issued a prospectus for the formation of an "ethnological" society—adopting the title of the Paris group, which was still new to English usage. The response to King's appeal was at first rather poor, but early the following year Hodgkin invited the group to meet in his home, and by the end of 1843 the new organization was on a firm enough footing to establish itself formally as the Ethnological Society of London. Exactly how much hard feeling was involved in all this is not clear. King spoke of the ethnologists as "disenfranchised" within the Aborigines Protection Society, but Hodgkin seems to have felt no difficulty in maintaining a dual affiliation, as did others, including Henry Christy. However, it seems clear that those who entered the Ethnological Society accepted an institutional division of labor between ethnological research and humanitarian purpose. Its prospectus suggested that "to complete the circle of Scientific Institutions" in the British metropolis, there was need of one "whose sole object should be the promotion and diffusion of the most important and interesting branch of knowledge, that of man—ETHNOLOGY," and the formal minutes of the Society's council are singularly lacking in discussion of issues of a specifically humanitarian character.[12]

The Emergence of Anthropology as an Alternative to Ethnology

For the first several years, the Ethnological Society led a marginal existence, publishing its papers irregularly in the *Edinburgh New Philosophical Journal*. But in the later 1840s the Society entered a period of heightened activity, and between 1848 and 1856 was able to publish four volumes of its own *Journal*. It took some time, however, to overcome the fear of some leading members of the British Association for the Advancement of Science that recognition of ethnology might compromise the pursuit of "pure science." Failing to win their own separate section in the Association in 1844, the ethnologists had to be satisfied in 1846 with recognition as a subsection of Section D (Zoology and Botany). Even after their successful session at Oxford in 1847, where Max Müller had listened to more than two dozen ethnological papers, there was still concern in the Association that ethnologists might introduce political or religious polemic, or that their emphasis might be too historical and literary. The ethnologists, on the other hand, chafed somewhat at their subordination to zoology—Prichard arguing that because ethnology dealt not with the present phenomena of nature, but with their past history, it should logically be associated with geology or archeology. Two years after Prichard's death the zoological subordination was ended when Sir Roderick Murchison, one of the Association's "magnates," who was himself vexed by the subordination of geography to geology, succeeded in establishing a separate Section E for Geography and Ethnology jointly.[13]

The abandonment of active humanitarian involvement and movement into the world of "science" should not imply, however, that the Ethnological Society had entirely cut off its roots in Quaker and Evangelical philanthropy. True, what was doctrine for the Aborigines Protection Society (their motto was the Latin phrase *ab uno sanguine*) was at least nominally problematic for the Ethnological Society. In inquiring into ''the distinguishing characteristics, physical and moral, of the varieties of Mankind which inhabit, or have inhabited, the Earth, . . . to ascertain the causes of such characteristics,'' the possibility was at least left open that these characteristics might result from differences in original hereditary makeup. But as the case of Prichard has already shown, the underlying commitment of most of the leading ethnologists to the unity of the human species was never in doubt.[14]

The continuity of this religiously based humanitarian and environmental approach is evident in an article by the Society's secretary, Richard Cull, in its *Journal* for 1854. One of the special treats the Society offered its members—whose ethnographic experience was largely second-hand—was the evening devoted to the examination of a living aboriginal, usually from the polyglot crew of some sailing vessel then in London. Describing three such Eskimo crewmen from a British whaler, Cull suggested that after only three weeks in England their ''dark, swarthy colour has subsided so as to admit of the vermillion hue of the European becoming apparent.'' He went on to argue that the ''poor degraded Esquimaux'' was a being of ''hopes, and fears, and aspirations for a future; in short, *a man*, capable of that true dignity and greatness which we all manifest when, as little children, we submit to receive the teachings of a superior power.''[15]

After its brief efflorescence at mid-century, the Ethnological Society went into decline, and Section E of the British Association passed largely under the sway of the geographers. Cull suggested that the Crimean War was a factor; later critics alleged the deadening influence of religion. Certainly the circumstances of ethnological research were not as propitious as they might have been. The attempt to tap new sources of data by the questionnaire method was not a success; Cull commented in 1855 that Prichard's ethnographic questions for the Admiralty's *Manual of Scientific Inquiry* had produced virtually nothing in six years and that the returns from the British Association's questionnaire had not been proportionate to the cost, despite the fact that the second edition of 1852 had been sent to every mission station in the world.[16] But even had the results been otherwise, it seems unlikely that the decline of ethnology would have been forestalled. Although it had only recently received its name, ''ethnology'' achieved a kind of fulfillment with the completion of the third edition of Prichard's *Researches* in 1848; and, as we have already seen, the next decade saw real signs of strain in the ethnological paradigm.

Toward the end of the decade, the Ethnological Society was reinvigorated by a group of anthropological scholars representing the newer trends in physical anthropology and archeology. Joseph Davis, Joseph Thurnam, and John Beddoe became fellows, and Robert Knox himself—after being blackballed in 1855—was made an honorary fellow in 1858. Although Thomas Wright, the secretary in this period, was rather conservative on archeological matters, he encouraged discussion of the new flint instrument finds, and by 1861 the Society's active members included several of the more prominent figures of the prehistoric movement, including Henry Christy, Lane Fox, and John Evans. The most dynamic new member, however, was a young man named James Hunt, who made his living treating stammerers by a method his father had developed, and who in the course of writing several books on human speech had become interested in "the great question of races and languages." Four years after joining the Society in 1856, Hunt became joint secretary along with Wright.[17]

The incorporation of these newer trends, however, was not accomplished without friction between the Society's older Quaker humanitarian element and the racialist current represented by several of the younger members—including Hunt, who later said his racial views had been "imbibed from the late Dr. Knox." Assigned to take the first steps toward the publication of a revived *Journal,* Hunt reported in March 1862 on the cost of engravings for an article on the inhabitants of Sierra Leone. After some discussion the matter was referred to a committee, on which Hunt was joined by two Quaker abolitionists, Hodgkin and Christy. Almost a year later, the minutes noted that "some differences of opinion" had arisen over the engravings, and the matter was referred to Wright—Hunt's resignation from the Society having been announced at the very same meeting. That the break should have occurred over an apparently trivial issue of iconography becomes more understandable when one recalls that the Sierra Leone colony of freed slaves had been a special concern of British humanitarians for over seventy years, and when one compares the soft and slightly romanticized lines of the engravings eventually published with the harsh and almost bestial representations of blacks in some of the racist works of this period.[18]

By the time this issue came to a head, Hunt had already founded his own competing organization, the Anthropological Society of London. Hunt gave various justifications for the new group: the need for a "publishing body"; for a group devoted primarily to "the anatomical aspects of ethnology"; and for "an arena for the free discussion of the various exciting questions which current events [notably, the American Civil War] were bringing into prominence." But he seems to have been driven largely by the need to create an active, vital organization as a forum for his own racialist views. In doing so he served as the institutional catalyst in a more general intellectual process, and he soon developed a philosophical justification for the institutional break, posing the matter in terms of the fundamental presuppositions for a scientific study of man.[19]

Following Paul Broca, whose recently organized Société d'Anthropologie de Paris was his institutional model, Hunt defined anthropology in the very broadest terms as "the science of the whole nature of man."

He posed it against ethnology, which was merely "the history or science of races"—and which, hamstrung by biblical dogma, had become mired in arguments over their unity or plurality. By contrast, anthropology would treat the great questions of man's relation to animals, his connection with the physical universe, the laws regulating his physical nature, and his psychological characteristics—in short, everything pertaining to his nature. While it would place heavy emphasis on the distinctions between human races and would in fact include ethnology as a subdivision, it would far transcend the ethnology of Prichard—whose works, to the "disgrace" of science, were "still the text-books of the day." Although it would be strictly empirical, rejecting unproven hypotheses and busying itself with the collection of facts, anthropology would also be practical—discovering the laws that were "secretly working for the development of some nations and the destruction of others." Ultimately, it would require government aid and university cooperation in the training of anthropologists, but for the present its growth would depend on the Anthropological Society of London.[20]

With such a vocation, and a leader of Hunt's evident dynamism, the Anthropological Society grew with amazing rapidity, despite the fact that its internal life was marred by dissension and by frequent resignations. Within two years there were over 500 members, and in 1866 constitutional provisions were established for local branches—at least one of which was founded in Manchester. The Society was also involved in an active publishing program, including its own *Memoirs,* a series of translations of foreign anthropological works, an *Anthropological Review* (which included the Society's *Journal*), and an abortive *Popular Magazine of Anthropology*—although the last two were in fact the personal organs of Hunt. During the decade when Darwinism made the nature of man a matter of general public intellectual concern, the growth of the Anthropological Society was so phenomenal that even unfriendly observers felt there "was nothing like it in any other scientific body in the country."[21]

The Darwinian Resistance to "Anthropology"

Given the common retrospective association of "anthropology" with Darwinism, it seems a bit odd that the men most closely identified with that viewpoint, including those we remember today as sociocultural evolutionists, were on the whole extremely antagonistic to the Anthropological Society. Although Tylor and Wallace belonged to it at the beginning, Tylor later on would have nothing to do with Hunt, and Wallace referred to the Society as "that *bête noire.*" Returning a proffered honarary diploma, Huxley spoke of it as "that nest of imposters"; Lubbock warned the French archeologist Morlot to steer clear. Hunt's resignation from the Ethnological Society in fact coincided with Lubbock's election as its president—which prompted Huxley to hope that "all the good men and true" would rally round. By and large they did, if not as regularly active members, then at least when called upon at moments of crisis. Knowledgeable contemporary observers were aware that "many of the most eminent of the Darwinians" were members of the Ethnological Society; and when Huxley became president in 1868, Hunt's journal feared it would become "little more than a sort of Darwinian club."[22] The fact that the Darwinians made the Ethnological Society the institutional vehicle for their "anthropological" interests, while vehemently rejecting that term—and joining in an eight-year struggle against Hunt's Anthropological Society—is an historical paradox worthy of some consideration.

At first glance, the important differences between the two groups do not command attention. The contents of their journals suggest a largely overlapping intellectual field, and throughout their conflict they met in the same building on different nights. Some men belonged to both societies, and some who belonged to one read papers to the other. Nor were all participants sensitive to the issues that divided them. John Beddoe later recalled how a paper he gave to the "anthropologicals" elicited inexplicable laughter—subsequently explained when he discovered that he had innocently but consistently used the tabu term "ethnological."[23] Nevertheless, there were in fact systematic differences that were much more than terminological.

Some of these differences were of a fundamental intellectual character. Despite the modern ring of many passages in Hunt's dissertations on the nature of anthropology, he made it a point to insist on his opposition to Darwinism, and that of his Society as well. Like Knox, he was influenced by German and French transcendental biologists, and while he was willing to hypothesize the "mutability of species," he would not accept the Darwinian mechanism. To Hunt, there was little difference between "a disciple of Darwin and a disciple of Moses—one calls in natural selection with unlimited power, and the other calls in a Deity provided in the same manner." Underlying this explicit anti-Darwinism was an anthropological approach in many respects uncongenial to a developmental study of man. In contrast to the broad vision of "the science of man" proclaimed in his presidential address, Hunt's primary scientific concern in practice was a rather narrow and static physical anthropology, well-illustrated in a paper on "anthropological classification" he gave to his Society soon after its founding. Rejecting the origin of man as an insoluble problem at present, Hunt proposed instead "merely to classify man as he now exists, or has existed since the historical period," on the basis of anatomical and physiological characteristics, and most especially "the form of the cranium." Leading physical anthropologists played a prominent role among the "anthropologicals," and more detailed comparison of the two societies' journals reveals three times as many physical anthropological articles in their *Memoirs* as were to be found in the *Transactions* of the "ethnologicals." The incompatibility of the typological assumptions of classical physical anthropology with evolutionism and the resistance of many leading physical anthropologists to Darwinism need not be reiterated here. Suffice it to say that many of them were (or had been) polygenists, and tended like Hunt to greet Darwinism as a disguised reassertion of the Prichardian doctrine of human unity.[24]

By contrast, the intellectual orientation of the Ethnological Society—save for its association with religious orthodoxy—was not incompatible with the sorts of questions evolutionists were interested in. Philologically oriented ethnologists were by no means totally antagonistic to the study of physical anthropology, or to the craniological differences between human races, but they viewed such matters in a more flexible framework. Whereas in Hunt's polygenetic view human races were basically unmodifiable over time, Prichardian ethnology placed great emphasis on the molding of human types to different environmental circumstances. Similarly, the historical and diffusionist orientation of the older ethnology was easily redirected toward a concern with the development of civilization—which in the earlier work of Tylor and Lubbock was still couched in diffusionist terms. The underlying compatibility of the old ethnology and the new evolutionism was in fact foreshadowed in a remark made by Richard Cull as early as 1851. Discussing the antagonistic relationship he saw between the "ethnologist" and the "naturalist," Cull suggested that the former studied "past history in order to trace descent and origin," going on to ask: "but who ever heard of a Naturalist studying fossils to trace descent and origin?" Within the decade, Darwin provided the answer to Cull's rhetorical question, and a number of naturalists concerned with "descent and origin" rallied around Lubbock in the Ethnological Society.[25]

This is not to say that all the "anthropologicals" were anti-Darwinian and polygenist, or that the "ethnologicals" were uniformly evolutionist and monogenist. Many of the almost 800 who joined Hunt's Society were attracted by his popularizing appeals and were merely nominal members—some of them later dropping out or resigning when they became more aware of the Society's character. Nor was the inner circle itself entirely homogeneous. Some, attracted by Hunt's plea for a broad-gauge science of man, merely tolerated his polygenist racialism. Neither were the young Darwinian naturalists and prehistorians the only group within the ethnologicals—the bulk of that Society continued to be made up of old-line philological ethnologists, traditional antiquarians, and others of rather diffuse interests. But if the monogenist C. S. Wake remained with the "anthropologicals," and if polygenist John

Crawfurd was a staunch champion of the "ethnological" cause, the contrast of dominant intellectual orientation is nevertheless clear enough.

Nor was this the only contrast between the two societies. Recent analysis of the characteristics of their leadership suggests important differences in social origin and status. The "anthropologicals" seem more likely to have come from traditionally established social backgrounds—but from marginal positions within them; the "ethnologicals" were from dissenting middle-class backgrounds, but of the sort from which in this period a new "intellectual aristocracy" was emerging. More of the "ethnologicals" were university educated, more were successful in established professions, more held office in other major metropolitan societies, more were members of the Athenaeum and the Royal Society. And whereas there were three Liberals for every Tory among the "ethnologicals," among the "anthropologicals" this ratio was reversed.[26]

The political differences between the two groups were quite strikingly manifest. Here, the tone of the Anthropological Society was set by Hunt in his first presidential address, which appeared in the first of the Society's *Memoirs*. Entitled, in obvious paraphrase of Thomas Huxley, "On the Negro's Place in Nature," Hunt's paper was a compendium of anatomical, physiological, and psychological evidence and opinion that might well stand as archetypical of the traditional racist view of blacks. Asserting that Negroes were a different species, closer to the ape than to the European, Hunt argued that they were incapable of civilization, either on their own or through the influence of others; indeed, they were better off as slaves in the Confederate States of America than as freemen in Sierra Leone. Nor was Hunt's paper an isolated manifestation. When Governor Eyre's ruthless suppression of a rising of black farmers on Jamaica roused a furor among liberals and humanitarians in 1866, the response of the Anthropological Society was a public meeting at which Captain Bedford Pim gave a paper on "The Negro and Jamaica." Pim's racist diatribe was greeted "with loud cheers" and a unanimous vote of thanks, after which one member of the audience after another got up to offer comments on "the true art of governing alien races"—one even advocating killing savages as "a philanthropic principle": when trouble broke out, there was "mercy in a massacre."[27]

Nor were the political concerns of Hunt and the "anthropologicals" limited to issues of colonial policy. Closer to home, they felt that "much of the misery we see around us" could be attributed to the illusion that "our fellow countrymen" were "beings so advanced in the scale of humanity as to be able to be left to themselves," rather than racial types with inherent psychological peculiarities that a wise government would take into consideration. Characteristically, leading "anthropologicals" were opposed to Bentham, Mill, and the Westminster philosophy, to

Bright, Gladstone, and the Liberal party, to missionaries and "social science" reformers—in short, to all who would not see basic issues of politics, economics, and philanthropy in racial terms. And often, quite vitriolically: for Hunt, "opponents of comparative anthropology" were simply people of "arrested brain growth" and "deficient reasoning power" who suffered respectively from "the religious mania, and the rights-of-man mania."[28]

The politics of the "ethnologicals" are less evident in that Society's publications—a fact itself distinguishing the two groups. But Lubbock was a Liberal M. P., and Huxley a leader of the attack on Governor Eyre; and many of the rest held just those humanitarian, utilitarian, and liberal views Hunt so scathingly attacked. True, like most Victorians, they tended to regard a darker skin as sign of both physical and cultural inferiority, and some of them—including Galton, who replaced Hunt as secretary in 1863—in fact held racial views in some respects as extreme as those of the "anthropologicals." But in contrast to Hunt, Galton felt that the "political value" of anthropology was that it taught us to sympathize with other races, and to regard them "as our kinsmen, rather than as aliens"; and even old John Crawfurd, who in fact argued the diversity of human races on linguistic grounds, was a staunch opponent of slavery. In general, it seems clear that on matters of race, the Ethnological Society continued to be conditioned by its origin in the humanitarian movement, as well as by the liberal political orientation of many of its members.[29]

In addition to these intellectual, social, and political differences, the two societies were sharply differentiated in tone and style. It was not simply that the "ethnologicals" were irritated by the kind of lampooning they received in the pages of the *Anthropological Review*; more generally, Hunt and the leading "anthropologicals" violated the canons of behavior appropriate to a scientific society composed of respectable gentlemen. The inner clique of the Anthropological Society ate together regularly in a group in some respects not unlike the "X Club," or the "Red Lions" of the British Association—of which several leading "ethnologicals" were members. But the "anthropological" group called itself "The Cannibal Club" and were gavelled to order by a mace in the form of a Negro head. Despite the complaints of the Christian Union across the street, the Anthropological Society displayed in its front window an articulated savage skeleton. Nor was the Christian Union the only religious body the "anthropologicals" provoked. According to Hunt, "most of the missionary societies" were "in arms" against the Anthropological Society after it devoted four consecutive meetings in 1865 to often sharply critical discussion of "the benefits of missionary work among savage races." It is in this context of free-wheeling discussion of a wide range of controversial topics that one must understand the issue which by some accounts provoked the separation of the two societies: the admission of women to the meetings of the Ethnological Society. For the "anthropologicals," who sought a "liberty of thought and freedom of speech" unrivaled by any other scientific society, the presence of women made it impossible to discuss freely matters of human anatomy and physiology, or such questions as phallic worship and male and female circumcision.[30]

This difference in style is archetypified in the personality of Richard Burton—who chaired the first meeting of the "anthropologicals," served as their president, and is the only one save the poet Swinburne who is still widely known today. The first of those venturous Victorians to disguise himself as an Arab in order to travel to the Moslem holy city of Mecca, Burton's life was a fugue on themes of cultural marginality and psychological dualism. At once fascinated and repelled by non-European cultures, he authored diatribes against the "abnormal cruelty" of the Africans after having joined the King of Dahomey in a *pas de deux* at a ritual decapitation dance. A latent homosexual who maintained a virtually asexual relationship with his morally rigid Catholic wife, Burton was at the same time a close friend of such "other Victorians" as Monckton Milnes and H. S. Ashbee, and risked prosecution to publish works his wife and most of his contemporaries thought pornographic. At once coveting and despising the conventional trappings of gentility, projecting in his own split personality all the tensions underlying the Victorian notion of gentlemanly respectability, Burton was a kind of Victorian outcast-hero, ultimately both knighted and notorious. Such a figure could not in a strict sense be "representative" of the "anthropologicals," whose membership lists included many fellows "canvassed for among general practitioners and clergymen in the country." But that Burton should have been regarded as the Anthropological Society's shining ornament clearly tells something of its character. From the point of view of the contemporary world of science, the "anthropologicals" were marginal men, and they saw themselves as such—cheering Burton as "the great destroyer of the scientific mock-modesty of this age."[31]

By contrast, the leading Darwinians—Huxley, Lubbock, Lane Fox Pitt Rivers, Evans, and Galton—were part of an emerging "intellectual aristocracy" which, intermarrying among themselves, was to endure for generations. Far from being marginal to the world of science, they were young men in the process of entering the scientific establishment. They were committed to one large heterodoxy—the "ape-theory" of the origin of man—and they took fairly "advanced" positions on theological questions. But they were confident that their heterodoxy was on its way to scientific orthodoxy, and they were not inclined to complicate matters unnecessarily by adopting extreme positions on other issues, proclaiming themselves a forum for the unrestricted discussion of unseemly topics, or otherwise violating the canons of respectable behavior. And if they favored the widespread diffusion of scientific knowledge and perhaps a certain democratization of its internal organization, they drew the line when it came to the Anthropological Society of London, which outnumbered them by more than two to one, and at one point considered canvassing a list of 8,000 names for prospective members.[32]

Organizational Struggle and Institutional Compromise

Throughout the decade of the Darwinian revolution relations between the Anthropological Society and the Ethnological Society were characterized by conflict, recrimination, and the failure of several attempts at reconciliation. The major arena of dispute was the annual meeting of the British Association, where the "anthropologicals" sought recognition for their new conception of the science of man. In 1864 they tried to get Section E renamed to include anthropology as well as ethnology and geography, but failed when the Association's leaders rallied to the support of John Lubbock, who argued that ethnology was "an older and prettier word"—thereby stimulating a considerable amount of historical research by the "anthropologicals" to show that theirs was actually the older term. The following year, Hunt's followers came in force to Birmingham to win a separate section, but were defeated by what they called "one of the most disgraceful pieces of cliquism ever known in the British Association." Fearing that the power of the scientific establishment would no longer suffice against the sheer force of "anthropological" numbers, Huxley succeeded in convincing Lubbock before the 1866 meetings that they should acquiesce in the formation of a Department of Anthropology within Section D, which was reorganized that year and named "Biology," while ethnology continued to be associated with geography in Section E.[33]

The relative success of the two groups that year made it clear that the "anthropological" conception of a broad-gauged natural science of man (articulated on this occasion by Alfred Russel Wallace) did in fact have considerable scientific appeal when it was not so closely tied to the personality and institutional activities of James Hunt. Even so, the "anthropologicals" suffered a serious setback at Dundee in 1867, when the leadership of the Association, apparently anticipating hostility to the brash new science in the conservative Scottish milieu, cancelled the anthropological department at the last moment, forcing Hunt and his colleagues to hold an impromptu "Dundee Anthropological Conference" instead. In 1868, most of the anthropological activity was again shifted to a parallel conference, when the International Congress of Prehistoric Archaeology met with the British Association in Norwich. By this time, however, the general committee of the Association had recommended that in the future "Ethnology" be omitted from the name of Section E; and in 1869, when anthropological papers were again presented in large numbers, they were again given to a "department" in Section D (Biology). In 1871, the name of that department was finally settled as "Anthropology," and that same year the general committee rejected an attempt by the original founder of the Ethnological Society, Richard King, to reestablish a subsection of "Ethnology."[34]

Within the British Association, the outcome of the conflict was thus a kind of compromise. To the extent that the "anthropologicals" were in harmony with the movement of British science, they won their point. The Darwinian revolution had not only placed dark-skinned savages in an evolutionary framework; at least in principle it required mankind in general to be viewed as part of the natural world. It was therefore quite appropriate that the subject matter of ethnology should be incorporated into a broader "science of man," and that, after a lapse of two decades, it would resume an affiliation with the biological sciences in the British Association. But if the Darwinians thus accepted the idea and even the name of "anthropology," they did not allow it to be conceived solely in physical anthropological terms; nor did they yield effective institutional control to a group of scientific and political mavericks.

In this context, a reunion was eventually effected between the two competing societies, although not until after the failure of several attempts to heal their breach. In acknowledgment of Huxley's peacemaking role at the British Association in 1866, the Anthropological Society, unanimously expressing willingness to consider amalgamation, asked him to become their president. Although negotiations were cut short by the resistance of John Crawfurd, then president of the "ethnologicals," they were resumed after Crawfurd's death, when Huxley agreed to succeed him only on condition that the "ethnologicals" support his efforts to end a separation that was becoming something of a "scientific scandal." At the last minute, however, the proposed union broke down when the "anthropologicals" refused to accept the rather cumbersome compromise name agreed on by Huxley and Hunt: "The Society for the Promotion of the Science of Man."[35]

In the aftermath of this failure there was a long and nasty exchange in the *Athenaeum* in which one of the negotiators for the "ethnologicals" (who, like some others, belonged to both groups) charged the leadership of the Anthropological Society with "charlatanism, puffery and jobbery" in the handling of its membership and finances. Membership had been inflated by nonpaying fellows, some of whom were elected without having applied; and since they received gratis the *Anthropological Review*, the paying fellows were in effect subsidizing what was in fact a private publishing venture of Hunt's, at a time when the Society was more than £1,000 in debt. Furthermore, the domination of the "cannibal clique" made it impossible for the "independent" members to remedy the situation—with the result that a steady stream of resignations had finally produced a net decline in membership. In 1869, the "independents" reopened the question of union, proposing another cumbersome compromise name: the "Society for the Study of Man in its Widest Interpretation." This time, it was Hunt who became suspicious that Huxley intended to take advantage of dissension to "crush us," and the "cannibal clique" voted to reject any proposal that violated the integrity of the Anthropological Society's name.

In the meantime, Huxley had turned his attention to reinvigorating the Ethnological Society, which had suffered under the aging Crawfurd's leadership. The internal structure was modified; the annual *Transactions* were converted to a quarterly *Journal*; and a distinction was introduced between special meetings, at which more "popular" topics would be discussed, and ordinary meetings, where "scientific" subjects would be treated in more technical terms, and "ladies will not be admitted." During this period, the "anthropologicals" continued to be plagued by dissension: in the last months before his death in 1869, even Hunt was at odds with the "cannibal clique." While things seem to have been more peaceful under his mild-mannered successor, John Beddoe, the organization's finances and membership continued to decline.

Although Huxley persisted in pushing amalgamation, it was not until after the Liverpool meeting of the British Association in 1870, where for the first time the two groups met in relative harmony within the same subsection ("Ethnology and Anthropology"), that the basis for rapprochement was laid by electing Beddoe to the Association's council. Early the next year final negotiations were undertaken at a meeting between Huxley, Lane Fox, and four from the "anthropological" side. The name was still a problem, but Huxley came up with a form that recognized the science but not the society of his antagonists: The Anthropological Institute of Great Britain and Ireland. Council membership and six vice-presidencies were evenly divided; and when several "anthropologicals" balked at Huxley for president, he convinced Lubbock to accept instead.

It took another half decade for the embers of controversy to cool. The "anthropologicals" were more regular in attending the Institute's meetings than the "ethnologicals," whose scientific activities cut a wider swath; on several occasions the latter called special meetings to reverse defeats suffered when some of their more broadly-ranging colleagues had been absent. Matters came to a head in the preparation of the house list for 1873, when Huxley, on Lubbock's behalf, proposed John Evans for president. Having assumed that there would be rotation in this office, the "anthropologicals" succeeded instead in nominating one of the more active of the old "cannibal clique." Back in force at the next meeting, the "ethnologicals" revised the house list by nominating George Busk (a physical anthropologist, but a Darwinian), claimed four of the six vice-presidencies, and introduced a new policy for council membership that virtually wiped out the "anthropological" representation—a victory facilitated by the refusal of ten "anthropologicals" to participate in an "illegal" meeting. When this coup was sustained by a vote of three to one at the next annual meeting, a group of "anthropologicals" withdrew to reorganize as the London Anthropological Society; but although they continued to meet for over a year, and published one volume of a journal, the recalcitrants eventually succumbed from limited support. Petitioning to rejoin the Institute, they were (on the principle of "the survival of the fittest") allowed to do so as individuals, but not in a body. From that time forward, the minutes indicate no further traces of controversy, although the private correspondence of several leading figures suggests continuing concern with recurring "symptoms of Cannibalism."

Retrospectively, it seems quite appropriate that the controversy was resolved by the founding of an *Anthropological* Institute in the same year that *The Descent of Man* was published. The intellectual issues of the preceding decade—which Huxley had defined as *Man's Place in Nature*—seem much more adequately reflected by "anthropology" than by "ethnology." Had the former term not been preempted by a scientific upstart for a controversial and somewhat disreputable group, the Darwinians might well have chosen to adopt it themselves. As it was, when the possibility developed that Lubbock might become president of an amalgamated group in 1867, Huxley cautioned him that the title "President of the Anthropological Society" might hinder his attempt to gain a seat in Parliament. And once the name had become focus for such bitter conflict, it was very hard for some to swallow. The difficulty is suggested in a letter Mrs. Lubbock wrote to Mrs. Darwin in 1873, asking if Mr. Darwin would head a subscription to pay off the Institute's inherited debt of £700. That done, they could drop the "horrid" word "anthropological" and "go back to the Ethnological, which was the root of the whole thing." But the resistance to "anthropology" had by this time almost passed: when a redemption fund liquidated the debt the following year, no one seems to have thought to raise the issue of the name. On the contrary, Lane Fox's presidential address for 1875 referred quite casually to "the progress of anthropological science." By then, anthropology, if not a household word, had at least achieved scientific respectability.[36]

The Anthropology of the Anthropological Institute

Despite the stirring of embers in 1873, there was a general sense in British anthropology in the early 1870s that the period of institutional and intellectual controversy and self-definition had passed, and that it was possible to turn to a more normal form of scientific activity. The sectional addresses of the British Association, which had focused on definitions of the field, began to treat specific substantive anthropological matters. As Lane Fox suggested in 1872, certain major issues had been settled: the antiquity and descent of man, his ultimate monogenetic origin, and the progressive character of the growth of civilization. What was needed now were more and better data. At the same meeting, a committee was set up, with Lane Fox as secretary, to draw up brief forms of instruction "for travellers, ethnologists and other anthropological observers." By 1874, the committee, in which Tylor played the dominant intellectual role, had produced the first edition of *Notes and Queries on Anthropology, for the Use of Travellers and Residents in Uncivilized Lands.* Although the dropping of "ethnologists" from the intended audience of *Notes and Queries* suggests a settling back into the armchair, the men who in that little volume proudly labeled themselves "anthropologists" clearly anticipated a period of hard work and slow progress within an accepted framework, one that would be remembered as having established the new science on a solid empirical, theoretical, and institutional footing—a period, perhaps, of "normal science."[37]

Although the serious history of later-nineteenth-century British anthropology has barely been begun, it seems on first glance a rather dry and dull period, of interest primarily for the light it casts back on the intellectual and institutional effort of the earlier evolutionary generation, and forward on the surge of activity out of which modern British social anthropology emerged after 1900. Dryness and dullness—qualities perhaps characteristic of the scholarly journal as genre—are of course not inconsonant with "normal science." Nevertheless, an analysis of the contents of the *Journal of the Anthropological Institute* during its first two decades reveals relatively little that one might call, even by loose analogy, "normal science" within an evolutionary paradigm.[38]

True, in discussing the work of the *Notes and Queries* committee in 1874, Lane Fox had suggested that the transformation of ethnology into anthropology reflected the emergence of "sociology," which gave every work of man's hand and brain social evolutionary significance, just as in natural history every variety of organism and every organic part was now studied in relation to the evolution of species. But when he subsequently analyzed the Institute's papers for 1881, his category "sociology" was to say the least somewhat heterogeneous. Its seven articles included one on Thomas Aquinas, one on cranial deformation (assuredly a work of hand on brain), one on Andamanese bone necklaces, one on Fijian riddles, and one by Tylor on the Asiatic relations of Polynesian culture. This is not to say that there was nothing sociological to be found in the *Journal*. Retrospectively, its most historically significant content is perhaps a series of papers on Australian social organization by Lorimer Fison and A. W. Howitt, who were ethnographic correspondents first of the American evolutionist Lewis Henry Morgan and then of Tylor. Their work contributed in a significant way to the later evolutionary period's single most important theoretical essay: Tylor's 1888 article on marriage and descent. In general, however, the *Journal* contained relatively little ethnographic material clearly bearing directly on theoretical issues of sociocultural evolutionism.[39]

It might be argued that an atheoretical ethnography was just what the Institute's leaders wished, since they envisioned a sharp division of labor between those abroad who would supply the necessary observations—but who "are not anthropologists"—and those at home who would use that data "for the scientific study of anthropology." Fittingly from this point of view, there is relatively little overt theory manifest in *Notes and Queries*. Those already familiar with *Primitive Culture* may easily see its categories and assumptions giving structure to Tylor's queries on religion, myth, magic, and superstition; and attitudinal assumptions of a broadly evolutionary sort are evident here and there throughout. But the emphasis was on detailed and careful observation, and the prefatory orientations seem intended largely to counteract prior assumption that might be present in the mind of an untrained observer.[40]

In this context, it is revealing to look at the "first fruits" of *Notes and Queries*, which did not arrive until 1882, when E. H. Man, who had spent twelve years as Assistant Superintendent of the Andaman and Nicobar Islands, presented his ethnographic observations to the Institute in three evening meetings. For the most part, Man's material was straightforwardly descriptive, following closely the categories of *Notes and Queries*. Where he went beyond these categories—as in his discussion of Andaman religion—the influence of prior assumption is immediately evident; however, it was not Tylorian evolutionary theory, but traditional Christian belief that governed Man's personal interpretations.[41]

Man's example suggests something about the general character of the ethnographic data in the *Journal*. Although *Notes and Queries* was sent to colonial governors throughout the empire for distribution to those who might be "brought into contact with natives," the major works of the evolutionary writers were not easily obtainable out on the ethnographic periphery, where the most active intellectual influence was likely to be missionary Christianity. If men on the spot brought with them from the intellectual center prior anthropological knowledge, it was more likely to have been ethnological than evolutionary. If, like Fison and Howitt, they established epistolary contact with anthropologists back in England, these contacts could also be with nonevolutionary writers—notably Max Müller, whose linguistic interests made him one of the most active anthropological correspondents back home. It is not surprising, therefore, that insofar as the pages of the *Journal* reflected paradigmatic assumptions, these were more likely to be those of traditional ethnology, since the problems of ethnic origin and relationship (who were these people? where did they come from?) were perhaps the most likely to command the immediate attention of ethnographic observers. In this context, the most likely "theoretical" ground against which ethnographic observation would be made was a rather generalized body of ethnocentric assumption, which could have an evolutionary aura insofar as it was cast in culturally or racially hierarchical terms, but whose specific anthropological content, if any, was more likely to be traditionally ethnological.[42]

The *Notes and Queries* committee no doubt assumed that data provided by such ethnography could be synthesized by evolutionary theorists in Britain. But much of the impetus of social evolutionary theorizing seems to have been spent in the initial revolution. Lubbock largely withdrew from anthropology; McLennan became bogged down in belaboring Henry Maine on the priority of patriarchy; Spencer was preoccupied with the completion of his *Synthetic Philosophy*; and save for his synthesizing paper on problems of marriage and descent in 1888, Tylor's later anthropology seems mostly a rehashing of themes defined early on. The great unfinished work of his later years was an extensive reconsideration of the problem of "natural religion," which was simply an elaboration and defense of the argument of *Primitive Culture*.[43]

This is not to say that there were no attempts in the 1870s and 1880s to present ethnographic accounts in terms of social evolutionary categories, or to follow up significant theoretical issues arising from the works of the classical evolutionary writers. Although Everhard Im Thurn's book about his travels *Among the Indians of Guiana* was written before he attended Tylor's early Oxford lectures, Tylorian assumption was clearly evident in his discussion of their religious beliefs. Within folklore, Andrew Lang was carrying the Tylorian banner against the Müllerians. And although it reflected also the influence of more traditional historical and philological scholarship, William Robertson Smith's *Kinship and Marriage in Early Arabia* may be thought of as a conscious attempt to demonstrate McLennan's "matriarchal" theories in a critical ethnographic case (the presumably patriarchal early Semites). Similarly, Smith's discussion of totemism in the *Religion of the Semites* was heavily influenced by both McLennan and Tylor. But although James Frazer published his little volume of that name in 1887, the anthropological debate on totemism did not really get going until after Baldwin Spencer and Frank Gillen published their account of the Arunta *intichiuma* ceremonies in 1896. Retrospectively, it is possible to construct—although not in the publications of the Institute—a debate between McLennan and Morgan on such presently relevant issues as the biological or social significance of kinship terms. But at the time there was perhaps more widespread interest in such matters as "primitive promiscuity," "marriage by capture," and the relative priority of "matriarchal" and "patriarchal" marriage—issues that in retrospect seem much more conditioned by ulterior motive. It may have been this preoccupation, rather than (as has been suggested) the influence of Tylor's preoccupation with rationalistic interpretations of primitive religion, that diverted classical evolutionism from realizing its "sociological" potential. Be that as it may, it seems likely that social evolutionism, rather than functioning as a puzzle-generating paradigm for "normal science," may have had more day-to-day anthropological significance as a kind of groundwork of ideological assumption pervading the later-nineteenth-century anthropological scene.[44]

But whatever its relationship to evolutionary theory, ethnography seems not to have bulked so large in the *Journal* as the authors of *Notes and Queries* might have wished. Rarely did it fill more than a quarter of the total pages and often rather less than that. Indeed, viewed in terms of the geography of its subject matter, the *Journal* had a remarkably Europocentric and even Anglocentric focus—a reflection of the fact that in this period the Institute's activities were largely dominated by archeologists and physical anthropologists.

For the first decade of its existence, during which Lane Fox was the leading figure, the *Journal* was so heavily archeological that presidents of the Institute (themselves predominantly archeologists) were occasionally somewhat apologetic. When an exploration committee was founded in 1875, it was for archeological inquiries, and a number of the research committees organized by the anthropological section of the British Association were also archeological. Toward the end of the decade, however, the Institute had gone into an obvious decline, which the physical anthropologist William Flower—looking to the flourishing state of French and German anthropology—attributed to the neglect of problems of race. In 1874, Lane Fox had been willing to relegate racial issues to paleontology and geology for determination in the distant future; but in 1882 Flower argued that structure was more urgent than origin because of its practical importance in a multiracial empire (if Englishmen abroad knew more about what race *really* meant, they would not apply "the same contemptuous epithet"—"nigger"—indiscriminately to Kaffirs, Hindus, Australian aborigines, and even Maoris!). An anthropometric committee had been in existence in the British Association since 1876, and soon spawned a separate committee to obtain photographs of the "typical races of the British Isles." When the Institute did in fact begin to revive somewhat in the mid-1880s, it was under the leadership of a series of physical anthropologists, among whom Francis Galton played the dominant role.[45]

Again, the predominance of archeology and physical anthropology in the 1870s and 1880s casts retrospective light on the transformation of anthropology in the Darwinian revolution. In contrast to linguistics, which had provided the intellectual backbone of traditional ethnology, but which represented only a tiny fraction of the total contents of the Institute's *Journal*, archeology and physical anthropology were two of the major contributing forces to the crisis of pre-Darwinian ethnology. In contrast to ethnography, which was pursued far afield by men who had at best tenuous ties to the world of British science, archeology and physical anthropology could be carried on in relation to bodies of data available close at hand at home. Furthermore, both were susceptible to a degree of technical elaboration, and were closely tied to well-established fields of scientific inquiry (geology and biology) that were in fact the primary foci of Darwinian scientific activity. Given the somewhat abortive development of Lane Fox's category "sociology," and the fact that after 1878 the Folk-Lore Society provided an alternative institutional focus for the intellectual energies of Tylorian scholars, it is not surprising that archeologists (Lubbock, Lane Fox Pitt Rivers, and Evans) and physical anthropologists (Busk, Flower, Galton, Beddoe, Macalister) were the dominant figures in the Institute during its first two decades.[46]

Nor is it surprising that the evolutionists who had led in its founding should accept these developments as normal to the "anthropology" of the Institute. The artifacts of British barrows and the cranial characters of visitors to Galton's Anthropometric Laboratory were as much the subject matter of a general "science of man" as the details of Australian social organization. And if they did not all clearly articulate in a coherent paradigm, they were nonetheless encompassable within a broadly evolutionary perspective—in which traditional ethnological questions of racial genealogy could find a place alongside those of a more strictly sociocultural evolutionary character, and both were enveloped in a pervasive ethnocentric aura of racial and cultural hierarchy.

The Limits of Institutionalization in Victorian Anthropology

The rather diffuse and unfocused character of postevolutionary anthropology may reflect also the limits of its institutionalization in this period. With very few exceptions, the members of the Anthropological Institute were men for whom anthropology was an occasional or avocational activity. The day was just dawning when a university student could choose science as a professional career; and while several who did (including Alfred Cort Haddon, who was trained in Sir Michael Foster's Cambridge school of physiology, and Baldwin Spencer, who attended Tylor's lectures at Oxford) chose in the end to make anthropology their scientific specialty, it was only in the generation of *their* students that it began to be possible to receive systematic university training as an "anthropologist." Others whose vocation was more literary than scientific were similarly constrained; Andrew Lang felt he might have been a "really big 'swell' in anthropology," if there had been any money in it. For both men of science and of letters—as well as those of independent means—anthropology was likely to be only one intellectual interest among several: just as Lang was largely occupied with reviews and poetry and fairy tales, men like Galton, Huxley, Lubbock, and Wallace all had other scientific irons in the fire. Still others were lawyers first, or doctors; Tylor was unusual in that he had no prior occupational commitment and his bibliography consists almost entirely of writings on anthropological topics.[47]

Even so, the institutional base of anthropology was beginning to extend a bit beyond such voluntary scientific associations as the Anthropological Institute and the British Association (where anthropology finally won full section status in 1884). The establishment of the Crystal Palace as a permanent museum was part of a broader Victorian museum movement that by mid-century had produced numerous local historical, antiquarian, and natural historical museums, and was transforming the British Museum from a place "intended only for the amusement of the curious and the rich" into "the largest and most popular educational center in the Kingdom." Many of these museums contained objects of anthropological relevance—primarily, of course, those of local archeology, although in the case of the British Museum there were also large ethnographic collections originating from the expeditions of Captain Cook. In a period when not only anthropology, but science generally, was much more "object"—or specimen—oriented than today, the existence of such collections became a significant inertial factor impelling anthropology toward further institutionalization, and even to a limited extent toward "professionalization," as full-time paid curators began in some of the larger or more specialized institutions to see their emergent curatorial professional identity in specifically anthropological terms.[48]

By this time natural scientists had become concerned that the scientific functions of museums were suffering relative to those of "rational amusement" and the "diffusion of knowledge," and had begun to emphasize the dual nature of the museum and the importance of separate research collections. As natural science instruction began to be established in the universities, they too, became foci of museum activity. When Henry Christy died in 1865, and the disposition of his ethnological collection was placed in the hands of John Lubbock and three other trustees, George Rolleston—who as Linacre Professor did the only teaching of biology at Oxford's recently established museum of natural history—proposed that it be given to Oxford. With Max Müller in language, Rawlinson in history, and himself in natural history, all that was needed was prehistoric archeology "to fill up the foundations we are laying for adequate study of Man's origin and beginnings." But although an Anthropological Society was formed at Oxford at about this time, the Christy collection was given instead to the British Museum, and it was more than a decade before Rolleston's hopes for anthropology at Oxford were to be realized.[49]

In 1880, after illness and accident had overtaken twelve intervening heirs, Lane Fox—by then a Major General—inherited the 29,000-acre estate that had once belonged to his great uncle, George Pitt, second Baron Rivers. Adopting the name Pitt Rivers, he now found a new outlet for his anthropological energies in the systematic excavation of the estate's numerous prehistoric remains. By this time, his ethnological collection, which had been removed from his home to the Bethnal Green Museum in 1874, and thence to the South Kensington Museum in 1878, was once more threatening to burst the limits of its space, and Pitt Rivers offered it to the British Museum. In contrast to the Christy collection, which had been organized on geographical principles compatible with those of the British Museum (and of diffusionary ethnology), Pitt Rivers' collection had from the beginning been organized in typological developmental terms; despite his continuing interest in tracing the origin of particular species to particular geographical locations, his collection was specifically "evolutionary" in character. But although a review committee (including Lubbock and Huxley) was willing to accept conditions Pitt Rivers attached to his gift to preserve the integrity of his arrangement, the responsible parliamentary committee overruled the review committee's unanimous recommendation and rejected the offer. Pitt Rivers had to turn elsewhere, and in March 1882 he wrote to H. N. Moseley, Rolleston's successor as Linacre Professor, offering the entire collection to Oxford University. Over the next few months, the terms of the gift were more precisely worked out to guarantee the collection's principle of arrangement and to provide its separate housing in an annex to be constructed to the University Museum.[50]

In the meantime, the internal push to establish anthropology at Oxford had been restimulated, largely by Max Müller. In February 1883, as the result of a formal petition on his behalf by twenty Oxford professors, Tylor gave two public lectures on anthropology at the university, and when the Keeper of the University Museum died early that very month, Tylor was chosen to replace him. In this context, Pitt Rivers—perhaps recalling Tylor's role in facilitating his election to the Royal Society in 1875—seems to have had further thoughts about the terms of his bequest. Although a deed of gift had already been drawn up and agreed to by the University, negotiations were reopened, and when an amended deed was finally approved in 1884, it included the stipulation that a lecturer be appointed to give regular instruction in anthropology. By that time Tylor—whose Quaker connection was no longer a bar to university teaching after the reforms of the 1870s—had been granted an M.A. and appointed Reader in Anthropology. Within the next two years, the "anthropological" personnel of the university were further increased by the appointment of Arthur Thomson as Lecturer in Human Anatomy and the hiring of Henry Balfour to assist Moseley (who as Linacre Professor had primary responsibility) in cataloguing and arranging the Pitt Rivers materials.[51]

If the Pitt Rivers bequest gained a foothold in the academy for anthropology, it remained throughout the century a narrow and precarious one. Tylor's position was structurally anomalous, and his lectures usually drew rather small and heterogeneous audiences, many of them nonacademics. Thomson did not lecture on physical anthropology until 1895, and Balfour's position only became permanent in 1890, when the cataloguing and setting up of the Pitt Rivers collection, much to the general's irritation, had dragged on for six years. During this period, a series of attempts to gain recognition for anthropology as an honors subject were unsuccessful—due to a lingering *odium scientificum* it carried for the still numerically dominant clerical and traditional humanist elements in the faculty.[52]

Developments at Cambridge, where an earlier attempt to get McLennan a teaching post had failed, despite the support of Maine, were similar to those at Oxford, but without the stimulus of Pitt Rivers' involvement or Tylor's commitment to anthropology. The basis for the later Museum of Archaeology and Ethnology was established in 1883 by the acquisition of the collections of the Cambridge Antiquarian Society, which included Oceanian ethnological material collected by Sir Arthur Gordon and by Alfred Maudsley. But the museum was underfunded, and despite the fact that he had accompanied Maudsley to the Pacific, the curator, Baron Anatole von Hügel, paid little attention to ethnology. Similarly, the anthropological interests of the new Professor of Anatomy, Alexander Macalister, remained secondary to his strictly anatomical work; it was only with the appointment of Haddon to lecture in physical anthropology in 1895 that anthropology gained what was to become a permanent place in the teaching curriculum.[53]

In short, anthropology benefitted only in the most marginal way from the university reforms of the 1870s, and it was only at the end of the century that an effective endogenous impulse for the development of academic anthropology began to make itself felt. Prior to that time, it was primarily the sheer physical inertia of museum collections, which required custodial care, that gave the impetus to the rather fortuitous and very limited institutionalization anthropology achieved outside the Anthropological Institute.[54]

When considered in terms of commonly used sociological indicators of institutionalization, the marginality of the anthropological enterprise in later Victorian England becomes even more striking. True, a rather broad area of knowledge had been roughly delineated, and there was a disciplinary organization meeting monthly for most of the year, with further annual meetings at the British Association. A regular *Journal* served as a channel of communication within the field and in 1881 there was published what was in effect the first textbook: Tylor's compact synthesis of evolutionary *Anthropology*. In contrast to the social research of the period, anthropology—although heavily laden with unexamined ideological assumption—had been largely purged of "non-scientific" humanitarian concerns. But despite some specialization of research activity and systematization of method in particular areas—notably physical anthropology—for the most part there was not the degree of technical complexity that might mark off anthropological inquiry from the participation of the layman or the gentleman amateur.[55]

Nor can one point to any significant social demand for anthropological research. Certainly, anthropologists were on occasion given to arguing the social utility of their endeavor—witness Tylor's "reformer's science" rooting out illiberal survivals, or Pitt Rivers' assurance that his typological arrangement, by impressing the popular mind with "the slow growth" and continuity of evolutionary development, would make the working classes less likely to respond to revolutionary enthusiasts. And it may be that the racial surveys of the British population undertaken in the British Association were an attempt (adopting a methodology previously utilized by geologists and statistical societies) to win support for "research in the national interest"—although the pattern seems more likely to have been adopted for reasons of scientific availability than ostensible social utility. But there was little success in translating programmatic or rhetorical assertions of utility into real social demand sustained by significant resources.[56]

There was virtually no governmental consciousness of any serious need for anthropology either at home or abroad. It was only after considerable effort that Lubbock was able to get Parliament to act to preserve ancient monuments under the supervision of Pitt Rivers as Inspector-General. Overseas, some individual colonial administrators, like Alfred Lyall in India or Arthur Gordon in Fiji, were influenced by anthropological writings; and in India, the census activities of the British administration involved the collection of ethnographic information. But the Colonial Office seems to have done little more than from time to time forwarding to the Institute data collected by colonial officials incidentally to their regular duties, and in other ways facilitating communication with the ethnographic periphery.[57]

Beyond the government, the museum, and the academy, as potential sources of a social demand for anthropological research, one thinks of the missionary movement and the general literate public. But missionaries were more likely to be suppliers of ethnographic data than consumers of anthropological interpretation. And insofar as one might regard popular interest in the culturally exotic as a stimulant to anthropological research, it was probably forestalled by incipient professionalization, which made the *Journal* something less than a literary attraction. If travel accounts, or particular works by leading "armchair" anthropologists, were more widely read, this did not contribute to the support of institutionalized anthropological research.

In this context, the most significant demand for anthropological research was internal to the scientific community itself. On the one hand, it came from segments of that community who felt the importance of anthropological issues to their own scientific concerns, or who were simply willing to support the anthropological activities of their colleagues; on the other, from the somewhat various community of those who chose to regard themselves as "anthropologists." Correspondingly, the money from institutional sources specifically allocated for anthropological activities—probably totalling no more than several hundred pounds a year—came primarily from small grants from the British Association and from the subscriptions of the Anthropological Institute's members.[58]

In the absence of any significant social demand for anthropological research, the community of anthropologists continued throughout the century to be composed primarily of gentleman amateurs, or professionals in some other area of scientific or scholarly activity. Although certain portions of the general intellectual tradition passed on in the universities and some of the instruction in specialized inquiries (comparative anatomy or comparative philology) were particularly useful to anthropology, there was no institutional framework that could provide systematic specialized training for any aspect of the discipline until the 1880s, when several figures who were to be important to early-twentieth-century anthropology received training in the biological sciences at Cambridge and Oxford. But until nearly 1900, there were probably no more than a dozen men whose professional life was given over solely to anthropological activity, and with the qualified exception of Tylor none of them was regularly involved as an anthropologist in training men who would later devote their own professional lives to anthropology. In this context, there could scarcely be any "patterned recruitment of talented people" into the discipline, or any meaningful distinction between "researchers," "practitioners," and "cultivators"—except insofar as some "anthropologists" were practitioners in other scientific fields and may therefore have taken anthropological research more seriously. But by the same token, the interest of such persons in anthropology was likely to be spasmodic, and their interactive contribution to its institutionalization correspondingly limited.[59]

Although many of the same statements could be made about the institutionalization of anthropology in other countries in this period, there were places where it seemed to be on a somewhat surer institutional footing. In France, where the dominance of physical anthropology may have provided a closer approximation to a unified research paradigm, an Ecole d' Anthropologie with six professorial chairs was established by Paul Broca in 1876. In the United States, where John Wesley Powell managed to convince Congress that anthropology might be useful in dealing with American Indians, a Bureau of Ethnology was established in 1879. Furthermore, British anthropologists were by no means unaware of these developments, and later used the American and French examples as models for emulation.[60]

This overall institutional situation was of course reflected in the fortunes of the Anthropological Institute. Until the end of the century, its finances were always precarious, its membership fluctuating, and its leadership spasmodic. The intellectually most important figures often turned their attention elsewhere, and the stable core tended to be made up of men of more limited reputation and ability who were willing to devote themselves more regularly to the organization. For better or worse, however, the Institute remained the focal institution of British anthropology, and its character as an institution seems clearly related to the character of the anthropology manifest in its *Journal*.[61]

Viewing anthropology in institutional terms, as an activity carried on within a community of investigators rather than in terms of the intellectual contributions of a few leading figures, it is thus not surprising that the paradigm metaphor, which helped to illuminate the intellectual reorientation from ethnology to evolutionary anthropology, does not adequately characterize the day-to-day anthropological activity of the post-revolutionary period. True, the pervasive intellectual atmosphere within the broader community constituted by the Institute was in a general sense ''evolutionary,'' and sociocultural evolutionism in a stricter sense may appropriately be spoken of as its theoretical ''cynosure.'' And from the stereotyping perspective of later critics of social evolutionism, and of historians of the anthropological reorientation precipitated by their criticism, that viewpoint may seem to take on a retrospectively paradigmatic character. But although there was a consciousness of revolutionary change in 1870, the group of thinkers whom we associate with it did not at the time constitute an effective continuing paradigmatic community. Diverse in both personnel and intellectual outlook, the institutionalized anthropological community that emerged from the intellectual revolution of the 1860s was marginal to the world of science and the traditional institutions of learning, and lacked the resources to sustain a coherent research endeavor or the means to train reseachers to a single viewpoint. In this context, it is not surprising that, viewed from the perspective of its daily practice, later-nineteenth-century anthropology in Britain turned out to be an extremely various and multifocal inquiry, for which the term "discipline" seems appropriate only in a rather loose sense.[62]

The Victorian Anthropological Compromise

With the emergence of modern social anthropology in Great Britain in the early twentieth century, the broader tradition embodied in the Institute began to seem to some anthropologists less a means of self-definition than an obstacle to it. Although their primary subject matter remained the same, the range of questions they asked of it both narrowed and shifted focus. When the boundary relations of their inquiry were redefined, so were their myths of origin. Insofar as these myths treated the early nineteenth century, Prichard's long empty niche was filled now by August Comte.[63] And yet as the relationship of adjective and noun suggests, social anthropology remains to this day associated with the broader tradition of anthropology in Britain, and some of its most general characteristics perhaps reflect this link. From this point of view, as well as from a more purely historical one, it may be worthwhile to offer some more general comments on the way in which "anthropology" was institutionalized in nineteenth-century Britain.

Some previous accounts have tended to minimize the significance of the controversy out of which the Anthropological Institute emerged. The pattern was set as early as 1875, when the Institute's president spoke of the episode as "entirely of a merely personal character"; more recently, it has been interpreted as evidence of the "crisis and confusion" that followed when "old boundary posts of thought were uprooted."[64] But it can also be viewed more significantly, as embodying the general intellectual development of anthropology in this period. We have distinguished in mid-nineteenth-century British anthropology three intellectual orientations toward a common subject matter: the "ethnological," which drew upon a wide body of ethnographic data to solve the historical problem of relating all human groups to a single original root; the "anthropological," which, giving priority to the physical differences among men, sought to classify them into distinct types in the context of pre-Darwinian comparative anatomy; and the "evolutionary," which treated ethnographic and archeological data in the developmental context provided by the Darwinian revolution. At various points along the way, we have seen post-Darwinian evolutionary anthropology as a compromise formation, synthesizing elements of the ethnological and the physical anthropological orientations. So, too, may we see this process reflected in an institutional dialectic, in which the Ethnological Society (itself a kind of dialectical outgrowth of the Aborigines Protection Society) was thesis, the Anthropological Society antithesis, and the Anthropological Institute synthesis.

From this point of view, the Anthropological Society of London represents something more than "that most neglected of factors in the history of ideas, the losing side." When Tylor in 1884 reviewed the development of British anthropology since mid-century, he noted that this had been the period of the rise and fall of polygenism, which had made an important contribution to the development of evolutionary theory by its careful discrimination of racial varieties existing in "comparative permanence." Far from dismissing polygenism out of hand, the evolutionists had come to terms with it. Thus Huxley had argued that Darwin's theory was capable of "reconciling and combining all that is good in the Monogenistic and Polygenistic schools." That Hunt found their compromise unacceptable should not obscure the fact that Darwinians incorporated a good bit of racial thinking into what he called their "new form of monogenism." And although the Darwinians were less boisterous in their heterodoxy, they too had called into question the religious assumptions underlying the old ethnology; like Hunt, they saw man as part of the natural world and the study of man as a natural science among natural sciences. In the end, they even accepted Hunt's name for their inquiry.[65]

But if the term Hunt adopted from Broca's Société prevailed in Britain, "anthropology" soon came to have a very different meaning from the one it had in France. There, Broca's Société and the Société d'Ethnographie remained distinct into the next century—the former giving priority to the physical study of man; the latter, tied to the philological and the biblical traditions, remaining diffusely descriptive and markedly amateur in style. Broca's Ecole d'Anthropologie had chairs in ethnology and linguistics from the beginning, and after 1885 one in sociology as well. But the term "anthropology" in France always had primarily a physical reference (as it did on the Continent generally), and the dominant French tradition until the 1920s was strongly biological (though not in the first instance Darwinian) in orientation. By contrast, when George Busk referred to physical anthropology as "anthropology proper" in his presidential address in 1874, he was rebuked the following year by Lane Fox, who insisted that the term had been "born anew" with the founding of the Institute, and that it embraced the whole range of the Institute's activities.[66]

Despite the role played by archeologists and physical anthropologists in the Institute, neither group attempted to give its own definition to the field as a whole. Anthropology, in Great Britain as in the United States, remained for a long time a loosely defined field embracing various forms of inquiry on more or less equal terms—although in Britain the linguistic researches associated with the ethnological tradition fell into desuetude. This embracive anthropological viewpoint was sustained by evolutionary assumption, which saw the development of mankind as a physical being, the growth of human culture, and origin and differentiation of human languages as parts of a single evolutionary process. But the origin of this embracive viewpoint may be traced back beyond evolutionism to the attempt of Prichardian ethnology to reconstruct the historical process of human differentiation. Furthermore, its continued strength in the Anglo-American tradition reflects the failure of physical anthropology either to replace or fully to separate itself from the older ethnological orientation. And over the longer run, this broad-gauge conception of anthropology, sustained by a considerable institutional inertia, retains even today a more than nominal power, not only in Britain, but in all the areas influenced by the Anglo-American tradition (including, lately, even France).[67]

Turning from matters of substance and scope to matters of scientific style, here, too, one can see the character of later British anthropology as a reflection of the controversies of the 1860s. If the nominal breadth of the British anthropological tradition reflects the influence of its ethnological roots, it is also true that its relationship to the earlier ethnological tradition is more disjunctive than in the United States. Perhaps because in Britain there was no reinfusion of German historical thought to match the influence of Franz Boas in the United States, the later history of British anthropology evinces relatively little of the epistemological ambivalence reflected in Prichard's hesitancy to include ethnology in the natural history section of the British Association because it was more allied with history than with natural science. The ''scientific'' status of anthropology, asserted by Hunt and the Darwinians alike, was still insisted upon in the early twentieth century, both by the leaders of the ''ethnological'' reaction against evolution and of the emerging functionalist social anthropology.[68]

On the other hand, the scientism of the Anthropological Institute was less strident than Hunt's had been. In reviewing Tylor's *Researches into the Early History of Mankind,* one writer suggested that ''thanks to the moderation of the author's views and the propriety of his style, the work is free from those objections which exclude almost every book on 'anthropology' from the household library.'' This moderation extended to other issues as well. Tylor later referred to the 1860s as one in which anthropologists had taken to ''cultivating their science as a party-weapon in politics and religion,'' and suggested that the attempt had been ''not only in the long run harmful to the [practical] effect of anthropology in the world, but disastrous to its immediate position.'' Tylor went on to say that ''my recommendation to students is to go right forward, like a horse in blinkers, neither looking to the right hand nor to the left.''[69]

Here we return to the broader context of colonial expansion and racial contact with which this discussion of institutionalization began. Organized anthropology in England started out as part of a Christian philanthropic movement to protect the aborigines of the world from the ravages of colonization. In the early 1840s, as this wave of humanitarian concern began to ebb, the "scientific" impulse within the anthropological movement separated itself gradually from practical philanthropy, although not immediately from biblical assumption. The 1860s witnessed the collapse of the biblical framework and the emergence of what might be called the misanthropic alternative of an applied anthropology shot full of racial assumption. The Darwinian "ethnologicals" were far from regarding all the races of men as presently equal in capacity; neither did they view their science as totally lacking social and political relevance. But their liberal political commitment, their assumption of human psychic unity, and their notions of scientific respectability would not permit them to embrace the blatantly racialist scientific activism symbolized by the Cannibal Club. Having rejected the left hand of philanthropy in the 1840s and the right hand of political racism in the 1860s, organized British anthropology remained for the most part unconcerned with practical colonial matters until after the emergence of the "new" imperialism later in the century.[70]

Many of those who published in the Institute's *Journal* were indeed men who as missionaries or colonial administrators had been actively involved in the day-to-day experience of racial contact, and their accounts frequently reflected this—though as often in the defense of savage capacity or the criticism of British colonial policy as in any heightening of the pervasive paternalistic Victorian racialism. But their treatment of issues of race contact was almost always incidental to descriptive ethnographic purpose, and the Institute as such was little concerned with the application of anthropology to colonial problems. An early committee "on the relation of savage to cultured races" seems to have lapsed after two years of inactivity. The same topic was treated in 1881 by Sir Bartle Frere, late governor of Cape Colony and victor in the Zulu War. But when General Pitt Rivers in his annual summary created the category "applied anthropology" for Frere's paper, suggesting that its neglect was the cause of the Institute's recent decline, this did not lead to a greater interest in colonial problems. On the contrary, practical anthropological interests in the 1880s focused on the physical anthropology of the British Isles. And as far as active humanitarian involvement in the uplift or defense of savages was concerned, the policy of the Institute seems clear: when a correspondent wrote to them in 1881 complaining of a massacre of aborigines in Queensland, the assistant secretary was instructed to refer the writer to the Aborigines Protection Society.[71]

In general, then, the outcome of the institutional dialectic seems, appropriately, to have been a Victorian compromise. Traditional ethnology and the newer physical anthropology were both accommodated into an anthropology born anew; active humanitarianism and political racism were both rejected by a "science" which was to be kept separated from the arena of party strife—and from the actual present life of its dark-skinned savage subject matter. As it was institutionalized in the mid-Victorian period, the study of British anthropology looked less toward social theory than to antiquarianism and natural history, transformed as prehistory and Darwinian evolution. Although its data were by no means limited to stones and bones, its orientation was toward the distant past and toward the animal realm. Its living human subjects could only be approached from a distance. On the one hand, one could study their artifacts, which were often preserved in museums of "natural history" along with other objects from the vegetable, mineral, and animal realms. Alternatively, they might be approached through the mechanism of the ethnographic questionnaire, in which the complexities of active human agency were reduced to the simplicity of recorded rule. In either case, the integral complexity of their specific cultural existences had been fragmented into discrete material and behavioral "elements" lacking any meaningful conceptual unity except through their subordination to a general evolutionary process—an ideological dismantling that has been analogized to the actual despoliation of historical cultural life then occurring on the ground of colonial expansion. But without indulging in retrospective interpretive hyperbole, there can be little doubt that a pervasive evolutionary racism contributed to the dehumanization and objectification of anthropology's human subject matter, from which an actively protectionist concern had been previously withdrawn.[72]

This is not to say that anthropological scholars had abandoned entirely their moral concern for savages. As his successor at Oxford later suggested, "Tylor was ever a kindly soul, as indeed every good anthropologist must be." If few in this period seriously questioned the white European's evolutionary mission, many anthropologists continued in kindly scholarly fashion to play the roles of defender of savage ways of life and explicator of savage modes of thought—roles clearly premised on a sense of moral obligation. Nevertheless, their attempt to collect and record the data of savage life for science and for posterity took for granted, and was largely impelled by, the impending extermination of savages (or at the least, of savagery as a social form) throughout the world. Furthermore, the content of their anthropology could easily be interpreted as providing a moral as well as a scientific justification for the often bloody process. When, in the last quarter of the nineteenth century, the juggernaut of European expansion began its final push into the darker regions of the world, evolutionary anthropology provided a portion of the ideological motive power. And when, a half century later, it began its retreat, evolutionary anthropology remained a part of the white man's ideological burden.[73]

Epilogue: The Extinction of Paleolithic Man

George Robinson and Truganina (seated with arm extended), persuading Tasmanians that "Europeans wished only to better their condition"—c. 1833
James Bonwick, *The Last of the Tasmanians: or The Black War of Van Dieman's Land* (London, 1870), facing p. 210.

OF the 349 groups of items exhibited at the Crystal Palace Exhibition by the inhabitants of what was then still called Van Dieman's Land, only four represented the handiwork of its aboriginal population. Sent along by a Hobart Town physician who was to become the leading authority on Tasmanian linguistics, these consisted of shell necklaces, simple reed and fiber baskets, a model of a broad-leaved kelp water carrier, and four small replicas of the grass-bound bundles of tree bark that served as the Tasmanians' only means of navigation.[1] Had the good Dr. Joseph Milligan succeeded in collecting samples of every material form of aboriginal Tasmanian culture, he would have added only a few more: unground and unhafted stone implements, fire-drills and notched throwing sticks, fire-hardened spears, kangaroo skins for carrying children or covering shoulders from the cold, fiber ropes to aid in climbing trees, and perhaps the tentlike tombs of bark in which some Tasmanians buried the ashes and the bones of their dead. The habitations of the living were crude and temporary windbreaks, and the temperate climate normally required no more covering than the grease and charcoal with which the Tasmanians coated their short and heavily scarified bodies. Subsisting on game, shellfish, and natural vegetable products on a heavily forested island the size of Ireland, they probably never totaled more than a few thousand persons. These were divided by mutually unintelligible dialects into four or five major groups, each consisting of a number of acephalous subgroups roaming over particular portions of the rugged mountainous terrain and engaging each other in frequent but relatively bloodless warfare. Separated by 150 miles of open sea from their equally land-loving Australian neighbors, the Tasmanians survived in more or less stable adaptation for untold centuries, until their antipodal isolation was broken by their first encounter with Europeans in 1772.[2]

Although this first contact precipitated a brief fray in which several natives were killed or wounded, relations with Cook, Bligh, D'Entrecasteux, and other early explorers were generally friendly. Moved by the "frankness of their manners" and "the touching ingenuousness of their caresses," François Péron, the self-styled "anthropologist" of the Baudin expedition in 1802, later described them as "the realization of those brilliant descriptions of happiness and simplicity of the state of nature of which I had so many times in reading felt the seductive charm."[3] Such echoes of the Noble Savage tradition were little heard among the colonists sent the following year by the Governor of New South Wales in an attempt to forestall French influence in the area. The forty-nine persons who sailed from Port Jackson to found Hobart Town included twenty-four "incorrigible" convicts, eight soldiers instructed to search them every morning for knives, an overseer, a military governor, a surgeon, and a dozen other free settlers, half of them women. From the beginning, social order among the intruding white population was precarious, and when a large group of aboriginals came near the settlement in hot pursuit of kangaroos in the fall of 1804, the anxious and disgruntled military responded with a barrage that became notorious as the "Risdon Massacre." Carrying their dead and wounded back into the hills, the Tasmanians kept well away from the convict colonists for the next few years.

They were followed into the interior, however, by runaway convicts who lived by hunting kangaroos, for which the government offered a bounty in the early days when the colony was often close to starvation. Until these gangs of "bushrangers" were brought under control by Lieutenant Governor Sorell around 1820, they inflicted inhuman cruelties on the Tasmanians, killing them for their women, or to feed their own dogs, even roasting them alive. One often-quoted account tells of a bushranger called "Carrots" who killed a Tasmanian for his *gin* and then forced the woman to wear her dead husband's bloody head suspended from her neck.[4]

In the beginning, the Tasmanians seem to have suffered such depredations with little retaliation. But after 1820, when transportation and emigration from England swelled both the convict and the free settler population, the spread of farmers and herdsmen began to exert a mortal pressure on tribal hunting grounds. Unable to retreat into the territories of antagonistic tribal groups, the natives were forced to help themselves to the settlers' livestock and provisions; settlers in turn treated them as animal predators, hiding steel traps in flour barrels and shooting natives out of trees. The Tasmanians responded by attacking outlying farms and herdsmen's huts in force. Led by a partially acculturated Australian aboriginal called "Mosquito," one group terrorized the herdsmen of the eastern coastal area until Mosquito was captured and executed in 1825. Increasingly, the settlers clamored for military protection, and although both Sorell and his successor, Colonel George Arthur, were inclined to regard native attacks as a just response to "aggression [that] originated with the white inhabitants," the government gradually adopted a more active policy.[5]

By this time, important economic interests were at stake. London speculators had invested one million pounds in the Van Dieman's Land Company headed by the lieutenant governor of the island. The company owned more than half a million acres, from which kangaroos were exterminated and replaced by sheep. The island's white population was doubling almost every five years, and over half were now free settlers. Feeling little responsibility for the earlier inhumanities of convicts, and even less sense of brotherhood with naked blacks who threatened their farms and herds, the newer settlers had no difficulty clothing self-interest in righteous indignation. As the editor of the *Colonial Times* said in 1826: "We make no pompous display of philanthropy. . . . The Government must remove the Natives; if not they will be hunted down like wild beasts and destroyed." Destruction was in fact proceeding at a rapid pace. The following July the *Times* reported the killing and wounding of sixty Tasmanians in retaliation for a settler's murder; in another incident that year a party of constables trapped a "mob" of seventy among some rocks, "dragging the women and children from crevices . . . and *dashing out their brains.*"[6]

Forced thus to implement the alternative of removal, Governor Arthur early in 1828 established a line of military posts to keep the natives isolated on the harsh and sterile western fringe of the island. Those in the east who could not be "induced by peaceable means to depart" were to be expelled by force. "Roving parties" of convicts promised emancipation were sent into the bush to round up natives; and though a bounty of £5 was instituted for those brought back alive, some observers felt nine were killed for every one taken living. Even so, the "Black War" continued to drag on and to exact a slowly mounting toll of whites as well; in one district, ninety-nine settlers were killed in "farm fights" between 1826 and 1831.

When all else seemed to have failed, Arthur in the fall of 1830 embarked on one of those tragicomic undertakings that in the next hundred years were occasionally to reduce imperial domination to a kind of ultimate absurdity. Mobilizing a total of 3,000 soldiers, convicts, and civilian volunteers, he attempted to drive the natives from the settled areas toward a small peninsula on the southeast coast, like game upon a great estate. When after some weeks of arduous tramping through the rugged mountains of the central region the Tasmanians were presumed to have been flushed toward the coast, the force was arrayed at forty-five yard intervals in one continuous "Long Black Line" that gradually closed upon the neck of the peninsula. But when—at a cost of £30,000 and four British soldiers accidentally killed along the way—the trap was finally sealed and searched, not one native was to be found!

Not surprisingly, Arthur was subjected to some rather caustic treatment in the *Colonial Times,* which recalled the old verse about the King of France marching up and down the hill with forty thousand men. Arthur later managed to insist to his superiors in London that it had all been worthwhile: "evidently awed by the force which was then put in motion," the Tasmanians had since "conducted themselves in a far more peaceable manner."[7] As it later turned out, there were by this time less than 300 of them still alive, and the Black Line's show of force may well have been a factor in convincing these to accept what turned out to be Arthur's final solution to the Tasmanian problem: the single-handed and single-minded force of Christian love.

The man who accomplished Arthur's goal was George Augustus Robinson, a large-nosed, heavy-set, and florid figure who had come from out of Dickens with his wife and seven children to make his living as a bricklayer in Hobart Town. A zealous Wesleyan Methodist, Robinson spent his spare time trying to convert convicts, and worrying about the fate of the natives. When Arthur advertised in 1829 for a "steady man of good character" to reside on Bruni Island and take charge of Tasmanians brought in by bounty hunters, Robinson seems to have been the sole applicant. Early the following year, before Arthur had conceived his cordon, Robinson proposed his own plan for ending the Black War. Convinced that the Tasmanians were rational creatures, he would simply go unarmed into the bush and by the voice of sweet reason "persuade them that the Europeans wished only to better their condition," so that they "might become civilized, and rendered useful members of society, instead of the bloodthirsty ferocious beings they were represented to be."[8]

Accompanied by seven Bruni Island aborigines, Robinson tramped through the West and North for months without success. Eventually, however, the smiles and trinkets distributed by his female interpreters enabled him to establish contact. There were many anxious moments at the brink of violence, and one dramatic incident in which he was saved from drowning by his companion Truganina, but in the end Robinson's Christian voice of reason—reinforced by the promptings of aboriginal despair—accomplished its mission. By early 1835 he had brought in the last of some 200 Tasmanian holdouts—for which noble effort of conciliation he was rewarded a total of about £8000 in money and grants of land, as well as the post of commandant of the Christianizing concentration camp to which his captives were remanded.

After several earlier reserves proved mortally inhospitable, Governor Arthur had decided late in 1831 to place all captured Tasmanians on Flinders Island—a large and agriculturally useless body of land sufficiently supplied with kangaroos that "the amusement of hunting would occupy their minds," but far enough from the northeast tip of Tasmania that they could not fulfill any idling dreams of escape.[9] By the time Robinson took charge, the island camp had just achieved a modicum of order after an extended period of intertribal feuding, military misgovernment, and open rebellion. Throwing himself into the work of reformation with all his methodical missionary zeal, Robinson devised a plan to enforce the Protestant ethic upon his helpless band of wornout hunters. The way to civilize savages was to entangle them in the cash nexus. By "establishing a circulating medium amongst them," paying them for their labor, eliminating rations, putting a price on everything, and holding a weekly market, Robinson would inspire "an interest in the acquisition of property" and "the habits of civilized life."[10]

If one may judge from Robinson's report for the first half of 1837, "the work of Christian instruction and civilization" was succeeding "beyond the most sanguine expectation." Instead of "wandering about the settlement with listless and careless indifference," the Tasmanians were now wholly employed in useful labor, harmless amusements, religious exercises, and attendance at school. No longer "idle spectators, but actors and ready agents," they had given up their grease and ochre for dresses and frockcoats—bought at ten and fifteen shillings each out of savings from their daily shilling wage. They all performed their "daily ablutions," and those who could afford them now ate with knives and forks. Order was maintained by an Aboriginal Police chosen by the full assembly, and "nocturnal orgies"(corroborees) had long since ceased—their "wild intonations" superseded by "sacred melody." They could all, when catechized, tell who made the world and to what purpose, and they knew what would happen to those of God's children who went to hell. Although commonly thought to be no more than "a link between the human and brute species," they had demonstrated such "precocity of intellect" as to surpass "by far" the majority of "the humbler grades of European inhabitants in Tasmania—and "forever put to silence the cavils of the most skeptical and prejudicially minded."[11]

Robinson did admit one "serious drawback to the success of the establishment." Though "every advantage of civilized life" had been afforded them, the Tasmanians persisted in dropping off like flies.[12] In the six-month period of his report, seven had died of acute or chronic visceral inflammation, four of pneumonia, one from "general debility," and seven from no recorded cause—which one is tempted to translate as the effects of European diet, clothing, industry, and sheer despair. Be that as it may, there were now less than one hundred left, and Robinson predicted they would become extinct, unless they could be transported to New Holland, where they would intermix, and the "declension would not be observed." When that option was overruled by the Governor and the Colonial Secretary in London, Robinson himself accepted an offer of £500 a year as Protector of Aborigines in South Australia, where he served fifteen years before retiring to England in 1853 to enjoy the fruits of his missionary endeavors. Six years previously, the forty-five then surviving Tasmanians had also been retired to their final home: "a miserable collection of huts and out-buildings" at Oyster Cove near Hobart Town, where they were brought in close contact with the scum of white Tasmanian society.[13] Deprived by his death of the dubious solicitude of their last missionary superintendent, they were given over to the frank neglect of an absentee administrator, under whom they rapidly declined into a rum-sodden desuetude.

By the time of Darwin's *Origin,* the extinction of their ill-favored race had been irrevocably guaranteed, since the nine surviving women were well beyond the age of bearing children. The last man, William Lanney, who had left Oyster Cove to become a seaman, died of choleric diarrhea in 1869. Although the government refused the request of the Royal Society of Tasmania that his body be given to their museum, Lanney's skull was stolen even before his burial (allegedly for the Royal College of Surgeons in London) and his body was robbed from its grave soon afterwards. To forestall a repetition of this outrage, the government kept secret the funeral arrangements for the last woman, Robinson's lifesaving companion Truganina. It was not until some years after her death in 1876 that Truganina's body was exhumed so that her skeleton might be displayed in the Tasmanian Museum.

Literally "civilized off the face of the earth" within a few short decades of European settlement, the Tasmanians did not leave much trace upon the ethnographic record. The early explorers' accounts, the tales of settlers, and a few more serious efforts by such men as Dr. Milligan (who had superintended their removal to Oyster Cove), as well as the artifacts and bones of the natives themselves, did, however, provide some material bearing on contemporary anthropological issues. Ethnologists, physical anthropologists, and sociocultural evolutionists all made what use they could of the residue of the Tasmanians' tragic history. Insofar as they concerned themselves with its ethical implications, it was for the most part to "join with philanthropists in regretting their unhappy fate"—which, as Tylor noted, had robbed anthropologists of material of great "scientific value."[14] Even so, their speculations had a certain latent apologetic character, and may be read as offering a kind of scientific bleach for the recrudescent moral stain of the Tasmanians' extermination.

For the traditional ethnologist, the origin of the Tasmanians was something of an enigma. Geographically distant from any group save the Australians, and lacking any means of navigation adequate for open seas, they nevertheless differed from their geographically most likely relatives in certain critical respects—including the lack of any knowledge of the boomerang. Prichard was inclined on physical and cultural grounds to relate them to the Papuans; but Latham, who had done research on their language, found affinities both with the Australians and the New Caledonians, and felt it was an open question whether they had reached Tasmania from South Australia, Timor, or New Caledonia.[15] Such issues continued to be debated in a post-Darwinian context, with Huxley arguing that they were a Negrito type that had come from New Caledonia "by means of broken land in the form of a chain of islands now submerged," and Sir William Flower favoring their arrival from Australia before the advent of the "existing native race."[16] In part perhaps because it implied that their recent extinction had not been without precedent, the notion that the Tasmanians had been isolated in

Van Dieman's Land by an invading neolithic Australian race seemed by the end of the century to suggest "a definite settlement" of the "Tasmanian Problem"—though in fact it is still moot today.[17]

Because they were so few and so far away and burned the bodies of their dead, the Tasmanians provided scant material for the physical anthropologist. It was not until very late in their decline that "the importance of preserving their osteological remains" was recognized, and means "taken to secure what specimens were still available"—one of them apparently being that offending skeleton in the window of the Anthropological Society. Knox had access to only one Tasmanian skull, and as late as 1900 the "most extensive series of observations" were those by Parisian physical anthropologists on eight skulls in the Musée d'Histoire Naturelle. Although even one was enough to demonstrate to some observers the "wild and sinister appearance which invests the whole physiognomy," and the seventy collected by 1900 seemed to distinguish them from their Australian neighbors, the limited evidence of Tasmanian osteology was of less general anthropological interest than certain circumstances surrounding their extinction.[18]

The most important of these were the sexual relations of European men with aboriginal women. Many writers were struck by the alleged failure of a population of "athletic and unscrupulous English males" not only to "produce an intermediate race, but to leave more than one or two adult specimens of their repugnant unions." The French polygenist Paul Broca used such anecdotal evidence to support the notion that various human races were distinct species, between which complete "eugenesic" hybridity was impossible.[19] Others, by contrast, were impressed by the Polish traveller Strzelecki's statement that Tasmanian women who had borne half-caste children were thenceforth unable to produce children by aboriginal males. Although Darwin concluded that such evidence was "almost valueless," he later used the "remarkable" infertility of Tasmanian women to argue the impact of racial competition on the human reproductive system. Darwin himself was inclined to regard the "profligacy of women" as less important than "changed habits of life" in inducing Tasmanian sterility, but other writers saw it as one more instance of the truth that "prostitution, all the world over, vitiates the powers of females." In the Victorian context, the impact of such speculation could only be to lighten the moral burden of the Tasmanians' fate. By showing that "the absence of births even more than the frequency of deaths completed the destruction of the people," it was possible to convert their extermination into "decline" or even "degeneration"—in which they were implicated by their own "licentiousness."[20]

For sociocultural evolutionists, such decline was clearly not to be taken as evidence that the Tasmanians had once been civilized. Quite the contrary, they stood very near the bottom of the scale of human progress—and (according to Wallace) might have stood even lower, if Mr. Robinson's civilizing efforts had not operated retrospectively to raise the estimate of their aboriginal capacity, which was sometimes argued to be higher than the Australians'. Herbert Spencer offered a systematic tabular summary of their cultural status in the volume of his *Descriptive Sociology* devoted to "lowest and negrito races." Although their "development of military tactics against the whites" was evidence of their improvability, the Tasmanians were for the most part characterized negatively. They had "no general conceptions, even of the simplest order"; "very few laws or established customs"; no chieftainship "except in time of war"; scarcely any "aesthetic sentiments"; and their moral nature was "not so much positively repugnant as negatively unattractive." On the basis of Dr. Milligan's account of their language, Spencer (or his hired abstracter David Duncan) suggested that it was so irregular that meaning had to be "eked out in an extraordinary way by tone, manner, and gesture."[21]

By contrast, Tylor was somewhat dubious of Milligan's linguistic evidence. But if he was uncertain whether the Tasmanians in fact offered an example of the gradual supercession of gesture language by oral speech, he was certain that they were "among the lowest tribes known to Ethnology." In *Primitive Culture* he drew frequently on the popular ethnographic accounts of James Bonwick to document the various features of early animistic religion. Max Müller, however, later used the Tasmanians to illustrate "The Untrustworthiness of the Accounts of the Religious Ideas of Savages," arguing that every stage or form of religious belief, including monotheism, could be documented from the contradictory data included in an authoritative summary of Tasmanian ethnography published under Tylor's sponsorship in 1890.[22] Tylor, however, remained confident that any trace of monotheistic belief was the result of "intercourse with civilized foreigners." In 1893, he recalled with some self-satisfaction how, on the basis of one artifact brought to the Somerset Archaeological Society and a conversation with Dr. Milligan in London in 1862, it was he who made "the earliest mention" of the similarity between Tasmanian tools and those of the Somme River drift. Although Milligan pursued the matter when he returned to Tasmania, the Somerset specimen was the only one available in England until the early 1890s, when Tylor was able to get sent from Tasmania a collection of about 150 for the Pitt Rivers Museum. On the basis of this and other evidence, Tylor concluded that the earlier piece was not exceptional, but that the Tasmanians "habitually used stone implements shaped and edged by chipping, not ground or polished." They were thus "living representatives of the early Stone Age, left behind in industrial development even by the ancient tribes of the Somme and the

Ouse.'' In them, paleolithic man ''ceases to be a creature of philosophic inference, but becomes a known reality.''[23]

One gets a sense of the apologetic function of this equation in the two books James Bonwick published in 1870 after returning to England from a long residence in Tasmania. Although balancing ''The Cruelties of the Whites'' by ''The Outrages of the Blacks,'' Bonwick had no doubt that the English had stolen the Tasmanians' land, deprived them of all rights, and inflicted on them the grossest inhumanities. Not insensitive to the irony of Robinson's civilizing efforts, he was in fact something of a latter-day Rousseauist, contrasting aboriginal ''freedom of movement in the Bush'' with ''the grooves of modern civilization.'' But although he wrote with the expressed wish of exciting ''some benevolent desire to bless the rude tribes left beneath our sway,'' Bonwick saw the Tasmanians on the other side of an almost unbridgeable cultural gap: ''physically, we have relations with them which excite common sympathies, and we seem to know them; but mentally and morally our position as Europeans is so different, and our means of studying them so slight, that we are unable to comprehend our identity with them.''[24]

The emergence of an anthropological style that might have facilitated that comprehension was by and large a twentieth-century phenomenon. In the evolutionary worldview of Victorian anthropology, the comprehension of human unity was fundamentally compromised by the paleolithic equation. True, Tylor, always the monogenist, saw the equation as breaking down ''any imaginary line of severance between the men of the Drift and the rest of the human species.''[25] But if it brought the Drift men closer, the paleolithic equation did quite the opposite for the Tasmanians. Left behind long since by the ancestors of the Europeans, they had outlived their time by many thousands of years. And when the two ends of the cultural time-scale were finally forced into spatial contact there at the furthest reaches of the antipodes, extinction was simply a matter of straightening out the scale, and placing the Tasmanians back into the dead prehistoric world where they belonged. Not only did the paleolithic equation help to distance the horror of the Tasmanians' extinction; it seemed even to set the seal of anthropological science upon their fate.*

*The ''extinction'' of the Tasmanians, which seemed a clearly defined ''event'' to Victorians inclined to construe ''race'' in quasi-polygenetic terms, seems rather more problematic in the present very different anthropological and political context. Europeans and Tasmanian Aboriginals did in fact produce numerous offspring, who survived primarily on the islands in Bass Strait to the north of Tasmania. On several occasions in the century after Truganina's death, there were disputes over rights to land and the taking of mutton birds. In 1978, the report of a committee of inquiry stated that there were then between 4,000 and 5,000 descendants ''from a mixture of ethnic groups including Tasmanian and Australian Aborigines and European and Maori stock, all of whom are eligible to claim land rights in Tasmania and in the adjacent islands'' (Ellis 1981:164; Mansell 1981).

A Prospective Retrospect: The Historical Significance of Victorian Anthropology (1880–1980)

Professor A. R. Radcliffe-Brown, with research students and staff of the Institute of Social Anthropology—Oxford University, 1946

Left to right, front row: K. T. Hadjioannou, Phyllis Puckle (secretary and librarian), A. R. Radcliffe-Brown, Meyer Fortes (Reader, 1947–50), K. A. Busia; back row: L. F. Henriques, W. Newell, W. Brailsford, A. A. Issa, M. N. Srinivas (courtesy of the Institute of Social Anthropology).

FRAMED by the Crystal Palace and the death of the "last" Tasmanian, the "multiple contextualizations" attempted in *Victorian Anthropology* have been offered in the spirit of "historicism"—using that somewhat problematic term to refer to the privileging of the questions to which the thinking of Victorian anthropologists provided answers, rather than questions that might be asked about related issues by anthropologists today. But like everything historical, "historicism" is a relative concept. In schematizing long ranges of intellectual history to provide background for the questions asked by Victorian anthropologists, we may have wrenched the thinking of their predecessors loose from the context of *their* questioning. And in imposing a late-twentieth-century interest in ulterior motivation or ideological determination on the thinking of Victorian writers whose anthropology was self-consciously rationalistic, we have surely qualified the sense in which the questions to which their thinking provided answers may be characterized as "theirs." Beyond this, the very decision to study their thinking in the first place must reflect our own present interests, whether these be "historicist" or "presentist" in motivation.[1] For in addition to providing answers to the questions they were asking, their thinking may provide answers to questions that we ask, whether these have to do primarily with what it was that they were thinking, or what it is that we think today about similar issues—or, perhaps, why it was that they were preoccupied with certain questions and neglected to consider others that have interested anthropologists since. Having treated a series of contextual constraints on Victorian anthropological inquiry, we may still ask: What were the limits of an anthropology so constrained? How did it help to shape later anthropology in Great Britain and elsewhere? How did it contribute to our understanding of the enduring central concerns of the discipline, and more generally, to our understanding of humankind?

One might in fact argue that in raising such issues, we are trying to answer a question that classical evolutionists themselves surely considered: What was the historical significance of their anthropological thinking? What was its place in the development of anthropological thought? And while they could perhaps suggest answers to this question in relation to what had gone before them, it necessarily remained an open one as far as the future development of anthropology was concerned—one that only history could answer *for* them. Were their works *merely* historically significant, to be read perhaps for a few years by inhabitants of their own intellectual milieu, later to be rediscovered by intruders from thought worlds less or more alien, who, if they did not attempt to recontextualize their ideas, must evaluate them by very different standards? Or would their works perhaps continue to be read (or later rediscovered) as *really* historically significant, whether as sources of the thinking of subsequent generations, or as milestones or turning points on the road to scientific understanding of the human species?[2]

Whether conceived in relativistic or universalistic terms, the question of the historical significance of Victorian anthropology can only be considered in relation to some later phase of the history of anthropology, or some standpoint of anthropological theory and method in the present. Without presuming to review systematically either the subsequent historical development or the current status of anthropological thinking about all the matters implicated in sociocultural evolutionary inquiry, we may pursue the issue of historical significance along several different lines. If we do no more than open some of the issues hinted at here, the attempt may nevertheless suggest yet another context for understanding the historical phenomenon of Victorian anthropology.

The Anthropological Reputation of Victorian Anthropology

Reputation and significance suggest a very different chronicity: the one, evanescent estimation; the other, enduring meaning. But since there is overlap as well as tension in their relationship, a brief review of the way Victorian sociocultural evolutionism has been perceived and evaluated by subsequent anthropological generations and by previous historiographers of anthropology within the Anglo-American tradition may provide the background for some thoughts on its historical significance. And since these phases of anthropological and historiographical evaluation in turn reflect the major transitions in the history of the discipline since the revolution of the 1860s, we must begin with a thumbnail schematization of its subsequent history.

During the latter third of the nineteenth century, classical evolutionism may be regarded, if not as a paradigm, then as the "cynosure" of anthropological inquiry. While the full range of day-to-day anthropological practice requires further investigation, and there was, as we shall see, a counter-evolutionary undercurrent, evolutionism provided the dominant interpretive metaphor and the major focus of theoretical speculation for those anthropologists since regarded as historically significant. In the United States, the leading evolutionist was Lewis Henry Morgan, who was particularly interested in the analysis of kinship and social organization, and whose *Ancient Society* was for twenty years the standard theoretical reference work for the anthropologists of the U.S. government Bureau of Ethnology founded by John Wesley Powell in

1879.[3] In Britain, one may distinguish two subsequent "generations" of sociocultural evolutionists after that of the 1860s. Coming on the anthropological scene around 1880, when evolutionism was no longer an intellectual innovation but an established viewpoint, Andrew Lang and William Robertson Smith published works that were heavily influenced by Tylor and McLennan respectively. And the end of that decade saw the first edition of James G. Frazer's *Golden Bough,* whose massively accumulating volumes were to carry a relatively pristine Tylorian viewpoint well into the twentieth century—long after the reaction against it had begun.[4]

Although it reflected changes in the colonial situation and domestic ideological contexts of anthropology, this antievolutionary reaction was part of the more general "revolt against positivism" in European social thought. It involved both a reassertion of the role of "irrational" factors in human social life, and a critique of the methodological and epistemological grounding of prevailing scientific determinisms. Within anthropology, the most important figure was the German émigré Franz Boas, whose intellectual viewpoint was shaped in the tension between the *Natur-* and the *Geisteswissenschaften,* as these were reflected in his own training in physics, psycho-physics, and geography. Settling in the United States after two ethnographic expeditions to Canada in the 1880s, Boas was a pioneer in the modern tradition of intensive fieldwork among particular groups. In a number of cases, such research produced results conflicting with evolutionary assumptions, and—in the context of changing attitudes toward European "civilization"—encouraged a more positive view of the dark-skinned others who had so long been stigmatized as "savages." Although Boas had begun his career accepting such evolutionary assumptions as the priority of maternal social forms, his studies of the historical diffusion of cultural elements led him to question evolutionism on both methodological and empirical grounds. In the years around 1900, he developed a systematic critique of the racial, psychological, and cultural assumptions of nineteenth-century evolutionary anthropology.[5]

Drawn together in 1911 in *The Mind of Primitive Man,* Boas' critique provided the essential intellectual groundwork for the modern pluralist and relativist view of culture, with its characteristic rejection of racial hierarchies and biological determinism, and its focus on the body of traditional meanings that condition the behavior of every individual growing up in a particular cultural milieu. Under the dominance of Boas, whose own orientation included both an historical and a psychological tendency, American anthropology moved gradually after 1920 from the diffusionist reconstruction of the history of cultures—which had been the focus of his early work—to the study of their psychological integration and their impact on the individual human personality. Although his student Robert Lowie and several others kept alive the Morganian interest in kinship and social organization, the Boasian approach to the study of cultural wholes, reflecting its Germanic *geisteswissenschaftliche* origins, tended to emphasize descriptive integration rather than systematic analysis, and in this respect contrasted dramatically with the outcome of the antievolutionary reaction in Great Britain.[6]

British anthropology, too, had what may be called a neo-ethnological phase—although shorter and more distinctly marked. It began when the psychologist-cum-ethnologist William Rivers (who had previously done important work in the Morganian analysis of social organization) announced his "conversion" from evolution to diffusion in 1911. During and after World War I Rivers' disciples Grafton Elliot Smith and William Perry carried diffusionism much further, and in the early 1920s British anthropological circles were set agog by Perry's accounts of seafaring Egyptians carrying sun worship, monoliths, and various other cultural elements to the corners of the earth—a diffusionist fantasy in fact foreshadowed in pre-Prichardian biblical anthropology.[7]

Other British anthropologists, under the influence of Durkheimian sociology, moved directly from evolutionism toward a more holistic analysis of the contemporary tribal groups that they had studied in the field. Rejecting the evolutionist assumption that there were many customs in contemporary societies that could be understood only in terms of the "survival" of primitive belief, they sought to understand the "function" of customs and beliefs in sustaining the ongoing existence of the group. But these "functionalist" critics retained a certain positive identification with evolutionary thought, and reacted sharply against the conjectural historical reconstructions of Rivers and the "heliolithic" diffusionists. Initially, the new functional anthropology also moved in the direction of a cultural psychology, especially in the work of the Polish émigré Bronislaw Malinowski, who came under the influence of Freudian psychoanalysis in the aftermath of his path-marking fieldwork in the Trobriand Islands during World War I. But although the other leading functionalist, A. R. Radcliffe-Brown, had been Rivers' student in psychology before going to the Andaman Islands in 1906, his interest in systematic analysis of social organization was to prevail over the longer run. And despite the fact that his early work was cast in a "cultural" idiom, Radcliffe-Brown came to reject the possibility of a psychological science of human culture, arguing instead that social anthropology should be a comparative natural science of "social systems." By the later 1930s, when he had succeeded Malinowski as its most influential figure, British anthropology was moving from its "functionalist" to its "structural-functional" phase.[8]

Although the reaction against evolutionism took a somewhat different course in the United States and in Britain, the outcome in each case may be seen as a variant of a single development. First, there was a reassertion of the historical concerns of the older "ethnological" tradition. This was followed by an attempt to explore the integration of particular cultures in either psychological or sociological terms. In the context of the further development of ethnographic fieldwork as the distinguishing feature of anthropological method, the outcome was a general "dehistoricization" of Anglo-American anthropological inquiry. American "cultural" anthropology continued to show certain distinctive markings of the Germanic Boasian tradition, and British "social" anthropologists followed Radcliffe-Brown in abandoning the idiom of "culture." But with the internationalization of American ethnography after World War II, the transatlantic exchange of scholars, and the pervasive influence of functionalist social science, followed by the impact in both countries of structuralist influences emanating from France, there was by 1960 a considerable convergence in the two traditions. Historical interests never disappeared entirely from either tradition during the "classic" period of modern anthropology (roughly, 1920–1960). But in relation to the evolutionary or diffusionary periods that preceded it, historical issues were clearly subordinated to those of the functioning of cultures or societies in the present.[9]

This dehistoricization and—if one may be forgiven a further barbarism—"ethnographicization" of anthropology was a reorientation at least as important as that of the 1860s. It was sustained by certain features of the discipline's historical situation after World War I. Anthropology, which already had a certain marginality to the rest of the human sciences, became by methodological self-definition and also to a considerable extent by recruitment a kind of immigrant science, culturally marginal to its own society as well as to the groups that were the subject of ethnographic fieldwork. Although anthropologists did their fieldwork under an umbrella of colonial power, they tended to identify with the tribal cultures they studied, and to dissociate themselves from the changes these cultures were undergoing, which were seen as imposed from without. In sharp contrast to the evolutionary period, when the characteristic posture of anthropologists toward surviving primitive peoples was one of progressivist assimilationism, a romantic preservationism with strong undertones of "Noble Savagery" became the attitudinal norm of sociocultural anthropology. Despite a questioning of relativism in the aftermath of World War II and despite the involvement of anthropologists in development programs and modernization studies in the postwar period, this romantic tendency to view the societies they study as outside the historical processes of modern civilization has continued strong until the present.[10]

Since World War II, with the rise of national liberation movements, the termination of colonial rule, and four decades of colonial and postcolonial wars, the non-European "others" who traditionally provided the substantive focus of anthropological inquiry have not only commanded the role of actors in their own history, but have moved to the center stage of world historical processes. As active agents of national development and modernization, they are themselves assisting in the demise of "savage" or "primitive" man—which since Prichard has been a major stimulus of anthropological inquiry. Often unfriendly to a discipline long dependent on European colonial power and traditionally devoted to the study of a state they are in the process of transcending, postcolonial governments have restricted fieldwork by European anthropologists, and have themselves tended to reject anthropology for sociology—which in the European tradition has been the human science devoted to the study of "civilized" societies.[11]

By the end of the first postcolonial decade, there were signs of a more general questioning—resonant of the late-nineteenth-century "revolt against positivism"—of many of the assumptions of contemporary Western social science. In the United States, where the Boasian tradition had sustained an interest in problems of meaning, the movement has been called the "interpretive" or "hermeneutic turn"; in Britain the shift from "function to meaning" was felt by some in rather sharper terms, as an "epistemological break."[12] Coming at a time when anthropology as an institutionalized discipline was showing signs of Malthusian demographic crisis after a generation of explosive growth, the outcome of what some have seen as a general "crisis of anthropology" is by no means sure, and there are those who wonder whether the discipline may not share the long-anticipated demise of its traditional subject matter.[13] But there seems little doubt that the ahistorical ethnographic observation and synchronic interpretation of tribal cultures and social structures, which for fifty years provided the methodological and theoretical "cynosure" of the discipline, will have to compete for disciplinary attention with more historically oriented and textually based approaches during whatever period lies before it.

Against this frankly sketchy panorama of the discipline's history since 1880, the perception and evaluation of classical evolution by later sociocultural anthropologists may be briefly outlined. Boas, who shared reservations his mentors Adolph Bastian and Rudolf Virchow held about Darwinism, and who still had ties to pre-Darwinian currents in the German anthropological tradition, saw classical evolutionism as a transformation, "principally through Darwin's powerful influence," of a prior historical tradition in anthropology. Writing in 1904, he argued that "the regularity in the processes of evolution became the center of attraction even before the processes of evolution had been observed and understood"; the result had been those "premature theories of evolution based on observed homologies and supposed similarities" that he devoted a large portion of his anthropological energies to criticizing. Having served an apprenticeship under Bastian and done ethnographic research for Tylor, Boas retained a sense of the diversity of the writers who were later classed together as "evolutionist." But among his students—for whom the battle against evolutionism was the starting point of their own anthropological training—one can see emerging the picture of the "unilinear" evolutionist that conditions informal scholarly opinion down to the present. Thus although Alexander Goldenweiser was aware that "in his better moments, the evolutionist was, of course, aware of the presence of cultural diffusion," such qualified judgments of particular writers were always posed against an implicit stereotype of "the evolutionist of the old school." And while Morgan and Powell have by no means faded completely from the disciplinary memory, the folk history of American cultural anthropology has found in Boas its "founding father"—to a degree that has disturbed neo-evolutionists, and has recently provoked a certain amount of historical revisionism.[14]

Although such stereotyped views of past paradigms have their basis in a particular historical context of disciplinary polemic, they may become part of the conceptual and methodological ideology of a particular school, and in modern academic disciplines are likely to be transmitted through the oral or the pedagogical tradition. When countercurrents later reassert themselves, they are often accompanied by a relegitimating historiography, which seeks out the textual evidence of the rejected ancestor's "better moments" to disprove the accepted stereotypic picture. One can see evidence of this pattern in more recent American anthropology. Although some Boasians—notably Margaret Mead—maintained an interest in broader evolutionary issues, during the interwar decades the Morganian evolutionary tradition was carried forward in American anthropology largely in the work of Leslie White, who devoted a considerable effort also to biographical research on Morgan. More recently, a student of White's has reviewed the fundamental assumptions of evolutionary thought, emphasizing textual evidence that calls into question the "unilinear" stereotype.[15]

In the aftermath of World War II, there was a renewal of interest in cultural universals, developmental regularities, and the comparative study of civilizations, and—coincident with the Darwin centennial—a resurgence of evolutionary interest in physical anthropology and paleoarcheology. With the radicalization of anthropology during the Vietnam War, evolutionary tendencies were augmented by the long-delayed academic legitimation of Marxism—itself a form of evolutionary theory, into which Morgan's developmental sequence had been incorporated by Friedrich Engels. By 1968, this neo-evolutionary movement had produced an account of *The Rise of Anthropological Theory,* in which the exclusion of Marx from anthropology and the virtues of a techno-environmental evolutionism were the major themes. But although a substantial number of anthropologists today would no doubt characterize their interests as "evolutionary," neo-evolutionism still represents a minority movement in American anthropology, and the bulk of the history of sociocultural anthropology is written from points of view critical of sociocultural evolutionism.[16]

If we have devoted disproportionate attention to the fate of evolutionary assumption in American cultural anthropology, it is because developments in Britain are less revealing of the ambiguities that complicate its present reputation. Despite the Boasian struggle against biological determinism, American cultural anthropology always remained one of the "four fields" of the embracive general science of "anthropology" that emerged in the evolutionary period—two of which (archeology and physical anthropology) are, in their modern forms, in principle congenial to evolutionary assumption. And despite the predominant influence of Boas, the variegated structure of American academic life has encouraged a plurality of intellectual currents within the discipline. By contrast, British social anthropology was to become a much more sharply delineated, intellectually coherent, and tightly knit field, largely independent of a somewhat attenuated and weakly institutionalized general anthropological tradition. The battles of social anthropology for conceptual and methodological independence were fought primarily against neo-ethnological diffusionism rather than against evolutionism. And the critique of racialist assumption and biological determinism, which in the United States was formative of the modern discipline, was in Britain instead an episode stimulated by the threat of Nazism in the 1930s.[17]

These differences are evident in the developing historical consciousness of British anthropologists. Early historical retrospection still strongly reflected the inclusive nineteenth-century tradition. In the account of A. C. Haddon, who had been trained as a Darwinian zoologist, "sociology" was only half a chapter in the history of a much broader anthropology "slowly becoming a coherent and organised science." Similarly, the history by T. K. Penniman, longtime curator of the Pitt Rivers Museum, was cast in embracive, evolutionary terms: "With the publication of the *Origin of Species* in 1859, the Constructive Period of Anthropology as a single, though many-sided discipline, begins."[18]

But by the time Penniman's book was published in 1935, the functionalist "revolution in anthropology" was virtually accomplished. Although still in some instances occupying the same academic precincts as the other inquiries traditionally included within the general rubric, "social anthropology" was on its way to becoming virtually a distinct discipline, which leading proponents came to regard as the branch of sociology that "chiefly devotes itself to primitive societies" by the method of intensive fieldwork. It had been effectively founded in 1922, when major publications of its methodological and theoretical progenitors, Malinowski and Radcliffe-Brown, had appeared; the oppositional terms of its foundation were clarified the following year, when Radcliffe-Brown sharply distinguished "The Methods of Ethnology and Social Anthropology."[19]

Although he felt that the failure of classical evolutionism to decide definitely "whether it was seeking to make a reconstruction of the history of [the origins and stages of] culture, or to discover the general laws of culture as a whole" had led to a "fundamental vice of method." Radcliffe-Brown, like Malinowski, was by no means unsympathetic to the aims of the evolutionists. Indeed, at the end of his career, he spoke of himself as one "who has all his life accepted the hypothesis of social evolution as formulated by Spencer as a useful working hypothesis in the study of human society," and belabored the "anti-evolutionists" for their "amazing confusion of thought and ignorance of the theory of social evolution." His purpose in 1923 had been to make clear the separation of social anthropology from the various neo-ethnological schools in England, Germany, and the United States, to insist on its differentiation from any individualistic psychology, and to turn it from the misguided search for origins—so that when the quite legitimate application of "the idea of evolution" to social anthropological inquiry was later undertaken, it might take the form of a statement of "principles from the continuous action of which the various past and present forms of society have resulted."[20]

In the event, this evolutionary task was indefinitely delayed. For Radcliffe-Brown as well as Malinowski, the important distinction was not that between conjectural historical reconstructions in the evolutionist and in the diffusionist modes, but that between diachronic studies of either sort and synchronic (or functionalist) studies. And as that battle for a broadly functionalist social anthropology was won, classical evolutionism receded gradually into the disciplinary memory—although its "intellectualist" psychological assumptions and its "conjectural" reconstructions continued to be criticized by social anthropologists. Tylor and his confreres and successors marked a major phase in the history of social anthropology, standing between its eighteenth-century precursors in France and Scotland and the modern functionalist school, which derived largely from Durkheim. But after the general dehistoricization of the discipline, they were no longer so clearly differentiated from the neo-ethnological diffusionists. Thus Evans-Pritchard—who by 1950 had himself turned away from Radcliffe-Brown to insist that social anthropology was a form of historiography—saw the quarrel between the two earlier diachronic perspectives simply as "a family quarrel between ethnologists" and no affair of "functionalist anthropologists."[21]

Although the questioning of structural-functional assumption during the 1960s and 1970s has led a number of social anthropologists to look again at the past of their discipline, the closest analogue to American neo-evolutionism has been the renewed interest in the rationalistic intellectualist interpretations of Tylor and Frazer. In 1964, this "neo-Tylorian" trend was reflected historiographically in a frankly caricatured account of *The Revolution in Anthropology,* which pitted Malinowski in patricidal conflict against Frazer. More recently, the reaction against functionalism has produced what may be the beginnings of a reconceptualization of the disciplinary past—most notably, in a book recounting the failure of British social anthropologists to pay adequate attention to language, and in an essay reevaluating "the philological anthropology of Friedrich Max Müller" as a forerunner of many of the concerns of those who would now encourage a shift from "a positivistic functional social science" to "a semantic style of investigation." Nevertheless, the most serious general study of the history of British social anthropology treats it almost as if it had begun in 1922—as in a sense it must have in the memory of the elder generation of modern British social anthropologists, who were trained under Malinowski and Radcliffe-Brown in the years from then until World War II.[22]

The Historical Reputations of Victorian Anthropologists

In this context, we may review the major tendencies in the more serious historiography of classical evolutionism—keeping in mind the distinction between sociocultural and biological evolutionism, the historiography of which is a separate although not unrelated matter. In the first place, there is a tendency, perhaps most widely evident in more general historical works, to subsume classical evolutionism under the rubric "social Darwinism," or to treat it as a footnote to the history of biological evolutionism.[23] By contrast, there is the tradition that emerged during the antievolutionary reaction in the work of the American historical sociologist Frederick Teggart, and was carried forward by several of his students. Motivated by the desire to ground comparative sociological inquiry on a sounder historical method, they attacked the notion that social evolutionism derived from Darwin by tracing its methodological assumptions proximately to the French and Scottish Enlightenments and ultimately to the Greeks.[24]

In contrast to those who saw classical evolution in terms of transference of Darwinism or continuity of developmental assumption, the British historian John Burrow focused on the neglected period between

1800 and 1860, interpreting the reemergence of social evolutionary speculation as a response to a "crisis" in the dominant British philosophical tradition, along lines that we have discussed at several previous points. Writing in the mid-1960s, before the critique of structural-functionalism had progressed far enough to motivate the retrospective interests of nonanthropologist historians, Burrow felt it necessary to explain the failure of social evolutionary writers, despite some promising beginnings, to develop a functional social anthropology—which he interpreted in terms of their ulterior interest in buttressing utilitarianism and providing a reassuring substitute for traditional religious belief.[25]

Although Burrow's is the only previous published monographic study of the classical evolutionary group, its major figures have been the subject of varying amounts of retrospective interpretation by historically oriented anthropologists or by historians of anthropology. As a way of moving closer to the problem of historical significance, we may offer a few reflections on the anthropological reputations of the five writers treated by Burrow who figure also in the present account—considered, as reputation might suggest, in the ascending order of the number of their citations in several recent general histories of anthropology.[26]

Of the five, Lubbock is the least known today among sociocultural anthropologists—although archeologists are likely to remember him as the first to distinguish between paleo- and neolithic. While *Prehistoric Times* and *The Origin of Civilisation* were never so widely read as Lubbock's popular homiletic essays—which sold more than a half million copies—they continued to appear in new editions until the end of his life; and he was for a time thereafter the subject of considerable biographical interest. But his last anthropological work, *Marriage, Totemism and Religion: An Answer to Critics,* anchored him firmly in an era that by 1911 was passing. While he will no doubt remain of interest to historians of the Darwinian era, his editor in the recent series *Classics of Anthropology* was hard put to justify Lubbock's inclusion: "it is extremely difficult to identify within modern anthropology a single one of his ideas or explanations . . . which has given rise to a tradition of anthropological thought." From the perspective of modern sociocultural anthropology, Lubbock seems thus a likely nominee for the permanent status of "*merely* historically significant."[27]

The reputation of Maine—the only one of the five *not* to be included in the *Classics in Anthropology* series—is more problematic. In distinguishing societies organized on the basis of kinship from those organized on the basis of territory, he in fact marked off what was later to be the main subject area and focus of social anthropology—although its immediate exploration was carried on in large part by the American evolutionist Lewis Henry Morgan. Being, however, by his own profession, little interested in "savages," and having taken what, in the short run, turned out to be the "wrong" (patriarchal) side in the debate on the nature of primitive society, Maine was easily excluded from the disciplinary pantheon, despite the incorporation of aspects of his historical reconstructions into the later stages of the evolutionary sequence. As late as 1929, one of the elder figures of the field argued that Maine had in fact held the development of anthropology back by his reliance on comparative philology rather than prehistoric archeology.[28]

But Maine had continued to be read, though criticized, by comparative jurisprudents, and his influence on certain late-nineteenth-century figures who strongly shaped the modern social anthropological tradition—notably Emile Durkheim—was not insignificant. The early 1930s saw a direct reinfusion of his thought on the nature of corporate groups into the thinking of Radcliffe-Brown, and through the latter's students, into modern British social anthropology (as well as, through Robert Redfield, and along somewhat different conceptual lines, into the American tradition).[29] With the integration of Indian studies—which, like India in the British Empire, had always had a somewhat separate status—into modern social anthropology, Maine's ideas on "village communities" took on renewed relevance, although they have tended to be criticized as empirically flawed and ideologically constituted. But despite a recent full-length biographical treatment, Maine's place in past and present anthropology remains somewhat problematic. Although it has in fact been argued that the dominant "paradigm" of modern British anthropology—lineage theory—is a "transformation" of Maine's model, the case was made in the course of calling for its rejection. However, insofar as anthropology is now turning once again to history, one might expect that Maine, the most historically minded of our figures, is unlikely to recede into the shadows of merely historical significance.[30]

McLennan's anthropological reputation follows a pattern which is in some respects the obverse of his antagonist's. Despite his institutional marginality, McLennan remained a significant figure in the British anthropological tradition throughout the prefunctionalist period. By nature a controversialist, he was involved in continuing debate not only with Maine, but also with the American social evolutionist Lewis Henry Morgan. Morgan criticized his understanding of the nature of the marital practices McLennan had denominated endogamy and exogamy; McLennan in turn disputed the significance of the "classificatory system" of kinship terms which Morgan had used to reconstruct the history of human marriage, and which McLennan insisted were not indicative of "blood-tie," but were merely "a system of mutual salutations for use in social intercourse." Although McLennan's position on the latter issue was to be picked up by later critics of Morganian assumption, it was Morgan's mode of kinship analysis—adopted by his Australian ethnographic collaborators Lorimer Fison and William Howitt, and subsequently embraced by Rivers—that was to become orthodoxy for British social anthropology in its Radcliffe-Brownian phase.[31]

A somewhat similar fate was to befall the concept of totemism, which McLennan had introduced into anthropology in 1869, but which became a topic of serious anthropological concern only twenty years later, after his disciple William Robertson Smith asked James Frazer to write an article on the topic for the "T" volume of the ninth edition of the *Encyclopedia Britannica.* According to McLennan's original definition, tribes in the totem stage believed themselves descended from, or of the same breed, as some species of animal or plant, which was their "symbol and emblem," and "religiously regarded" or "taboo"; recognizing kinship only through the mother, they also followed "exogamy as their marriage law"—so that one could not marry a member of the same totem. Without offering a systematic theory of origins, McLennan had thus linked a specific form of animistic religious belief with two social phenomena—to which Smith, in speculating on the nature of the early *Religion of the Semites,* had added the notion of the totem sacrifice and communal meal.[32] When Baldwin Spencer and Frank Gillen's fieldwork among the Arunta in 1896 provided Frazer with the first ethnographic evidence that modern "primitives" actually did upon occasion eat species that were normally subject to totem taboo, the topic became the major focus of anthropological debate until World War I. By that time, however, Boasian critique had called into question the presumed ethnographic correlation of the various defining features, and "totemism" as an ethnological category threatened for a time to prove a figment of the later Victorian anthropological imagination. When discussion was subsequently resumed by Radcliffe-Brown and Claude Lévi-Strauss, it was on a somewhat different basis, and McLennan's role as "inventor of totemism" was given only brief acknowledgement.[33]

Thus it was that McLennan's influence on the development of later British social anthropology was forestalled first by Morgan, and then—after the rejection of the priority of matrilineal forms in the 1920s—by a revival of interest in the ideas of his antagonist Maine. When the systematic critique of both Morgan and McLennan that C. Staniland Wake had authored in 1889 was rediscovered in 1967 as a *Classic in Anthropology,* it seemed possible that McLennan might be forced into Wake's vacated place in anthropological oblivion. But despite the fact that McLennan "was almost entirely wrong and that to the modern reader his arguments may appear ridiculous," his own book soon appeared in the same series. He was there reclaimed as a "founder" of social anthropology—perhaps more deserving than Tylor of the title "father of anthropology," because "it is with him that the continuing topics of anthropological concern such as marriage forms, incest, exogamy . . . and totemism originated."[34]

The anthropological reputation of Herbert Spencer is complicated by the fact that his interests were so broad-ranging and his influence so diffusely pervasive—and by the fact that for a half century after his death he was confined to an intellectual historical purgatory from which he is only now emerging. In 1870, Darwin expected that "hereafter he will be looked at as by far the greatest living philosopher in England; perhaps equal to any that have lived." But in 1933, Crane Brinton could ask "Who now reads Spencer?" and Talcott Parsons—after affirming that "Spencer is dead"—could then, ostensibly, devote perhaps the most influential single modern work on social theory and its history to explaining the death of Spencer's reputation, without quoting a single passage directly from his work.[35]

But as we have already seen, Spencer had been somewhat marginal to anthropology from the beginning. The anthropological aspects of his sociological thought were systematically pursued only after classical evolutionism had emerged; his more significant contribution to classical evolutionism was probably in the area of psychological assumption. Thus while Spencer belonged to no major anthropological society, either as ordinary or (like Darwin) honorary fellow, he was once asked to give a lecture to the Anthropological Institute on "The Comparative Psychology of Man"; and Boas' later critique of evolutionary views of *The Mind of Primitive Man* was in fact largely directed against the viewpoint Spencer had advanced in "Primitive Man—Emotional" and "Primitive Man—Intellectual." Although A. L. Kroeber used Spencer's notion of "The Superorganic" as the title of a major programmatic pronouncement in 1917, it was to the anti-Spencerian end of affirming the autonomy of the cultural realm. When his colleague Robert Lowie published a *History of Ethnology* in 1937, Spencer's name was not even mentioned.[36]

While Spencer's reputation suffered a similar decline in Britain, his influence on British social anthropology was considerable, if somewhat indirect. Evans-Pritchard, in reviewing late-nineteenth-century theoretical developments, suggested that "Spencer's use of the biological analogy of organism, dangerous though it has proved to be, did much to further the use of the concepts of structure and function in social anthropology." While Evans-Pritchard's references suggest that this acknowledgment was merely honorific, his one-time mentor Radcliffe-Brown did indeed get a heavy dose of Spencer in the Moral Science Tripos at Cambridge in 1904. It seems likely, however, that the more important influence of Spencer's thought came indirectly through Durkheim, who was, through Radcliffe-Brown (and to a lesser extent, Malinowski), the major theoretical influence on modern social anthropology. Although Durkheim's earlier work was largely a critique of Spencer's views on the nature of contract, a considerable body of Spencerian assumption was in the process incorporated into Durkheim's thinking, and thence into social anthropology. Given Talcott Parsons' unexplored but evident debts to Malinowski and Radcliffe-Brown, a very likely line of intellectual influence may be "from Spencer to Durkheim to British and British-influenced functional anthropology to structural-functional sociology in the United States." Be that as it may, by the end of his life Parsons had begun reading Herbert Spencer and had turned to evolutionary questions.[37]

While the active disciplinary memory of social evolutionism in American anthropology was long tied to Morgan, more recent neo-evolutionary writings have resurrected Spencer—although not without a certain ambivalence. Thus, although Marvin Harris credited him with being the evolutionist "who approached most closely to the understanding of sociocultural phenomena in terms of evolving systems, each of whose parts contributed to each other and to the continuity and change of the whole," he also used "Spencerism" (rather than "social Darwinism") as the general category for the distasteful ideological functions of nineteenth-century evolutionary thought ("the utility of this position for an empire or a corporation on which the sun never sets needs no special emphasis"). Other neo-evolutionists seem more unqualifiedly positive: rejecting the general view that Spencer has "only [merely] historical significance," the editor of the selections included in *Classics in Anthropology* insisted that his "indirect influence on contemporary anthropology and sociology is by no means negligible."[38]

In British social anthropology, where neo-evolutionism has not been a significant current, the revival of interest in Spencer has been less present-oriented. Thus the recent biography by a British social anthropologist concluded by suggesting that despite our inheritance from Spencer, "his interest for us now lies in how different he was from us." Nevertheless, it seems unlikely that a writer who wrote so much on so many topics, who was so widely acknowledged in his day, only to be criticized, stereotyped, and then dismissed unread, should not contain much material for "rediscovery." If there are today in sociocultural anthropology no neo-Lubbockians or neo-McLennians, neo-Spencerian seems a much more likely category—quite aside from the sociobiologists who are sometimes (not inappropriately) so described.[39]

In contrast to the other four, Tylor's name has never faded from the disciplinary memory of anthropology; and although his sole paternity might be disputed by those in the lineages of Morgan or of Boas, few would dispute his status as a "father of anthropology." A number of factors have contributed to this, including longevity and institutional centrality. Although he was suffering from senility by the time his *festschrift* appeared in 1907, and never completed the anticipated "magnum opus" that was to have eventuated from the Gifford Lectures of 1889 and 1890, Tylor survived until 1917—by which time anthropology in both England and the United States had achieved a foothold in a number of major academic institutions. From the 1880s on, Tylor had been a focal figure in the incipient institutionalization of the discipline, as president of the Anthropological Institute, chairman of the British Association Committee on the Northwest Tribes of Canada—which supported much of the early fieldwork of Franz Boas—and, most importantly, as the first Reader and then Professor of Anthropology at Oxford. The effective institutionalization of social anthropology was the work of later anthropological generations—Haddon and Rivers at Cambridge, Seligman and then Malinowski at the London School of Economics, and Marett and later Radcliffe-Brown at Oxford. But when the fourth generation looked back along the institutional lineage, it was possible, as Evans-Pritchard was wont to do, to trace a straight descent in the chair at Oxford: from Tylor to Marett to "R-B" down to "E-P" himself.[40]

If Tylor's institutional position made it unlikely that his paternity would be challenged by British anthropologists, his methodological sobriety and conceptual resonance enhanced his paternal status on both sides of the Atlantic. Most would have agreed with Evans-Pritchard that Tylor was "more cautious and critical than most of his contemporaries and avoided their stage-making proclivities." Tylor's early and continuing interest in diffusion, his caution regarding the disputes over matriarchal priority, his similar self-distancing from the discussion of totemism, all encouraged a diffuse retrospective solidarity. True, the diffusionists of the 1920s found it necessary to argue that his evolutionary turn in the late 1860s had been motivated by extraneous religious considerations. But for all those who conceived anthropology as "the science of culture," the opening line of *Primitive Culture* had an almost inescapable conceptual resonance—especially in the American tradition, given the failure of Franz Boas to offer a similarly apothegmatic statement. There, inscribed on the foundation stone of the discourse, was what read like a definition of its central concept: "Culture or Civilization, taken in its wide ethnographic sense, is that complex whole which includes knowledge, belief, art, morals, law, custom, and any other capabilities and habits acquired by man as a member of society."[41]

Although his own intellectual lineage led back to Durkheim and to Spencer, Radcliffe-Brown in 1923 still used that definition as evidence of Tylor's undisputed right "to the title of father of the science." But in the 1930s this attribution began to seem a bit anomalous to British social anthropologists. During his Chicago interlude Radcliffe-Brown found it necessary to distinguish more sharply his social anthropological enterprise from that of American cultural anthropologists; in defending his "Natural Science of Society" in 1937, he in fact asserted the impossibility of a comparative science of "culture." By this time, Evans-Pritchard had elaborated more systematically the critique of "The Intellectualist (English) Interpretation of Magic" that those in the Durkheimian tradition had been making since 1908—although in deference to Tylor's paternal status, it had always been directed primarily against Frazer.[42] Although Marett published a brief biography focusing especially on that part of Tylor's work "which touches Sociology," references to Tylor in the later historical accounts by Evans-Pritchard and Radcliffe-Brown were rather perfunctory, and the role of Comte, Morgan, Spencer, and other more "sociological" writers was accentuated. If long-institutionalized tradition would not allow Tylor's paternity to be denied, paradox allowed it to be placed in an appropriate perspective. Meyer Fortes, who reflected in person as well as in print on the history of his inquiry, was upon occasion given to suggest that whereas Tylor had in fact been the founder of American cultural anthropology, the true founder of British social anthropology was the American Lewis Henry Morgan—whose "rediscovery" by Rivers "was the beginning of a method and theory of research which took deep root in British anthropology."[43]

Even so, Tylor's interest today seems much more than "merely historical." With appropriate deletions of material not easily recontextualized in terms of present anthropological concerns, one of his books was included in the *Classics in Anthropology* series as a study in "signs, symbols and communication"—and was proclaimed as lying "at the foundation of all later work" on the process of symbolization in human life. And just as there has been a Morganian countercurrent in American cultural anthropology, so has there been a "neo-Tylorian" current in British social anthropology—not as a reassertion of evolutionism, but rather of the centrality of belief and purpose against the post-Durkheimian social anthropological insistence on the priority of ritual and function.[44]

In tracing the rise and fall of Victorian anthropological reputations, we are thus pulled toward issues of historical significance—the merely historical significance of Lubbock suggesting by opposition the real historical significance of Tylor. But none of the figures we are treating has the obvious world historical significance of a Marx, or the general intellectual historical significance of a Freud—though Spencer's reputation was once as great. Nor have they the discipline-forming historical significance of a Weber or a Durkheim; none of them offers today a general theoretical standpoint (although one could no doubt be derived from Spencer's oeuvre). Nor would they be regarded today, like each of the four just mentioned, as major investors in the general intellectual capital of the modern human sciences. From the perspective of the history of anthropology as a discipline, their enduring historical significance may better be sought in their collective representation of some of the more general characteristics of the British anthropological tradition.

Classical Evolutionism and the Idea of Culture

To explore further the historical significance of classical evolutionism, we may do well to start with the Tylorian half of Fortes' paradox—leaving aside for the moment the issue of Morgan's fatherhood of British social anthropology. Tylor's presumed status as founder of American cultural anthropology is predicated on the assumption that the "culture" he wrote of in *Primitive Culture* is essentially the same as that studied by modern cultural anthropologists. But the assertion that Tylor was "deliberately establishing a science by defining its subject matter" has been seriously questioned since 1952, when Alfred Kroeber and Clyde Kluckhohn offered it in their encyclopedic inventory of the culture concept.[45]

Without reviewing an argument developed at length elsewhere, suffice it to say that, once past that opening definition—in which the anthropological character of the concept was compromised by its equation with "civilization"—Tylor's actual usage of the term "culture" lacked a number of the features commonly associated with the modern anthropological concept: historicity, integration, behavioral determinism, relativity, and—most symptomatically—plurality. For although it still is spoken of as "the science of culture," modern cultural anthropology might be more accurately characterized as the "science of cultures." And in contrast to the variety of putatively equal human cultures studied by modern anthropologists, Tylor's culture was singular and hierarchical—as his frequent references to "uncultured" savages suggest. Although he may appropriately be regarded as having made traditional humanist culture evolutionary, the opening line of Tylor's *Primitive Culture* was not, if judged by subsequent usage in the same volume, a definition of culture in the anthropological sense. As evidenced by the long temporal gap Kroeber and Kluckhohn found between Tylor's and succeeding anthropological definitions, the modern anthropological usage was developed somewhat later, in the work of anthropologists with closer ties to the German tradition.[46]

It is not an easy matter, however, for the intruding historian of disciplines to disturb the conventional disciplinary historical wisdom. Anthropologists still sometimes refer to Tylor as the "father" of the anthropological culture concept; and recently, a considerable historical effort has been offered in support of "the older view." There it has been argued that although Tylor's use of the term approximated "post-Boasian American usage" only "in a few contexts," his definition was nevertheless an important landmark "in the introduction of 'culture' as a modern anthropological term in English"—from German sources on which he heavily relied.[47]

If we pursue the issue here, it is not simply to reaffirm an argument made previously, but because the nature of Tylor's conception of culture, and his relation to the German intellectual tradition, are matters bearing closely on the broader historical significance of British classical evolutionism. In 1968, it was somewhat rashly suggested that the issue might be "reformulated in terms of a testable hypothesis": the appearance or nonappearance of plural usages of the word "culture." And while it is unlikely that any matter of cultural meaning can be disposed of by a simple grammatical test, the results of an attempted rebuttal are worthy of note: a search of the surviving residue of Tylor's career has produced only two rather dubious instances of the plural, neither of them in a published work by Tylor.[48]

If a similar review of German anthropological sources produced more instances of plural usage, this is not inconsistent with the argument that the modern concept emerged in the work of early Boasian anthropologists, whose debt to the Germanic tradition is indisputable. More critical for our understanding of Tylor's conception of culture is the way he reacted to such plural usages. Although it was apparently overlooked in the dedicated rebutting effort, some evidence on this point is contained in a review Tylor published in 1876 of a "History of Culture" written by the German Darwinist Friedrich von Hellwald. Agreeing with Hellwald that culture should be treated as "varying according to the regions where it is formed and to which it is adapted"—so that "the culture of America will always be American and that of Europe European"—Tylor went on to note Hellwald's suggestion that properly speaking, the ethnologist should refer not to "civilisation" but to "civilisations." But although he felt that "this caution against the common plan of measuring all nations by an exact cosmopolitan standard is much to be approved," Tylor went on in the same review to do just that, speaking of customs prevailing "at different stages of civilization," and suggesting that "cultured man is perceptibly superior to savages in both the material quantity of his brain and in his power of reasoning." In short, whatever impulse Tylor may have had to embrace the idea of cultural plurality and relativity was constrained by his evolutionary commitment.[49]

As a matter of fact, Tylor himself, on at least one prior occasion, had used the word "civilization" in the plural—in the passage previously quoted (page 159) regarding the mutual influences of the "civilizations of many races.'' However, the fact that he should nevertheless have reacted to Hellwald's suggestion as if it were a novel one may be taken as sustaining the general thrust of the present interpretation. The passage at issue occurs in *Researches into the Early History of Mankind,* at a point when Tylor was still operating in terms of the more Germanic Prichardian paradigm; in the context of the immediately following reference to the ''civilization of the whole world,'' the passage can be read as reflecting his shift, then in process, from an ethnological to an evolutionary paradigm. Once in the latter mode, Tylor found the plurality of civilization an interesting anomaly, but it did not open him up to a modern anthropological relativism. A similar argument might be offered regarding the incipient plurality of Mill's suggestion (page 38) that even ''unmitigated savages'' had ''their own education, their own culture'': it reflects the Germanic moment in Mill's thought, which, like his ''ethology,'' was not a very live intellectual option within the post-Darwinian tradition of evolutionary positivism.

Had Tylor been employing ''culture'' in a sense radically different from the contemporary English usage of his day, one might expect him to have insisted on legitimating his innovative scientific definition when he advised Leslie Stephen on the anthropological terms to be included in the Oxford *New English Dictionary.* But though he ''argued at length with [Stephen] about the entry for 'couvade' in the same volume, and would probably have been able to have had inserted an anthropological definition of 'culture' and an example of his own use of it, if he had tried,'' it was not until fifteen years after Tylor's death in 1917 that the opening line of *Primitive Culture* was inserted in the supplementary volume—to illustrate an evolutionary (rather than a relativistic) usage.[50]

Similarly, although the comprehensive review of Tylor's German readings contributes to our more detailed understanding of his relationship to the German intellectual tradition, it does not change the major outlines. He began in the English empiricist tradition, and after an excursion into German thought—stimulated by his early ethnological interest in comparative philology—he turned again, in the context of the Darwinian debate, to more congenial sources: the Enlightenment and utilitarian traditions, and the contemporary natural sciences, which were the dominant intellectual influences on *Primitive Culture.* In this context, the fundamental opposition between Tylor's characteristic mode of inquiry and another more characteristic of the German tradition becomes clearly evident. But to appreciate this disjunction, one must move beyond cataloging Tylor's German readings and consider his reaction to the German tradition as it was manifest in the British polemical context.[51]

The more systematic investigation of anthropological debate at different historical moments and over periods of time may in fact provide a means by which committed ''historicists'' can approach issues of historical significance in a manner which, still privileging the questions their historical subjects were addressing, nevertheless seeks to cast light on their relation to those that have concerned subsequent writers, down to the present. Because intellectual groupings bear some analogy to the lineage groups studied by modern social anthropology, the range of issues thus illuminated may depend on the parties drawn together in any particular debate. By studying debates among advocates of a single general viewpoint, we may perhaps best illuminate its theoretical potentialities—the issues which, freed to some extent from their original ideological determination, could become the subject of more autonomous intellectual investigation, insofar as they elicited the systematic elaboration of argument or the collection of evidence. On the other hand, if we are interested in the limitations rather than the potentialities of a viewpoint, we may find more useful those debates that unite lineage members against outsiders, since here fundamental assumptions are more likely to be at issue. A dissenting critic may be free to explore the latent significance of arguments which, by virtue of their ideological overdetermination, seem compelling to those who initially advocate them. Thus Maine, as we have had occasion to note, raised issues anticipating criticisms made of evolutionary comparison a half century later, and still made today. Alternatively, in defending themselves against someone with incommensurable assumptions, advocates may reveal what is really essential to their own viewpoint.[52]

From this point of view, it is worth considering the relation of the classical evolutionists to Friedrich Max Müller, who was the most influential representative of the German intellectual tradition in post-Prichardian British anthropological circles. Throughout the last half of the nineteenth century Müller played the role of an accommodating but resolutely determined missionary to "Ante-Kantian or Ante-Copernican" English empiricists, maintaining through much of that time a peculiarly marginal but illuminating relationship to Victorian anthropological writers. Though his reputation was based to a considerable extent on his activities as an intellectual popularizer, and had already fallen considerably before his death, in the 1860s Müller was a figure to be reckoned with on any issue relating to language, and every one of the major classical evolutionary writers in fact felt it necessary to disagree with him.[53]

In the case of Tylor, the confrontation was muted by the considerable intellectual debt that Tylor's early thinking did indeed owe to Müller—who later played an influential role in winning Tylor his academic appointment at Oxford. But if Tylor's ideas about the early mental condition of man reflect to some extent Müller's romantic "mythopoeic" age, and if both men saw the content of mythology in terms of analogies discovered in nature, there was a profound epistemological opposition underlying Tylor's appropriation of substantive and conceptual specifics. In one of the few passages in which he confronted the matter directly, Tylor himself suggested the nature of this difference: "For myself, I am disposed to think (differing here in some measure from Professor Max Müller's view of the subject) that the mythology of the lower races rests especially on a basis of real and sensible analogy, and that the great expansion of verbal metaphor into myth belongs to more advanced periods of civilization. In a word, I take material myth to be the primary, and verbal myth to be the secondary formation. But whether this opinion be historically sound or not, the difference in nature between myth founded on fact and myth founded on word is sufficiently manifest."[54]

As recent analysis has suggested, Tylor here "rather inconspicuously delineates a radically different set of epistemological principles," the implications of which "compound and ramify" in many directions. For Tylor, the fundamental units of mythology, like those of language, of religion, of science—and indeed, of all culture—were to be derived "ultimately from associations of physical sense impressions" of the material world (and thereby "founded on fact"). Thus it was that he insisted that the "resemblances" or "analogies" on which mythology was based "thrust themselves directly on the mind, without any necessary intervention of words. Deep as language lies in our mental life, the direct comparison of object with object, and action with action, lies yet deeper."[55]

By contrast, Müller's "myth founded on word" reflected a radically different epistemology, in which language and thought were inseparable, and "language exercised a distinctive constitutive function in human knowledge": "Now the first step towards this real knowledge, a step which, however small in appearance, separates man for ever from all other animals, is *the naming of a thing,* or the making a thing knowable. All naming is classification, bringing the individual under the general; and whatever we know, whether empirically or scientifically, we know it only by means of our general ideas." For Müller, the "several hundred Indo-European 'roots' that comparative analysis had isolated [were] an irreducible set of concepts in terms of which this 'naming' or 'making a thing knowable' proceeded"; and this ultimate conceptual nature of language made it a "distinctly human capacity that could not have been built up from mere sense experience." Myth was a special development of processes that were "essentially linguistic and non-derivable from any other order of phenomenon"—of capacities which were, ultimately, God-given. Whereas Tylor, like Darwin, "sought the universals of human mentality in terms of principles *general* enough that they would . . . show man to be continuous with the rest of the animal kingdom," Müller sought them "in terms of principles *specific* enough that they would . . . demonstrate man's distinctiveness from the rest of the animal kingdom." Thus it was that language was also a Rubicon separating the two theorists; while Tylor congratulated Müller for having pursued its development on Lyellian principles, he quickly added that "below the problem of the Development of Language" lay "the problem of the Origin of Language, the question of how these simple root-forms came into existence." To cross that Rubicon, Tylor was willing if necessary to carry his argument on the reeds of gesture, interjection, and onomatopoeia.[56]

Having bridged the Rubicon of language, Tylor recognized "no impediment to the attainment of perfect 'positive knowledge' other than the 'practical ones' of enormous complexity of evidence, and imperfections of methods of observation." By contrast, Müller echoed Kant's insistence that knowledge was "inherently and always limited by its own forms," and even suggested that Western scientific concepts like ether and gravity were in a sense mythological in character. Like many others in the Germanic tradition, Müller assumed that the universe contained two components ("spirit" and "matter") and therefore required "two distinct kinds of intellectual disciplines": "historical" or "moral" sciences and "physical" or "natural sciences." By contrast, Tylor's universe "was ultimately composed of a single [materialist] principle," so that all knowledge could "ultimately be comprehended within a single science."[57]

To varying degrees, similar oppositional themes are manifest in the work of the other major evolutionary figures. Thus Lubbock quoted at length "my friend Professor Max Müller" on the "original roots" of language as having been created "by the hand of God"—but went on to suggest that onomatopoeia (Müller's "bow wow" theory) would in fact provide a "satisfactory" alternative explanation of their origin. Similarly, McLennan—after expressing his surprise that "a man of the acknowledged ability and great learning of Professor Müller" should cast "ridicule upon the views of others respecting so important a point"—insisted that "as ideas came gradually, and therefore words . . . came after ideas, we are led back to a time when man, as regards his power of communicating with his fellows, was undistinguishable from any other animal. . . ." So also Lane Fox: "words are the outward signs of ideas in the mind."[58]

But it was Spencer, for whom epistemological assumptions were a matter of systematic concern, who treated Müller's work at greatest length. Again, we find the insistence on the distinction between the "growth of ideas" and the "growth of words," and on the priority of the former: because "a more special science cannot be fully understood until the more general science including it is understood . . . philological proofs are therefore untrustworthy unless supported by psychological truths.'' In the study of mythology, one must start by ''arguing from the phenomena symbolized'' rather than ''the phenomena which the symbols present.'' Müller's error was to start from the complex, and to ''get from it the factors of the simple.'' Beginning with ''the ideas and feelings possessed by the civilized,'' he carried these along in the study of the semicivilized Aryans, and then descended ''by inference to the ideas and feelings of the uncivilized.'' Assuming that men originally ''had certain verbal symbols for abstractions [notably, that of a Universal Power]; and having, by implication, had a corresponding power of abstract thinking; it is alleged that the barbarian thereupon began to deprive these verbal symbols of their abstractness''—to make their meanings concrete, and thus to create myths. But this implied, contrary to everything known of savage thought and language, that ''the progress of thought is from the abstract to the concrete.'' The proper order was that of ''ascending evolution,'' which moved from the concrete to the abstract, from the simple to the complex. ''Lacking words even for low generalities and abstractions, it is utterly impossible that the savage should have words to frame a conception uniting high generality with high abstractness.'' There was no such thing as a primitive ''mythopoeic tendency.'' It was rather that lacking imagination, and ''having only rude speech'' which was, of necessity, ''full of metaphor,'' the savage created the marvelous ''unawares''; from there he gradually progressed toward factual narrative by a ''slowly increasing ratio of truth to error.''[59]

Spencer insisted that Müller's position was in fact based on a ''theological'' assumption: the postulation of an innate human ''intuition of God.'' Similarly, he charged that Müller's ''science of language'' was based on ''the Hebrew legend of the creation,'' since it required us to go behind the evolutionary processes evident in existing languages to a ''special creation'' of original ''linguistic capital in the shape of roots having abstract meanings.'' And when Müller, in his assimilating missionary mode, tried to show that Spencer was actually a Kantian, Spencer argued at some length that the true evolutionary view was simply an extension of the ''experiential'' view of Locke, against that of Kant, which was ''absolutely unexperiential.''[60]

Certain themes recur throughout this confrontation between Kant's self-professed ambassador to the empiricists and the empiricist defenders of sociocultural evolutionism. There is a series of differentially related and prioritized oppositions—thing (or fact) vs. symbol, material vs. verbal, idea vs. word, thought vs. language, concrete vs. abstract, simple vs. complex—all of which imply a different conception of the way the human mind works, how it relates to the external world, and how it has developed through time. To note this is simply to reemphasize the fact that Tylor and his confreres did indeed belong to a different intellectual/philosophical tradition from Müller. But in doing so, we suggest also that this identification—reinforced by certain other aspects of their intellectual orientation, and of their "ulterior motivation"—had consequences for their anthropology, placing limitations on the conception of culture that it could develop.

For the classical evolutionists, human mental activity was an attempt, on the principles of associationist psychology, to develop useful knowledge—a realistic picture of the external world that would enable human individuals to achieve adaptive utilitarian ends. Viewed in developmental terms, it was an ever-closer correlation of the ideal (or mental) and the real (or material). While the principle of mental activity was assumed to be the same for all humans, they differed in how far they had gotten in this process of correlation. In an undeveloped state, all human reason was subject to a fatal flaw: the tendency to respond too immediately to the outside world, and to be misled by the apparent similarities of ideal images of it—thereby substituting an ideal for a real connection, or being misled by a verbal similarity. Although in the first instance extremely concrete and literal minded, savages accidentally created a world of false metaphors and analogies, producing myth and religion instead of scientific knowledge.

With the progress of culture, these errors were gradually overcome, and a more perfect correlation of the ideal and the real was achieved, by straightening out erroneous connections and moving from limited concrete ones to more general and abstract ones. (Paradoxically, progress was facilitated in certain areas—notably language, but also economics, where money was substituted for barter—by processes of conventionalization and arbitrary symbolization.) Culture was conceived in diachronic and vertical (if not linear) terms, so that people were more or less cultured rather than living in different cultures; since culture was essentially one, differences tended to be conceived as erroneous superstition or irrational survival. Except insofar as it was accumulated, either as knowledge or as inherited mental capacity, culture was primarily a consequence rather than a condition of human activity. While groups differed in their degree or stage of culture, culture was not the conditioning medium in which individuals came into being, but the expression in them of the progress in refinement achieved by the group. What constrained human behavior was not culture, but tradition, or survival in culture (what had once been rationally purposive but was now "merely" symbolic or ritual); alternatively, behavior could be constrained by character, which was the embodiment in the individual of the degree of moral progress that the group had attained.

Similarly, rather than being in any meaningful sense culturally constituted, the natural world existed "out there" as a determinant and reference point of all psychological and by extension of all cultural processes. Things preceded ideas, which in turn preceded words—establishing a hierarchy of sciences, all based on similar principles. Insofar as Tylor created a "science of culture [or civilization]" it was not constituted on any fundamental difference of subject matter or epistemological assumption, but rather in an attempt to bring the accumulative development of human knowledge, belief, art, morals, law, and custom within the same realm of "regular causation" that governed the natural world, and through increasing knowledge of its laws, to bring it similarly under greater human control.

While empiricism, positivism, and materialism were also manifest in mid-nineteenth-century Germany, other more characteristically German intellectual currents emphasized the inherent internal constraints on human knowledge. Although in Kant these had been argued in generic human terms, there was also a strong orientation in the German tradition toward the study of human cultural variety, which was reinforced by a tendency to insist on a distinction between a variously manifest spiritual culture and a uniformly progressive material civilization. The German orientation toward human variety had of course a strong racialist potential. But in the context of the German scholarly interest in the phenomena of language it also encouraged an approach to human cultural differences in constitutive rather than consequential terms. For one obvious way to a more meaningful cultural plurality is through language—through the notion, suggested in Herder and elaborated by Wilhelm von Humboldt, that different languages somehow constitute different worlds of thought.[61]

Although Müller was a product of this tradition, he did not in fact offer a viable substitute for Mill's abortive science of character. Müller did stimulate the collection of linguistic data by missionaries, and continued to regard his writings on language, thought, and religion as fundamentally "anthropological." But his role was rather that of critical gadfly than cultural theorist. And his criticisms of evolutionary assumptions had an ambiguous double thrust—on the one hand, anticipating issues that were to be raised by his intellectual countryman, Franz Boas; on the other, echoing themes of traditional Christian degenerationism.[62] But if the linguistic alternative was only hinted at in Müller's work, to be followed up later in the Boasian tradition, this route to a more anthropological culture was in effect shut off to the classical evolutionists, whose approach to language was essentially reductive, and who tended to associate its study with the biblical anthropology they were combating.

This is not to suggest that one may not find in English writers occasional approaches to a more "anthropological" view of culture—although such thinking is perhaps more likely to be found in Maine, who had strong ties to the Germanic tradition. Nor is it to deny that Tylor's "science of culture" was in its own terms a contribution to the development of later British anthropology; for the study of "culture"—gradually pluralized in the context of the modern ethnographic tradition and the resurgence of historical ethnology—continued to be a focus of British anthropological inquiry until Radcliffe-Brown succeeded in redefining that inquiry in sociological terms in the late 1930s. Nor is it to suggest that the project of a cognitive or evolutionary study of culture may not still be worth pursuing. But it is to argue that the traditional attribution to Tylor of the invention of anthropological culture is a somewhat misleading basis for an appreciation of the historical significance of Victorian anthropology.

From the point of view of the later development of the culture concept, especially in its more recent idealist forms (as a "system of symbols and meanings"),[63] the historical significance of British classical evolutionism may lie rather in its turn away from German thought. Prichardian ethnology, which privileged the study of language, had been closely tied to that tradition. In 1847, Müller had joined his mentor Bunsen with Prichard at the ethnological discussions of the Oxford meetings of the British Association. Forty years later, when he returned to chair the anthropological section at the Cardiff meetings, it was as an outsider, looking back to a time when philology and anthropology had stood in a more constructive relationship. Although in the interim the German idealist tradition was by no means without influence in certain corners of British intellectual life, it was never again to have a major direct influence on British anthropology (except perhaps in the work of William Robertson Smith, who began as and always in a fundamental sense remained a theologian). When, in the early twentieth century, the influence of German idealism was felt again in British anthropology, it came via France and the sociology of Emile Durkheim, which, although it allowed a more constitutive role for culture (in the form of the *conscience collective*), nevertheless kept it within the realm of a unified scientific discourse.[64]

In turning away from German influences, classical evolutionary writers strongly reasserted characteristic themes of the English utilitarian tradition in its later-nineteenth-century positivist mode. In the study of the evolution of social structure, some of them followed Maine in conceiving a prior time when the individual atoms of modern society had not yet been differentiated out of larger familial or tribal entities. And in general, they saw the evolution of culture as an ideational phenomenon: cultural progress consisted primarily in the production of new and better ideas. But in treating questions of human motivation, they tended to think in terms of individual actors pursuing pleasurable or adaptive goals according to the best knowledge that was available to them. The ideas that they produced were ideas provoked by the external world, and intended to bring it under control; ultimately, the progress of culture and the progress of science were one and the same.[65]

From this perspective, the historical significance of classical evolutionism may be further illuminated by considering its interesting oblique relationship to the dominant human science in the British tradition: classical political economy. It has been suggested that Darwinian evolutionism was the expression in scientific thought of the ideology and practice of Victorian economic life: unrestricted competition and the survival of the economic fittest being projected into the biological realm as the law of evolutionary development. In these terms, "social Darwinism" might similarly be regarded as a projection, via biology, of the competitive ethos of contemporary social life into the realm of social theory.[66] But as we have argued, classical sociocultural evolutionism bore a more indirect relationship to Darwinism, and similarly, to economic life. Classical evolutionists were, in fact, relatively little concerned with the economic realm, except in its most limited technological sense, where it provided the objective standard by which progress in culture could be measured. In contrast to Maine, whose ultimate concern might be defined as the historical derivation of the cultural foundations for Victorian economic life, they took those foundations largely for granted. Instead, the classical evolutionists dealt primarily with myth, religion, marriage, and kinship, at reaches of time that removed them from a direct relationship to the life of their own day—except by the principle of the survival of the unfit: the irrationally persistent and now culturally inappropriate, which the reformer's science would identify and mark out for elimination.

In doing so, however, classical evolutionists may perhaps be regarded as refracting the economic assumptions of their own culture through the medium of time—thereby creating, by a kind of inversion, a discipline complementary to the dominant human science of their era. For if classical political economy was the science of rational behavior directed toward manifestly utilitarian goals, then classical evolutionism was the counterscience of behavior that seemed, by the standards of the culture of political economy, to have no rational utilitarian justification. In addition (and prior) to the task of present cultural reformation—which came, after all, as a kind of afterthought in *Primitive Culture*—the task of anthropology was to explain how such irrationality could have existed in the first place. It did so by arguing that what seemed irrational, nonutilitarian, or apparently purposeless customs and beliefs, when judged by present standards, had in fact been rationally purposeful, utilitarian, and even adaptive in some prior evolutionary phase, and could thus be incorporated into the march of cultural progress.

Recalling our prior suggestion that anthropology-cum-ethnology had been the science of leftovers or residues, insofar as the methodological elaboration and differentiation of the human sciences in the early nineteenth century was excluding the "savage" from the discourse of disciplines treating the phenomena of civilized life, we may see this complementarity of Victorian anthropology in another perspective of significance. It has been suggested that what was being excluded from the human sciences in this process of disciplinary differentiation was the realm of the irrational—whether defined in pathological, paranormal, or developmental terms—and that it was only in the revolt against positivism that this residue became again the subject of serious investigation by students of human mental phenomena. Insofar as one accepts this interpretation, then Victorian anthropology may perhaps be understood as the residuary legatee not only of the savage, but also of the irrational in human existence. By equating the irrational with the primitive, it was possible to bring it under the control of cultural progress.[67]

From a broader perspective, the classical evolutionist preoccupation with the irrational may be regarded simply as a variant of a more general Western anthropological concern. For at the ethnographic or experiential level of direct cultural confrontation, the question "why do they do this crazy thing?," albeit fundamentally ethnocentric, is at the same time perhaps the most fundamental anthropological question: "Why do these human Others do things which to Us seem manifestly irrational?" And immediately implicated in it is what Clifford Geertz has spoken of as anthropology's deepest theoretical dilemma: how is the manifest variety of human cultural forms to be "squared with the biological unity of the human species"?[68]

The major orientations of the Western anthropological tradition constitute a series of approaches to these questions. Most of them, like Geertz's formulation of the dilemma, have privileged an essential likeness of humankind, which is in fact one of the founding ethnocentric assumptions of the Western cultural tradition. Thus for Christian degenerationism, idolatry was potential to all mankind in its fallen state, just as for Enlightenment progressionism all mankind in the early stages of refinement were victims of superstition. Similarly, in the twentieth century, there has been a series of answers which, although differing in their approach to the variety of cultural forms, each start from the presupposition of biological unity: notably Boasian culturalism, British functionalism, and French structuralism.

In the nineteenth century, however, the assumption of ultimate biological unity was seriously called into question by polygenist racialism, which saw different groups of mankind as aboriginally distinct and irreducibly unequal. Although classical evolutionism was not primarily concerned with the physical differentiation of humankind, it nevertheless incorporated a substantial body of racialist assumption—in effect preserving the biological unity of mankind by accepting the substantial differentiation of human races in evolutionary time. At the same time, it was still strongly influenced by the unitarian assumptions of the Christian and Enlightenment traditions and took for granted that the cumulation of racial mental differences had not destroyed the fundamental unity of human mental process. But in thus limiting the significance of racial difference, classical evolutionism also reduced the significance of the variety of cultural forms. Itself the product of an era of unparalleled cultural self-confidence, it interpreted cultural variety in terms that, to a rather greater degree than subsequent anthropological viewpoints, privileged the assumptions of its own culture (which in Tylor's case provided an explicit standard of cultural evaluation). Judged in such terms, the variety of cultural forms represented flawed or imperfect manifestations of the processes of Western practical cultural rationality, produced by small-brained primitive men—and by their contemporary savage representatives—in the attempt to understand and control the external world.

It was possible in this context to establish a "science of culture." And indeed the establishment of that science marks one of the major turning points in the development of anthropology; it was an event of unquestionable historical significance. But given the variety of contextual constraints that conditioned its formation, the evolutionary "science of culture" differed in historically significant ways from later cultural anthropology. As Fortes suggested, disciplinary development in Britain was to proceed along quite different lines.

Classical Evolutionism and Disciplinary Discourse

Maintaining a disciplinary perspective on the matter, one might argue that it is a defining characteristic of the *really* historically significant in the anthropological past that it somehow escapes the constraints of the cultural context in which it was formed, and enters into the formation of subsequent disciplinary inquiry, even to the present. One might wish to distinguish between ancestral totem emblems chosen to legitimize a particular present viewpoint, and more substantively constitutive influences—between Tylor's mythic status as the "inventor of the culture concept," or his symbolic status as "founding father" of British (or American) anthropology, on the one hand, and the substantive influence of his widely quoted definition of culture, or of positions he took on issues of human rationality now discussed as "neo-Tylorian," on the other. However, it would be claiming too much for historicism to make the historian the final arbiter of such matters. One hopes historical inquiry may influence anthropological opinion; but if enough present anthropologists continue to regard Tylor as the inventor of culture, or attempt to claim him for the camp of "cultural idealism" or "cultural materialism,'' then the fact of those claims (regardless of their historical validity) must be taken as a measure of Tylor's *real* historical significance. Conversely, a measure of *mere* historical significance might be the fact that a figure is not regarded as worth claiming or fighting over—as in the case of C. Staniland Wake, who remains a marginal figure even after the discovery that he was ''right'' on many issues that McLennan (or Morgan) got ''wrong.''[69]

To have put quotation marks about these two evaluative terms was in fact a choice of some historiographical significance. They symbolize the historian's ambiguous temporal stance and marginal relation to disciplinary discourse; implicitly calling into question the epistemological status of anthropological knowledge, they are also an implicit admission of the limitations of the historian's ability to judge what is *really* historically significant in certain areas of the history of anthropology. (For how is a nonspecialist in kinship and social organization to judge a matter about which social anthropologists might disagree, if more than one of them were ever to take the time to do a close reading of both Wake and McLennan?)

Nevertheless, the fact that Wake was able to get things ''right'' raises questions for historical speculation. Perhaps his personal, institutional, and paradigmatic marginality—or the influence of somewhat different ''ulterior motives''—may have given him greater freedom to judge certain issues ''on their merits.'' Or perhaps, writing at a later moment in the debate, when some issues had developed a greater degree of relative cognitive autonomy, he was able to treat them more ''objectively.'' For it is surely a characteristic of disciplinary traditions that issues that are in varying ways exogenously motivated nonetheless become the subject of disciplined inquiry, where they are submitted to the standards of logical argument and judged by bodies of empirical evidence.

No doubt in some cases such inquiry may lead into what are later perceived to be intellectual dead ends. One approach to the historical significance of classical evolutionists might have been to treat systematically all the cases where anthropology was later seen to have been led astray by their having treated as scientific categories what came to be regarded as projections of ethnocentric concern—starting with ''primitive promiscuity'' and continuing right through to the very notion of ''kinship'' itself, which some present anthropologists have called into question as a comparative analytic category on the grounds that it is based on the false assumption that ''relatedness'' is everywhere thought of ultimately in biological terms. From this perspective, McLennan was ''right'' when he dismissed the ''classificatory'' terminology as mere ''terms of address''—although he would perhaps have been a little surprised to discover that kinship itself was not ultimately a matter of ''blood'' relationship.[70]

Alternatively, one might approach historical significance by showing how a writer who was "wrong" nevertheless provided arguments for subsequent scholars to push against; or how, within a nexus of "wrong" positions, there were some that generated lines of inquiry that came to be regarded as constructive. Thus while McLennan's preoccupation with laws of incest as a defining characteristic of the human species reflected a cultural and perhaps personal preoccupation with certain issues of human sexuality, his concepts of "exogamy" and "endogamy" were nonetheless susceptible to logical and empirical clarification. Once Morgan's critique made it clear that endogamous and exogamous groupings frequently existed within the same society, the two terms became part of the permanent conceptual armory of social anthropology, and continue to this day to be subjects of systematic inquiry. Similarly, the universal evolutionary significance of "female infanticide," "marriage by capture," and "polyandry" was called into question very quickly after their formulation and now seems perhaps to have been—like "primitive promiscuity" and "matriarchy"—largely a fantasy of the Victorian male anthropological imagination. But the analysis of "heterogeneous societies" resulting from matrilineal kinship nevertheless became a continuing preoccupation of social anthropologists.[71]

Perhaps because his own ulterior motivation manifested itself in relation to the evolution of religious belief and because he was somewhat marginal to the discussion of sociological issues, Tylor offers the best evidence of the way the latter issues, embedded originally in particular contexts of intellectual polemic and cultural ideology, could in some cases achieve a degree of relative cognitive autonomy. Despite his feeling that the study of social organization should be left to lawyers, Tylor published occasional articles and reviews in this area, and as early as the 1860s had begun to collect systematic comparative data on customs relating to "the development of institutions." In 1888, he presented to the Anthropological Institute the results of his inquiries, in a paper which stands in the same exemplary relation to the later development of social evolutionary debate as McLennan's "Early History of Man" does to its emergence.[72]

Like Herbert Spencer, Tylor had compiled comparable data on a large number of societies; but whereas Spencer published tabular summaries for a series of societies representing different types, along with the ethnographic extracts on which they were based, Tylor attempted a systematic statistical treatment, but without presenting specific ethnographic data. (Spencer may thus be regarded as the ultimate source of the later Human Relations Area Files; Tylor, of the systematic comparative cross-cultural study of the data they contain.) Although he spoke of "social arithmetic" rather than "statistics," and of "adhesions" rather than "correlations," Tylor attempted to find out whether, in his sample of "between three and four hundred peoples," particular customs appeared among the same peoples to a greater degree than one would expect "following the ordinary law of chance distribution." Thus if the apparently "absurd" custom of mutual avoidance between the husband and his wife's relatives was to be expected in nine cases among the sixty-five in which the husband resided with the wife's family, but actually appeared in fourteen, then there must be "a causal connexion of some kind between [the] two groups of phenomena."[73]

Studying the adhesions of a series of such customs—avoidance, residence, teknonymy (renaming the parent after the newborn child), the levirate (the remarriage of a widow to her husband's brother), the couvade (the father's ceremonial pretense of being the mother of his child), marriage by capture, exogamy, and Morgan's classificatory system of relationship (the classification of groups of collateral relatives by the same kinship terms used for lineal ones)—Tylor plotted their distributions on charts representing three developmental stages. He found the results "only compatible with a tendency of society to pass from the maternal to the paternal systems"—since the maternal stage, unlike the paternal and the transitional, manifested no adhesions that could be explained as "survivals." Tylor felt he had thus established "on an enlarged and firm basis the inference as to the antiquity of the maternal system arrived at by the pioneers of the investigation, Bachofen and McLennan, and supported by the later research of a generation of able investigators"—a list headed by Morgan and Lubbock.[74]

The central substantive point of Tylor's methodological demonstration was thus to reaffirm an exogenously motivated evolutionary sequence that was soon to come under criticism and eventually to be rejected by the overwhelming consensus of Anglo-American social anthropologists down to the present. But in the process, he made permanent contributions to the definition or clarification of important concepts, and opened up lines of investigation that have been similarly long-lived. Rejecting the commonly used terms "matriarchal" and "patriarchal," he indicated a differentiation between the components of authority (which in the maternal system was actually in the hands of male relatives), descent, succession to rank, and inheritance of property. Drawing on data provided him by several ethnographic correspondents (Fison and Howitt in Australia, and Codrington in Melanesia), Tylor brought together the phenomena of exogamy and classificatory relationship through the pattern of marriage in Australian section systems—which prohibited the intermarriage of the children of sisters, or of brothers, but allowed that of what Tylor was the first to call "cross-cousins." And though he cast it in evolutionary terms, he offered what was in effect a functional explanation of exogamy: "by binding together a whole community with ties of kinship and affinity, and especially by the peacemaking of the women who hold to one clan as sisters and to another as wives, it tends to keep down feuds and to heal them when they arise, so as at critical moments to hold together a tribe which under endogamous conditions would have to split up.''[75]

Again, Tylor saw his contribution in evolutionary terms as a synthesis and summation—a demonstration that ''my old friend McLennan'' and his adversary Morgan ''were all the while allies pushing forward the same doctrine from different sides.'' In general, he felt that he had shown that ''the institutions of man . . . succeed each other in series substantially uniform over the globe, independent of what seem the comparatively superficial differences of race and language, but shaped by similar human nature acting through successively changed conditions in savage, barbaric, and civilised life.'' But he professed himself less interested in this evolutionary argument than in the usefulness of his method for future anthropological inquiry. And although the method was by no means unproblematic, the article itself was probably the most historically significant paper to emerge from British classical evolutionism, if frequency of subsequent citation may be used as a measure.[76]

Paradoxically, however, it had the immediate result of stimulating research on what were to be antievolutionary lines. Many of the later citations are in fact not to the paper itself but to the brief discussion that followed, in which Francis Galton, then the Institute's president, raised a question that has gone into the literature as ''Galton's Problem'': ''the degree in which the customs of the tribes and races which are compared together are independent''—or, in words Galton did not use, whether Tylor's ''cases'' were the results of ''independent invention'' or ''diffusion.'' For if any two instances had in fact ''been derived from a common source,'' they would be simply ''duplicate copies of the same original'' and—though Galton did not say so in as many words—not properly counted as separate cases in any tabulation. Galton argued that each observation must therefore be carefully ''weighted,'' and suggested a mapping of their geographical distribution. Provoked by Tylor's article—and even more by Galton's criticism—Franz Boas was to pursue studies of the diffusion of cultural elements which led him to a general critique of ''The Limitations of the Comparative Method of Anthropology.'' So also, Edward Westermarck and Fritz Graebner, along somewhat different lines, followed Tylor's lead to conclusions that called into question traditional evolutionary assumptions.[77] While these critiques of evolutionism were no doubt impelled and shaped by their own exogenous influences, they were directed toward issues that had achieved a certain degree of cognitive autonomy since the 1860s, when classical evolutionism had first emerged—out of a similar interplay of the cognitively autonomous and the exogenously motivated.

In Britain, however, Tylor's paper stimulated no systematic critique of evolutionary assumption. There, the reaction against evolutionism came more than a decade after it began in the United States, and the significance of Tylor's paper is to be seen in less discontinuous terms. On the one hand, it suggests that the influence of Lewis Henry Morgan had been felt in England before Rivers "rediscovered" him after 1900—through Fison and Howitt, who had been Morgan's ethnographic correspondents before they became Tylor's and who had established a Morganian approach to the problem of Australian social organization as early as 1880. On the other, it suggests how, under Morgan's influence, the disciplinary debate of particular issues began to transform an exogenously motivated interest in the evolution of marriage into a more technically oriented study of kinship and social organization.[78]

The shift from marriage to kinship was of course a movement toward the characteristic substantive foci of twentieth-century British social anthropology; however, the parallel movement in the religious sphere—from belief to ritual—was slower to develop. In part, this may have been a matter of longevity. McLennan died in 1881, leaving a mass of unfinished manuscripts on the priority of matrilineal kinship and the origin of exogamy which were eventually published by his executors—but which had little or no influence on the debate Tylor drew together in 1888. By contrast, Tylor remained an active participant in disciplinary discussion until after 1900, and as late as 1907, anthropologists were awaiting the "magnum opus" that was to have eventuated from his Gifford Lectures of 1889 and 1890. But although Tylor's later writings on religion included some characteristically cautionary thoughts on the problem of totemism, there was little modification of his fundamental position. Indeed, just as McLennan's posthumous publications suggest that he remained entangled in the debates of the 1860s and 1870s, so also do the remnants of Tylor's "magnum opus" suggest that there was little evolution in his thinking on the evolution of religion.[79]

By the turn of the century, however, Tylor's doctrine of animism had begun to come under attack within British anthropological circles. The missionary ethnographer Codrington (who was influenced by Max Müller) had found the groundwork of Melanesian religion in the much less rationalistic notion of "mana" (the pervasive unseen presence of a "supernatural power" that "attaches itself to persons and to things"). In 1900, Tylor's young Oxford colleague R. R. Marett used Codrington's data to propound the notion of "pre-animistic" religion. Focusing on "those residual phenomena which a strictly animistic interpretation of rudimentary religion would be likely to ignore," Marett suggested that the essence of religion lay in the "specific emotion whereby man is able to feel the supernatural precisely *at the point at which his thought breaks down.*" Tylor, however, seems to have been more concerned with the arguments of Andrew Lang, who in the 1880s had been the apostle of Tylorian folklore against Müllerian Aryanism, but who by 1900 had fallen into apostasy on matters of religion. Arguing that animism was based not on flawed reason but on actual supernatural experience, Lang used Australian aboriginal data to argue that savages actually had a belief in a Supreme Being. In several chapters of his magnum opus which were actually set in galleys, Tylor argued against Lang that the ethnographic evidence for non-animistic beliefs was in fact the result of missionary influence.[80]

A more clear-cut presaging of the shift from belief to ritual had been manifest in 1889 in Robertson Smith's *Religion of the Semites*, which argued that myths were not primitive philosophical speculations, but rather secondary attempts to explain preexisting customary rituals; the ritual of sacrifice was not, as Tylor thought, a utilitarian attempt to win favors from a god, but rather "an act of communion, in which the god and his worshippers unite by partaking together of the flesh and blood of a sacred victim." However, the impact of Smith's "ritualism" in anthropology was delayed by his death, and by the fundamentally Tylorian position of his disciple Frazer. Cast in rather extreme intellectualistic terms, Frazer's massive writings on magic and religion were very influential in the first years of the twentieth century, when anthropological debate swirled around his three "theories" of totemism. The eventual turn to "ritualism" was due largely to the influence of Emile Durkheim (who had in turn been influenced by Smith) on Marett, and of both on Radcliffe-Brown.[81]

That turn was part of the more general movement from evolutionism to functionalism in British anthropology, which took place in three phases—an initial reassertion of the ethnological tradition by Rivers, followed first by the "pure" functionalism of Malinowski, and then by the "hyphenated" structural-functionalism of Radcliffe-Brown. Although the details of this rough schematization lie outside the range of the present study, there are certain aspects of the development which, approached through each of the three major figures involved, retrospectively illuminate both the character of classical evolutionism and its relation to the more general British anthropological tradition.[82]

Coming from medicine, neurophysiology, and experimental psychology at the moment when British anthropology was moving from the armchair to the field, Rivers joined the Torres Straits Expedition organized by his Cambridge University colleague Alfred Haddon in 1898 and went on to help establish the role model of the academically trained ethnographic fieldworker who collected the data for his own ethnological analyses. At first Rivers rather consciously enculturated himself to still prevailing evolutionist assumptions. After having done fieldwork among the Todas in 1902, he attempted to interpret their customs in Tylorian evolutionary terms, looking for the "motives" that led to their origin; he also devoted considerable effort to sifting out the "chaff from the wheat" of Morgan's evolutionary approach to kinship terms. By 1911, however, his analysis of data collected in Melanesia in 1908 led to what he spoke of as his "conversion" from evolutionism to diffusionism: before one could attempt to find general laws of evolutionary development, there must be an historical analysis "of the cultures . . . now spread over the earth."[83]

Rivers' "conversion" did not, however, mark a complete break from evolutionary assumption. His posture remained staunchly determinist; his orientation was still diachronic; his reconstruction blatantly "conjectural." If fieldwork in a number of different groups and the influence of German diffusionist writers led him thus to speak of "cultures" in the plural, his basic approach to culture remained Tylorian insofar as he continued to fragment it for analytic purposes into a series of cultural elements, related to each other not in synchronic systemic terms, but rather in stratified diachronic terms as the layered residues of different episodes of cultural contact. Similarly, while he did adopt a much more systematic and even functionalist approach in his studies of social structure, his historical analysis of the sequence of social structures in any given area continued to be heavily dependent on the doctrine of survivals—customs which had no function in the present, but could only be explained in terms of their utility in some prior social state. Finally, while his psychiatric work in World War I led Rivers to explore the possibilities of psychoanalysis, during the period of his "conversion" he was unable to conceive of an alternative to the rationalistic individualistic psychological assumptions of Tylorian anthropology.[84]

Similar continuities of evolutionary assumption may be found in the work of Malinowski, who was in fact wont to attribute his own shift from the natural sciences to anthropology to his reading of Frazer's *Golden Bough* and who wrote his doctoral dissertation on the evolutionary epistemology of Ernst Mach. Although influenced by Rivers' ethnographic method, Malinowski was more endebted theoretically to Durkheim and Westermarck; his own intensive fieldwork in the Trobriand Islands—which became the primary ethnographic exemplar for modern British social anthropology—led him toward an antihistorical analysis of culture focusing on its "functional" integration in the present. But although he conceived his enterprise as a venture in social psychology, and was heavily influenced by Freudian psychoanalysis, Malinowski remained in some respects very much within the British evolutionary tradition. Despite a synchronic and pluralist approach to cultural variety, he continued to see the Trobrianders as archetypical representatives of "savage" society; and although critical of matriarchal assumption, he still attributed to them an ignorance of the mechanism of physiological paternity. More importantly, he still tended to interpret human action in pragmatic and individualistic utilitarian terms and to see culture in deterministic terms as (in the first instance) a means of satisfying seven basic individual biopsychological needs. And in the analysis of kinship and social organization, he adopted an "extensionist" viewpoint which saw social structure as a generalization of individual kinship relationships, rather than providing the systemic milieu in which they were constituted.[85]

In Radcliffe-Brown's case, the break with his early evolutionary assumptions was in some respects more strongly marked—although, paradoxically, it came in resisting his mentor Rivers' attempts to push him toward conjectural diffusionist explanations of the ethnographic material he had collected during fieldwork in the Andaman Islands and Western Australia. Having come under the influence of Durkheim in 1910, Radcliffe-Brown was already inclined to functionalist explanation, and when Rivers several years later offered alternative diffusionist interpretations of phenomena he had been trying to explain in evolutionary terms, Radcliffe-Brown decided that the issue of independent invention versus borrowing was no longer of interest to him. Any approach to "dynamic" (or diachronic) problems of social change depended on solutions of "static" (or synchronic) problems; specifically, any argument that a custom was a "survival" depended on a hypothesis as to the "function that such a custom fulfills (or on the nature of the necessary connections between such customs and the other institutions of the society)." It was no longer enough to appeal, as defenders of the persistence of nonutilitarian survivals were wont to do, to "the mental disposition which we call conservatism," since the conservatism of human culture was precisely what had to be explained. In contrast to his own explicitly Durkheimian approach to problems of social psychology, which emphasized the constraining force of the *conscience collective* acting from without upon the individual, he suggested that Rivers was still operating implicitly on the basis of "the associationist intellectualist psychology of thirty years ago."[86]

Having rejected individualist, rationalist psychological assumptions, the notion of nonfunctional survivals, and (at least for present purposes) the diachronic framework of inquiry, Radcliffe-Brown eventually went on to reject, as a subject appropriate for comparative scientific inquiry, the study of culture itself, restricting himself instead to the comparative study of "social structure." Nevertheless, as he himself recognized, Radcliffe-Brown remained *au fond* very much within the evolutionary tradition. Although his ties were more to Spencer than to Tylor and his thinking reflected the influence of twentieth-century philosophers, Radcliffe-Brown's *Natural Science of Society* was nonetheless conceived in the spirit of Tylor's "science of culture." Just as Tylor had assumed that "our thoughts, wills, and actions accord with laws as definite as those which govern the motion of waves, the combination of acids and bases, and the growth of plants and animals," so also was Radcliffe-Brown's enterprise modeled on the physical and biological sciences. Through the comparative empirical study of concrete social phenomena, it, too, sought to establish "scientifically exact formulations of significant and probable generalizations."[87]

The functionalist movement led by Malinowski and Radcliffe-Brown has been described as a "revolution in anthropology"—and while he was still in the Trobriands Malinowski in fact spoke of his ambition in these terms. Although a preliminary historical account suggests that the process was more complex than disciplinary mythology (either retrospective or prospective) would have it, the emergence of functionalism was in some respects a change quite as revolutionary as that in which classical evolutionism emerged in the 1860s, involving as it did a redefinition of causal assumption, a radical restructuring of temporal perspective, a shift in psychological assumption, a remodeling of methodological approaches, and a reorientation of guiding concepts.[88]

Even so, the continuities in British social anthropology are also notable. Having achieved a degree of cognitive autonomy, certain issues (notably in the area of kinship) remained the subject of disciplinary inquiry that was more or less continuous, even through radical changes in the surrounding framework of assumption. Others, like the problem of the rationality of "primitive" beliefs, although pushed into the background by functionalist assumptions, continued to be enduring options of disciplinary inquiry, in terms of explanatory orientations no longer the cynosure of disciplinary attention.[89] And aside from the continuity of substantive issues or explanatory alternatives, there are also important continuities of underlying assumption.

In both its evolutionary and its functionalist phases, British anthropology was characterized by an orientation that may be called, broadly, "positivistic." It was staunchly empirical, assuming that anthropological phenomena, like butterflies and other phenomena of the natural world, can be collected and subjected to comparative inductive study in an objective manner, which will eventually produce deterministic laws of the same sort as those of the natural sciences. It remained, in a broad sense, utilitarian, if not at the level of the rationally motivated pragmatic individual, then at the level of the adaptive functional requirements of the society as an entity.[90]

Even in the areas of most obvious change—assumptions regarding history, psychology, and culture—there was a certain negative continuity. Despite the radical difference of temporal framework, evolutionism and functionalism share an attitude toward the concrete particulars of history and the processes of historical change—the one subordinating them to generalized diachronic developments; the other to generalizations about synchronic relationships. Similarly, it might be argued that the abstractly conceived rational individual of evolutionism and the externally constraining social milieu of Durkheimian functionalism have in common the neglect of the full phenomenological reality of the human actor—the brevity of the opening toward psychoanalysis around 1920 and the failure of Malinowski's more actor-oriented psychological projects simply confirming the general trend. Finally, evolutionism and functionalism seem to have had in common an attitude toward culture—on the one hand minimizing the significance of specific cultural systems; on the other, the study itself of culture as a system of symbols and meanings.

While it seems unlikely that this common ground of assumption was equally shared by every British anthropologist in the evolutionary and functionalist periods, from the difference blurring perspective of the national and disciplinary outsider it seems generally characteristic of British anthropology in the century after the Darwinian revolution. As the previous discussion suggests, it may be the reflection of a more deeply rooted British intellectual orientation—strongly contrasting with the Germanic orientation which through Boas has strongly influenced American cultural anthropology. If so, it remains to be seen whether there really was an "epistemic break" around 1970, or whether "the curious strength of positivism" in British intellectual life will continue to be manifest in British social anthropology.[91]

The Ambiguous Heritage of Evolutionary Anthropology

If all disciplines ultimately originate in and return to questions of general human concern, this is especially so in the case of anthropology, where the nature of humankind is explicitly at issue. Thus while the present study is primarily one of the formation of British anthropology as a disciplinary tradition, the question of the historical significance of classical evolutionism cannot be left in a narrowly disciplinary context. With the possible exception of Tylor, the writers we have been discussing would not in fact have defined themselves as "anthropologists." And even when they wrote in an anthropological vein, they did not necessarily write for audiences that may be thought of as specifically "anthropological." At times, they wrote for a general scientific audience within which they sought equal status for anthropological inquiry; at others, for an undifferentiated audience of Victorian intellectuals and educated people. Nor did they do so simply in a popularizing vein: the *Fortnightly*

Review published essays by the major sociocultural evolutionists which, in terms of their content and style of argument, could just as well have appeared in the *Journal of the Anthropological Institute* (though the reverse could not be said of much of the material in the latter publication).[92] While their names—save Spencer's—figure only briefly, if at all, in the cultural or intellectual histories of their era, British sociocultural evolutionists thought of themselves as contributing to an intellectual transformation as historically significant as the Copernican revolution.

And surely it was—for just as that earlier revolution permanently redefined mankind's place in the cosmos, so did the Darwinian revolution permanently redefine not only "man's place in nature," but also his place in time—as well as the relationship of God both to nature and to humankind. It also marked a transition in the human studies—what might be called their entry into the "positive" phase. Explicitly "theological" assumptions (of the sort that had conditioned biblical anthropology) were henceforth excluded from disciplinary discourse, and empirical natural science henceforth provided the dominant model for inquiry and the standard for its evaluation. On the other hand, the outcome was not as clear-cut as Comte might have envisioned, insofar as there continued to be significant diversity of "metaphysical" assumption in the "sciences" that had been called "moral" and would be called "social," "behavioral," or "human"—even, in the German tradition, to the point of insistence on their fundamental epistemological differentiation. And it was by no means the case that inquiry in these discourses was to be systematically evolutionary.[93]

Classical evolutionism did indeed contribute to this intellectual revolution insofar as it sustained a natural rather than a supernatural origin and development of human capacities. But as we have already had numerous occasions to note, it often did so by drawing on assumptions and elaborating arguments that were pre- or even un-Darwinian—including the "comparative method," traditional stage theories of human social development, polygenist racial typologies, and the method of reasoning from opposites or stripping away the characteristics of civilized man to arrive at a presumed starting point of cultural development. And in doing so, it provided reassurance that human life on earth was not governed by randomly motivated Darwinian processes, but had an overall progressive direction. Indeed, in a sense it might even be said that while Darwinism gave man a new place in nature, classical sociocultural evolutionism reasserted a traditional one; for if in origin man was part of nature, and controlled by it, the progress of civilization removed him from nature and won him control over it.

It might also be argued that classical evolutionism involved little change in assumptions about human nature and social order; for the most part these were drawn from a centuries-old repertoire, and even the more extreme materialist views had pre-Darwinian precursors (as in the case of phrenological assumptions about the mind and brain). Indeed, despite its presumption of human psychic unity, and its relative lack of explicit concern with racial differentiation, the impact of classical evolutionism on the European image of man had perhaps less to do with reshaping thinking about the commonalities of human nature than with regrounding assumptions about human differences. The traditional hierarchy of culture and color existed now in an entirely different temporal and biological context: the present differentiation of humankind was ranged upon a scale of cosmic rather than merely historical time; the "primitive" and the "savage" were now associated with the apelike and the animal not simply by analogy but by derivation. And while in principle the processes of human differentiation were governed by universal deterministic laws, the reconstruction of their operation was in fact conjecturally constituted on an explicitly ethnocentric basis.

In this context, the early-twentieth-century reaction against evolutionism within anthropology may be seen as part of a third general intellectual revolution, as fundamental and far-reaching as that in which classical evolution had been formed. For the most part, this revolution did not in the first instance involve a systematic questioning of evolutionary assumption; the major figures were products of the post-Darwinian intellectual milieu that classical evolutionists had helped form, and they drew heavily on classical evolutionary thought—as Freud's *Totem and Taboo* makes abundantly clear. But if this revolution did not call into question the fact of human evolution, it did undermine the compensatory consolations that had enabled classical evolutionists simultaneously to give direction to human history and to distance themselves from the "primitive" and the "savage" in human animal nature. On the one hand, there was a strong assertion, not only in Freud, but in other areas of psychology and the social sciences, of the power of the "primitive" and the irrational within the psyche of civilized man. On the other, there was a questioning—most strikingly, but not solely, in Boasian anthropology—of the network of ethnocentric and racialist assumptions in which classical evolutionary progressivism was entangled. The cultural values by which progress had been measured were seen increasingly in relative terms; the moral and mental differences between the peoples that held them were no longer seen as indicators of inherited cultural capacity, but rather as the result of experience in different cultures.[94]

In the context of methodological criticism of evolutionary assumption, of a more general shift toward the analysis of human behavior in the present, and of a changing sociopolitical milieu manifest in the response to the rising threat of Nazi racialism, this reorientation was eventually to leave evolutionism in a rather ambiguous position in the human sciences, and especially in anthropology. Just as theological assumption had once provided the unquestioned grounding for discourse about humankind, so now did evolutionary assumption, in the general sense that a natural origin and development of human capacity were taken for granted. But except in areas such as paleoanthropology, or among some individual writers who may be viewed as a disciplinary countercurrent, explicitly "evolutionary" argument receded from the foreground of concern. Most disciplinary discourse was directed to problems with no explicit evolutionary implications; and some of it was carried on in terms of assumptions that were implicitly antievolutionary.[95]

Thus a century after the Darwinian revolution, the status of evolutionism in anthropology is today more than a bit paradoxical—insofar as one may judge the matter on the basis of the situation in the United States. From the point of view of the general reading public, the discipline has never lost its evolutionary aura, and there are important currents of popularizing anthropological literature which still sustain this image. For many who might have been readers of the *Fortnightly Review,* had they lived in Britain in the 1860s and 1870s, anthropology today would no doubt be epitomized either by the fossil man discoveries of the Leakeys, or by the cultural exoticism of Margaret Mead, with her Samoans and New Guineans placed on a temporal continuum extending backward to Lake Rudolf—or perhaps, to some, by one of the manifestations of what has recently been called "sociobiology." But as the internal disciplinary response to the recent sociobiologically oriented critique of Mead's Samoan ethnography suggests, the matter is more complicated when viewed from the inside looking out.[96]

When confronted by a neobiblical anthropology in the form of creationism, modern anthropologists would no doubt endorse an evolutionary view of human origins with virtual unanimity (as indeed American anthropologists actually have by formal resolution at the annual meeting of their professional association). On the other hand, a great many of them are equally disturbed by the potential effect on public attitudes and social policy of the sociobiologists' attempt to explain many aspects of human cultural behavior in terms of the evolution of "fitness." In the minds of many anthropologists, sociobiology is simply nineteenth-century racialist evolutionism reincarnated—and threatening now to undermine the critique of biological determinism which, a half century ago, was an essential contribution to the establishment of modern cultural anthropology. Thus it is that we witness now the paradox of American anthropologists, many themselves critical of Mead's ethnography (and little sympathetic to her own occasional neo-evolutionary speculations), leaping to her defense in the recent controversy over Samoan culture and personality.[97]

Within the American discipline itself, the present situation is similarly paradoxical. Although evolutionary assumptions are essential to biological anthropology and the earlier reaches of archeology, much of linguistic and sociocultural anthropology is unconcerned with evolutionary issues, and even antagonistic to evolutionary interpretations. Thus the response to efforts to investigate the language capacities of domesticated apes suggests that many linguistic anthropologists would still join Max Müller in regarding language as a Rubicon no ape may ever cross. And within cultural anthropology, the most influential tendencies of the recent "hermeneutic turn" are on the whole epistemologically and methodologically antithetical to evolutionary assumption. Thus it is that neo-evolutionists now see themselves as a "minority voice" of dissent against a resurgent idealism that has retreated "from the promise of recent advances in the objective comparative analysis of cultural similarities and differences which had begun to place the study of human behavior and thought within the framework of a general evolutionary tendency"; by contrast, their antagonists tend to see themselves as defenders of the true cultural faith against the populist threat of adaptational, ecological, utilitarian, or otherwise evolutionary assumptions—which are in fact widely shared by large numbers of anthropologists, the more so perhaps as one moves from elite departments toward the institutional margins of the academic discipline.[98]

More than a century after Darwinism posed the questions for which classical evolutionists attempted to provide answers, the status of evolutionary argument in anthropology and its relationship to more general intellectual discourse remain thus somewhat ambiguous. Although the span of hominid existence is now measured in millions of years, the fossil gap seems not nearly as imposing now as it did in 1860, and a great deal of archeological evidence on human cultural development has been accumulated in the interim. But despite the anthropological reluctance to speak of any present population as "primitive," the "comparative method" has by no means passed entirely out of use. Thus, the Bushmen of the Kalahari, with appropriate antiracialist admonitions, have for thirty years provided evidence on the nature of early hunter/gatherer existence, in a way that Tylor would surely have appreciated—although he might have found the occasionally Rousseauistic rhetoric a bit archaic. Which is simply to suggest that some of the questions posed by Darwinism are by no means closed today, and that if we have many good reasons for rejecting the classical evolutionary assumption that present cultural differences between human "racial" groups can provide a systematic basis for reconstructing "primitive" human development, we may nonetheless appreciate how, in the absence of even a small portion of the archeological and human paleontological data now available, serious anthropological thinkers might have thought this a viable approach. Similarly, while it seems unlikely that all anthropologists will soon agree that the significant issues of cultural discourse can be resolved within either a ''positivist'' or a ''hermeneutic'' framework, it seems equally unlikely that the classical evolutionary goal of a deterministic ''science of culture'' will be abandoned, or—whatever the historical fates of individual Victorian anthropologists—that classical evolutionism itself will soon be reduced to *merely* historical significance.[99]

Notes

For full titles, consult the alphabetical listing under ''References Cited.''

Preface (pp. xi–xvii)

1. Stocking 1968a. Cf. Stocking 1974a, 1974b, 1974d, 1976, 1978b, 1979.
2. Stocking 1973b.
3. Stocking 1971a & b, 1973a, 1974e, 1975, 1983b, 1984b, 1985b.
4. Stocking 1968a, 1974a, 1983a, 1984a, 1985a, 1986a.
5. Kuhn 1962; Cedarbaum 1983.
6. Stocking 1965 (cf. 1974c); 1982b:xvii–xviii.
7. Cf. G. Jones 1980; Sahlins 1976b.
8. Cf. Banton 1967; Kiernan 1969.
9. Stocking 1979.
10. As quoted in Stocking 1974a:10.
11. Cf. Schneider 1984.

Prologue (pp. 1–6)

1. Hardy 1894:152; Whewell 1852:6. On the Great Exhibition see, among others, Beaver 1970; Briggs 1953; Ffrench 1950; Gibbs-Smith 1950; Tallis 1852.
2. Mayhew 1851:155; Prince Albert, quoted in Ffrench 1950:22; Mayhew 1851:137.

3. Engels 1845; Disraeli 1845:I, 149; *Punch* quoted in Ffrench 1950:193.
4. Mayhew & Cruikshank 1851:17, 54; Fay 1951:73.
5. *Official Catalogue* 1851:I, 104.
6. *Official Catalogue* 1851:III, 1169.
7. Mayhew & Cruikshank 1851:134, 137.
8. Quoted in *Official Catalogue* 1851:I, 3–4.
9. Whewell 1852:16–19; Mayhew & Cruikshank 1851:137, 155–56 (cf. Yeo & Thompson 1971).
10. Mayhew & Cruikshank 1851:129; Palmerston, quoted in Briggs 1965:404. Cf. Burn 1965, and chapter 6 of the present book.
11. Burn 1965:332, 41; Clark 1962:62, 60.
12. Laslett 1965:xiii.
13. *Official Catalogue* 1851:II, 642: [Christy] 1862 (cf. Anon. 1965); Chapman 1985 (cf. Pitt Rivers 1874b).
14. Whewell 1852:13–14.
15. Himmelfarb 1959:287; Cannon 1964b:176–91. Cf. chapter 1, pp. 37–38, of the present book.

CHAPTER 1: The Idea of Civilization (pp. 8–45)

1. Radcliffe-Brown 1958:143–65; Evans-Pritchard 1950:21–42; Lowie 1937; Harris 1968; Voget 1968. For recent sources on the history of anthropology, see Stocking 1973–.
2. Burrow 1966:xv (cf. p. 232 and pp. 294–295 of the present book).
3. Jones 1971; Johnson 1959; Lovejoy & Boas 1935.
4. Sinclair 1977; Tinland 1968; Bernheimer 1952; White 1972.
5. Cole 1967; Guthrie 1957; Huppert 1971.
6. Bury 1932 (cf. Nisbet 1980); Hay 1957; Talmor 1980.
7. Febvre 1930; Benveniste 1966; Elias 1939; Williams 1976; Rothblatt 1976.
8. Bryson 1945; Duchet 1971; Manuel 1962, 1965; Meek 1976; Sher 1985.
9. Lovejoy 1936; Bock 1956; Manuel 1959; Richter 1973.
10. Rossi 1979.
11. Lowith 1949; Stocking 1983d (cf. Harris 1968:25–26); Gliozzi 1976.
12. Quoted in Allen 1949:133 cf. Rossi 1979:132–36; Johnson 1962; Ryan 1981.
13. Allen 1949:137; cf. Rossi 1979: passim.
14. Lafitau 1724:I, 107, 75, 81 (cf. Certeau 1980, Fenton 1969); Rossi 1979:152, 246–48, 254–55.
15. Tagliacozzo & White 1969:147–223; Locke, as quoted in Meek 1976:3; Warren 1921; Aarsleff 1982:42–83; Fraser 1977; MacPherson 1962; Zengotita 1984.
16. Montesquieu 1748:276, 269; cf. Hervé 1907; Shackleton 1961:318–19; Stark 1961d; Meinecke 1959:121; Glacken 1967.

17. Turgot 1750:42; Meek 1971, 1973.
18. Turgot 1751 (cf. Meek 1976:68–76).
19. See, among others, Baker 1975; Bryson 1945; Cloyd 1972; Duchet 1971; Forbes 1954; Gossiaux 1984; Hoebel 1960; Kettler 1965; Lehmann 1960, 1971; Lemay 1984; Lovejoy 1948; Manuel 1965; Meek 1976; Skinner 1967; Stocking 1975; Swingewood 1970; Van Gennep 1914.
20. Ackerknecht 1954; Hoenigswald 1963; Hodgen 1964; Meek 1976.
21. Cf. Bryson 1945; Aarsleff 1982:210–24.
22. Gay 1969; Meek 1954; Pascal 1939; Skinner 1967.
23. Allen 1949; Baudet 1965; Harris 1949; Hodgen 1964; Starn 1975; Trompf 1979.
24. Willey 1940. Cf. Gay 1969:56; Lowith 1949; Tuveson 1964.
25. Lovejoy 1948. Cf. Kassem 1974; Vyverberg 1958.
26. Snyder 1923:69–86; Heilbroner 1973.
27. Lovejoy 1934; Chinard 1913; Fairchild 1961; Reichwein 1925; Forbes 1951:19–20.
28. Gay 1969:99; Trompf 1979; Stocking 1975; Cloyd 1972; Baker 1975; Lehmann 1960.
29. Robertson 1777:I, 288.
30. Voltaire, as quoted in Hazard 1946:437; Hay 1957.
31. Lovejoy 1936; Gerbi 1955; Sloan 1973.
32. Pagliaro 1973; Stocking 1975.
33. Stocking 1968a:29–31; Cunningham 1908; Coleman 1964:60–62; Slotkin 1965; Topinard 1885.
34. Rousseau 1755:121, 103; Haber 1959:159; Bowler 1974; Greene 1959a:55–59, 74–75.
35. Febvre 1930; Lochore 1935; Pflaum 1961.
36. LeClerc 1972; Duchet 1971:12ff.
37. See, among others, Bauer 1952; Bruford 1962; Elias 1939; Hartog 1938; Kroeber & Kluckhohn 1952; Pflaum 1961.
38. Bruford 1962:194, 197; Clark 1955:177. Cf. Pascal 1939.
39. Herder 1784:141–45, 151, 197–201, 348–49. Cf. Manuel 1959:299; Meinecke 1959:295–372; Poliakov 1971; Simar 1922:94–96.
40. Walzel 1932; Acton 1886:346.
41. Reill 1975; Iggers 1983; Feisel 1927.
42. Niebuhr 1811–32:I, ix, xxiii; Savigny, as quoted in Small 1924:52, 56–57; Kantorowicz 1937.
43. Niebuhr 1811–32:I, xxiii.
44. Niebuhr 1811–32:I, 83, 54; cf. Niebuhr 1854:49–50.
45. Butterfield 1955:32–61; Iggers 1983; Krieger 1977; Meinecke 1911; cf. Reill 1975.
46. Jones, as quoted in Mukherji 1968:95; Kopf 1969; Schwab 1950; Said 1978.

47. Schlegel 1808:439, 472–73, and as quoted in Hoenigswald 1963:1; Gerard 1963:72, 113–14, 120; Schwab 1950:74–86.
48. Peppard 1971:87; Hymes 1972; Jespersen 1922.
49. Jespersen 1922:71–76, 85–88; Borst 1957–63.
50. Humboldt 1836; Jespersen 1922:54–55, 320–22; see pp. 48–53 of the present book.
51. Fichte 1808:45–62; Poliakov 1971:183–99.
52. Manuel 1965; Gusdorf 1960.
53. Manuel 1956b:408; Stocking 1968a:35–41.
54. Manuel 1956b:297–98; Cabanis 1802:III, 450; Ackerknecht & Vallois 1956; Young 1970a:8–53.
55. Broberg 1983; Cunningham 1908; Topinard 1885:1–145; Blumenbach 1776.
56. Cuvier, as quoted in Stocking 1968a:35; Coleman 1964:143–46, 156–57; Blanckaert 1981.
57. Hall 1969:II, 121–32; Coleman 1971; Manuel 1956a; Nisbet 1943, 1944.
58. Comte 1822:88, 91, 97, 101, 107, 118, 124–25; cf. Manuel 1956b, 1962:252–61.
59. Comte 1822:130–32, 137, 158, 160.
60. Comte 1822:200–206; cf. Comte 1853: II, 80–91.
61. Comte 1822:194–97; Turner 1985:60–89; Comte 1853: I, 393; II, 66–67, 93, 455; cf. Greene 1959b.
62. Comte 1853:I, 344–45; II, 93, 155, 173, 213.
63. Comte 1853:II, 3; Guizot 1829 (cf. Lochore 1935).
64. Foucault 1966:250–302; Schumpeter 1954:382; Blaug 1958.
65. Burke 1790:III, 320, 335–36; Paine 1791:I, 357–61, 398; cf. Cobban 1929.
66. Veitch 1877:X, xlviii–xlix, lxx–lxxv; Stewart 1811:34–36; Lehmann 1960:148. Cf. Burrow 1966:15–16, 54–58; Davie 1964.
67. Halevy 1928:5–34, passim; Stephen 1876:II, 1900:I, 169–326; LeMahieu 1976.
68. Burrow 1966:29–42, esp. 35–36.
69. Smith 1776:Book IV (cf. Campbell 1971:79–85).
70. Stewart 1855; Ricardo 1817:87, 152 (cf. Halevy 1928:266; Foucault 1966:254–57).
71. James Mill 1817:II, 107–64, esp. 109, 114 (cf. Forbes 1951; Stokes 1959); James Mill 1824:23, 72.
72. Wilberforce 1797:284–85, 289, 298–311, 315, 317, 319, 375 (cf. Brown 1961).
73. Sumner 1816:I, 45–50; II, 34–35, 44, 407.
74. Soloway 1969:104; Malthus 1798:4, 138–39; 1806:I, xiii; II, 74–75, cf. II, 301–35; cf. Godelier 1983
75. Senior, as quoted in Eversley 1959:94, 108, 203, 216; cf. Smith 1951.
76. Schumpeter 1954:570; Ricardo 1817:129; James Mill 1826:231; Halevy 1928:341–42; Blaug 1958:29–34.

77. Halevy 1928:364; James Mill 1824:241–42.
78. Williams 1958:55–56; 1976:48–50, 76–82; Young 1936:17.
79. LeClerc 1972; cf. Fairchild 1961.
80. Coleridge, as quoted in Williams 1958:67; cf. Forbes 1952:6, 118; Cannon 1964a:66.
81. Forbes 1952:12, 29, 95.
82. Whewell 1847:I, 640.
83. Whewell 1847:I, 679, 681–82; 1849:266; cf. Rickman 1967.
84. J. S. Mill 1843; Stephen 1900:I, 76; Packe 1954:272.
85. J. S. Mill 1873:29, 39, 41, 89, 93; 1838:132; Packe 1954:271, passim.
86. J. S. Mill 1873:134–38, 164; 1835; Mueller 1956.
87. J. S. Mill 1865:63–66; 1843: 530–37, 540, 545–47; cf. Warren 1921:81–94.
88. J. S. Mill 1843:547, 558–60, 565, 569, 570, 574, 579–83; 1838.
89. J. S. Mill 1843:550, 575; Leary 1982.
90. J. S. Mill 1838:130; 1843:584–86.
91. J. S. Mill 1843:574–75; 577–78, 586.
92. Hamburger 1965:239 ff. Cf. Abrams 1968; Annan 1959; Burrow 1966; Parsons 1937.
93. Milhauser 1959.
94. Chambers 1844:234; Sedgwick, as quoted in Gillispie 1951:150–51 and in Bynum 1974:372.
95. Glass et al. 1959; Bowler 1984; Foucault 1966.
96. Newman 1975 (cf. Schilling 1950; Morrell 1971); Garfinkle 1955.
97. Gillispie 1951; Bynum 1974.
98. Bynum 1974; Lawrence 1819 (cf. Goodfield-Toulmin 1966, 1969).
99. E. Darwin 1803.
100. Hooykaas 1956; cf. Bynum 1974.
101. Bynum 1974; cf. Taylor 1841. On biblical anthropology, cf. Allen 1949; Browne 1983; Gliozzi 1976; Rossi 1979.
102. Cf. Burrow 1966.

CHAPTER 2: Ethnology on the Eve of Evolution (pp. 46–77)

1. Latham 1854; Wallace 1905:II, 322–24; Prichard 1836–47.
2. Stocking 1973a; cf. Bynum 1974.
3. Hymes 1972; Hoebel et al. 1982; Fabian 1983; Gruber 1970.
4. Bryson 1932; Stocking 1978a, 1981a, 1983c; Ryding 1975.
5. The discussion that follows is based on Stocking 1973a, and fuller documentation may be found there.
6. Stocking 1968a:38–39; Popkin 1976; Blanckaert 1981.

7. Stocking 1973a:xii–xxiv; 1975.
8. Prichard 1819; Grafton 1975; Johnson 1962.
9. Prichard 1808.
10. Stocking 1973a:xlix–lxi, lxxx; Bynum 1974. Cf. Browne 1983.
11. Prichard 1813:233; Stocking 1973a:liv–lv, lxv–lxvi.
12. Prichard 1819:1–11.
13. Stocking 1973a:lxxxv–lxxxvi, xci.
14. Prichard 1847:231.
15. Prichard 1848:302, 304.
16. Latham 1850, 1854, 1859, 1862 (cf. Watts 1888).
17. Prichard 1836–47:III; Dorson 1968a.
18. Evans 1956; Kendrick 1950, 1927; Piggott 1968, 1976; Gomme 1883–1904.
19. Brand & Ellis 1873:I, xi, xv; III, 14; cf. Dorson 1968a:13–26.
20. Scott, as quoted in Dorson 1968a:53; Keightley, as quoted in Dorson 1968a:55; cf. 45, 54, 109–18.
21. Thoms, as quoted in Dorson 1968b:53, 55; cf. Dorson 1968a:84.
22. Thoms, as quoted in Dorson 1968b:57; cf. Cocchiara 1952; Feldman & Richardson 1972; Peppard 1971.
23. Burrow 1967; Aarsleff 1967.
24. Müller 1901:49, 66, 97, 305; Chaudhuri 1974:69–91; Harris 1973.
25. Müller 1901:194; 1868; Chaudhuri 1974:38–68.
26. Chaudhuri 1974:61–62, 112, 211, 220–30; Wilson 1860:57–102.
27. Prichard 1831; Latham 1862 (cf. Taylor 1890:20); Bunsen 1854:II, xi; Müller 1851:VI, 3.
28. Bunsen 1847; Latham 1847; Müller 1847; Prichard 1847; Muller 1891a:787.
29. Bunsen 1847:295–99.
30. Müller 1854:478, 480.
31. Müller 1856, 1861, 1864; Taylor 1890; Poliakov 1971; Leopold 1974.
32. Müller 1891a:786–87 (cf. 1851); as quoted in Taylor 1890:5 and in Chaudhuri 1974:90; Biddiss 1970.
33. Müller 1901:194; 1851:I, 12; 1856:9, 15, 19; 1861:273; cf. Haber 1959:265–69.
34. Müller 1856:52ff, 72; 1864:392–93.
35. Müller 1864:565; 1856:107, 140.
36. Dorson 1968b:I, 66; Dasent 1859:3; Kissane 1962.
37. Müller 1856:7; 1861:343, 403, 439–40; cf. Darwin 1903:II, 45; Chaudhuri 1974:257.
38. Müller 1901:3, 1861:438; Chaudhuri 1974:193–94; Hutchinson 1914:I, 62; Lyell 1863:454ff.
39. Tylor 1866a:410. Cf. Schrempp 1983; Dorson 1955; pp. 163 and 305–307 of the present book.
40. Briggs 1966; MacDougall 1972; Aarsleff 1967:182–210; cf. Poliakov 1971.

41. Prichard 1836–47: III, 175, 178–79, 342; II, 349; cf. Curtis 1968; Lebow 1976.
42. Kingsley, quoted in Horsman 1976:410; Hodgkin 1850:182; Metcalf 1964:290–97; Edwardes 1973:156–65. Cf. Bolt 1971.
43. Zirkle 1946; Odom 1967; Stocking 1969.
44. Burke 1848; Knox 1850.
45. Lonsdale 1870; Rae 1964; Biddiss 1976.
46. Knox 1850:7–8, 23, 53, 57, 464, 496.
47. Knox 1850:591.
48. Retzius 1846; Larsen 1924; cf. Erickson 1974.
49. Davis 1845–60; Davis & Thurnam 1865:3; Beddoe 1910:205; De Giustino 1975.
50. Beddoe 1847–48; 1851–52; 1910:204; 1885:xv, 5.
51. Stanton 1960; Blanckaert 1981; Schiller 1979:136–64.
52. Wagner and Darwin, quoted in Stocking 1968a:40, 46.
53. Cf. Nott & Gliddon 1854 with Prichard 1836–47; Latham 1859:II, 66.
54. Broca 1862.
55. Renan 1855; Tylor 1864; Chaudhuri 1974:181.
56. Stocking 1973a:lv–lvi, passim.
57. Knox 1850:564; Davis & Thurnam 1865:5; Stewart 1959.
58. Whewell, as quoted in Cannon 1960:12; Lyell, as quoted in Bynum 1974:292; Gillispie 1951; cf. Young 1985a:126–63.
59. Cooter 1984; De Giustino 1975; Young 1970a; Haber 1959; Crowther 1970:40–81; Storr 1913:160–95; Brontë, as quoted in Houghton 1957:68.
60. Whewell, as quoted in Cannon 1960:27.
61. Carpenter 1950; cf. Daniel 1950.
62. Levine 1986; Evans 1956:263–67; 1950:5; 1949:1–5; Pitt Rivers as quoted in Daniel 1950:63.
63. Clark 1961:14, 75; Lyon 1970.
64. Lyell, as quoted in Gruber 1965:381; Bynum 1974:228–304; Grayson 1983:122, 172; Laming-Emperaire 1964.
65. Worsaae 1849:24, 127–49; Daniel 1950:78 (cf. 1943, 1964); Rodden 1981.
66. Daniel 1950:83–84; Wilson 1851:5; Trigger 1966.
67. Wilson 1851:193, 22–27, 696, 102–3, 701, 160.
68. Lyell and Evans, as quoted in Gruber 1965:383, 395; Evans 1943:100–108; cf. Grayson 1983.
69. Stocking 1973a, 1983b; cf. Erickson 1974.
70. Kuhn 1962; Cedarbaum 1983.
71. Taylor 1890.
72. Prichard 1836–47:I, 8–9; King 1868:cxi.
73. Lyell 1863:386.
74. Stocking 1968a:44–68.
75. Cf. pp. 270–71 of the present book.

Chapter 3: Travelers and Savages (pp. 78–109)

1. Stocking 1973a:cxix–cxliv.
2. Prichard 1836–47:V, 283; [Prichard et al.] 1839; Prichard 1849; *J. Roy. Geog. Soc.* 1853 (23):xxvii–xlii. Cf. Tylor 1871a; Frazer 1890.
3. Rutherford 1961; Collier 1909.
4. Rutherford 1961:5–7; Semmel 1970:100–29.
5. Grey 1841:I, 152, 381; II, 30.
6. Grey 1841:I, 301–3, 278, 279.
7. Grey 1841:II, 225–32; Prichard 1838; Gallatin 1836:109–10; Radcliffe-Brown 1931b:216–19; Mulvaney 1964.
8. Grey 1841:II, 227, 217–25, 230.
9. Grey 1841:II, 217, 248–49.
10. Grey 1841:II, 224, 200–201.
11. Grey 1841:II, 297–98, 366–67, 371.
12. Grey 1841:II, 372ff; Austen 1971.
13. Rutherford 1961; Morrell 1930; Miller 1966; Wards 1968.
14. MacMillan 1928:296–300; Rutherford 1961.
15. Grey 1855:preface; Biggs 1952.
16. Grey, as quoted in Rutherford 1961:330–31; MacLean 1858; Bleek 1858; Bunsen, as quoted in Thornton 1983:88.
17. Grey 1869a; Lubbock 1869; Grey 1869b; cf. p. 154 of the present book.
18. Warren 1967; Neill 1964:297; cf. Boutilier 1978; Koskinen 1953; Berkhofer 1965.
19. Williams 1840–53:introduction; Semmel 1973.
20. Williams & Calvert 1859:216, 232–33; Williams 1840–53:xxvi; Findlay & Holdsworth 1921–24:III.
21. Williams & Calvert 1859:241, 248; Williams 1840–53:191, 243, 356.
22. Williams 1840–53:416, 456, 561, 573, 582; Henderson 1931:242–61.
23. Williams 1840–53:266 (cf. Clammer 1976); Williams & Calvert 1859:22, 45, 105, 81.
24. Williams & Calvert 1859:107, 46, 87–88, 107, 209.
25. Williams & Calvert 1859:88, 161–68, 145, 171.
26. Williams & Calvert 1859:140–42.
27. Williams & Calvert 1859:13, 14, 41, 46, 65, 82, 94; Williams 1840–53:511; Pickering 1851; Stanton 1975:185–215.
28. Williams & Calvert 1859:196, 170, 154.
29. Williams 1840–53:387; Williams & Calvert 1859:239, 441; Henderson 1931: 161–73; Findlay & Holdsworth 1921–24:III, 431–68; France 1969.
30. Williams & Calvert 1859:551.
31. Pearson 1914–30:I, 198, 200, 203; Galton 1908:97; Forrest 1974; Fancher 1983a.
32. Galton 1908:110; Fancher 1983b.

33. Galton 1853:292–93, 72, 82, 134 (cf. Lubbock 1870:275; Spencer 1855:350) 232, 228–29.
34. Galton 1853:209, 236, 93.
35. Galton 1853:88, 69, 187–94; Latham 1854:79; 1859:164–66.
36. Galton 1855:60; Forrest 1974:84; Galton 1863:123, 138.
37. Forrest 1974:85; Galton 1869:vi; Galton 1865:157; Keith 1920; Blacker 1952.
38. Galton 1865:320–21, 325–26; cf. Fancher 1983b.
39. Galton 1865:166, 326–27; 1869:344–45, 350.
40. Galton 1869:347, 352–53, 356, 361–62; 1865:326, 165, 319.
41. Galton 1869:362; Fancher 1983a; Cowan 1977.
42. McKinney 1972; Brooks 1984.
43. Wallace 1905:I, 254–57; Williams-Ellis 1966:23–30; cf. George 1964.
44. Wallace 1905:I, 256–57; McKinney 1972:12; Wallace 1853.
45. Wallace 1905:I, 322–23; 1853:330–61; Latham 1854:79.
46. Wallace 1853:331, 336, 189–91, 200, 342, 347, 348, 360.
47. Wallace 1905:I, 269; 1853:6, 265, 261, 263, 231–32, 83, 180.
48. Wallace 1853:190; 1905:I, 288–89.
49. Wallace 1869:171, 351, 359.
50. Wallace 1869:343, 186, 198, 195, 197, 223, 455.
51. Wallace 1869:282, 455–57.
52. Wallace 1905:I, 366; 1864a:214; 1869:15.
53. Wallace 1869:318, 332, 317–18.
54. Wallace 1905:I, 361; 1869:243; and as quoted in McKinney 1972:82.
55. McKinney 1972:80–95; cf. Brooks 1984:181, 200ff.
56. Prichard 1836–47:V, 266–71; Stocking 1973a:lxxxiii–iv, lxxxix–xc.
57. Latham 1850:viii, xi, 561; 1854:71; 1859:I, 1–2; Ritterbush 1964:61–71; cf. Rehbock 1985.
58. Latham 1859:I, 80, 44; II, 502–5.
59. Latham 1859:I, 114.
60. Wallace 1869:360, 367.
61. Williams & Calvert 1859:24–26, 184.
62. Cf. Berkhofer 1965.
63. Darwin 1839:213.
64. Darwin 1839:215–16.
65. Cf. Stepan 1982:xvi.
66. Cf. Stepan 1982:20–47.
67. Darwin 1839:474.
68. Cf. Burrow 1966; Cullen 1975.
69. Tylor 1868:121; Ethnological Society of London 1869.
70. Herschel 1849; cf. Cannon 1978:152.

CHAPTER 4: The History of Civilization (pp. 110–43)

1. Quoted in Haltern 1971:351.
2. Burrow 1966.
3. St. Aubyn 1958; cf. Taylor 1872, Huth 1880.
4. Taylor 1872:xxvii–viii; Huth 1880:24.
5. Buckle 1872:II, III.
6. Buckle 1861:258; 1872:I, 144, 148.
7. Buckle 1872:III, 429–30; Buckle, as quoted in St. Aubyn 1958:6; Buckle 1857:42; Taylor 1872:xv; Huth 1880:55.
8. Taylor 1872:xxx; Buckle 1872:I, 37, 210–11, 8–16.
9. Taylor 1872:xxxv.
10. Buckle 1857:29, 87–93.
11. Buckle 1857:131, 50, 110, 162.
12. Buckle 1857:109, 84–85, 59, 168–69.
13. Buckle 1857:181–82, 242–43.
14. St. Aubyn 1958; Buckle 1861; Benn 1906:II, 183.
15. Stephen 1880:672; Mill 1872:607–8; Benn 1906:II, 185; Himmelfarb 1959:283; cf. Robertson 1895.
16. See the present book, pp. 295–96.
17. Feaver 1969; Rothblatt 1971; Annan 1955.
18. Galton 1908:66; Brookfield 1906:8; Feaver 1969:15.
19. Feaver 1969:19.
20. Dicey 1914:411–12; Kantorowicz 1937; Brown 1872; Hallifax 1836; Pollock 1893.
21. Maine 1855:35–37; cf. Savigny 1849:57–64 ("Race and territory as grounds of the subjection of a person to a particular positive law").
22. Maine 1856a:336, 332; Colquhoun 1858.
23. Duff 1892:11–13, 66; Maine 1886b; 1856a & b (see Feaver 1969:332–34 for the attribution of Maine's unsigned articles).
24. Maine 1858d; cf. 1858b.
25. Maine 1857b (cf. Edwardes 1973); 1858c; 1857c; 1858a (cf. Dumont 1966; Dewey 1972).
26. Maine 1858c; 1886a:193.
27. Derrett 1959:42; Tupper 1898:400; Maine et al. 1856; Müller et al. 1856; Maine 1871:210–11.
28. Maine 1861:21, 29, 27.
29. Maine 1861:84, 110, 113, 114–15.
30. Maine 1861:118, 116.
31. Schochet 1975; Maine 1861:119, 142–44, 121–22.
32. Maine 1861:123, 124.

33. Maine 1861:162, 215, 163–65.
34. Maine 1861:252, 161.
35. Tupper 1898; Gopal 1965:33–34.
36. Stokes 1959:309–15; Maine 1892:90; Maine 1871:231, 271, 28.
37. Maine, as quoted in Feaver 1969:217, 319; cf. Maine 1886b:166.
38. Maine 1861:10, 15–16, 18, 66–67, 297–98; cf. Buckle 1857:109.
39. Dewey 1972:302; Maine 1871:6; 1883:197; 1861:118–19; 1875:306; 1883:195.
40. Maine 1875:304, 166; 1886b; 1888.
41. Maine 1875:310, 142–43; 1883:232; 1875:67–70.
42. Maine 1861:21, 246–47; 1871:133, 7, 158, 148; 1883:160, 197.
43. Burrow 1966:162–64; Maine 1886a:197–98; 1875:313–14.
44. Hodgen 1936; Maine 1875:275; see the present book, pp. 162–63.
45. Maine 1883:192, 218–19; cf. Bock 1974 and Kuper 1985.
46. Maine 1875:307; 1883:207–9; 1886b:passim; Stephen 1893:346.
47. Spencer 1899:551; cf. Bowler 1975.
48. Peel 1971:52.
49. Peel 1971:52, 10.
50. Spencer 1904:I, 209; Peel 1971:64–68, 75.
51. De Giustino 1975:136–45; Combe 1828:196–97; Young 1970b:157–58; Spencer 1904:I, 200, 306, 540–44.
52. Duncan 1911:418; Spencer 1851:81, 13, 326, 329.
53. Spencer 1851:29, 30–31, 123, 79, 471.
54. Spencer 1851:73, 78–80, 45, 51.
55. Spencer 1851:447, 121, 208–9, 82–83, 266, 277, 504.
56. Spencer 1851: 264, 209, 483–88.
57. Stark 1961b; Perrin 1976; Spencer 1851:264.
58. Spencer 1879:6; 1851:91, 192, 352, 413, 490, 503, 476.
59. Spencer 1899:545; Eisen 1967; Spencer 1904:I, 377.
60. Spencer 1904:I, 373; 1852b.
61. Spencer 1904:I, 384–85; II, 166; I, 176; 1852a:481; 1904:II, 12.
62. Spencer 1899:546–47; 1904:I, 470; 1855:523–30, 577–83; 1904:II, 89.
63. Spencer 1904:I, 499, 467; 1855:v–vi (cf. 1870–72, which begins with a section on the structure and functions of the nervous system); 1857.
64. Spencer 1857:3, 4, 32, 34; 1904:II, 167, 14–15, 479–84.
65. Spencer 1899:559; 1904:II, 100; 1854a:64–65, 109; 1857.
66. Spencer 1855:349–50; 1854b:147; 1904:II, 165; 1860:400.
67. Tylor 1873a:545.
68. Spencer 1904:II, 172–73; 1873–81; 1873b; 1876–96; McLennan 1877b:894 (cf. 1877a); Tylor 1877a, and succeeding correspondence between Spencer and Tylor in *Mind* 2 and *Academy* 11.

69. Eisen 1967.
70. Forbes 1952:144; cf. Burrow 1966.
71. Stephen 1880:678–79, 687.
72. Stephen 1900:III, 256, 360–61; I, 29–30.
73. Buckle 1857:29; cf. 1872:I, 152–54; Leary 1982.
74. Cf. the present book, pp. 222–23.
75. Buckle 1857:128.
76. Maine 1861:67.
77. Spencer 1855:573–74.
78. Spencer 1855:583, 574–75; 1876–96:I, 100.
79. Young 1970b:150–51; Darwin 1859:488 (cf. 1959:757).
80. Mill, as quoted in Duncan 1911:114–15, and in Packe 1954:433, 80; Leary 1982.

Chapter 5: The Darwinian Revolution (pp. 144–85)

1. Goldman 1959:55; Kardiner & Preble 1961:36; Penniman 1935:93; Carr 1962:50–51.
2. Greene 1959b; Jones 1980; Caplan 1978; Kitcher 1985; Bock 1955; Burrow 1966; Murphree 1961.
3. Conry 1983; Bannister 1979; Halliday 1971; Freeman 1974; Ruse 1982; Young 1970b:15; Schweber 1980, 1985.
4. Rogers 1972; Greene 1977; Bagehot 1867:78, 80, 133–34.
5. Blacker 1952; McKenzie 1976; Searle 1976; Stark 1961c.
6. Peckham 1959; Collingwood, as cited in Stocking 1968a:5.
7. For entry into the immense Darwin literature, see Greene 1975, Churchill 1982, and Kohn 1985.
8. Darwin 1859:488; Bibby 1959; Himmelfarb 1959:274–78; Ellegård 1958:24, 294.
9. Lyell 1863:407–54; Gruber 1965; Grayson 1983; Haber 1959.
10. Kingsley, as quoted in Bibby 1959:83; Ellegård 1958:337; Huxley 1863; Desmond 1984:74–81.
11. Huxley 1863:144, 207–8.
12. Huxley 1863:208, 107 (cf. Huxley 1874); Eiseley 1958:255–86; Holtzman 1970.
13. Wallace 1864b:clxvi, clviii, clx, clxiii.
14. Wallace 1864b:clxvi, clxiv–v, clxix–xx.
15. Eiseley 1958:308, 278; Holtzman 1970.
16. Argyll 1863:567–68; Whately, as quoted in Himmelfarb 1959:259.
17. Cf. Gillespie 1977.
18. Ghiselin 1969; Vorzimmer 1970; Hull 1973.
19. Duff 1924:14; Lubbock Papers, British Museum: Huxley/Lubbock n.d. Cf. Hutchison 1914 for biographical details.

20. Lubbock 1894, 1895; Smithells 1927; Lubbock 1865:590–91.
21. Lubbock 1865:2–3; Grayson 1983:200.
22. Lubbock 1865:56, 59, 545.
23. Lubbock 1865:410, 412, 416.
24. Lubbock 1865:583.
25. Lubbock 1882:26–27; 1869:354.
26. Lubbock 1867:326, 329; 1869:341; Gillespie 1977.
27. Lubbock 1870:1–2, 70, 119.
28. Lubbock 1912:1–2; 1870:14, 140.
29. Lubbock 1870:192, 323; 1912:2.
30. Lubbock 1912; the continuity of Lubbock's later work is evident in his "answer to critics" of 1911.
31. Burrow 1966:257; cf. Opler 1964. My own present reading of Tylor represents a reconsideration of that embodied in Stocking 1968a, where, in arguing (I think correctly) against Opler's attribution to Tylor of "a considered utilization of Darwin's 'natural selection'" (94), I did not adequately appreciate the extent to which Tylor was nevertheless responding to issues raised by the Darwinian debate.
32. Leopold n.d.; Stocking 1968b; Marett 1936; Hardy 1887; Bonney 1898; Marett 1927; Tylor 1870:13n.
33. Tylor papers, Pitt Rivers Museum, Oxford: notebooks, 1858–99; Tylor 1861:iii–iv, 192, 308, 329, 339.
34. Tylor notebooks.
35. Tylor 1865:140, 4; for contrasting readings of this volume, and of its place in Tylor's work, consult Bidney 1953, Bohannon 1964, Leopold 1980, Lowie 1937, Radin 1933, Smith 1933, as well as unpublished papers by several of my students (Parmentier 1976; M. Taylor 1980).
36. Tylor 1865:3, 4, 5, 332, 376–77.
37. Tylor 1865:370; cf. the present book, pp. 250–51.
38. Tylor 1863; 1865:150, 193.
39. Tylor 1865:377–78.
40. Wallace 1870; Tylor 1865:12.
41. Argyll 1868; Hannah 1869.
42. Leopold 1980; Tylor 1869:105; 1871a:I, 2.
43. Tylor 1871a:I, 5, 6, 7, 158–59, 6.
44. Tylor 1871a:I, 15, 25, 26, 27, 31.
45. Tylor 1871a:I, 158, 94, 71.
46. Tylor 1871a:I, 32; Hodgen 1936; Dorson 1968b.
47. Tylor 1871a:I, 240, 299. Cf. Schrempp 1983, and the present book, pp. 305–307.
48. Tylor 1871a:I, 234; Tylor papers, British Museum: Darwin/Tylor 9/24/71.
49. Rivière 1970; McLennan 1860.

50. Tylor 1881d.
51. McLennan 1857:255–56, 259, 262–67.
52. McLennan 1861:204–5.
53. McLennan 1863:393, 419, 421, 409.
54. Lubbock papers, British Museum: McLennan/Lubbock 10/11/67, 10/28/67.
55. McLennan 1865:20, 23, 58, 61–62.
56. McLennan 1865:107.
57. McLennan 1865:6.
58. Burrow 1966:233; Maine 1861:116–17; McLennan 1865:6–10.
59. Bachofen 1861; McLennan 1865:63–114.
60. McLennan 1865:115.
61. McLennan 1869a:276, 278; Lubbock papers, British Museum: McLennan/Lubbock 9/12/67, 10/15/67.
62. Cf. Carneiro 1973.
63. Cf. Burrow 1966:32.
64. McLennan 1876c:420; Tylor 1871a:I.
65. Maine 1883:205.
66. Cf. Stocking 1968a:93–109.
67. Cf. Opler 1964; White 1949; Harris 1968.
68. Maine 1886a:197–201; Galton 1888.
69. White 1945; Carneiro 1973.
70. Darwin 1859:210; McLennan 1865:7.
71. Maine 1886a:200–201.
72. Carneiro 1973:75; Tylor 1893:148; cf. 1894, 1895, 1898, 1900.
73. McLennan 1865:67.
74. McLennan 1865:67; Darwin 1871:II, 362; McLennan 1896:51; W. R. Smith papers, Camb. Univ. Library: McLennan/Gibson 5/11/77.
75. Lane Fox 1874a:216; McLennan 1896:55; Maine 1883:206; Westermarck 1891.
76. Carneiro 1973:90, 78–80; McLennan 1896:57; 1869b:288.
77. Tylor, pref. 2nd ed. 1871a:vii; Darwin 1871:passim.
78. Wilson 1862:I, 1–16; II, 455–75; Tylor 1876a; Trigger 1966.
79. Wake 1863:252, 263, 271, 291ff, 315–16; 1878:I, 1–61; II, 433–442; 1888:278ff; cf. Needham 1967.
80. Lane Fox 1867:54; 1874a:10; Pitt Rivers n.d.; 1874b:18, 7, 15; Chapman 1985.
81. Chapman 1985:20; Trigger 1966; Needham 1967, 1975.
82. Lane Fox 1867:55ff.; cf. Carneiro 1973:82–86.
83. Boas, as quoted in Stocking 1974a:134.
84. Tylor 1879; 1881b; 1896a; cf. Huxley 1865, and the present book, pp. 258–60.
85. Cf. Stocking 1968a:43–68.
86. Lane Fox 1867:49–50.

87. Morgan papers, Rush Rhees Library, Rochester, N.Y.: Maine/Morgan, 2/24/79, 10/29/80.
88. Tylor 1871b:178; Lubbock 1878.
89. Lane Fox 1875c:187; Hymes 1974b:19–23; cf. Kuhn 1962, Scholte 1983.

CHAPTER 6: Victorian Cultural Ideology (pp. 186–237)

1. Tylor 1877a:144.
2. Burrow 1966:251, 97; 1969; Harris 1968:106, 108.
3. Lubbock 1870:50–256; McLennan 1865; Tylor 1871:II.
4. Symondson 1970; Tylor 1871a:I, 156; Young 1985a:23, 126; Spencer 1904:I, 152. Cf. Chadwick 1966:I, 527–572; Crowther 1970:40–66; Meacham 1963; Storr 1913:362–97.
5. Cockshut 1964:48; Robertson 1929; Smith 1967; Wood 1955; H. B. Wilson 1860:453, 6, 215, 160, 167.
6. Chadwick 1966:II, 75–96; cf. Cockshut 1964; Crowther 1970; Glover 1954.
7. Lubbock manuscripts, British Museum:1861, passim (correspondence regarding Wilson 1860).
8. Young 1970b:25; Cockshut 1959:82, 1, 32; Lang & Tylor 1883; Lang 1907:15; see also Tylor 1877a:142. For contrasting views of Tylor's revolutionary impulses, cf. Peckham 1970 and Baker 1980:77–104.
9. Tylor, as quoted in Stocking 1971a:100; cf. Turner 1974.
10. Tylor 1871a:II, 107; Stocking 1971a:100; Gauld 1968:32–65.
11. Tylor 1871a:I, 424–25; cf. Stocking 1971a:90.
12. Tylor 1871a:I, 22–23, 428–29.
13. Tylor 1866b:82–83; cf. Stocking 1968a:80–81.
14. Tylor 1871a:II, 362, 393, 376, 397.
15. Locke 1690:161.
16. Eliot, as quoted in Wood 1955:104; Tylor 1871a:II, 107, 360–61, 450; cf. 1873b & c.
17. Tylor 1871a:II, 443–44, 448, 452.
18. Tylor 1871a:II, 453.
19. Tylor 1871a:I, 428, 23; II, 358, 451–52; cf. Baker 1980:46–104, and rather more questionably, Smith 1933.
20. Max Müller, as quoted in Lang 1907:13; Lane Fox 1868:92; Lubbock 1869:349; 1870:256, 116, 121 (cf. 1865:455; 1912:184); Duff, ed. 1924:14, 206; McLennan 1869b; Spencer 1904:II, 467–69; 1876–96:I, 285; Duncan 1911:324.
21. Lubbock 1870:125–26; McLennan 1869b:416, 422–23; Tylor 1877a & b; Spencer 1877; cf. subsequent correspondence between Tylor and Spencer in *Academy* 11 (1877).
22. Evans-Pritchard 1933 (cf. Marett 1908); Heelas 1974.
23. Spencer 1904:II, 466–67; Tylor 1871a:II, 362, 359.

24. Clay 1848:217; Graveson & Crane 1957:32; McLennan 1861.
25. Stone 1975; Mitterauer & Sieder 1982; Shorter 1975; Smith 1977; Trudgill 1976; Weeks 1981.
26. Laslett 1965; Roberts 1979; Maine 1861:154; Blackstone 1765–69:430; Graveson & Crane 1957:2–3; Reiss 1934:45–47; Dunbar 1953:25.
27. Ruskin, as quoted in Houghton 1957:343, and in Banks & Banks 1964:59; S. Ellis, as quoted in Banks & Banks 1964:58–59; Houghton 1957:348; Pinchbeck 1930:303. Cf. Davidoff 1974; Vicinus 1972.
28. Alexander Walker, as quoted in Banks & Banks 1964:22; Marshall Hall, as quoted in Smith-Rosenberg & Rosenberg 1973:334; Alaya 1977; Fee 1976; Gorham 1983; Klein 1946.
29. Smith-Rosenberg 1974:24; Edwin Hood, as quoted in Houghton 1957:352; William Acton, as quoted in Basch 1974:9; *Westminster Rev.*, as quoted in Thomas 1959:215. Cf. Auerbach 1982; Cominos 1972.
30. Trudgill 1976:159–73, 204–18; Weeks 1981; Jaeger 1956; Quinlan 1941. Cf. Comfort 1967, Gay 1984, Foucault 1978.
31. Haley 1978:107–19; Thomas 1959; Marcus 1966; Houghton 1957:204, 354; Rosenberg 1973:140; Walkowitz 1980:13–31; Gay 1984; Branca 1975; Davidoff 1973; Haight 1971; Vicinus 1972; Cominos 1963.
32. Banks 1964:12, 29–30, 86–87 (cf. 1954, 1982); Horn 1975; McCrone 1972; O'Neill 1969; Holcombe 1977; Langer 1974; Walkowitz 1980.
33. McGregor 1957; Wolfram 1955; Graveson & Crane 1957.
34. Coward 1983:17–74; Fee 1974; McLennan 1865:28, 90, 107, 66, 72–73.
35. McLennan 1865:69; McLennan to Darwin, in McLennan 1896:51–52; 1865:31–32, 35–36, 12; 1896:74–76; 1865:81–82.
36. McLennan 1865:63–64, 95–99; McLennan 1877a:702.
37. McLennan 1865:27–28; McLennan to Darwin, 2/3/74, in McLennan 1896:55; McLennan 1896:45.
38. Lubbock 1870:100–101, 70–72; Spencer 1876–96:I, 626, 639; Tylor 1881c:266; 1885a:68.
39. Tylor 1885a:67; 1881c:265.
40. Tylor manuscripts, Pitt Rivers Museum: Fison to Tylor, 7/15/81, 8/23/82, 9/29/93; Westermarck 1891; Tylor 1896b:82.
41. Schneider & Gough 1961; Gough 1975; Webster 1975.
42. Fee 1974:88; Spencer 1876–96:I, 725; 1873b:340–48.
43. Bachofen 1861; McLennan 1876c:411; Maine 1875:326–27, 339; Feaver 1969:302; Tylor 1881d.
44. Spencer to Huxley 2/6/88, in Duncan 1911:281 (cf. 137–39); Peel 1971:224–37; McLennan 1866:306.
45. Fee 1974:88; Hutchinson 1914:I, 70; Lubbock, as quoted in Duff 1924:233; Lubbock 1895:107, 132–33 (cf. 1865:557; 1870:50).
46. Cf. Mill 1869.
47. Maine 1875:340.

48. Quoted in Houghton 1957:3; cf. Clark 1962:60.
49. Polanyi 1944; Bendix 1967; Nisbet 1966; Laslett 1965.
50. Laslett 1965:xiii.
51. Perkin 1969:117; Clark 1962:113; Chambers & Mingay 1966:54; Bushaway 1982:107–110; Horn 1980:13–35.
52. Laslett 1965:7, passim.
53. Laslett 1965:19–21, 170, passim; Perkin 1969:17–62.
54. Laslett 1965:passim; Perkin 1969:17–62; Wagner 1960; F. Thompson 1963.
55. Bushaway 1982:22–23; Malcolmson 1973; E. Thompson 1974; Brand & Ellis 1873.
56. Roberts 1979; Perkin 1969:97, 94, 61, 52, 78.
57. Perkin 1969:109, 117–18; Habbakuk 1965; Landes 1969:4–123. Cf. Thomas 1983.
58. Perkin 1969:176–217, passim; Horn 1980:38–95. Cf. Briggs 1956; Neale 1972; F. Thompson 1963.
59. Perkin 1969:218–307; Best 1972:256–63; Semmel 1973; Annan 1955.
60. E. Thompson 1967; 1963:189–213, 429–44; Bushaway 1982:138–48; Horn 1980; Poynter 1969.
61. Hechter 1975; Bushaway 1982:10–12, 14–16, 168–70 (cf. Wigley 1980); Dorson 1968; Cullen 1975; Engels 1845:104–5, 139; Mayhew, as quoted in Himmelfarb 1984:324, 327, 527.
62. Houghton 1957:394–430, passim.
63. Harrison 1971; Perkin 1969:134–49; Clark 1962:95–107; Donajgrodzki 1977; Hearn 1978.
64. Perkin 1969:391; Tobias 1967; Chesney 1972:369; Cooper 1974. Cf. Bailey 1981; Philips 1977.
65. Woodward 1938:426–54; Perkin 1969:413–28; Mason 1962:11; Bushaway 1982:265–73; Girouard 1971:21; Horn 1975:109–132; Chadwick, as quoted in Himmelfarb 1984:357.
66. Clark 1962:65–83; Perkin 1969:273–89.
67. Raven 1961; Perkin 1969:288.
68. F. Thompson 1963:144–50; Baldick 1965:199–200; Smiles 1859:374; Clark 1962:253–74.
69. Cominos 1963 (Mill, as quoted on 36–37).
70. Trudgill 1976; Smith 1951; Himmelfarb 1984:143; Poynter 1969; Smiles 1859:282.
71. Smiles 1859:282; Best 1972:256–64; Spencer 1851:504.
72. Lubbock manuscripts, British Museum: McLennan to Lubbock, 1/6/70; John W. Lubbock to Lubbock, 5/17/65; Hutchinson 1914; Marett 1936; Leopold n.d.
73. Lubbock 1870:323; Tylor manuscripts, Oxford: undated fragment; Tylor 1867:91.

74. McLennan 1869a:286–88; Gould 1977:76–85.
75. Malthus 1798; Smith 1951; Young 1985:23–55.
76. Malthus 1806:I, 19 (ft. a).
77. Lubbock 1865:582; McLennan 1896:81.
78. Spencer 1904:I, 384; 1852a.
79. Spencer 1904:I, 370–71; 1852a.
80. Darwin 1838:29.
81. Burrow 1966:xv, passim.
82. McLennan 1869a:279; Lubbock 1870:269, 261; 1865:561.
83. Tylor 1871a:I, 31.
84. Tylor 1871a:I, 29; 1873a:704, 708–9, 72.
85. Spencer 1876–96:I, 612.
86. Burrow 1966:98.
87. Spencer 1876–96:I, 73, 61, 68, 70, 71.
88. Spencer 1876–96:I, 77, 79, 83–4, 85, 86, 87, 90, 59.
89. Spencer 1876–96:I, 89, 99, 100, 109, 122, 123.
90. Spencer 1870–72:I, 456, 466–67.
91. Spencer 1870–72:I, 456, 443, 581.
92. Spencer 1876–96:I, 54–55.
93. Spencer 1861:60–61.
94. Gould 1977:2–4, 184–85.
95. Spencer 1870:II, 537–38.
96. Cf. Houghton 1957:186–87; Harvie 1976:117–18.
97. Houghton 1957:93, passim; Kern 1974; Mazlish 1975; Taylor 1958; Weinstein & Platt 1969; Wolf 1965.
98. Cf. Cominos n.d.
99. Burrow 1969.
100. Spencer 1851:141; Duncan 1911:218, 229, 336; Harvie 1976; Roach 1957; Pitt Rivers 1891:116; cf. Van Keuren 1984.
101. Galton 1865; Halliday 1971; Jones 1980.
102. Frazer 1909:170; Briggs 1965:397.
103. Spencer 1904:I, 88; Curtin 1964:318–42; Talmadge 1980:328–29.
104. Semmel 1970:107–24; Hechter 1975; Lebow 1976.
105. Brantlinger 1985; Curtis 1968; Kiernan 1969; Street 1975; Spencer 1874.
106. Tylor 1871a:I, 27.
107. Bagehot 1867:60–81.
108. Spencer 1870:I, 422; Duncan 1911:320–23.
109. France 1968:27 (cf. Owen 1973:224–28); Fison & Howitt 1880:361; Fison, as quoted in Stern 1930; 419; Codrington 1891:123 (cf. Stocking 1980).
110. Brantlinger 1985; Kiernan 1969.

CHAPTER 7: Evolutionary Ideas and Anthropological Institutions (pp. 238–73)

1. Cf. Shils 1970:763; Cannon 1978:137–65; Larsen 1977; Oberschall 1972; Reingold 1976.
2. APS 1838:7–9; APS 1899:9. The present chapter is an elaboration of Stocking 1971b, most of which is incorporated here, with the gracious permission of the Royal Anthropological Institute of Great Britain and Ireland. More complete documentation on many points will be found in the original version, and some of the issues treated are dealt with more systematically in Van Keuren 1982.
3. Schuyler 1945; Gallagher & Robinson 1953:11; Semmel 1970; Eldredge 1978.
4. Grey 1853 (cf. Morrell 1930); Mellor 1951; Koebner & Schmidt 1964; Farwell 1972; Huttenback 1976; McIntyre 1967.
5. Knaplund 1953; MacMillan 1928; Temperly 1972; cf. Stocking 1971b:369–70.
6. Aborigines Select Committee 1836–37:part II, 44–45, 73–74, 76; Warren 1967: chapt. 1; Dachs 1972; Comaroff & Comaroff 1986.
7. Aborigines Protection Society documents, as quoted in Stocking 1971b:370.
8. Hodgkin 1835. Cf. Burrow 1967; Curtin 1964:329–32.
9. Prichard, as quoted in Stocking 1971b:371; Prichard 1839:169–70; Hodgkin 1841; BAAS 1841.
10. Keith 1917; E. Williams 1983: chapt. 2; APS documents, as quoted in Stocking 1971b:371.
11. Gallagher 1950; Curtin 1964:298–303; Tinker 1974; APS documents, as quoted in Stocking 1971b:371.
12. King, and ESL minutes, as cited in Stocking 1971b:372. The Aborigines Protection Society had a long and honorable history (APS 1899); its papers, now lodged at Rhodes House, Oxford, contain almost no materials relating to this episode.
13. BAAS Repts. 1844–51, esp. 1844:xxxiii, 1848:xxxv (cf. MacLeod & Collins 1981); Geikie 1875:II, 121.
14. ESL 1850.
15. Cull 1854:215, 225.
16. Cull 1855; Prichard 1849.
17. Stocking 1971b:375–76.
18. Hunt 1866:336; Brantlinger 1985; Curtin 1964; Stocking 1971b:376.
19. Burke 1865–66:4–5.
20. Hunt 1863a:2, 8, 9, 12.
21. Burke 1865–66:91–93; Stocking 1971b:377.
22. Tylor et al., as quoted in Stocking 1971b:377; Burke 1865–66:194.
23. Beddoe 1910:209.
24. Hunt 1867b:77; 1867a:116; 1863b:382; Stocking 1968a:42–68 (cf. Stewart 1959).

25. Cull 1851:105.
26. Van Keuren 1982:17–43.
27. Hunt 1863c:51–52, 54, 57; Pim 1866:50–51, 63; Semmel 1962.
28. PMA 1866:7–8; AR 1866a:113ff.; Hunt 1867b:lix.
29. Hutchinson 1914; L. Huxley 1903:I, 300; Galton 1885; Crawfurd 1866:223.
30. Keith 1917:20; AR 1865a:175; Burton 1864.
31. Brodie 1967:211–15, 337; AR 1865a:181.
32. Annan 1955; Stocking 1971b:381.
33. AR 1864:294–99 (cf. Bendyshe 1865; Hunt 1865); AR 1865b:224–29; AR 1865c; AR 1866b:386.
34. AR 1868a; AR 1869; BAAS 1871:lxix.
35. For the manuscript sources which form the basis of this and the next four paragraphs, see Stocking 1971b:382–84.
36. Manuscript sources, as cited in Stocking 1971b:369, 387; JAI 1874:506–7; JAI 1875:473–75, 500.
37. Lane Fox 1879a:158, 171; BAAS Repts. 1872:xlvi; BAAS 1874. Cf. Stocking 1983b; Urry 1972.
38. Cf. Jones 1984, Kuklick 1984, Urry 1984. In addition to my own research in the *Journal* throughout this period, I am indebted to my research assistant, Lawrence Carucci, and to students in my undergraduate classes for content analyses of its contents (cf. Bloxam 1893).
39. Lane Fox 1874a:217; Pitt Rivers 1882:502–7; Fison 1879; Howitt 1882; Howitt & Fison 1882, 1884; Tylor 1888; Stern 1930; Mulvaney 1970; Walker 1971.
40. BAAS 1874:iv.
41. Evans 1883:563; Man 1882.
42. Urry 1972:13; Chaudhuri 1974; cf., e.g., Moseley 1876; Wake 1882.
43. Stocking 1981b.
44. Im Thurn 1883:341–70; Lang 1884; Smith 1885, 1889; Frazer 1887; Spencer & Gillen 1899; Service 1985:59–74; Burrow 1966:238–41 (cf. Baker 1980).
45. Evans 1878:529–30; 1879:419; Flower 1881:682, 688; BAAS 1876, 1882.
46. Dorson 1968:203.
47. Quiggin 1942; Mulvaney & Calaby 1985; Geison 1978; Lang, as quoted in DeCocq 1968:43 (cf. Gross 1969:131–39); Freire-Marreco 1907.
48. Van Keuren 1982:157; cf. Stocking 1985a.
49. Lubbock papers, British Museum: Rolleston/Lubbock, 6/23/65; Braunholtz 1970:38; cf. Van Keuren 1982:211.
50. Chapman 1985:35–36; cf. Van Keuren 1982:173–82.
51. Tylor papers, British Museum: Lane Fox/Tylor 1/29/75; Müller/Tylor, 11/8/81; Tylor/Müller 11/11/81; Tylor 1883; Chapman 1981:177–86; Van Keuren 1982: 210–11.
52. Van Keuren 1982:216–41; Chapman 1985:37–38.
53. Rivière 1970:ix, xii, xv; Van Keuren 1982:184–92, 241–54.
54. Roach 1959; Rothblatt 1968; Ward 1965; Stocking 1985b:112–16.

55. Oberschall 1972:4–5, passim; Tylor 1881a.
56. Pitt Rivers 1891:116; Van Keuren 1982:110–40.
57. Chapman 1981:454–63; Owen 1973; France 1968:27; Risley 1911; Müller 1891b; Roy. Anth. Inst., Manuscript Council Minutes, passim.
58. BAAS Repts., passim; Van Keuren 1982:111.
59. Van Keuren 1982:96–110; Reingold 1976:38.
60. E. Williams 1985; Hinsley 1981; Van Keuren 1982:133–49.
61. Cf. Van Keuren 1982:273–87.
62. Cf. Hymes 1974:9–23; Graham et al. 1983; Lemaine et al. 1976; Whitley 1976.
63. Evans-Pritchard 1981; Stocking 1984a; cf. the present book, p. 293.
64. JAI 1875:500; Burrow 1966:133; cf. Rainger 1978.
65. Burrow 1966:133; Tylor 1880:444; Huxley, as quoted in Hunt 1866:321, 327.
66. Stocking 1984d; E. Williams 1985; Harvey 1983; Lane Fox 1876:470. Cf. Scholte 1980.
67. Tylor 1975; Boas 1904; Stocking 1984a; Henson 1974; Stocking 1984d.
68. Cf. Stocking 1984c; Stocking 1984a:passim; see the present book, pp. 321, 323.
69. *Geological Magazine* 1865:175; Tylor 1885c:94.
70. Cf. Van Keuren 1982:133–39; Semmel 1960.
71. Roy. Anth. Inst., Manuscript Council Minutes, 3/18/73, 4/26/81; Frere 1881; Pitt Rivers 1881:507; Reining 1962.
72. Cf. LeClerc 1972:15–39.
73. Marett 1920:83; Morris 1978.

Epilogue (pp. 274–83)

1. *Official Catalogue* 1851:IV, 992.
2. Roth 1899. For Tasmanian bibliography, see Plomley 1969.
3. François Péron, as quoted in Bonwick 1870a:27. Other sources on the history of European/Tasmanian relations include Walker 1902; Davies 1974; Travers 1968; Turnbull 1948.
4. Bonwick 1870a:61.
5. Travers 1968:148.
6. Quoted in Bonwick 1870a:241; Davies 1974:64.
7. Great Britain 1834:153.
8. Quoted in Bonwick 1870a:212, 216.
9. Great Britain 1834:159.
10. Quoted in Bonwick 1870:254.
11. Great Britain 1839:6–21.
12. Quoted in Bonwick 1870a:255.
13. Bonwick 1870a:274.

14. Tylor 1899:vii.
15. Prichard 1855:467–68; Latham 1851:222.
16. Quoted in Roth 1899:182, 221.
17. Roth 1899:223; Plomley 1969:xii.
18. Roth 1899:191–92, 197, Cf. Knox 1850; Davis 1874.
19. George Gliddon, quoted in Bonwick 1870a:316, 386–87; Broca 1864:45–49.
20. Darwin 1874:170, 184, 187; Calder 1874:13; Bonwick 1870a:386.
21. Wallace 1879:249; Spencer 1874:table V.
22. Tylor 1865:78–80, 194–98, 334; 1873 passim; cf. Bonwick 1870b; Müller 1892:428–35.
23. Tylor 1892:283; 1893:141, 142, 147; 1899:ix. Cf. Milligan 1863:128.
24. Bonwick 1870a:iv, 71, 255, 327, 334; 1870b:1.
25. Tylor 1893:142.

Prospective Retrospect (pp. 284–329)

1. Cf. Stocking 1965.
2. Levenson 1965:85, 90.
3. Resek 1960; Hinsley 1981:133.
4. Lang 1884; Smith 1885; Frazer 1890; cf. Jones 1984.
5. Hughes 1958; Stocking 1968a:133–234; 1974b & d; 1978b.
6. Stocking 1976.
7. Stocking 1984b; Langham 1981:118–99; Bryant 1774.
8. Stocking 1984b, 1986b; Kuper 1973.
9. Stocking 1978a; Murphy 1971:15–17 (cf. Diamond 1980, Harris 1980).
10. Stocking 1978a & 1982a; Murphy 1976; cf. Marcus & Fischer 1986.
11. Brockway 1973; Fahim 1982; Stocking 1983c.
12. Rabinow & Sullivan 1979 (cf. Geertz 1983; Marcus & Fischer, 1986); Ardener 1971.
13. Stocking 1982a; Hymes, ed. 1972; Worsley 1970; cf. Gruber 1970.
14. Boas 1904:25–26; Goldenweiser 1925:220; Lowie 1937:41; White 1966; Mark 1980.
15. White 1948; Carneiro 1973.
16. Murphy 1976; Stocking 1979 & 1981a; Harris 1968 & 1980; Stocking 1973–.
17. Kuper 1973:147–48; Stocking 1984a.
18. Haddon 1910:154; Penniman 1935:93.
19. Evans-Pritchard 1950:11; Kuper 1973; Malinowski 1922; Radcliffe-Brown 1922 & 1923.
20. Radcliffe-Brown 1923:11, 19; 1958:189.
21. Radcliffe-Brown 1930 (cf. 1931a); Evans-Pritchard 1933; 1950:47.

22. Jarvie 1964; Henson 1974; Crick 1976a:2; Kuper 1973.
23. Carr 1962:50–51 (cf. Bock 1955).
24. Teggart 1925; Bryson 1945; Hodgen 1964; Bock 1956.
25. Burrow 1966.
26. Harris 1968; Honigmann 1976; Leaf 1979; Service 1985; Voget 1975.
27. Lubbock 1865, 1870, 1911; Hutchinson 1914; Duff 1924; Rivière 1978:lxii.
28. Myres 1929:27.
29. Pollock 1893; Evans 1896; Vinogradoff 1904; Landman 1930; Lukes 1973:140; Radcliffe-Brown 1935; Redfield 1950.
30. Dumont 1966; Dewey 1972; Burrow 1974; Feaver 1969; Kuper 1982.
31. Service 1985:59–68, 113–15; McLennan 1876b:367; Fortes 1970; Schneider 1984.
32. McLennan 1869b; Frazer 1887; Smith 1889 (cf. Jones 1984).
33. Spencer & Gillen 1899; Frazer 1910; Goldenweiser 1910; Radcliffe-Brown 1929; Lévi-Strauss 1962:13.
34. Wake 1889; Rivière 1970:xl, xliv, vii.
35. Darwin 1891:II, 301; Parsons 1937:3.
36. Spencer 1876; Boas 1911; Kroeber 1917; Lowie 1937.
37. Evans-Pritchard 1950:51; Lukes 1973:82–84, 392–93; Stocking 1984d; Becker 1954:132; Parsons 1962.
38. Harris 1968:208, 108–41, 134; Carneiro 1967:xlix.
39. Peel 1971:265; Caplan 1978; Sahlins 1976b.
40. Thomas 1907; Stocking 1981b; Evans-Pritchard, personal communication, 5/2/73.
41. Evans-Pritchard 1950:31; Smith 1933; Tylor 1871:I, 1; Kroeber & Kluckhohn 1952.
42. Radcliffe-Brown 1923:3–4; Stocking 1984b:172; Evans-Pritchard 1933.
43. Marett 1936:11; Evans-Pritchard 1950; Radcliffe-Brown 1958; Fortes 1970:3.
44. Bohannan 1964:x (cf. White 1960); Wilson 1970; Hollis & Lukes 1982.
45. Kroeber & Kluckhohn 1952:150.
46. Stocking 1968a:69–90, 195–233.
47. Leopold 1980:67.
48. Stocking 1968a:92; Leopold 1980:113, 177 (note 253).
49. Leopold 1980:96; Tylor 1876b.
50. Leopold 1980:115.
51. Leopold 1980:155 (note 30); Schrempp 1978 & 1983.
52. Cf. Stocking 1984b:134; Service 1985.
53. Müller 1896:xxxvi.
54. Tylor 1871:I, 299.
55. Schrempp 1983:96–97, 94; Tylor 1871:I, 298.
56. Schrempp 1983:95–97; Müller 1861:433; Tylor 1866a:423.

57. Schrempp 1983:97–98.
58. Lubbock 1870:289–90; McLennan 1869a:283; Lane Fox 1875a:25.
59. Spencer 1870–72:I, 831–33, 837, 841.
60. Spencer 1870–72:I, 849; 1873a (cf. 1871).
61. Penn 1972; Brown 1967.
62. Müller 1901:19; 1885.
63. Schneider 1976 (cf. Geertz 1973a; Sahlins 1976; Keesing 1974).
64. Collini 1978; Richter 1964; Lukes 1973.
65. Annan 1959; Parsons 1937.
66. Schweber 1985; Young 1985a; Sahlins 1976b.
67. Stocking 1986b; Ryding 1975; Weber 1974.
68. Geertz 1973b:22.
69. Pouillon 1980; Stocking 1968a:91–109; Needham 1967.
70. Schneider 1984.
71. Service 1985.
72. Tylor 1888 (cf. 1871b, 1873b, 1877a, 1878).
73. Tylor 1888:246, 248.
74. Tylor 1888:256.
75. Tylor 1888:252, 263, 268.
76. Tylor 1888:265, 269.
77. Galton 1888:270 (cf. Naroll 1970; Driver & Chaney 1970); Boas to Tylor, 3/6/89, in Stocking 1974a:134; Boas 1896; Westermarck 1891:4; Graebner 1911:66.
78. Fortes 1970; Langham 1981.
79. McLennan 1885; 1896; Lang 1907; Stocking 1981b.
80. Codrington 1891:118–19; Marett 1914:viii; 1900:28; Lang 1901; Stocking 1981b.
81. Smith 1889:226–27; Jones 1984; Stocking 1984b:137–38.
82. Stocking 1984b.
83. Rivers, as quoted in Stocking 1984b:138–42.
84. Stocking 1984b:142–43; Langham 1981.
85. Stocking 1986b.
86. Radcliffe-Brown, as quoted Stocking 1984b:150–56.
87. Tylor 1871a:I, 2; Radcliffe-Brown 1937:3.
88. Malinowski 1967:289; cf. Stocking 1984b.
89. Langham 1981; Kuper 1982; Hallpike 1979; Hollis & Lukes 1982.
90. Leach 1961; Stocking 1984b:180–84; Kuper 1973.
91. Annan 1959; Ardener 1971; Kuper 1983.
92. McLennan 1877a & b; Spencer 1879.
93. Cf. Gusdorf 1960.

94. Hughes 1958; Stocking 1968a; Geertz 1966.
95. Stocking 1981a; Greenwood 1984.
96. Leakey 1969; Freeman 1983; Caplan 1978.
97. *Anthropology Newsletter* 22(1981):#1; Spuhler 1985; Sahlins 1976b; Brady 1983.
98. Hill 1978; Ross 1980:xv; Stocking 1981a.
99. Boaz 1979; Pilbeam 1979; Konner & Shostak 1983; Service 1985:287–319.

A Note on Manuscript Sources

Although the vast majority of sources cited are published books and articles, this volume is also founded on and occasionally refers to a considerable body of research in manuscript sources, including manuscripts and papers of the following individuals and organizations (cf. Stocking 1973b):

Aborigines Protection Society (Rhodes House, Oxford)
Anthropological Society of London (R.A.I. Archives)
John Beddoe (University of Bristol)
Franz Boas (American Philosophical Society)
Charles Darwin (University Library, Cambridge)
Joseph B. Davis (R.A.I. Archives)
Ethnological Society of London (R.A.I. Archives)
James G. Frazer (Trinity College, Cambridge)
Francis Galton (University College, London)
Alfred C. Haddon (University Library, Cambridge).
Thomas Henry Huxley (Imperial College of Science and Technology)
John Lubbock, Lord Avebury (British Museum)
Henry Maine (London School of Economics)
Bronislaw Malinowski (London School of Economics; Yale University)
Lewis Henry Morgan (Rush Rhees Library, Rochester, N.Y.)
Friedrich Max Müller (Bodleian Library, Oxford)
Pitt Rivers Museum (Oxford)
William Robertson Smith (University Library, Cambridge)
Royal Anthropological Institute (R.A.I.), London
Edward B. Tylor (Pitt Rivers Museum, Oxford; British Museum)

References Cited

Sources are cited and listed by the date of the original edition. In cases where another edition was consulted, the date of the original edition is here placed within brackets; but the place of publication is that of the later edition, the date of which is indicated at the end of the entry.

Aarsleff, Hans

1967 *The study of language in England, 1780–1860.* Princeton.

1982 *From Locke to Saussure: Essays on the study of language and intellectual history.* Minneapolis.

Aborigines Committee

[1836–37] *Report from the Select Committee on Aborigines (British Settlements) with minutes of evidence.* 2 vols. Capetown: 1966.

Abrams, Philip

1968 *The origins of British sociology.* Chicago.

Ackerknecht, E. H.

1954 On the comparative method in anthropology. In *Method and perspective in anthropology,* ed. R. F. Spencer, 117–25. Minneapolis.

Ackerknecht, E. H. & H. Vallois

1956 *Franz Joseph Gall (1758–1828), inventor of phrenology and his collection.* Madison, Wis.

Acton, J. E. D.

[1886] German schools of history. In Acton, *Historical essays and studies,* 344–92. London: 1907.

Allen, D. C.

[1949] *The legend of Noah: Renaissance rationalism in art, science, and letters.* Urbana, Ill.: 1963.

Annan, N. G.
1955 The intellectual aristocracy. In *Studies in social history*, ed. J. H. Plumb, 243–87. London.
1959 The curious strength of positivism in English political thought. In *Hobhouse memorial lectures, 1951–1960*. London.

Anon.
1965 Exhibition: Henry Christy, a pioneer of anthropology. British Museum (mimeographed).

APS [Aborigines Protection Society]
1838 *First annual report*. London.
1899 *The Aborigines Protection Society: Chapters in its history*. London.

AR [unsigned articles in *Anthropological Review*]
1864 Anthropology at the British Association. A.D. 1864. 2:294–335.
1865a Farewell dinner to Captain R. F. Burton. 3:167–82.
1865b On the prospects of anthropological science at the British Association of 1865. 3:224–29.
1865c Anthropology at the British Association. 3:354–71.
1866a Race in legislation and political economy. 4:113–35.
1866b Anthropology at the British Association. 4:386–408.
1868a The Dundee anthropological conference. 6:71–88.
1869 Anthropology at the British Association. 7:414–32.

Ardener, Edwin
1971 The new anthropology and its critics. *Man* 6:449–67.

Argyll, Duke of
1863 Professor Huxley on man's place in nature. *Edin. Rev.* 117:541–69.
1868 *Primeval man: An examination of some recent speculations*. London.

Asad, Talal, ed.
1973 *Anthropology and the colonial encounter*. London.

Auerbach, Nina
1982 *Women and the demon: The life of a Victorian myth*. Cambridge, Mass.

Austen, Ralph
1971 Varieties of trusteeship: African territories under British and French mandate. In *France and Britain in Africa: Imperial rivalry and colonial rule*, ed. P. Gifford & W. R. Lewis, 515–42. New Haven.

Alaya, Flavia
1977 Victorian science and the 'genius' of woman. *J. Hist. Ideas* 38:261–86.

BAAS [British Association for the Advancement of Science]
1841 Varieties of the human race. Queries respecting the human race, to be addressed to travellers and others. *Rept.* 11:332–39.
1871 [Decision of the General Committee]. 41:lxix.
1874 *Notes and queries on anthropology, for the use of travellers and residents in uncivilized lands*. London.
1876 Report of the Anthropometric Committee. *Rept.* 46:266.
1882 First report of the committee appointed for the purpose of obtaining photographs of the typical races in the British Isles. *Rept.* 52:270–74.

Bachofen, J. J.
1861 *Das Mutterrecht: Eine Untersuchung über die Gynaikokratie der alten Welt nach ihrer religiösen und rechtlichen Natur.* Stuttgart.

Bagehot, Walter
[1867] *Physics and politics: Or, thoughts on the application of the principles of 'natural selection' and 'inheritance' to political society.* Boston: 1956.

Bailey, Victor, ed.
1981 *Policing and punishment in nineteenth century Britain.* New Brunswick, N.J.

Baker, Keith
1975 *Condorcet: From natural philosophy to social mathematics.* Chicago.

Baker, P. G.
1980 The mild anthropologist and the mission of primitive man: Sir Edward Tylor and the anthropological study of religion in the Victorian era. D. Phil. diss. University of Cambridge.

Baldick, Robert
1965 *The duel: A history of duelling.* London.

Banks, J. A.
1954 *Prosperity and parenthood: A study of family planning among the Victorian middle classes.* London.
1982 *Victorian values: Secularism and the size of families.* London.

Banks, J. A. & Olive Banks
1964 *Feminism and family planning in Victorian England.* New York.

Bannister, R. C.
1979 *Social Darwinism: Science and myth in Anglo-American social thought.* Philadelphia.

Banton, Michael
1967 *Race relations.* New York.

Barnes, Barry
1982 *Thomas Kuhn and social science.* New York.

Basch, Francois
1974 *Relative creatures: Victorian women in society and the novel.* New York.

Baudet, Henri
1965 *Paradise on earth: Some thoughts on European images of non-European man.* Trans. E. Wentholt. New Haven.

Bauer, Isolde
1952 Die Geschichte des Wortes 'Kultur' und seiner Zusammensetzungen. Inaug. diss. Munich.

Beaver, Patrick
1970 *The Crystal Palace, 1851–1936.* London.

Beddoe, John
1847–48 Manuscript diary. University of Bristol Library.
1851–52 Comparative anatomy and zoology: Notes from Dr. Grant's lectures. University of Bristol Library.

1885 *The races of Britain: A contribution to the anthropology of western Europe.* Bristol.
1910 *Memories of eighty years.* Bristol.

Becker, Howard
1954 Anthropology and sociology. In *For a science of social man,* ed. J. Gillen, 102–59. New York.

Bendix, Reinhard
1967 Tradition and modernity reconsidered. *Comp. Stud. Soc. & Hist.* 9:292–346.

Bendyshe, Thomas
1865 The history of anthropology. *Mem. Anth. Soc. London* 1:335–458.

Benn, A. W.
1906 *The history of English rationalism in the nineteenth century.* 2 vols. London.

Benveniste, Emile
1966 Civilisation: Contribution à l'histoire du mot. In *Problèmes de linguistique générale,* 336–35. Paris.

Berkhofer, Robert
1965 *Salvation and the savage: An analysis of protestant missions and American response, 1787–1862.* Lexington, Ky.

Bernheimer, Richard
1952 *Wild men in the Middle Ages.* Cambridge, Mass.

Best, Geoffrey
1972 *Mid-Victorian Britain, 1851–1875.* New York.

Bibby, Cyril
1959 Huxley and the reception of the 'Origin.' *Victorian Stud.* 3:76–86.

Biddiss, Michael
1970 *Father of racist ideology: The social and political thought of Count Gobineau.* New York.
1976 The politics of anatomy: Dr. Robert Knox and Victorian racism. *Proc. Roy. Soc. Med.* 69:245–50.

Bidney, David
1953 *Theoretical anthropology.* New York.

Biggs, Bruce
1952 The translation and publishing of Maori material in the Auckland Public Library. *J. Polyn. Soc.* 61:177–91.

Blacker, C. P.
1952 *Eugenics: Galton and after.* Cambridge, Mass.

Blackstone, William
[1765–69] *Commentaries on the laws of England.* Chicago: 1979.

Blanckaert, Claude
1981 Monogénisme et polygénisme en France de Buffon à P. Broca (1749–1880). Thèse de doctorat de 3e cycle. Sorbonne.

Blaug, Mark
1958 *Ricardian economics: An historical study.* New Haven.

Bleek, Wilhelm
1858 *The library of his excellency Sir George Grey, K.C.B. Philology.* London.

Bloxam, George
1893 *Index to the publications of the Anthropological Institute of Great Britain and Ireland (1843–1891).* London.

Blumenbach, J. F.
[1776] On the natural variety of mankind. In *The anthropological treatises of Johann Friedrich Blumenbach.* Trans. T. Bendyshe. London: 1865.

Boas, Franz
1896 The limitations of the comparative method of anthropology. *Science* 4:901–8.
1904 The history of anthropology. In Stocking, ed., 1974a:23–35.
1911 *The mind of primitive man.* New York.

Boaz, N. T.
1979 Hominid evolution in eastern Africa during the Pliocene and early Pleistocene. *Annu. Rev. Anth.* 8:71–85.

Bock, Kenneth
1955 Darwin and social theory. *Phil. Sci.* 22:123–34.
1956 *The acceptance of histories.* Berkeley.
1966 The comparative method of anthropology. *Comp. Stud. Soc. & Hist.* 8:269–80.
1974 The comparison of histories: The contribution of Henry Maine. *Comp. Stud. Soc. & Hist.* 16:232–62.

Bohannon, Paul
1964 Introduction. In Tylor 1865 [abridged ed.]:vii–xvii. Chicago.

Bolt, Christine
1971 *Victorian attitudes to race.* London.

Bonney, T. G.
[1898] Alfred Tylor. *Dict. Natl. Biog.* 19:1349. 1917.

Bonwick, James
1870a *The last of the Tasmanians.* London.
1870b *Daily life and origin of the Tasmanians.* London.

Borst, Arno
1957–63 *Der Turmbau von Babel.* 4 vols. Stuttgart.

Boutilier, J. A., D. T. Hughes, & S. W. Tiffany, eds.
1978 *Mission, church, and sect in Oceania.* Ann Arbor, Mich.

Bowler, Peter
1974 Evolutionism in the Enlightenment. *Hist. Sci.* 12:159–83.
1975 The changing meaning of 'evolution.' *J. Hist. Ideas* 36:95–114.
1984 *Evolution: The history of an idea.* Berkeley.

Brady, Ivan, ed.
1983 Speaking in the name of the real: Freeman and Mead on Samoa. *Amer. Anth.* 85:908–47.

Branca, Patricia
1975 *Silent sisterhood: Middle class women in the Victorian home.* London.

Brand, John & Henry Ellis

1873 *Observations on the popular antiquities of Great Britain.* [Enlarged by Henry Ellis.] 3 vols. London.

Brantlinger, Patrick

1985 Victorians and Africans: The genealogy of the myth of the dark continent. *Critical Inquiry* 12: 166–203.

Braunholtz, H. J.

1970 *Sir Hans Sloane and ethnography.* London.

Briggs, Asa

1953 The Crystal Palace and the men of 1851. In Briggs, *Victorian people.* New York.

1965 *The making of modern England, 1783–1867.* New York.

1966 *Saxons, Normans and Victorians.* Bexhill-on-Sea, Sussex.

Broberg, Gunnar

1983 Homo Sapiens: Linnaeus's classification of man. In *Linnaeus: The man and his work,* ed. T. Frangsmyr, 156–94. Berkeley.

Broca, Paul

1862 La linguistique et l'anthropologie. *Bull. Soc. d'anth. Paris.* 3:264–319.

1864 *On the phenomenon of hybridity in the Genus Homo.* Trans. & ed. C. C. Blake. London.

Brockway, Fenner

1973 *The colonial revolution.* New York.

Brodie, Fawn

1967 *The devil drives: A life of Sir Richard Burton.* London.

Brookfield, F. M.

1906 *The Cambridge 'Apostles.'* London.

Brooks, J. L.

1984 *Just before the origin: Alfred Russel Wallace's theory of evolution.* New York.

Brown, Archibald

1872 *Epitome and analysis of Savigny's treatise on obligations in Roman Law.* London.

Brown, Ford K.

1961 *Fathers of the Victorians: The age of Wilberforce.* Cambridge, England.

Brown, R. L.

1967 *Wilhelm von Humboldt's conception of linguistic relativity.* The Hague.

Browne, Janet

1983 *The secular ark: Studies in the history of biogeography.* New Haven.

Bruford, W. H.

1962 *Culture and society in classical Weimar, 1775–1806.* New York.

Bryant, Jacob

1774 *A new system, or, an analysis of ancient mythology.* 3 vols. London.

Bryson, Gladys

1932 The emergence of the social sciences from moral philosophy. *Int. J. Ethics* 42:304–23.

1945 *Man and society: The Scottish inquiry of the eighteenth century.* Princeton.

Buckle, H. T.

1857 *The history of civilization in England*. Vol. I. London.

1861 *The history of civilization in England*. Vol. II. London.

1872 *Miscellaneous and posthumous works*. Ed. Helen Taylor. 3 vols. London.

Bunsen, Christian

1847 On the results of the recent Egyptian researches in reference to Asiatic and African ethnology, and the classification of languages. *Rept. Brit. Assn. Adv. Sci.* 17:254–301.

1854 *Outlines of the philosophy of universal history, applied to language and religion*. 2 vols. London.

Burke, Edmund

[1790] *Reflections on the revolution in France*. In *Works*, vol. III. Boston: 1865.

Burke, Luke

1848 Outlines of the fundamental doctrines of ethnology: Or, the science of human races. *Ethnol. J.* 1:1–8, 129–141, 235–39.

1865–66 *The ethnological journal: a monthly record of ethnological research and criticism*. London.

Burn, W. L.

1965 *The age of equipoise*. New York.

Burrow, J. W.

1966 *Evolution and society: A study in Victorian social theory*. Cambridge, England.

1967 The uses of philology in Victorian England. In Robson 1967:180–204.

1969 Evolution and society: Second thoughts. Seminar paper. King's College, Cambridge.

1974 'The village community' and the uses of history in late nineteenth-century England. In *Historical perspectives: Studies in English thought and society*, ed. N. McKendrick, 255–84. London.

Burton, Richard

1864 Notes on certain matters connected with the Dahoman. *Mem. Anth. Soc.* 1:308–21.

Bury, J. B.

1932 *The idea of progress: An inquiry into its growth and origin*. New York.

Bushaway, Bob

1982 *By rite: Custom, ceremony and community in England, 1700–1880*. London.

Butterfield, Herbert

[1955] *Man on his past: The study of the history of historical scholarship*. Boston: 1960.

Bynum, W. F.

1974 Time's noblest offspring: the problem of man in the British natural historical sciences, 1800–1863. Ph.D. diss. University of Cambridge.

Cabanis, P.

[1802] *Rapports du physique et du moral de l'homme*. Vols. 3 & 4 of *Oeuvres complètes*. Paris: 1823.

Calder, J. E.

1874 Some account of the wars of extirpation and habits of the native tribes of Tasmania. *J. Anth. Inst.* 3:7–28.

Campbell, T. D.
1971 *Adam Smith's theory of morals.* London.

Cannon, S. F.
1978 *Science in culture: The early Victorian period.* New York.

Cannon, Walter
1960 The problem of miracles in the 1830s. *Victorian Stud.* 4:5–32.
1964a Scientists and broad churchmen: An early Victorian intellectual network. *J. Brit. Studies* 4:65–88.
1964b William Whewell, F.R.S. (1794–1866) II. Contributions to science and learning. *Notes Rec. Roy. Soc. Lond.* 19(2):176–91.

Caplan, A. L., ed.
1978 *The sociobiology debate: Readings on the ethical and scientific issues concerning sociobiology.* New York.

Carneiro, R. L.
1967 Editor's introduction. In *The evolution of society,* by H. Spencer, ix–lvii. Chicago.
1973 Classical evolution. In *Main currents in cultural anthropology,* ed. R. Naroll & F. Naroll, 57–122. Englewood Cliffs, N.J.

Carpenter, E. S.
1950 The role of archeology in the nineteenth-century controversy between developmentalism and degenerationism. *Penn. Archeol.* 20:5–18.

Carr, E. H.
1962 *What is history?* New York.

Cedarbaum, D. G.
1983 Paradigms. *Stud. Hist. Phil. Sci.* 14:173–213.

Certeau, Michel de
1980 Writing vs. time: history and anthropology in the works of Lafitau. *Yale French Stud.* 59:37–64.

Chadwick, Owen
1966 *The Victorian church.* 2 vols. New York.

Chambers, J. D. & G. E. Mingay
1966 *The agricultural revolution, 1750–1880.* New York.

Chambers, Robert
[1844] *Vestiges of the natural history of creation.* Leicester, England: 1969.

Chapman, W. R.
1981 Ethnology in the museum: A. H. L. F. Pitt Rivers (1827–1900) and the institutional foundations of British anthropology. D. Phil. diss. University of Oxford.
1985 Arranging ethnology: A. H. L. F. Pitt Rivers and the typological tradition. In Stocking, ed. 1985d:15–48.

Chaudhuri, N. C.
1974 *Scholar extraordinary: The life of Professor the Rt. Hon. Friedrich Max Müller, P.C.* New York.

Chesney, Kellow
1972 *The Victorian underworld.* New York.

Chinard, Gilbert
1913 *L'Amerique et le rêve exotique.* Paris.

[Christy, Henry]
1862 *Catalogue of a collection of ancient and modern stone implements and other weapons, tools and utensils of the aborigines of various countries.* London.

Churchill, F. B.
1982 Darwin and the historian. *Biol. J. Linnaean Soc.* 17:45–68.

Clammer, J. R.
1976 *Literacy and social change: A case study of Fiji.* Leiden.

Clark, G. K.
1962 *The making of Victorian England.* London.

Clark, L. K.
1961 *Pioneers of prehistory in England.* London.

Clark, R. T.
1955 *Herder: his life and thought.* Berkeley.

Clay, W. K., ed.
1848 *The book of common prayer,* as reprinted in *Liturgies and occasional forms of prayer set forth in the reign of Queen Elizabeth.* Cambridge, England.

Cloyd, E. L.
1972 *James Burnett, Lord Monboddo.* Oxford.

Cobban, Alfred
[1929] *Edmund Burke and the revolt against the eighteenth century.* New York: 1960.

Cocchiara, Giuseppe
[1952] *The history of folklore in Europe.* Trans. J. N. McDaniel. Philadelphia: 1981.

Cockshut, A. O. J.
1964 *The unbelievers: English agnostic thought, 1840–1890.* London.

Codrington, R. H.
1891 *The Melanesians: Studies in their anthropology and folk-lore.* Oxford.

Cole, Thomas
1967 *Democritus and the sources of Greek anthropology.* Cleveland.

Coleman, William
1964 *Georges Cuvier, zoologist: A study in the history of evolution theory.* Cambridge, Mass.
1971 *Biology in the nineteenth century: Problems of form, function, and transformation.* New York.

Collier, James
1909 *Sir George Grey, governor, high commissioner, and premier: An historical biography.* Christ Church, New Zealand.

Collini, Stefan
1978 Sociology and idealism in Britain, 1880–1920. *Arch. Europ. Sociol.* 19:3–50.

Collini, S., D. Winch, and J. Burrow
1983 *That noble science of politics: A study in nineteenth-century intellectual history.* Cambridge, England.

Colquhoun, Patrick
1858 The rise and progress of the Roman civil law. Traces of the Roman law in the barbaric codes. In *Papers read before the Juridical Society, 1855–1858,* 331–359, 480–504, 505–30. London.

Comaroff, Jean & John L.
1986 Christianity and colonialism in South Africa. *Amer. Ethnol.* 13:1–22.

Combe, George
[1828] *The constitution of man considered in relation to external objects.* Edinburgh: 1847.

Comfort, Alex
1967 *The anxiety makers: Some curious preoccupations of the medical profession.* London.

Cominos, Peter
n.d. The late Victorian revolt: 1859–1895. D. Phil. diss. Oxford.
1963 Late-Victorian sexual respectability and the social system. *Int. Rev. Soc. Hist.* 8:1–65.
1972 Innocent femina sexualis. In Vicinus 1972:155–72.

Comte, Auguste
[1822] Plan of the scientific operations necessary for reorganizing society. In *Early essays on social philosophy,* trans. H. D. Hutton, 88–217. London: n.d.
1853 *The positive philosophy of Auguste Comte.* Trans. H. Martineau. 2 vols. London.

Condorcet, M. J.
[1795] *Sketch for a historical picture of the progress of the human mind.* Trans. J. Barraclough. London: 1955.

Conry, Yvette
1983 Le darwinisme social existe-t-il? *Raison Présente* 66:17–39.

Cooper, D. C.
1974 *The lesson of the scaffold: The public execution controversy in Victorian England.* Athens, Ohio.

Cooter, Roger
1984 *The cultural meaning of popular science: Phrenology and the organization of consent in nineteenth-century Britain.* Cambridge, England.

Cowan, Ruth S.
1977 Nature and nurture: The interplay of biology and politics in the work of Francis Galton. *Stud. Hist. Biol.* 1:133–208.

Coward, Rosalind
1983 *Patriarchal precedents: Sexuality and social relations.* London.

Crawfurd, John
1866 On the physical and mental characteristics of the Negro. *Trans. Ethnol. Soc. Lond.* 4:212–39.

Crick, Malcolm
1976a *Explorations in language and meaning: Towards a semantic anthropology.* New York.
1976b The philological anthropology of Friedrich Max Müller. In Crick 1976a:15–35.

Crowther, M. A.
1970 *Church embattled: Religious controversy in mid-Victorian England.* Newton Abbot, Devon.

Cull, Richard
1851 Remarks on the nature, objects, and evidences of ethnological science. *J. Ethnol. Soc. Lond.* 3:103–11.
1854 A description of three Esquimaux. *J. Ethnol. Soc. Lond.* 4:215–25.
1855 On the manual of ethnographic inquiry. *Rept. Brit. Assn. Adv. Sci.* 25:141.

Cullen, M. J.
1975 *The statistical movement in early Victorian Britain: The foundations of empirical social research.* New York.

Cunningham, D. J.
1908 Anthropology in the eighteenth century. *J. Roy. Anth. Inst.* 38:10–35.

Curtin, P. D.
1964 *The image of Africa: British ideas and action, 1780–1850.* Madison, Wis.

Curtis, L. P., Jr.
1968 *Anglo-Saxons and Celts: A study of anti-Irish prejudice in Victorian England.* Bridgeport, Conn.

Dachs, A. J.
1972 Missionary imperialism—the case of Bechuanaland. *J. African Hist.* 4:647–58.

Daniel, Glyn
1943 *The three ages: An essay on archaeological method.* Cambridge, England.
1950 *A hundred years of archaeology.* London.
1964 *The idea of prehistory.* Baltimore.

Darwin, Charles
[1838] M notebook. In *Metaphysics, materialism, and the evolution of mind,* ed. P. H. Barrett, 8–45. Chicago: 1980.
[1839] *Journal of researches into the natural history and geology of the countries visited during the voyage of H.M.S. "Beagle."* London: 1891.
[1859] *On the origin of species.* Cambridge, Mass.: 1966.
[1871] *The descent of man, and selection in relation to sex.* Princeton: 1981.
[1874] *The descent of man, and selection in relation to sex.* 2nd. ed. New York: 1883.
1891 *The life and letters of Charles Darwin.* 2 vols. New York.
1903 *More letters of Charles Darwin.* Ed. F. Darwin and A. C. Seward. 2 vols. London.
1959 *On the origin of species: A variorum text.* Ed. M. Peckham. Philadelphia.

Darwin, Erasmus
1803 The temple of nature, or the origin of society. In *The essential writings of Erasmus Darwin,* ed. D. King-Hele. London.

Dasent, G. W.
1859 *Popular tales from the Norse.* Edinburgh.

Davidoff, Leonore
1973 *The best circles: Women and society in Victorian England.* Totowa, N.J.
1974 Mastered for life: Servant and wife in Victorian and Edwardian England. *J. Soc. Hist.* 7:406–28.

Davie, G. E.
1964 *The democratic intellect: Scotland and her universities in the nineteenth century.* Edinburgh.

Davies, David
1974 *The last of the Tasmanians.* New York.

Davis, J. B.
1845–60 Manuscript diary. Archives of the Royal Anthropological Institute. Museum of Mankind, London.
1874 *On the osteology and peculiarities of the Tasmanians, a race of man recently become extinct.* Haarlem, The Netherlands.

Davis, J. B. & J. Thurnam
1865 *Crania Britannica: Delineations and descriptions of the skulls of the aboriginal and early inhabitants of the British Islands.* London.

De Brosses, Charles
1760 *Du culte des dieux fétiches, ou parallèle de l'ancienne religion de l'Egypte avec la religion actuelle de Nigritie.* Paris.

DeCocq, A. L.
1968 *Andrew Lang, a nineteenth-century anthropologist.* Tilburg, The Netherlands.

De Giustino, David
1975 *Conquest of mind: Phrenology and Victorian social thought.* London.

Derrett, J. D. M.
1959 Sir Henry Maine and law in India, 1858–1958. *Jurid. Rev.* 4:40–55.

Desmond, Adrian
1984 *Archetypes and ancestors: Paleontology in Victorian London, 1850–75.* Chicago.

Dewey, Clive
1972 Images of the village community: A study in Anglo-Indian ideology. *Mod. Asian Stud.* 6:291–328.

Diamond, Stanley
1980a Anthropological traditions: The participants observed. In Diamond 1980b:1–18.
——, ed.
1980b *Anthropology: Ancestors and heirs.* The Hague.

Dicey, A. V.
1914 *Lectures on the relation between law and public opinion in England during the nineteenth century.* London.

Disraeli, Benjamin
1845 *Sybil, or, the two nations.* 3 vols. London.

Donajgrodzki, A. P.
1977 'Social police' and the bureaucratic elite: A vision of order in the age of reform. In *Social control in nineteenth century Britain*, ed. Donajgradzki, 51–76. London.

Dorson, Richard
1955 The eclipse of solar mythology. *J. Amer. Folklore* 68:393–416.
1968a *The British folklorists: A history.* Chicago.
——, ed.
1968b *Peasant customs and savage myths.* 2 vols. Chicago.

Driver, H. & R. P. Chaney
1970 Cross-cultural sampling and Galton's problem. In Naroll & Cohen, eds., 1970:990–1003.

Duchet, Michele
1971 *Anthropologie et histoire au siècle des lumières: Buffon, Voltaire, Rousseau, Helvetius, Diderot.* Paris.
1985 De l'histoire morale à la description des moeurs: Lafitau. In *Le partage des savoirs: discours historique et discours ethnologique,* 30–52. Paris.

Duff, M. Grant
1892 Sir Henry Maine: A brief memoir of his life. In Maine 1892:1–84.

Duff, Ursula Grant, ed.
1924 *The life-work of Lord Avebury (Sir John Lubbock) 1834–1913.* London.

Dumont, Louis
1966 The 'village community' from Munro to Maine. *Cont. Indian Sociol.* 9:67–89.

Dunbar, Janet
1953 *The early Victorian woman: Some aspects of her life, 1837–57.* London.

Duncan, David
1911 *The life and letters of Herbert Spencer.* London.

Edwardes, Michael
1973 *Red year: The Indian rebellion of 1857.* London.

Eiseley, Loren
[1958] *Darwin's century: evolution and the men who discovered it.* Garden City, N.Y.: 1961

Eisen, Sydney
1967 Herbert Spencer and the spectre of Comte. *J. Brit. Stud.* 7:48–67.

Eldridge, C. C.
1978 *Victorian imperialism.* London.

Elias, Norbert
[1939] *The civilizing process: The history of manners.* Trans. E. Jephcott. New York: 1978.

Ellegård, A.
1958 *Darwin and the general reader: The reception of Darwin's theory of evolution in the British periodical press, 1859–1872.* Göteborg.

Ellis, V. R.
1981 *Trucanini: Queen or traitor?* Canberra.

Engels, Friedrich
[1845] *The condition of the working class in England.* Trans. W. O. Henderson & W. H. Chaloner. Stanford, Calif.: 1958.

Erickson, Paul
1974 The origins of physical anthropology. Ph.D. diss. University of Connecticut.

ESL [Ethnological Society of London]
1850 *Regulations.* London.
1869 Classification committee. Bound in *J. Ethnol. Soc. Lond.* 1:332.

Evans, Joan
1943 *Time and chance: The story of Arthur Evans and his forebears.* London.
1949 The Royal Archaeological Institute: A retrospect. *Archaeol. J.* 106:1–8.
1950 Archaeology in 1851. *Archaeol. J.* 107:1–6.
1956 *A history of the Society of Antiquaries.* Oxford.

Evans, John
1878 Anniversary address. *J. Anth. Inst.* 7:515–34.
1879 Anniversary address. *J. Anth. Inst.* 8:402–25.
1883 Anniversary address. *J. Anth. Inst.* 12:563–66.

Evans, M. O.
1896 *Theories and criticisms of Sir Henry Maine.* London.

Evans-Pritchard, E. E.
1933 The intellectualist (English) interpretation of magic. *Bul. Fac. Arts, Cairo* 1:1–21.
[1950] Social anthropology. In Evans-Pritchard, *Social anthropology and other essays,* 1–134. Glencoe, Ill.: 1962.
1981 *A history of anthropological thought.* Ed. A. Singer. New York.

Eversley, D. E. C.
1959 *Social theories of fertility and the Malthusian debate.* Oxford.

Fabian, Johannes
1983 *Time and the other: How anthropology makes its object.* New York.

Fahim, Hussein, ed.
1982 *Indigenous anthropology in non-western countries.* Durham, N.C.

Fairchild, Hoxie
1961 *The noble savage: A study in romantic naturalism.* New York.

Fancher, Raymond
1983a Biographical origins of Francis Galton's psychology. *Isis* 74:227–33.
1983b Francis Galton's African ethnography and its role in the development of his psychology. *Brit. J. Hist. Sci.* 16:67–79.

Farwell, Byron
1972 *Queen Victoria's little wars.* New York.

Fay, C. R.
1951 *Palace of industry, 1851.* Cambridge, England.

Feaver, George
1969 *From status to contract: A biography of Sir Henry Maine 1822–1888.* London.

Febvre, Lucien
  1930 Civilisation: Evolution d'un mot et d'un groupe d'idées. In *Civilisation: Le mot et l'idée,* ed. L. Febvre, M. Mauss, et al., 3–45. Paris.

Fee, Elizabeth
  1974 The sexual politics of Victorian social anthropology. In Hartman & Banner 1974:86–102.
  1976 Science and the woman problem: Historical perspectives. In *Sex Differences: Social and biological perspectives,* ed. M. S. Teitelbaum, 175–223. New York.

Feisel, Eva
  1927 *Die Sprachphilosophie der deutschen Romantik, 1801–1816.* Tübingen.

Feldman, B. & R. Richardson, eds.
  1972 *The rise of modern mythology: 1680–1860.* Bloomington, Ind.

Fenton, William
  1969 J. F. Lafitau (1681–1746), precursor of scientific anthropology. *Southwest. J. Anth.* 25:173–87.

Ffrench, Yvonne
  1950 *The Great Exhibition, 1851.* London.

Fichte, J. G.
  [1808] *Addresses to the German nation.* Ed. G. A. Kelly. New York: 1968.

Findlay, G. G. & W. W. Holdsworth
  1921–24 *The history of the Wesleyan Methodist Missionary Society.* 5 vols. London.

Fison, L.
  1879 Australian marriage laws. *J. Anth. Inst.* 9:354–57.

Fison, L. & A. W. Howitt
  [1880] *Kamilaroi and Kurnai: Group-marriage and relationship, and marriage by elopement, drawn chiefly from the usage of the Australian Aborigines.* Oosterhout, The Netherlands: 1967.

Flint, Robert
  1874 *The philosophy of history in France and Germany.* Edinburgh.

Flower, W. H.
  1881 Address to section H. *Rept. Brit. Assn. Adv. Sci.* 51:682–89.

Forbes, Duncan
  1951 James Mill and India. *Camb. J.* 5:19–33.
  1952 *The liberal anglican idea of history.* Cambridge, England.
  1954 'Scientific Whiggism': Adam Smith and John Millar. *Camb. J.* 7:643–70.

Forrest, Derek
  1974 *Francis Galton: The life and works of a Victorian genius.* London.

Fortes, Meyer
  1970 *Kinship and the social order: The legacy of Lewis Henry Morgan.* Chicago.

Foucault, Michel
  [1966] *The order of things: An archaeology of the human sciences.* New York: 1970.
  1978 *The history of sexuality: Volume I, an introduction.* Trans. R. Hurley. New York.

France, Peter
1968 The founding of an orthodoxy: Sir Arthur Gordon and the doctrine of the Fijian way of life. *J. Polyn. Soc.* 77:6–32.
1969 *The charter of the land: Custom and colonization in Fiji.* Melbourne.

Fraser, Russell
1977 *The language of Adam: On the limits and systems of discourse.* New York.

Frazer, J. G.
1887 *Totemism.* Edinburgh.
1890 *The golden bough: A study in comparative religion.* London.
[1909] *Psyche's task: A discourse concerning the influence of superstition on the growth of institutions.* London: 1913.
1910 *Totemism and exogamy: A treatise on certain early forms of superstition and society.* 4 vols. London.

Freeman, Derek
1974 The evolutionary theories of Charles Darwin and Herbert Spencer. *Curr. Anth.* 15:211–21.
1983 *Margaret Mead and Samoa: The making and unmaking of an anthropological myth.* Cambridge, Mass.

Freire-Marreco, B. W.
1907 A bibliography of Edward Burnett Tylor from 1861 to 1907. In Thomas, ed. 1907:375–99.

Frere, Bartle
1881 On the laws affecting the relations between civilized and savage life, as bearing on the dealings of colonists with aborigines. *J. Anth. Inst.* 11:313–54.

Gallagher, J.
1950 Fowell Buxton and the new African policy, 1838–1842. *Camb. Hist. J.* 10:36–58.

Gallagher, J. & R. Robinson.
1953 The imperialism of free trade. *Econ. Hist. Rev.* 6:1–15.

Gallatin, Albert
[1836] *A synopsis of the Indian tribes within the United States east of the Rocky Mountains and in the British and Russian possessions in North America.* New York: 1973.

Galton, Francis
1853 *The narrative of an explorer in tropical South Africa.* London.
1855 *The art of travel: Or, shifts and contrivances available in wild countries.* London.
1863 The first steps toward the domestication of animals. *Trans. Ethnol. Soc. Lond.* 3:122–38.
1865 Hereditary talent and character. *Macmillan's Mag.* 12:157–66, 328–27.
[1869] *Hereditary genius: an inquiry into its laws and consequences.* New York: 1870.
1885 Remarks made at the commencement of the session. *J. Anth. Inst.* 15:336–38.
1888 Comment on Tylor 1888:270–71.
1908 *Memories of my life.* London.

Garfinkle, Norton

1955 Science and religion in England, 1790–1800: The critical response to the works of Erasmus Darwin. *J. Hist. Ideas.* 16:376–88.

Gauld, Alan

1968 *The founders of psychical research.* New York.

Gay, Peter

1966 *The Enlightenment: An interpretation. I. The rise of modern paganism.* New York.

1969 *The Enlightenment: An interpretation. II. The science of freedom.* New York.

1984 *The bourgeois experience: Victoria to Freud. I. The education of the senses.* New York.

Geertz, Clifford

1966 The impact of the concept of culture on the concept of man. In Geertz 1973a:33–54.

1973a *The interpretation of cultures.* New York.

1973b Thick description: Toward an interpretive theory of culture. In Geertz 1973a:1–30.

1983 Blurred genres: The refiguration of social thought. In Geertz, *Local knowledge: Further essays in interpretive anthropology,* 19–35. New York.

Geikie, Archibald

1875 *Life of Sir Roderick I. Murchison.* 2 vols. London.

Geison, Gerald

1978 *Michael Foster and the Cambridge school of physiology: The scientific enterprise in late Victorian society.* Princeton.

George, Wilma

1964 *Biologist philosopher: A study of the life and writings of Alfred Russel Wallace.* London.

Gerard, René

1963 *L'orient et la pensée romantique allemande.* Paris.

Gerbi, Antonello

[1955] *The dispute of the new world: The history of a polemic, 1750–1900.* Trans. Jeremy Moyle. Pittsburgh: 1973.

Ghiselin, Michael

1969 *The triumph of the Darwinian method.* Berkeley.

Gibbs-Smith, C. H.

1950 *The Great Exhibition of 1851.* London.

Gillespie, Neal

1977 The Duke of Argyll, evolutionary anthropology, and the art of scientific controversy. *Isis* 68:40–54.

Gillispie, Charles

[1951] *Genesis and geology: A study in the relations of scientific thought, natural theology and social opinion in Great Britain, 1790–1850.* New York: 1959.

Girouard, Mark

1971 *The Victorian country house.* Oxford.

Glacken, Clarence
1967 *Traces on the Rhodian shore: Nature and culture in western thought from ancient times to the end of the eighteenth century.* Berkeley.

Glass, H. B. et al. eds.
1959 *Forerunners of Darwin: 1745–1859.* Baltimore.

Glick, T. F., ed.
1972 *The comparative reception of Darwinism.* Austin, Tex.

Gliozzi, Giuliano
1976 *Adamo e il nuovo mondo: La nascita dell'antropologia como ideologia coloniale: dalle genealogie bibliche alle teorie razziali (1500–1700).* Florence.

Glover, W. B.
1954 *Evangelical nonconformists and higher criticism in the nineteenth century.* London.

Godelier, M.
1983 Malthus and ethnography. In *Malthus past and present,* ed. A. Dupâquier et al., 125–50. London.

Goldenweiser, A. A.
1910 Totemism, an analytical study. *J. Amer. Folklore* 23:178–298.
1925 Cultural anthropology. In *The history and prospects of the social sciences,* ed. H. E. Barnes, 210–55. New York.

Goldman, Irving
1959 Evolution and anthropology. *Victorian Stud.* 3:55–75.

Gomme, G. L., ed.
1883–1904 *The Gentleman's Magazine library: Being a classified collection of the chief contents of the Gentleman's Magazine from 1731 to 1868.* London.

Goodfield-Toulmin, J.
1966 Blasphemy and biology. *Rockefeller Rev.* Sept.:9–18.
1969 Some aspects of English physiology, 1780–1940. *J. Hist. Biol.* 2:283–320.

Gopal, S.
1965 *British policy in India, 1858–1905.* Cambridge, England.

Gorham, Deborah
1982 *The Victorian girl and the feminine ideal.* Bloomington, Ind.

Gossiaux, P. P.
1984 Séquences de l'histoire dans l'anthropologie des lumières: Problèmes et mythes. In Rupp-Eisenreich 1984:67–85.

Gough, Kathleen
1975 The origin of the family. In Reiter 1975:51–76.

Gould, S. J.
1977 *Ontogeny and phylogeny.* Cambridge, Mass.

Graebner, Fritz
[1911] *Methode der Ethnologie.* Osterhout, The Netherlands: 1966.

Grafton, A. T.
1975 Joseph Scaliger and historical chronology: The rise and fall of a discipline. *Hist. & Theory* 14:156–85.

Graham, L., W. Lepenies, & P. Weingart, eds.
1983 *Functions and uses of disciplinary histories.* Dordrecht.

Graveson, R. H., & F. R. Crane, eds.
1957 *A century of family law, 1857–1957.* London.

Grayson, Donald
1983 *The establishment of human antiquity.* New York.

Great Britain Parliamentary Papers (House of Commons)
1834 *Aboriginal tribes (North America, New South Wales, Van Diemen's Land, and British Guiana).* Vol. 44, No. 617, August 14.
1839 *Australian aborigines. Copies or extracts of despatches relative to the massacre of various aborigines of Australia in the year 1838, and respecting the trial of their murderers.* Vol. 34, No. 526, August 12.

Greene, John
1959a *The death of Adam: Evolution and its impact on western thought.* Ames, Iowa.
1959b Biology and social theory in the nineteenth century: Auguste Comte and Herbert Spencer. In Greene 1981:60–94.
1975 Reflections on the progress of Darwin studies. *J. Hist. Biol.* 8:243–73.
1977 Darwin as a social evolutionist. In Greene 1981:95–127.
1981 *Science, ideology, and world view: Essays in the history of evolutionary ideas.* Berkeley.

Greenwood, D. J.
1984 *The taming of evolution: The persistence of nonevolutionary views in the study of humans.* Ithaca, N.Y.

Grey, Earl
1853 The colonial policy of Lord John Russell's administration. 2 vols. London.

Grey, George
1841 *Journal of two expeditions of discovery in northwest and western Australia during the years 1837–39.* 2 vols. London.
[1855] *Polynesian mythology and ancient traditional history of the Maori, as told by their priests and chiefs.* New York: 1970.
1869a On the social life of the ancient inhabitants of New Zealand, and on the national character it was likely to form. *J. Ethnol. Soc. Lond.* 1:333–62.
1869b Anthropology at the British Association. *Anth. Rev.* 7:418–19.

Gross, John
1969 *The rise and fall of the man of letters: Aspects of English literary life since 1800.* London.

Gruber, Jacob
1965 Brixham Cave and the antiquity of man. In *Context and meaning in cultural anthropology,* ed. M. E. Spiro, 393–402. New York.
1970 Ethnographic salvage and the shaping of anthropology. *Amer. Anth.* 72:1289–99.
1973 Forerunners. In *Main currents in cultural anthropology,* ed. R. & F. Naroll, 25–56. Englewood Cliffs, N.J.

Guizot, François
[1829] *General history of civilization in Europe.* New York: 1880.

Gusdorf, Georges
1960 *Introduction aux sciences humaines: Essai critique sur leurs origines et leur développement.* Paris.

Guthrie, W. K. C.
1957 *In the beginning: Some Greek views on the origins of life and the early state of man.* Ithaca, N.Y.

Habbakuk, H. J.
1965 The economic history of modern Britain. In *Population in history,* ed. D. Glass & D. Eversley, 147–58. London.

Haber, Francis
1959 *The age of the world from Moses to Darwin.* Baltimore.

Haddon, A. C.
1910 *History of anthropology.* London.

Haight, Gordon
1971 Male chastity in the nineteenth century. *Cont. Rev.* 219:252–62.

Halévy, Elie
[1928] *The growth of philosophical radicalism.* Trans. M. Morris. Boston: 1960.

Haley, Bruce
1978 *The healthy body and Victorian culture.* Cambridge, Mass.

Hall, T. S.
1969 *Ideas of life and matter: Studies in the history of general physiology.* 2 vols. Chicago.

Halliday, R.
1971 Social Darwinism: A definition. *Victorian Stud.* 14:389–405.

Hallifax, Samuel
1836 *An analysis of the civil law in which a comparison is occasionally made between the Roman laws and those of England.* Cambridge, England.

Hallpike, C.
1979 *The foundations of primitive thought.* Oxford.

Haltern, Utz
1971 *Die Londoner Weltausstellung von 1851.* Münster.

Hamburger, Joseph
1965 *Intellectuals in politics: John Stuart Mill and the philosophical radicals.* New Haven.

Hannah, J.
1869 Primeval man. *Cont. Rev.* 11:160–77.

Hardy, Thomas
1894 The fiddler of the reels. In Hardy, *Life's little ironies.* London.

Hardy, W. J.
[1887] Henry Christy. *Dict. Natl. Biog.* 4:295–96. 1921.

Harris, Horton
1973 *David Friedrich Strauss and his theology.* Cambridge, England.

Harris, Marvin
1968 *The rise of anthropological theory: A history of theories of culture.* New York.
1980 History and ideological significance of the separation of social and cultural anthropology. In Ross 1980:391–407.

Harris, Victor
1949 *All coherence gone.* Chicago.

Harrison, Brian
1971 *Drink and the Victorians: The temperance question in England, 1815–1872.* London.

Hartman, M. & L. Banner, eds.
1974 *Clio's consciousness raised: New perspectives on the history of women.* New York.

Hartog, Philip
1938 'Kultur' as a symbol in peace and in war. *Sociol. Rev.* 30:317–45.

Harvey, Joy
1983 Evolutionism transformed: Positivists and materialists in the Société d'Anthropologie de Paris from Second Empire to Third Republic. In *The wider domain of evolutionary thought,* ed. D. Oldroyd & I. Langham, 289–310. Dordrecht, The Netherlands.

Harvie, Christopher
1976 *The lights of liberalism: University liberals and the challenge of democracy, 1860–86.* London.

Hay, Denis
1957 *Europe: The emergence of an idea.* Edinburgh.

Hazard, Paul
[1946] *European thought in the eighteenth century: From Montesquieu to Lessing.* Trans. J. L. May. Cleveland: 1965.

Hearn, Francis
1978 *Domination, legitimation, and resistance: The incorporation of the nineteenth-century English working class.* Westport, Conn.

Hechter, Michael
1975 *Internal colonialism: The Celtic fringe in British national development, 1536–1966.* Berkeley.

Heelas, P. L. F.
1974 Intellectualism and the anthropology of religion. D. Phil. diss. Oxford University.

Heilbroner, R. L.
1973 The paradox of progress: decline and decay in *The Wealth of Nations. J. Hist. Ideas.* 34:243–62.

Henderson, G. C.
1931 *Fiji and the Fijians, 1835–1856.* Sydney.

Henson, Hilary
1974 *British social anthropologists and language: A history of separate development.* Oxford.

Herder, J. G.
[1784] *Outlines of a philosophy of the history of man.* Trans. T. Churchill. London: 1800.

Herschel, J. W., ed.
1849 *A manual of scientific enquiry, prepared for the use of Her Majesty's Navy and adapted for travellers.* London.

Hervé, G.
1907 Montesquieu: L'ethnographie dans 'L'Esprit des lois'; la théorie des climats. *Rev. Ecole d'Anth.* 17:337–53.

Hill, Jane
1978 Apes and language. *Annu. Rev. Anth.* 7:89–112.

Himmelfarb, Gertrude
1959 *Darwin and the Darwinian revolution.* Garden City, N.Y.
1984 *The idea of poverty: England in the industrial age.* New York.

Hinsley, Curtis
1981 *Savages and scientists: The Smithsonian Institution and the development of American anthropology, 1846–1910.* Washington, D.C.

Hodgen, Margaret
1936 *The doctrine of survivals: A chapter in the history of scientific method in the study of man.* London.
1964 *Early anthropology in the sixteenth and seventeenth centuries.* Philadelphia.

Hodgkin, Thomas
1835 On the importance of studying and preserving the languages spoken by uncivilized nations, with a view of elucidating the physical history of man. *Lond. & Edin. Phil. Mag. & J. Sci.* 7:27–35; 94–106.
1841 On inquiries into the races of man. *Rept. Brit. Assn. Adv. Sci.* 11:52–55.
1850 Obituary of Dr. Prichard. *J. Ethnol. Soc. Lond.* 2:182.

Hoebel, E. A.
1960 William Robertson Smith: An eighteenth century anthropologist-historian. *Am. Anth.* 62:648–55.

Hoebel, E. A. et al., eds.
1982 *Crisis in anthropology: View from Spring Hill, 1980.* New York.

Hoenigswald, H. M.
1963 On the history of the comparative method. *Anth. Ling.* 5:1.

Holcombe, Lee
1977 Victorian wives and property: Reform of the married women's property law, 1857–1882. In Vicinus 1977:3–28.

Hollis, M. & S. Lukes, eds.
1982 *Rationality and relativism.* Cambridge, Mass.

Holtzman, S. F.
1970 History of the early discoveries and determination of the Neanderthal race. Ph. D. diss. University of California, Berkeley.

Honigmann, J. J.
1976 *The development of anthropological ideas.* Homewood, Ill.

Hooykaas, R.
1956 The principle of uniformity in geology, biology and theology. *J. Trans. Victoria Inst.* 88:101–16.

Horn, Pamela
1975 *The rise and fall of the Victorian servant.* New York.
1980 *The rural world, 1780–1850: Social change in the English countryside.* New York.

Horsman, Reginald
1976 Origins of racial Anglo-Saxonism in Great Britain before 1850. *J. Hist. Ideas* 37:387–410.

Houghton, Walter
1957 *The Victorian frame of mind, 1830–1870.* New Haven.

Howitt, A. W.
1882 Notes on the Australian class systems. *J. Anth. Inst* 12:496–512.

Howitt, A. W. & L. Fison
1882 From mother-right to father-right. *J. Anth. Inst.* 12:30–46.
1884 On the deme and the horde. *J. Anth. Inst.* 14:142–69.

Hudson, K.
1981 *A social history of archaeology: The British experience.* London.

Hughes, H. S.
1958 *Consciousness and society: The reorientation of European social thought, 1890–1930.* New York.

Huizer, G. & B. Mannheim, eds.
1979 *The politics of anthropology: From colonialism and sexism toward a view from below.* The Hague.

Hull, David
1973 *Darwin and his critics.* Cambridge, Mass.

Humboldt, W. von
[1836] *Linguistic variability and intellectual development.* Trans. G. C. Buck and F. A. Raven. Coral Gables, Fla.: 1971.

Hunt, James
1863a Introductory address on the study of anthropology. *Anth. Rev.* 1:1–20.
1863b On anthropological classification. *Anth. Rev.* 1:382–83.
1863c On the Negro's place in nature. *Mem. Anth. Soc.* 1:1–64.
1865 President's address. *J. Anth. Soc. Lond.* 3:lxxx–cxii.
1866 On the application of the principle of natural selection to anthropology. *Anth. Rev.* 4:320–40.
1867a On the doctrine of continuity applied to anthropology. *Anth. Rev.* 5:110–120.
1867b President's address. *Anth. Rev.* 5:xliv–lxx.

Huppert, George
1971 The idea of civilization in the sixteenth century. In *Renaissance studies in honor of Hans Baron,* ed. A. Molho & J. Tedeschi, 759–69. Florence.

Hutchinson, H. G.
1914 *The life of Sir John Lubbock, Lord Avebury.* 2 vols. London.

Huth, A. H.
1880 *The life and writings of Henry Thomas Buckle.* New York.

Huttenback, R. A.
1976 *Racism and empire: White settlers and colored immigrants in the British self-governing colonies, 1830–1910.* Ithaca, N.Y.

Huxley, T. H.
1863 *Man's place in nature.* In Huxley 1910:1–208.
1865 On the methods and results of ethnology. In Huxley 1910:209–52.
1874 Note on the resemblances and differences in the structure and the development of the brain in man and apes. In Darwin 1874: 199–206.
[1900] *Life and letters of Thomas Huxley.* Ed. L. Huxley. 3 vols. New York: 1916.
1910 *Man's place in nature and other anthropological essays.* London.

Hymes, Dell
——, ed.
1972 *Reinventing anthropology.* New York.
——, ed.
1974a *Studies in the history of linguistics: Traditions and paradigms.* Bloomington, Ind.
1974b Introduction: Traditions and paradigms. In Hymes, ed., 1974a:1–40.

Iggers, Georg
1983 *The German conception of history: The national tradition of historical thought from Herder to the present.* Rev. ed. Middletown, Conn.

Im Thurn, E. F.
1883 *Among the Indians of Guiana: Being sketches chiefly anthropologic from the interior of British Guiana.* London.

Jaeger, Muriel
[1956] *Before Victoria: Changing standards and behavior.* Harmondsworth, Middlesex: 1967.

JAI [*Journal of the Anthropological Institute*]
1874 Annual general meeting. 3:499–527.
1875 Annual general meeting. 4:469–502.

Jarvie, I. C.
1964 *The revolution in anthropology.* London.

Jespersen, Otto
[1922] *Language: Its nature, development and origin.* New York: 1964.

Johanson, D. & M. Edey
1981 *Lucy: The beginnings of humankind.* New York.

Johnson, James
1959 The Scythian: His rise and fall. *J. Hist. Ideas* 20:250–57.
1962 Chronological writing: Its concept and development. *Hist. Theory* 2:124–45.

Jones, Greta
1980 *Social Darwinism and English thought: The interaction between biological and social theory.* Brighton, Sussex.

Jones, R. A.
1984 Robertson Smith and Frazer on religion: Two traditions in British social anthropology. In Stocking 1984a: 31–58.

Jones, W. R.
1971 The image of the barbarian in medieval Europe. *Comp. Stud. Soc. Hist.* 13:376–407.

Juliard, P.
1970 *Philosophies of language in eighteenth century France.* The Hague.

Kantorowicz, Hermann
1937 Savigny and the historical school of law. *Law Quart. Rev.* 211:326–43.

Kardiner, A. & E. Preble
1961 *They studied man.* Cleveland.

Kassem, Badreddine
1974 *Décadence et absolutisme dans l'oeuvre de Montesquieu.* Paris.

Keesing, Roger
1974 Theories of culture. *Annu. Rev. Anth.* 3:71–97.

Keith, Arthur
1917 How can the Institute best serve the needs of anthropology? *J. Roy. Anth. Inst.* 47:12–30.
[1920] Galton's place among anthropologists. *Eugenics Rev.* 60 (1968):12–24.

Kendrick, T. D.
1927 *The Druids: A study in Keltic prehistory.* London.
1950 *British antiquity.* London.

Kern, Stephen
1974 Explosive intimacy: Psychodynamics of the Victorian family. *Hist. Childhood Quart.* 1:437–61.

Kettler, David
1965 *The social and political thought of Adam Ferguson.* Columbus, Ohio.

Kiernan, V. G.
1969 *The lords of human kind: European attitudes towards the outside world in the imperial age.* London.

King, Richard
1868 Comments on Darwinism and anthropology, by H. Schaaffhausen. *Anth. Rev.* 6:cxi.

Kissane, James
1962 Victorian mythology. *Victorian Stud.* 6:5–27.

Kitcher, Philip
1985 *Vaulting ambition: Sociobiology and the quest for human nature.* Cambridge, Mass.

Klein, Viola
1946 *The feminine character: History of an ideology.* London.

Knaplund, Paul
1953 *James Stephen and the British colonial system, 1813–1847.* Madison, Wis.

Knoll, Elizabeth
1986 The science of language and the evolution of mind: Max Müller's quarrel with Darwinism. *J. Hist. Behav. Sci.* 22:3–22.

Knox, Robert
[1850] *The races of men: A philosophical enquiry into the influences of race over the destinies of nations.* London: 1862.

Koebner, R. & H. Schmidt
1964 *Imperialism: The story and significance of a political word, 1840–1960.* New York.

Kohn, David, ed.
1985 *The Darwinian heritage.* Princeton.

Konner, M. & M. Shostak
1983 Ethnographic romanticism and the idea of human nature: Parallels between Samoa and the Kung San. Paper presented to the Amer. Anth. Assn., 11/18, Chicago.

Kopf, David
1969 *British orientalism and the Bengal renaissance.* Berkeley.

Koskinen, A. A.
1953 *Missionary influence as a political factor in the Pacific islands.* Helsinki.

Krieger, Leonard
1977 *Ranke: The meaning of history.* Chicago.

Kroeber, A. L.
1917 The superorganic. *Amer. Anth.* 19:163–213.

Kroeber, A. L. & Clyde Kluckhohn
1952 *Culture: A critical review of concepts and definitions.* Cambridge, Mass.

Kuhn, Thomas
1962 *The structure of scientific revolutions.* Chicago.

Kuklick, Henrika
1984 Tribal exemplars: Images of political authority in British anthropology, 1885–1945. In Stocking 1984a:59–82.

Kuper, Adam
1973 *Anthropologists and anthropology: The British school, 1922–1972.* London.
1982 Lineage theory: A critical retrospect. *Curr. Anth. 11:71–95.*
1983 *Anthropology and anthropologists: The modern British school.* London.
1985 Ancestors: Henry Maine and the constitution of primitive society. *Hist. & Anth.* 1:265–86.

Lafitau, J. F.
[1724] *Customs of the American Indians compared with the customs of primitive times.* Ed. & trans. W. N. Fenton & E. L. Moore. 2 vols. Toronto: 1974.

Laming-Emperaire, A.
1964 *Origines de l'archéologie préhistorique en France des superstitions médiévales à la découverte de l'homme fossile.* Paris.

Landes, David
1969 *The unbound Prometheus: Technological change and industrial development in western Europe from 1750 to the present.* Cambridge, England.

Landman, J. H.
1930 Primitive law, evolution and Sir Henry Maine. *Michigan Law Rev.* 28:404–25.

Lane Fox [see under Pitt Rivers]

Lang, Andrew
1884 *Custom and myth.* London.
1901 *Magic and religion.* London.
1907 Edward Burnett Tylor. In Thomas 1907:1–15.

Lang, A. & E. B. Tylor
1883 Double ballade of primitive man. In Lang, *XXXII ballades in blue china,* 44–46. London.

Langer, W. L.
1974 Infanticide: A historical survey. *Hist. Childhood Quart.* 1:353–65.

Langham, Ian
1981 *The building of British social anthropology: W. H. R. Rivers and his Cambridge disciples in the development of kinship studies.* Dordrecht.

Larsen, B.
1924 Anders Adolf Retzius. *Ann. Med. Hist.* 6:16–24.

Larsen, M. S.
1977 *The rise of professionalism: A sociological analysis.* Berkeley.

Laslett, Peter
1965 *The world we have lost.* New York.

Latham, R. G.
1847 On the present state and recent progress of ethnological philology. *Rept. Brit. Assn. Adv. Sci.* 17:154–229.
1850 *The natural history of the varieties of man.* London.
1851 *Ethnology of the British colonies and dependencies.* London.
1854 *The natural history department of the Crystal Palace described. Ethnology.* London.
1859 *Descriptive ethnology.* 2 vols. London.
1862 *Elements of comparative philology.* London.

Lawrence, William
1819 *Lectures on physiology, zoology and the natural history of man.* London.

Leach, Edmund
1961 *Rethinking anthropology.* London.

Leaf, Murray
1979 *Man, mind and science: A history of anthropology.* New York.

Leakey, L. S. B. & V. M. Goodall
1969 *Unveiling man's origins. Ten decades of thought about human evolution.* Cambridge, Mass.

Leary, David
1982 The fate and influence of John Stuart Mill's proposed science of ethology. *J. Hist. Ideas.* 43:153–62.

Lebow, R. N.
1976 *White Britain and black Ireland.* Philadelphia.

LeClerc, Gerard
1972 *Anthropologie et colonialisme: Essai sur l'histoire de l'africanisme.* Paris.

Lehmann, W. C.
1960 *John Millar of Glasgow, 1735–1801: His life and thought and his contributions to sociological analysis.* Cambridge, England.
1971 *Henry Home, Lord Kames, and the Scottish Enlightenment: A study in national character and the history of ideas.* The Hague.

LeMahieu, D. L.
1976 *The mind of William Paley: A philosopher and his age.* Lincoln, Nebr.

Lemaine, G., R. Macleod, M. Mulkay, & P. Weingart, eds.
1976 *Perspectives on the emergence of scientific disciplines.* The Hague.

Lemay, Edna
1984 Le monde extra-européen dans la formation de deux révolutionnaires. In Rupp-Eisenreich 1984: 117–32.

Leopold, Joan
1974 British applications of the Aryan theory of race to India 1850–1870. *Engl. Hist. Rev.* 89:578–603.
1980 *Culture in comparative and evolutionary perspective: E. B. Tylor and the making of Primitive Culture.* Berlin
n.d. Early life and letters of E. B. Tylor: The man behind the country gentleman's mask. Unpub. ms.

Levenson, Joseph
1965 *Confucian China and its modern fate. III. The problem of historical significance.* Berkeley.

Levine, Philippa
1986 *The amateur and the professional: Antiquarians, historians and archaeologists in Victorian England.* Cambridge, Eng.

Lévi-Strauss, C.
[1962] *Totemism.* Trans. R. Needham. Boston: 1963.

Lochore, R. A.
1935 *History of the idea of civilization in France.* Bonn.

Locke, John
[1690] *An essay concerning human understanding.* Ed. P. H. Nidditch. Oxford: 1975.

Lonsdale, Henry
1870 *A sketch of the life and writings of Robert Knox, the anatomist.* London.

Lovejoy, A. O.
1934 Foreword. In *Primitivism and the idea of progress in English popular literature of the eighteenth century,* by Lois Whitney, xi–xix. Baltimore.
1936 *The great chain of being: A study of the history of an idea.* Cambridge, Mass.
1948 The supposed primitivism of Rousseau's *Discourse on Inequality.* In Lovejoy; *Essays in the history of ideas,* 14–37. Baltimore.

Lovejoy, A. O. & George Boas
1935 *Primitivism and related ideas in antiquity.* Baltimore.

Lowie, R. H.
1937 *The history of ethnological theory.* New York.

Lowith, Karl
1949 *Meaning in history.* Chicago.

Lubbock, John (Lord Avebury)
[1865] *Pre-historic times, as illustrated by ancient remains, and the manners and customs of modern savages.* London: 1869.
1867 The primitive condition of man. Part I. In Lubbock 1870:326–37.
1869 The primitive condition of man. Part II. In Lubbock 1870:337–62.
[1870] *The origin of civilisation and the primitive condition of man.* Ed. Peter Rivière. Chicago: 1978.
1878 Review of L. H. Morgan, *Ancient Society. Sat. Rev.* 45:19–21.
1882 *Ants, bees and wasps: A record of observations on the habits of the social hymenoptera.* London.
1894 *The use of life.* London.
1895 *The origin of civilisation and the primitive condition of man.* 5th ed. London.
1896 *The scenery of Switzerland and the causes to which it is due.* London.
1911 *Marriage, totemism and religion: An answer to critics.* London.
1912 *The origin of civilisation and the primitive condition of man: Mental and social condition of savages.* 7th ed. London.

Lukes, Steven
1973 *Emile Durkheim: His life and work.* London.

Lyell, Charles
[1863] *The geological evidences of the antiquity of man, with remarks on theories of the origin of species by variation.* Philadelphia: 1870.

Lyon, John
1970 The search for fossil man: Cinq personnages à la recherche du temps perdu. *Isis* 61:68–84.

McCrone, Kathleen
1972 The assertion of women's rights in mid-Victorian England. Canadian Hist. Assn. *Hist. Papers* 5:39–53.

MacDougall, H. A.
1972 *Racial myth in English history: Trojans, Teutons, and Anglo-Saxons.* Hanover, N.H.

McGregor, O. R.
1957 *Divorce in England, a centenary study.* London.

McIntyre, W. D.
1967 *The imperial frontier in the tropics, 1865–75: A study of British colonial policy in West Africa, Malaya and the South Pacific in the age of Gladstone and Disraeli.* London.

McKenzie, D.
1976 Eugenics in Britain. *Soc. Stud. Sci.* 6:499–532.

McKinney, H. L.
1972 *Wallace and natural selection.* New Haven.

MacLean, John
[1858] *A compendium of Kafir laws and customs including genealogical tables of Kafir chiefs and various tribal census returns*. London: 1968.

McLennan, J. F.
1857 Law. *Encyclo. Brit.*, 8th ed. 13:253–79.
1860 Some reflections on an old street. *Macmillan's Mag.* 1:431–39.
1861 Marriage and divorce—the law of England and Scotland. *No. Brit. Rev.* 35:187–218.
1863 Hill tribes in India. *No. Brit. Rev.* 38:392–422.
[1865] *Primitive marriage*. Ed. Peter Rivière. Chicago: 1970.
1866 Kinship in ancient Greece. In McLennan 1876a:233–309.
1869a The early history of man. *No. Brit. Rev.* 50:272–90.
1869b The worship of animals and plants. *Fort. Rev.* 6:407–27, 562–82; 7:194–216.
1876a *Studies in ancient history*. London.
1876b The classificatory system of relationships. In McLennan 1876a: 329–407.
1876c Bachofen's 'Das Mutterrecht.' In McLennan 1876a: 411–21.
1877a The levirate and polyandry. *Fort. Rev.* 27:694–707.
1877b Exogamy and endogamy. *Fort. Rev.* 27:884–895.
1885 *The patriarchal theory, based on the papers of the late John Ferguson McLennan*. Ed. D. McLennan. London.
1896 *Studies in ancient history: The second series, comprising an inquiry into the origin of exogamy*. Ed. Eleanora McLennan & A. Platt. London.

MacLeod, Roy & P. Collins, eds.
1981 *Parliament of science: The British Association for the Advancement of Science, 1831–1981*. Northwood, Middlesex.

MacMillan, W. M.
1928 *Bantu, Boer and Briton: The making of the South African native problem*. London.

MacPherson, C. B.
1962 *The political theory of possessive individualism: Hobbes to Locke*. Oxford.

Maine, H. S.
1855 The conception of sovereignty and its importance in international law. In *Papers read before the Juridical Society, 1855–1858*, 26–45. London.
1856a Roman law and legal education. In Maine 1871:330–86.
1856b Circumlocution vs. circumvention. *Sat. Rev.* 2 (Nov. 22):649–50.
1857a Eothen in the southwest. *Sat. Rev.* 3 (Jan. 17):45–46.
1857b Wild justice. *Sat. Rev.* 4 (Aug. 8):121–22.
1857c Indian statesmen and English scribblers. *Sat. Rev.* 4 (Oct. 24):361–62.
1857d European opinion on Bengal. *Sat. Rev.* 4 (Nov. 21):457–58.
1858a The new Indian department. *Sat. Rev.* 5 (Jan. 2):1–2.
1858b The middle classes and the abolition of the East India Company. *Sat. Rev.* 5 (Jan. 9):31–32.
1858c Thirty years of improvement in India. *Sat. Rev.* 5 (Feb. 6):129–30.
1858d Administrative Brahmanism. *Sat. Rev.* 5 (Mar. 13):259–60.

[1861] *Ancient law, its connection with the early history of society and its relation to modern ideas.* London: 1873.
[1871] *Village communities in the east and west.* London: 1876.
1875 *Lectures on the early history of institutions.* New York.
1883 *Dissertations on early law and custom.* New York.
1886a The patriarchal theory. *Quart. Rev.* 162:181–209.
1886b *Popular government: Four essays.* London.
1888 *International law: The Whewell lectures.* London.
1892 *Indian speeches and minutes.* Ed. W. Stokes. London.

Maine, H. S., et al.
1856 *Cambridge essays, contributed by members of the university.* Cambridge, England.

Malcolmson, R. W.
1973 *Popular recreations in English society, 1700–1850.* Cambridge, England.

Malinowski, Bronislaw
[1922] *Argonauts of the western Pacific.* New York: 1961.
1967 *A diary in the strict sense of the term.* Trans. N. Guterman. New York.

Malthus, T. R.
1798 *An essay on the principle of population, as it affects the future improvement of society with remarks on the speculations of Mr. Godwin, M. Condorcet, and other writers.* London.
1806 *An essay on the principle of population: Or, a view of its past and present effects on human happiness with an inquiry into our prospects respecting the future removal or mitigation of the evils which it occasions.* 3rd ed., 2 vols. London.

Man, E. H.
1882 On the aboriginal inhabitants of the Andaman Islands. *J. Anth. Inst.* 12:69–175, 327–434.

Mansell, Michael
1981 Tasmania. In *Aboriginal landrights: A handbook,* ed. N. Peterson, 128–39. Canberra.

Manuel, Frank
1956a From equality to organicism. *J. Hist. Ideas* 17:54–69.
1956b *The new world of Henri Saint-Simon.* Cambridge, Mass.
1959 *The eighteenth century confronts the gods.* Cambridge, Mass.
1962 *The prophets of Paris.* Cambridge, Mass.
1965 *Shapes of philosophical history.* Stanford, Calif.

Marcus, G. E. & M. Fischer
1986 *Anthropology as cultural critique: An experimental moment in the human sciences.* Chicago.

Marcus, Stephen
1966 *The other Victorians: A study of sexuality and pornography in mid-nineteenth-century England.* New York.

Marett, R. R.
1900 Pre-animistic religion. In Marett 1914:1–28.
1908 A sociological view of religion. *Sociol. Rev.* 1:48–60.

1914 *The threshold of religion.* 2nd ed. London.
1920 *Psychology and folklore.* London.
1927 E. B. Tylor. *Dict. Natl. Biog. 1912–1921.*
1936 *Tylor.* New York.

Mark, Joan
1980 *Four anthropologists: An American science in its early years.* New York.

Mason, Philip
1962 *Prospero's magic: Some thoughts on class and race.* London.

Mayhew, H. & G. Cruickshank
1851 *1851: Or, the adventures of Mr. and Mrs. Sandboys and family who came up to London to enjoy themselves, and to see the great exhibition.* London.

Mazlish, Bruce
1975 *James and John Stuart Mill: Father and son in the nineteenth century.* New York.

Meacham, Standish
1963 The evangelical inheritance. *J. Brit. Stud.* 3:88–104.

Meek, Ronald
1954 The Scottish contribution to Marxist sociology. In *Democracy and the labour movement,* ed. J. Saville, 84–102. London.
1971 Smith, Turgot and the 'four stages' theory. *Hist. Pol. Econ.* 3:9–27.
——, trans. and ed.
1973 *Turgot on progress, sociology and economics.* Cambridge, England.
1976 *Social science and the ignoble savage.* Cambridge, England.

Meinecke, Friedrich
[1911] *Cosmopolitanism and the national state.* Trans. R. Kimber. Princeton: 1970.
[1959] *Historism: The rise of a new historical outlook.* Trans. J. E. Anderson. London: 1972.

Mellor, G. R.
1951 *British imperial trusteeship, 1783–1850.* London.

Metcalf, Thomas
1964 *The aftermath of revolt: India, 1857–1870.* Princeton.

Milhauser, Milton
1959 *Just before Darwin: Robert Chambers and* Vestiges. Middletown, Conn.

Mill, James
[1817] *History of British India.* 5th ed., 10 vols. London: 1858.
[1824] *Essay on government.* New York: 1937.
[1826] *Elements of political economy.* In *James Mill: Selected economic writings,* ed. D. Winch. Chicago: 1966.

Mill, J. S.
1835 Guizot's lectures on European civilization. *Lon. Rev.* 2:306–36.
[1838] *John Stuart Mill on Bentham and Coleridge.* Ed. F. R. Leavis. New York: 1962.
[1843] *A system of logic.* New York: 1850.
[1865] *Auguste Comte and positivism.* Ann Arbor, Mich.: 1961.
[1869] *The subjection of women.* Cambridge, Mass.: 1970.

1872 *A system of logic.* 8th ed. London.
[1873] *Autobiography.* New York: 1964

Miller, Harold
1966 *Race conflict in New Zealand, 1814–1865.* Auckland.

Milligan, J.
1863 Note on the shell-mounds of the Tasmanians. *Trans. Ethnol. Soc. Lond.* 2:128.

Mitterauer, M. & R. Sieder
1982 *The European family: Patriarchy to partnership from the middle ages to the present.* Trans. K. Osterveen & M. Horzinger. Chicago.

Montesquieu, Baron de
[1748] *The spirit of the laws.* Trans. T. Nugent. New York: 1966.

Morrell, J. B.
1971 Professors Robison and Playfair, and the Theophobia Gallica: natural philosophy, religion and politics in Edinburgh, 1789–1815. *Notes Recs. Roy. Soc. Lond.* 26:43–63.

Morrell, W. P.
1930 *British colonial policy in the age of Peel and Russell.* London.

Morris, James
1978 *Farewell the trumpets: An imperial retreat.* New York.

Moseley, H. N.
1876 On the inhabitants of the Admiralty Islands. *J. Anth. Inst.* 6:379–425.

Mueller, Iris
1956 *John Stuart Mill and French thought.* Urbana.

Mukherji, S. N.
1968 *Sir William Jones: A study in eighteenth-century British attitudes to India.*Cambridge, England

Müller, F. M.
1847 On the relation of the Bengali to the Arian and aboriginal languages of India. *Rept. Brit. Assn. Adv. Sci.* 17:319–50.
1851 My first course of eight lectures in comparative philology. Müller papers, Bodleian Library, Oxford.
1854 The last results of the researches respecting the non-Iranian and non-Semitic languages of Asia or Europe, or the Turanian family of language. In Bunsen 1854:I, 267–521.
[1856] Comparative mythology. In *Chips from a German workshop,* II, 1–140. New York: 1876.
[1861] *Lectures on the science of language.* [first series] London: 1885.
[1864] *Lectures on the science of language.* [second series] London: 1885.
[1868] Bunsen. In *Chips from a German workshop,* III, 343–89. New York: 1876.
1885 The savage. *Nineteenth Cent.* 17:109–32.
1891a Presidential address to section H. *Rept. Brit. Assn. Adv. Sci.* 61:782–96.
1891b On the work of Major J. W. Powell, Director of the U. S. Ethnological Bureau. *Rept. Brit. Assn. Adv. Sci.* 61:798.
1892 *Anthropological religion.* London.

[1896] Translator's preface. *Critique of pure reason,* by I. Kant, xxvii–lxxx. New York: 1920.
1901 *My autobiography: A fragment.* New York.
1902 *Life and letters of the Rt. Hon. Friedrich Max Müller.* Ed. Georgina Müller. 2 vols. New York.

Müller, F. M., et al.
1856 *Oxford essays, contributed by members of the university.* Oxford.

Mulvaney, D. J.
1964 The Australian Aborigines, 1606–1929: Opinion and fieldwork. In *Historical Studies, Australia and New Zealand, Selected Articles,* ed. J. J. Eastwood & F. B. Smith, 31–56. Melbourne.
1970 The anthropologist as tribal elder. *Mankind* 7:205–17.

Mulvaney, D. J. & J. H. Calaby
1985 *'So much that is new': Baldwin Spencer, 1860–1929.* Melbourne.

Murphree, Idus
1961 The evolutionary anthropologists: The progress of mankind. The concepts of progress and culture in the thought of John Lubbock, Edward B. Tylor, and Lewis H. Morgan. *Proc. Amer. Phil. Soc.* 105:265–300.

Murphy, Robert
1971 *The dialectics of social life: Alarms and excursions in anthropological theory.* New York.
1976 A quarter century of American anthropology. In *Selected papers from the American Anthropologist 1946–1970,* ed. R. Murphy, 1–22. Washington, D.C.

Myres, J. L.
1929 The science of man in the service of the state. *J. Roy. Anth. Inst.* 59:19–52.

Naroll, Raoul
1970 Galton's problem. In Naroll & Cohen, eds., 1970:972–89.

Naroll, R. & R. Cohen, eds.
1970 *A handbook of method in cultural anthropology.* New York.

Neale, R. S.
1972 *Class and ideology in the nineteenth century.* London.

Needham, Rodney
1967 Editor's introduction. In Wake 1889:v–xlvii.
1975 Charles Staniland Wake, 1835–1910: A biographical record. In *Studies in social anthropology,* ed. J. Beattie & R. G. Lienhardt, 354–87. Oxford.

Neill, Stephen
1964 *Christian missions.* Harmondsworth, Middlesex.

Newman, Gerald
1975 Anti-French propaganda and British liberal nationalism in the early nineteenth century: Suggestions toward a general interpretation. *Victorian Stud.* 18:385–418.

Niebuhr, B. G.
[1811–32] *The history of Rome.* Trans. J. C. Hare & C. Thirlwall. 3 vols. London: 1855.
1854 *Life and letters of Barthold George Niebuhr, with essays on his character and influence by the Chevalier Bunsen.* Trans. Miss Winkworth. New York.

Nisbet, R. A.
1943 The French revolution and the rise of sociology in France. *Amer. J. Sociol.* 49:156–64.
1944 De Bonald and the concept of the social group. *J. Hist. Ideas* 5:315–31.
1966 *The sociological tradition.* New York.
1980 *History of the idea of progress.* New York.

Nott, J. C. & G. Gliddon
1854 *Types of mankind: Or, ethnological researches, based upon the ancient monuments, paintings, sculptures, and crania of races.* Philadelphia.

Oberschall, A., ed.
1972 *The establishment of empirical sociology: Studies in continuity, discontinuity, and institutionalization,* New York.

Odom, Herbert
1967 Generalizations on race in nineteenth-century physical anthropology. *Isis* 58:4–18.

Official catalogue
1851 *Official descriptive and illustrated catalogue of the great exhibition [of] 1851.* 3 vols. London.

O'Neill, W. L.
1969 *The woman movement: Feminism in the United States and England.* London.

Opler, Morris
1964 Cause, process and dynamics in the evolutionism of E. B. Tylor. *Southwest. J. Anth.* 20:123–44.

Owen, Roger
1973 Imperial policy and theories of social change: Sir Alfred Lyall in India. In Asad 1973:223–44.

Packe, M. St. J.
1954 *The life of John Stuart Mill.* London.

Pagliaro, H. E., ed.
1973 *Racism in the eighteenth century.* Cleveland.

Paine, Thomas
[1791] *The rights of man.* Part II, in *The complete writings.* Ed. P. S. Foner. New York: 1945.

Parmentier, Richard
1976 An archaeology of E. B. Tylor. M.A. diss. University of Chicago.

Parsons, Talcott
1937 *The structure of social action: A study in social theory with special reference to a group of recent European writers.* New York.
1962 Introduction. In Spencer 1873b:v–x.

Pascal, Roy
1939 Herder and the Scottish historical school. *Pub. Eng. Goethe Soc.* 14:23–42.

Passmore, John
1970 *The perfectability of man.* London.

Pearson, Karl
1914–30 *The life, letters and labours of Francis Galton.* 4 vols. Cambridge, England.

Peckham, Morse
1959 Darwinism and Darwinisticism. *Victorian Stud.* 3:19–40.
1970 The romantic birth of anthropology. In Peckham, *Victorian revolutionaries: Speculations on some heroes of a culture crisis,* 175–234. New York.

Peel, J. D. Y.
1971 *Herbert Spencer: The evolution of a sociologist.* New York.

Penn, Julia
1972 *Linguistic relativity and innate ideas: The origins of the Sapir-Whorf hypothesis in German thought.* The Hague.

Penniman, T. K.
[1935] *A hundred years of anthropology.* London: 1952.

Peppard, Murray
1971 *Paths through the forest: A biography of the brothers Grimm.* New York.

Perkin, Harold
1969 *The origins of modern English society: 1780–1880.* London.

Perrin, R. G.
1976 Herbert Spencer's four theories of social evolution. *Am. J. Sociol.* 81:1339–59.

Pflaum, G. M.
1961 Geschichte des Wortes 'Zivilisation'. Inaug. diss. University of Munich.

Philips, David
1977 *Crime and authority in Victorian England: The black country, 1835–1860.* London.

Pickering, Charles
1851 *The races of man and their geographical distribution.* London.

Piggott, Stuart
1968 *The druids.* London.
1976 *Ruins in a landscape: Essays in antiquarianism.* Edinburgh.

Pilbeam, David
1979 Recent finds and interpretations of Miocene hominoids. *Annu. Rev. Anth.* 8:333–52.

Pim, Bedford
1866 *The Negro and Jamaica.* London.

Pinchbeck, Ivy
1930 *Women workers and the industrial revolution, 1750–1850.* New York: 1969.

Pitt Rivers, A. H. Lane Fox [all titles through 1880 were published under the name Lane Fox]
1867 Primitive warfare, I. In Pitt Rivers 1906:45–88.
1868 Primitive warfare, II. In Pitt Rivers 1906:89–143.
1872 Address to the Department of Anthropology. *Rept. Brit. Assn. Adv. Sci.* 42:157–74.
1874a Report on the anthropological notes and queries for the use of travellers. *Rept. Brit. Assn. Adv. Sci.* 44:214–18.
1874b Principles of classification. In Pitt Rivers 1906:1–19.
1874c *Catalogue of the anthropological collection lent by Colonel Lane Fox for exhibition in the Bethnal Green Branch of the South Kensington Museum.* London.
1875a On the evolution of culture. In Pitt Rivers 1906:20–44.
1875b Excavations in Cissbury Camp, Sussex; Being a report of the Exploration Committee of the Anthropological Institute for the year 1875. *J. Anth. Inst.* 5:357–90.
1875c On early modes of navigation. In Pitt Rivers 1906; 186–232.
1876 Anniversary address. *J. Anth. Inst.* 5:468–88.
1882 Anniversary address. *J. Anth. Inst.* 11:488–508.
1891 Typological museums, as exemplified by the Pitt Rivers Museum at Oxford, and his provincial museum at Farnham, Dorset. *J. Soc. Arts* 40:115–22.
1906 *The evolution of culture and other essays.* Ed. J. L. Myres. Oxford.
n.d. Arrangement and object of this collection [poster preserved in the Pitt Rivers Museum, Oxford]

Plomley, N. J. B.
1969 *An annotated bibliography of the Tasmanian aborigines.* Roy. Anth. Inst. Occasional Paper No. 28. London.

PMA [Popular Magazine of Anthropology]
1866 Anthropology a practical science. 1:6–9.

Polanyi, Karl
[1944] *The great transformation: The political and economic origins of our time.* Boston: 1962.

Poliakov, Leon
[1971] *The Aryan myth: A history of racist and nationalist ideas in Europe.* Trans. E. Howard. New York: 1974.

Pollock, F.
1893 Sir Henry Maine as jurist. *Edin. Rev.* 177:100–121.

Popkin, R. H.
1973 The philosophical basis of racism. In Pagliaro 1973:245–62.
1976 The pre-Adamite theory in the renaissance. In *Philosophy and humanism: Renaissance essays in honor of Paul Oskar Kristeller,* ed. E. P. Mahoney, 50–69. New York.

Pouillon, Jean
1980 Anthropological traditions: Their uses and misuses. In Diamond 1980b:35–52.

Poynter, J. R.
1969 *Society and pauperism: English ideas on poor relief. 1795–1834*. London.

Prichard, J. C.
1808 *De generis humani varietate*. Edinburgh.
[1813] *Researches into the physical history of man*. Chicago: 1973.
1819 *An analysis of the Egyptian mythology: To which is subjoined a critical examination of the remains of Egyptian chronology*. London.
1826 *Researches into the physical history of mankind*. 2nd. ed. London.
1831 *The eastern origin of the Celtic nations proved by a comparison of their dialects with the Sanskrit, Greek, Latin and Teutonic languages. Forming a supplement to* Researches into the physical history of mankind. Oxford.
1836–47 *Researches into the physical history of mankind*. 3rd. ed., 5 vols. London.
1838 Letter to Albert Gallatin, 10/26. Gallatin Collection, New-York Historical Society.
1839 On the extinction of human races. *Edin. New Phil. J.* 28:166–70.
1847 On the various methods of research which contribute to the advancement of ethnology, and of the relations of that science to other branches of knowledge. *Rept. Brit. Assn. Adv. Sci.* 17:230–53.
1848 On the relations of ethnology to other branches of knowledge. *J. Ethnol. Soc. Lond.* 1:301–29.
1849 Ethnology. In Herschel 1849:423–40.
1855 *The natural history of man*. 4th ed. London.

[Prichard, J. C., et al.]
1839 *Queries respecting the human race, to be addressed to travellers and others, drawn up by a committee of the British Association for the Advancement of Science, appointed in 1839*. London.

Quiggin, A. H.
1942 *Haddon the headhunter: A short sketch of the life of A. C. Haddon*. Cambridge, England.

Quinlan, M. J.
1941 *Victorian prelude: A history of English manners, 1700–1830*. New York.

Rabinow, Paul & W. M. Sullivan
1979 The interpretive turn: Emergence of an approach. In *Interpretive social science: A reader*, ed. Rabinow & Sullivan, 1–24. Berkeley.

Radcliffe-Brown, A. R.
1922 *The Andaman islanders*. Cambridge.
1923 The methods of ethnology and social anthropology. In Radcliffe-Brown 1958:3–31.
1929 The sociological theory of totemism. In Radcliffe-Brown 1952:117–32.
1930 Applied anthropology. *Rept. Aust. & N. Z. Assn. Adv. Sci.* 20:267–80.
1931a The present position of anthropological studies. In Radcliffe-Brown 1958:42–95.
1931b *The social organization of Australian tribes (Oceania Monographs* 1). Melbourne.
1935 Patrilineal and matrilineal succession. In Radcliffe-Brown 1952:32–48.
[1937] *A natural science of society*. Chicago: 1956.

[1952] *Structure and function in primitive society.* New York: 1965.
1958 *Method in social anthropology.* Chicago.

Radin, Paul
1933 *The method and theory of ethnology: An essay in criticism.* New York.

Rae, Isobel
1964 *Knox, the anatomist.* Edinburgh.

RAIN
1974–84 *RAIN: Royal Anthropological Institute News.* London. [continued as *Anthropology Today,* 1985–].

Rainger, Ronald
1978 Race, politics, and science: The Anthropological Society of London in the 1860s. *Victorian Stud.* 22:51–70.

Raven, Simon
1961 *The English gentleman: An essay in attitudes.* London.

Redfield, Robert
1950 Maine's *Ancient Law* in the light of primitive societies. In Redfield, *Human nature and the study of society,* 254–68. Chicago.

Rehbock, P. F.
1985 *The philosophical naturalists: Themes in early nineteenth-century British biology.* Madison, Wis.

Reichwein, Adolf
1925 *China and Europe: Intellectual and artistic contacts in the eighteenth century.* London.

Reill, P. H.
1975 *The German enlightenment and the rise of historicism.* Berkeley.

Reingold, Nathan
1976 Definitions and speculations: The professionalization of science in America in the nineteenth century. In *The pursuit of knowledge in the early American republic,* ed. A. Oleson & S. Brown, 33–69. Baltimore.

Reining, Conrad
1962 A lost period in applied anthropology. *Amer. Anth.* 64:593–600.

Reiss, Erna
1934 *Rights and duties of English women: A study in law and opinion.* Manchester, England.

Reiter, Rayna, ed.
1975 *Toward an anthropology of women.* New York.

Renan, Ernest
1855 *Histoire générale et système comparé des langues sémitiques.* Paris.

Resek, Carl
1860 *Lewis Henry Morgan: American scholar.* Chicago.

Retzius, Anders
1846 On the ethnographic distribution of round and elongated crania. *Rept. Brit. Assn. Adv. Sci.* 16:116.

Ricardo, David
[1817] *On the principles of political economy and taxation.* Ed. R. M. Hartwell. Harmondsworth, England: 1971.

Richards, Robert
n.d. *Darwin and the emergence of evolutionary theories of mind and behavior.*

Richter, Melvin
1964 *The politics of conscience: T. H. Green and his age.* Cambridge, Mass.
1968 Montesquieu. *Int. Encyclo. Soc. Sci.* 10:467–76.
1973 Despotism. *Dict. Hist. Ideas* 2:1–18.

Rickman, H. P.
1967 Geisteswissenschaften. *Encyclo. Phil.* 3:275–78.

Riggs, J. M.
[1894] John F. McLennan. *Dict. Natl. Biog.* 12:654–55. 1921.

Risley, Herbert
1911 The methods of ethnography. *J. Roy. Anth. Inst.* 41:8–19.

Ritterbush, Philip
1964 *Overtures to biology: The speculations of the eighteenth-century naturalists.* New Haven.

Rivière, Peter
1970 Editor's introduction. In McLennan 1865:vi–xlviii.
1978 Editor's introduction. In Lubbock 1870:xii–lxiv.

Roach, J. P. C.
1957 Liberalism and the Victorian intelligentsia. *Camb. Hist. J.* 13:58–81
1959 Victorian universities and the national intelligentsia. *Victorian Stud.* 3:132–50.

Roberts, David
1979 *Paternalism in early Victorian England.* New Brunswick, N.J.

Robertson, J. M.
1895 *Buckle and his critics: A study in sociology.* London.
1929 *A history of freethought in the nineteenth century.* 2 vols. London.

Robertson, William
[1777] *The history of America.* 3 vols. London: 1824.

Robson, Robert, ed.
1967 *Ideas and institutions of Victorian Britain: Essays in honour of George Kitson Clark.* London.

Rodden, Judith
1981 The development of the three age system: Archaeology's first paradigm. In *Towards a history of archaeology,* ed. G. Daniel, 51–68. London.

Rogers, J. A.
1972 Darwinism and social Darwinism. *J. Hist. Ideas* 33:265–80.

Rosenberg, Charles
1973 Sexuality, class and role in 19th-century America. *Amer. Quart.* 25:131–53.

Ross, E. B., ed.
1980 *Beyond the myths of culture: Essays in cultural materialism.* New York.

Rossi, Paolo
[1979] *The dark abyss of time: The history of the earth and the history of nations from Hooke to Vico.* Trans. L. G. Cochrane. Chicago: 1984.

Roth, H. Ling
1899 *The aborigines of Tasmania.* 2nd ed. Halifax, England.

Rothblatt, Sheldon
1968 *The revolution of the dons: Cambridge and society in Victorian England.* London.
1971 Review of Feaver 1969. *J. Mod. Hist.* 43:156–59.
1976 *Tradition and change in English liberal education.* London.

Rousseau, J.-J.
[1755] *Discourse on the origin and foundations of inequality among men.* In *The first and second discourses,* ed. R. D. Masters, 77–248. New York: 1964.

Rupp-Eisenreich, Britta, ed.
1984 *Histoires de l'anthropologie (xvi*[e]–xixe *siècles).* Paris.

Ruse, Michael
1979 *The Darwinian revolution.* Chicago.
1982 Social Darwinism: The two sources. *Riv. Fil.* 73:36–52.

Rutherford, James
1961 *Sir George Grey, K.C.B., 1812–1898: A study in colonial government.* London.

Ryan, M. T.
1981 Assimilating new worlds in the sixteenth and seventeenth centuries. *Comp. Stud. Soc. Hist.* 23:519–38.

Ryding, James
1975 Alternatives in nineteenth-century German ethnology: A case study in the sociology of science. *Sociologus* 25:1–28.

Sahlins, Marshall
1976a *Culture and practical reason.* Chicago.
1976b *The use and abuse of biology: An anthropological critique of sociobiology.* Ann Arbor, Mich.

Said, Edward
1978 *Orientalism.* New York.

St. Aubyn, G. R.
1958 *A Victorian eminence: Life and works of Henry Thomas Buckle.* London.

Savigny, K. F. von
[1849] *Private international law, and the retrospective operation of statutes: A treatise on the conflict of laws, and the limits of their operation in respect of place and time.* Trans. W. Guthrie. Edinburgh: 1880.

Schiller, Francis
1979 *Paul Broca: Founder of French anthropology, explorer of the brain.* Berkeley.

Schilling, B. N.
1950 *Conservative England and the case against Voltaire.* New York.

Schlegel, F. W.
[1808] On the language and wisdom of the Indians. In *The aesthetic and miscellaneous works of Frederick Schlegel.* Trans. E. J. Millington. London: 1860.

Schneider, D. M.
1976 Notes toward a theory of culture. In *Meaning in anthropology,* ed. K. H. Basso & H. A. Selby, 197–220. Albuquerque, N.M.
1984 *A critique of the study of kinship.* Ann Arbor, Mich.

Schneider, D. M. & K. Gough, eds.
1961 *Matrilineal kinship.* Berkeley.

Schochet, G. J.
1975 *Patriarchalism in political thought: The authoritarian family and political speculation and attitudes especially in seventeenth-century England.* New York.

Scholte, Bob
1972 Toward a reflexive and critical anthropology. In Hymes, ed., 1972:430–57.
1980 Anthropological traditions: Their definition. In Diamond 1980b: 53–88.
1983 Cultural anthropology and the paradigm-concept: A brief history of their recent convergence. In Graham et al. 1983:229–80.

Schrempp, Greg
1983 The re-education of Friedrich Max Müller: Intellectual appropriation and epistemological antinomy in mid-Victorian evolutionary thought. *Man* 18:90–110.

Schumpeter, J. A.
1954 *A history of economic analysis.* New York.

Schuyler, R. L.
1945 *The fall of the old colonial system: A study in British free trade, 1770–1870.* New York.

Schwab, Raymond
1950 *La renaissance orientale.* Paris.

Schweber, Sylvan
1980 Darwin and the political economists: divergence of character. *J. Hist. Biol.* 13:195–289.
1985 The wider British context in Darwin's theorizing. In Kohn 1985:35–70.

Searle, G. R.
1976 *Eugenics and politics in Britain, 1900–1914.* Leyden.

Semmel, Bernard
1960 *Imperialism and social reform: English social-imperial thought, 1895–1914.* London.
1962 *The Governor Eyre controversy.* London.
1970 *The rise of free trade imperialism: Classical political economy and the empire of free trade and imperialism, 1750–1850.* Cambridge, England.
1973 *The Methodist revolution.* New York.

Service, E. R.
1985 *A century of controversy: Ethnological issues from 1860 to 1960.* Orlando, Fla.

Shackleton, Robert
1961 *Montesquieu: A critical biography.* London.

Sher, Richard
1985 *Church and university in the Scottish enlightenment: The moderate literati of Edinburgh.* Princeton.

Shils, Edward
1970 Tradition, ecology and institution in the history of sociology. *Daedalus* 99:760–825.

Shorter, Edward
1975 *The making of the modern family.* New York.

Simar, Théophile
1922 *Etude critique sur la formation de la doctrine de races au xviii*[e] *siècle et son expansion au xix*[e] *siècle.* Brussels.

Sinclair, Andrew
1977 *The savage: A history of misunderstanding.* London.

Skinner, Andrew
1967 Natural history in the age of Adam Smith. *Pol. Stud.* 15:32–48.

Sloan, P. R.
1973 The idea of racial degeneracy in Buffon's *Histoire Naturelle.* In Pagliaro 1973: 279–92.

Slotkin, J. S., ed.
1965 *Readings in early anthropology.* Chicago.

Small, Albion
1924 *Origins of sociology.* Chicago.

Smiles, Samuel
[1859] *Self-help: With illustrations of conduct and perseverance.* London: 1958.

Smith, Adam
[1776] *An inquiry into the nature and causes of the wealth of nations.* New York: 1937.

Smith, F. B.
1967 The atheist mission, 1840–1900. In Robson 1967:205–35.
1977 Sexuality in Britain, 1800–1900: Some suggested revisions. In Vicinus 1977:182–98.

Smith, G. E.
1933 *The diffusion of culture.* London.

Smith, Kenneth
1951 *The Malthusian controversy.* London.

Smith, W. R.
1885 *Kinship and marriage in early Arabia.* London.
[1889] *The religion of the Semites: The fundamental institutions.* New York: 1956.

Smithells, A.
1927 Sir John Lubbock. *Dict. Natl. Biog. 1912–21.*

Smith-Rosenberg, C.
1974 Puberty to menopause: The cycle of femininity in nineteenth-century America. In Hartman & Banner, eds., 1974:23–37.

Smith-Rosenberg, C. & C. Rosenberg
1973 The female animal: Medical and biological views of woman and her role in nineteenth-century America *J. Amer. Hist.* 60:332–56.

Snyder, E. D.
1923 *The Celtic revival in English literature, 1760–1800.* Cambridge, Mass.

Soloway, R. A.
1969 *Prelates and people: Ecclesiastical social thought in England, 1783–1852.* London.

Spencer, Herbert
[1851] *Social statics; Or, the conditions essential to human happiness specified and the first of them developed.* New York: 1865.
1852a A theory of population deduced from the general law of animal fertility. *Westm. Rev.* 57:468–501.
1852b The development hypothesis. In Spencer 1873c:377–83.
1854a Manners and fashion. In Spencer 1873c:61–115.
1854b The genesis of science. In Spencer 1873c:116–93.
1855 *The principles of psychology.* London.
1857 Progress: Its law and cause. In Spencer 1873c:1–60.
1860 The social organism. In Spencer 1873c:384–428.
[1861] *Education: Intellectual, moral, and physical.* New York: 1911.
[1870–72] *The principles of psychology.* 2nd. ed., 2 vols. London: 1890.
1871 Specialized administration. *Fort. Rev.* 10:627–54.
1873a Replies to criticisms. *Fort. Rev.* 14:581–95, 715–39.
[1873b] *The study of sociology.* Ann Arbor, Mich.: 1961.
1873c *Illustrations of universal progress: A series of discussions.* New York.
1873–81 *Descriptive sociology; Or, groups of sociological facts, classified and arranged.* 8 vols. London.
1874 *Descriptive sociology: Lowest races, Negrito races, and Malayo-Polynesian races.* London.
1876 The comparative psychology of man. *J. Anth. Inst.* 5:301–16.
[1876–96] *The principles of sociology.* 3 vols. New York: 1898–99.
1877 A rejoinder to Mr. McLennan. *Fort. Rev.* 21:895–902.
[1879] *The data of ethics.* New York, n.d.
1899 The filiation of ideas. In Duncan 1911:533–76.
1904 *An autobiography.* 2 vols. London.

Spencer, W. B. & F. Gillen
1899 *The native tribes of central Australia.* London.

Spuhler, J. N.
1985 Anthropology, evolution, and 'scientific creationism.' *Annu. Rev. Anth.* 14:103–33.

Stanton, William
1960 *The leopard's spots: Scientific attitudes toward race in America, 1815–59.* Chicago.
1975 *The great United States exploring expedition of 1838–1842.* Berkeley.

Stark, W.
1961a *Montesquieu: Pioneer of the sociology of knowledge.* Toronto.
1961b Herbert Spencer's three sociologies. *Am. Sociol. Rev.* 26:515–21.
1961c Natural and 'social selection.' In *Darwinism and the study of society: A centenary symposium,* ed. M. Banton, 49–61. London.

Starn, R.
1975 Meaning levels in the theme of historical decline. *Hist. & Theory* 14:131.

Stepan, Nancy
1982 *The idea of race in science: Great Britain, 1800–1960.* London.

Stephen, Leslie
1876 *The history of English thought in the eighteenth century.* 2 vols. New York.
1880 An attempted philosophy of history. *Fort. Rev.* 27:672–95.
[1893] Sir Henry James Sumner Maine. *Dict. Natl. Biog.* 12:787–90. Oxford: 1921.
1900 *The English utilitarians.* 3 vols. New York.

Stern, Bernhard
1930 Selections from the letters of Lorimer Fison and A. W. Howitt to Lewis Henry Morgan. *Amer. Anth.* 32:257–79, 419–53.

Stewart, Dugald
[1811] *Biographical memoirs of Adam Smith, William Robertson and Thomas Reid.* In *Collected works,* ed. Sir William Hamilton, vol. X. Edinburgh: 1877.
[1855] *Lectures on political economy.* 2 vols. New York: 1968.

Stewart, T. D.
1959 The effect of Darwin's theory of evolution on physical anthropology. In *Evolution and anthropology: A centennial appraisal,* ed. Betty Meggers, 11–25. Washington, D.C.

Stocking, G. W., Jr.
1963 Matthew Arnold, E. B. Tylor, and the uses of invention. In Stocking 1968a:69–90.
1965 On the limits of 'presentism' and 'historicism' in the historiography of the behavioral sciences. In Stocking 1968a:1–12.
1966 Franz Boas and the culture concept in historical perspective. In Stocking 1968a:195–233.
1968a *Race, culture and evolution: Essays in the history of anthropology.* New York.
1968b Tylor, Edward Burnett. *Int. Encyclo. Soc. Scis.* 10:170–77.
1969 The nineteenth-century concept of race. Unpublished ms.
1971a Animism in theory and practice: E. B. Tylor's unpublished 'Notes on spiritualism.' *Man* 6:88–104.
1971b What's in a name? The origins of the Royal Anthropological Institute: 1837–1871. *Man* 6:369–90.

1973a From chronology to ethnology: James Cowles Prichard and British anthropology, 1800–1850. In Prichard 1813: ix–cx.

1973b Notes on manuscript sources in British anthropology. In Stocking 1973– :1 (#1).

——, ed.

1973– *History of Anthropology Newsletter.* Chicago.

——, ed.

1974a *The Shaping of American Anthropology, 1883–1911: A Franz Boas Reader.* New York.

1974b The basic assumptions of Boasian anthropology. In Stocking 1974a:1–20.

1974c Some comments on history as a moral discipline: 'Transcending textbook chronicles and apologetics.' In Hymes 1974a:511–19.

1974d The Boas plan for the study of American Indian languages. In Hymes 1974a:454–84.

1974e Some problems in the understanding of nineteenth century cultural evolutionism. In *Readings in the History of Anthropology,* ed. R. Darnell, 407–25. New York.

1975 Scotland as the model of mankind: Lord Kames' philosophical view of civilization. In *Toward a science of man: Essays in the history of anthropology,* ed. T. Thoresen, 65–89. The Hague.

1976 Ideas and institutions in American anthropology: Thoughts toward a history of the interwar years. In *Selected Papers from the American Anthropologist, 1921–1945,* ed. G. W. Stocking, 1–53. Washington, D.C.

1978a Die Geschichtlichkeit der Wilden und die Geschichte der Ethnologie. *Geschichte und Gesellschaft: Zeitschrift für Historische Sozialwissenschaft* 4:520–35. Trans. W. Lepenies.

1978b Anthropology as *kulturkampf:* Science and politics in the career of Franz Boas. In *Anthropology and the Public,* ed. W. Goldschmidt, 33–50. Washington, D.C.

1979 *Anthropology at Chicago: Tradition, discipline, department.* Chicago.

1980 Two styles of missionary ethnography: Lorimer Fison and R. H. Codrington. Unpublished conference paper.

1981a Apes, grandfathers and Rubicons: Some thoughts on an enduring tension in anthropology. Unpublished paper.

1981b Books unwritten, turning points unmarked: Notes for an anti-history of anthropology. The Morris Fishbein Lecture. Unpublished.

1982a Anthropology in crisis? A view from between the generations. In Hoebel et al. 1982:407–19.

1982b Preface to reprint ed. of Stocking 1968a (Chicago).

——, ed.

1983a *Observers observed: Essays on ethnographic fieldwork. (Hist. of Anth.* 1). Madison, Wis.

1983b The ethnographer's magic: Fieldwork in British anthropology from Tylor to Malinowski. In Stocking 1983a:70–120.

1983c Afterword: A view from the center. *Ethnos* 47(1–2):172–86.

1983d The 'Genesis' of anthropology: The discipline's first paradigm. Unpublished paper.

——, ed.
1984a *Functionalism historicized: Essays on British social anthropology. (Hist. of Anth.* 2). Madison, Wis.
1984b Radcliffe-Brown and British social anthropology. In Stocking 1984a:131–91.
1984c Qu'est-ce qui est en jeu dans un nom? ("What's in a name?" II.): La "Société d'Ethnographie" et l'historiographie de l' "anthropologie" en France. In Rupp-Eisenreich 1984:421–31.
——,ed.
1984d Dr. Durkheim and Mr. Brown: 'Comparative Sociology' at Cambridge in 1910. In Stocking 1984a:106–30.
——,ed.
1985a *Objects and others: Essays on museums and material culture. (Hist. of Anth.* 3). Madison, Wis.
1985b Philanthropoids and vanishing cultures: Rockefeller funding and the end of the museum era in Anglo-American anthropology. In Stocking 1985a:112–45.
——, ed.
1986a *Malinowski, Rivers, Benedict and others: Essays on culture and personality. (Hist. of Anth.* 4). Madison, Wis.
1986b Anthropology and the science of the irrational: Bronislaw Malinowski's encounter with Freudian psychoanalysis. In Stocking 1986a:13–49.

Stokes, Eric
1959 *The English utilitarians and India.* Oxford.

Stone, Lawrence
1975 The rise of the nuclear family in early modern England: The patriarchal stage. In *The family in history,* ed. C. Rosenberg, 15–39. Philadelphia.

Storr, Vernon
1913 *The development of English theology in the nineteenth century: 1800–1860.* London.

Street, Brian
1975 *The savage in literature: Representations of 'primitive society' in English fiction, 1859–1920.* London.

Sumner, J. B.
[1816] *A treatise on the records of creation and on the moral attributes of the creator.* 3rd ed., 2 vols. London: 1825.

Swart, Koenraad
1964 *The sense of decadence in nineteenth-century France.* The Hague.

Swingewood, Alan
1970 Origins of sociology: The case of the Scottish Enlightenment. *Brit. J. Soc.* 21:164–80.

Symondson, Anthony, ed.
1970 *The Victorian crisis of faith.* London.

Tagliacozzo, G. & H. White, eds.
1969 *Giambattista Vico: An international symposium.* Baltimore.

Tallis, John
1852 *Tallis's history and description of the Crystal Palace, and the exhibition of the world's industry in 1851.* London.

Talmadge, John
1983 From chronicle to quest: The shaping of Darwin's "Voyage of the Beagle." *Victorian Stud.* 23:325–46.

Talmor, E., ed.
1980 *The rise and development of the idea of Europe. (Hist. Eur. Ideas* 1.)

Taylor, G. R.
1958 *The angel-makers: A study in the psychological origins of historical change, 1750–1850.* London.

Taylor, Helen
1872 Biographical notice. In Buckle 1872: I:ix-xlviii.

Taylor, Isaac
1890 *The origin of the Aryans.* London.

Taylor, Mark
1980 Naiveté in a father of anthropology: The negative critique and reappropriation of Tylor's 'rational ethnography' in social anthropology. Unpublished ms.

Taylor, W. Cooke
1841 *The natural history of society in the barbarous and civilized state: An essay towards discovering the origin and course of human improvement.* 2 vols. New York.

Teggart, F. J.
1925 *Theory of history.* New Haven.

Temperly, Howard
1972 *British anti-slavery, 1833–1870.* Columbia, S.C.

Thomas, Keith
1959 The double standard. *J. Hist. Ideas* 20:195–216.
1983 *Man and the natural world: A history of the modern sensibility.* New York.

Thomas, N. W., ed.
1907 *Anthropological essays presented to Edward Burnett Tylor in honour of his seventy-fifth birthday.* Oxford.

Thompson, E. P.
1963 *The making of the English working class.* New York.
1967 Time, work-discipline, and industrial capitalism. *Past & present* 38:56–97.
1974 Patrician society, plebian culture. *J. Soc. Hist.* 7:382–405.

Thompson, F. M. L.
1963 *English landed society in the nineteenth century.* London.

Thornton, Robert
1983 The elusive unity of Sir George Grey's library. *African Stud.* 42:79–89.

Tinker, Hugh
1974 *A new system of slavery: The export of Indian labour overseas, 1830–1920.* New York.

Tinland, Franck
1968 *L'homme sauvage: Homo ferus et homo sylvestris de l'animal à l'homme.* Paris.

Tobias, J.
1967 *Crime and industrial society in the nineteenth century.* New York.

Topinard, Paul
1885 *Eléments d'anthropologie générale.* Paris.

Travers, Robert
1968 *The Tasmanians.* Cassell, Australia.

Trigger, Bruce
1966 Sir Daniel Wilson: Canada's first anthropologist. *Anthropologica* 8:3–28.

Trompf, G. W.
1979 *The idea of historical recurrence in western thought from antiquity to the Reformation.* Berkeley.

Trudgill, Eric
1976 *Madonnas and Magdalenes: The origins and development of Victorian sexual attitudes.* New York.

Tupper, Charles
1898 India and Sir Henry Maine. *J. Soc. Arts.* 46:390–405.

Turgot, A. R. J.
[1750] A philosophical review of the successive advances of the human mind. In Meek 1973:41–59.
[1751] On universal history. In Meek 1973:61–118.

Turnbull, Clive
1948 *Black war.* Melbourne.

Turner, F. M.
1974 *Between science and religion: The reaction to scientific naturalism in late Victorian England.* New Haven.

Turner, S. P.
1985 *The search for a methodology of social science: Durkheim, Weber, and the nineteenth-century problem of cause, probability, and action.* Dordrecht.

Tuveson, E. L.
1949 *Millenium and utopia: A study in the background of the idea of progress.* New York.

Tylor, E. B.
1861 *Anahuac: Or Mexico and the Mexicans, ancient and modern.* London.
1863 Wild men and beast-children. *Anth. Rev.* 1:21–32.
1864 Pott on myths of the origin of man and language. *Anth. Rev.* 2:24–30.
[1865] *Researches into the early history of mankind and the development of civilization.* 2nd. ed. London: 1870.
1866a The science of language. *Quart. Rev.* 119:394–435.
1866b The religion of savages. *Fort. Rev.* 6:71–86.
1867 On traces of the early mental condition of man. *Proc. Roy. Inst.* 5:83–93.
1868 Remarks on language and mythology as departments of biological science. *Rept. Brit. Assn. Adv. Sci.* 38:120–21.
1869 Review of Lubbock 1865. *Nature* 1:103.

[1871a] *Primitive culture: Researches into the development of mythology, philosophy, religion, language, art, and custom.* 2 vols. London: 1873.
1871b Maine's Village Communities. *Quart. Rev.* 131:176–89.
1873a Review of H. Spencer's *Descriptive Sociology. Nature* 8:544–47.
1873b Primitive society. *Contemp. Rev.* 21:701–718; 22:53–72.
1873c On the relation of morality to religion in the early stages of civilization. *Rept. Brit. Assn. Adv. Sci.* 43:148–50.
1875 Anthropology. *Encyclo. Brit.*:II, 107–123.
1876a Review of Wilson's *Prehistoric Man. Nature* 14:65–66.
1876b Review of von Hellwald's *Culturgeschichte. Acad.* 9:198–99.
1877a Review of Spencer 1876. *Mind* 2:141–56.
1877b Reply to Spencer 1877. *Mind* 2:419–23.
1878 Review of L. H. Morgan, *Ancient Society. Acad.* 14:67–68.
1879 The history of games. *Fort. Rev.* 25:735–47.
1880 Anniversary address. *J. Anth. Inst.* 9:443–99.
1881a *Anthropology: An introduction to the study of man and civilization.* London.
1881b Notice on the Asian relations of Polynesian culture. *J. Anth. Inst.* 11:401–4.
1881c Review of L. Fison & A. Howitt, *Kamilaroi and Kurnai. Acad.* 19:264–66.
1881d Obituary of J. F. M'Lennan. *Acad.* 20:9–10.
1883 Two lectures on anthropology. *Nature* 28:8–11, 55–59.
1885a Review of McLennan 1885. *Acad.* 28:67–68.
1885b How the problems of American anthropology look to the English anthropologist. *Trans. Anth. Soc. Wash.* 3:81–94.
1888 On a method of investigating the development of institutions, applied to laws of marriage and descent. *J. Anth. Inst.* 18:245–72.
1892 On the limits of savage religion. *J. Anth. Inst.* 21:283–301.
1893 On the Tasmanians as representatives of palaeolithic man. *J. Anth. Inst.* 23:141–52.
1895 On the occurrence of ground stone implements of Australian type in Tasmania. *J. Anth. Inst.* 24:335–40.
1896a On American lot-games, as evidence of Asiatic intercourse before the time of Columbus. *Int. Archiv für Ethnog.* 9:55–67.
1896b The matriarchal family system. *Nineteenth Century* 40:81–96.
1898 The survival of palaeolithic conditions in Tasmania and Australia. *J. Anth. Inst.* 28:199.
1899 Preface to Roth 1899.
1900 On stone implements from Tasmania. *J. Anth. Inst.* 30:257–62.

Urry, James
1972 *Notes and Queries in Anthropology* and the development of field methods in British anthropology, 1870–1920. *Proc. Roy. Anth. Inst.* 45–57.
1984 Englishmen, Celts, and Iberians: The Ethnographic Survey of the United Kingdom, 1892–1899. In Stocking 1984a:106–30.

Van Gennep, Arnold
1914 La méthode ethnographique en France au xviiie siècle. In Van Gennep, *Religions, moeurs et légendes: Essais d'ethnographie et de linguistique,* 93–215. 5th series. Paris.

Van Keuren, D. K.

1982 Human science in Victorian Britain: Anthropology in institutional and disciplinary formation, 1863–1908. Ph.D. diss. University of Pennsylvania.

1984 Museums and ideology: Augustus Pitt-Rivers, anthropological museums and social change in late Victorian Britain. *Victorian Stud.* 28:171–89.

Veitch, John

1877 Memoir of Dugald Stewart. In *Collected works of Dugald Stewart,* ed. Sir William Hamilton, vol. X. Edinburgh.

Vicinus, Martha, ed.

1972 *Suffer and be still: Women in the Victorian age.* Bloomington, Ind.

1977 *A widening sphere: Changing roles of Victorian women.* Bloomington, Ind.

Vinogradoff, P.

1904 *The teaching of Sir Henry Maine.* London.

Voget, Fred

1975 *A history of ethnology.* New York.

Vorzimmer, P. J.

1970 *Charles Darwin: The years of controversy. The* Origin of Species *and its critics, 1859–1882.* Philadelphia.

Vyverberg, Henry

1958 *Historical pessimism in the French enlightenment.* Cambridge, Mass.

Wagner, A. R.

1960 *English genealogy.* Oxford.

Wake, C. S.

1863 The relations of man to the inferior forms of life. *Anth. Rev.* 1:365–73.

1868 *Chapters on man, with the outlines of a science of comparative psychology.* London.

1878 *The evolution of morality: Being a history of the development of moral culture.* 2 vols. London.

1882 The Papuans and the Polynesians. *J. Anth. Inst.* 12:197–222.

1888 *Serpent worship and other essays, with a chapter on totemism.* London.

[1889] *The development of marriage and kinship.* Ed. Rodney Needham. Chicago: 1967.

Walker, M. H.

1971 *Come wind, come weather: A biography of Alfred Howitt.* Melbourne.

Walkowitz, J. R.

1980 *Prostitution and Victorian society: Women, class and the state.* Cambridge, England.

Wallace, A. R.

[1853] *A narrative of travels on the Amazon and Rio Negro, with an account of the native tribes.* London: 1889.

1864a On the varieties of man in the Malay archipelago. *Trans. Ethnol. Soc. London* 3:197–215.

1864b The origin of human races and the antiquity of man deduced from the theory of 'natural selection.' *J. Anth. Soc. London* 2:clvii–clxxxvii.

[1869] *The Malay archipelago: The land of the Orang-utan and the bird of paradise.* New York: 1962.
1870 The early history of mankind. *Nature* 2:350–51.
1879 *Australasia.* London.
1905 *My life: A record of events and opinions.* 2 vols. New York.

Walzel, Oskar
[1932] *German romanticism.* Trans. A. E. Lusskey. New York: 1966.

Ward, W. R.
1965 *Victorian Oxford.* London.

Wards, Ian
1968 *The shadow of the land: A study of British policy and racial conflict in New Zealand, 1832–1852.* Wellington.

Warren, Howard
1921 *A history of the associationist psychology.* New York.

Warren, Max
1967 *Social history and Christian missions.* London.

Watts, Theodore
1888 Dr. R. G. Latham. *Athenaeum* #3151 (3/17):340–41.

Weber, Gay
1974 Science and society in nineteenth century anthropology. *Hist. Sci.* 12:260–83.

Webster, Paula
1975 Matriarchy: A vision of power. In Reiter 1975:141–56.

Weeks, Jeffrey
1981 *Sex, politics and society: The regulation of sexuality since 1800.* London.

Weinstein, F. & G. Platt
1969 *The wish to be free: Society, psyche, and value change.* Berkeley.

Westermarck, Edward
1891 *The history of human marriage.* London.

Whately, Richard
1832 *Introductory lectures on political economy.* 2nd ed. London.

Whewell, William
1847 *The philosophy of the inductive sciences, founded on their history.* 2 vols. London.
[1849] *Induction with especial reference to Mr. J. Stuart Mill's system of logic.* In *William Whewell's theory of scientific method,* ed. R. Butts. Pittsburgh: 1968.
1852 The general bearing of the Great Exhibition on the progress of art and science. In *Lectures on the results of the Great Exhibition of 1851 delivered before the Society of Arts, Manufactures, and Commerce,* 3–34. London.
1857 *History of the inductive sciences.* 2 vols. New York: 1863.

White, Hayden
1972 The forms of wildness: Archaeology of an idea. In *The wild man within: An image in western thought since the Renaissance,* ed. E. Dudley & M. Novak, 3–38. Pittsburgh.

White, Leslie
1945 History, evolutionism, and functionalism: Three types of interpretation of culture. *Southwest. J. Anth.* 1:221–47.
1948 Lewis H. Morgan: Pioneer in the theory of social evolution. In *Introduction to the history of sociology,* ed. H. E. Barnes, 138–54. Chicago.
1949 Ethnological theory. In *Philosophy for the future: The quest of modern materialism,* ed. R. W. Sellars, et al. New York.
1960 Foreword. In Tylor 1881a [abridged reprint]. Ann Arbor, Mich.
1966 *The social organization of ethnological theory. Rice Univ. Stud.* 52 (#4).

Whitley, Richard
1976 Umbrella and polytheistic scientific disciplines and their elites. *Soc. Stud. Sci.* 6:471–97.

Whitney, Lois
1934 *Primitivism and the idea of progress.* Baltimore.

Wigley, John
1980 *The rise and fall of the Victorian Sunday.* Manchester.

Wilberforce, William
[1797] *A practical view of the prevailing religious system of professed Christians in the higher and middle classes contrasted with real Christianity.* New York: 1835.

Willey, Basil
1940 *The eighteenth century background: Studies in the idea of nature in the thought of the period.* London.

Williams, Elizabeth
1983 The science of man: Anthropological thought and institutions in nineteenth-century France. Ph.D. diss. Indiana University.
1985 Anthropological institutions in nineteenth-century France. *Isis* 76:331–48.

Williams, Raymond
1958 *Culture and society.* New York.
1976 *Keywords: A vocabulary of culture and society.* New York.

Williams, Thomas
[1840–53] *The journal of Thomas Williams, missionary in Fiji, 1840–1853.* Ed. G. C. Henderson. Sydney: 1931.

Williams, Thomas & James Calvert
1859 *Fiji and the Fijians.* Ed. G. S. Rowe. New York.

Williams-Ellis, Amabel
1966 *Darwin's moon: A biography of Alfred Russel Wallace.* London.

Wilson, A. L.
1964 *A mythical image: The ideal of India in German romanticism.* Durham, N.C.

Wilson, B. R., ed.
1970 *Rationality. Oxford.*

Wilson, Daniel
1851 *The archaeology and prehistoric annals of Scotland.* Edinburgh.
1862 *Prehistoric man: Researches into the origin of civilisation in the old and the new world.* 2 vols. London.

Wilson, H. B., ed.
[1860] *Essays and reviews.* London: 1865.

Wolf, H. R.
1965 British fathers and sons, 1773–1913: From filial submissiveness to creativity. *Psychoan. Rev.* 52 (#2):53–70.

Wolfram, Sybil
1955 The English concept of affinity. Unpublished manuscript.

Wood, H. G.
1955 *Belief and unbelief since 1850.* Cambridge, England.

Woodward, E. L.
1938 *The age of reform: 1815–1870.* Oxford.

Worsaae, J. J.
1849 *The primeval antiquities of Denmark.* Trans. W. Thoms. London.

Worsley, Peter
1970 The end of anthropology? *Trans. 6th World Cong. Sociol.* 3:121–29.

Yeo, Eileen & E. P. Thompson
1971 *The unknown Mayhew.* New York.

Young, G. M.
[1936] *Victorian England: Portrait of an age.* Garden City, N.Y.: 1954.

Young, R. M.
1970a *Mind, brain, and adaptation in the nineteenth century: Cerebral localization and its biological context from Gall to Ferrier.* Oxford.
1970b The impact of Darwin on conventional thought. In Symondson 1970:13–35.
1985a *Darwin's metaphor: Nature's place in Victorian culture.* Cambridge, England.
1985b Darwinism *is* social. In Kohn 1985:609–39.

Zengotita, Thomas de
1984 The functional reduction of kinship in the social thought of John Locke. In Stocking 1984a:10–30.

Zirkle, Conway
1946 The early history of the idea of the inheritance of acquired characters and of pangenesis. *Trans. Amer. Phil. Soc.* 35:91–151.

Index

Abbéville, 72, 74
Aberdeen, 117, 164
Aborigines, Parliamentary Select Committee on, 241–42, 244
Aborigines Protection Society, 240, 242–44, 269, 272
Acclimatization, 65, 66
Acquired characteristics, inheritance of, 63–64, 106, 134, 140, 141, 142, 222, 228, 235–36
Acton, Lord, 21
Adam, 12, 51, 189
Africa (Africans), 51, 63, 64, 80, 87, 92, 244
African Civilization Society, 244
Agrarian Revolution, 209
Albert, Prince, 1, 2, 3
Algiers, 164
Amazon River, 97, 99
Amazons, 205
American Indians, 12–13, 24, 26, 47, 49, 58, 83, 95, 97, 153, 268
Andamans, 234, 258, 259, 322
Anglo-Saxons, 54, 62–64, 81, 98, 99, 120, 235
Animism, 15, 159, 192–95, 196, 197, 237, 282, 297, 319
Annan, Noel, 117
Anthropogenesis, 146–50, 178
Anthropological Institute of Great Britain and Ireland, 263, 265, 298, 300, 316, 318
  anthropology of, 257–62, 270, 271, 272
  as compromise formation, 269–70
  decline of, 268, 272
  founding of, 256–57, 269
  Journal, 258–62, 266, 267, 268, 272, 325
  revival of, 261
Anthropological Society of London, 159
  anti-Darwinism of, 249
  contrasted with Ethnological Society, 249–54, 270
  founding of, 247–48
  growth of, 248
  and physical anthropology, 249–50, 255, 281
  publications of, 248, 250, 255
  struggle with Ethnological Society, 254–57
Anthropological Society of Oxford, 264
Anthropology; *see also* Biological evolution(ism); Cultural anthropology; Ethnography; Ethnology; Evolution(ism); Physical anthropology; Social anthropology; Sociocultural evolution(ism)
  Anglo-American, 47, 76, 185, 254, 270–71, 286, 289, 317
  anthropologists' attitudes toward native peoples, 272–73, 287, 289, 326
  applied, 242, 248
  armchair, 79, 108–109, 258, 267
  in classical period (1920–1960), 289, 290; in Great Britain, 249 (*see also* Social anthropology); in the United States, 287–88 (*see also* Cultural anthropology)

Anthropology (*cont.*)
colonial situation of, 287, 289
crisis of, 290
cynosure or focus of, 76–77, 180, 185, 248, 249, 268, 269, 290, 313, 323
and Darwinism, 146, 182, 248, 262, 290, 327
dehistoricization of, 289, 293, 321, 324
as a discipline, 268–69, 324, 327–29
early twentieth-century (1900–1925), 326; in Great Britain, 288, 289, 319, 320–22; in the United States, 287, 289
in the Enlightenment, 17–19, 50
ethnographicization of, 289
and ethnology, 240, 248
in France, 268, 270, 271, 289, 313; *see also* Physical anthropology; Structuralism
in Germany, 290; *see also* Physical anthropology
and government, 248, 266
historical dimension in, 76, 289
history of, ix, 9, 14, 44, 179, 239, 258, 286, 314; *see also* History; Sociocultural evolution(ism)
ideological function of, 273, 283, 285; *see also* Sociocultural evolution(ism)
institutionalization of, 239–40, 243, 247, 254, 262–69, 270, 273, 290, 300
intellectualist school, 196, 293, 294, 301
and the irrational, 313
later nineteenth-century; in Great Britain, 257–62, 263–69, 270–73, 287, 315–20; in the United States, 286, 318–19
limits of, 285
in museums, 263–65, 273
as natural science, 183, 247, 254, 255, 270, 271, 272, 273, 300, 323, 328–29
object orientation in, 263, 273
paradigms in, xiii–xiv, 44, 101, 258, 268, 286, 291; *see also* Bible; Developmentalism; Ethnology; Sociocultural evolution(ism)
philology as basis of, 58, 311
and politics, 252, 271, 272–73
professionalization of, 240, 262–63, 266, 267
radicalization of, 291
recent: in Great Britain, 290, 294; in the United States, 290, 327–28
rehistoricization of, 296
revolution in, 292, 323
as science of savages, 47, 185, 239, 290, 312
social demand for, 266–67
as social theory, 273
as term, 239, 248, 249, 254–55, 256, 258, 270
transitions in, 286, 289, 292, 314, 319, 320, 323, 324, 325, 327
unity of, 239
and universities, 248, 262–65, 267, 328
Anthropometric Laboratory, 262
Anthropometry, 26, 94, 262
Antiquarianism, 53–56, 62, 66, 71, 79, 113, 250, 263, 265, 273
Antiquity of man, 18, 44, 50, 69–74, 76–77, 126, 136, 140, 147–48, 152, 153, 167, 168–69, 173, 178, 179, 180, 182, 183, 258, 326, 328
Anti-slavery activities/sentiments, 234, 237, 241, 247, 252
Apes, 18, 42, 44, 51, 70, 76, 128, 146, 147, 148, 149, 154, 172, 176, 179, 225, 234, 253, 326, 328
Aquinas, Thomas, 258
Arabs, 92, 253, 260
Archaeologia, 54
Archaeological Institute, 71
Archeology, 37, 52, 59, 69, 74, 163, 245, 246, 292, 328; *see also* Brixham Cave; Bronze Age; Iron Age; Paleolithic Age/man; Prehistory; Stone Age
in Anthropological Institute, 261, 262, 270
and ethnology, 173
and geology, 172
in Great Britain, 70–73, 262
local, 263
neolithic/paleolithic, 152
revolution in, 69–74, 76, 126, 136, 147, 158
three age system, 72–73, 152
Argyll, Duke of, 149, 154, 160, 163–64, 172
Arnold, Thomas, 37, 62
Arthur, George, 276–77
Aru Islanders, 99, 104
Arunta, 260, 297
Aryans, 24, 58–60, 68, 75, 126, 127, 152, 167, 308, 320
Ashbee, H. S., 253
Asia; *see also* Orient
cradle of the race, 72, 75
despotism of, 13, 14, 19, 21–22, 32
as home of Aryans, 58, 75
precocious maturity of, 15
and Polynesian culture, 258
stationary civilization of, 3, 5, 32, 111, 125
Asiatick Society of Bengal, 22
Assimilationism, 80, 85
Associationism, 13, 20, 31, 37, 39, 41, 114, 134, 141, 142, 171, 174, 175, 185, 224, 226, 309, 322
Atheism, 43, 49, 155
Athenaeum, 251
Aufrecht, S. T., 169

Austin, John, 118, 137
Australia, 4, 82, 85, 91, 240, 317
Australians, 47, 58, 82–84, 153, 162, 175, 202, 207, 221, 234, 235, 258–59, 275, 280, 281, 283, 317, 319, 320, 322
Avebury, Lord: *see* Lubbock, John
Avoidance, 317
Aztecs, 162, 235

Babel, Tower of, 12, 50, 57, 91
Babylon, 71
Bachofen, Johann, 168, 205, 317
Bacon, Francis, 114
Bagehot, Walter, 145, 235
Bain, Alexander, 142
Balfour, Henry, 265
Balkans, 124
Bantu, 241
Barbarism, 3, 10, 14, 15, 32, 63, 79, 95, 96, 100, 124, 125, 126, 154, 156, 162, 184, 195, 308, 318
Bastian, Adolph, 290–91
Bateman, Thomas, 66
Bates, Henry, 97
Baudin, Nicolas, 275
Beagle, H.M.S., 82, 97, 107
Beddoe, John, 66–67, 246, 249, 256, 262
Bentham, Jeremy, 31, 37, 38, 39, 118, 119–20, 121, 122, 125, 129, 130, 137, 138, 212, 232, 251
Berbers, 92
Bethnal Green Museum, 264
Bible, 82, 112; *see also* Adam; Christianity; Flood; God; Ham; Noah
  as anthropological paradigm, 11–12, 22, 26, 44, 50, 51, 69, 73, 74–76, 83, 102, 122–23, 154, 161, 182, 248, 259, 270, 272, 325, 327
  chronology of, 12–13, 18, 50, 52, 53, 59, 71, 75, 76, 140
  and comparative philology, 24
  defense of, 42, 49, 189
  and early nineteenth-century science, 41–45
  the Fall, 12, 16, 91
  higher criticism of, 57, 70, 189
  historicity of, 12, 37–38, 50, 57, 70, 91, 122–23, 125, 190, 199
Bichat, M.-F.-X., 25, 28
Biological anthropology, 328; *see also* Physical anthropology
Biological determinism, 63–64, 235–36; *see also* Hereditarianism
  critique of, 286, 292, 327
Biological evolution(ism); *see also* Darwinian revolution; Darwinism
  emergence of, 94, 96, 101, 132, 172, 273
  in Enlightenment, 18
  of man, 68, 76, 80, 146–50, 178, 185, 327; *see also* Ape; Sociocultural evolution(ism)
  of nervous system, 134, 221, 225, 228
  in Prichard, 50
  relation to sociocultural evolutionism, 18, 29, 42, 150, 233, 326
  scholarship on, 42, 294
  Spencer and, 129, 135, 221, 224–28
  as synthesis of monogenism and polygenism, 102, 269
  tree image of, 173, 181, 183
  Whewell on, 6
Biology, 30, 133, 136, 228, 249, 262, 263, 267, 270, 312, 326
Birmingham, 92, 254
Blacks, 20, 25, 51, 64, 230, 247, 251
Blackstone, William, 198
Bleek, Wilhelm, 87
Bligh, William, 275
Blumenbach, Johann, 26, 50
Boas, Franz, xvi, 181–82, 271, 287, 288, 290–91, 298, 299, 300, 310, 318
Boasian anthropology, 289, 292, 297, 302, 303, 310, 313, 324, 326
Boers, 86, 241
Bonwick, James, 282–83
Bopp, Franz, 23, 57
Borneo, 98
Bory de Saint-Vincent, J. P., 27, 66
Boswell, James, 11
Boulanger, N.-A., 15
Bourne, Henry, 54
Bournouf, J. L., 57
Brain, human, 26, 29, 39, 43, 70, 134, 141, 142, 147, 148, 149, 221, 222, 226, 228, 302, 314, 326
Brand, Joseph, 54, 56, 163, 210
Brazilian Indians, 97–98
Bright, John, 252
Brinton, Crane, 298
British Archaeological Association, 71, 72
British Association for the Advancement of Science, 52, 57, 65, 69, 74, 79, 146, 147, 154, 243, 261, 263, 266, 267, 271, 300, 310
  sectional structure of, 245, 246, 254–56
British Empire, 81, 240, 296, 299; *see also* Colonialism; Imperialism
British Museum, 263, 264
Britons, ancient, 208
Brixham Cave, 73, 75, 111, 112, 140, 147, 172, 187
Broca, Paul, 67, 247, 268, 270, 281
Bronte, Charlotte, 70
Bronze Age, 72–73, 152, 153
Brooke, Charles, 63
Buckle, H. T., 112–17, 129, 137, 138, 140, 158, 223
Buffon, Comte de, 18

Bunsen, Christian, 57–58, 59, 75, 87, 189, 310
Bureau of Ethnology, U.S., 268, 286
Burke, Edmund, 30, 121
Burke, Luke, 64
Burke, William, 64
Burrow, John, xiii, 111, 170, 225, 232, 294–95
Burton, Richard, 253
Bushmen, 47, 94, 328
Busk, George, 256, 262, 270
Buxton, Thomas, 241, 242, 244

Cabanis, Pierre, 25–26
Calcutta, 124
Caledonians, 73
Cambridge Antiquarian Society, 265
Cambridge University, 1, 6, 37, 49, 62, 92, 118, 121, 126, 164, 262, 265, 267, 298, 300
Camper, Peter, 26
Canada, 180–81, 240, 287, 300
Cannibalism, 89, 90, 153, 252, 255, 256, 257, 272
Cape Colony, 64, 85, 240, 272
Cape Town, 82
Capitalism, 36, 187, 210
Catholicism, 54–55, 72, 81, 87, 113, 164, 189, 253
Celebes, 99
Celts, 53, 54, 55, 62–63, 65, 73, 121, 210, 213, 229, 234, 235
Chadwick, Edwin, 215
Chain of Being, 11, 16, 18, 43
Chambers, Robert, 41–45, 70, 97
Chartism, 2, 129, 214
Chinese, 2, 17, 24, 58, 162, 202, 235
Christianity; *see also* Bible; Religion
  apologetic writers, 12
  attack on, 19, 57, 69, 70, 190–91, 194–95, 207
  and civilization, 11, 30, 33, 35–36, 37, 84, 87, 92, 241, 242, 277–79
  conversion to, 88–89, 91, 234, 237, 277–79
  defense of, 189
  "muscular," 200
  as mythology, 190, 195
  and organized anthropology, 271–72
  orientalism and, 25
  orthodoxy of, 27, 36, 42–44, 49, 92, 116, 151, 209
  and race, 106–107
  revival of, 10, 33–34, 44, 49, 86, 87–88, 89, 105, 188, 197
  savage capacity for, 86
  and unity of man, 17, 313–14
Christy, Henry, 5, 152, 157–58, 245, 247, 263, 264
Chronology, study of, 12, 50
Chukchee, 202
Church of England, 49, 189–90, 209
Civil War, American, 63, 247
Civilization(s); *see also* Barbarism; Culture; Developmentalism; Progress; Savage(s); Sociocultural evolution(ism)
  in Britain, 30–36, 115, 210, 215, 219
  and Christianity, 30, 33, 35–36, 37, 84, 87, 92, 241, 242, 277–79
  comparative study of, 291
  crisis of, 27–28, 37, 49
  and culture, 20, 25, 36, 37, 300, 310
  defined, 162, 300
  and delay of gratification, 207, 217, 222
  development of, 158–64, 172, 258
  and European culture, 10, 19, 29, 32, 33, 115
  fragility of, 95, 96, 233
  and French Revolution, 30, 42
  hierarchy of, 17, 19, 32, 162, 183, 262
  idea of, 1, 9, 10–11, 15, 29, 35–36, 239
  inequalities within, 219, 229–30, 233
  last step to, 149, 154, 160
  and liberalism, 230
  Maine on, 124, 207
  material/spiritual, 20, 125, 153, 310
  middle-class, 36, 228–33
  natural selection and, 95, 145
  origin of, 37, 41, 43, 45, 49, 53, 70, 76, 221
  and property, 124
  race and, 18, 25, 159, 303–304
  reaction against, 287, 326
  scientific study of, 29, 36–41, 45, 76, 103, 115–16, 161
  as self-improvement, 217, 231
  singularity/plurality of, 18, 122, 159, 302, 303–304
  Spencer on, 131–32
  stages of, 61, 72, 100, 131, 155, 219, 303
  stationary and progressive, 3, 5, 32, 111, 115, 125, 127
  and utilitarianism, 31, 37
  vices of, 17, 36, 98
  Western, 11, 21, 140
  and women's status, 207
Clapham sect, 241
Classes
  aristocracy, 33, 36, 81, 119–20, 129, 132, 210, 212, 216, 217, 231, 232
  conflict of, 187, 212, 213, 214
  distance between, 215, 231
  emergence of, 211–12, 215, 231, 234
  lower, 95, 200, 214
  middle, 33, 34, 36, 96, 117, 120, 129, 130, 132, 191, 198, 199, 200, 210, 212, 227, 228–33, 251; ambivalent con-

sciousness of, 230–32; ethic of, 35, 213, 214, 216
and progress of civilization, 217–19, 228–33
ruling, 210–11, 230
upper, 199, 200, 215
working, 1, 4, 96, 129, 212, 217, 232, 266
Classical philology, 21, 22, 23
Cobden, Richard, 116, 151
Codrington, Robert, 236–37, 317, 319
Cole, Henry, 1
Colebrook, H. T., 23
Coleridge, Samuel, 36, 38, 39, 40, 41
Collections, ethnographic, 5, 263, 264–65
Colonial administrators, 85–87, 259, 266, 272
Colonial Office, 81, 85, 86, 241, 244, 266
Colonial Secretary, 82, 85
Colonialism, 35, 63, 65, 80, 81, 233–37, 240–42, 271, 272, 273, 287, 289; *see also* British Empire; Imperialism
Colonization, 81, 234, 240, 241, 242, 243, 272
Colquhoun, Patrick, 119
Combe, George, 130
Combination Acts, 211
Comparative anatomy, 18, 23, 24, 26–27, 30, 49, 50, 52, 65, 69, 75, 102, 133, 174, 267, 269
Comparative jurisprudence, 122, 296
Comparative method, 6, 14, 15, 19, 28, 51, 72, 125, 127, 136, 152, 154–56, 160, 161, 162, 167–68, 169, 170, 174–75, 177, 180, 183, 184, 236, 325, 328
Comparative mythology, 59–61, 121, 158, 159
Comparative philology, 21, 23–24, 30, 32, 37, 50, 52, 56–62, 68, 73, 74, 75, 87, 97, 100, 102, 121, 122, 150, 157–58, 165, 167, 174, 183, 267, 296, 304
Comte, Auguste, 9, 15, 27–29, 39, 40, 41, 107, 111, 114, 133, 137, 165, 196, 269, 301, 325
Condillac, Etienne de, 16, 26, 31
Condoret, Marquis de, 15, 17, 25, 27, 34, 39, 116
Confederate States of America, 251
Conservatism, 122, 162, 193, 206, 231, 254, 322
Contagious Diseases Acts, 201
Contract, 123, 124, 125, 184, 198, 203, 206, 299
Cook, James, 262, 275
Copernicus, Nicholas, 305, 325
Corn Laws, 116, 120, 212
Couvade, 304
Craniology, 26, 65–66, 68, 100, 221, 249, 250, 262
Crawfurd, John, 100, 250–51, 252, 255
Creationism, 327
Crime, 21, 123, 221, 223, 229
Crimean War, 66, 86, 119–20, 121, 241
Croker, Thomas, 55
Cromer, Lord, 124
Cross-cultural comparison, 316–18
Crystal Palace, 1–6, 9, 45, 47, 53, 76, 94, 97, 103, 111, 114, 133, 137, 157, 214, 233, 239, 263, 275, 285
Cull, Richard, 246, 250
Cultural anthropology, xi, 289, 292, 301, 302, 304, 314, 324, 327, 328
Cultural contact, 84, 98, 100, 106, 321
Cultural determinism, 138, 142–43, 235, 287, 302, 309, 322, 326
Cultural idealism, 311, 314
Cultural materialism, 314–15
Cultural psychology, 287, 288
Cultural relativism, 18, 20, 25, 37, 93, 105, 187, 287, 302, 304, 326
Cultural universals, 291
Culture; *see also* Civilization; Evolution(ism) (mental)
anthropological idea of, 19, 80, 106, 138, 140, 287, 302–304, 310, 314, 324
Boasian anthropology and, 303, 313
and civilization, 20, 25, 36, 37, 300, 310
and color, 235, 326
as constitutive, 309–10, 311
elements, 161, 273, 287, 321
Enlightenment idea of, 19
evolution of, 160–64, 309, 311, 328; *see also* Sociocultural evolution(ism)
folk, 55
German idea of, 20, 36, 302, 303, 310; *see also* German thought
hierarchy of, 80, 163, 177, 185, 192, 224, 235, 302, 303, 309, 326
holistic study of, 288, 324
integration of, 104, 175, 273, 287, 289, 302
material, 108, 273, 287
origin of, 176–77, 223, 293
and personality, 104, 327
plurality of, 287, 288, 302, 309, 310, 311, 313–14, 321, 324
and progress of science, 309, 311
race and, 25, 138–39, 142–43, 162, 314
Radcliffe-Brown on, 288, 293, 301, 311, 322–23
and reform, 194
scientific study of, 161–62, 194, 195, 288, 293, 300, 301, 302, 311, 314, 322, 323, 328
social evolutionary conception of, 309–10, 314
stages of, 161, 194, 219, 293; *see also* Progress

Culture (*cont.*)
  Tylor on, 159, 161–62, 192, 194, 300, 302–304, 314, 323
  working-class, 213
Cuvier, Georges, 26, 43, 64, 65

Dahomey, King of, 2, 253
Damaras, 93, 94, 136
Damascus, 116
Darwin, Charles, 12, 61, 67, 97, 189, 222, 257, 291, 294
  and Chambers, 41
  and comparative method, 175
  on Fuegians, 105–107
  and Galton, 94
  and inheritance of acquired characteristics, 106, 150
  and Lubbock, 151, 152, 179
  and Malthus, 101
  and McLennan, 176, 177, 179, 202
  and Prichard, 50, 108
  as Social Darwinist, 145
  and Spencer, 129, 142, 163, 298
  on Tasmanians, 279, 281
  and Tylor, 164, 178, 179, 224, 306
  and Whewell, 6
Darwin, Emma, 257
Darwin, Erasmus, 42, 43, 92, 129
Darwinian debate, 146, 149, 154, 161, 164, 181, 187, 304
Darwinian method, 149–50
Darwinian revolution, 94, 111–12, 116, 128, 129, 138, 142, 145, 147, 150, 164, 167, 168, 172, 178, 179, 180, 182, 183, 224, 239, 240, 255, 269, 324, 325, 327
Darwinism, 26, 41, 69, 70, 72, 76, 96, 103, 137, 139, 145, 171, 172, 231–32, 248, 270, 271, 312, 328
Darwinisticism, 146
Dasent, George, 61, 157
Davis, J. B., 66–67, 100, 246
de Bonald, Louis, 27
de Brosses, Charles, 15, 171, 196
D'Entrecasteux, Bruni, 275
de Maistre, Joseph, 27
de Pauw, Cornelius, 15
de Perthes, Boucher, 72, 74
Degenerationism, 12, 14, 15, 16, 17, 18, 22, 23–24, 26, 32–33, 44, 51, 58, 61, 71, 73, 80, 83, 87, 91, 106, 125, 154, 159–61, 173, 175, 185, 221, 228, 310, 313
Demeunier, J.-N., 15
Derby, 129, 130
Descartes, René, 114
Desmoulins, Antoine, 27
Developmentalism, 181, 264; *see also* Progress; Sociocultural evolution(ism)
  decline in early nineteenth century, 9, 48, 295
  eighteenth-century, 11, 111, 112, 171, 178, 210, 219–20
  in Greek thought, 10, 12
  naturalistic, 182; *see also* Naturalistic view of man
  nineteenth-century, 27, 111, 133, 150
  as paradigm, 12, 44, 183
  and revelation, 33
  McLennan and, 165–67
  and sociocultural evolutionism, 219–20
  Tylor and, 158–63, 194
Dickens, Charles, 278
Diffusionism, 15, 51, 55, 56, 72, 73, 74, 77, 152, 155, 156, 158–60, 166, 180, 181–82, 184, 250, 264, 287, 288, 291, 293, 300, 317, 321, 322
Disciplinary discourse, 314–15
  and cognitive autonomy, 315, 316, 317, 318, 323
  and theological assumption, 325
Disraeli, Benjamin, 1, 62
Divorce, 201, 202
Domestic servants, 201, 215, 230
Druids, 54, 208
Duelling, 215–16
Dugmore, H. H., 87
Duncan, David, 282
Dundee, 254
Durkheim, Emile, 288, 293, 298, 299, 300, 301, 311, 320, 321, 322
Dutch, 100
Dyaks, 47, 63

East India Company, 2, 57, 117, 120
Ecole d'Anthropologie, 268, 270
Economics, 13; *see also* Political economy
Eden, 73
Edinburgh, 31, 48, 49, 64, 73, 164, 169
Edwards, William, 27
Egyptians, 12, 50, 51, 58, 71, 73, 92, 115
Eimauk, 202
Eliot, George, 133, 134, 193
Elizabeth I, 114
Elphinstone, Mountstuart, 121
Empiricism, 61, 114, 141, 160, 161, 163, 174, 203, 226, 248, 304, 305–10, 323
Enclosure Acts, 213
Encyclopedia Britannica, 164–65, 297
Endogamy, 167, 296, 316
Engels, Friedrich, 1, 213, 291
Enlightenment, 9, 10–19, 21, 25, 50, 107, 112, 137, 156, 304, 313
Environmental determinism, 14, 18, 20, 26, 50, 64, 106, 113, 116, 125, 140, 142, 174, 235, 246, 250
Epistemology, 12, 25, 37, 80, 114, 134,

137–38, 157, 160, 203, 226–27, 271, 287, 305–10, 321, 324, 325, 328
Eskimos, 246
Essays and Reviews, 57, 189–90
Ethiopians, 12, 26
Ethnocentrism, 80, 87, 89, 104, 105, 153–54, 162, 175, 177, 202, 206, 224, 260, 262, 313, 314, 315, 326
Ethnography
Aborigines Protection Society and, 242
from classical sources, 79
classification of, 108, 136
by correspondence, 79, 87, 259, 317, 319
and ethnological theory, 102–109, 182, 260
and evolutionary theory, 167, 175, 177, 258–59, 261
and Indian census, 266
function of, 194
Galton's, 93–94
Grey's, 82–87
by missionaries, 79, 104, 204, 234, 267, 310, 320
modern, 289, 311; *see also* Fieldwork
by naturalists, 79, 104, 234
by nonscientists, 262
questionnaires, 66, 79, 243, 258–59, 261, 273
from printed books, 79, 136
by travelers, 79, 104, 105, 153–54, 175, 234, 267
Wallace's, 97–101
Williams's, 89–91
Ethnological Society of London, 87
Classification Committee, 108
contrasted with Anthropological Society, 249–54, 269
Darwinians in, 248–54, 256–57, 271, 272
founding, 244–45
heightened activity, 245, 246–47
publications, 245, 250, 256
religion and, 245–46, 250
struggle with Anthropological Society, 254–57
Ethnology, 73, 239, 264, 270
and anthropology, 240, 248, 269
and comparative philology, 24, 57, 59, 65, 68, 87, 250, 262
crisis in, 74–77, 80, 102–109, 166, 184, 262
defined, 47, 50, 52
and evolution, 183, 184, 268
monogenism of, 25, 68
as paradigm, 74–75, 80, 100, 102, 103, 104, 107, 108, 166, 179, 181, 184, 246, 260, 269, 304
persistence of, 182, 183, 185
and physical anthoropology, 67–68
Prichardian, 48–53, 58, 65, 68–69, 74–77, 79, 87, 100, 114, 142, 150, 157–60, 165, 166, 172, 179–80, 183, 184, 250, 271, 304, 305, 310
as science of savages, 48
and social anthropology, 293
Tasmanians and, 280–81
as term, 254, 257, 258
tree image of, 52, 77, 181, 183
in twentieth century, 271, 288, 289, 293, 311, 321
Tylor and, 158–60
Ethology, 39–40, 139, 142, 165, 172, 310
Eugenics, 80, 94, 145, 233, 235
Europe
cultural superiority of, 18, 20, 26, 33, 80
European image of man, 326
expansion of, 49, 102, 177, 187, 205, 237, 240, 242, 271, 273
as home of primeval man, 58, 75
idea of, 10, 11, 18
identity linked to civilization, 18, 19, 115
racial history of, 65, 74; *see also* Aryans
Evangelical Revival, 34, 35, 36, 86, 87, 105, 189, 199, 216, 231, 241, 245
Evans, John, 74, 152, 247, 256, 262
Evans-Pritchard, E. E., 293, 298, 300, 301
Evolution(ism); *see also* Biological evolution(ism); Sociocultural evolution(ism)
ambiguous heritage of, 324–29
"classical," xi, xiii, xv, 169–72, 177, 178, 179, 181, 183, 184, 239, 261, 285, 286, 290, 293, 295, 298, 302, 303, 309, 312, 313, 314, 315, 318, 320, 324, 326, 328; *see also* Sociocultural evolution(ism)
of distinctive human features, 149, 150, 172, 176
and embracive anthropology, 271, 292
mental, 69, 134, 141, 148, 160, 180, 181, 205, 225–28, 307; as correlation of external world and internal representation, 220, 225, 226, 227, 228, 306, 309, 311, 314; and individual freedom, 230
moral: *see* Morals
neo-evolutionism, 291–92, 294, 299
reaction against, 42, 287, 288, 319; as intellectual revolution, 326
Exeter Hall, 241
Exogamy, 83, 103, 155, 166–67, 196, 203, 204, 296, 297, 298, 316, 317, 319
Eyre, Edward, 251

Factory Acts, 214
Family, 122, 124, 167, 197–98, 200–201, 203, 209, 219
Feminism, 201, 205, 206
Ferguson, Adam, 15, 17, 31
Fetishism, 19, 29, 155, 196

Feudalism, 91, 119, 126, 127, 210, 232
Fichte, Johann, 25
Fieldwork, 108, 175, 287, 289, 290, 293, 297, 300, 320, 321, 322
Fiji, 88–92, 104, 157, 223, 236, 258, 266
Filmer, Robert, 13, 122, 210
Fison, Lorimer, 79, 204, 236, 259, 297, 317, 319
Flinders Island, 278
Flood, the biblical, 12, 13, 15, 33, 43, 70, 72, 180
Flower, William, 261, 262, 280
Folklore, 21, 23, 53–56, 62, 71, 73, 108, 127, 163, 213, 219, 260, 320
Folk-Lore Society, 262
Fortes, Meyer, 301, 302, 314
Fossil record, 147–49, 154, 172, 250, 328
Foster, Michael, 262
Foucault, Michel, 30
Frazer, James, 79, 233, 260, 287, 294, 297, 320, 321
Free trade, 1, 32, 35, 100, 119, 124, 151, 212, 240–41, 244
French progressivists, 11, 20, 33, 40, 137, 293, 295
  contrasted with Scottish, 15–18
  evolutionism of, 18
  nineteenth-century followers of, 25–30, 39
French Revolution, 10, 19, 21, 25, 27, 30, 31–32, 42–44, 49, 197, 211
Frere, Bartle, 272
Frere, John, 72
Freud, Sigmund, 221, 288, 301, 321, 326
Froude, James, 57
Functionalism, 39, 41, 104–105, 107, 271, 288, 289, 292, 293, 299, 300, 313, 320, 321, 322, 323, 324; *see also* Malinowski; Radcliffe-Brown; Social anthropology; Structural-functionalism
  reaction against, 294

Gall, Franz, 26
Gallatin, Albert, 83
Galton, Francis, 80, 92–96, 104, 118, 136, 145, 174, 233, 234, 235, 252, 253, 261, 262, 263, 318
Galton's problem, 318
Geertz, Clifford, 313
Geisteswissenschaften, 21–22, 38, 287, 307, 325
Gentleman, 30, 54, 56, 80, 92, 185, 191, 209, 210, 212, 215–16, 218, 233, 253, 266, 267
Gentleman's Magazine, 54
Geography, 52, 245, 287
Geological Society of London, 73–74, 151
Geology, 37, 43, 70, 72, 73, 127, 157, 158, 163, 245, 261, 262, 266
George, Henry, 86, 232
German thought; *see also Geistes-* and *Naturwissenschaften*
  and Boasian anthropology, 287, 289, 302, 303, 324
  historical school, 21–22, 27, 32, 37, 38, 118
  on history of culture, 20–25
  idealism, 21, 25, 57, 174, 311
  influence in Great Britain, 37, 38–39, 40–41, 44, 56, 61, 70, 111, 118, 140, 174, 189, 271, 303, 304, 305, 308, 311, 323
  on language and culture, 310
  reaction against Enlightenment, 20
  romanticism, 9, 10, 21, 22, 23, 29, 56, 222
  Tylor and, 157, 161, 164, 302, 304
Gibbon, Edward, 21, 113
Gillen, Frank, 260, 297
Gilolo, 101
Gladstone, William, 151, 164, 218, 232, 252
Glenelg, Lord, 241
Glorious Revolution, 211
Gobineau, Arthur de, 59, 64
God, 91, 199, 237, 320; *see also* Bible; Christianity; Monotheism
  as creator, 3, 42, 44, 51, 69, 133, 190, 192, 195, 197, 223, 228, 249, 308
  loss of belief in, 70, 92, 94, 96, 193, 195, 196; *see also* Religion (weakening of)
  and Jupiter, 13
  and language, 23, 61, 306, 308
  and marriage, 165, 197, 201, 206, 207
  and morality, 130, 193
  and nature, 133, 199, 325
  providential role in history, 4, 25, 36, 37–38, 41, 57, 70, 83–84, 149, 150, 154, 161, 168, 180, 189, 222, 228
  revelation by, 49, 189
Godwin, William, 129
Goguet, A.-Y., 15
Golden Age, 16, 23, 205
Goldenweiser, Alexander, 291
Gordon, Arthur, 236, 265, 266
Göttingen, 22, 114
Graebner, Fritz, 318
Grant, Robert, 66
Great Britain
  preindustrial society in, 208–11, 213
  problem of civilization in, 30–35, 112, 114, 210, 215
  scientific thought in, 41–45
  social change in, 1–5, 30, 32, 34–35, 53, 56, 95, 111, 125, 137, 201, 208, 213, 214, 219, 234
  social inequality in, 210, 212, 219, 229–30

social mobility in, 208–209, 210–11, 212, 214, 217–18, 231, 232
Great Exhibition of the Works of Industry of All Nations: *see* Crystal Palace
Greece, ancient, 9, 10, 12, 22, 60, 61, 207, 294
Grey, George, 80, 81–87, 92, 102, 104, 107, 207
Grey, Lord, 240
Grimm, Jacob, 23, 56
Grimm, Wilhelm, 23, 56
Guiana, 260
Guizot, François, 29, 39, 113
Gungorees, 202

Haddon, A. C., 262, 265, 292, 300, 320
Haeckel, Ernst, 219, 229
Ham, 24, 58
Hardy, Thomas, 1, 4
Hare, William, 64
Harris, Marvin, 299
Hartley, David, 31
Havana, 157
Haxthausen, A. von, 121
Hebrews, 24, 125, 308
Heeren, Arnold, 114
Hegel, G. W., 25
Hellwald, Friedrich von, 303–304
Herder, Johann, 20–21, 22, 25, 37, 310
Hereditarianism, 64, 93, 94, 107, 116, 130, 138, 141, 142, 235; *see also* Biological determinism; Phrenology; Racialism
Hermeneutics, 290, 328–29
Herschel, John, 108
Hindus, 32, 59, 120, 123, 261
Historicism, xv, 20, 21, 118, 285, 304, 314
History, 52, 113, 114, 128; *see also* Anthropology (history of)
  conjectural, 9, 16, 31, 43, 44, 128, 155, 161, 177, 178, 219, 288, 293, 321, 322
  contextualization in, xii–xiii, xiv, 170–71, 174, 177, 178, 179, 181, 182, 188, 205, 239, 285–86
  cyclical, 15, 16, 17, 37
  development in Germany, 21–22
  and evolution, 174–75, 183
  of gentile nations, 13, 14
  early history of man, 158–61, 165, 169, 173
  historical significance, 286, 295, 299, 300, 302, 304, 311, 314–15, 318, 329; and anthropological debate, 305, 314–16
  inadequacy of, 75, 153, 155, 160, 170, 173, 174, 181, 183
  intellectual, 9, 145–46, 169–71, 182, 187–88
  philosophy of, 38, 40, 58, 232
  and progress, 37
  psychohistory, 187–88, 231
  revisionism in, 291
  of social sciences, 145
  and written sources, 48, 127–28, 154, 155, 167, 174
Hobart Town, 275, 279
Hobbes, Thomas, 12, 13, 34, 94, 99, 220
Hodgkin, Thomas, 63, 242, 243, 244, 247
Hottentots, 18, 93, 94, 141, 153, 241
Howitt, A. W., 236, 259, 297, 317, 319
Human nature, 13, 17–18, 31, 33, 35–36, 37, 38, 39, 40, 111, 116, 122, 131, 138, 141, 170, 207, 219–28, 306–309, 318, 325, 326; *see also* Primitive mentality; Psychic unity; Race; Savage(s); Sociocultural evolution(ism)
Human Relations Area Files, 316
Human sciences, 13, 19, 21, 23, 25, 30, 48, 289, 312–13, 325, 326
Humanitarianism, 240–45, 246, 247, 251, 252, 266, 272
Humboldt, Alexander von, 97
Humboldt, Wilhelm von, 24, 58, 310
Hume, David, 16, 33, 113
Hunt, James, 247–48, 249–52, 254, 255, 270, 271
Hurons, 18
Hutcheson, Francis, 16
Huxley, Thomas, 41, 146, 147, 149, 151, 169, 190, 248, 249, 251, 252, 253, 254, 255, 256, 263, 264, 270, 280
Hymes, Dell, 185

Idealism, 21, 25, 57, 114, 134, 157, 174, 180, 311, 328
Ideology, 36, 105, 145, 187, 199, 205, 212, 215, 216–17, 221, 223, 227, 228–33, 239, 242, 261, 266, 273, 285, 287, 291, 299, 305, 316; *see also* Anthropology (ideological functions); Sociocultural evolution(ism) (ideological functions)
Im Thurn, Everhard, 260
Imperialism, 80, 81, 86, 124, 187, 240–42, 261, 272, 277; *see also* Colonialism; White man's burden
Incest, 176, 202, 204, 219, 298, 316
Independent invention, 51, 55, 73, 98, 102, 152, 154, 155, 158, 160, 162, 170, 173, 180, 181–82, 195, 318, 322
India, 2, 22, 23, 32–33, 51, 57, 115, 120–21, 124, 126, 127, 168, 240, 266, 296
Indian Mutiny, 63, 68, 119–20, 165, 234, 241
Individual agency, 209, 212, 213, 230, 231, 273, 279, 290, 311, 324
Individualism, 27, 30, 41, 93, 123, 131, 132, 198, 210
Industrial and military societies, 1, 19, 130

Industrial Revolution, 30, 36, 105, 129, 208–209, 211, 215, 217, 220
Infanticide, 34, 90, 105, 166, 201, 203, 204, 221, 316
Inns of Court, 118, 164
Instinct, 35–36, 70, 95, 105, 130, 139, 207, 219–28, 229, 233, 236
Institutionalization: *see* Anthropology (institutionalization of)
Intellectual aristocracy, 96, 117, 120, 212, 233, 251, 253
International Congress of Prehistoric Archaeology, 254
Irish, 63, 80, 81, 126, 151, 213, 221, 225, 229–30, 232, 234
Iron Age, 72, 73
Iroquois, 183
Israel, 102
Italians, 66, 162, 235

Jamaica, 251
Japanese, 236
Japheth, 24, 58
Jews, 20, 197
Johnson, Samuel, 11
Jones, William, 22–23, 32, 50, 121
Jupiter, 13
Juridical Society of London, 119
Jurisprudence, 118–19, 121–22

Kaffirs, 47, 86–87, 126, 241, 261
Kames, Lord, 15, 17, 18, 49, 171
Kant, Immanuel, 25, 37, 59, 133, 305, 307, 308, 310
Keightley, Thomas, 55
Kemble, John, 62
King, Richard, 244, 255
King George Tubou, 88
Kingsley, Charles, 57, 63, 147
Kinship, xvii, 83, 126, 155, 167, 197, 203, 204, 261, 286, 288, 322, 323; *see also* Marriage; Matriarchy; Matriliny; Patriarchy; Social organization
  classificatory system of, 296, 315, 317, 321
  and social anthropology, 105, 296, 319
  and territory, 117, 119, 123, 184
Kluckhohn, Clyde, 302
Knox, Robert, 64–65, 69, 246, 247, 281
Kroeber, A. L., 298, 302
Kuhn, Thomas, xiii

Lafitau, Joseph, 12–13
Lamarck, J. B., 64, 69, 106, 107, 133, 135, 141, 145, 224, 226, 228, 233, 235–36, 237
Lane Fox, A. H.: *see* Pitt Rivers, A. H. L. F.
Lang, Andrew, 190, 260, 263, 287, 320
Language(s); *see also* names of particular ethnic groups
  and civilization, 159
  disease of, 60, 125, 163
  evolution of, 58, 155, 159, 282
  genealogical classification of, 23, 24, 58, 68
  gesture, 159, 282, 307
  Indo-European, 22–23, 24, 58, 61, 62, 68, 121, 152, 235, 306
  morphological classification of, 24, 58, 68
  Müller on, 58–61, 306–307
  origin of, 13, 33, 61, 149, 163, 306–308
  and race, 51, 57–58, 65, 75, 100, 102, 108, 166, 235, 243, 247
  rude, 84
  Semitic, 24
  Spencer on, 308
  Tylor on, 157, 159, 163, 306–307
Lanney, William, 280
La Peyrère, Isaac de, 12, 18
Laplace, Pierre, 28, 141
Latham, R. G., 53, 58, 94, 97, 100, 103–104, 108, 158, 165, 280
Latin, 22
Law
  civil, 118, 119, 122
  common, 121, 165, 198
  evolution of, 121–23, 125, 149, 155, 156
  international, 126
  Maine on, 121–24
  McLennan on, 164–65
  natural, 122
  Roman, 21, 23, 118–19, 121, 123, 198, 203
  Scottish, 164
Lawrence, William, 43, 66, 97
Layard, A. H., 71
Leakey, Louis, 327
Lévi-Strauss, Claude, 297
Levirate, 203, 204, 317
Lewes, G. H., 133, 134, 164
Liberal Anglicans, 37, 57, 81, 87, 161, 189
Liberalism, 1, 27, 30, 35, 38, 81, 145, 151, 157, 193, 218, 230, 232, 251, 252, 272
Linguistic anthropology, 328
Linguistics, 23, 163, 262; *see also* Comparative philology; Language(s)
  as criterion of human diversity, 12, 27, 29, 59
  in later British anthropology, 270
Linnaeus, Carolus, 26
Liverpool, 256
Livingstone, David, 87, 92
Lobuk, Robert, 218
Locke, John, 13, 16, 26, 31, 116, 122, 193, 211, 308
London, 66, 73–74, 87, 92, 96, 108, 112,

113, 119, 124, 133, 151, 157, 164, 209, 213, 214, 223, 243
London School of Economics, 300
Louis XIV, 14
Lowie, Robert, 288, 298
Lubbock, John, 250, 260, 263, 264, 266
and Anthropological Institute, 256, 257, 262
and antiquity of man, 152–53
and Darwin, 151–52, 179
and Darwinian revolution, 136, 173, 224
and degenerationism, 87, 154, 168
and Ethnological Society, 249, 253
on evolution of marriage, 203, 317
on evolution of religion, 188, 194–95
on independent invention, 154–55, 156, 180
intellectual biography of, 150–56, 206
later reputation of, 295, 301
and Liberal party, 151, 218, 232, 252
and Maine, 184
and Malthus, 221
and McLennan, 166, 168, 169, 176
on moral progress, 223
and Müller, 307
on savages, 153–54, 155, 187
on stages of development, 155, 156
Lubbock, Mrs. John, 257
Lucretius, Titus, 13, 14
Lugard, Lord, 124
Lyall, Alfred, 266
Lyell, Charles, 61, 69, 72, 73, 74, 75–76, 82, 133, 147, 148, 151, 152, 168, 307

Macalister, Alexander, 262, 265
Mach, Ernst, 321
MacLean, John, 86–87
MacPherson, James, 17
McEnery, John, 72
Maine, Henry, 92, 236
on ancient law, 121–24
and Buckle, 116, 125
on comparative method, 121, 125, 126, 127, 154, 183, 305
and comparative philology, 121, 122, 296
and economic life, 312
and eighteenth-century thought, 121, 137
and evolutionism, 125–26, 128, 129, 172, 184, 305, 311
and German thought, 118–19, 310
on instinct and civilization, 207–208
intellectual biography of, 117–28
later reputation of, 295–96
and McLennan, 164, 165, 167, 168, 260, 265
on moral progress, 140
on patriarchy, 117, 122–24, 126, 127, 197–98, 204, 205–206, 296
Radcliffe-Brown and, 296
and social anthropology, 117, 295–96
and utilitarianism, 118, 121, 125
on village community, 120–21, 123–24, 296
Malay Archipelago, 82, 99, 101
Malays, 47, 58, 63, 100, 104
Malinowski, Bronislaw, 288, 290, 293, 294, 298, 299, 300, 320, 321–22, 323, 324
Malthus, Thomas, 34–35, 38, 81, 96, 97, 99, 101, 114, 133, 215, 217, 220–22, 233
Man, E. H., 259
Mana, 85, 319
Manchester, 2, 213, 248
Maoris, 47, 85, 86, 87, 261, 283
Marett, R. R., 300, 301, 319, 320
Marriage; *see also* Exogamy; Polyandry; Polygamy; Primitive promiscuity
among Australians, 83–84
by capture, 155, 166, 202–203, 204, 261, 316, 317
Christian, 197, 200
cross-cousin, 317–18
to deceased wife's sister, 201, 202–203
Divine founding of, 165, 167, 197, 201
English, 165, 197–200
evolution of, 155, 156, 166–68, 176, 178, 180, 188, 197–208, 316–18
among Fijians, 90
historiography of, 197
Lubbock on, 203–204
Maine on, 197–98
McLennan on, 166–67, 197, 200–206
origin of, 117, 149
postponement of, 34, 96, 200–201
Scottish, 165, 197
Spencer on, 204, 207, 221–22
Tylor on, 204, 316–18
Martineau, Harriet, 70
Marx, Karl, 16, 34, 291, 301
Materialism, 23, 42, 43, 70, 174, 180, 192, 307, 310, 326
Matriarchy, 201, 205, 261, 262, 300, 316, 317, 322
Matriliny, 83, 102, 167, 196, 203, 204, 297, 316, 317
Matrimonial Causes Acts, 201
Maudsley, Alfred, 265
Mauritius, 82
Mayhew, Henry, 3, 213, 219
McCulloch, J. R., 113, 164
McLennan, John
and comparative method, 136, 150, 167–68, 169, 219
and Darwin, 176, 177, 179, 202
and Darwinian revolution, 136, 150, 167–68, 173, 179, 224
and eighteenth century, 165, 168, 171

McLennan, John (*cont.*)
 on evolution of marriage, 166–67, 180, 188, 197, 200–204, 205, 316, 318, 319
 and feminism, 206
 intellectual biography of, 164–69
 later reputation of, 296–98
 and Latham, 103
 and Liberal party, 218, 232
 and Maine, 164–65, 167, 168, 174, 265, 296, 297
 and Malthus, 221
 on moral progress, 223
 and Morgan, 260–61, 296–97, 315, 316, 318
 and Müller, 307
 and Robertson Smith, 260, 287
 and social anthropology, 297–98
 on totemism, 195, 297
 and Tylor, 168, 195, 297, 318
 and utilitarianism, 164–65, 171–72, 221
 and Wake, 297, 315
Mead, Margaret, 291, 327
Mecca, 253
Medicine, 48, 53, 65–66, 68, 91, 114, 320
Melanesia, 317, 319, 321
Melanesian Mission, 236–37
Merrie England, 213
Merton, Ambrose, 55–56
Mesmerism, 97
Methodism, 80, 88, 92, 129, 212, 278
Mexico, 115, 157
Miall, Edward, 130
Middle Ages, 23, 27, 28, 29, 71, 113, 119
Middle East, 92, 116
Migration(s), 15, 24, 50, 51, 53, 58, 59, 73, 74–75, 77, 166, 184
Mill, J. S., 38–41, 107, 113, 114, 116, 118, 120, 138, 142, 163, 165, 171–72, 188, 206, 216, 251, 310
Mill, James, 31, 32–33, 35, 38, 39, 121
Millar, John, 15, 17, 20, 31, 171
Milligan, Joseph, 275, 280
Milnes, Monckton, 253
Missionaries, 34, 79, 80, 85, 87–92, 234, 236–37, 241, 242, 243, 252, 259, 266, 272, 310, 320
Monboddo, Lord, 17
Monogamy, 85, 168, 204, 219, 228
Monogenism, 25, 26, 49, 50, 52, 58, 66–68, 75–76, 80, 101, 102, 180, 250, 258, 270, 283; *see also* Unity of mankind
Monotheism, 22, 29, 92, 155, 228, 282
Montesquieu, Baron de, 13–14, 15, 17, 23, 114, 116, 137
Moral sciences, 31, 38, 114, 116, 165, 171–72, 298, 325
Morals
 degradation of, 91, 98
 evolution of, 149, 155, 161, 193–94, 224–25
 Lubbock on, 223
 McLennan on, 223
 of the poor, 217
 positive, 194
 progress of, 95, 100, 114, 122, 138, 139, 140, 141, 205, 222–25, 309
 relativism of, 165, 188, 222, 223–24
 revolution in, 33, 35, 42, 199–200, 214, 215, 220
 sexual, 217
 Spencer on, 130–32, 134, 224–25
 Tylor on, 193–94, 223–24
Morgan, L. H., 126, 183, 259, 260–61, 286, 288, 291, 295, 296, 297, 299, 301, 302, 315, 316, 317, 318, 319, 321
Morlot, A., 248
Morton, Samuel, 66, 67
Moseley, H. N., 264, 265
Müller, F. M., 158, 165, 166, 245, 259, 260, 263, 294, 310
 and Aryans, 58–59, 64, 320
 and comparative mythology, 60–61, 121, 306
 and disease of language, 60, 125, 163
 and German idealist philosophy, 57, 61, 189, 305, 311
 intellectual biography of, 67–62
 linguistic paleontology of, 59–60
 on origin of language, 61, 306–308, 328
 and religion, 57, 282, 319
 on Turanian philology, 58–59, 68
 and Tylor, 61–62, 160, 163, 195, 264, 305–306
Municipal Reform Act of 1835, 214
Murchison, Roderick, 245
Musée d'Histoire Naturelle, 281
Museum of Archaeology and Ethnology, Cambridge, 265
Museums, 263–65, 273
Muslims, 92, 253
Mythology, 20, 37, 59, 60, 86, 107, 159, 190, 195, 305–306, 320; *see also* Comparative mythology
Mythopoeic mentality, 21, 60, 160, 305

Nationalism, 32, 66, 145
Native policy, 81, 84–85, 100, 124, 242–43, 266, 276–79
Natural history, 52, 66, 69, 76, 97, 100, 103, 106, 108, 151, 244, 250, 258, 263, 273
Natural theology, 130, 189
Naturalistic view of man, 50, 68, 76, 135, 149–50, 161, 167, 168, 172, 177, 182–83, 191, 222, 247–48, 270, 325

Nature
conquest of, 3, 35, 113, 115, 148, 193, 211, 220, 228, 325
continuity of, 70, 173–74, 180, 232
internal to man, 220, 228
laws of, 115, 217
man's place in, 147, 176, 257, 325
and mythology, 305–306
savages at mercy of, 36, 84, 153, 154, 217, 220, 227
state of, 11, 121–22, 177–78
Naturphilosophie, 229
Naturwissenschaften, 21, 38, 287, 307, 325
Nazism, 292, 326
Neanderthal man, 73, 147
Negroes, 26, 93, 95, 97, 107, 251; *see also* Blacks
Nepal, 103
New Caledonia, 280
New English Dictionary, 304
New Guinea, 98, 173, 327
New Holland, 279
New South Wales, 275
New World, 12, 18, 80, 91, 179
New Zealand, 85, 86, 221
Newton, Isaac, 14, 17
Niebuhr, Barthold, 21–22, 37, 118, 123
"Niggers," 63, 101, 120, 261
Nile, 92, 116
Nineveh, 71
Noah, 12, 22, 50, 51, 52, 54, 179
Noble Savage, 17, 36, 86, 100, 153, 223, 275, 283, 289
Nonconformism, 189, 196
Normans, 62, 208, 235
Notes and Queries, 56
Notes and Queries in Anthropology, 258–61

Orient, 22, 74, 120; *see also* Asia
Ossian, 17
Otherness, 47–48, 80, 125, 141, 233–38, 290, 313
Ovampo, 93
Owen, Richard, 133, 147
Owenites, 96
Oxford University, 49, 57, 62, 121, 126, 146, 164, 181, 218, 260, 262, 263, 264, 267, 273, 300, 305, 311

Paine, Thomas, 30, 31
Paleoanthropology, 327
Paleolithic Age/man, 152, 282–83
Paleontology, 59–60, 76, 261
Paley, William, 31, 130
Palmerston, Lord, 4, 120
Papuans, 47, 58, 100, 101, 141, 280
Paracelsus, 49
Paris Commune, 232
Parsons, Talcott, 298, 299
Patans, 202
Patriarchy, 12, 13, 84, 91, 97, 117, 119, 122–24, 126, 127, 128, 168, 177, 184, 197–98, 200, 204, 205–206, 207, 210, 211–12, 215, 222, 260, 261
Patricide, 90, 223
Peasantry, 53, 81, 163, 210, 229, 234
Peel, Robert, 119
Pembroke College, Cambridge, 118
Penniman, T. K., 292
Perfectibility of man, 34
Péron, François, 275
Perry, William, 288
Peru, 115
Pessimism, 17, 64, 80, 96, 233, 244
Philological Society of London, 243
Philosophical radicalism, 29, 30, 232; *see also* Utilitarianism
Phrenology, 26, 29, 39, 65, 66, 68, 70, 92, 97, 130, 137, 191, 326
Physical anthropology, 73, 74, 292
and Anthropological Institute, 261, 270
and Anthropological Society of London, 249–50, 255
and anthropology in Britain, 269, 271
eighteenth-century, 18
emergence of, 26–27, 65
and evolution, 148, 172, 182, 250
in France, 67, 261, 268, 281
Galton's, 93
in Germany, 67, 261
in Great Britain, 65–68, 246, 265, 266, 270, 272
and polygenism, 68, 182
of Tasmanians, 280–81
in the United States, 67
Physiology, 25, 28–29, 39, 52, 114, 133, 199, 216, 320
Pim, Bedford, 251
Pinel, Philippe, 25
Pitt, George, 264
Pitt Rivers, A. H. L. F., 5, 71, 176, 180–81, 183, 195, 247, 253, 256, 258, 261, 262, 264–65, 266, 270, 272, 307
Pitt Rivers Museum, 181, 264–65, 282, 292
Plato, 61
Police, 214
Political economy, 30–32, 34–36, 37, 39, 40, 48, 113, 157, 216–17, 223, 312
Political science, 13, 48
Polyandry, 103, 136, 166, 168, 176, 202–203, 316
Polygamy, 84, 90, 97, 105, 165, 228
Polygenism, 12, 18, 26–27, 49, 64–69, 74, 80, 96, 97, 100, 101, 102, 107, 139, 148–49, 159, 179, 180, 182–84, 235, 237, 250, 270, 281, 283, 313, 325

Polygyny, 202
Polynesians, 58, 86, 87, 100–101, 107, 258
Polytheism, 22, 29, 43, 49, 228
Poor Law, 35, 213, 217
Population, 34–35, 113–14, 133, 209, 211, 215, 217, 220–21
Portuguese, 98, 99
Positivism, 9, 27, 42, 76, 80, 111, 127, 128, 133, 161, 163, 171, 190, 304, 307, 310, 323–24, 325, 328
  critique of, 287, 290, 294, 313, 324
Pott, August, 68
Powell, John W., 268, 286, 291
Prehistory, 41, 59, 72–74, 108, 126, 128, 136, 152, 157, 167, 172, 179, 180, 250, 264, 273, 282, 296
Pre-Raphaelites, 164
Prestwich, Joseph, 152
Prichard, James C., 47–53, 58, 63, 65, 68–69, 74–75, 97, 100, 102, 103, 108, 160, 181, 185, 242–43, 246, 271, 280, 290
Priestley, Joseph, 31
"Primitive," as a term, 328
Primitive mentality, 13, 16, 57, 59, 93, 159, 160, 225–28, 229, 234–35, 298, 307–308, 313, 314, 326; *see also* Savage(s) (capacities of; mind of)
Primitive promiscuity, 128, 167, 168, 176, 177, 184, 202–203, 315, 316; *see also* Marriage (evolution of)
Primitive society, 60, 122–23, 208, 224, 296
Primitivism, 17, 23, 25, 36, 80, 96, 98–99, 101, 205, 213
Professionalization, 240
Progress, 1, 9; *see also* Civilization; Developmentalism; Sociocultural evolution(ism)
  class vision of, 36, 216–17
  discontinuity in, 32–33, 34
  in Enlightenment, 10–19, 111
  French prophets of, 25–30
  German idea of, 25
  and Graeco-Roman tradition, 127
  of knowledge, 115–16, 161, 196, 220
  laws of, 161
  material/spiritual, 161, 162, 220, 223, 228; *see also* Morals (progress of)
  among savages, 154, 161
  and social mobility, 217–19
  Spencer on, 135
  stages of, 5, 14–15, 17, 19, 28, 40, 155, 168
  from status to contract, 123, 124
  summary view of, 169
  Tylor on, 161, 194
  unilineal, 14, 15, 28, 40, 111
  westward movement of, 37
Property, 16, 123, 124, 125, 126, 203, 209, 211, 216, 224, 278
Propriety, 203
Prostitution, 200, 201, 202, 281
Provincial radicalism, 129, 133, 137, 206, 232
Prudential restraint, 34–36, 96, 216–17, 220
Psychic unity of man, 17, 19, 51–52, 102, 127, 141–42, 155–56, 160, 161–62, 170, 173, 174, 224, 236, 309, 314, 326
Psychoanalysis, 288, 321
Psychology, 48, 320, 324–25, 326; *see also* Associationism
  common sense, 16, 31
  Comte's exclusion of, 28
  cultural, 287–88
  dynamic, 187
  experimental, 94
  humoral, 18, 26
  innatism, 38–39, 134, 141
  intellectualist, 186, 293, 294, 301, 321, 322
  Lockean, 13, 16, 32
  Mill's, 39–40, 142
  psychophysics, 287
  social, 322
  Spencer's, 134, 136, 142, 180, 224, 298, 307

Quakers, 49, 63, 92, 157, 159, 197, 218, 241, 242, 245, 247, 265
Queensland, 272
Quetelet, Adolphe, 28, 114

Race(s), 62–69; *see also* Monogenism; Polygenism; Unity of Man
  of Britain, 66–67, 261, 266, 272
  Buckle and, 138–39
  character of, 62–63, 89–90, 93, 95, 98, 101, 120, 138, 236
  and class, 213, 218
  classification of, 26, 51, 103, 104, 182, 184, 248, 249, 272, 325
  and culture, 64, 235
  definition of, 65
  differentiation of, 50–51, 100, 262, 313, 326
  dispersion of, 22, 24, 50
  essences of, 25
  evolution and, 101, 140, 142–43, 148, 170, 173, 236, 270
  Germanic, 21, 25, 63, 148
  hierarchy of, 26, 80, 84, 93, 106, 148, 153, 160, 172, 182, 194, 224–25, 234–35, 262, 272, 282, 313; critique of, 287
  Lamarckian view of, 106, 141, 224–25, 235

linguistic view of, 27, 29, 52, 57–59, 100, 235
mental differences among, 94, 106, 141, 142, 159, 314
Mill and, 137–38
mixture, 67, 85, 157, 236, 281
and nation, 235
neglect of, 261
prejudice, 153, 252, 279
and progress, 29, 64
relations, 63, 81, 86, 120, 251, 271, 272, 275–83
Tylor and, 235, 270
Racialism, 20, 36, 37, 59, 62, 106, 140, 142, 159, 185, 224, 235–36, 247, 250, 251, 272–73, 313, 326, 327
critique of, 287, 292, 326, 328
Radcliffe-Brown, A. R., 288, 289, 293, 294, 296, 297, 298, 299, 300–301, 311, 320, 322–23
Railroads, 2, 4, 71, 129, 208, 211
Ranke, Leopold von, 22
Rawlinson, Henry, 263
Reason, 16, 19, 35–36, 37, 39, 40, 69, 70, 107, 134, 141, 174, 181, 194, 196–97, 207, 219–28, 229, 230, 233, 309, 312, 314
Recapitulation, 174, 219, 228–29
Reform of 1832, 129, 156, 198, 212
Relativism: *see* Cultural relativism; Morals (relativity of)
Religion, 108; *see also* Animism; Bible; Catholicism; Christianity; God; Monotheism; Ritual; and specific sects
absence of, 104, 195
Andamanese, 259
Brazilian Indian, 98
and civilization, 25, 35
Damara, 94
essence of, 192
evolution of, 51–52, 149, 155, 161, 178, 188–97, 207, 208, 319, 320
Fijian, 90–91
functions of, 193, 195, 196
Judeo-Christian, 11
Lubbock on, 195–96
McLennan on, 195–96
and morality, 193–94, 195
natural, 193, 194, 260
Polynesian, 86
preanimistic, 319
Semitic, 260
and social anthropology, 105, 319
Spencer on, 189, 190, 195–96
Tasmanian, 282
Tylor on, 190–97, 207, 260, 261, 319
universal basis of, 57
weakening of, 187, 188–90, 194–95, 196, 199, 207, 222, 253
Renan, Ernest, 68
Respectability, 195, 196, 212, 216, 217, 221, 230, 253–54, 257
Revolution of 1848, 2, 45, 63, 66, 119
Ricardo, David, 32, 34–35, 37, 38
Ritual, 193, 195, 196, 210, 301, 309, 319, 320
Rivers, W. H. R., 288, 297, 300, 301, 319, 320–21, 322
Robertson, William, 15, 17, 33, 113
Robinson, George, 278–79, 283
Rolleston, George, 263, 264
Romans, ancient, 10, 12, 21, 183, 208; *see also* Law
Romanticism, 9, 10, 21, 29, 38, 55, 56, 222, 302
Rousseau, J.-J., 15, 17, 18, 121–22, 283, 328
Royal College of Surgeons, 280
Royal Geographical Society, 79, 82, 94, 99, 243
Royal Society of Arts, 1
Royal Society of London, 151, 251, 264
Royal Society of Tasmania, 280
Russell, Lord John, 85, 240
Russia, 121, 124, 157
Ruskin, John, 198

Saint-Hilaire, Geoffroy, 64
Saint-Simon, C. H., 25, 27, 39, 92
Samoa, 327
Sanskrit, 22–23, 57, 60, 124, 169
Sarawak, 63
Savage(s), 9
of America, 13, 18, 122
capacities of, 3, 83–84, 92, 142, 155, 160, 237, 272, 303, 308, 314, 326
character of, 113, 153, 217, 223, 225, 229, 234–35
as child, 94, 95, 100, 174, 223, 225, 226, 229
civilization of, 84, 90, 237, 242, 278–79
in Comte, 20
data of, 77, 132, 136, 140, 153–54, 172, 173, 175, 178, 183, 222, 234, 239, 273
defense of, 272–73, 287, 326; *see also* Aborigines Protection Society
defined, 10, 13, 36
double image of, 153–55, 187–88, 208, 219
economics of, 32
eighteenth-century view of, 18, 142
evolutionary view of, 185, 187, 237, 255, 273
extermination of, 64, 84, 100, 114, 148, 180, 234, 237, 240, 243, 251, 273, 275–83, 290
as fallen man, 36, 88, 107; *see also* Degenerationism

Savage(s) (*cont.*)
and Greeks, 13
ignoble, 153, 155
at mercy of nature, 36, 84, 153, 154, 217, 220, 227
mind of, 225–26, 235, 308
in Montesquieu, 13–14
objectification of, 273
as original human state, 19, 33, 51, 107, 176, 184
as philosopher, 192, 208, 219, 226, 227, 228, 320
in pre-evolutionary progressivism, 111, 115, 125, 132, 136, 140
sexuality of, 202, 217
as subject matter of anthropology, 47, 48, 184, 185, 239
as a term, xv, 322
treatment of women, 84–85, 90, 98, 99–100, 105, 225
variety among, 93, 100
as wanderers, 237
Savagery
as degenerative, 22, 34
horrors of, 92, 93, 99, 153
as system, 105
in Victorian society, 4–5, 164, 202, 210, 213–14, 217, 218
Savigny, Karl von, 21, 118–19, 123, 127, 165
Schlegel, August von, 23
Schlegel, Friedrich von, 23, 24
Schmerling, P. C., 72
Science
as assumption, 193
hierarchy of, 28, 30, 310
ideological functions of, 237
jurisdiction of, 161, 170, 190–92, 323, 325
methods of, 108, 194
and miracles, 70, 168
mythological aspect, 307
natural, 24, 25, 38, 50, 52, 183, 189, 321
orthodoxy, 253
palaetiological, 37, 42
progress of, 15, 28, 124, 136, 149, 169, 170, 192, 196–97, 307, 308, 309, 311
reassuring function of, 191, 196–97
Scientific Revolution, 12
Scots, Highland, 66, 219
Scott, Walter, 55
Scottish progressivists, 9, 11, 19, 33, 34, 38, 49, 114, 130, 134, 137, 165, 293, 294
contrasted with French, 15–18
decline of, 31, 32, 44
evolutionism of, 18
Scythians, 11, 12
Sedgwick, Adam, 41–42, 44
Selection
artificial, 94, 96
natural, 61, 95, 106, 135, 145, 148, 150, 173, 180, 222, 228, 237, 249
unnatural, 233
Self-help, 2, 129, 212, 216
Seligman, C. G., 300
Semites, 24, 58, 68, 126, 260, 297, 320
Setswana, 94
Sex, sexuality; *see also* Marriage; Primitive promiscuity; Women
continence, 216–17
double standard of, 200, 201
and economics, 216–17, 221, 233
evolution of, 208
female, 199, 202, 203
historiography of, 197
human, 201, 204, 220, 316
male, 200, 202, 203
relationships, 167, 176, 206–207
repression of, 34–35, 197, 199–200, 203, 207–208
among savages, 202
Shaftesbury, Earl of, 16
Shakespeare, William, 112
Sierra Leone, 247, 251
Simon, J. F., 114
Slavery, 49, 63, 93, 207, 241, 244
Smiles, Samuel, 216, 217
Smith, Adam, 14, 15, 17, 31, 32, 33, 116, 131, 137
Smith, G. Elliott, 288
Smith, W. Robertson, 260, 287, 297, 311, 320
Social anthropology; *see also* Functionalism; Structural-functionalism
continuity with evolutionism, 323–24
and culture, 289, 324–25
data of, 105
emergence of, 258, 269, 271, 288, 292, 294, 323
and ethnology, 293
and kinship, 295, 296, 316, 319, 323
and language, 294
and lineage theory, 296, 305
as historiography, 293
institutionalization of, 300
Maine and, 117, 296
McLennan and, 297–98
Morgan and, 301, 302
as natural science, 288, 323
precursors of, 13
and psychology, 293, 323–24
Radcliffe-Brown and, 288, 289, 293, 294, 299, 311
and ritual, 319, 320
Spencer and, 129, 298
as synchronic study, 293, 322, 324

Turgot and, 14
Tylor and, 300-301
Social contract, 13, 122, 178
Social Darwinism, 9, 95, 96, 128, 140, 145, 173, 233, 294, 299, 312
Social organism, 29, 39, 130, 132-33, 298
Social organization, 169, 258-59, 262, 286, 288, 315, 319, 322
Social sciences, 325, 326
Social structure, 117, 138, 311, 321, 322
Social system, 288, 299
Société d'Anthropologie de Paris, 247, 270
Société d'Ethnographie de Paris, 270
Société Ethnologique de Paris, 243
Society for the Promotion of the Science of Man, 255
Society for the Study of Man in its Widest Interpretation, 256
Society of Antiquaries, 54, 71, 72, 74
Sociobiology, xv, 145, 299, 327
Sociocultural evolution(ism); *see also* Barbarism; Comparative method; Developmentalism; Evolution(ism); History (conjectural); "Primitive"; Progress; Psychic unity of man; Savage(s); Survivals
anthropological reputation of, 286
assumptions of, 169-79, 239, 321
background of, 10
as compromise formation, 269, 272
in Comte, 28-29
critique of, 171, 177, 287, 290-91, 297, 298, 305, 317, 318, 319, 327
and culture, 309, 311, 314, 324
as cynosure of anthropology, 180, 185, 268
data of, 104-105, 107-108, 153-54, 167, 172, 177, 234, 239, 258, 260, 269, 273
defense of, 291-92, 325, 328
defined, 170-71
emergence of, 45, 48, 52-53, 80, 107-108, 111-12, 117, 138, 140, 145, 146, 150, 152, 156, 169, 180-81, 184, 239, 268, 295, 323
and ethnology, 77-77, 102-109, 259, 268
historical evaluation of, 290-94
historical significance of, 285-86, 311, 312, 314, 315, 318, 324, 325, 328-29
historiography of, 171, 294-302
as ideational, 174, 180, 203, 311
ideological functions of, 187-88, 218-19, 223-33, 266, 273, 280-81, 283, 285, 299, 312
as intellectual revolution, 325
and the irrational, 192-93, 312, 313
ladder of, 77, 177, 183
as law-governed, 125, 127, 158, 161, 162, 167-68, 170, 318, 321, 323
loss of impetus after 1870, 260
in Lubbock, 152, 154-56
Maine and, 125-26, 128, 174-75, 177-78
Malinowski and, 322
in McLennan, 167-69, 176-77, 219, 318
metaphorical extendibility of, 228-29
in Mill, 40-41
as normal science, 240, 258, 261
as paradigm, 183, 184-85, 239-40, 258, 260, 262, 304
and paternal authority, 231
and political economy, 312
polygenist assumptions in, 182-83
Prichard and, 51-52
process in, 173-74, 177, 181
race and, 236, 313, 318, 326
Radcliffe-Brown and, 293, 322-23
reassuring function of, 152, 187, 223, 228, 232, 295, 325, 326
Rivers and, 321
Spencer on, 135-37, 224-28
Tasmanians and, 280, 281-83
in Turgot, 14-15
in Tylor, 159-64, 175-76, 192, 218, 303-308, 318
ulterior motives of, 187-88, 205-206, 233, 261, 285, 309, 315, 316
un-Darwinian arguments and, 146, 150, 154, 176-77, 202
unilinear, 125, 128, 156, 173, 177-78, 183, 291, 318
Sociology, 18, 28, 40, 102, 103, 108, 132, 136, 138, 258, 261, 262, 270, 290, 292, 294, 298, 299, 301, 311
Somerset Archaeological Society, 282
Somme River drift, 152, 282
Sömmering, Samuel von, 26
Sorell, William, 276
South Africa, 85-86, 241
South Australia, 279
South Kensington Museum, 264
Spencer, Baldwin, 79, 260, 297
Spencer, Herbert, 233, 234, 235, 236, 282
and Buckle, 129
and cross-cultural comparison, 136, 282, 316
and Darwin, 298
and feminism, 205-206
evolutionism of, 133-36, 140-42, 260
intellectual biography of, 128-37
later reputation of, 298-99, 301, 325
and Maine, 129
and Malthus, 221-22
and McLennan, 165, 204
on moral progress, 205, 224
and Müller, 307-308
on primitive mind, 225-28, 298, 307-308
and provincial radicalism, 129-30, 232
psychology of, 134-35, 137, 140-42
and Radcliffe-Brown, 293, 298, 322

Spencer, Herbert (*cont.*)
 and religion, 189, 190, 195–96
 on social statics, 100, 130–32, 148
 and Tylor, 178, 187
 and utilitarianism, 130
Spinoza, Baruch, 12
Spiritualism, 191–92
Spurzheim, J. C., 26, 130
Statistics, 28, 94, 114, 213, 266, 316
Stephen, Fitzjames, 119
Stephen, James, 241
Stephen, Leslie, 116, 128, 138–39, 143, 304
Stephens, J. L., 71
Stewart, Dugald, 31, 32, 48, 49, 168, 171
Stokes, Whitley, 121
Stone Age, 72, 73, 154, 176, 282
Storch, H. F., 114
Strauss, David, 57
Structural-functionalism, 288, 299, 320
 critique of, 294, 295
Structuralism, 289, 313
Strzelecki, P. E., 281
Sumner, Archbishop J. B., 33–34, 44, 117–18, 125, 190
Survivals, doctrine of, 54, 127–28, 162–63, 165, 166, 168, 169, 170, 171, 175, 178, 193, 218–19, 266, 288, 309, 312, 317, 321, 322
Swing Riots, 213
Swiss lake dwellings, 73, 153, 173
Symbolic anthropology, xvi, 311, 324
Syria, 92

Taboo (tabu), 83, 94, 104, 199–200, 204, 297, 326
Tahiti, 2, 162, 235
Tasmanian Museum, 280
Tasmanians, 5, 176, 234, 275–83, 285
Taylor, Harriet, 206
Teggart, F. J., 294
Teknonymy, 317
Temperance, 214
Teutons, 59, 66, 73
Thackeray, William, 208
Thakombau, 91
Thoms, William, 55–56
Thomsen, Christian, 72
Thomson, Arthur, 265
Thorpe, Benjamin, 62
Thurnam, Joseph, 66, 246
Tibet, 175
Tierra del Fuego, 72, 105–107, 153, 234
Timor, 82, 280
Todas, 321
Tonga, 88, 90, 153
Torres Straits Expedition, 320
Toryism, 112, 119, 251
Totemism, 83, 102, 155, 195, 196, 260, 297, 298, 300, 314, 319, 320, 326
Trinity College, Cambridge, 1, 6, 92, 117, 164
Trobriands, 288, 321–22, 323
Truganina, 278, 280, 283
Trusteeship, 240, 242
Tübingen, 57, 121
Turanians, 58–59, 65, 68, 73
Turgot, Baron, 14–15, 17
Turkey, 165
Tylor, Alfred, 157
Tylor, Anna, 158, 230
Tylor, Edward B., 5, 168, 180, 181, 230, 266, 321, 322, 324
 and adhesions, 316–18
 and Anthropological Institute, 300, 316
 and Anthropological Society, 159, 248
 and Boas, 181–82, 291, 300, 318
 and Buckle, 158
 and cross-cultural comparison, 316–18, 328
 and cultural anthropology, 301, 302, 311
 on culture, 159, 161, 162, 192, 194, 300, 302–304, 310–11, 314
 and Darwin, 163–64, 178–179
 and Darwinian revolution, 136, 150, 173
 on degeneration, 160–61
 on diffusion, 159, 160, 163–64, 300
 on eighteenth century, 15, 171, 304
 and ethnography, 79, 108
 and ethnology, 157, 159, 160, 250, 303–304
 and evolution of marriage, 316–18
 and evolution of religion, 188, 190–97, 236–37, 261, 300, 319, 320
 and folklore, 56, 163
 and German thought, 157, 161, 164, 302, 304
 on independent invention, 158–59
 intellectual biography of, 156–64, 232
 on language, 157, 159, 163, 306–307
 later reputation of, 299–301, 314, 315
 magnum opus of, 260, 319
 and Maine, 127, 175, 184
 and McLennan, 168, 195, 297, 318
 on moral progress, 193, 223–24
 and Müller, 61–62, 158, 160, 163, 195, 305–307
 neo-Tylorianism, 294, 301, 314
 at Oxford, 236–37, 260, 263, 264–65, 267, 305
 on polygenism, 159, 270
 and social anthropology, 293, 300, 301, 319
 and Spencer, 178, 226–27
 on survivals, 127, 218, 317
 and Tasmanians, 176, 280, 282, 283
Tylor, Joseph, & Sons, 5, 157, 230

Uniformitarianism, 37, 69, 71, 72, 157, 163, 170–71, 172, 173, 177, 178, 180
Unitarian, 129
United States, 157
United States Exploring Expedition, 90
Unity of mankind, 3, 17, 25, 36, 44–45, 48, 49–53, 67, 74–76, 148, 159, 178, 181, 184, 225, 236, 245–46, 248, 250, 283, 313–14
Universities, 38, 251, 263–65
University College, London, 66
University Museum, Oxford, 264
University of London, 151
Utilitarianism, 9, 13, 31, 32–33, 34, 36, 38, 40, 111, 112, 118–19, 125, 129, 134, 137–38, 140–42, 152, 164, 165, 171, 175, 187, 193, 216, 217, 220, 221, 231, 232, 309, 311, 312, 321, 323, 328

Van Dieman's Land: *see* Tasmania
Van Dieman's Land Company, 276
Veda, 23, 57, 59
Veddahs, 153
Vico, Giambattista, 13, 17, 37
Vicq-d'Azir, Félix, 25
Victoria, Queen, 2, 199
Vietnam War, 291
Village community, 117, 120–21, 123–24, 126, 127, 184, 209, 210, 296
Virchow, Rudolf, 290
Völksgeist, 20
Voltaire, François, 18, 42, 43
Von Baer, Karl, 133–34, 229
von Hügel, Anatole, 265

Wagner, Rudolf, 67
Wake, C. Staniland, 179–81, 250, 297, 315
Wakefield, Edward, 81, 85
Wallace, A. R., 80, 96–101, 104, 148–49, 160, 173, 191, 234, 248, 254, 263, 282
Weber, Max, 301
Wellington, Duke of, 2
West Indies, 244
Westermarck, Edward, 177, 204, 318, 321
Westminister philosophy, 251
Whately, Archbishop Richard, 44, 81, 85, 87, 149, 154
Whewell, William, 1, 2, 5–6, 37, 42, 44, 69–70, 71, 118, 126, 128, 134, 163, 165, 188
White, Charles, 26
White, Leslie, 291
White man's burden, 237, 273
Wilberforce, Bishop Samuel, 146, 151
Wilberforce, William, 33, 241
Wilkinson, J. G., 71
Williams, Thomas, 80, 87–92, 102, 104, 107
Wilson, Daniel, 73, 179, 180
Wiseman, Nicholas, 44
Women
- admission to scientific societies, 253, 256
- character of, 198–99, 205, 206, 229
- equality of, 131, 206
- fallen, 199
- and progress of knowledge, 114, 199
- "redundant," 200, 202
- rights of, 201, 203, 205, 206
- in savagery, 84–85, 90, 98, 99–100, 105
- sexuality of, 199, 203
- status of, 198, 200, 203, 205, 206, 207

World War I, 289, 321
Worsaae, J. J., 72–73
Wright, Thomas, 55, 71, 73, 246, 247

Xhosa, 86

Zeus, 60
Zulu War, 272

Made in the USA
Lexington, KY
29 August 2014